Elgin and Churchill at the Colonial Office

Elgin and Churchill at the Colonial Office 1905-1908

THE WATERSHED OF THE EMPIRE-COMMONWEALTH

Ronald Hyam, M.A., PH.D.,

FELLOW AND LIBRARIAN OF MAGDALENE COLLEGE
AND ASSISTANT LECTURER IN HISTORY IN THE
UNIVERSITY OF CAMBRIDGE

Macmillan
LONDON · MELBOURNE · TORONTO
St Martin's Press
NEW YORK
1 9 6 8

© Ronald Hyam 1968

Published by
MACMILLAN AND CO LTD
Little Essex Street London W C 2
and also at Bombay Calcutta and Madras
Macmillan South Africa (Publishers) Pty Ltd Johannesburg
The Macmillan Company of Australia Pty Ltd Melbourne
The Macmillan Company of Canada Ltd Toronto
St Martin's Press Inc New York

Library of Congress catalog card no. 68–16801

Printed in Great Britain by
ROBERT MACLEHOSE AND CO LTD
The University Press, Glasgow

32575

DEDICATED TO

THOSE OF MY FRIENDS WHO,

THOUGH THEY WILL NOT READ

THIS BOOK, ENCOURAGED ME

TO PERSEVERE WITH IT,

ESPECIALLY

ANTHONY MILNER

MICHAEL HUGGAN

ROY POTTS

Contents

CONTENTS

viii

List of Illustrations

Preface

SINCE I have failed to think of a suitable catch-penny title for this book,[1] the present title as it stands needs little explanation. The book is concerned with the colonial policy of the British Liberal government during the colonial secretaryship of the 9th earl of Elgin. Winston Churchill was then in his first ministerial post as parliamentary under-secretary of state for the colonies. This period coincides with the premiership of Sir Henry Campbell-Bannerman, from 5 December 1905 to 6 April 1908. When Asquith succeeded him as prime minister, he replaced Elgin and Churchill at the colonial office by Lord Crewe and Col. Jack Seely.

This brief period is historically interesting in providing a fantastic clash of personalities, and important in determining the evolution of the commonwealth. It would be hard to envisage an official partnership so essentially incongruous as that which thrust together a former viceroy of India, a middle-aged, serious, disinterested and taciturn pillar of the Scottish establishment, and a brash, brilliant, audacious and voluble young politician, determined, as Churchill was, to make his mark. Their partnership was uneasy but fruitful, and represents a turning-point in British colonial history. I did not begin this study with a preconceived willingness to confirm the notion of the period as a watershed between the nineteenth-century empire and the twentieth-century commonwealth. But when I came across attitudes of mind and divergencies of outlook which could not readily be reconciled, it seemed right to

---

[1] 'British bulldog and Scottish spider: an imperial partnership' did not seem quite right, even though Elgin was descended from Robert de Bruce.

xi

recognise that they were irreconcilable, and to deduce the co-existence of some incompatible theories about imperial expansion and government, such as one would expect to find at a time when newer ideas were ousting older ones.

Although primarily concerned with the thoughts and ideas of Elgin and Churchill, and the evolution of colonial policy within their relationship, some attempt has been made to set this central theme in the wider contexts, both of the political career of Lord Elgin, and of the policy of the Liberal government towards the empire generally. As far as Elgin is concerned, the book is an exercise in rehabilitation. As far as the empire is concerned, the book is offered as a contribution towards the understanding of top-level British politics and policy-making in its colonial aspects. The object has been to establish what Liberal policy at the cabinet level was, how it was arrived at by discussion between ministers, what attitudes and opinions ministers had severally and in common, what the intention of their policy was, and what arguments were used in its defence. The study is not concerned with analysing the remoter origins of policies before they reached the cabinet level, with parliamentary and overseas pressures upon ministers. Nor is it concerned very much with the process by which policy was translated into practice, nor with criticisms of the policy offered at the time, except in so far as these served further to modify policy. The opinions of colonial governors and civil servants have been referred to where these are necessary to understand, or where they help to illuminate, ministerial policy: but the governors and civil servants remain shadowy figures on the periphery of these pages.

The research is based mainly upon more than 900 volumes of the original colonial office records, now in the Public Record Office, and the private papers of Lord Elgin, which are still at Broomhall, Dunfermline. This central core of material has been buttressed by reference to the Elgin Viceroy of India Papers in the India Office Library, and to more than one hundred volumes of other private papers, mainly in the British Museum, Public Record Office or Bodleian Library. The documentary basis of the study is not quite complete. The private papers of

Lord Crewe will not be made available in Cambridge University Library until 1973. Access to the private papers of Lord Selborne was refused, but fortunately the Elgin papers contain a nearly complete record of their private correspondence. The papers of the lord chancellor, Loreburn, were not traced.

The book analyses problems, rather than tells a story in a strict chronological narrative. It is a series of studies within the field covered by the title, rather than a comprehensive survey. The problems surrounding the presence of Indians in Natal, or Japanese in British Columbia, are omitted; British policy in Malaya is not discussed; the account of the work of the colonial conference of 1907 is incomplete. To have dealt with such questions more fully would have added length and tedium rather than illumination. The main body of the work is divided into three approximately chronological sections. Although all of these overlap, it is possible to trace three successive phases, each characterised by a different dominant preoccupation. The guiding themes constituting the main framework of the book are the attitudes and policies with respect to three things: the principle of continuity of policy, the principle of self-government, and the so-called native question. Much space is devoted to the Transvaal, not only because this was the most considerable and controversial imperial problem dealt with in the period, but also because these three themes are most closely interrelated in the Transvaal.

I am very deeply indebted to the 10th earl of Elgin and to Lord Bruce of Broomhall, Dunfermline, for allowing me unrestricted access to the private papers of the 9th earl relating to his colonial secretaryship. I am also grateful for their kindness and hospitality, and for their help in clarifying the personal and family background. It has not been possible to cite proper references to the Elgin papers, as the collection is still only in process of being sorted and arranged. Photocopies of Elgin's letters to Churchill have been added to the Elgin collection through the good offices of the Chartwell Trust. I should also like to thank the Hon. Randolph S. Churchill for his kindness in allowing me to see in draft the portions of the official life of Churchill which overlap with my own work. I am grateful to the Hon. Mark Bonham Carter for permission to use the Asquith Papers, and Mrs M. E. Campbell Fraser for permission to see the Haldane Papers. All quotations from Crown-copyright records in the Public Record Office appear by permission of the Controller of H.M. Stationery Office.

Professor P. N. S. Mansergh has guided my work on this project from the beginning, and I owe a great deal to him. My historical training as a scholar of St John's was supervised by Mr F. H. Hinsley, Dr R. E. Robinson, Mr (now Professor) E. Miller, and Mr J. A. Crook, to all of whom I also owe much. My text has benefited too from suggestions made by Professor J. Gallagher, Dr A. F. Madden, Mrs Mary Bull, the Rev. S. Barrington-Ward and Mr G. T. Greig. I remain responsible for all shortcomings.

I have tried to follow the conventions usual in historians' prefaces. There is one glaring and lame omission: I have no wife-typist to thank. Perhaps I shall make good this defect in my equipment before publishing my next book. Meanwhile, it is a pleasure to acknowledge that Fellows of the College of my adoption, and those to whom I dedicate this book, have given me kindly support.

Note on Abbreviations

Abbreviated reference to sources (example)	*Full reference would be:*
African (S) 804	Confidential print, colonial office, minute or memorandum, African (South), no. 804
Asq. 10/192	Asquith papers, box/file 10, folio 192
CAB. 41/30/15	Prime minister's cabinet letter-reports to the sovereign: photographic copies of original letters in royal archives, vol. 30, number 15
CB. 41207/18	Campbell-Bannerman papers, British Museum Additional MSS. [vol. no.] 41207, folio 18
CO. 291/87/1084	Colonial office records, Transvaal series, vol. 87, correspondence file number 1084 in the year
Cromer 13(ii)/48	Cromer Papers, vol. 13, part 2, folio 48
EP	Elgin papers, 1905–1908
GP. 7	Sir Edward Grey papers, vol. 7
MM. 1/274	Letters from Lord Morley to Lord Minto, viceroy of India, vol. i, folio 274
PD. 152/1427	[Hansard] Parliamentary Debates, 4th series, vol. 152, column 1427
PD/HC. 12/1008	[Hansard] Parliamentary Debates, 5th series, House of Commons, vol. 12, column 1008
PD/HL. 1/327	[Hansard] Parliamentary Debates, 5th series, House of Lords, vol. 1, column 327
VRP. 15/10	Elgin, viceroy of India papers, 1894–9, Elgin to secretary of state for India, vol. 15, part 1, page 10

For the location of these sources, see Bibliography, pp. 546–8

The following word abbreviations are used in the footnotes and index:

WSC	Winston S. Churchill
cab. memo.	Memorandum printed for the use of the cabinet
CB	Sir Henry Campbell-Bannerman, prime minister
CO	colonial office
desp.	despatch (official)
E	Lord Elgin
FO	foreign office
govr	governor
H.M.G.	His Majesty's Government
MAJ	W. S. Churchill, *My African Journey* (1908)
S/S	secretary of state (for the colonies, unless otherwise stated)
Selb.	Lord Selborne
tel.	telegram

Private letters to and from Elgin are indicated by using 'E', not 'S/S', which is used only for official correspondence.

In transcribing quotations, punctuation has occasionally been added, and abbreviations written out in full, *except* H.M.G.

Introduction

Introduction

WHEN the Liberal ministry was formed in December 1905 the ultimate responsibility for the government of nearly a quarter of the world resided in London. The new government found itself in charge of 'one continent, a hundred peninsulas, five hundred promontories, a thousand lakes, two thousand rivers, ten thousand islands'. At this time, moreover, 70 per cent of all the ships on the seas flew the Union Jack.[1] The British empire was at its apogee. True, confidence in perpetual progress and the automatic perfectibility of mankind was much diminished. The rose-coloured spectacles of Macaulay and Palmerston had already been widely exchanged for the blinkers of Milner and Curzon. Britain no longer swayed the fortunes of the greater part of the globe unchallenged or alone. But London was still the most important city in the world. The men who ruled there believed that it was the centre of civilisation. Perhaps also, they were tempted to imagine, the new Jerusalem really had been built in England's green and pleasant land? Here, maybe, true wisdom was to be found. 'The culture of London seemed so polished that it was hard to treat with perfect seriousness the aspirations of Toronto or Auckland, Lagos or Belize'.[2] The mandarins of the colonial office, and many politicians too, held colonial and non-European societies in contempt. Smuts, Gandhi, Deakin, Mullah Muhammad of Somaliland: the significance of each of them in the history of their own peoples was underestimated. They were regarded in Whitehall merely

[1] See W. S. Adams, *Edwardian Heritage* (1949), p. 18, quoting *St. James Gazette*, 1901.
[2] R. B. Pugh in *Cambridge History of the British Empire*, iii (1959), 768.

3

as 'cunning', 'half-mad', 'boring' and 'mad' respectively. Colonial nationalism was not yet shaping the destinies of the empire. The sharpest criticism still came from anti-imperialists, such as J. A. Hobson and W. S. Blunt, at the centre, and not from new national leaders at the periphery. All this began to change after 1905, but for the time being the problems of the empire continued to come to London, to be seen from London and conquered in London. The colonial office staff performed annually a gigantic bottling operation, distilling (and partly distorting) the essence of 50,000 incoming despatches and telegrams into manageable minutes and recommendations for the delectation and usually the decision of the colonial secretary.

The imperial policy of the Liberal government after 1905 has to be seen against this general cultural and administrative background. It has also to be seen in a more particular context of party politics. The Liberals thought that the Unionists from 1895 to 1905 had abused their power, widening the scale of British territorial responsibilities while weakening the scope of moral ones. It was up to the Liberals, therefore, to 'cleanse the body of this empire' and to 'solace all its wide dominion'[1] with the healing power of renewed freedom, love and truth. It was of course easy enough for the Liberals to surround themselves with an aura of superior virtue. Circumstances favoured them in three ways. First, it was the Unionists who had to superintend the forcible injection of European conceptions of law and order into most of the newly acquired African territories. 'Pacification', with its inherent tendency towards embarrassing incidents, rapidly became a residual problem after 1905. Second, in making a South African settlement, it was highly convenient for the Liberals that the Unionists had annexed the Transvaal during the Boer War. The Liberals could thus play from strength. The Transvaal had been acquired in a war which they had opposed: this was an ace put up their sleeve, if not by God, at least by Milner. They could appear magnanimously to return something which they had in fact never particularly

[1] These lines are from Henry Scott Holland's hymn 'Judge eternal, throned in splendour', written in 1906.

4

wished to possess. Third, it was, as Professor Mansergh has pointed out,[1] very fortunate for them that in the matter of granting the franchise to the natives in South Africa, their hands were tied by their predecessors' action. They could denounce the Unionists for having sold the pass by a clause in the peace treaty which ended the Boer war: a clause which, if they had themselves then been in office, they would have found very difficult to escape, and which, when they took office, absolved them from tackling the thorny problem.[2]

The Liberals thus had an easier row to hoe than the Unionists. This difference in situation and circumstance was one of the major reasons for the difference between their policies. The difference was not simply the academic one of basic theoretical principle and preconception, though their propaganda may have made it seem to be so. At the same time, at least as far as method was concerned, the difference between them was partly one of the degree to which each believed in the efficacy of political means to ensure two things: the loyalty of Australians, Boers or Indians, and the elevation of Bantu, Kikuyu or Hindu. Liberals had less faith than Unionists in the power of politics alone to effect change. They still believed in free trade imperialism, that is to say, in a process whereby British economic expansion might, for example, eventually assimilate and conciliate the Boers, with the employment of few political safeguards.[3] By contrast, the Unionists, many of whom had abandoned free trade, believed that constructive political action by the British government was needed to make South Africa loyal, to control the reconstruction and development of the Transvaal economy. Because of their scepticism about the power of political action, the Liberals were increasingly deferential to the principle of responsible government in the colonies, adamantly opposed to schemes of imperial federation, and willing to encourage as much African economic

[1] N. Mansergh, *South Africa, 1906–1961: the price of magnanimity* (1962), pp. 65 and 71.

[2] This clause promised that the franchise question would not be decided until after the introduction of self-government in the Transvaal and Orange River Colony.

[3] See R. E. Robinson and J. Gallagher, *Africa and the Victorians* (1961), p. 419.

5

development as the ethos of the times allowed. These policies, together with growing appreciation of colonial nationalism, were the essential prerequisites for the transformation of the empire into the commonwealth. After the first world war, the empire of Britain became the empire in Britain; the proprietor was reduced to being a participant.

The Liberal government between 1905 and 1908 provided the point of departure for this process. This is why we call the period under scrutiny the watershed of the empire–commonwealth. It would not be possible for any later period to orientate a study of colonial policy as this one is orientated: from London looking outward. In 1908, though the habit had begun to decrease, the colonial secretary still made *ex cathedra* pronouncements and still might, should occasion seem to him to require it, issue directions to colonial governments. Consultation was not yet the normal guiding principle of imperial administration. A far greater proportion of work, including trivial matter, appeared on the colonial secretary's desk than it did later in the century.[1]

The personality and capabilities of the colonial secretary were therefore highly important in determining policy. Lord Elgin's poor reputation as colonial secretary is intimately connected with the misconception that the Liberals had no interest in, or contribution to make to, the empire outside South Africa. This study will reveal, however, Liberal concern and activity in Trinidad as well as in the Transvaal, in Fiji and Somaliland as well as in the Free State, in Ceylon, Cyprus and Kenya as well as in Cape Colony, in Newfoundland, Nigeria and the New Hebrides as well as in Natal. If the South African policy of the Liberal ministry has been reckoned an exception to general indifference and ineffectiveness, it has been assumed that the credit could not possibly belong to Elgin, but must go exclusively to the prime minister. The amount of distinction (or lack of it) in British colonial policy in the years 1905 to 1908 can only be evaluated correctly if Elgin himself is assessed fairly. To this problem we turn first.

[1] Cosmo Parkinson, *The Colonial Office from within, 1909–1945* (1947), pp. 34 and 142.

1 The Career and Reputation of Lord Elgin

IF Balliol College Hall is to qualify for the title of the Valhalla of the British Empire, it lacks one portrait which it ought to have. Viceroy of India (1894–9), colonial secretary (1905–8): surely Elgin should be represented? All others of its alumni who became proconsuls of the empire are honoured there. The omission of Elgin is hardly accidental. His reputation has suffered a total eclipse.

THE GENESIS OF AN UNFAVOURABLE REPUTATION

There is no doubt at all what the orthodox view of Elgin has been hitherto. There is almost as little doubt that it is partly wrong. Ever since 1911 at least, Elgin has had the reputation of being, as Sir Richard Jebb then described him, a 'weak and unimaginative administrator'.[1] He is generally thought to have been 'the weak link' in the chain of successive colonial secretaries active in imperial and African development in the twenty years before 1914.[2] 'Worthy but undistinguished', 'lethargic and pedestrian', 'dull and solid', 'timid and hesitant', 'dithering but well-meaning', 'acquiescent and unimaginative', 'detached and unemphatic': these are typical views among historians.[3] Harshest of all, and the most damaging, was the

[1] R. Jebb, *The Imperial Conference* (1911), ii, 25, quoted by R. B. Pugh in *C.H.B.E.*, iii, 737. The entry in *Dictionary of National Biography 1912–21*, pp. 71–4: 'Bruce, Victor Alexander, 9th earl of Elgin', is very critical of Elgin.

[2] A. F. Madden in *C.H.B.E.*, iii, 382.

[3] E. Huxley, *White Man's Country* (1953), i, 193; H. Tinker, *Foundations of Local Self-government in India, Pakistan and Burma* (1954), p. 60; S. Gopal, *British Policy in*

judgment of Arthur Berriedale Keith in his standard work *Responsible Government in the Dominions* (1928), in which Elgin is repeatedly characterised as feeble, weak, vacillating and maladroit.[1] These views and judgments in part reflect the gossip of some of the major figures in empire history: Deakin, Lugard, Jameson and Curzon. Deakin disliked Elgin's chairmanship of the colonial conference, and found him 'dull and inferior in every way'.[2] Lugard disliked being overruled, and so complained that Elgin was 'both weak and interfering'.[3] Curzon, forming a retrospective opinion of Elgin's performance as viceroy of India, alleged that Elgin had resigned himself into the hands of his official advisers, become a puppet of the soldiers, and had been found totally lacking in ideas or initiative. His predecessor's régime was, he said, 'the apotheosis of bureaucracy'.[4]

The unfavourable image was moulded at the time by Curzon and Lugard, Deakin and Jameson, and written up fairly quickly by Jebb and Keith. Later historians have simply repeated the received doctrine more from thoughtlessness and ignorance than from malice or partisanship. Charges of partisanship must, however, inevitably stick to those who moulded the unfavourable image. The very list of their names is proof enough: these were not the men who looked to the commonwealth ideal. They were the grand imperialists. Elgin was naturally cursed by those who saw only too well that his conception of imperial development was one which would

---

India, 1858–1905 (1965), pp. 180, 213; J. Pope-Hennessy, *Lord Crewe, 1858–1945* (1955), pp. 63–4; J. A. La Nauze, *Alfred Deakin: a biography* (Melbourne, 1965), ii, pp. 449, 500, 506–7.

[1] i, pp. 193, 220, ii, pp. 828, 870.

[2] Deakin, Lugard and Jameson expressed their opinions to Austen Chamberlain: see A. Chamberlain, *Politics from inside 1906–1914* (1936), pp. 79–80; C. Petrie, *Life and Letters of Sir Austen Chamberlain* (1939), i, 198.

[3] M. Perham, *Lugard*, ii, 267. On the other hand Lugard took the trouble to write to Elgin, 30 Dec 07: 'A rumour has appeared in the papers that we are to lose you at the colonial office. I trust that it has no foundation at all' (EP).

[4] H. L. Singh, *Problems and Policies of the British in India 1885–1898* (1963), p. 5; S. Gopal, *British Policy in India*, pp. 180–1, both quoting Hamilton papers, Curzon to Hamilton, 5 Apr 1900, 26 Oct 02, and Gopal quoting Curzon papers, Curzon to Selborne, 1900.

thwart theirs. They have something else in common too, something which also reduces the value of their opinion. With the single exception of Keith, none of them had anything more than fleeting opportunities to watch Elgin at work. Only Keith can be reckoned an informed critic. Against this we must set the fact that he was not merely partisan, but actuated by malice. Keith worked in the colonial office throughout this period, and there is no doubt that of all the officials then at work, he was more worrying to his superiors than any of the others, and that he was the only official to be seriously reprimanded by his political chiefs. He was made to feel unusually uncomfortable. He took a savage revenge in the guise of an authoritative historian.[1]

[1] Keith also criticised Churchill sharply (*Responsible Government in the Dominions*, i, 217, ii, 1181). On 31 Mar 06 Keith compared the disturbances in Natal (see below, p. 239 ff.) with the Morant Bay rising in Jamaica under Governor Eyre, commenting, 'whereas the Jamaica revolt was a real and serious one, the Natal, so far as overt action has gone, has been a trifle. Natal desires with the aid of British troops to terrify by executions its native population, and the threat of removing the battalion from Pietermaritzburg would be effective in reducing them to commonsense.' Cox rebuked him: 'I consider this statement an outrage on a population which is quite as humane as Mr Keith and has more knowledge of the circumstances. . . . The line he takes, of absolutely discrediting the views and feelings of the men on the spot, if put into action, will lose us not only South Africa, but every colony we possess.' Elgin added: 'I recognise Mr Keith's ability, but the line he has taken here, not I think for the first time, detracts from the usefulness of his minutes.' In justification, Keith pleaded that the colonial secretary of Natal had said that if there was to be bloodshed, it should be at once, and that the despatch of the telegram of 28 March 1906 requesting suspension of executions till more information had been received, was an action 'hardly consistent with a belief in the man on the spot'. This only made matters worse, and Elgin told him bluntly that his interpretation was certainly wrong (CO. 179/233/11034, minutes by E, 15 and 26 Apr 06). Meanwhile Churchill was conducting a private war with Keith on the score of the illegibility of his handwriting, a very necessary campaign. After two formal complaints, Churchill wrote: 'Great inconvenience is caused by this kind of writing to all who have to study it, and I hope we may claim a little more consideration in future from Mr Keith.' Keith made an abject reply, hoping that it would not be thought he had been deliberately writing in an illegible way (CO. 291/88/44764, CO. 224/18/10335, minute by WSC, 9 Apr 06). Keith was transferred out of the South African department, and given less controversial work. Elgin wrote to Churchill about this: 'As to Keith, I may just say that I should never have wanted him moved if he could have restrained his propensity for smart sayings and attended a little more to the correctness of his law: but the position was getting awkward' (EP, 6 Jun 06). Keith, of course, remained a marked man. He was dealing with Newfoundland questions in the autumn of 1907, a ticklish time;

Everything conspired against Elgin's reputation. His work was unfavourably commented on by powerful enemies. As viceroy he was overshadowed by Curzon, who followed him; as colonial secretary by Churchill, who stole the limelight. In the former capacity, he had sharp differences of opinion with the Liberal ministry in 1895 over the future defence of North-West India; in the latter, he was unceremoniously dropped by Asquith on the formation of his ministry in April 1908, and never again returned to politics.

Elgin's fate is indeed a cautionary tale about the penalties of silence in politics. He never defended himself. He was temperamentally silent on social occasions. In the cabinet he was always brief in introducing his own business, and rarely opened his mouth on subjects outside his departmental concern. J. A. Spender, a very astute commentator, felt sure that Elgin must have been an able man, and he realised that he was certainly a dutiful one, 'but no one ever made on one quite the same impression of complete passivity'.[1] Such silence makes other men feel uncomfortable, even when, as in Elgin's case, the silence was companionable and not boorish. Politicians are inclined to jump to the conclusion that a silent tongue implies an empty head. When Morley was trying to assess support for his Indian policy, he felt able to overlook Elgin's lack of enthusiasm: 'Elgin does not open his mouth on any subject, so I leave him out of account'.[2] Elgin apparently owed his extrusion from the Asquith ministry in large measure to his silence in the cabinet and his unwillingness to speak in the House of Lords on non-colonial subjects. He lacked the gift of eloquence, which, though perhaps over-valued by the Victorian and Edwardian public, necessarily counted for much in a country supposedly governed by discussion. His manner of

owing to reshuffling of staff, Keith was writing the principal minutes and tele-grams. Elgin was anxious about this. Keith, he wrote, 'with all his ability is not, in my judgement, a very safe guide' (EP, E to WSC, 25 Sep 07). See further, p. 267, n. 5, below.

[1] J. A. Spender, *Life, Journalism and Politics* (1927), i, 213.

[2] MM. 2/79, 17 Apr 07. Like Ripon, Elgin was opposed to an Indian member's sitting on the viceroy's executive council, mainly on grounds of security (ibid. p. 211, 3 May 07); see also J. Morley, *Recollections*, ii, 208, 28 Mar 07.

speaking was dry, plain and matter-of-fact, his delivery often halting. And so he preferred not to make speeches if he could avoid them. His silence was not, however, merely temperamental. In controversy, dignified silence was a political principle. Rather than say unpleasant things, Elgin preferred to eschew public utterance. He disapproved of the Boer War,[1] but was too patriotic to denounce it. No man courted popularity less. He refused to cultivate a public image. He was totally lacking in the urge to justify himself before the public. In this respect he might be said to stand in politics at one opposite extreme to the earl of Chatham, who never lost an opportunity of ingratiating himself with the public, even if it involved telling a lie. Elgin lacked the will to press his own programmes for the sake of his reputation. As viceroy he wrote:

I have never been able in public matters to give to that side of any question the importance which is usually attributed to it. If things can be done in my time, well and good; if not, it is enough for me, or for any man, that we have not failed to advocate what we deemed to be in the public interest. . . .[2]

He never publicly refuted misrepresentations, never answered critics. A less tolerant and modest man would have found it easy enough to deflate Churchill's presumptuous and juvenile conceit that he, the under-secretary, was really running the colonial office. Elgin had written testimony from both Curzon and Churchill to suggest that their implied denigrations of Elgin were selfish and did not genuinely reflect their real and private opinions. Had not Curzon requested to be left a copy of the printed volume of Elgin's Indian speeches, 'many of which, even in the imperfect form in which I have seen them in the newspapers, I have admired from a distance'? And had Curzon not told Elgin that he hoped on laying down his own office he might 'have earned one half of the credit and distinction which in times of great emergency, and even peril, you have done. I shall find in your courage and coolness of judgement the

---

[1] This is necessarily a speculation, an argument from silence.
[2] VRP. 14/212, E to S/S for India, Hamilton, 23 Dec 96.

best of examples.'[1] Had not Churchill written to him most appreciatively?[2]

No one could ever have had a more trustful and indulgent chief than I have been most lucky to find on first joining a government: and I have learned a very great deal in the conduct of official business from your instruction and example which I should all my life have remained completely ignorant of, if I had gone elsewhere.

The essential prerequisite of a proper assessment of Elgin as colonial secretary is to rescue his reputation as a viceroy of India. But first a personal sketch.

CHARACTER AND EARLY CAREER

One of the central facts about Elgin's character was his incapacity for social leadership, reflected in his reputation for shyness and inaccessibility. Family circumstances go a long way towards explaining this. The family estates of the Bruce family in Dunfermline were comparatively small, some four thousand acres. Until the 1890s they were saddled with the debt which had been incurred mainly on the rescue of the marbles of the Parthenon by Thomas, the 7th earl.[3] Victor Alexander, the 9th earl of Elgin (1849–1917), was therefore brought up in more straitened circumstances than might otherwise have been supposed. The suppression of vivacity in Elgin's personality may be traced to the results of his father's death in November 1863, when he was fourteen. His father, James, the 8th earl (1811–63), had achieved enormous distinction: he was governor of

[1] VRP. 33/56(1), Curzon to E, 21 Sep 1898; 47, 12 Aug 1898.
[2] EP, 30 Dec 06.
[3] Thomas Bruce, 7th earl of Elgin, 1766–1841; ambassador to the Ottoman Porte, 1799–1803. The Elgin marbles were shipped from Athens 1803–12; some of them had to be recovered from shipwreck. They were bought for the nation for £35,000 in 1816, but Elgin had spent £74,000 on the description, formation, removal and arrangement of the collection. The 7th earl's debt also included large sums spent on buying mineral rights, building Broomhall, and financing his diplomatic missions.

Jamaica, governor-general of Canada (1847–54),[1] envoy to China (1857, 1859) and died in India as viceroy. Thereafter, the atmosphere in the home was one of perpetual mourning. Young Elgin and his brothers and sisters were not allowed to speak above a whisper outside the nursery, out of respect for their dead father. Insistence on a rather mawkish adulation by the widowed mother (herself the daughter of the famous Lord Durham), and the grandmother, undoubtedly had an inhibiting effect on children who seem to have had some talent for theatricals and singing. Victor Alexander was not naturally a gloomy person, and later in life he was capable of being sparked off into lively conversation if stimulated by his companion. Moreover, he later enjoyed being the compère at parties for the villagers on his estate. He was a very good mimic and sang well.

Victor Alexander married Lady Constance Carnegie, daughter of the 9th earl of Southesk, in 1876. His wife's health showed signs of weakness even before they went to India in 1894. For this reason he became disinclined to shoulder the burden of duties which might take him away from home. Elgin doubted whether his wife could take the strain of going to India. However, once out there, she appears to have thrown herself fully into social activity. Her eleventh confinement took place in India in difficult circumstances. But Lady Elgin's poor health was now permanently impaired. During the period of his colonial secretaryship Lady Elgin became virtually bedridden. There could be no question of her entertaining. Elgin treated the matter firmly and insisted that there must be no afternoons 'at home', which were being pressed upon them by society hostesses. The doctors advised against it. Even if Lady Elgin had not been in such bad health, social leadership would have been impracticable from domestic considerations. With eleven children to provide for, an expensive domestic establishment was needed, and left little physical space at Broomhall for the entertainment of guests.

Behind all this, Elgin was never happy in London society.

---

[1] Victor Alexander was born in Canada, 16 May 1849.

The ebullience of the Edwardian era dismayed him. Until he became colonial secretary he had managed without visiting cards, but had some printed for the first time in 1906.[1] Some weeks after taking office he wrote a melancholy note about dining with the Reays:

Even with several people I knew, Sandhurst, Birrell, Crewe, I felt as if I was once more learning to swim – and on my own side I feel that I must have a season fairly quiet in which to acclimatise in this respect.

Hospitality was all very well in its way, but work must come first, and there was plenty of that.[2] More than a year later, after dining at the Harcourts' he reported that although Mrs H. seemed 'pleasant and conversible', he did not suppose that they would ever have much in common with them, adding that he had not realised that 'they would be so smart'.[3] Official dinners he loathed. The Mansion House dinner in 1906 he described as 'intolerably dull . . . No-one could make himself heard properly'.[4] At about this time he brought himself to give a dinner for the thirty or forty Liberal peers at the National Liberal Club; but only because several other cabinet ministers had done this sort of thing, and only because the manager of the club handled all the arrangements.[5] This was about the limit of his social activity. Elgin drew a distinction between the social responsibilities of being viceroy of India and colonial secretary, deciding that a colonial secretary could dispense with undue entertaining. But his decision was probably damaging to his political career in a governing *élite* which set such store by social contact. His predecessor as colonial secretary, Alfred Lyttelton, was a notable practitioner of it, and one of his later successors, Leopold Amery, attached enormous significance to entertaining as part of the function of a colonial secretary.[6]

---

[1] E. Marsh, *A Number of People* (1939), p. 150.
[2] EP, to Lady E 17 Feb 06.   [3] Ibid., 8 Jun 07.
[4] Ibid., 10 Nov 06.   [5] Ibid., 14 Nov 06.
[6] The Amerys made their London home a centre for colonial officials on leave, for dominion statesmen and visitors; crowded receptions were held every week (L. S. Amery, *My Political Life*, ii (1953), 370).

As colonial secretary, whilst in London, Elgin often dined quietly alone at Brooks's. Week-ends and all other possible times were spent in Scotland, not simply because of his ailing wife, whose death he now feared, but also because he thought the pavements of London a poor substitute for the heather of Scotland.[1]

To his wife he was indeed deeply devoted:

It is to your dear companionship that I owe everything and above all the atmosphere of affection and peace which so gladdens our home. It is hard, even for me with the distractions of work to be parted so much just now.[2]

Lady Elgin died in 1909.

Elgin loved a vigorous outdoor life. A glimpse of this is provided in a letter to his wife in April 1906, when he was at home at Broomhall and she was away for medical care. He described

A splendid afternoon's exercise – cutting trees near the Secret Path from lunch to tea. Then digging on the road for an hour. Topping up with a big bath (hot). – N.B. I am *not* overdoing.[3]

Like Gladstone he was an expert forester, and when he sprained a leg while hewing a tree in February 1908 the newspapers had some fun pointing out that this sort of activity was not entirely unknown among Liberal cabinet ministers. Elgin was better at cutting and felling trees than any of his retainers. He also enjoyed pruning bushes. He valued regular walking, and found that official tours as viceroy tended to upset him because they interfered with his habit. He disliked horse-riding, and on public occasions even objected to driving in a carriage, which struck members of Anglo-Indian society as very odd.[4] He learned to drive a motor-car during his time as colonial secretary. For many years he took an attractive estate at Dunphail, Morayshire, which had a fishing and a dogging grouse moor. The whole family moved there with him each

[1] VRP. 31/41.
[3] Ibid., 14 Apr 06.
[2] EP, 9 Nov 06.
[4] See *D.N.B. 1912–21*, p. 73.

summer between 1899 and 1905. But he never liked the ritual 'blood bath' slaughter of game. He was very keen on archery, cricket and curling, and founded clubs for all three on his Broomhall estate.

He once described himself as an 'opponent of extravagance and...a foe to display'.[1] He kept meticulous accounts of expenditure, both personal and estate, and habitually recorded the reasoning behind his decisions. He refused to have a telephone at Broomhall lest he should commit himself on the spur of the moment. There was no conspicuous consumption. In public life he had a high sense of seriousness and duty, forcing himself into the service of the state against his own inclination. Henry Lawrence's epitaph, 'who tried to do his duty', inspired him.[2]

Elgin was educated at Glenalmond, Eton and Balliol. He graduated with a second class in *literae humaniores* in 1873, and captained the Balliol cricket XI. After coming down from Oxford he was, as a result of his father's early death, plunged at once into the problems of estate management, and especially into financial rehabilitation and expansion. He developed a strong interest in, and an intense regard for, the history of his distinguished family. He read through the archives at Broomhall, and made notes of their contents. But he seemed to show no signs of wishing to follow his father and grandfather in playing a part in affairs of state. Since his grandfather had been so much vilified and so much out of pocket in his dealings with the state, and since his father had suffered shipwreck, lost his first wife in Jamaica, and been buried in an Indian grave, there was no reason why a political career should seem attractive. In any case, he found ample satisfaction in taking a very active part in local affairs, especially in education. In the years immediately before he went to India, he became increasingly concerned with university affairs. For many years he sat on the University Court, the governing body of St Andrews, the most ancient Scottish university, and studied the problems of

[1] VRP. 88/194, 10 Nov 96. [2] Ibid., 501, 2 Jan 99.

The 9th earl of Elgin

Lord Elgin and his eldest children, c. 1889

higher education as a member of the Committee of the Council on Education in Scotland. He was particularly interested in two problems: how to maintain the benefits of a classical education whilst meeting 'the imperative requirements of our own practical age', and how to make sure that the poor man was not denied the fullest opportunity to develop his faculties.[1] From 1886 until his death, he was Lord Lieutenant of Fife. There were business connections too: he was a director of the North British Railway and the Royal Bank of Scotland. He was chairman of the executive committee of the Scottish Liberal Association for a long spell, and drafted its prospectus. Quite a lot of thought was devoted by him to the problems of constituency organisation in an age threatened by the development of the caucus.

Elgin's first public appointment was as treasurer in the Queen's household during Gladstone's third ministry, between February and July 1886. The Queen objected to him because he was not talkative. Elgin acted as spokesman for Scottish affairs in the House of Lords. He was disappointed when Lord Dalhousie was appointed to the vacant Scottish Office. In order to keep his allegiance, Gladstone offered Elgin the ministry of works in succession to Morley. Elgin acted as first commissioner of works from April to August 1886, when Gladstone's third ministry ended.[2] In the great political issue of his generation, Elgin followed Gladstone on Home Rule for Ireland, and into the political wilderness.

During his fourth return to power, Gladstone had to appoint a viceroy of India. He recommended Elgin to the Queen on 11 August 1893. The Queen expressed doubts about Elgin's appointment. She had regard for him as a member of 'that most distinguished family of Bruce', but

she hardly thinks him well suited for this important post. He is very shy and most painfully silent, has no presence, no

[1] VRP. 88/10 and 101. E was also a member of first school board created in Scotland.
[2] A. Ramm (ed.), *Political Correspondence of Mr Gladstone and Lord Granville 1876–1886* (1962), ii, 428, 439, n. 4.

experience whatever in administration. He would not command the respect which is necessary in that office.

In any case, she predicted that Elgin might well refuse on the grounds of the delicacy of his wife's health. Gladstone reconsidered the question with some of his leading colleagues. They conceded all the Queen's objections, but they still found that they wished to recommend Elgin, because the testimonies to his character and capacity from those members of the cabinet who knew him and Scotland best – Lord Rosebery, Campbell-Bannerman and Marjoribanks – were very strongly on his side. Gladstone wisely thought that his political inexperience was compensated for by his very large unofficial experience of Scottish business. Elgin refused the offer. Family considerations were decisive. The cabinet then passed over the Queen's suggestion of Lord Carrington and made the offer to Sir Henry Norman, governor of Queensland, who at first seemed inclined to accept. After he withdrew, Rosebery, urged by Gladstone, saw Elgin again, and for more than an hour on 2 October, walked with him round Arthur's Seat in Edinburgh, and persuaded his friend to accept the viceroyalty. Next day Gladstone reported to the Queen that Elgin had 'overcome the honourable and modest diffidence, never shared by his friends'. The appointment was made, and the Queen saw Elgin on 26 November, prior to his departure. She found him very sensible.[1]

---

[1] G. E. Buckle (ed.), *The letters of Queen Victoria*, 3rd Series, ii (1931), 300–4, 309, 315–16. R. R. James, *Rosebery* (1962), p. 290, n. 1, quotes Rosebery's letter to the Queen, 4 Sep 93, in which Rosebery remarked: 'it seems positively sad to Lord Rosebery that more fit and aspiring men should not be found for this splendid position', as if it were a comment on Lord Elgin. This is not so. It was rather a comment upon the fitness of Sir Henry Norman, whom Rosebery presumed had accepted. The portion quoted by Mr James is immediately preceded by a sentence which makes this quite clear: 'Lord Rosebery knows nothing of the new Viceroy, who is obviously too old to undertake the post with safety. . . .' The misconception which Mr James's footnote invites, has, unhappily, misled the author of the most recent study of British policy in India: 'Rosebery had no high opinion of Elgin's abilities, and presumably urged him to go to India because no one better suited was available' (S. Gopal, *British policy in India, 1858–1905* (1965), p. 180. Dr Gopal also gives the impression that Elgin was made an offer only after Sir Henry Norman had declined).

THE CAREER AND REPUTATION OF LORD ELGIN

VICEROY OF INDIA, 1894–1899

There are two reasons why some account of Elgin's vice-royalty is a necessary part of the introduction to this book. The first is the absence of a full-scale study of it which might correct the impression that Elgin was a weak and uninteresting viceroy; the most recent short account of it creates a one-sided picture by dwelling upon its constitutional aspects.[1] The second reason is that Elgin's Indian experience left so decisive a mark on him, that a knowledge of his viceroyalty helps to illuminate his performance as colonial secretary, a performance which was in many ways 'the turning of an Indian lantern upon colonial problems', to adapt a phrase by Fitzjames Stephen.

The Cotton Duties.[2] The first controversial problem confronting Elgin was the cotton duties. It was rather a shock to him, with his rooted conviction in favour of free trade, that his first important task was to introduce a measure imposing duties, however moderate, on imports, and even if only for urgent revenue purposes. It took three years of multiple conflict to settle the arrangements.

In March 1894 the government of India found a 5 per cent import duty necessary to raise enough revenue to cope with an increasing deficit. Cotton was exempted under pressure from the British government in Whitehall. However, Indian agitation and Elgin's support eventually made it necessary to include cotton among the duties. Then the British government, still acting on behalf of Lancashire interests, required a counter-vailing excise to be established in order to remove the supposed protective value of the duty to Indian cotton goods. When Lancashire interests complained that there were iniquities in working this, the government of India was obliged in 1896 to make further concessions, exempting cotton yarn from all taxes

---

[1] Gopal, *British policy in India*, chap. 4. Dr Gopal does not discuss Elgin's administrative achievements in railway and famine management.

[2] See P. Harnetty, 'The Indian Cotton Duties Controversy', *English Historical Review*, vol. 77 (1962).

and reducing the import and excise duties to $3\frac{1}{2}$ per cent. These arrangements then remained in force until after the first world war.

Indian historians regard the tariff measures of 1896, acting protectively on British cotton exports to India, as some of the most iniquitous in the whole British record. Elgin is thought not to have defended Indian interests forcefully enough.[1] It is difficult, however, to see what more he could have done against a determined cabinet and parliament. His deference to the views of the secretary of state for India has been commented on as if it were a peculiar personal weakness, whereas it sprang from a fairly orthodox conviction that, if co-operation broke down, the viceroy must, constitutionally, in the last resort submit to the secretary of state who was responsible to parliament. When the import duties were being arranged in 1894, the British government had wished to exclude cotton goods, but Elgin had opposed this emphatically, by pointing out that the exclusion could be defended 'by no real argument, certainly by no argument that will be accepted here as valid'. And so he insisted that this indefensible point, a flagrant concession to Lancashire, be reconsidered.[2] Nevertheless, Elgin was severely criticised for seeming to propound on 27 December 1894 the doctrine that the secretary of state could legislate for India by an over-riding mandate. It was not an exact interpretation of his attitude. On reflection[3] he was not prepared to withdraw anything he had said. He claimed for the government of India the fullest right to be heard, but admitted, or rather asserted, the supremacy of the British parliament, coupling this with the opinion that the secretary of state was the only proper exponent of what parliament intended.

During heated controversy, there were violent attacks on

[1] Gopal, op. cit., pp. 212–13. It should be remembered that Elgin protested against Indians being used in Egypt to defend imperial interests of concern to Australia and other colonies, who, he urged, might make at least a financial contribution (VRP. 14/75, 2 Jun 96).

[2] VRP. 12/8 and 13, to S/S Fowler 20 Feb and 7 Mar 94.

[3] VRP. 13/6, 9 Jan 95. He later complained of charges of 'a subservience I never professed founded on a phrase I never used', VRP. 88/500, 2 Jan 99.

Elgin in the Anglo-Indian press, based mainly on the mis-representation of his phrase about the mandate, and consisting partly in a desire to vindicate the fiscal liberty of the Indian government and partly in a liking for protection. Anglo-Indian opinion on the cotton duties always seemed to him 'quite unreasonable and unreasoning'.[1] He was convinced that wherever there was a real competition between mills and hand-looms, the latter must be driven out of the field. He doubted too whether mere exemption from duty could save them, even supposing that the mill-owners in Lancashire or Bombay were determined to reach the rural markets. He did not believe that the 5 per cent duty made any material difference to the trade, and a remission to $3\frac{1}{2}$ per cent, he said, could have 'but an infinitesimal effect'.[2]

Chitral. By 1893 a British agency was established at Gilgit in Kashmir territory, with an outpost in Chitral, on the extreme north-west frontier, between Kashmir and Afghanistan, and near the Russian border. The Mehtar (ruler) of Chitral was assassinated in January 1895. Robertson, the British agent at Gilgit, was besieged in Chitral by the rebellious chiefs. These troubles forced Elgin to change his mind about the wisdom of a policy, already planned, of withdrawal from Chitral. The Dir road would have to be opened permanently and guarded by levies along its whole length, as in Khyber. This would enable Chitral to be held cheaply and Gilgit garrison to be greatly reduced. Elgin's decision was of some historical importance, as has been pointed out by Dr Alder: 'Behind this important change of view lay some fundamental and, it must be admitted, long overdue re-thinking of the whole strategic problem of the Northern frontier.' It recognised as fallacious the defensive scheme which, based on Gilgit to the east, was intended for the defence of Chitral, 220 miles to the west, reachable in only five months of the year by a bad road, a pass of 12,000 feet, and a dangerous defile. Elgin recognised that the defensive centre of gravity on the northern frontier lay in Chitral and not at

[1] Ibid. 13/13, 25 Jan 95.   [2] Ibid. 18 Dec 95; and 14/9, 5 Feb 96.

Gilgit. Essentially the settlement he arrived at was one which remained unchanged. By 1895 a measure of frontier stability was achieved after a search of thirty years' duration, and it lasted until 1947.[1]

Elgin had hoped that by establishing a right of access from Peshawar they might give the death-blow to the intrigues of the Amir of Afghanistan in these mountainous regions, and effectively limit his sphere of influence.[2] Although he felt that in the unlikely event of a Russian advance on India, Britain could seize the necessary points of vantage first, mild Russophobia was involved in his anxiety about the stability of Afghanistan in the face of 'the Russian bogey'.[3] If withdrawal from Chitral took place, and British India were to 'await Russia on the Indus', Elgin believed that the whole frontier would be in a blaze. Moreover, there were obligations beyond the line of the frontier on the map, resulting from Lytton's virtual guarantee to Kashmir in 1876 of its suzerainty over Chitral, and from the Durand treaty. The implication of the Durand convention was that the tribes between the frontier and Afghanistan were in the British sphere of influence. These obligations might be regretted, but Britain could not afford 'in dealing with these Oriental peoples', to let it be thought that she was unable or unwilling to observe them. He hesitated to use the word prestige, but it really did count for a good deal, he thought. If it were damaged by a withdrawal from Chitral, it was by no means certain where the mischief would stop.[4]

Elgin's argument was not accepted by the Liberal cabinet (now led by Rosebery), who had commissioned him. Perhaps they thought it too much influenced by the forward policy of his military advisers. Elgin's disappointment was soon followed by Rosebery's fall from power. Extraordinarily enough, the

[1] G. J. Alder, *British India's Northern Frontier 1865-95* (1963), pp. 286-98.
[2] VRP. 13/38, 13 Mar 95.
[3] Ibid. 69 and 48, 24 Apr and 10 Apr 95.
[4] VRP. 30/51-3, E to prime minister Rosebery, 7 Jul 95; this letter is reprinted, except for its final paragraph, in C. H. Philips (ed.), *The evolution of India and Pakistan 1858-1947* (1962), pp. 464-6; see also VRP. 13/48-51, E to S/S Fowler 10 Apr 95.

new Unionist government of 1895 decided to reverse the decision of their predecessors to withdraw from Chitral, and to uphold the view of the Liberal viceroy whom the Liberal government had overruled. This reconsideration of cabinet policy took place in August 1895. In a debate on the subject in October 1895, the former ministers were hotly on the defensive. Fowler, the former Liberal secretary of state for India, alleged that Elgin's recommendations had been rejected by the Liberals because of promises made 'in an opposite direction'. This assertion rested upon an unfair interpretation of a proclamation issued in March 1895 promising certain tribes that their territory would not be occupied. This promise was, however, confined to the Swatis and Bajauris who were not partisans of Umra Khan, the tribal chief who had invaded Chitral. Fowler had never made this point in official correspondence.[1] Two years later the Liberal Opposition returned to the charge that Elgin's policy contradicted promises that Chitral would not be occupied. The phrase then used by the Liberals, 'Lord Elgin's breach of faith', was paraded in Reuter's telegrams throughout the world. Elgin resented this intensely,[2] as he had every right to. It was a misrepresentation. The Indian tribes who were concerned never themselves complained of any breach of faith.[3]

Policy towards the tribes. An agreement had been signed with the Amir of Afghanistan in November 1893, delimiting his frontier from the tribes of Waziristan, to which region the Amir

[1] VRP. 13/133–4, E to S/S Hamilton, 2 Oct 95.

[2] VRP. 14/162–3, 28 Oct 97; 192, 2 Dec 97. 'A viceroy is of course fair game and an excellent person to attack. As a rule he cannot defend himself without indiscretion, and assailants in England no doubt count on his being at a distance, which makes a prompt refutation of falsehoods or misrepresentations out of the question. I do not think that the position of "Aunt Sally" annoys me more than most men; but I must honestly confess I did not expect to see my former friends on the front bench again entering the booth with the very battered bludgeon labelled "Chitral breach of faith". . . .'

[3] Elgin's experience in the Chitral affair was to have influence on his attitude to Lugard (see p. 208), and to Selborne: having himself been overruled, he was the better able to understand how Selborne must have felt in being overruled on Transvaal policy (EP, E to Selborne 6 Sep 06).

relinquished his claims. The boundary between the Amir and the government of India was worked out by a commission in 1895 and 1896. Frequent raids and outrages took place. It was extremely difficult to get reparations. In existing conditions it was absolutely impossible for the Waziristani headmen to coerce their recalcitrant tribesmen. Elgin concluded that the policy of controlling them entirely from outside by tribal subsidies and levy-posts, without military backing, had failed. In July 1894, therefore, he proposed that there should be a permanent garrison and a political officer appointed to explain to the tribes the reasons for the work of the boundary delimitation commission. He was strongly opposed to punitive expeditions. His reflections upon this subject were to be re-stated when, as colonial secretary, he was confronted with the problems of pacifying West Africa:

I detest the idea of punitive expeditions. Undoubtedly we get in this way the least possible return for our money. Even the moral effect of which one hears so much, is a gradually vanishing quantity; but this is the smallest of the objections. Because we cannot catch a robber or a murderer, we march through a whole country, burn villages and destroy crops and march out again, leaving ruin behind, having killed a number of innocent people and, as likely as not, left the guilty untouched.

He was well aware that it was necessary in all government to use measures against which 'our feelings of humanity rebel'. He did not mean that he would never authorise a punitive expedition, but he would only do so as a last resort; he would not subscribe to a policy which included them as a probability.[1]

Since Britain had established with Russia and Afghanistan boundaries beyond which the tribes should not pass, Elgin realised that Britain must improve the condition of the tribes. He would not intrude British influence ostentatiously. He adhered to the classical theory of informal control through indigenous collaborators:

[1] VRP. 12/60, E to S/S Fowler 10 Jul 94; see also Edith Fowler, *Life of H. H. Fowler, first viscount Wolverhampton* (1912), pp. 356–63.

I see no reason whatever why all that is necessary should not be done without undertaking local government or any definite control beyond a general keeping of the peace . . . their form of society does not give sufficient protection. What we should give would be that protection; and we should have all the well-disposed with us, who would be able, if backed, to deal with disorder under their own laws and customs.[1]

There can be no doubt that Elgin thought of himself as engineering a change in frontier and tribal policy of some significance. Both in Chitral and Waziristan the same experiment, essentially, was attempted. In Elgin's own words:[2]

We have gone into the tribal country, not as of old to punish by fire and sword and come away again, but offering an amicable settlement on the conditions which we thought the necessities of the case required. We have gone in such strength that the tribes recognised the impossibility of resistance; we have kept our troops thoroughly in hand, so that no fresh feelings of resentment or injury have been excited; and we have offered terms so clearly preserving autonomy and in other respects so liberal, that self-interest, the most powerful motive for a Pathan, was at once enlisted on our side; and we have then retired, in strict accordance with our proclaimed intentions, in both cases without a shot fired at our retreating troops, in both cases followed by petitions from the tribesmen that we would allow them to remain.

This was the early Victorian theory of the regenerative power of enlightened self-interest, brought up to date by the substitution of persuasive for coercive methods. There was to be no interference with tribal customs in Waziristan. If the opening up of certain routes and the prevention of outrages made some administrative interference necessary, then Elgin proposed to use 'the laws of the people and not our own'. If the rulers would not co-operate in 'putting the tribal machinery in motion' to deal with outrages, and if eventually this involved going into the country once more,

[1] VRP. 13/74, 8 May 95. [2] Ibid. 152–3, 29 Oct 95.

we ought to go in force, to abstain as much as possible from hostile acts and the idea of punishment, and to aim at consolidating and strengthening native authorities in alliance with us, rather than at superseding it.[1]

From these remarks, it is clear that Elgin, just as much as Lugard, came to apply a policy of ruling through chiefs in Africa on the basis of Indian experience.

Elgin admitted that the tribes in fact disliked certain features of British rule, especially court fees and land revenue, and probably would continue to do so for many years to come.

But . . . they are the means which the more civilised portion of mankind universally adopt for the regulation of their affairs; and their presence or absence indicates the stage which the community has reached in its progress towards civilisation . . . the premature introduction of the adjuncts of the more advanced stages of civilisation is unwise, but I confess I am sanguine enough to believe that the time will come when it may be desirable to substitute even the pleader in tribal territory for the Pathan knife, as, on the whole, the better instrument for securing the ends of justice.

His idea, therefore, was that anything by which they could encourage the outward flow of civilising influences must ultimately make for permanent peace:

I hold that the forces of civilisation are even now beginning to penetrate into the Hills; and that if we do not unduly check them, the gradual extension of our institutions will come, and may be brought about for the benefit of the weak rather than the strong, as an act of incorporation rather than annexation.[2]

Such optimism can only appear to us excessive. Too many of his contemporaries held similar views for us to call them old-fashioned. The persistence of early and mid-Victorian doctrines about the automatic progress of civilisation, in the face of what one would have thought conclusive evidence to the contrary, is remarkable.[3]

[1] VRP. 13/152–4, 29 Oct 95.   [2] VRP. 16/153–4, 22 Sep 98.
[3] Elgin's policy and guiding principles were adopted by Curzon, and reaffirmed in 1904: there was to be no extension in tribal country and no interference whatever

Indian nationalism: the press and Congress. Elgin's appraisal of Indian nationalism was a little more sympathetic than the assessments made both by earlier viceroys and by Curzon, his successor. This did not pass unnoticed at the time. The journal *India* wrote at the beginning of 1896 that there was good reason to believe the government of India to be adopting a more friendly and sensible attitude.[1] Elgin was not afraid of Congress, but even anxious to encourage it, and to cultivate friendly relations. He spoke in 1894 of holding the scales as evenly as possible between the Bombay government and their Indian critics in Poona.[2]

The Madras Congress sought to take advantage of the more liberal attitude, and requested Elgin to receive a deputation. Congress had never asked such a favour before. Elgin refused their request, not from any aversion to Congress, its methods or motives, but on the ground that it was 'entirely contrary to precedent', and might give colour 'to the assertion that I wished to dissociate myself from my predecessors'.[3] He did not, as others in his position might, refuse on grounds of the insufficient standing of Congress, but on grounds of a prior political loyalty to the British ruling *élite*.

Elgin understood that Indian politicians were bound to use 'a little spicy language', but he did not think that they meant

---

with the tribes if it could possibly be avoided. The Liberal government after December 1905 adhered to this policy, as Elgin declared in 1908, after the cabinet approved an expedition against the Zakka Khels, a tribe of raiding and aggressive Pathans (CAB. 41/31/41, 10 Feb 08). In defending government policy on this occasion, Elgin repeated his view that 'Even without operations for containing territories, we may do a good deal, by helping the promotion of trade and communications, to bring the people to a state of mind and body in which they will not be so liable to make sudden attacks on our posts and garrisons' (PD. 184/1728–1730, 26 Feb 08). Optimism did not solve the problem of the north-west frontier. In the 1930s Waziristan was the main trouble-spot on the north-west frontier; the tribes were still nomadic, truculent and prone to violence on a major scale. The conventional methods of settlement and control failed consistently when applied to them. A costly and protracted campaign was launched in 1936 to subdue widespread unrest (J. Connell, *Auchinleck, a biography* (1959), p. 66).

[1] H. L. Singh, *Problems and policies of the British in India*, p. 241.
[2] Gopal, *British policy in India*, p. 203.
[3] VRP. 13/10–11, 16 Jan 95.

to be offensive or disloyal. Some of the Congress leaders were on the imperial or provincial councils; this, he thought, was the right place for them. Not because they had much claim to representative character, but because 'they are men of intelligence and can do good work when they are not led away by the temptations of irresponsible oratory.'[1] No responsible person, he said, would propose the prohibition of Congress, even though it was 'a red rag' to many Anglo-Indians and it not infrequently trespassed on the borderland 'of what is permissible'.[2] Elgin refused to declare war on the press.[3] Talk was not in itself dangerous, and an extreme dislike of the 'agitator' could look a little ridiculous.[4]

Elgin kept his sense of proportion. He penetrated to the fundamentally moderate nature of the early Congress movement. He encouraged the Conservative and Unionist secretary of state for India, Lord George Hamilton, to take a less gloomy prospect of the future. Elgin took a broad-minded view of advanced Indian politicians who sat on the councils which had been reformed in 1892. These men were anathema to civil servants who had grown old in the traditions of the service, but as far as Elgin was concerned, he hoped that they would appear on the councils for Burma and the Punjab which he was establishing:

if these men do not find their way in by election, I should like to nominate them. . . . They are compelled, in order to justify themselves with their supporters, to speak out, and to show their hand; and that is exactly the sort of information that otherwise in India it is so difficult to get at. If excluded, we do not shut their mouths . . .[5]

Indians were perhaps a little disappointed that Elgin's viceroyalty did not bring more dramatic political advance. In reality the time was not ripe. It was only in 1892 that the Indian Councils Act had been passed, and its principles were still being worked out in practice. Elgin merely, as he said,

[1] VRP. 15/63, 21 Apr 97. [2] VRP. 15/App. 67, 27 Jul 97.
[3] VRP. 15/App. 94, 7 Sep 97. [4] VRP. 15/125–6, 25 Aug 96.
[5] Ibid.

brought 'history up to date' by extending to Burma and the Punjab[1] the principle of provincial councils; he recommended following through the idea of decentralisation so as to reduce restrictions on the conduct of local legislation in the more advanced provinces.[2]

Railways. Of the 25,000 miles of railway track in India in 1900, something like one fifth had been constructed or planned in Elgin's viceroyalty.[3] In his opinion, nothing in the past thirty years had so materially affected and improved the condition of the Indian people, and nothing would do so much in the next thirty, as the extension of railways.[4] His knowledge of railways was a very useful asset in a viceroy, as it was also to be in a colonial secretary.[5] He considered that the greatest improvement achieved in his term as viceroy was in the planning of railways.

After his arrival in India, and casting an experienced eye on the railways department, he had very soon come to the conclusion that it was not working smoothly. The delays were intense, and almost fatal to the introduction of private enterprise.[6] 'If there are difficulties ahead, where can we look for additional revenue except to the increase in the general prosperity of the country, to secure which the further construction of railways is essential?' Hamilton, the secretary of state, completely agreed.[7]

Elgin instituted a system under which schemes were approved and sanctioned 'with the express object of avoiding hasty and

[1] VRP. 14/126, 25 Aug 96.

[2] Ibid. 143–4, 23 Sep 96. In general my discussion in this section on Indian nationalism is closely parallel to that of Singh, *Problems and policies*, pp. 130–1, 246–50.

[3] About 3000 miles were constructed, 3000 more sanctioned; the total completed when he left India was 22,000 (VRP. 88/480).

[4] VRP. 88/155, speech, 25 Oct 95.

[5] 'I have never known any class of questions to which a man without technical knowledge is more hopelessly at sea than those presented by engineering and railway management' (Sir Charles Eliot, *East Africa Protectorate* (1905), p. 215); VRP. 15/132, 4 Aug 07.

[6] VRP. 12/26a, 17 Apr 94.

[7] VRP. 14/17, 19 Feb 96.

rash decisions and yet of giving a definite reply to all applications within a reasonable time'.[1] The management of the
railways should be improved by entrusting the working to
substantial companies. He wanted to get rid of promoters, who
he thought had caused untold trouble and confusion, and get
nearer to the *bona fide* investor.[2] Private enterprise should be
encouraged by putting out to tender the construction of
planned lines. A few schemes deliberately put forward on
government authority, taken up by responsible businessmen,
and carried out successfully, would do more than anything
else, he thought, to encourage the flow of private capital to
India. He introduced such measures as he could to make the
construction of new lines less hedged with complications.[3]

Famine and plague. As if there had not been troubles enough,
Elgin's viceroyalty was marked by widespread famine after the
failure of the rains in 1896. Plague made its appearance in 1896
in Bombay and spread with alarming rapidity. The famine of
1896–7 proved to be one of the worst of the century. The loss of
food crops was estimated at 18 to 19 million tons. Three-
quarters of a million people died. As soon as the stress of famine
relief was over, a commission of engineering and medical experts
was set up by Elgin to ascertain the points in which the system
needed modification, and to formulate other lessons which had
been learned. The commission of 1898 reported that the success
actually attained in the relief of distress and the saving of
human life was, 'if not complete, far greater than any that has
been recorded in famines that are at all comparable to it in
extent, severity and duration'. The cost of relief measures was
remarkably moderate.[4] Although Elgin probably at first underestimated the magnitude of the trouble, he responded to its full
challenge effectively. The administration of charitable relief
funds was most carefully organised, and relief given to more

[1] VRP. 88/494.
[2] VRP. 84/31/ii/6, E to Sir Charles Crosthwaite, 19 Feb 96.
[3] Railway minute, VRP. 84/132b.
[4] L. C. A. Knowles, *The economic development of the British overseas Empire* (1924),
p. 361.

than four million people. Elgin's energetic railway policy provided a contribution to a more long-term solution of the famine problem. The recuperation of the famine-stricken areas by the time of his departure was remarkable.[1] His famine organisation gave the government confidence for the future.[2] Dufferin, ex-viceroy, complimented Elgin on the way he dealt with the famine and saved so many millions of lives; it was 'one of the most remarkable achievements' of British rule in India.[3]

After the famine had been attended to deftly, the government was confronted with an outbreak of plague. The problems presented by methods of control and the prevention of the disease were less familiar than those involved in famine administration, but here too the difficulties were met by Elgin and his government with resourcefulness.[4] The secretary of state praised the vigour and wide scope of his preventive measures, his tact in applying new powers of inspection in the face of religious objection.[5]

Assessment. Elgin's rule was, more than any other in the half century after the Indian mutiny, disturbed by shocks and misfortunes of divers kinds. Difficulties taxed every branch of Indian administration. Without resort to heroics, Elgin surmounted all the successive and manifold challenges. Some mistakes were made. Maybe he did not always press his views as forcefully as he might have done. It may be conceded that in his first year of office his grip was not as firm as it later became.[6]

Elgin was not bound by his civil service, and thought out things for himself.[7] He was well regarded both in India and in England. As far as opinion at the Indian end is concerned, the

---

[1] *Quarterly Review*, vol. 189 (1899), 325–7, 'India under Lord Elgin'.
[2] VRP. 15/ii/23–4, Hamilton to E 19 Feb 97.
[3] VRP. 33/App. 1, Dufferin to E 6 Jan 98.
[4] *The Times*, 19 Jan 17, p. 31, obituary of E.
[5] VRP. 15/ii/32 Hamilton to E 12 Mar 97.
[6] P. E. Roberts, *A historical geography of the British dependencies*, ed. C. P. Lucas vol. 7, *India*, pt. 2 (1920), 501–2.
[7] *Quarterly Review*, vol. 189, 313–36.

commander-in-chief of the army, Sir George White, may be cited. He took a 'strong liking' to Elgin, describing him as 'very industrious and capable, and I believe, thoroughly honest and public spirited'. Just before the end of their connection, he wrote of his regard for Elgin – 'straight, clever and considerate'.[1]

The letters of the Unionist secretary of state for India, Lord George Hamilton, abound in congratulations to Elgin both on particular and on general points.[2] He admired the 'personal ability and courage' which Elgin had shown throughout five years of 'hard and successful government'. The Queen had written to him appreciatively of Elgin, of his quiet and effective management. Hamilton considered that this reflected the universal feeling.[3] Even the Prince of Wales went out of his way to make complimentary remarks, which Hamilton felt all the more significant 'as he does not often speak of the serious side of politics'.[4] The prospect of a new viceroy was one which Hamilton contemplated with dislike and regret:

there has been, although I did not know you personally, from the first, an ingrained feeling of confidence in your judgment and action that has, during the more troublous periods of this year, been of great solace. Confidence is a plant of slow growth, and without flattery, I do not think I shall find easily another viceroy who will give to us all the same sense of security and strength. What I am writing is felt by all inside this Office, by my colleagues and notably by the prime minister, who expressed himself very strongly as to your conduct and management of recent difficulties.[5]

There were many who thought that search might be made for a successor with characteristics similar to those which had served Elgin so well.[6] But when the prime minister chose flamboyance

---

[1] Sir Mortimer Durand, *The Life of Sir George White* (1915), pp. 435–6.
[2] For example, Hamilton paid tribute to the value of the material collected and considered by Elgin concerning the grave problem of agricultural indebtedness, one of the most difficult and complicated questions of the day.
[3] VRP. Hamilton to E 15/ii/101, 17 Dec 97 and App. 73, 28 Oct 97.
[4] VRP. Hamilton to E 16/ii/App. 48, 22 Apr 98.
[5] Ibid. 15/App. 98, 23 Dec 97.
[6] Earl of Ronaldshay, *The Life of Lord Curzon* (1923), i, 293.

in the person of George Nathaniel Curzon, instead of Lord Balfour of Burleigh, Hamilton hoped that Curzon would at least seek Elgin's opinion on many matters, for, in his assessment, Elgin had safely steered India through the most serious crises of the last thirty years, and could speak not only with authority, but with a success behind him 'such as no viceroy of modern days can command'.[1]

On his return to England, Elgin was fêted by the Northbrook Society. At this occasion, Rosebery recalled Elgin's 'rooted objections' to believing that there was in him a potentially great viceroy of India, remarking upon the 'diffidence in his own powers which is his only drawback'. He trusted that his residence in India had completely cured the defect.[2]

Elgin had indeed enjoyed his work.[3] A man could not, he said, lay down the viceroyalty without feeling that he had lived the best part of his life. A sense of anticlimax, even of unreality, did perhaps afflict him thereafter. He never seemed so happy at the colonial office, where he was pitched more into the cut and thrust of political exchange. He found the loneliness and isolation of his position in India quite different from anything which could be experienced in England.[4] This did not worry a man of his temperament in the least.

Ex-viceroy. Five years of ruling India qualified Elgin practically as an elder statesman. As was only to be expected, he became in demand for impartial exercises at the highest level of state. His first appointment as ex-viceroy was as chairman of the strong Royal Commission appointed in September 1902 to inquire into the military preparations for the South African War, and into

[1] VRP. Hamilton to E 16/76, 14 Sep 98.

[2] Quoted by *The Times*, 19 Jan 1917, p. 31, obituary notice.

[3] By the time he was firmly in the saddle, Elgin never doubted his ability to see the job through to its conclusion. The work never got him down, even after an illness: at the end of 1897 he wrote: 'The utmost I can say is that I think I am rather more easily tired by a long spell, especially of Council. But I shall last out my term all right' (VRP. 15/195, 16 Dec 97 and App. 135, 1 Dec 97).

[4] VRP. 16/217, 5 Jan 99; VRP. 88/424, speech 14 Oct 98. In Jun 07 he repeated his opinion that the viceroyalty, 'Whatever might befall him in life, must remain the greatest of his experiences.'

various logistical questions relating to its conduct. He carried through the inquiry with despatch and judgment. A unanimous and fairly drastic report was presented in July 1903. Its unanimity was one of the achievements of his life which he always recalled with the greatest satisfaction. Nor was the report on the whole ever seriously challenged, although the investigation was full of controversial matter. It contained one possibly classic sentence. The true lesson of the war was that 'No military system will be satisfactory which does not contain a power of expansion outside the limits of the Regular Forces of the Crown, whatever that limit might be'. This was the major observation of the report bearing upon the future. Methods of home defence were suggested which later became embodied in the system of territorial forces. Elgin supported Haldane's army reforms of 1907 as the first attempt to provide the expanded framework on which the organisation desired by the Commission could be built, especially by drawing on a reserve of military strength and turning it to account without converting it into a vast standing army.[1]

After this conspicuous success in committee chairmanship, he was called upon to solve the thorny problems arising out of the ecclesiastical crisis involving the Free Churches of Scotland.[2] In

[1] For an account of the work of the Commission see *C.H.B.E.*, iii, chap. 15, 'Imperial defence 1897–1914' by W. C. B. Tunstall; PD. 176/1266, 26 Jun 07.

[2] See the *Annual Register for 1904*, 235–8; *for 1905*, 189–91, 241–4; *for 1906*, 256–7; *for 1907*, 261–2; *for 1908*, 254. The Free Church of Scotland was a small minority group, mainly in the Highlands, who in 1900 opposed unsuccessfully the union of the body formerly bearing that name with the United Presbyterian Church to form a national Presbyterian body, the United Free Church; it was a fusion of funds under elastic formularies of belief. The dispute was over the transfer of funds and property to the new United Free Church. The Free Church of Scotland appealed to the House of Lords in two cases, on grounds that the United Free Church had departed from the original beliefs of the Free Church of Scotland; the House of Lords reversed the decision of the Scottish Court of Session. The commissioners were Elgin, Lord Kinnear and Sir Ralph Anstruther, Bt; their report, issued 19 Aug 05, recommended a commission constituted by act of parliament to make a division of funds. The original commissioners were then reinforced by two more. By 19 Oct 06, about 1000 congregations had their cases decided. The chief difficulty was that the Free Church of Scotland (the 'Wee Frees') was too small in numbers to sustain the task of carrying on the religious and missionary work appropriate to its funds; nevertheless, it was treated very liberally.

December 1904 he was made chairman of the important Royal Commission to take evidence and to divide property, as necessitated by the decision of the House of Lords in the unsuccessful appeal of the Free Church of Scotland against the union in 1900 of the two large non-established presbyterian bodies in Scotland. The recommendations of the commission were embodied in the Scottish Churches Act passed a few months later, in July 1905. Elgin then became chairman of a second commission, the Statutory Executive Commission, charged with giving detailed effect to the recommendations of the first. *The Times* later commented that it was a high testimony to his judgment and impartiality that in a dispute of peculiar bitterness and exceptional complication neither side seriously questioned or even criticised the decisions of the commission.[1] Work on this commission absorbed quite a deal of time while Elgin was colonial secretary.[2]

Elgin obviously had talent as a chairman and negotiator. One can imagine him at work: calm, quiet, not saying too much himself, showing that he understood and appreciated the necessities of others and was ready to satisfy them as far as he could, ensuring loyal teamwork.[3]

[1] *The Times*, 19 Jan 1917.

[2] For example, in April, June and October 1906, January and April 1907, the commission met in Edinburgh, sometimes two or three days in a week.

[3] Once reports were issued, Elgin never allowed himself to speak in public upon their interpretation: for single members of such commissions to arrogate such authority to themselves would be 'beside the mark' (PD. 176/1266, 26 Jun 07).

2 The Formation of the Liberal Ministry, December 1905

THE resignation of Mr Balfour's Unionist ministry was announced on 4 December 1905. Sir Henry Campbell-Bannerman, leader of the Liberal party since 1898, became prime minister on the next day. Lord Selborne, recently appointed high commissioner in South Africa, had begged Balfour to carry on until February or March of the following year, but to no purpose.[1] Balfour had resigned, rather than seek a dissolution of parliament. This meant that another ministry could be formed before a general election could be held. In this way he avoided the embarrassment of a Conservative and Unionist ministry being defeated at the polls, and he hoped to give the electors the policy of a Liberal government to attack. The procedure conceivably led to the formation of a more right-wing Liberal government than might have been the case if an election had preceded the formation of a ministry:[2] once free trade had been secured by an overwhelming electoral decision in its favour, Grey would almost certainly not have taken office.

Some of his colleagues urged Campbell-Bannerman to take up the challenge of forming a ministry after the resignation, but some did not. Herbert Gladstone disliked the idea of having 'to formulate a policy to the country without any knowledge of our strength'.[3] Bryce, Morley, Ripon and others advised accepting, lest Chamberlain or Rosebery should be

[1] Balfour papers 49721/231.
[2] J. E. Tyler, 'Campbell-Bannerman and the Liberal Imperialists 1906–1908', *History*, xxiii (1938), 257.
[3] CB. 41217/277.

36

asked to form a ministry instead, lest the Radicals be infuriated, lest the electors mock at any refusal to take power after all the clamour they had made against their opponents, lest the Tories taunt them with disunity. Campbell-Bannerman needed little persuading. He had always felt that refusal would be 'ascribed to divisions or to cowardice' and would disappoint party stalwarts.[1]

The formation of the Liberal ministry is chiefly interesting for an attempt by R. B. Haldane, H. H. Asquith and Sir Edward Grey ('the Liberal Imperialists') to force Campbell-Bannerman to take a peerage, so that he should not combine the premiership with the leadership of the House of Commons. Their pact is sometimes referred to as the Relugas compact, after the name of Grey's fishing lodge, at which they met to plan their strategy. King Edward VII was secretly aware of their plans. The three friends did not intend to join the ministry except on their own terms. In particular Grey wanted Asquith to lead the Commons, and Asquith wanted Haldane to have the Woolsack. Contrary to their expectations, Campbell-Bannerman was perfectly prepared to form his ministry without them. He could not be blackmailed, especially as his wife had firmly counselled 'no surrender' to the Liberal Imperialists. He was therefore able to form his ministry according to his own wishes; the three plotters capitulated in order to form as strong a defence of free trade as possible.[2] Grey became foreign secretary, Asquith chancellor of the exchequer, and Haldane secretary for war. Lord Ripon, formerly viceroy of India and colonial secretary 1892–5, became lord privy seal. John Morley took the India Office, James Bryce the Irish Office.

Like Disraeli, Campbell-Bannerman reached the top of the greasy pole too late. His energies were flagging, and his best work for the party was nearly over. He nursed a dying invalid

[1] CB. 41211/316, 41223/162–3, 172–5, 41225/65–8, 41220/194.
[2] All the biographers of the participants in this episode give accounts of it. Among the unpublished papers, the Asquith collection is probably the best place for studying it,

wife for the first eight months of his premiership, and never had a full night's sleep. After an interval of one month from her death, he himself became dogged with fatal illness. Despite these handicaps, he held his team together successfully, and attracted the affection and loyalty of an unusually clever cabinet. He was not an outstanding prime minister, but he was an adequate one, which is more than can be said for some of those who succeeded him in that office. His collected speeches make dull reading. Though well educated, he had little of the intellectual brilliance or reflectiveness of John Morley, little of the passion or perversity of Gladstone. His letters are more lively, being punctuated with a rather quaint style of humour and ingenious nicknames for his political acquaintances. His strength was an unquestioning and courageous faith in the inspiration of Gladstonian liberalism. This enabled him to preserve a singularly optimistic outlook on affairs, an outlook hardly characteristic of his colleagues. He rather cultivated the impression of being merely a worthy man of the second rank, a rough but amiable Scotsman. The impression of a simple geniality was but an item of his political equipment. In fact he could be intolerant of those he disliked; he was also a cosmopolitan, an epicure of the first rank, and a considerable humorist.[1] John Morley rightly described him as sagacious and experienced, 'cool, acute, straight, candid, attentive to affairs, considerate'.[2] He was skilful in the minor arts which disarm and conciliate. He was rather contemptuous of precedent, and irritated the court by his perfunctory reports upon cabinet meetings. Campbell-Bannerman was bored by the duty of writing to his sovereign. It was fortunate he was not serving Queen Victoria. Edward VII scarcely bothered to protest, because he liked Campbell-Bannerman personally, especially in comparison with Balfour, who was too intellectual to appeal to royalty.

The prime minister will not, however, figure very prominently in these pages. He was anxious to settle the South African problem, and keen to spread the panacea of self-government

[1] A. M. Gollin, *Proconsul in politics* (1964), p. 59.
[2] *Recollections* (1917), ii, 84, 143.

among white men. But he left the work of planning and drafting the Transvaal constitution to others, and in Asquith's words, 'never bothered his head about it'.[1] Then again, he was far too close to the personal tradition of Gladstone ever to be interested in India,[2] or the administration and development of the tropical dependencies of the empire. His interest in the orient did not in practice extend much further than alertness to the necessity of defending the Suez Canal from the encroachments of the Sultan of Turkey in the Sinai peninsula in 1906. As far as Africa was concerned, he seemed a bit doubtful about the wisdom of constructing a railway in Northern Nigeria.

It was clear from the start that Campbell-Bannerman would insist on giving Elgin high office, though there were many other claimants. He had known Elgin a long time, and recently had been impressed with Elgin's conduct of the inquiry into the Scottish ecclesiastical crisis.[3] In November 1905 he had been planning to make Elgin foreign secretary. Grey apparently had no objection to this. Asquith thought he had persuaded Campbell-Bannerman that Grey would be a better choice, and that Elgin would do well at the colonial office. When the new prime minister began cabinet-making in earnest, *The Times* declared that Elgin and Grey 'suggest themselves at once for the foreign and colonial secretaries, though the distribution may be left open'. No other Liberal, *The Times* added, was equipped to meet foreign statesmen and ambassadors on equal terms.[4] Characteristically, Elgin's ambitions did not run so high. He wanted the Scottish Office, because this would enable him to spend plenty of time at home with his ailing wife. His second choice would have been the war office, also a natural wish in view of his work for the South African War Inquiry. The Foreign Office was only third best to Elgin, and the colonial

[1] Asquith to J. A. Spender, 15 Jun 1912, quoted by B. B. Gilbert, *Historical Journal*, vol. x, no. 3 (1967), 458.

[2] It was said of Gladstone that the only Indian subject which warmed him to something like enthusiasm was the question how best Cook's tourists could be encouraged to travel there.

[3] J. A. Spender, *The Life of Sir Henry Campbell-Bannerman*, ii, 178. See also CB. 41225/36, 18 Jan 04.

[4] *The Times*, 7 and 8 Dec 05.

office less attractive still. The India office was never considered.[1]

The prime minister got in touch with Elgin on 6 December and asked to see him the next day, when he offered him the colonial office. Elgin accepted after some hesitation:

I have carefully considered the proposal which you made to me this morning. As I said then, so far as personal inclination and interests are concerned, I have no desire to seek office. But the nature of your proposal and the manner in which it was made, was such, that I am forced to the conclusion that I cannot allow personal considerations to prevail.

In common with several others, he had one reservation. It was about Ireland. He hoped that the problem would be allowed to sleep for a while, from a conviction that any renewal of Home Rule legislation, as it took shape in the past, or an alliance with an Irish party for that end, would be fatal to the usefulness of the Liberal party.[2] His chief personal anxiety was about his duties in the House of Lords, for he was quite unused to debating. 'I don't think that I am "afraid",' he wrote to Lady Elgin, 'but I am certainly uneasy – for it is all a very new experience – much more so than most people can realise'.[3] He took up office on 11 December.

Campbell-Bannerman may well have prided himself on this appointment. Elgin was well equipped by his previous experience to deal with colonial problems. If the problems of empire were those of estate management writ large, he came from the right background. In addition, he knew about India, and had plenty of experience of business and chairmanship. His very name would be a commendation to the Canadians and the South Africans, because his father had made responsible government in Canada a living reality. A peer as colonial secretary might be able to take colonial problems out of an embittered popular arena and lend a little more dignity to

---

[1] Ripon was, however, so impressed with a letter about India that he had received from Elgin, he sent it to Campbell-Bannerman, remarking: 'It is very clear and good' (CB. 41225/36, 18 Jan 04).

[2] CB. 41214/13–14, 7 Dec 05. [3] EP, 19 Feb 06.

imperial deliberations. Elgin was acceptable to the Unionists, and warmly welcomed by *The Times*, chiefly because his record was clear of partisan speeches. He had never joined in denunciations of Chinese Labour on the Rand, or made the sort of remark which offended 'our brethren beyond the seas'. *The Times* described him as a statesman, 'a man of high position who has filled the great place of Viceroy of India, besides doing much good work at home'. The most satisfactory appointments in the new cabinet, said *The Times*, were to the foreign office and the colonial office.[1] Elgin's presence in the cabinet also gave reassurance to the civil servants who had known his work in India.[2]

It certainly could not be argued that Elgin began work with any ineradicable prejudice against him. Haldane defended him against possible detractors. He admitted that Elgin was likely to make an unfavourable impact on people meeting him for the first time, but he had qualities of shrewdness, ability, grasp of his own subject and tenacity of will, which made him, Haldane thought, a far more serious man, and likely to be a much better colonial secretary, than Lyttelton, from whom Elgin took over.[3]

Campbell-Bannerman apparently offered the financial secretaryship of the treasury and the under-secretaryship at the colonial office to Reginald McKenna and Winston Churchill, leaving the two of them to decide who should take which.[4] The treasury appointment on paper looked the more important, but whereas Churchill knew little about finance, he had experience of South Africa which was obviously going to be useful, and so he opted for the colonial office. Maybe he also

[1] *The Times*, 11 Dec 05. These editorial views contrast strangely with the reaction ascribed by Dame Margery Perham to Flora Lugard, a prominent member of the staff: 'Elgin! The very name gave her a shock from its very lack of significance' (*Lugard*, ii, *The years of authority* (1960), p. 237; see also p. 279, and compare with pp. 241–2).

[2] Sir Arthur Godley of the India Office had 'such a high opinion of his good sense and judgment that I am always ready to take my hat off to him' (Minto papers [National Library of Scotland], M. 1005/24). Sir Almeric Fitzroy, clerk to the privy council, wrote that with Grey, Haldane and Elgin 'the principal places will not be badly filled' (*Memoirs*, p. 272). Hugh Gunn, of the educational department, Bloemfontein wrote to B. Holland: 'I have confidence in Lord Elgin's exceptional experience and breadth of mind' (EP, 16 Jul 06).

[3] M. Perham, *Lugard*, ii, 241.   [4] Spender, *Life, journalism and politics*, i, 162.

calculated that with Elgin in the House of Lords, the colonial office offered a clear field for the exposition of government policy in the House of Commons. Elgin was not very enthusiastic about the appointment. A certain notoriety clung to Churchill. After all, he showed renegade tendencies towards the ruling class into which he had been born. According to the standards of the men who were to be his colleagues, he had been very inadequately educated: it was a surprise to him to be told that Aristotle had anticipated some of his ideas. Blenheim, Harrow and Sandhurst had not tamed him. Although only just thirty-one years old, and as yet totally untried in government, Winston Churchill was far from being unknown, and he was no greenhorn. By this time, he had seen fighting in three continents, and he had a larger experience of wars than any man of his years. He had been in Cuba, the Sudan and South Africa. He had visited America in 1901. He had been in the Indian army for three years, whilst Elgin was viceroy; they met once. The first biography of Churchill had already appeared.[1] He himself had written more books than any soldier living, including a novel, and a book on the Malakand field-force which was spoken of as 'a subaltern's hints to generals'. His public criticisms of Kitchener and the Unionist secretary of state for war had been fearless, even impudent. He had stood up to Joe Chamberlain, and rivalled Balfour in subtlety. Lord Randolph Churchill, his father, had not been popular in British politics, and Winston was known to follow the patterns of his father's thought and action. He had already published a long and remarkably scholarly biography of his father,[2] a work which enabled him to hold his own in a generation of gifted biographer-politicians. Elgin realised that this formidable, swashbuckling tyro would be difficult to manage, but accepted him with good grace.[3]

Unabashed confidence, unsquashable resilience, push, dash,

---

[1] A. MacCallum Scott, *Winston Spencer Churchill* (1905), Methuen, 266 pp. 'Already he has won for himself a foremost place among the politicians of the day' and was 'confidently spoken of by his admirers as a future prime minister.' (p. 1).

[2] WSC, *Lord Randolph Churchill* (1905).

[3] EP, to Crewe, 7 May 1908.

flair, contempt for humdrum conformity – so Baroness Asquith summed him up.[1] He had courage, originality, magnetism. A statesman sprang instantaneously to life, fully developed and mature, from the equivocal personality of Winston Churchill, soldier, journalist and politician, in December 1905. From the first he cultivated the attributes of an elder statesman. He even began writing minutes on the colonial office files in red ink, a privilege hitherto arrogated to himself only by a full secretary of state, or by the archbishop of the Autocephalic Church of Cyprus.[2]

Nevertheless, Churchill had been lucky to obtain office. He had been a member of parliament only since 1901, and a Liberal for an even shorter period. His transition from a protectionist Conservative and Unionist to a free trade Liberal in 1904 had lost him friends on one side of politics without gaining him many on the other. The Tories ostracised him for shamelessly pursuing power. His new colleagues did not trust the genuineness of his Liberal conversion – one spoke a year or two later of the 'aboriginal and unchangeable Tory in him'. Campbell-Bannerman was fully alive to his faults ('a young man in a hurry'), and kept him out of the cabinet during his lifetime – 'very recent convert, hardly justifying cabinet rise'.[3]

At the general election in January 1906 Churchill was returned as a Liberal for north-west Manchester, and thereafter settled down to his departmental work with energetic enthusiasm. It is sometimes said of Churchill that he suffered all his life from never having been controlled or guided or disciplined by older and more experienced colleagues.[4] This is to overlook

---

[1] Violet Bonham Carter, *Winston Churchill as I knew him* (1965), p. 15.

[2] C. Parkinson, *The Colonial Office from within, 1909–45* (1947), p. 29.

[3] It is almost unbelievable, but Churchill was considered for the Board of Education in December 1906. Campbell-Bannerman decided against the appointment on the grounds that he ought to stay where he was, especially as much was happening in the colonial office, that he was a recent convert, and that he would be quite unsuitable for the delicate business of the Education office (Asq. 10/222, CB to Asquith, 5 Jan 07). See also EP, E to Lady E, 23 Aug 07, and M. V. Brett (ed.), *Journals and Letters of Reginald, Viscount Esher*, ii, 1903–10 (1934), 215–16.

[4] E.g. Lord Beaverbrook, *Politicians and the war, 1914–16*, p. 234.

the contribution Elgin made to Churchill's development. The relationship between these two was significant for Churchill because it was the only one in his political career in which Churchill experienced a restraining hand from above.

3 The Liberal Ministry and the Empire

M OST Liberal ministers believed generally in the desirability of maintaining, as far as possible, continuity of external policy through changes of government. By 1905 a 'bi-partisan' foreign policy was virtually established. Shortly before the new Liberal government took office in December 1905, Sir Edward Grey emphasised the need for continuity of foreign policy. He would not say that they were always bound at all costs to advocate continuity, but at that time he thought it important to adhere to the principle, if only to reassure foreign governments that Britain was a trustworthy and reliable friend.[1] Shortly after taking office, Sir Henry Campbell-Bannerman emphatically reaffirmed his adhesion to the policy of the Entente Cordiale.[2] Despite his dislike of some features of Unionist foreign policy, particularly the renewed Anglo-Japanese Alliance (a dislike shared by Ripon and Morley),[3] no fundamental changes occurred during his ministry. Indeed the Liberal government actually extended the principles laid down by their predecessors and soon began working for an agreement with Russia, to the disgust of their Radical supporters. The prime minister also accepted the non-party status of Indian questions,[4] and the new secretary of state for India, John Morley, refused to reconsider the recent partition of Bengal. Although he thought it a 'sad mistake',[5] and although

[1] Sir E. Grey, *Speeches on Foreign Affairs 1904–1914*, ed. P. Knaplund (1931), p. 31. Once in office he did indeed take the principle seriously.
[2] Sir H. Campbell-Bannerman, *Speeches 1899–1908*, selected and reprinted from *The Times*, p. 179, 21 Dec 05.
[3] CB. 41225/43 and 52; MM. 1/274.   [4] Campbell-Bannerman, *Speeches*, p. 177.
[5] MM. 1/163, 6 Aug 06.

some of his colleagues thought that it should have been reversed, he proceeded on the assumption that it was 'a settled fact'.[1]

The contrast with colonial policy is striking, and was the subject of frequent comment at the time. As Churchill observed, although the questions with which the colonial office dealt were perhaps almost as critical as those with which the foreign office was concerned, it stood at the centre of the fiercest partisanship and controversy in 1905/6.[2] It was generally expected that the new government would introduce changes in South African policy. When the first of these was announced, the government was challenged for infringing the principle of continuity. In reply to Unionist critics, government spokesmen paid at least lip service to the principle even in colonial policy. They would not make changes merely for the sake of change, and they admitted that it might be desirable to some extent to continue a policy they believed wrong, but they would not bind themselves to continue any policy without consideration. To deny an incoming government a free hand would, they said, be destructive of the proper management of the nation's affairs. Unionists could not hope to secure continuity if, in declaring their policy whilst in power, they 'stood to the ultimate end of their extreme rights' and used the whole weight of their majority to crush all protest against their policy.[3]

There had been some difference of opinion among Liberal leaders about the extent of possible continuity in South African policy. For some years Haldane had been anxious that the Unionists should follow a policy which Liberals could continue absolutely.[4] Campbell-Bannerman was much less worried about maintaining continuity. Morley told Haldane in 1902 that he was not sure whether Campbell-Bannerman appreciated as much as he did the necessity for continuity in South African policy.[5] The 'Liberal Imperialist' wing of the party, led by

---

[1] PD. 152/844, 26 Feb 06.
[2] PD. 154/496, 21 Mar 06; see also Lansdowne, PD. 152/41, 19 Feb. 06.
[3] PD. 152/167, CB 19 Feb 06; PD. 152/940, Loreburn, 27 Feb 06.
[4] C. Headlam, ed., *The Milner Papers – South Africa 1897–1905* (1933), ii, 187; Haldane to Milner, 31 Mar 01.
[5] F. Maurice, *Haldane* (1937), i, 119; Haldane to Rosebery Aug 02.

Haldane, Asquith and Grey, was not so critical of Unionist policy as the Gladstonian wing, and therefore found it easier to accept the idea of continuity in colonial affairs. Nevertheless, the division of the Liberals into two wings appears to have almost no bearing on the formulation of the imperial policy of the government.[1] The Gladstonians never admitted that there was any real difference of opinion between the two wings about the empire. It was as 'imperialists' that they condemned the South African war, just as it was as 'imperialists' that they advocated Home Rule for Ireland. They condemned the former because it weakened the empire; they advocated the latter because it would strengthen it. Campbell-Bannerman had no objection to the views of the 'Liberal Imperialists'; indeed so far as those opinions were not coloured by what he called 'extraneous sympathies', he felt that he shared them. Hence he and his friends tended to dismiss the attitude of the 'Imperialists' as purely personal and self-interested in character.[2] The Haldane-Asquith-Grey pact had not been motivated by doubts about the soundness of Campbell-Bannerman's imperialism, but by doubts about his qualities of leadership, about his strength and decisiveness of character. They were more concerned with foreign policy and defence than imperial policy. The new cabinet met for the first time on 14 December, and soon found itself unexpectedly harmonious. Apprehensions about the prime minister's capabilities were rapidly dispelled. Neither Haldane at the war office, nor Grey at the foreign office had much time for South African affairs, which dominated the first year. Of the 'Liberal Imperialists' only Asquith served on the cabinet committees to deal with South African problems, and he had perhaps always been closer to Campbell-Bannerman than the other members of his group.

Most of January 1906 was taken up with the general election. No full statement of government policy was made until the King's Speech at the beginning of the new parliament on 19 February 1906. Election speeches did not throw much light on

[1] Haldane spoke of full co-operation (*Autobiography* (1929), p. 139).
[2] CB. 41211/193, 206, 41218/17.

47

Liberal attitudes towards imperial problems, apart from Chinese Labour. 'Free trade versus protection' was the main issue of the election. 'Chinese slavery on the Rand' was the second main Liberal party cry. The issues had been forecast by Churchill in 1904 in describing Unionist policy as 'dear food for the millions, cheap labour for the millionaire'. The importation of Chinese Labour to work the Rand mines was seen rather as a labour question than an African or imperial one.[1] From the point of view of the underlying attitudes which the election revealed towards African and imperial problems, perhaps the most striking feature was the denunciation of capitalists. The real foundation for the cry of 'Chinese slavery' seems to have been the feeling of resentment in Britain that the Transvaal mine-owners had been permitted by the Unionist government to import an unfree form of labour over which they had complete control, and the disappointment born of this result of the South African war, which had cost Britain so dear.[2] Protection was denounced as 'a sop to capitalists' – only capitalists would make anything out of it.[3] In his election address, Herbert Gladstone, the home secretary, described the South African gold companies as 'the favoured class to whom has been given the privilege of cheap Chinese labour', which he had always opposed. He hoped that in a very short time power would be given to the people of the Transvaal to deal with the matter themselves.[4] But Chinese Labour was not mentioned in Haldane's election address,[5] and he had abstained from voting in the division on Chinese Labour on 21 March 1904. His view was: 'there have been abuses in the compounds of the Rand which can and must be remedied, but these abuses are being grossly exaggerated by our people for party ends'.[6] It is true that the excesses of the

[1] Morley noted the strength '– I might say the violence – of the currents now racing in the House of Commons on all labour questions' (MM. 1/15 Mar 06).
[2] PD. 129/1519, H. Samuel, 16 Feb 04; PD. 152/210–2, Mr Paul, 19 Feb 06.
[3] Dr Rutherford, speech at Brentford, *Middlesex Chronicle*, 2 Dec 05.
[4] Viscount Gladstone papers 46063/257, 'To the electors of West Leeds', Dec 05.
[5] Haldane papers 7/12, 'To the electors of East Lothian', 9 Jan 06.
[6] Maurice, *Haldane*, i, 145.

48

Secretary of State's room, Colonial Office

Elgin at his desk in the Colonial Office

The Liberal Cabinet, December 1905

Back row left to right: Home Secretary, Mr P. Gladstone; Lord President of the Council, Earl of Crewe; War Secretary, Mr Haldane; President, Board of Trade, Mr Lloyd George; Postmaster-General, Mr Sydney Buxton; Chancellor of the Duchy of Lancaster, Sir H. Fowler; President, Board of Agriculture, Earl Carrington; President, Board of Education, Mr Augustine Birrell; First Lord of the Admiralty, Lord Tweedmouth; Secretary for Scotland, Mr John Sinclair

Mr Bryce, Prime Minister and First Lord of the Treasury.

election campaign created a good deal of embarrassment for Liberal ministers.

During the early years of the century, the revelation of abuses in Leopold's Congo also powerfully influenced the growth of anti-capitalist and anti-concessionaire sentiment. There was strong feeling against mining magnates even in Johannesburg itself, and fearless hostile criticism of the capitalists even by men who raised no objection to the principle of Chinese Labour, and who repudiated the allegations of bad treatment.[1] Official opinion was no less emphatic. There was bitter opposition in the colonial office to the South African capitalist and speculator, in so far as he made money by financial jugglery and company promotions.[2] Ministerial opinion was reflected in Elgin's remark that, like his colleagues, he had no partiality for the Rand magnates or the capitalist companies, both of whom he thoroughly distrusted.[3]

The hatred of Chinese Labour and of capitalists was also a symptom of more general moral indignation over the trend of Unionist imperial policy. When Campbell-Bannerman and his friends took office, it was with the strong belief that the previous twenty years had witnessed an aberration from the sensible principles of British expansion and from the spirit of justice and fair play in the conduct of imperial affairs, an aberration from what Dilke as well as Campbell-Bannerman had labelled 'the true as against the bastard imperialism'.[4] Despite the misgivings of some of their followers, Liberal leaders had not always been absolutely opposed in principle to any territorial expansion of British rule. They were not in the least ashamed of the empire; even Morley spoke of it as 'a wonderful thing'. They valued it chiefly as an instrument of peace and progress, justice and co-operation between all sorts of men throughout the world. They valued British power only as it was used in the cause of justice. They thought of the empire as 'a great moral

---

[1] CO. 291/96/4253, Selb. to S/S, tel. 3 Feb 06.

[2] African (S) 837 (a), memo by Graham 1 Apr 06.

[3] EP. Cab[inet] memo[randum] 12 Feb 06.

[4] S. Gwynn and G. M. Tuckwell, *Life of Sir Charles Dilke* (1918), i, 68; CB, *Speeches*, p. 148.

force on the side of progress', as the most effective agency yet devised for combating oppression and for spreading enlightenment. Those who, like Churchill, looked forward to 'larger brotherhoods and more exact standards of social justice', cherished it as a model of what they hoped the whole world would one day become.[1] The Liberal leaders believed their predecessors had cheapened the name of the empire. Campbell-Bannerman repeatedly spoke of the degradation wrought upon national life by neglect of the old standard of moral principle.[2] 'The old ideals of justice, liberty and humanity as they were cherished from 1840 to 1880', observed Bryce, 'seem to have become obscured . . . [by] the Jingo whirlwind'.[3] Most of the Liberal ministers came into office believing that their task was nothing less than the moral regeneration of British imperialism. They realised that it might be difficult to reverse Unionist policy to any considerable extent, but they could at least try to ensure henceforth a change of spirit and atmosphere in the management of imperial affairs, and they could attempt to apply once again the traditional Liberal principles.[4] 'The policy and spirit which would govern the action of the present government', promised Campbell-Bannerman, 'would be the very antithesis of that of their opponents. It would be based on justice and liberty, not privilege and monopoly'.[5] That set the keynote. The Liberals took to heart what the president of the United States had said: that the greatness of England and her high estate in the world depended first on the administration of justice all over the world. There must be no 'methods of barbarism', not merely in South Africa, but in any sphere of

---

[1] H. A. L. Fisher, *James Bryce* (1927), i, 24; H. Samuel, *Liberalism, its principles and proposals* (1902), pp. 323 and 335; W. S. Churchill, *Liberalism and the Social Problem* (1909), p. 122, speech, 15 Jul 07.

[2] CB, *Speeches*, p. 187, 16 Jan 06; also pp. 61, 82 and 91.

[3] Fisher, *Bryce*, i, 317, Bryce to Goldwin Smith, 12 Apr 01. In 1904, WSC took issue with Chamberlain's opinion that the future rested with great territorial empires: if the British empire held together, said WSC, it would be not because of its size or soldiers, but 'because it is based upon the assent of free peoples, united with each other by noble and progressive principles; because it is animated by respect for right and justice . . . an agent of human progress and of international peace' (quoted by A. MacCallum Scott, *Winston Spencer Churchill*, p. 259).

[4] CB. 41224/118, 136, 186, 189.   [5] CB, *Speeches*, p. 188.

imperial administration. Africans must be treated in accordance with the rules and notions of civilised humanity.[1] European colonists must receive self-government step by step with their progress in education and political capacity. The empire as a whole must transcend Anglo-Saxon allegiance and conduce to the well-being of all mankind.[2]

[1] As Lugard quickly discovered in discussing discipline in the West African Frontier Force. 'I suggested the pillory and stocks, but they want to deal with a primitive people on the lines of 20th century England instead of on the lines of 15th century England' (Perham, *Lugard*, ii, 199; CO. 446/53/11875, Lugard to S/S, 7 Mar 06).

[2] H. Samuel, *Memoirs* (1945), p. 33.

Inherited Problems and Continuity of Policy

It was ten years since there had been a Liberal government, and more than twenty since there had been a strong one. Much had happened during this period. In December 1905, only three and a half years had elapsed since the Anglo-Boer war (October 1899– May 1902) had been brought to an end by the treaty of Vereeniging. Only a few years had passed since the last British acquisitions in the partition of Africa had been made. Meanwhile, with the notable exception of the West Indies, most of the other parts of the empire had been neglected. The Liberals thus inherited some big problems, a triple aftermath of war or partition or neglect. A legacy from their predecessors confronted them everywhere during the whole of their first year in office. In every case they had to determine how much of the inheritance they would perpetuate in deference to the principle of continuity of policy through a change of government. South Africa was the most serious and the most urgent problem, and attempts to deal with it dwarfed all other aspects of imperial policy throughout 1906. Since the points of divergence between Liberals and Unionists were widest over the Transvaal, the differences in policy between the two parties were greater at the very beginning of our period than at any other time.

4 South Africa: Aftermath of the Boer War

THE LIBERAL APPROACH TO THE SOUTH AFRICAN PROBLEM

GLADSTONE had spoken of the South African question in 1881 as 'the one great unsolved, perhaps unsolvable problem of our colonial system'. This strain of pessimism was never far away from Liberal thinking about South Africa. Long before the end of the nineteenth century, there was an underlying realisation that South Africa had already receded beyond imperial control. It was for this reason that Liberals regarded Sir Alfred Milner as a dangerous high commissioner (1897–1905). The day had long passed when a policy of vigour could be safely indulged. Persistence in such a course must lead inevitably to the creation of another Ireland, a Teutonic not a Celtic Ireland. Any attempt to repeat the policy of 'the pale' in Ireland was foredoomed to failure because of the numerical preponderance of the Dutch.[1]

The Liberals believed that the South African problem had been seriously aggravated by Dr Jameson's foolish raid into the Transvaal in January 1896. Loyalty to the British connection was thought actually to have been growing before this catastrophe: the raid created a deep and bitter breach in trust and good feeling between Briton and Boer, which, they feared, threw into a dim and distant future all hope of permanent reconciliation and fusion.[2] The Liberal view was that Milner and Chamberlain were directly responsible for the South African war, because in their desire for victory over president

[1] The Dutch were more than 54% of the white population in 1911. See L. M. Thompson, *Unification of South Africa* (1960), p. 498.
[2] J. Bryce, *Impressions of South Africa* (3rd ed., 1899), pp. x–xi, xliii; Asq. 9/95, Ripon to Asquith 29 Dec 97.

Kruger's will, they bungled negotiations and so blundered into war.[1] In examining the causes of the Boer war, not much importance was attached to what Campbell-Bannerman called the 'silly franchise question'.[2] Denial of the vote to British immigrants in the Transvaal was only one issue among several. They did not imagine that the Boers were blameless: Campbell-Bannerman thought that Kruger by his methods had done much to invite sharp treatment.[3]

Chiefly, however, the Liberals made Milner the scapegoat for all South African evils. Their detestation of him was very marked.[4] They were much relieved when he was replaced as high commissioner in May 1905 by Lord Selborne, formerly first lord of the admiralty, but not particularly partisan in his politics.[5]

The note of pessimism was at its peak during and immediately after the war. Ripon became convinced in 1901 that the condition of Cape Colony was 'very bad indeed', and that the final loss of it to Britain was not impossible.[6] Even in 1906 Morley still spoke of the war as a 'very bad, false step' which had landed Britain in 'inextricable confusion'.[7] Self-government was the traditional Liberal solution, but would the panacea work in South Africa? In 1901 Ripon thought that the adoption of the Canadian or Australian system was 'only a question of time, if any remedy is to be found or can be found for the existing

---

[1] CB. 41211/61–4.   [2] CB. 41211/29.   [3] CB. 41230/16.

[4] Bryce wrote to Campbell-Bannerman 12 Nov 99 that Milner 'has shewn himself so wanting in tact, coolness and even in the art of preserving the semblance of impartiality, as to destroy all one's confidence in his judgment' (CB. 41211/67); the 'first requisite to better things in South Africa is to get that gentleman out of it' (ibid. 124, 27 Oct 1900). Campbell-Bannerman thought that Milner was 'the worst man possible for his position . . . sensible and solid people regard him and his influence with the gravest mistrust' (CB. 41224/132, CB to Ripon 7 Nov 1900). To Morley, Milner stood 'for all that is shallow, violent, sentimental, crude, unsound and dangerous' (MM. 3/35, 30 Jan 08); 'Milner has many qualities, but he is at the end of them all, a *Bismarck manqué*' (MM. 4/165, 29 Jul 09). Elgin rarely referred to Milner, but he certainly thought his bureaucratic system in the Transvaal very extravagant (EP, E to WSC, 21 Feb 08, photocopy).

[5] Selborne was deliberately chosen for his presumed acceptability to the Liberals. 'As a peer without constituents, and in a great, comparatively speaking, non-contentious administrative office, he has had less conflict with the Opposition than most ministers' (Balfour papers 49775/29, Balfour to Lyttelton, 20 Jun 05).

[6] CB. 41224/189, Ripon to CB 23 Oct 01.   [7] PD. 161/572, 30 Jul 06.

terrible evils. Of this I am sorry to say, I am becoming seriously doubtful. . . . But if one can reasonably take a less hopeless view of the situation, the only hopeful policy will be found in the speediest possible establishment of a real self-governing system in the two new colonies'.[1] Campbell-Bannerman in 1904 thought that the grant of full self-government to the Transvaal was the only policy offering 'a ray of hope'.[2] Full self-government, and trust – these alone, said Campbell-Bannerman, might redeem an almost irredeemable situation.

Like Gladstone confronted with the Irish problem, Campbell-Bannerman got much of his inspiration from the example of Canada, 'the greatest triumph of British statesmanship'. The real encouragement to be derived from the Canadian analogy was that South Africa did not look so insoluble when this comparison was made. The appointment of an Elgin to the colonial secretaryship was not without symbolic significance. One Lord Elgin had helped to make a loyal Canadian dominion, another might do the same for South Africa. Elgin had studied his father's Canadian papers thoroughly. When Selborne, welcoming Elgin's appointment, referred to Canada and mentioned that he had read the Durham Report, Elgin replied:

I quite admit that there are essential differences between the case then and what we have to face now. Those to which you refer may make our task more difficult. On the other hand, I think I could show you from unpublished papers, if it does not sufficiently appear in those which were published, that the feeling between the British and French was more hostile than that between British and Boer. You tell me that you are well received by the Boers – and I am not surprised, for even during the war there there were many instances of good feeling. I do not overlook the possible results of the influence of leaders if exerted in a hostile manner, but still what you have seen indicates the natural disposition of the people.[3]

[1] CB. 41224/156, to CB 19 Jan 01. The South African Republic and the Orange Free State were annexed by Britain as the Transvaal and Orange River Colony in 1900, with Crown Colony status.

[2] CB. 41243A/93.

[3] EP, E to Selb. 12 Jan 06.

Unlike Elgin's father, Selborne had not had stones thrown at him. Elgin's view was not unsupported. In 1890 Sir Charles Dilke had thought that the hatred for the British even among the most extreme Boers was less than that of the French of Lower Canada in the 1840s.[1] But of course, a great deal had happened since 1891, and any attempt to compare the two situations in 1905–6 was a speculation rather than an inspiration. Elgin sent Churchill a copy of his father's memoirs[2] because he thought 'in the chapters dealing with his experience in Canada you may find a good [deal] that has a bearing on the present'. The book showed the results of the adoption of the principles of the Durham report: 'can we follow them in South Africa is the question?'[3] There was no certain answer. All that can be said is that Elgin had a personal interest in the Liberal decision to grant responsible government to the Transvaal, and that he derived encouragement from the knowledge that he was following the principles professed by his father and his maternal grandfather Lord Durham, principles which resulted in the 'prosperous and great and loyal dominion of Canada'.[4]

Nevertheless, the strain of pessimism did not entirely disappear from Liberal thinking. Sometimes it was doubtless expressed to impress electors with Unionist iniquity, but Ripon's private opinions suggest that much of it was sincere. Even Churchill, notably optimistic, and not easily deterred by apparent limitations to government action, sometimes despaired of finding acceptable solutions in South Africa. Warned by officials that repatriation of Chinese labourers would create an outcry, he asked whether there was anything that they could do which would not create an outcry in South Africa.[5] His successor as under-secretary, Colonel Seely, admitted frankly in 1908 that he had always believed that Boer sentiment would increasingly prevail in South Africa.[6] This opinion is the more striking in view of the fact that he was also confident that native

[1] C. Dilke, *Problems of Greater Britain* (1890), i, 543.
[2] T. Walrond (ed.), *Letters and Journals of James, 8th earl of Elgin* (1872).
[3] EP, E to WSC 22 Jan 06 (copy).   [4] PD. 152/748, 26 Feb 06.
[5] CO. 291/95/2402, 22 Jan 06.   [6] CO. 48/597/28129, 12 Aug 08.

policy would improve under the Union government. 'The unification of South Africa', writes Professor Thompson, 'was one of the last creative expressions of the age of optimism which was brought to a close by the first world war'.[1] The evidence in the British archives scarcely sustains this assertion. There was very little genuine optimism in the Liberal approach to the South African problem in 1905–6. Unification in 1909 was home-made, and there was optimism where it mattered, in South Africa itself. But colonial optimism was conveyed to, rather than shared by, the imperial government.

CHINESE LABOUR[2]

During their last two years in office, the Unionist government, with Milner's advice, had taken two major policy decisions for the Transvaal. They had introduced indentured Chinese labour to work the Rand mines, and they had issued letters patent establishing representative institutions.

The Unionist colonial secretary who approved these measures was Alfred Lyttelton. A schoolboy whose career at Eton was of heroic proportions, a fine all-round sportsman, a cricketer whose play was described by W. G. Grace as 'the champagne of cricket', a barrister who would not enter parliament, because of his opposition to Home Rule, until his maternal uncle William Gladstone had retired, a cabinet minister who had never previously worked in a government office or had any administrative experience, Lyttelton succeeded Joseph Chamberlain in 1903. He was noted for his charm. He was adept at enriching personal relationships, and universally loved.[3] The key to Lyttelton as a politician is that he aspired to be Milner's *alter ego*, his metropolitan mouthpiece. He thought of himself as subordinate to Milner, rather than the

[1] Thompson, *Unification of South Africa*, p. vi; see also p. 480.

[2] In the interests of clarity, the Chinese Labour problem is treated in a separate section from the Transvaal constitution, but it is important to remember that the two issues were interrelated, and that no such separation of issues was made by ministers at the time.

[3] E. Lyttelton, *Alfred Lyttelton* (1917).

other way round. He was nearly as deferential to Lugard. As a result he was constantly in opposition to his permanent officials, but apparently impressed and charmed them out of bearing any malice against him on this score.[1]

Milner looked on the Chinese labourers as the key to the success of his entire South African policy.[2] He had recourse to every other expedient first, but by 1903 he was already convinced that the labour shortage in the mines could not be met from South African sources. By January 1904 Lyttelton was satisfied that Milner's desire to import Chinese labourers was supported by Transvaal public opinion, and he therefore permitted the experiment. An ordinance,[3] sanctioned by the colonial office, was passed by the Transvaal council. The labourers began to arrive in June 1904. Thereafter, the plain duty of the colonial office, as Lyttelton saw it, was, by amendment and advice to make the Labour Ordinance 'as good as possible, and by vigilant criticism to secure that it should not exceed the moderate professions of its authors'.[4] His permanent officials were not so easily convinced that they had obtained the

---

[1] R. B. Pugh in *C.H.B.E.*, iii, 746.

[2] Milner was convinced that Chinese were necessary, because his reconstruction programme would collapse if mining profits did not increase, and because it was necessary to anticipate an alliance of British and Boers in demanding compulsory labour for Africans, and white self-government to put it into force (G. H. Le May, *British supremacy in South Africa, 1899–1907* (1965), p. 161). In the event, the Chinese Labour episode ended Milner's personal immunity from criticism by Liberal Imperialist leaders, divided the British in the Transvaal and provided the occasion for the return of the Boers to organised politics (ibid. p. 158).

[3] The ordinance provided that the Chinese were to come for a fixed term of years only. During their stay in the Transvaal they were to live in compounds which they were forbidden to leave, save under a permit limited to 48 hours, and restricted to the district around the mines. The Chinese were not allowed to own any real property or mineral rights, nor allowed to engage in any business. They were required to work ten hours a day, six days a week. They were not permitted rights of access to the courts of law. The ordinance defined fourteen particular offences, for which there were special penalties, different from those usually sanctioned by the law. They were not explicitly forbidden to bring their families, but the conditions were such that it would be impossible. At first no minimum wage was guaranteed, but later a minimum of two shillings a day was fixed. During the years 1905 to 1906, 47,639 of the total of 161,327 workers employed in the mines were Chinese (see Thompson, *Unification of South Africa*, p. 498).

[4] CO. 291/68/534, minute 7 Jan 04.

real feeling of the Transvaal outside Johannesburg and the Chamber of Mines. Sir Montagu Ommanney, the permanent under-secretary, predicted 'very strong anti-Chinese feelings', which might take 'an inconvenient and even a violent form'. He believed in the wisdom of 'applying the drag to the impetuosity of Johannesburg'.[1] Retrospectively Graham (head of the South African department of the office) wrote: 'It was because we believed that Chinese Labour was demanded merely for the purpose of creating a "boom in the Kaffir market", that I and others in this department opposed the demand to the last'.[2]

Helped by the vigilance of sceptical officials, Lyttelton lived up to his professions. He always spoke of the introduction of Chinese labour as an experiment, he tried to ensure that Chinese wages should not be lower than existing African wages, he repeatedly asked for information to answer questions in parliament. He reminded Milner of the necessity for continued vigilance in observing the effects of the experiment, with the object on the one hand of preventing it from undercutting African wages, and on the other of ensuring that it was plainly within the government's powers of supervision and control.[3] He constantly enjoined circumspection and care in the administration of all regulations especially those of an unusual character. Lyttelton also tried to keep the experiment from expanding too quickly. In January 1905 he was considering whether, pending the result of experience and the introduction of representative government, it would be desirable to impose any limitation on the monthly shipments of Chinese.[4] On 27 October he commended voluntary limitation to the mineowners.[5]

Chinese Labour: policy. Liberals felt immensely strongly about Chinese Labour. Looking back on fifty years of public life, Lord Samuel, for example, could think of no movement in which he

---

[1] Ibid. minute 5 Jan 06.　　　　　　　[2] African(S) 837(*a*), 1 Apr 06.
[3] CO. 291/80/2252, S/S to Milner tel. 10 Feb 05.
[4] CO. 291/92/1673, S/S to Milner 19 Jan 05.　　　[5] CO. 291/86/37652.

61

took part, in which he had rendered more definite service to the state than in the opposition to Chinese Labour. It was 'highly detrimental to the prestige of British colonial rule; and it was wholly unnecessary'.[1]

The Chinese Labour problem has an important place in this book. It was recognised as a test question[2] of the imperial policy of the Liberal government. The attempt to end Chinese Labour on the Rand was the only major attempt completely to reverse Unionist policy. The process demonstrated the truth of Asquith's objection when the experiment was introduced: the worst of taking a step of this kind, he said, was that it would be very difficult to retrace.[3] The question is one which shows not only how the pressure of public opinion and election pledges created embarrassment for the government, but also how difficult it was to translate the principles of many Liberal supporters into practical politics. And Chinese Labour was the first subject of imperial affairs upon which the Liberal government took action.

Why did Liberal ministers dislike Chinese Labour so much? Ripon felt that if real responsible government existed in the Transvaal, and if a bill for the admission of Chinese labour were to be passed by an *elected* legislature, it ought to be allowed to come into operation. But so grave a question ought not to have been decided by anything short of a really representative body. A mere Crown Colony government was quite unfit to deal with such a matter.[4] His chief objection to the ordinance governing the system, was to the attempt to regulate the position of the coolies outside the places where they worked, that is to say, to the restrictions which were laid upon their general relations with the community, especially by confining them to compounds. Grey had four main objections: to the restriction of the Chinese to unskilled work, to the compound system, to the total separation from their families, and to the compulsory return to China upon termination of their con-

[1] Viscount Samuel, *Memoirs* (1945), p. 46.   [2] *The Times*, 11 Dec 05.
[3] PD. 132/358, 21 Mar 04.
[4] CB. 41225/22, Ripon to CB 18 Jan 04.

tracts. (The contracts were for three years and might be renewed after the first term.) Grey agreed with Ripon that the 'secret of all these special restrictions' was the prevention of living contact with the community for whom they worked. It was this that made it different from other labour ordinances operating in the empire.[1] Even wider implications were discerned by Bryce. The ordinance, he said,

intensifies the sense of separation and antagonism between different races, and it also intensifies the scorn and contempt which a superior race feels for an inferior race. It creates a class who are debarred from the ordinary civil rights which every man ought to enjoy. . . . The effect of these provisions will be to degrade labour, and in degrading labour you go some way to degrade humanity itself.[2]

The Liberals looked upon Chinese Labour as the greatest infraction of traditional policy that the Unionists had made, because it was a 'flagrant denial on all points, of the principles of freedom and equity', representing the negation of the old social, economical and political principles which they believed had given Britain her position in the world. They were not satisfied that the supply of African, or even white, labour was inadequate. What sort of imperialism was it, that acted apparently at 'a signal from Johannesburg'? As a result, men were being treated as if they were implements rather than human beings. Campbell-Bannerman denounced it as 'a system indistinguishable in many of its features from slavery'.[3]

From the very first they heard of it, the Liberals had thought it a bad scheme.[4] They consistently opposed it, and when they came to power, gave high priority to an attempt to remove this stain on the empire.

One of Lyttelton's last decisions as colonial secretary was not to disallow an amendment to the original Labour Importation Ordinance of 1904, since it was considered necessary in the Transvaal to tighten the disciplinary arrangements in the interests of the labourers themselves and of the community

[1] PD. 169/32, 180, 12 Feb 07.   [2] PD. 132/314, 364, 21 Mar 04.
[3] CB, *Speeches*, pp. 135–51.   [4] CB. 41211/262, Bryce to CB 30 Dec 03.

generally. He observed in a despatch of 2 December, that some of the provisions of the amendment were unusual; 'it must unavoidably be of the nature of an experiment . . . its administration will require to be carefully watched'.[1] He recognised that regulations under the revised ordinance would have to be framed to 'check the over-zealous white'.[2] The revised code of regulations came before Elgin; although with one exception the office was satisfied, he refused to initial it: 'even if I merely approved, as being a matter of routine, which indeed it is, the fact, if it got out, might be taken as a deliberate approval of the system, a misrepresentation no doubt, but still awkward, especially at the election'. The prime minister accepted his suggestion of telegraphing to the high commissioner that they needed time to consider the whole question.[3] Meanwhile there seemed no alternative but to allow tentative and judicious application of the ordinance, emphasising the desirability of not enforcing penalties which Ommanney described as of 'questionable justice and distinctly dangerous'.[4] Churchill, however, recorded his opinion that the amending ordinance ought not to have been sanctioned, even on trial, and that the despatch of 2 December ought to have been cancelled by telegraph. He singled out five objectionable points, and concluded:

It is absolutely indefensible in principle. It will lead to gross abuses and perhaps cruelties in practice. It is satisfactory at this stage to observe that the objections to it have been clearly and tersely stated in this department from the first and that no inconsistency or change of view, or any substantial division of opinion can be discovered from a careful study of the minutes.[5]

Selborne had written to Grey on 24 November 1905, arguing that a third of the mining industry would at once cease to operate if the Chinese were withdrawn. Grey passed the letter to Elgin, commenting:

[1] CO. 291/86/41962, S/S to Selb. 2 Dec 05. The new penalties came into force in Oct 05.
[2] CO. 291/85/33624, minute 20 Sep 05.   [3] CB. 41214/16, E to CB 12 Dec 05.
[4] CO. 291/90/43490, 19 Dec 05.   [5] Ibid. minute 21 Dec 05.

It still seems to me to be essential that we should stop any further importation of Chinese. I have always held that it was a bad foundation on which to build up the mining industry. We cannot immediately repatriate the Chinese who are there, but we can prevent the thing going any further.[1]

Elgin replied; 'I think on the papers there is an opportunity for calling a halt in the importation of coolies: (to repatriate them at once is surely out of the question) . . . I think the stories have been exaggerated, but to simply say so would not convince.'[2] On 18 December, Asquith set down six reasons for his opinion that on the whole, Selborne's statement was 'very unconvincing'.[3]

By 18 December the colonial office staff had completed a memorandum, prepared at Elgin's request, to help the cabinet to decide 'whether further importation should or should not be stopped for the present'.[4] The memorandum stated that the alternatives appeared to be, either to end the system entirely and repatriate the Chinese at once, or to leave the whole matter to the elected Assembly and meanwhile do nothing, or to leave it to the Assembly and meanwhile stop importation and see that the labourers were efficiently controlled and fairly treated. The objections to immediate repatriation were as follows: that a reversal of policy without consulting the colony would be bitterly resented throughout South Africa; it would be disastrous to the mining industry; it would not be feasible to replace Chinese by African labourers from the tropics, for their mortality was likely to be over a hundred per thousand; it would imply a breach of contract with the labourers; and it would involve the government in large claims for compensation. Officials also pointed out that the mine-owners would allege a breach of faith, for the Unionist government had led them to believe that they would be safe at least until a Transvaal elected Assembly decided the matter.[5]

---

[1] EP, Grey to E 16 Dec 05.   [2] GP. 52, E to Grey 17 Dec 05.
[3] EP.   [4] African (S) 797.
[5] CO. 291/88/45336, minutes by Ommanney 24 and 26 Dec 05; CO. 291/88/76, minute by Just 1 Jan 06.

On 20 December, after cabinet decision, the colonial secretary told Selborne by telegraph:

H.M.G. consider that the experiment of the introduction of Chinese labourers should not be extended further, until H.M.G. can learn through an elected and really representative legislature, the opinion of the Colony, and the Cabinet has accordingly decided that the recruitment embarcation and importation of Chinese coolies shall be arrested pending decision as to grant of responsible government.

It was therefore desirable that every available step should be taken to prevent the shipment from China of 14,700 coolies already licensed.[1] Next day the same message was repeated, prefaced by the remarks that His Majesty's Government were 'not prepared in all the circumstances to be responsible for further importation' and that they reserved 'their opinion and freedom of action in the whole matter'; their decision was arrived at after careful consideration, and they took special cognisance of the fact that the system had always been accepted in Britain as an experiment. The government observed that there were 47,000 Chinese on the Rand, and 96,000 Africans, which represented an increase of nearly 20,000 since 1904, bringing the total of Africans almost to its pre-war maximum. Campbell-Bannerman himself was believed to have been responsible for wording the telegram, which Selborne did not find easy to interpret.[2] On the evening of 21 December the prime minister announced at a party rally in the Albert Hall that it had been decided 'to stop forthwith – as far as it is practicable to do it forthwith – the recruitment and embarcation of coolies in China and their importation into South Africa; and instructions have been given to that effect'.[3] The King, fearing Selborne's resignation, criticised the precipitancy of a decision which would be regarded as a reversal of policy. Campbell-Bannerman discussed the complaint with Elgin, remarking: 'This was a case of sudden action being required.

[1] CB told the king he considered this a startling number (CAB. 41/30/36).
[2] CO. 291/88/44878.   [3] CB, *Speeches*, p. 178.

The large number of licences applied for constituted ample proof of concerted plan which it was necessary to stop. And we could not wait for criticism and argument even in the highest quarter'.[1]

When the announcement was made, the government was not in possession of exact facts about the 14,700 coolies for whom licences were granted but who had not yet left China. Qualifying the word 'forthwith' by the condition as to practicability proved to be very necessary. Further inquiry showed that 13,199 licences were granted before 18 November, despite the fact that Lyttelton had on 27 October expressed the opinion that mine-owners would do well voluntarily to suspend recruiting for six months. His suggestion was ignored; Selborne did not even reply to it. It was now suggested that the licences could be revoked legally only by *ex post facto* legislation. The attorney general of the Transvaal declared that a special Order-in-Council would be *ultra vires*. Asquith agreed with Elgin that they should avoid *ex post facto* legislation; public opinion neither demanded nor would approve such a step.[2] Haldane did not believe that much harm would be done to the reputation of the government if it declared that it could not undo the past, and at the same time stopped all fresh licences.[3] The lord chancellor, however, was not convinced that local action in the Transvaal would not suffice in law; but the proper method of stopping the importation of the 14,000 (the exact number was not clear) would, he thought, be by Order-in-Council.[4] Asquith pressed his opinion on the prime minister. 'I think that the effect of the announcement' he wrote, 'has been excellent, and that it has completely satisfied our friends'. *Ex post facto* legislation 'would raise a tremendous hubbub both here and there, would involve the British taxpayer (who is without available funds) in indefinitely large claims for compensation, and would not be regarded as necessary to fulfil your pledge. The whole responsibility for this addition to the number

[1] EP, CB to E 26 Dec 05, Knollys to E 22 Dec 05, E to Knollys 24 Dec 05 (copy).
[2] EP, Asquith to E 27 Dec 05.   [3] Asq. 10/195, Haldane to Asquith 28 Dec 05.
[4] EP, Reid to E 29 Dec 05.

ought to be thrown on the late government. I believe that anti-Chinese opinion here would quite acquiesce in this course'.[1] Campbell-Bannerman agreed

that the Chinese Labour matter goes well, but that it will be ticklish and may appear *small* to meddle in any wholesale way with the new licences. . . . I am of course receiving lots of letters denouncing me as bringing ruin to mine shareholders.[2]

Elgin refused to believe in any collusion between the governor and the mine-owners in issuing these licences. He told Campbell-Bannerman that as the licences were issued before any immediate prospect of a change of government, 'sharp practice – which some suspected' could not be made out.

As in your speech at the Albert Hall you introduced the qualification of the word 'forthwith', which always seemed to me prudent – we can state with absolute accuracy that we do interfere immediately the law enables us to do so – and that for all else the late government is responsible. And if we couple this by some such provision as Mr Samuel . . . thinks will abolish the charge of slavery, our whole policy, it seems to me, becomes coherent.[3]

The essence of Herbert Samuel's proposal (submitted in a memorandum, 22 December) was that those Chinese who wished to return should be given facilities by executive action for doing so. The prime minister passed the suggestion to Elgin with the commendation that Samuel was 'a very level-headed fellow'.[4] Elgin at once began preparing a case on these lines, feeling that if practicable it would take the sting out of the slavery argument.[5] By 1 January he had a memorandum ready for the cabinet on the proposal for repatriation. In it he stated, very properly, that they must not be guided by exclusively moral considerations:

---

[1] CB. 41210/256–7; Asquith to CB 27 Dec 05.
[2] Asq. 10/192, CB to Asquith, 28 Dec 05.
[3] CB. 41214/35–7; E to CB 28 Dec 05, partly quoted in J. A. Spender, *Life of Rt. Hon. Sir Henry Campbell-Bannerman*, ii (1923), 230. In his reply, CB expressed pleasure 'that the South African matters are shaping so well' (EP, 29 Dec 05).
[4] EP.   [5] GP. 52, E to Grey 28 Dec 05.

The matter is one which affects peace, order and good government, and ought to be dealt with on that basis, not from philanthrophic motives; and ought therefore to be the care of the Transvaal government and of the mineowners themselves.

He suggested that inspectors might be asked whether there were people deserving repatriation because they had not understood the conditions of labour to which they were being sent; they should state to what extent under existing arrangements the discontented were being repatriated. If the government got a satisfactory answer it might obviate the necessity of making a direct offer to the coolies, 'a course surrounded with much difficulty and open to strong local objection'. Did many really desire repatriation?[1]

Selborne expressed his opinion that if the licences already issued were allowed to stand, the decision to issue no fresh licences until the opinion of the elected representatives of the Transvaal could be taken on the subject, would be loyally accepted, and there would be no feeling of injustice.[2] The cabinet decided on 3 January that it was not worthwhile to excite tremendous ill-feeling for the small practical result of preventing the addition of 14,700 labourers, a step which in itself could hardly do much to satisfy those who alleged 'slavery', and might present the government with strong claims for compensation.[3] A telegram of 5 January conveyed the decision that the licences would be respected as valid, adding first a word of regret that the approval of the secretary of state had not been sought for them in November, and stressing that from the day on which the Liberals assumed office nothing would be done to add to the number under contract until Transvaal opinion was properly declared.[4] The Liberals were not able, or not willing, to put the clock back, only to stop its hands.

---

[1] EP, cab. memo: CAB. 37/82/2.   [2] CO. 291/95/197, tel. 1 Jan 06.
[3] CAB. 41/30/37. Haldane wrote to E, 6 Jan 06: 'How well you managed the Chinese question in the cabinet. The result was remarkable. Winston Churchill said to me: "We have got a great administrator at the head of the office and all goes well in consequence" ' (EP).
[4] CO. 291/88/77, S/S to Selb.

69

Herbert Gladstone wondered whether it would be possible to lay down a time limit of two months for the further importation of the Chinese already under licence. The lord chancellor quashed the idea, because it would be in effect a cancellation of the licences, which were unlimited as to time; therefore the old objections would apply. Assuming that they were going to grant responsible government, 'and leave the whole thing to them', it did not seem worthwhile to fix a time limit only for the interval between April and July, the month in which it was assumed that the new Assembly would meet.[1]

Officials were sceptical about the repatriation proposals. As the good order of the Transvaal was involved, there seemed no justification for meeting the cost from imperial funds. It was equally difficult to saddle a new Transvaal legislature with the expense, by an Order-in-Council. Above all, the major difficulty seemed to be the risk of imposture on the part of the coolies. Churchill brushed all objections aside brusquely:

First we take our stand upon the letter of the law,[2] in strict accordance with our attitude upon outstanding business. Secondly, Lord Selborne is convinced that the numbers of coolies thus repatriated would be small. If so, the expense will be small.

He did not think that the argument that the Chinese would try to take a 'short holiday' lent itself to serious treatment, and suggested that three applications on the first day of three successive months should be accepted as the test of a real desire to return, 'and no passing freak of passion.'[3] Some weeks later Churchill firmly recorded the opinion he had been pressing upon Elgin, that unless this 'moderate and reasonable' reform were adopted, the indignation of the House of Commons at the continued employment of 'armed compulsion to maintain an immoral contract', would assuredly lead to some far more drastic measure.[4]

[1] Visc. Gladstone papers 45988/215–16, Loreburn to CB 22 Jan 06, enclosed on CB to Gladstone 23 Jan 06.
[2] The ordinance permitted the repatriation of coolies if they could find £17.
[3] CO. 291/95/2402, minute 22 Jan 06.   [4] Ibid. 4947, 14 Feb 06.

The advice of the colonial office was as follows:

> In the interests of South Africa, the most desirable policy is to leave the whole question as to Chinese Labour to a responsibly governed Transvaal, and to do everything that can be done *administratively* to remove any blots and to improve it, in the interval, the assumption being that the Transvaal will do the right thing and must be allowed to have its way, like any other self-governing Colony....[1]

On the whole the Liberals did not differ much from this conclusion. They were not inclined to base their policy upon moral grounds (it was difficult to develop moral arguments in a despatch), though the doubtful features about the employment of Chinese Labour would naturally be referred to in debate, but upon the principle that Chinese Labour was a matter for the Transvaal to settle for itself. The government could argue, suggested one of the officials, that not to have stopped importation would have tended to prevent the Transvaal from having a free hand.[2]

Elgin considered the Unionist government's handling of the Chinese Labour problem inept. The burden of his criticism was that their management of the whole transaction was so loose and inaccurate that it gave an opportunity for the introduction into what was, or ought to have been, an experimental stage, conditions which gave a far greater amount of permanency than they probably were aware of.[3] This does indeed seem a fair criticism. In minutes and despatches Lyttelton had always used the word 'experiment', but failed to secure acceptance of this view by people in South Africa, including Lord Selborne.[4]

Elgin was anxious to avoid precipitate action with respect to Chinese Labour. He had always believed that 'if our friends only have a little patience, they may see it more than likely fall by its own weight'.[5] He certainly did not think that the

[1] African (S) 825, memo. by Just, 6 Feb 06.

[2] CO. 291/95/2635, minute by Just 24 Jan 06.

[3] PD. 160/345, 6 July 06.

[4] EP, Selb. to E 26 Jun 06; African (S) 829 quotes seven instances when Lyttelton used the words 'experiment' or 'temporary' (CO. 879/72, memo. by Just 7 Feb 06).

[5] EP. Undated note.

government could be called upon to sweep away all they objected to at one moment. There were plenty of precedents for not doing so. He recognised that a ruthless course of action would be grievously injurious to the mining industries. Moreover, he reminded the cabinet, they could not altogether ignore the fact that Lord Selborne might feel the abrupt termination of a system carefully elaborated by him as fatal to his continuance in office:

without suggesting that this is a reason for our declining to act where we deem the honour of the Imperial Government is concerned, it appears to me only common prudence that we should not precipitate an event, which in my judgment might have very serious consequences, on an issue where we stand on thin ice.

Their intention was to modify the regulations under the ordinance so as to secure the publicity of all trials, reversion to the ordinary procedure of courts of law, and the abolition of special penalties. Elgin still thought that, subject to proper precautions to prevent 'precipitate action' by the coolies, it would be very useful in amending the ordinance to include a provision for assisting the repatriation of coolies who could prove a genuine desire to return home, and who did not possess sufficient means. If properly managed, no large sum of money need be involved. This policy still worried him a little. Chinese Labour, in many of its characteristics, he disliked quite as much as any of his colleagues; but

there are honest investors, and there are honest and free workers, both of whom depend on the working of the mines. A general financial crisis would indisputably spell ruin to many individuals, and also must in great measure affect the prosperity, and endanger the peace of the Colony.[1]

Rather than modify the regulations, Elgin assured Lord Selborne, personally he would have preferred to rely on his careful administration of the ordinance, but

[1] EP. Cab. memo. 12 Feb 06.

If the publicity of an ordinary Court is secured, which can be done by the Lt. Governor appointing another place than a mine, and if penalties, which you have reported practically inoperative, are openly abandoned, I see no reason why you should not retain the essentials of a system which you have so carefully constructed.[1]

A few days later he referred to the matter again, and asked Selborne to remember that the government had to secure the assent of a party, 'a large proportion of which approaches the subject under undue prepossessions which make our task arduous'. He repudiated the calumnies expressed during the election.

But it is not those only who may be subject to such influences with whom we have to deal. There is a genuine dislike of Chinese Labour and the conditions under which it has been introduced; and I cannot, even if I would, cut aloof from that. It is from no want of appreciation of your efforts to secure 'justice and humane treatment' (your telegram of Feb. 20th) that we put forward proposals for amending the regulations, but from the positive necessity of the case. If we do not show in some such way that we are in earnest our whole policy of respecting contracts might be in danger.[2]

The repatriation scheme was designed to meet the demand for compulsory repatriation which Elgin imagined was put before the electors by many candidates but which they as a government recognised to be impossible.[3]

Churchill summed up government policy on 24 February:

In short it amounts to this – that the Chinese will have to go, but that all reasonable time – even perhaps six years – will be given for their gradual and I trust comparatively painless extinction. There may therefore be good ground for depression and depreciation of already vastly inflated stock, but there is no ground for panic. If anything can be done to let the Banks of South Africa down gently and to make them let their clients down gently, I should rejoice. Any suggestions to stop a sudden crash should be carefully considered. But crash or no crash, the

---

[1] EP, E to Selb. tel. 18 Feb 06 (copy).   [2] Ibid. 22 Feb 06.
[3] Ibid. 28 Apr 06.

policy will have to go forward, and the sooner this is realised, the better for all concerned.[1]

Elgin was anxious to establish some degree of continuity of policy. For this reason he attached great importance to, and frequently quoted from Lyttelton's telegram[2] of 27 October 1905, in which he enjoined caution in expanding the 'experiment', and expressed the hope that mineowners would voluntarily limit their importation for a while.

Much time and attention was devoted to the parliamentary exposition and justification of government policy, especially during debates between 19 and 28 February. Elgin declined responsibility for the use of the term 'slavery'. He went further perhaps than any other government spokesman by adding: 'I wish to express my deep regret – I have no hesitation in using that word – that this particular term has been used.' He thought that there were provisions in the ordinance which were not consistent with the liberty of free men; the more he studied the problem, the more convinced he became that there was a departure from the traditions of the British empire. The ordinance created crimes 'which are not crimes under the ordinary law and in my opinion, that does constitute a difference from the point of true liberty which every free man ought to possess under the British flag'. His basic objection was to limiting liberty; compulsory repatriation when contracts ran out lay 'at the very essence of the matter'. He argued that in their policy there was no want of continuity. He quoted several Unionist declarations containing the word 'experiment', and concluded:

We honoured all the Bills of the late government. . . . But surely we were entitled to take the whole question of the 'experiment' into consideration before it crystallised and became permanent.[3]

[1] CO. 291/96, 24 Feb 06.
[2] EP, E to Selb. 12 Jan 06 (copy).
[3] PD. 152/735–45, 26 Feb 06. Fitzroy could not stay for the whole of Elgin's speech but described it as opening well (*Memoirs*, p. 284). See also PD. 160/345–7, 6 Jul 06.

Elgin's speech was calm, frank, firm, unaffectedly moderate. He could be as solemn as any judge, and, at his best, seem nearly as authoritative. There was no resort to the words that burn or the phrase that stings. The Tories cheered his expression of regret over the use of the word slavery, but did the lord chancellor listen to it with mixed feelings? Elgin was staunch in his dislike of the system, but could never take the strong line against it which those who had taken part in the electoral controversy had assumed. He knew that he could never satisfy the Liberal fanatics without using language which 'could be taken up by the other side', and so he did not try.[1]

Ripon said that they had felt deeply and had strong, clear convictions: they had rightly not decided the question 'out and out' for themselves, because there was no more difficult question in connection with responsible government than the management of non-European races, a matter upon which a colonial secretary had no really effective means of control.

You can veto their bills, but you cannot control their executive action. The moment you attempted to do anything of the kind, you would be involved in infinite difficulty. Therefore it is from no wish to shift responsibility from ourselves, but from a desire to leave to the people of the Transvaal the decision of a great question deeply concerning the future interests of that country, that the step referred to has been taken.[2]

He denied ever having spoken of 'slaves', but the Chinese were, he said, exactly in a 'condition of semi-slavery'.

Campbell-Bannerman now described the conditions of the Chinese as 'servile'. Many of the conditions were more than servile; they were either cruel in themselves or led readily to the perpetuation of cruelty. He felt quite acutely the difficulty of reversing policy. 'There are many cases', he said, 'where an evil having been done, or an evil practice established, it is impossible, without a possibly greater evil almost, to put an end to it abruptly.' They proposed to remove as much cruelty and servility as possible from the conditions of the Chinese

[1] EP, E to WSC 27 Dec 05 and 10 Jan 06 (photocopies).
[2] PD. 152/51–6, 19 Feb 06.

labourers, and at the same time give those who disliked the life an opportunity to escape from it.[1]

Churchill also mentioned the difficulty of retracing a 'wrong step in politics', and denied the slavery charge in a famous passage:[2]

A labour contract into which men enter voluntarily for a limited and for a brief period, under which they are paid wages which they consider adequate, under which they are not bought or sold, and from which they can obtain relief . . . may not be a desirable contract, may not be a healthy or proper contract, but it cannot in the opinion of H.M.G. be classified as slavery in the extreme acceptance of the word without some risk of terminological inexactitude.

But alternative epithets were not spared – it was an 'evil inheritance', a 'sordid experiment'. The government's object was 'gradual withdrawal' – the experiment would be forced to peter out by the natural process of exhaustion. The purpose of the repatriation proposal was 'to undercut cruelty' by a 'conscience clause'.[3]

Asquith repeated two of the major government themes; he disclaimed responsibility for use of the term 'slavery', and explained why their action was of a limited kind – 'It is quite clear, I think, to anybody of reasonable intelligence and experience, that they could not simply take a wet sponge and wipe the whole thing off the slate in a moment'.[4]

In summary, it may be said that by the end of February, the government had evolved a four-point policy. First, they would respect existing licences, but issue no more. Second, they would modify regulations to remove, in Churchill's phrase 'all danger of cruelty, of impropriety or of gross infringement of liberty'.[5] Third, they would repatriate those who wished to go. Fourth, and most important, they would allow the Transvaal itself to take the final decision whether Chinese Labour should or should not be continued, after it had obtained self-government.

[1] Ibid. 170–4.
[2] His cool withdrawal of the offending phrase enraged the Opposition (A. M. Gollin, *Proconsul in power*, p. 77).
[3] PD. 152/554–72, 22 Feb 06.   [4] Ibid. 668–77, 23 Feb 06.
[5] PD. 152/570, 22 Feb 06.

But supposing the Transvaal decided to import more Chinese, or passed an ordinance to which Liberals took exception – what would the government do? According to Ripon, a self-governing Transvaal must be allowed to have its way.[1] But Crewe said that there was a point 'when Imperial considerations must in our view override even the express wishes of any responsibly governed Colony'. He and Asquith threatened the use of an imperial veto.[2] Churchill shared their view. Believing that 'the maxim "Trust the People" ought to follow the flag', he found considerable evidence that the Transvaal would decide to terminate the system; but it should not for a moment be taken for granted, he warned, that while the conditions of Chinese labour continued to be repugnant to the opinions and feelings of the British public, imperial sanction for its continuation would be forthcoming.[3] Elgin confirmed the impression that the veto would be used: if the Transvaal voted for Chinese Labour, it would be the duty of the government

to endeavour to adjust conditions satisfactory to both parties; but it will also undoubtedly equally be their duty not to shrink from advising His Majesty to exercise his right of veto if that effort failed, or if in their judgment, the right of freedom in any part of the Empire was infringed.[4]

In no sense could it be said that the government's policy was to terminate Chinese Labour.[5] Indeed, it was not, apart from repatriation, an impressive policy. Immediate application for further licences was unlikely, so that prohibition was little more than nominal. Modifications in the ordinance in practice

[1] See p. 62. [2] PD. 152/677, 1002, 22 and 27 Feb 06.
[3] Ibid. 561–71, 22 Feb 06. [4] Ibid. 741, 26 Feb 06.
[5] Churchill asked Elgin to vet his election address. Elgin commented: 'It seems to me that to say the Government must do its utmost to *terminate* such a system will invite the retort, you are doing nothing to *terminate* it, if your policy is to leave the system for the Transvaal legislative assembly to decide' (EP, E to WSC 27 Dec 05, copy). H. W. Just was about right when he wrote: 'The broad fact is patent that they do not propose to put an end to Chinese Labour *in toto*, and that they are prepared, on the whole, to accept what has been done as a *fait accompli* for the time being' (African (S), 825, 'Chinese Labour: policy of His Majesty's Government', 6 Feb 06, CO. 879/92).

77

scarcely affected the features described as servile. Rigid segregation in the mine compounds continued.

Chinese Labour: administration. Once the major policy decisions had been taken, the main Chinese Labour problems which came before the colonial secretary related to the working out of the repatriation policy, the supervision of disciplinary problems on the Rand, and the legislative decisions of the new Transvaal government with respect to termination.

(*a*) *Repatriation problems.* The terms of the notice announcing the availability of State-aided repatriation were discussed at considerable length, and not finally approved by the secretary of state until 1 May 1906. Notices were posted about 12 May. By 27 May only twelve applications were received; a revised notice was posted early in July. By 1 January 1907, 1550 applications were received: 766 were repatriated.[1]

On 12 April 1906 Selborne telegraphed the opinion of the Chamber of Mines: to post notices in compounds would lead to more than a third of the coolies petitioning to go. This telegram prompted a long minute by Churchill, for it raised the question 'are we to keep our pledges given to Parliament or not?' He felt sure that parliament would insist on a public announcement to the coolies. 'Mere mutterings by the mine inspectors' would not suffice. The government had to face the fact that all the Transvaal authorities admired the system they administered and were deeply concerned to protect it from what they regarded as the foolish intervention of the British government. Churchill did not therefore trust them for any anti-Chinese purpose. The government had always been assured that the Chinese were content, but the confession that one-third might go fortified all their suspicions about the impropriety and even harshness of the industrial system on the Rand. The explanation they were asked to accept was that the Chinese wanted to go back to China,

[1] CO. 291/116; memo. by Vernon 20 Feb 07.

not because they are unhappy in South Africa, but because they are so happy in South Africa, that they want to go back to China in the hopes of coming back again to South Africa. Such fantastic humbug was never before offered upon official papers.

This caustic analysis was followed by curt recommendations:

The announcement should be public and immediate. The process of examination among the labourers applying should be elaborate and gradual. In any case two or three months' notice should be required with reduced pay. This should be made known at the same time. The first result to a Chinaman of an application should be *not* a free passage home, but a spell of hard work with no pay. Make that clear and there will be no unmanageable rush.

Elgin supported Churchill, though with misgivings. Throughout he had acted on the hypothesis that the number of *bona fide* cases would not be excessive, nothing like one-third. He described himself as now in 'a horrible dilemma', and inclined to consult the cabinet. 'I do not pretend', he wrote, 'to any intimate knowledge of the nature of Chinamen, but I have had some opportunity of framing an opinion', and he could not reject as impossible the effect on the mind of a coolie which had been forecast as resulting in one-third demanding repatriation. If they were starting afresh he could have enquired more fully: but they had gone too far already to abandon public announcement; he wished that he could take a different view, 'for I cannot shut my eyes to the fact that if . . . one-third of the coolies demand repatriation – a very serious commercial, and perhaps political, situation may develop'.[1] Public notification, therefore, could not be abandoned. Elgin repeated justifications for their policy to Selborne. He reminded him that as soon as the House of Commons reassembled, Churchill was challenged on the subject of repatriation; their scheme was not free from

---

[1] CO. 291/98/12925, minutes 17 and 19 Apr 06; EP, E to WSC 17 and 19 Apr (photocopies); privately he wrote: 'As I think you know, I have never been quite sure that there was a necessity for public notices – and I should not like to be responsible for either an industrial collapse at this moment or an excessive Imperial charge' (EP, E to WSC 16 Apr 06, photocopy).

difficulties, but it would be 'an error in tactics' not to meet those difficulties at once.[1] Repatriation was urgent, he suggested, from a consideration of Selborne's own interests:

You probably do not realise strength of feeling for [immediate] compulsory repatriation. We have with difficulty managed compromise on basis of our scheme. But continued delay in giving effect to it prejudices our position, and increased number of offences in last returns may give opportunity for renewed attack on whole system.... I hold entirely to restricting operation of scheme to cases ascertained to be genuine by full enquiry and probation, both on principle, and because this was essential condition of assistance from Imperial funds.[2]

The attempt to imitate the language of Chinese proclamations in the wording of the repatriation notice excited some adverse comment.[3] Elgin thought it extraordinary that people would not give them some discretion in wording such documents, 'but it is some evidence of the truth of my contention that there is considerable latent feeling which might easily be blown up into a flame.'[4] Elgin was irritated by House of Commons naïvety.

[1] EP, E to Selb. 28 Apr 06 (copy).   [2] Ibid. tel. 24 Apr 06.

[3] The repatriation proclamation explained to the Chinese that payment of costs under existing repatriation provisions would no longer be insisted upon: 'An exceptional act of benevolence of this kind ought to command your gratitude. ... It must be understood that no-one who has not served in the Transvaal for at least six months need apply: for you all know that beginnings are not easy, and anyone undertaking work partaking of a novel character cannot be in a position to judge whether or not he is fit for it until he has given it a fair trial. The obvious duty of all who desire to return to China is to save money . . .' for their return, but, 'I am willing to consider genuine applications with a view to rendering assistance. I solemnly warn you that any attempts to deceive me by misrepresentations which are punishable by the law of the Transvaal will be dealt with accordingly.' Churchill announced the terms of this proclamation to the House of Commons on 3 May 06. On 7 May Mr Chiozza Money asked why the word 'benevolence' was used. Churchill replied that the object was 'to assure the Chinese coolies that the Imperial Government, while willing to provide relief in exceptional cases, had no desire to incite them to leave their work, and will bear no malice against those who do not avail themselves of the facilities offered. In view of the fact that it is the British taxpayer who will bear any charges which may be involved, the word "benevolence" does not seem to me to be ill-chosen; nor would gratitude be wholly ill-placed on the part of the Chinese thus enabled by the intervention of a distant community to return unexpectedly to their native land' (PD. 156/706–7).

[4] EP, E to Selb. 7 May 06 (copy).

Unless we could transport the House of Commons to the East it would, I admit, be useless to attempt [to] explain the etiquettes which there prevail. But that they *do* differ from our notions everybody who has experience of the East knows well.[1]

Resolutions and remonstrances poured on Selborne from every side. This did not surprise him. Although his private opinion was that there would not be a great exodus of Chinese, owing to the fact that the great majority of them were contented with their lot, 'nobody can disguise the fact that it is a leap in the dark. The Chinese character is so different from ours that it is impossible to say beforehand how they will take it.'[2] By the beginning of June Elgin was hopeful of being able to use the action taken on the notices, even though the number of applications was small, to steady some of the impatient members of the Liberal party.[2] Feeling against the terms of the proclamation, which were thought to be deterrent rather than encouraging, grew in the House of Commons. Elgin thought it was probably based largely 'on misunderstanding of Oriental custom and therefore difficult to dispel'. It was most undesirable to allow the agitation to continue. Alterations would have to be made. Suggested alterations were communicated to Selborne on 28 June, Elgin explaining:

We want to effectually remove what is proving dangerous demonstration, and this is result of careful enquiry by Churchill into feeling of House. I should have preferred to do less, but it is difficult to make same language equally intelligible to British and Chinese. While new notice will reassure British, I hope it will not convey idea of change of policy to Chinese after full explanation they have already received.[4]

Churchill's reflections on the necessity for a new notice were as follows:

The existing notice was defended by me as being a fair fulfilment of our pledges; but I did not and do not feel convinced that it would prove to be so. All depended on the working.

---

[1] CO. 291/98/17941, minute 4 Jun 06.   [2] EP, Selb. to E 7 May 06.
[3] EP, E to Selb. 1 Jun 06 (copy).   [4] EP, E to Selb. tel. 28 Jun 06 (copy).

If it had been fairly worked, I am sure more Chinamen would have gone. I cannot tell what secret pressures have operated. Anyhow my plea has been treated with disdain by all political parties in this country. The notice is universally described as a hoax. The Prime Minister has described it as a 'burlesque' of our intentions. The results of it have been lamentably small.[1]

The Chinese translation of the new proclamation was a literal one and no effort was made to render it in Chinese official style. In order to remove all possible doubt or suspicion as to government intentions 'all minatory and hortatory sentences' contained in the original proclamation were omitted.[2] The new notice clearly specified that the coolie was to give half his wages for one month towards the expenses of repatriation. In practice no distinction was made between applicants under the two proclamations.

On 4 August Selborne reported that 375 coolies had been approved for repatriation, but the majority of them were unable to contribute anything towards their expenses. The original arrangement was that the British government should provide £17.0.0., the payment of which sum under the ordinance entitled a coolie to be repatriated by his employer. Elgin hoped that nothing would be done to hinder, much less to prevent, the repatriation of all coolies who met the conditions of the proclamation, even though the expense exceeded £17.0.0. He did not, however, understand the statement that the majority of the 375 applicants professed inability to contribute to the cost of repatriation by working:

If they are able-bodied they ought to work; if not, they ought to be repatriated by mine-owners at their own expense as unfit and sickly. . . . It should be clearly understood that H.M.G. do not intend to relieve mine-owners of their proper responsibilities of bearing expense of repatriation of sickly, useless or dangerous characters, and whenever possible the test of making applicants work for a month should be employed.[3]

Then on 18 August Selborne telegraphed that before the

[1] CO. 291/99/22581, minute 29 Jul o6.
[2] CO. 291/110/23986, S/S to Selb. 5 Jul o6.
[3] CO. 291/101/28886; S/S to Selb. 11 Aug o6.

first batch of coolies could sail, the Labour Importation Agency required payment of their expenses, which amounted to £10,000. Elgin authorised this, 'for it would never do not to get the first batch of repatriated coolies off'.[1]

Another snag was discovered in January 1907. Although the actual number of licences issued was 63,043, as a result of a series of clerical errors, there were altogether 63,302 Chinese expected to arrive; that is to say, 259 more than the official number.[2] These must be returned to China at once, said Churchill. The House of Commons had been assured that the limit had been reached. Rectification of the mistake was a clear duty. Inconvenience was no reason for breaking a promise: nor did a clerical error legalise a breach of law. There might have been a clerical error, said Elgin, but it showed 'extraordinary carelessness' in keeping the record on a matter where accuracy was obviously needed.[3] Elgin thought it a stupid blunder, but the cost of repatriating the 259 would be excessive, and probably borne by the British tax payer; the House of Commons would surely understand that it was an accident and that they were not bound to act.[4] In view of the obvious difficulty, and Selborne's very strong and repeated pleas against repatriating the 259 coolies, the request to rectify the accident was not pressed. The colonial office simply trusted that the 259 excess would pass undetected.[5]

The new Transvaal government took office under Botha on 21 March 1907. In August 1907 they proposed to remove the

[1] CO. 291/102/30784, minute 24 Aug 06.   [2] CO. 291/115/159.
[3] Ibid. minutes 3 and 4 Jan 07. On 3 Jan 07 WSC wrote to E: 'I must most strongly and earnestly appeal to you to enable me to keep faith with the House of Commons on this point. . . . I had to promise that if any had been shipped beyond the licensed number they should be repatriated at once.
'I never dreamed that such would prove the case: and I am quite sure you never intended it to happen. But it has; and we ought to act up to our words – unless the currency of Colonial Office pledges is to be seriously depreciated'; and again on 8 Jan: 'I do not want to be unreasonable about the 259 extra Chinese and if great difficulties are encountered in repatriating them I suppose they will have to stop. But it is important that we should have a try. I daresay the House of Commons will be content with that and will recognise that the mistake was pure accident' (EP).
[4] EP, E to WSC 4 Jan 07 (photocopy).
[5] EP, WSC to E 11 Jan 07. The fact did not escape notice, but a row was avoided.

notices. Elgin admitted that as the last arrivals came into the Transvaal in January 1907, there was foundation for the opinion that a sufficient period of time had elapsed for those who wished to avail themselves of the offer of repatriation to do so. On the other hand, he felt that the retention of the notice would constitute a safeguard for the Administration, as well as for the labourers themselves. Its value was not to be measured merely by the numbers of those who applied to be repatriated under it. He therefore urged ministers to weigh carefully the expediency of not withdrawing the notice.[1]

(b) *Disciplinary problems.* Particularly before responsible government was established in the Transvaal in 1907, general supervision of the administration of the system, especially in its disciplinary aspects, was a matter to which the Liberal government had inevitably to pay considerable attention, if only because of the large number of questions asked in the House of Commons about the treatment of the Chinese. In order to cope with anticipated parliamentary questions, a telegram was despatched to Selborne on 16 January asking for full information on various points – for example, the working of the new system of magisterial jurisdiction exercised by the superintendent and inspectors, the investigation of Chinese complaints, the precise functions of the Chinese compound police, a comparison of Chinese and African wage-earnings and ration supplies. In addition, Lyttelton's warning that irregular and illegal punishment could not be tolerated, was repeated. Conclusive evidence that such practices were effectually prohibited by all concerned, was required.[2]

The question of illegal flogging burst on the political scene. Lyttelton had remonstrated with Milner for having in 1904 authorised the corporal punishment of Chinese without the safeguards of the law and without reference to him. Lyttelton and Balfour were amazed at Milner's carelessness. 'A bad business', 'extraordinary stupidity', 'this amazing blunder' –

---

[1] CO. 291/119/30475, S/S to Selb. 28 Aug 07.
[2] CO. 291/88/649.

these were some of the phrases they used in private.[1] On being asked by them to give an explanation, Milner had no recollection of the incident, now nearly a year old. He imagined that he must have regarded the matter as of no great importance. Lyttelton had not tried to suppress the incident, especially as it was bound to leak out.[2] When the relevant parliamentary paper was published, it was revealed that Milner had not objected to illegal flogging.[3] Churchill described Milner as guilty of a grave dereliction of duty. A motion of censure on Milner was debated in the Commons on 21 March 1906. Churchill's pompous and patronising speech on this occasion won him little credit.[4] He called Milner 'a guilty Parnell'. Lord Halifax then proposed in the Lords a motion approving of Milner's services to the empire. This proposal was discussed by the cabinet. Ministers thought it undesirable to revive the old controversy when a new constitution was to be established and feeling was running high. They wished to prevent a debate on this 'acrimonious subject'. Reasons were put to Halifax for abandoning his motion, but he persisted.[5] The debate took place on 29 March. Elgin would not say anything which might grate on the ear or unintentionally seem unjust. Milner had done his work 'strenuously, faithfully and disinterestedly'. More than this he would not say. The government would not examine the policies of Milner and the late government, because it would involve 'the use of language which might aggravate difficulties or create new ones'. Real discussion of the

[1] Gollin, *Proconsul in politics*, pp. 70–2. Balfour papers, 49775/51, 49708/93, Oct and Sep 05.

[2] CAB. 37/80/160, cab. memo. by Lyttelton 19 Oct 05, with annexure, Milner to Lyttelton 8 Oct 05.

[3] Cd. 2786.

[4] PD. 154/493–9. Marsh describes this speech as one of WSC's failures: it was 'generally felt to be unbecoming in its tone and was long remembered against him ... the fault was one of manner, not of feeling ... harshness of utterance ... he appeared to be taunting a discredited statesman with the evil days on which he had fallen' (*A number of people*, p. 152).

[5] CAB. 41/30/51, CB to the king 26 Mar 06: if intemperate speeches were made in the Lords, the Commons would not be slow to take up the challenge: 'a mischievous and unseemly, and wholly unnecessary conflict between the Houses would thus arise, with the worst effect.'

motion would only raise up further obstacles to the progress of peace and good will in South Africa.[1]

When Selborne reported in April 1906 that more coolies had been flogged, Churchill wrote in despair: 'What are we to do with people so reckless of their own interests as to continue these floggings and malpractices after all that has happened?' Abuses seemed widespread. Elgin was more patient. He detected an evident desire to meet their wishes:

It must be remembered that the system which, for good reasons, we are altering, was worked out by Lord Selborne avowedly in the interest of the coolies. It is the duty of the Transvaal Government to preserve any provisions in the interest of the coolies if at all compatible with our requirements – and we should not discourage the attempt.[2]

Early in June the government had before them the report of a committee which had considered measures to control lawless Chinese. Churchill would not have allowed any aggravation of the restrictions upon the Chinese, except by means of increased police supervision at the importers' expense, during the time in which the Liberal government was responsible for the administration of the ordinance. Elgin likewise thought it dangerous to tighten up restrictions:

I do not think it possible [he minuted], to defend the position of H.M.G., unless we maintain the status quo, so far as the liberties of the Chinese are differentiated from ordinary workmen, either by provisions of special laws, or erection of barriers and the like. Even that position is challenged in the House of Commons, and if we begin to alter the conditions in one direction, we shall have an immediate, and possibly irresistible, demand for alterations in the other. . . . It is just because the whole state of affairs is provisional that we cannot do these

[1] PD. 154/1414–94, 29 Mar 06. Sir Almeric Fitzroy recorded in his diary: 'Elgin had little to say, but said it well' (*Memoirs*, i, 288). Halifax moved 'that this House desires to place on record its high appreciation of the services rendered by Lord Milner in South Africa to the Crown and the Empire'. Dr Gollin suggests that the censure of Milner in the Commons was not an isolated or meaningless incident, but a symbol of the different approaches to imperial problems between the two parties (Gollin, op. cit. p. 99).

[2] CO. 291/98/12750, minutes 16 and 21 Apr 06.

things. It is like a house of cards – if you touch one card the whole edifice tumbles.[1]

It was Elgin's fixed determination to do everything possible to assimilate the conditions of the Chinese to those of other labourers. The main change made in August 1906, modifying the regulations, therefore, was to prohibit certain forms of punishment, viz, the deduction of fines from wages, fining a 'head boy' who did not report offences, and collective punishment of gangs. Trials by inspectors were to be held in public, not in the compounds.

But the tendency to punish Chinese harshly was hard to eradicate. In the summer of 1907 Churchill was disturbed by the punishment of Chinese for visiting white prostitutes and brothel-keeping in Johannesburg. His minute on the subject reflected hatred of the entire system:

In my opinion the whole responsibility for this and other occurrences rests with those who have brought about this horrible experiment; and they have no right to try to clear their own consciences by imposing ferocious sentences upon the unhappy victims of their greed.[2]

The absence of Chinese women on the Rand was a considerable source of disciplinary trouble. There were allegations of 'unnatural practices', which Elgin thought they ought not to show any disinclination to investigate. It was one of the most serious 'moral' difficulties of the situation. He assured Selborne that he did not wish

to use it as a lever for other ends. Nothing, however, would more inevitably lead to such use, than the discovery that warnings such as those now before us had been received – had been neglected – and *had been founded on fact.*

That was why he pressed the matter on Selborne's attention. A report by Mr Bucknill was eventually laid before the secretary of state, but not surprisingly, its contents were considered

[1] CO. 291/99/20208, minutes 9 and 10 Jun 06.
[2] CO. 291/117/18568, minute 2 Jun 07.

unprintable.[1] Churchill enjoyed himself enormously in tackling the subject in the House of Commons, where partial disclosures aroused a great stir. His relish, and his command of the appropriate vocabulary, were unusual in the days before M.P.s became more accustomed to hearing allegations of homosexuality.[2] Administratively, Elgin urged the view that any coolie against whom any suspicion of 'professionalism' could be entertained, should be immediately treated as undesirable, and repatriated by the mine-owners: men convicted of a crime entailing such severe punishment were surely 'disorderly'.[3]

Elgin agreed with Churchill that the only real remedy for outrages committed by coolies, was to try to convert public opinion in the Transvaal to the policy of repatriation.[4] The key to understanding Elgin's handling of the routine admini-

[1] E to Selb. 27 Oct 06: 'I have seen and partially read the Report on Chinese immorality. It is not pleasant reading, but surely will disprove the worst charges'; tel. E to Selb. 22 Nov 06: 'I accept Bucknill's report but its publication alone would have certainly been followed by demand for evidence, which I hope has been avoided by my statement'; see also E to Selb. 23 Nov 06 (EP, copies). The matter was discussed by the cabinet (EP, E to Lady E 15 Nov 06).

[2] Mr Lehmann alleged in the House of Commons that 'a great moral disaster' was occurring on the Rand. It was 'a disagreeable, nay, a detestable and horrible matter', namely, 'systematic unnatural vice'. Many of the coolies, he said, were dressed, and wore their hair, in a special fashion intended to show that they might be used for this purpose. Churchill took all this in his stride. First he referred to suspicions that there was a prevalence of a specific disease of a peculiar nature to which he need 'not specifically refer'. Then, he said, it was true that there was a percentage of proved catamites in all compounds. (The word 'catamite' was rendered 'Amalekite' by the mystified and innocent shorthand writer, who must have thought Churchill had got a biblical allusion wrong.) Some expert witnesses, Churchill continued, said they could detect a person affected by sodomy (another word nobody else had dared to use); others said that they could not, and the 'indications would in any case be of a very minute kind, perhaps only of a character to be understood by those who dealt in such matters and not by others who had no sympathy or agreement with them'. Having made this reply, Churchill proclaimed privately that he 'smote the Radicals hip and thigh from Sodom to Gomorrha' (PD. 165/191–219, 15 Nov 06; C. Hassall, *Edward Marsh, a biography* (1959), 163). The episode is an early example of Churchill's skill in exploiting the theme of homosexuality for humorous purposes: for later examples, connoisseurs may be referred to M. Davidson, *The world, the flesh and myself* (1962), p. 282. For House of Commons excitement, see the *Annual Register for 1906*, pp. 235–6, 400.

[3] EP, E to Selb. 14 July; tel. 10 Nov 06, 7 Jun 07.

[4] CO. 291/93/44963, minutes 2 Jan 06.

strative problems of Chinese labour, and to much of his anxiety to get the repatriation scheme working properly, seems to lie in his conviction that it was imperative to ward off criticism in the House of Commons. This criticism might have developed into a demand for summary curtailment of the whole system.

(c) *Termination problems*. In February 1907 Churchill wrote:

Our duty is quite clear. Chinese Labour under the compound system must be brought to an end . . . any Ordinance of an objectionable character will have to be vetoed – no matter what majority is behind it [in the Transvaal].[1]

It was decided in July 1906, that the last day of November 1906 should be the day upon which the issue of licences to recruit in China for the mines would be stopped.[2] The letters patent granting responsible government to the Transvaal stipulated that the Labour Importation Ordinances were to be repealed, and were to cease to have effect at the end of one year from the opening of the Transvaal legislature. Thereafter the main question was – would the new Transvaal government renew existing contracts? Churchill's nervousness on this point emerges from a minute recorded on 28 April 1907. The present House of Commons would not, he believed, sanction renewal, but

on the other hand, a conflict with the new Transvaal Government, and still worse with a unanimous and far less friendly Transvaal legislature, might lead very quickly into unfathomed waters. It appears therefore to be a most important object of State policy to avoid altogether, and at an early stage, becoming committed to such unpromising alternatives. . . . So many verbal assurances have already been given upon the subject of Chinese Labour, that considerable sympathy may be extended to those supporters of the Government who desire that something tangible and solid should at last be done. This can only take the form of real ships steering Eastwards with live Chinamen on board. The sooner that spectacle is exhibited, and

[1] CO. 291/106/2459, 8 Feb 07.
[2] CO. 291/110/23986.

the larger its scale, the better it will be for all concerned. . . . Once the serious and actual repatriation of the Chinese was in progress, we should be ready to discuss with the Transvaal Government the speed at which that repatriation should continue, in a spirit of mutual accommodation – provided always that the diminution of Chinese upon the Rand was constant and their extinction certain.

If the gold industry was becoming seriously disorganised, he could quite believe 'that there would be a very strong case for some spinning out of the process'.[1]

When the relevant clauses of the Transvaal Constitution were being framed, Elgin recorded his impression that the existing ordinance would come to an end soon enough to prevent renewal of contracts under its conditions, at any rate for the great majority of the coolies.

If however the right of renewal is an essential part of the contracts, the sacredness of which, especially in the minds of the coolies it is . . . important not to disturb, it is difficult to press this point too far, and I should prefer to allow the system to expire without more risk of convulsions than is necessary.[2]

While in England for the colonial conference in 1907, Botha avowed a determination not to import any more Chinese, and completely to abolish the system as soon as possible. However, he asked Elgin to undertake to consider proposals, if made by him, for some form of renewal of the contracts, because he foresaw a possible difficulty in filling up all places, if repatriation on expiry of contracts were insisted upon. Under these circumstances, Elgin hoped that Botha would allow all those whose contracts expired during 1907 to be repatriated without question. If this could be achieved, fresh legislation (to deal with the coolies whose contracts did not expire after the one year allowed in the constitution for the continuation of the ordinances) would not be required till January 1908. By this time Botha might be in a position to propose nothing more than was

[1] African (S), 880.
[2] EP, Cab. memo. 12 Nov 06.

necessary for the protection of life and property. 'Those who know the position in the House of Commons assure me that it would be dangerous to attempt more'.[1] In writing to Botha, Elgin said:

It will be the desire of H.M.G. to consider in a fair and impartial spirit, any provisions which may be required to secure the peace and good order of the country. But it is my duty to warn you, that we must act up to the pledges which we have given, and we do not see how, consistently with that obligation, we could agree to the renewal of the contracts entered into under the present Ordinance.[2]

At the end of August an amendment act was passed by the Transvaal legislature, keeping the ordinance and regulations alive until the expiry of the existing contracts of three years. This surprised Elgin, for his preliminary discussions with Botha in London left him with the impression that Botha had accepted the proposition that if the British government were asked to assent to an extension of the ordinance, there could be considerable modification of the provisions most objected to in Britain. Elgin had given no advance promise of assent. There was no bargain. Now, to avoid friction and the appearance of difference of opinion, he asked the Transvaal government to consider introducing modifications of practice by administrative action, and thereby strengthen the Liberal government's position in defending the course taken. Their pledges to *repeal* the ordinance were 'very specific'; its re-enactment with the omission only of one sub-section, could scarcely at first sight be reconciled therewith. He admitted that in defending the Transvaal proposal it would be possible to point out that the amending ordinance of 1905 improved the system, that the definite object of the new bill was to terminate it, and so forth: but Elgin earnestly hoped that Botha would not object to bringing the Chinese, so far as it could safely be done, into the position of other men. After all, he argued, by March 1908 (when the existing ordinance expired), the numbers would be

[1] EP, E to Selb. 4 May 07 (copy).   [2] EP, E to Botha 4 May 07 (copy).

considerably decreased, and they would steadily decrease every month. Police difficulties would lessen correspondingly.[1]

Elgin secured the assent of the cabinet to his final determination not to disallow the renewed ordinance. His despatch stated that the government recognised,

while maintaining their objections, that the declaration of your Ministers that it is their fixed policy to make an end of the Chinese Labour experiment now governs the whole position.

Yielding to the distinct opinion of your Ministers, H.M.G. have decided not to press at present for the administrative changes which they suggested to assimilate treatment of Chinese to that of natives, and they will not advise His Majesty to disallow the Act.

They however reserve the right to make further suggestions in administrative matters connected with the Act hereafter, if it should appear to them expedient to do so, and they confidently expect that your Ministers, having associated themselves with condemnation of whole system will readily remove, so far and so soon as public convenience permits, all that is objectionable in practice.[2]

Botha did not re-enact the labour ordinance; so the Chinese departed on expiry of the renewed contracts.

Thus earlier threats of imposing Liberal principles on a self-governing Transvaal did not entirely materialise. Respect for the principle of self-government was recognised as almost the predominant consideration, as Ripon had always said it must be. Ministers had apparently discovered that the situation on the Rand was not perhaps as evil as they may have imagined when they were out of office, or as their supporters continued to allege. Pressure from the House of Commons, brought to bear upon the cabinet partly by Churchill, may have compelled them to declare that Liberal principles must prevail, and that the system should not only be mitigated, but ended as soon as possible. But it seems that in the last resort, the cabinet must

[1] EP, E to Selb. 30 Aug 07 (copy).
[2] CO. 291/120/38741, S/S to Selb. tel. 27 Nov 07.

have come near to agreeing with the opinion of one of their advisers, Mr Keith, who wrote: 'No-one could really hold that Chinese Labour is so serious as to discredit the Empire, or justify a breach of the policy of non-interference with self-governing Colonies'.[1] The difficulty was that Chinese Labour had become a symbol of Unionist and capitalist iniquity and greed. As such it had to be attacked. Although Campbell-Bannerman had once described Chinese Labour as 'the biggest scheme of human dumping since the Middle Passage was adopted',[2] ministers plainly did not regard the question in the same light as the Atlantic slave trade was regarded a century earlier. Such action as they took was, to a considerable extent, the result of House of Commons pressure.[3]

Aftermath: problems of indentured labour. Because they found that they could not regard Chinese Labour as irredeemably bad, the Liberals did not become adamantly opposed to every form of indentured labour. It appeared in the New Hebrides under government sponsorship in 1906, and the government was much abused.[4] On the other hand, the various examples of indentured Asiatic labour everywhere became subject to cautious scrutiny. One of the most fascinating facets of the study of imperial policy is to see the way in which situations in one part of the empire affected policy towards parallel situations elsewhere. Chinese Labour provides a whole crop of examples. The problem of indentured labour was discussed with reference to Canada and Australia, to Hong Kong and British Honduras.

[1] CO. 291/95/2635, minute 24 Jan 06.   [2] CB, *Speeches*, p. 144, 21 Mar 04.

[3] On 10 Feb 06, Selborne reported a serious faction fight between Africans of two mines. This received little publicity because they were not Chinese. He also observed that the condition of indentured Indians in Natal was worse than that of the Chinese in the Transvaal: only 12% had wives, there was more deliberate desertion, average wages were less, food and accommodation worse. But this attracted little governmental interest. Ommanney dismissed the report shortly with the remark that 'The Natal coolies are not at present a factor in domestic politics' (EP, minute on Selb. to E 10 Feb 06, Mar 06). Public opinion, it seems, could determine the particular issues on which government chose to fight general principles.

[4] See p. 309.

The governor-general of Australia, Lord Northcote, felt that the opposition to Chinese and Japanese labour there was selfish and short-sighted, and was led by the Labour party who feared that wages would be lowered. To keep immigration within bounds, in 1905 he was thinking of suggesting the issue of 10,000 licences to Chinese traders and others to work for a fixed term of years in Australia. This was before he learned of Liberal policy on Chinese Labour. Elgin swiftly checked him. The mention of licences for Chinese, he wrote, caused a perceptible shudder:

I don't say the circumstances are at all the same as those in South Africa, but you know how much a 'cry' once established is apt to dominate a situation. And I venture to think that, however much coloured labour may be required, and I can quite see that in no other way can you hope to develop parts of your territories, still it would be wise to put forward proposals that cannot be associated in the public mind with those that have given and are still giving us so much trouble in the Transvaal.[1]

Elgin also warned Lord Grey, governor-general of Canada, that he had heard criticism of a speech made by Grey at the Canada Club about the need for cheap labour to develop British Columbia, as the cheap labour would be Chinese. While Elgin's hands were still full of the South African controversy, the entire question of cheap labour needed to be treated with great caution and reserve.[2]

There was prolonged discussion about labour emigration from Hong Kong. An ordinance of 1889 made it illegal for Hong Kong coolies to be recruited for work outside the British empire, but in 1906 a British trader named Dodwell requested an amendment which would enable him to tender for shipping coolies to Panama. Churchill saw no reason to question the wisdom of the policy of 1889, especially as a change might quite unnecessarily add to the many difficulties which Chinese indentured labour had brought upon the government, and

---

[1] EP, 2 Feb 06 (copy).   [2] EP, 7 Jan 06.

tend to prejudice the conduct of far more important matters in South Africa. Elgin, on the other hand, pointed out that a decision had been taken in 1905 not to object to the despatch of coolies to the Panama Canal. Although it had been then over-looked that the decision would be illegal, Elgin was much inclined to follow it, since the Chinese government was not likely to submit much longer to any interference with the emigration of its subjects. He was not prepared to condemn all labour under contract, though he objected to the conditions of the contract in South Africa. All the same, it was an incon-venient moment to make a change in the direction suggested. He refused to create possible Chinese Labour complications just for the sake of a single British trader. Dodwell must be told that the moment was inopportune. His proposal must stand over, without any prejudice to its being reconsidered later.[1] Churchill went even further: the regulations governing Hong Kong migrant traffic ought not, he said, even to allow British subjects to carry Chinese coolies in British ships to foreign countries unless they had ascertained that the conditions of future employment in Mexico and America would be so far superior to Rand conditions as to be wholly unobjectionable. If the British government stopped Chinese Labour in South Africa – the evil conditions of which were, at least, superior to any conditions prescribed hitherto by foreign countries in such cases –

all the more are they bound to abstain themselves from any participation in the profits arising from the conveyance of coolies to conditions of servitude, not less and possibly more 'tainted with slavery' than those which have been denounced upon the Witwatersrand.[2]

His view was confirmed by the conduct of the Opposition on the New Hebrides convention,[3]

which shows very clearly the sort of use that will be made of the action to which we are asked to commit ourselves; and whereas

---

[1] CO. 129/335/31440, minutes 31 Aug and 4 Sep 06, S/S to govr. 7 Sep 06.
[2] CO. 885/8/*Eastern*, 105, 26 Oct 06.   [3] See p. 309.

in the case of the New Hebrides Convention there were no real grounds for a charge of inconsistency, there appears to me to be considerable ground in this matter, of which full advantage will be taken in the House and in the country.

Personally Elgin thought the circumstances so completely different from those in South Africa that it was unfair to condemn a carrying trade, in which Britain had nothing whatever to do with either the previous engagement or subsequent employment of the coolie.

But no doubt the debate on the New Hebrides shows once more that any stick is good enough to beat a dog with. If however, H.M.G. were of opinion that in view of the serious loss to British shipping and the stimulus to foreign competition which will result if no steps are taken in the matter, the instructions should be modified, I am disposed to think that the best course would be to lay down, that having regard to the abuses which formerly existed, H.M.G. are not prepared to authorise the governor to issue any such licences except under the most stringent regulations – regulations which must be carefully prepared by the Colonial Office in consultation with the Governor of Hong Kong and approved by H.M.G.[1]

Once the Transvaal had declared against continuation of Chinese Labour, it was felt in some quarters that alteration of the law might be easier. Elgin was ready to take the matter to the cabinet. Lloyd George, who was chiefly concerned, as president of the board of trade, was not inclined to move.[2] After several discussions, Elgin and Lloyd George decided not to act. Churchill agreed. A few months after Crewe came into office as colonial secretary, he decided against reopening the question, though there were, he thought, strong arguments in favour of relaxing the law.[3]

Elgin did not believe that all indentured labour was necessarily bad. With reference to the Pacific Phosphate Company's desire for Asiatic labour for Ocean Island he wrote:

[1] CO. 885/8, *Eastern*, 106, minutes 16 Feb 07.
[2] CO. 129/336/46689 and 340/23339 and 342/31506.
[3] CO. 129/347/20856, 27 Jun 08.

I am not sure that I feel so positive that this is 'indentured labour' – in the sense of the Chinese in Africa – as some of the minutes above. The Japanese – and the Japanese government – are well able to look after themselves, and until we know more I would not assume that proper arrangements cannot be made . . . I have thought for some time that the specialising of the term 'industrial labour' was inconvenient. There is surely no dispute of the fact that some forms of indentured labour are reasonable and proper. To my mind the 'indenture' is not the point at all – it is the 'power' invoked to enforce its conditions. Where that power is 'force' outside the ordinary law, the presumption is against the arrangement. But so far as I know the Company in this case has no 'force': and the position given to the Inspector (himself a Japanese) sounds exactly like that of a foreman in any gang of platelayers.[1]

Although in 1908 Seely estimated that in the House of Commons there was a majority of three to one in favour of the proposition that all indentured labour was bad, and ought to be put an end to as soon as possible,[2] ministers and officials had no such prejudice, though they were always wary about particular manifestations. Hence Balfour could taunt them by saying that in Africa indentured labour was regarded as slavery, elsewhere as social reform.

---

[1] CO. 225/77/45133, minute 4 Jan 08.

[2] CO. 137/668/16229, minute 13 May 08. The government was in favour of supplying labour deficiencies from India, both to ease congestion in India, and to placate Indians by showing them that parts of the empire were open to them (CO. 42/921/33369, minute by Hopwood 16 Sep 08). In 1907, however, when the governor of British Honduras submitted the necessity of importing East Indian labourers because of the shortage of agricultural labour, Hopwood, Churchill and Elgin agreed the matter must be left alone, whatever the business arguments. As the Hong Kong problem was unsolved, and the House of Commons was still keeping a close watch on all questions affecting indentured labour, a crusade against indentured labour in general might be launched. The possible lamentable results of such an event no-one could fairly estimate (CO. 123/256, minutes 24 and 26 Jul 07).

THE TRANSVAAL CONSTITUTION

The Unionist Legacy.[1] On 31 March 1905 the Unionist government issued letters patent granting to the Transvaal a
representative constitution,[2] known almost at once, and to
history, as the Lyttelton Constitution. This constitution never
came into operation. It was abrogated by the new Liberal
government.

Milner had not taken up proposals for representative
institutions in the Transvaal in response to a strong popular
demand. The unpopularity of Crown Colony government in
the Transvaal, however, was obvious.[3] Colonial office officials
thought of Crown Colony government as a failure in the
Transvaal.[4] It was bitterly resented by the British settlers. The
demand for self-government was spreading widely in 1904.
Milner thought that the only way in which he could hope to
control this tendency was to humour it to some extent. If the
government itself took the initiative it might be able to retard
the pace and perhaps to provide against some of the dangers.
Milner did not deny that with an overwhelmingly British
majority, responsible government would be by far the best
system, but it was his policy, in the absence of that majority, to
defer responsible government until either the Boers had learned
to acquiesce in membership of the empire, or the British
element had become so strengthened by immigration as to make
separation impossible.[5] He would have preferred to let several
years elapse before entering the path of constitutional change,
but he admitted that adherence to Crown Colony government

[1] The standard account of the Milner-Lyttelton constitution is by G. H. L. Le
May, *British supremacy in South Africa, 1899–1907* (1965), chap. 7; the account given
in the present work is prior and independent.
[2] A 'representative' constitution is one in which the executive council, partly
nominated by the governor, is not responsible to the elected representatives of the
people in the legislative assembly. A 'responsible' government constitution is one
in which the executive is responsible to the elected representatives.
[3] Balfour papers 49775/28, Lyttelton to Balfour 20 Jan 05.
[4] CO. 291/70/19079, minute by Graham 7 Jun 04.
[5] CO. 291/70/18245, Milner to S/S 2 May 04; in Liberal eyes this meant
deferring to the Greek Kalends.

would tend to alienate the affections of a large number of loyal people. Before granting responsible government, he wanted to have some experience of what popular election might produce; a period in which representative institutions would be a reality and in which, 'within very wide limits, "the people" should "manage their own affairs" ', was, he thought, reasonable in itself, and would lead 'gradually and without convulsions to complete self-government'.[1]

The Unionist government expected constitutional change to have two advantages. It would cut away the ground from under the feet of the opposition to Chinese Labour in the House of Commons, and it would forestall an incoming Liberal government in dealing with the question. Expecting electoral defeat, Lyttelton asked Milner whether it would not be wise to take the first step towards self-government 'under your and our guidance', rather than to leave the initiative to 'men who seem very reckless of the essential interests of South Africa'.[2]

Officials disliked the scheme, which involved placing the government in a minority in the Legislative Assembly. In their view, the first step should be merely that of introducing an elected minority, as opposed to an elected majority, and this should be the only step between Crown Colony government and self-government. Milner's proposal, dividing power and responsibility, was, they thought, vicious, and experience had proved it impossible to provide adequate safeguards against a paralysis of administration. They feared that with the government official members in a minority, the mining industry would have everything its own way, combining with the government against the Boers, and with the Boers against the government, just as suited its interests and convenience. Their argument was: 'If we can keep Cerberus quiet for a year or so by the sop of an elected minority, circumstances may have changed so much as to admit of complete self-government being given. But in less time than a year, we may hope that financial prosperity will have returned to the Transvaal, and in that case, the cry for

[1] CO. 291/74/43435, Milner to S/S 5 Dec 04.
[2] Headlam, *The Milner Papers*, ii, 520, Lyttelton to Milner 26 Apr 04.

self-government will be much less heard'.[1] But Lyttelton and the cabinet accepted a 'moderate elected majority' of elected members, wishing 'to concede the utmost liberty compatible with safety'. No change was contemplated for the Orange River Colony.[2]

In a despatch dated 5 December 1904, Milner said that there would be disappointment unless there were not less than thirty nor more than thirty-five elected members as against six to nine official members, and so he recommended an increase. This could hardly be described as a 'moderate elected majority'. The colonial office officials predicted that on all questions, except measures involving a charge on public funds, the government would be at the mercy of the elected members. Ommanney commented shortly: 'Government will be an impossibility'. On certain questions of imperial importance, South African opinion of all shades was known to be in absolute opposition to the policy of the British government; for these questions, 'the process would be very much like putting leading members of the Opposition into the Cabinet'.[3] Lyttelton asked for more information about Milner's views and recommendations. Public expectation of thirty elected members, he said, 'in itself hardly appears to be a sufficiently convincing ground' for providing so many. Twenty 'would have been more in accordance with the views originally expressed by H.M.G., and would have presented less difficulties and fewer risks of deadlock.' 'But', Lyttelton added, in a phrase revealing his ingrained deference to Milner's views, 'you are probably right in thinking such a number insufficient. . . . Assuming that the number of elected members is fixed at 30 or 35, it would be essential to adopt safeguards for the purpose of ensuring that the King's government could be carried on'.[4]

Milner's draft constitutional proposals arrived in January 1905. Officials found them 'bristling with questionable points'.[5]

[1] CO. 291/70/19079, minutes by Ommanney, Graham and Just June 04.
[2] CO. 291/71/23839, S/S to Milner 20 Jul 04.
[3] CO. 291/74/43435.
[4] Ibid. 43435, S/S to Milner 23 and 24 Jan 05.
[5] Ibid. 1376, minutes by Ommanney and Graham 19 Jan 05.

Almost immediately Milner himself began to have doubts whether the scheme would command adequate popular support. However, in their anxiety to move beyond Crown Colony government, the cabinet disregarded the objections of the colonial office and Milner's own misgivings, and issued the letters patent embodying what became known as 'the Lyttelton Constitution' on 31 March 1905, destined, as we have already noted, never to come into operation.[1]

The carefully prepared government despatch covering the promulgation of the new constitution expressed the Unionist belief that 'some time, though not they hope, a very long time, must still pass before the people of Colonies recently annexed after a long war should be entrusted with so great a control of their destinies' as full self-government gave. Responsible government implied, and in practice involved, party government:[2] parties in the Transvaal must for some time yet mainly coincide with the line of races. Party government would most probably mean government by one race or the other. It would become more practicable – Lyttelton himself drafted the remainder of the sentence – 'when the two races have, with equal rights of citizenship, lived and acted somewhat longer together and when bitter memories have become softened by the healing effect of time.' The Canadian analogy was alluded to, in order to point out the differences. Not the least of these was the presence of a coloured population, numerically much

[1] The Lyttelton Constitution provided that the Legislative Assembly was to have 6–9 officials and 30–35 elected members; white male British subjects over 21, with a specially defined monetary qualification (ownership of property worth £100 p.a., or a £10 p.a. rental or £100 p.a. wage), could vote, provided they were not descended 'from any of the aboriginal races or tribes of Africa'. The voters' roll was to be compiled on the principle of 'one vote one value', i.e. a voters basis as opposed to a population basis. This favoured the town-dwelling, English-speaking section of the population which contained an unusually large proportion of adult males (see p. 154). Equal distribution of single-member constituencies formed the basis of the electoral system, with automatic redistribution every four years. English was to be the language of debate, discussion and record, but Dutch could be spoken in the Assembly with the permission of the chairman.

[2] The very discussion of the constitution gave rise to the formation of parties in 1904: Het Volk by the Boers, the Progressive Association and the Responsible Government Association by the British.

in excess of the white South African population, which made it necessary 'to move with greater caution in the direction of political change'. The government were aware of the difficulties attending a system in which the Transvaal obtained effective control of legislation. Experience had frequently shown how much friction could occur. 'On the other hand, a system of this kind proved in Cape Colony and in Natal to be a school for self-government, a means of bringing citizens together in political co-operation, and a sphere for the natural selection of the men most fit to lead and ultimately to undertake the responsibility of administration.'[1]

The Lyttelton Constitution was not well received. Het Volk announced that it was unacceptable, and the Responsible Government Association threatened to do their best to make it unworkable. The Progressive Association at first appeared grateful, but by November they were convinced that they would win the elections. Their leaders then declared that if, when the Assembly met, the British government was not in sympathy with their views, it would require only the slightest inducement to lead the Progressives into an immediate agitation for full self-government.[2]

Two flaws in the letters patent were discovered. The vote was to be given to men who had been 'enrolled on the latest list of burghers', which was that of 1898, and by then notoriously defective. The secretary of state regretted debarring anyone entitled to vote, but as he refused to amend the letters patent, he could only hope that the number of those who were excluded by reason of deficiencies in the old burgher rolls, and not otherwise qualified for the franchise, was very small.[3] The second difficulty was that nobody had remembered to disqualify the soldiers of the British garrison from voting. Lyttelton did not

---

[1] CO. 291/91/10049. 'The two races' means British and Boers.
[2] CO. 291/87, Selb. to S/S 27 Nov 05. The Progressive Association and the Responsible Government Association were both English-speaking parties; the leaders of the former were connected closely with the mining industry, and the leaders of the latter, with the professions and commerce. Het Volk was the Boer party, advocating in particular, a population as opposed to a voters basis.
[3] CO. 291/84/30863, S/S to Selb. 1 Dec 05.

think that the registration of soldiers could be properly or justly maintained, but he did not wish to amend so solemn an instrument as the letters patent. A mere declaration of the government's intention and policy would, he thought, ease friction.[1] Besides these two points, Het Volk and the Responsible Government Association, in a joint deputation to the high commissioner, made five other recommendations. Selborne himself recommended an amendment which would increase the number of constituencies and seats.

All these issues came before the new Liberal ministers. Together they provided a convenient excuse to reconsider from the beginning the merits of the policy embodied in the despatch of 31 March 1905.[2] The failure of Crown Colony government and the unpopularity of the proposed Lyttelton constitution[3] gave the Liberals their chance to consider an alternative.

Initial consideration of the Transvaal problem, December 1905 and January 1906. One of the first exchanges of opinion between ministers on the subject of the Transvaal constitutional question was between the colonial secretary and a 'Liberal Imperialist'. In his letter to Elgin dated 16 December, already referred to,[4]

[1] CO. 291/83/20141, S/S to Selb. tel. 14 Jun 05.

[2] See minute by WSC 18 Dec 05, probably the first one he wrote as a minister: 'The question of the military vote is of small practical importance, but has acquired considerable sentimental significance. To the British, or Progressive Party, it is a trifle which cannot affect their electoral position. To the Dutch it not unnaturally presents itself as a menace. The increase in the number of constituencies is plainly desired by the Progressives to secure them possible minority representation, and also because, expecting to secure a majority, they are anxious to double it for working purposes.

'Both these questions make it desirable to amend the Letters Patent. The moment seems to have therefore come when H.M.G. may review and reconsider the position adopted by Mr Lyttelton in his despatch of March 31' (CO. 291/88/44104).

[3] It was not, however, as unpopular as Le May suggests: it was not quite a 'dormant constitution which no-one wanted and which the Colonial Office had heartily damned' (*British supremacy*, p. 183). Selborne would not have agreed with that assessment; Elgin thought it well supported (by the British) and Loreburn merely said opinion upon it locally was divided. A deputation representing the mining interest visited England in 1906 to support the Lyttelton Constitution, but it did not have the united support of those for whom it purported to speak (the *Annual Register for 1906*, 398).

[4] EP. See p. 65.

Grey declared that further importation of Chinese Labour should be stopped, and added: 'It looks too as if responsible government were the only way out of the impasse: it has its risks, but is not the risk of deferring it still greater?' In reply, Elgin said that had there been no decision and action upon the constitution by their predecessors, he would be

inclined to the side of the larger measure. There are no doubt difficulties in the uncertainties which now exist, but I quite see the force of your observation that the risk of deferring may be greater – for surely the certainty of a majority one way or the other will in itself raise awkward questions. I had been a little inclined on the papers as they stood, to take the stand which Lord Ripon suggested, i.e. that the thing had been done and must in the meantime run its course.[1]

If the view ascribed to Ripon was that the Lyttelton Constitution should be allowed to come into operation for a brief period, it is hard to reconcile it with his memorandum advocating immediate responsible government, written about ten days later.[2] Ripon might have been misunderstood, or he might have changed his mind.

A memorandum on the question was prepared by the colonial office staff at Elgin's request, and dated 16 December. It stated the issue:

To introduce responsible government at once would practically involve introducing it also into the Orange River Colony at once. . . . It must be admitted that in neither Colony does there seem to be any really strong body of opinion in favour of representative government. . . . The main question is, whether a fair trial is to be given to the Transvaal representative Constitution (with or without a larger number of members), or whether H.M.G. will adopt the alternative of the immediate grant of self-government.[3]

Apparently no very clear cabinet decision was come to. Obviously further consideration was needed, and accordingly a cabinet committee was set up at the end of December; the

[1] GP. 52, E to Grey 17 Dec 05.   [2] EP. Cab. memo. 26 Dec 05.
[3] African (S) 796, 16 Dec 05.

members were Loreburn (chairman), Ripon, Elgin, Asquith and Bryce.

Selborne at once began questioning the new government by telegraph. Would they amend the letters patent in response to any of the demands which were being made? Het Volk and the Responsible Government Association protested against Lyttelton's franchise qualification. They objected that 'one vote one value' gave inadequate representation to sparsely populated rural districts. The Progressive Association wanted an increase in the number of constituencies, a change also favoured by Selborne. On 20 December Selborne was informed that consideration of the question of responsible government involved delay in replying to his telegrams regarding amendments in the letters patent. He was asked to forward the opinions of the Responsible Government party and of Het Volk on the proposed increase of seats, and invited to make any observations for the guidance of the Liberal government in considering how far responsible government, if granted, could follow the lines of the letters patent.[1] Elgin intended this telegram to show Selborne that they did not wish to overlook him.[2]

Throughout December and much of January, Elgin assumed that the representative Constitution would come into force. Modifications to it therefore formed the basis of discussions he had during that time. In the interests of the Boers, as well as of the colony as a whole, Elgin thought that it would be far better to have the first government with a British majority, and a strong Boer minority, than the other way round. He therefore inclined to retaining 'one vote one value', as it seemed likely to produce that result. As regards the increase of seats, he did not think that Selborne in suggesting it had any intention of favouring one side or the other. Undoubtedly an Assembly of thirty-five did not, he thought, provide scope for a government and an opposition under responsible government. Perhaps it would be possible to obtain early cabinet sanction for the proposed increase to sixty seats. If they could quickly determine

---

[1] CO. 291/88, tel. 20 Dec 05.   [2] CB. 41214/20, E to CB 26 Dec 05.

the two points of the number of seats and the franchise qualification, the commission to delimit constituencies could begin
work in February as originally planned. The other details of the
constitution could then be adjusted later with due deliberation.
On the other hand, if there was likely to be much discussion on
these points, 'we might fall back on Ripon's suggestion at the
first Cabinet and let the "representative" Constitution be
established in May, if only for a few months'.[1]

Ripon agreed that it would be best to have a British majority
with a strong Boer minority in the first legislature, provided
that there was no attempt to bring this about by any exceptional
measure.

As for the increase of seats, on the present system proposed by
Selborne, I do not object to it in itself, if the Lyttelton Constitution is to be brought into operation at all; on the contrary
I think it would be an improvement; but my idea was that we
were going to let that Constitution drop altogether and to
establish responsible government in its place with as little delay
as possible.[2]

The cabinet on 3 January decided that the question of
granting responsible government had to be postponed pending
receipt of further information from Selborne, and consideration
of the views which Smuts wished to place before them. They
did not expect a full decision of the constitutional question much
before the end of February. The election occupied most of
January, and made it impossible for the cabinet committee to
meet and for the cabinet to decide. In the meantime, Elgin and
his staff did everything possible to prepare for a submission of
the case at the earliest opportunity. An important telegram was
sent to Lord Selborne on 11 January:

In considering the question of the modification of the Letters
Patent of 31st March 1905, H.M.G. will deliberate whether
responsible government should be introduced at once, and will
no doubt be considerably influenced by the statement [of

___

[1] Ripon papers 43552/22–5, Elgin to Ripon 28 Dec 05; Bryce papers, E. 27, Elgin
to Bryce 31 Dec 05.
[2] EP; Ripon papers 43552/26, Ripon to Elgin 29 Dec 05.

Farrar and Fitzpatrick] that representative government is likely to be of such short duration [months rather than years], and by the feeling of the Progressives, seeing that if that party ceases to advocate representative government there will be no political section in favour of it.[1]

Elgin explained privately to Selborne his feeling that the real difficulty was to determine whether 'one vote one value' was to be retained as the basis,

if and when responsible government is introduced. If that were decided in the affirmative, it might perhaps be our best course to accept your recommendation for an increase of seats, to allow the present Letters Patent to take effect and your Assembly under it to meet in July.

It would surely be most inconvenient to change, after a short interval, from the principle of 'one vote one value' under representative government, to that of population or any other, under responsible government.[2]

Selborne became increasingly impatient to learn what action the Liberals proposed to take with regard to the suggested amendments to the letters patent. Elgin told him of their need for time to study matters which were complicated and controversial in themselves, and entirely new to them. Any government was entitled, he felt, to state its case as a whole, and to declare its policy at the time it thought suitable.[3] These considerations meant that their conclusions would not be announced until parliament met. At the end of January Selborne telegraphed twice in three days, asking if any alteration in the basis of the constitution was proposed. Churchill minuted: 'No reply can be sent to Lord Selborne until the Cabinet have decided. He must wait like everybody else.'[4] Elgin warned Selborne that several of his colleagues who were 'sincerely desirous' of retaining his co-operation, were becoming

---

[1] CO. 291/111/1324. Sir G. Farrar and Sir J. Fitzpatrick, both with mining interests, were leaders of the Progressive Association.

[2] EP, E to Selb. 12 Jan 06 (copy).

[3] EP, E to Selb. 15 Dec 05; tel. 2 Feb 06 (copy).

[4] CO. 291/95/3279, 3409, minute 30 Jan 06.

as he was himself, 'a little anxious lest it should be said that you were pressing us too hard'.[1]

Uncertainty remained for much of January. As late as 15 January Ommanney considered it to be 'assuming a good deal' to think that self-government must come soon.[2] On 19 January, Keith minuted that he gathered the only question now to be 'whether responsible government will be given at once, or whether the representative Assembly will be allowed to sit for a session and pass the legislation establishing responsible government'.[3]

Early in the second half of January, Elgin told Mr H. B. Cox, the colonial office legal expert, that the lord chancellor wished to see him about the preparation of a scheme giving responsible government to the Transvaal at once. On 21 January, Loreburn reported to Elgin that he had seen Cox and Just, and asked them to make a 'purely tentative' draft amending the Lyttelton Constitution on the footing of responsible government, with the electoral basis unchanged (i.e. one vote one value), and the number of seats increased to sixty; he did not include anything about a Second Chamber. The purpose of this provisional draft was to enable the lord chancellor 'to supply if required a draft in legal shape which could be cut and carved into its final form very rapidly, and so no time lost'.[4] The two officials met Loreburn with their draft on 24 January. He dictated the substitution of certain clauses from the Australian constitution for those drawn from the Natal Act. Prints of the Lyttelton letters patent were used, and manuscript alterations made.[5] Certain words and clauses irrelevant to a grant of responsible government were altered or deleted as necessary. Loreburn settled a third revised draft on 30 January. The cabinet committee met on the same day and approved the draft constitution, which was then circulated to the other ministers. The fourth and final draft, headed 'Draft prepared under the directions of the lord chancellor' was then laid before the full cabinet on 8 February, together with a memorandum, dated

---

[1] EP, E to Selb. 2 Feb 06 (copy).　　[2] CO. 291/88/1604.　　[3] CO. 291/95/2011.
[4] EP, Loreburn to E 21 Jan 06.　　[5] CO. 291/111/2847, minute by Cox 24 Jan.

4 February, written by Churchill at Elgin's request,[1] 'A summary of the reasons influencing the decisions of the cabinet committee'. This memorandum recorded the conviction of Loreburn, Elgin, Ripon, Asquith and Bryce, that the Lyttelton Constitution would be unworkable:

for under it a nominated Executive of six to nine members, devoid of parliamentary experience and not possessed of any ascertained parliamentary capacity, would have to face a dissatisfied Assembly without the support either of a nominated majority or of an organised political party. His Majesty's Government therefore resolve on granting full responsible self-government – namely a Representative Assembly with an Executive responsible thereto ...

The question must be regarded as urgent:

Both races and all parties in the Transvaal have now been looking forward for nearly a year to the privilege of electing a Representative Assembly. . . . It is important that that change [the decision to grant full responsible government] should involve no delay in the date of the elections. First, because the people of the Transvaal are already impatient of a costly and none too efficient or well-informed bureaucratic regime. Secondly, because the difficulties of the House of Commons situation may be considerable if H.M.G. are forced for a prolonged or indefinite period to be *responsible* for the day-to-day administration of the Chinese Labour Ordinance, with its various objectionable features and possible recurrence of improper incidents. Time is therefore a factor which must powerfully influence, if indeed it should not govern, Cabinet policy.[2]

In its details, the draft submitted to the cabinet differed substantially from the letters patent of 31 March 1905 only by disallowing the soldiers' vote, by establishing equality between the two languages, and by increasing the number of members of the legislative assembly.[3]

[1] WSC had asked to attend the final meeting of the committee and E welcomed this (EP, E to WSC 30 Jan 06, photocopy).
[2] CAB. 37/82/16 (Lord chancellor's draft), African (S) 823: CO. 879/92.
[3] Ibid. covering note by Loreburn 31 Jan 06.

The Liberal reasoning. The Liberal ministers had plenty of expert advice before them when they decided to grant immediate self-government to the Transvaal.

Milner had declared against it, and his successor, Lord Selborne, agreed: the time was not yet ripe. Selborne hoped that it would be deferred for some years, but he admitted that indefinite postponement was impossible.[1] In general, Selborne accepted the argument of the despatch of 31 March 1905. Selborne quickly sent three memoranda to the new ministers, in which he set forth at length his reasons for advising unhesitatingly against the grant of immediate self-government. His reasons may be summarised as follows. In the first place, he followed Milner in disliking a 'leap in the dark'. His 'first and principal reason' for advocating a representative government stage, however brief, was that, as a matter of caution, they should know exactly what the balance of power was before committing themselves to self-government. It could even be, that if the British and Boers were found to be fairly equally balanced, both parties might unite in desiring to postpone responsible government.[2] In the second place, he believed the generation of Boers who fought in the war to be irreconcilable. All the Boer generals, including Botha, had

an ideal which is never absent from their thoughts, and which governs all their policy. It is to form a United Republic of South Africa, to which British colonials will be gladly admitted, but only on condition that it is a Republic with its own flag, and that the predominant influence is Boer not British. . . . Their policy at the present moment is exactly what mine would be in similar circumstances – that is to acquire power under a system of full responsible government at the first opportunity, and then to use it remorselessly to diminish British influence in every way. . . . Now, given time and education, the new generation will not be animated by these feelings.[3]

In the third place, he was worried by the political inexperience

[1] CO. 291/83/22917, Selb. to S/S 12 Jun 05.
[2] African (S) 813, memo. Selb. to E 14 Dec 05.
[3] African (S) 812, memo. Selb. to E 14 Dec 05.

of the population. Selborne considered that no comparison was possible between the type of self-government the Boers had exercised in the past, and the type Britain would grant them. Under their old constitution, except in municipal affairs, the only part the people played was in the election of the president, who acted as an autocrat for the period of his office. The Boer voter had comparatively little influence in the administration. He had had no training for responsible government in the British sense. The Transvaal British were 'an unimaginative people', and were also largely without political experience. Neither side could be relied upon in power not to be selfish and exclusive, although 'Boer misgovernment of the British would be greater in degree and more dangerous in its effect, than the British misgovernment of the Boers'.[1]

Selborne's opinion was in accordance with that of all the South African governors and lieutenant governors. Sir H. Goold-Adams of the Orange River Colony, for instance, declared in November 1905 that immediate responsible government 'would be a dire calamity to the people of the Colony'.[2] Local opinion was supported from within the colonial office. In Ommanney's opinion, the arguments of the despatch of 31 March 1905 had 'lost none of their cogency'.[3] He and Just thought it impossible to ascertain the consent, or to gauge the wishes, of the Transvaal on the constitutional question without an elected assembly or a duly elected *ad hoc* convention. The alternative was for the government, 'in deference to views which are of necessity based on very partial knowledge', to assume the very grave responsibility of acting arbitrarily, and arrogating to themselves a knowledge and a capacity to judge, unsupported by, and indeed in defiance of, the judgment of Milner and Selborne, whose objections as a whole 'must be allowed to have considerable weight', as voicing the opinion 'of a large number of prudent and thoughtful men upon a complicated situation'. They were inclined to stress the desirability of following the usual precedent of a stage of representative government during

[1] CO. 291/88/1604, memo. 23 Dec 05.   [2] CO. 224/18/42959.
[3] CO. 291/88/44104, 15 Dec 05.

which the colony would appeal for the grant of full self-government.[1] Graham arrived at a similar conclusion from different reasons, closer to Selborne's line of argument. It seemed to him impossible that the grant of complete self-government at that time could lead to the welfare and contentment of the masses. Perhaps the strongest argument against immediate responsible government was that it would mean party government, based on racial lines. Even if the Boers were in a small minority, their leaders, who were 'very "slim" in political jugglery', would find means of detaching a sufficient number of votes to turn the scale. Graham very much doubted whether the Boer farmer would be taught the gospel of reconciliation; 'for all the smooth words of General Botha and others we must lay our accounts with any Boer ministry containing a strong element of irreconcilables' such as Beyer and Smuts, who made no secret of their antipathy to Britain. Like Selborne and Lyttelton, he hoped that time would be given for the forces of conciliation to have effect, so that responsible government might result in party divisions on non-racial lines.[2]

The course generally favoured by the civil servants was to allow one short session under representative government, during which the Transvaal could decide the Chinese Labour question and pass resolutions in favour of responsible government. They believed that the advantages of this course were considerable. First, it was in conformity with precedent that responsible government was appealed for. Secondly, the same course could be followed in the Orange River Colony. Thirdly, serious difficulties arising out of the clashing of the functions of the Inter-Colonial Council and the legislatures under responsible government could be settled in advance:

it must here be borne in mind, that if the Transvaal receives responsible government at once and the Orange River Colony lags behind, the two Colonies will be prevented for the time being from going into conference on the subject of the Inter-

[1] CO. 291/88/1604, minute by Ommanney 19 Jan 06; CO. 291/95/2011, minute by Just 19 Jan 06.
[2] African (S) 796 (c) 30 Dec 05.

Colonial Council, and H.M.G. will be subject to criticism for appearing not to decide to grant self-government on its merits, but solely or mainly for the purpose of getting rid of all responsibility for Chinese Labour.

Fourthly, continuity of policy in regard to the constitution would be formally maintained:

> If H.M.G. act of their own motion now . . . they will be liable to be attacked both in the Colony and in Parliament for being ready to allow the Boer to regain by the ballot-box what he lost by the sword. The sting will, however, really be taken out of this charge by having 'one vote one value' as the basis of the Constitution. Nevertheless, the cry will be raised that the 'British' in the Transvaal, like another Ulster, have been betrayed.[1]

Fifthly, it would avoid a drastic remodelling of the Lyttelton Constitution. Such a remodelling would please the Boers at the expense of the English-speaking population. Finally, it would allow time to consider a second chamber, which Lyttelton left over, as he did not contemplate the early advent of responsible government.[2]

By what reasoning did the Liberals persuade themselves that they could afford to set aside such weighty advice? The experts had not, of course, been able to formulate a completely watertight case against granting immediate responsible government.[3] Nor had a really strong defence of the imperfect and unpopular Lyttelton Constitution been made in the colonial office, although this did not rule out advocacy of a short stage of representative government. If officials by and large apparently preferred the Lyttelton Constitution to immediate self-government, the force of their pleading was somewhat weakened by their former minutes criticising that constitution. Furthermore, Graham, in a typical minute doubtless originally written in turquoise ink with much alteration and crossing-out, admitted that if self-government had got to come soon, it might be better

---

[1] African (S) 815, memo. by Just 25 Jan 06.   [2] African (S) 796(*b*), Dec 05.
[3] CO. 291/95/2011, 19 Jan 06; see N. Mansergh, *South Africa 1906–1961: the price of magnanimity* (1962), p. 26.

to grant it at once in the Transvaal, though not in the Orange River Colony. Graham admitted that if in response to a demand from the colony, responsible government were to be granted within a year or so, their arguments fell to the ground. Unless the British government were prepared to resist such a demand, it would, in his view, be better to give it at once on their own terms. He did not think that this would be an arbitrary procedure, for the circumstances were without precedent.[1]

Even Selborne accepted one compelling argument in favour of immediate responsible government. The Liberals had decided to prohibit any further importation of Chinese labourers. He thought that responsible government would probably be a necessary measure in compensation for a blow at the 'industrial and economical existence, and even daily bread, of such a large proportion of the British population'. He would prefer to run the risk 'inseparable from the immediate introduction of responsible government', rather than let the British South Africans think that they had been wronged politically as well as economically, a combination which would excite a feeling he would regard with grave apprehension. Premature self-government, he added, would be 'a small evil compared with the alternative of the creation of a breach so wide and so grave' as he apprehended between the British population of the Transvaal and His Majesty's Government.[2] Hence the Liberal ministers might reasonably convince themselves that their advisers, despite hesitations and gloomy predictions, had virtually conceded the necessity of granting immediate responsible government.

In any case, many Liberals considered themselves to be entitled, especially after their overwhelming electoral victory, to a free hand. Churchill, for example, seized at once upon the argument that established precedent should be followed, with the aggressive, slightly exultant and perhaps ill-advised retort:

[1] Ibid.   [2] CO. 291/88/1604, memo. by Selb. 23 Dec 05.

Precedents in other Colonies need not be followed in a Colony whose history is wholly different. We may grant any form of responsible government we choose, without following any settled pattern, and what is necessary to Imperial interests can be reserved, even though no similar reservation has been made elsewhere.[1]

All other colonies, it was argued, had an intermediate stage of representative government only because in every case they were unused to political institutions. This was not true of the Transvaal or the Orange River Colony: both had formerly had their own governments.

Churchill's contribution to the Liberal reasoning was considerable. The first memorandum ever written by Churchill which can really be called a state paper was dated 2 January 1906. This eloquent and cogent memorandum made a valuable contribution to the government decision by focusing the issue and by steering the under-secretary's superiors towards responsible government. All the stylistic paraphernalia which were to become typical were deployed:

We have therefore abandoned one practical and defensible position, viz, Crown Colony Government. . . . When one crest line is abandoned it is necessary to retire to the next. Halting at a 'half-way house' midway in the valley is fatal. What is the next defensible position? I submit that it will not now be possible to deny the Transvaal a representative Assembly with an Executive responsible thereto. . . .

He pointed out that responsible government would be demanded with 'ever-increasing vehemence', while the government would already have surrendered all that was necessary to enable the rest to be extorted:

In the end, which may come quite soon, the Lyttelton Constitution will be recognised as unworkable, and we, or our successors, will be forced to concede full responsible self-government. The control of events will then have largely passed from our hands. We may not be able, without the employment of force, to prescribe the electoral basis of the new

[1] CO. 291/88/1604, minute 20 Jan 06.

Constitution, or even to reserve the functions necessary to the maintenance of public order and the King's authority. What we might have given with courage and distinction, both at home and in South Africa, upon our own terms, in the hour of our strength, will be jerked and twisted from our hands – without grace of any kind – not perhaps without humiliation – at a time when the government may be greatly weakened, and upon terms in the settlement of which we shall have only a nominal influence....

This was a classic statement of the primary principle of political conduct of the Victorian and Edwardian ruling *élite*, the principle of timely concession to retain an ultimate control. Churchill regarded it as indispensable that Britain should herself prescribe the basis of the responsible constitution whenever it did come, 'so to shape our policy as to keep the British party well together, and so to frame the Constitution as to give it a fair chance of securing the balance of power' –

But Mr Lyttelton's proposals will, if carried out, have the effect, first of dividing the British party . . . into Responsibles and Progressives, secondly, of putting the Transvaal Government into a large minority, and thirdly, converting the Legislative Assembly into a kind of constituent body, which will begin by agitating the demand for responsible government, and very possibly proceed to dictate its exact basis. In all this the *beau rôle* is assigned to the Boers, who, in their exertions for responsible government, are admittedly voicing the opinions of men outside their own party organisation, and appear as the champions of the Colony as a whole; while the Imperial Government can only fall back to that foundation of mere force from which we have laboriously endeavoured to raise it.[1]

The paper combines a freshness of presentation with a firm grasp of purely British interests. Military metaphor, which Churchill frequently used for major matters, was seldom employed more appositely than in the opening passage here, or made so integral to the argument. The ruthless logic, the

[1] African (S) 804, 'A note upon the Transvaal Constitution as established by Letters Patent' by WSC 2 Jan 06.

foresight, the polished phrases, the arresting words (jerked, twisted, humiliation), the favourite thematic words (courage, grace) – all these features stamp it unmistakably as a memorable piece of Churchilliana. Here is Churchill at his best, expressing the thoughts of older colleagues better than they could themselves. This superlative passage reads like the work of the years when he was an elder statesman, yet it was written when he was a mere under-secretary who had held political office for only three weeks.

To act now, Churchill argued in a supplementary paper, would place the British government in the position of Grand Elector. As they resolved, so would the balance of power be struck, and the future of the British throughout South Africa be determined, for the politics of the Transvaal were the politics of South Africa, and Johannesburg the nerve centre of the whole.[1]

Loreburn, the lord chancellor, who combined immense gifts with a Scottish shrewdness and common sense,[2] was impressed by Churchill's statement. He agreed that it was better to give way constitutionally as a matter of duty, than gracelessly under constraint.

[1] African (S) 817, 'A note upon the Transvaal Constitution question', WSC 30 Jan 06. He stated the issue in a striking passage: 'Differences of class, and occupation, differences of religion, loyalty and language, race-hatred still red hot from war, vital material interests, passionate national ambitions, divide parties and predetermine votes. Upon such moulding, ordinary political argument is mere varnish. We may airily talk of taking the sense of the inhabitants on this or that grave matter, but the only question that can in fact be decided by Transvaal electors will be which party has got most names on the register. Everything depends on the basis selected. H.M.G. are therefore in the position of Grand Elector.'

Selborne wrote to Haldane on 5 Mar 06: 'I have been sent from the Colonial Office the two memoranda of Winston Churchill about the Transvaal Constitution. I think they are most admirable documents. Of course I do not agree with everything in them, but with the backbone of his contentions I absolutely agree, viz, that the Witwatersrand is the key to the Transvaal and the Transvaal is the key to South Africa. If the Transvaal has a Boer Government, then, in my opinion, sooner or later – and of course these things never work themselves out at once, but take years to do so – we shall lose South Africa' (Haldane papers, 5907/7/35).

[2] Loreburn was at Balliol, got firsts in Mods and Greats, and was awarded a blue; he won the Ireland Scholarship – a much better record than any of his colleagues had (R. F. V. Heuston, *Lives of the Lord Chancellors, 1885–1940* (1964), p. 134).

The Lyttelton Legislature may refuse supplies on some occasion of discontent. What is to happen if they do? The power of the purse settles everything short of violence, and I think Lyttelton's Constitution almost invites a revolutionary movement, unless the so-called independent executive gives way whenever it is squeezed.

This consideration, however, pointed only to an early introduction of responsible government in the following year. Loreburn was led to favour granting immediate responsible government, first from concern about the unrest of having two constitutional changes within six months, and secondly from the belief that the Liberal government must rid itself of responsibility for the Chinese Labour problem as soon as possible. Until self-government was instituted, His Majesty's Government would 'incur the odium and have to take the responsibility' for the day-to-day administration of the Chinese Labour ordinance. If a representative assembly should decide to continue the system, Loreburn argued,

it would be impracticable for us to administer that system having regard to the feeling at home, and to my mind, it would be intolerable that an Imperial Executive should be called upon to carry out a practice detestable to the great majority of our people in obedience to the vote of a Colonial legislature.

On the other hand, if the Transvaal decided to abolish Chinese Labour,

our officials would have to do the work, and likely enough, we should be called upon to find the money for repatriation....
   If this view is sound, the one question of Chinese Labour makes it necessary that responsible government should be installed in the Transvaal by the month of July [1906] .... July is about the end of the tether.

While representative government continued, His Majesty's Government would have upon their shoulders not merely the problem of Chinese Labour, but also the impossible duty of having to take one side or the other on every question that acutely divided the [Transvaal] Chamber. In my opinion we have a duty to the United Kingdom in this matter as well as to the Transvaal, and we ought to insist upon divesting ourselves of duties which we cannot satisfactorily discharge, when the result of trying to execute them must be continually to place us in the false position of partisans in regard to controversies, where we ought to be neutral. It is in the interest of the United Kingdom to stand aside from the internal controversies of the Transvaal, and we ought not to give them the chance of compelling us still to interfere. Accordingly in my view, the proper course is to announce at once that responsible government will come into effect in June or July . . . under fresh Letters Patent containing the amendments necessary to transform representative into responsible government.

He was not blind to the real risk there was in this course. But he said:

It must come soon under the Treaty of Vereeniging. I think the risk will be greater the longer we wait. It arises from the step taken when the new Colonies were annexed, and it is too late to recall what was then done. But, danger for danger, I believe the preferable course is to let the different sections find their own level and shape their own destiny. . . .[1]

The letter was very lucid in its analysis, as befits a lord chancellor. His observations were unquestionably to the point. In the same letter, Loreburn mentioned that he had arranged for the preparation of a draft responsible government constitution on the footing of the existing letters patent. Elgin, therefore, read the radical lord chancellor's letter with a sense of relief, and was substantially in accord with him throughout.

I entirely agree with him as to the extreme importance of *an* Assembly meeting in July [1906] . . . and I also am certain that to secure this we must accept the 'one vote one value' principle.[2]

[1] EP, Loreburn to E 21 Jan 06.

[2] CB. 41214/39–40, E to CB 23 Jan 06. Loreburn acquired the reputation of making the most radical speeches from the Woolsack since Brougham (A. G. Gardiner, *Prophets, priest and kings*, p. 199), and of being the most advanced Radical in the cabinet (Brett, *Journals and Letters of Esher*, ii, 335).

Elgin did not come into office with his mind made up. He approached the constitutional question rather cautiously. Despite strong instincts in favour of responsible government, he doubted whether it would in fact be feasible to change the policy the Unionist government had so recently announced. He assumed that the representative constitution would have to come into operation for a brief period. Thus far he was in accord with civil service opinion. Sometime in January he seems to have been persuaded by Loreburn and Churchill that an alternative procedure would be possible. The intermediate stage of representative government could be dispensed with, but, by way of compromise, and to avoid undue delay, the Lyttelton Constitution could be largely retained. This method commended itself to Elgin and others because it seemed likely to give the Boers what they wanted and to satisfy traditional Liberal principles, without upsetting those who favoured the Lyttelton Constitution. Elgin welcomed it as a means of avoiding the administrative difficulties with which, as colonial secretary, he would have to cope, consequent upon a complete break in continuity of policy.

The Liberals were quite certain that representative government would not work properly. Basing themselves on Lord Durham's diatribes against representative institutions, and observing not only historically their failure in various parts of the globe, but also the by no means favourable reception accorded the Lyttelton Constitution in the Transvaal, they came to see the issue as a choice, not between representative and responsible government at all, but between Crown Colony and responsible government.[1] It was clearly not possible to continue with Crown Colony government. Even Milner and Lyttelton, the Liberals reminded themselves, had admitted that. In September 1906 Elgin wrote: 'I always said Lyttelton's Constitution would never be more than a paper one, and that

---

[1] EP, E to Selb. 16 Aug 06: 'I am more and more convinced that the alternative [to responsible government] was not representative government, but the Crown Colony system you now have.'

its proper place was in a glass case in the British Museum.'[1] There was a faint touch of hindsight about this, but belief that it would prove abortive was real enough. When the Lyttelton Constitution was first published, Haldane wanted 'to follow out the historical cases of failure of merely representative government'; he asked a friend to look out some literature and make some notes for him.[2] The inevitable failure of representative government was probably the major theme in the parliamentary exposition of government policy. In this connection, a passage of Lord Durham's report was quoted repeatedly, for example by Campbell-Bannerman (27 July 1905), Elgin (26 February 1906), and Churchill (17 December 1906). Campbell-Bannerman copied the passage into his notebook.[3] In view of its importance as a Liberal text, providing them with a basis for their reasoning, it should be quoted at least in part here: Durham found it difficult to understand how any English statesman could have imagined that representative and irresponsible government could be successfully combined. Crown nomination of the officers of government was a 'complete nullification of representative government', making it

a mockery and a source of confusion. For those who support this system, have never yet been able to devise, or to exhibit in the practical working of colonial government, any means for making so complete an abrogation of political influence palatable to the representative body. . . .

Such a system supposed, said Durham, that 'Englishmen renounce every political opinion and feeling when they enter a colony'.[4]

Nor did the Liberals attach much importance to the theory that educative values resided in representative constitutions. The assumption that representative government would be a 'convenient educative stage' was refuted, said Churchill, by the whole experience of British colonial policy.[5] Elgin considered

---

[1] EP. Note on a letter from Sir R. Solomon to Hopwood, forwarded to E by Hopwood 6 Sep 06.

[2] Haldane papers 6/163, to Ashley 28 Apr 05.   [3] CB. 41243A/119.

[4] See extracts from Durham Report in Keith, *Speeches and Documents*, i, 130–1.

[5] PD. 167/1066, 17 Dec 06.

representative government the natural form to be given perhaps to colonies which had come into existence as commercial settlements, but the South African colonies had formerly enjoyed a form of self-government.[1] Campbell-Bannerman described responsible government itself as the best form of political education, 'if education is wanted'.[2]

For the purpose of making a clear explanation of Liberal policy, the Chinese Labour question has been discussed separately from the constitutional problem. No such separation was possible for ministers at the time. Both issues were discussed at each of the early cabinets. Chinese Labour policy was in fact decided first. How then did the decision to stop further importation of Chinese influence the decision about the timing of the grant of responsible government? From passages which have been quoted already, it is clear that Grey, Loreburn and Churchill, as well as officials, were conscious of the connection between the two decisions.[3] Grey described responsible government explicitly as the way out of the impasse on Chinese Labour. This was exactly the attitude that Balfour had predicted the Liberals would take.[4] Churchill remarked on 30 January:

The question of the Constitution ought not to be prejudiced by the desirability of terminating Chinese Labour. It should be settled with reference to the general future of South Africa and not with reference to any particular question of South African politics.[5]

It is significant that Churchill felt it necessary to make a warning of this kind. Moreover, as we have seen, the cabinet committee believed it important that the decision to grant full responsible government should involve no delay in holding elections in the Transvaal, scheduled for July 1906. This was partly because it would then be forced to be responsible for a

[1] PD. 152/747, 26 Feb 06.   [2] PD. 152/168, 19 Feb 06.   [3] See pp. 104, 109, 112–13
[4] 'They will be confronted with their dishonest and insincere utterances about Chinese Labour by the ignorant and sincere of their followers, and I am convinced that they will extricate themselves from a painful dilemma by granting self-government to the new colonies *sans phrase*' (Balfour to Lyttelton, quoted by E. Lyttelton, *Alfred Lyttelton*, p. 320).
[5] African (S) 817, 23 Dec 05.

longer period for the day-to-day administration of the Chinese Labour ordinance. Despite his opposition to immediate self-government, Selborne nevertheless believed it to be desirable as a measure 'compensating' the Transvaal for the prevention of further importation of Chinese labourers. The situation was seen by one of the officials like this:

The declared object of H.M.G. is to refuse to accept responsibility for the continuance of the system of importation of Chinese Labour into the Transvaal, and to throw the responsibility upon the inhabitants of the Transvaal.

. . . as long as representative government lasts, responsibility for the administration of the system, if it is continued, will be incurred by H.M.G. It would therefore be the wish of H.M.G. to escape all responsibility, by advising His Majesty to grant responsible government to the Transvaal at the earliest possible moment, assuming that there are no other considerations which compel delay. . . .

In the face of this situation, and of the certainty that the policy of H.M.G. to disclaim responsibility for Chinese Labour will be accentuated when Parliament meets, it would appear that it must be taken for granted that the advent of responsible government cannot be delayed beyond the present year.[1]

Mr Just's observations were perceptive and mildly prophetic.

It may perhaps therefore be concluded, that while no doubt responsible government would soon have been granted if the Chinese had never been brought to the Rand, the Chinese Labour policy of the new government had implications exercising a very considerable influence on the timing of the grant of responsible government. Elgin openly admitted that the Orange River Colony Constitution had not 'the same urgency in the conditions of labour'.[2] The exercise of the imperial factor in the economic sphere was balanced by its withdrawal in the political. The Liberals were not of course merely prisoners of circumstance.[3] They made a positive choice between real alternatives.

[1] African (S) 815, memo. by Just 25 Jan 06.   [2] PD. 162/615.
[3] As Le May, *British supremacy in South Africa*, p. 186, implies.

The cabinet decisions of February 1906. Until the opening of the government and private archives in the last few years, the accounts of the part played by the prime minister at the cabinet on 8 February, and of the supposed influence upon him of General Jan Smuts, have necessarily been largely based on hearsay, and been inflated to somewhat heroic dimensions. Something approaching a mythology has tended to surround these events. This mythology views the Smuts mission as 'the climax in the drama of the South African settlement'.[1] It assumes that Smuts convinced Campbell-Bannerman that immediate responsible government should be granted, and that the prime minister then persuaded a reluctant cabinet, on 8 February, to take a step which all but two of the ministers had not, apparently, hitherto dared to support or contemplate.[2] The mythology ignored the part played by Elgin, and was content to imagine that he was a dull cypher whom the prime minister overrode. Smuts was convinced he had exercised decisive influence. It is now possible to check against documents this rather interesting piece of oral tradition in British political history.

Smuts almost certainly exaggerated his own influence. He

[1] See for example, G. B. Pyrah, *Imperial policy and South Africa, 1902–1910* (1955); the author wrote this book before the relevant documents were made available. The process of de-mythologising was begun by W. K. Hancock, *Smuts*, i, *The sanguine years, 1870–1919* (1962), and P. N. S. Mansergh, *South Africa, 1906–1961* (1962); it was continued by G. H. L. Le May, *British supremacy in South Africa, 1899–1907* (1965). Each of these three books was written before the cabinet memoranda and the Elgin papers were available to historians: the conclusions suggested by a perusal of these further sources were presented by R. Hyam, 'Smuts and the decision of the Liberal Government to grant responsible government to the Transvaal, January and February, 1906', *Historical Journal*, viii (1965), 380–98, which gives a slightly more detailed discussion of Smuts' influence than is possible here, though I am indebted to the editor for permission to reproduce much of my article. Further supporting evidence for the view it advanced has been adduced from the Spender papers by B. B. Gilbert, see communication in *Historical Journal*, vol. x, no. 3 (1967), 'The grant of responsible government to the Transvaal: more notes on a myth'.

[2] A vague statement by Lloyd George to Lord Riddell is the source of this misconception: 'At the outset, only two of us were with him, John Burns and myself. But his speech convinced the whole cabinet' (Lord Riddell, *More pages from my diary* (1934), 144–5, 27 Apr 13. It will be noted that the question at issue was not precisely stated).

did not perhaps realise how intensely suspicious of him ministers and officials were. Because Smuts later became the very paragon of a loyal commonwealth statesman, it is all too easy for us to forget that in 1906 he was regarded by the British as the most dangerous of the Boer leaders. Selborne telegraphed a warning as soon as Smuts departed for London:

He is a very clever, well-educated man, agreeable to meet, and personally I much like him; but please remember that he is an absolutely unreconciled Afrikander Republican, and that he has an ultimate ideal of a Boer South African Republic always before him, and all that he says or does politically has that ultimate end in view.[1]

After Smuts had gone, when Elgin wrote to Selborne reviewing the decisions taken and the reasons for them, he referred only parenthetically to Smuts:

I and many of my colleagues saw him; I am sure he cannot complain of any want of attention; he was as you foretold very pleasant and plausible; but so far as I can judge he did not leave behind him any undue impression.[2]

Smuts argued the case for granting immediate self-government to the Transvaal in a long and elaborate memorandum,[3] nicely calculated to appeal to Liberal sympathies and predilections. This memorandum was not, however, printed until March 1906, a whole month after the cabinet decision had been taken, so it is not at all certain how many ministers had read it before they took their decision.[4] Over and above this, the very persuasiveness of his argument ought to have put them on their guard against accepting some of its main contentions without corroboration. It was perilously close to being too clever by half. When this memorandum was eventually printed, it was circulated with a commentary by Graham, one of the most

[1] EP, Selb. to E, tel. 28 Dec 05.   [2] EP, E to Selb. 22 Feb 06 (copy).
[3] African (S) 837, CO. 879/92. For full text, see *Selections from the Smuts Papers*, ii, 1902–10, edited by W. K. Hancock and J. van der Poel (1966), pp. 216–27; extensively quoted in Pyrah, op. cit. and Hancock, op. cit. 207–10.
[4] Smuts certainly sent a copy to Bryce (see EP, Bryce to E 5 Feb 06), and to WSC (see acknowledgement, 1 Feb 06, *Selections from the Smuts Papers*, ii, 278).

senior members of the colonial office staff, who warned readers: 'Mr Smuts is a Boer and a lawyer. His Memorandum ... exhibits all the cunning of his race and calling.' Generally it contained nothing about Boer views that they were not already familiar with. Reference to dislike of Chinese Labour and to concern for African interests was not genuine, Graham thought, but simulated to enlist sympathy. In at least two cases in the published blue books, Graham saw Smuts as appearing in 'a shady light'. For these reasons he urged ministers to look suspiciously both on the honesty and the motives of the memorandum.[1]

Although the assumption of the traditional mythology of the Smuts mission is that Smuts devoted his energies to persuading the Liberals to grant immediate responsible government, he was clearly at least as concerned with more specific constitutional points. These were irrespective of whether the constitution was on the basis of representative or responsible government. In particular he was anxious, as Selborne realised,[2] to try to induce the government to depart from the principle of 'one vote one value' in the delimitation of the Transvaal constituencies. He failed to impose his view in this crucial matter.

Smuts found his meetings with Liberal ministers,[3] in contrast to that with the prime minister, disappointing. Elgin had an hour with him on 31 January. His disappointment cannot be used as evidence that ministers were not in favour of immediate responsible government. Their reticence may be explained by the necessity of preserving a very proper discretion upon a matter so controversial. It is not clear whether or not Campbell-Bannerman actually gave Smuts a hint of what would be done, but if he did say: 'Smuts, you have convinced me' (as Smuts sometimes alleged), it should be remembered that he alone, within a few hours of the cabinet that would decide, was perhaps in a position to take Smuts rather more into his confidence. Some of his colleagues when they saw Smuts may

[1] African (S) 837(a), 1 Apr 06, CO. 879/92.   [2] EP, Selb. to E, tel.28 Dec 05.
[3] Smuts saw Churchill on 26 January. He had an hour with Elgin on 31 January, and also met Morley and Lloyd George.

have wanted to do the same, but could not. There is evidence that Morley at least would have liked to tell Smuts 'what it is in my heart to say'.[1]

On the fundamental policy decision, whether or not to grant immediate responsible government, although he could not know it, Smuts had no need to persuade Liberal ministers. He was in fact preaching to the converted. The issue was virtually settled before the cabinet met, and there was no dispute on the principle. The ground had been thoroughly prepared by the committee of the cabinet, and other key ministers, such as Sir Edward Grey, were known to agree with their conclusions. Ripon, the ministry's unconventional Roman Catholic elder statesman, indeed, had produced the first memorandum in favour of immediate responsible government, on 26 December. He did not argue the case for it, but rather took it for granted that it was an agreed policy, and argued only contingent points.[2]

There can be no doubt, therefore, that however bleak Smuts may have found them, the leading ministers had already made up their minds to grant immediate responsible government, not only before 8 February, but before he met them. From the Liberal point of view, the arguments in favour of such a policy were strong. Smuts had nothing to add to the compelling reasons which had already decided them. The cabinet decision was a foregone conclusion, and it had only to be formally agreed. Therefore, when Lloyd George, years later, spoke of only two ministers supporting the prime minister at the cabinet meeting he could not have been referring, as the mythology supposes, to the principle of granting immediate responsible government. Asquith in 1912 dismissed the story of opposition in the cabinet as 'a ridiculous fiction': there was, he added, 'never the faintest difference of opinion about it'.[3]

And yet this cabinet meeting was undoubtedly marked by some cleavage of opinion. This must have been upon an issue other than that of principle or timing. And it must have been

[1] Hancock, *Smuts*, i, 213. [2] CAB. 37/81/85, 'Constitution of the Transvaal'.
[3] Asquith to Spender 15 Jun 12, quoted by Gilbert, loc cit.

raised unexpectedly. For Elgin, and all those who had worked with him, it was a distressing session. Immediately after the meeting he wrote a crestfallen note to his wife: 'Rather a disappointing cabinet – but one cannot always have one's own way. I shan't know for a day or two how things are to go.'[1] The prime minister had warned them about divulging cabinet secrets to wives, but Elgin was able to be more explicit in writing to Ripon:

The result of Thursday's cabinet was unexpected, and as it stands there is no very clear decision, while it is more than ever necessary that anything we say should be well considered. I do not know that the duty distinctly lies on me – for the prime minister rather took it out of my hands. But it may be convenient that I should state my views and I shall try, though it is not exactly an easy thing to do, to draw up a short memorandum for circulation on Monday.[2]

What had happened? The prime minister had made a speech which intervened in the deliberations of ministers in a way which took them wholly by surprise. As the basic policy decision to grant immediate responsible government had already been accepted by Elgin and those working with him, Campbell-Bannerman's speech can only have been concerned with the method of giving effect to the decision. An unexpected proposal about procedure made the cabinet meeting into a famous and dramatic occasion. It was only upon the procedure to be followed, the method of introducing responsible government, that ministers entertained the initial misgivings implied by Lloyd George. Campbell-Bannerman did not convince them there and then. The cabinet broke up in confusion, without reaching the final settlement everyone had expected. There was what would nowadays be called 'an adjourned decision'. Ministers had to meet again on 13 and 16 February before the method of proceeding could be determined.[3] In view of Campbell-Bannerman's action it is interesting to compare his

[1] EP, E to Lady E 8 Feb 06.
[2] Ripon papers, 43552/28–9, E to Ripon 10 Feb 06, draft in EP.
[3] CAB. 41/30/41 and 42.

account of the cabinet, written for the King, with Elgin's. The prime minister wrote as follows:

The desire of the Cabinet was to introduce fully responsible government into that Colony [the Transvaal] at the earliest possible time. Examination and discussion however disclosed the fact that much information is lacking as to the actual facts upon which any scheme of franchise and organisation must be based, and the Cabinet concluded that it would be necessary, by a Commission or otherwise, to ascertain these data before framing a plan of government, even although this will cause some delay in bringing it into operation. A matter so important as the introduction of a new Constitution for the permanent government of the Colony ought not to be prejudiced by a hurried decision. The precise reference to the Commission could not well be settled today, and was deferred to an early Cabinet.[1]

Elgin's interpretation of the proceedings of the cabinet was far less determinate. He felt that the circulation of his memorandum was 'rather a risk' but it might save some time at the next cabinet meeting.[2] He explained the situation as he saw it, beginning with this observation:

The result of the discussion of the draft Constitution ... [prepared by the cabinet committee] submitted to the Cabinet on the 8th is that it has been determined not to proceed further with that draft, but no arrangement was made as to the lines on which the discussion is to be resumed. ...

It was agreed, as he understood, that the draft constitution should be dropped, not on account of 'a final determination adverse to the principles on which it was founded', but because His Majesty's Government were of opinion:

(1) that responsible and not representative government should be given to the Transvaal, and (2) that further consideration of the forms under which responsible government ought to be given was required. It was also agreed, following upon this conclusion, that, in as much as a period of representative government was not desirable, the Constitution granted under the existing Letters Patent should be withdrawn and the Colony

---

[1] CAB. 41/30/39.   [2] EP, E to WSC 11 Feb 06.

should continue under Crown Colony government during the interval necessary for the preparation of a Constitution for the establishment of responsible government.

He believed that nothing further was definitely determined, but if he was incorrect in this or in any particular of his statement, he would wish to be corrected, for it seemed to him 'essential that the reason for delay and also for annulling the Lyttelton Constitution should be stated with great precision'.

Another proposal was mentioned, but was not finally determined upon, i.e. that the decision to take time for consideration should be accompanied by the announcement that a Commission, presumably a Royal Commission, would be sent to South Africa as part of the machinery for the further examination of the whole subject. I venture to hope that this question may be reconsidered.

He felt a much closer definition of its objects and of the terms of reference under which such a commission would act 'ought to be given to us, before we can form any judgment upon it or make it a part of an accepted policy'. Elgin saw no advantage in inquiry by a Royal Commission, and thought a simpler method of inquiry would not only suffice, but be more convenient.[1]

It appears, therefore, that two suggestions about procedure, neither of them recommended by the cabinet committee, were pressed unexpectedly upon the cabinet by the prime minister. Thus, the cabinet of 8 February is historically important because it was not until then that the Lyttelton Constitution was finally abandoned. Indeed, until then it had not seriously occurred to any of the ministers that it ought to be abandoned. Campbell-Bannerman's tear-jerking eloquence[2] was devoted, not to persuading his colleagues to grant immediate responsible government, but rather to stop trying to adapt the Lyttelton Constitution as the basis for responsible government. In so urging them, he was repudiating the procedure planned

[1] CAB. 37/82/23, cab. memo. 12 Feb 06; also in EP.
[2] 'The speech moved at least one member of the Cabinet to tears' (Riddell, *More pages from my diary*, p. 145).

departmentally, in the colonial office, and in cabinet committee, under the guidance of the lord chancellor. The prime minister had apparently never given a hint previously that he would make such a recommendation, which suggests that if Smuts had any influence on Campbell-Bannerman, it was upon these two points – scrapping the Lyttelton Constitution and holding an inquiry. Both points were urged by Smuts in his memorandum.[1] Perhaps even at this late moment Campbell-Bannerman had of his own accord come to the same conclusions as Smuts, but independently of him, and then very cleverly had allowed Smuts to gain the impression that he had decisively influenced him. The two proposals were sensible in themselves and would probably have occurred naturally to anyone with Campbell-Bannerman's political flair. The party political consideration seems strong enough to have indicated the advisability of doing these two things even if Smuts had not advocated them. On the other hand, if the prime minister had come to these conclusions independently of Smuts some days before the cabinet, why did he not tell his colleagues that his mind was moving differently from those who were specially concerned with devising the policy for the Transvaal? The prime minister could hardly have been unaware of the preparation of a draft constitution on the basis of the Lyttelton constitution, or of the opinions of the cabinet committee, since both had been printed and circulated some days before 8 February. It does not, perhaps, seem very good management to have sprung an alternative arrangement on them without warning, if it could be given. Maybe he did not bother to tell them because he underestimated the possible opposition. Or perhaps at the very last moment, he really was influenced by Smuts? If so, he could never admit it, because, in view of the horror in

[1] Smuts Memorandum, paras. 15 and 16. The Boers 'wish it to be clearly understood that responsible government granted on the basis of the present Constitution will only make matters worse and is strongly disapproved of by them'. If the British were still apprehensive, 'It would be better by far to delay the grant of a Constitution until the truth has been fully ascertained, either by an impartial commission, or in any other way.' On the other hand, the possibility of a Royal Commission had already been raised in Whitehall: it had been mentioned to Campbell-Bannerman by Herbert Gladstone, 26 Oct 05 (CB. 41217/269).

which Smuts was held, to have done so would have been sure to bring fatal opposition to his proposals.

The prime minister's unexpected suggestions raised starkly the issue of how far the Liberal ministry should maintain some semblance of continuity in British colonial policy through a change of government. This worried the 'Liberal Imperialists', and the more mandarin-minded of his colleagues. Elgin was alarmed by the prospect of a complete and undisguised break in the continuity of policy. As he reminded his colleagues more than once, it might lead to the resignation of Lord Selborne as governor of the Transvaal and high commissioner in South Africa. This would be embarrassing. Elgin's memorandum was very much a piece of self-justification, which is most un-characteristic. Obviously he must have felt very deeply that highest reasons of state required a stand against the prime minister. In his attempt to regain the initiative from the prime minister after the startling intervention of the latter, and also, in his view, to counteract some of the damage likely to occur from Campbell-Bannerman's plan, Elgin insisted at the next cabinet meeting that there should be a declaration in parlia-ment that the revocation of the letters patent was entirely without prejudice to the consideration of the basis upon which the Lyttelton Constitution was framed, to every particular of which they would give their attention. He succeeded, though only after making ministers late for lunch. 'I think on the whole I am satisfied with the results of keeping them', he wrote to Lady Elgin, 'though I had at one time to show a little fight.'[1] Campbell-Bannerman agreed to make this careful reservation. Perhaps repenting a little of the embarrassment he had caused, he assured Elgin in a conciliatory letter that in his announce-ment he would 'avoid anything that commits us to any particular line, beyond a clear stage for consideration. This comes the more naturally as it expresses my own opinion.'[2] Elgin believed:

if we state in firm but conciliatory language that we are resolved not to allow a form of Government to come into force which we

[1] EP, E to Lady E 16 Feb 06.
[2] Ripon papers 43552/30131, CB to E 19 Feb 06; E passed this letter to Ripon.

consider insufficient and inappropriate, but with an open mind to carefully consider by what means we can establish responsible government on a sure foundation, we shall carry with us the assent of reasonable men. They will not ask us by what steps we intend to proceed.

But Elgin was still apprehensive about adopting the procedure urged by the prime minister:

I must add in justice to myself, that I do not mean thereby that I am free from the apprehension of serious consequences, both at the moment and in the future, if the British party, speaking of them in the largest sense, are carried away by the disappointment of the loss of a Constitution for which they have so strongly declared.[1]

Selborne was informed of the cabinet decisions by an official telegram of 18 February. The government expressed the hope that the change to responsible government, without an intermediate stage of representative government, would 'be accomplished as speedily as possible, subject to such enquiry as may be necessary'. The Orange River Colony was also to have a constitution, 'similar in character'.[2]

With his misgivings, Elgin probably felt some genuine regret that they had thought it their duty to differ from Selborne's advice, and wrote privately:

I am conscious that you may think that in forming our own view of the necessities of the situation we are departing from the policy which you recommend. I do not think the departure goes so far as might at first sight appear. . . .[3]

There was nothing to prevent final adoption of the main features of the Lyttelton Constitution, 'if enquiry establishes your view'.[4] In a further letter, Elgin asked Selborne to accept his assurance

---

[1] Cab. memo. 12 Feb 06. It is possible Elgin may have exaggerated support for the Lyttelton Constitution by relying too closely on Selborne. He was challenged at the cabinet on 8 Feb for relying too exclusively on official reports, but he was not inclined to withhold his trust in the accuracy of these reports as narrations of fact, because in some instances, 'they may seem tinged with some of the local colour', and circulated with his memorandum two letters (African (S) 826; CO. 879/92) from non-official sources, which seemed to him to corroborate his argument.

[2] CO. 291/111/6082.　[3] EP, E to Selb. 17 Feb 06 (copy).　[4] Ibid. tel. 18 Feb 06.

that not I only, but those associated with me in preparing the case, did our very utmost to minimise the divergence. We examined with great care the methods by which the provisions of the present Letters Patent could be adapted to the introduction of responsible government – and Mr Cox, whose ability in these matters you no doubt know well, did his very best. But when we came to the opinion that working on this system must result in a scheme which we could not recommend as free from imperfections, it seemed to us that it was our duty to say so. I will not attempt to support that contention with arguments, but I may give as an illustration that we found it impossible within the time to construct a scheme for a Second Chamber...

... so far as I am concerned, nothing would please me more than to find myself at the end in substantial agreement with you.[1]

Undoubtedly Elgin would have preferred to adapt the Lyttelton Constitution to responsible government. He wished to move cautiously both on the constitutional question and on Chinese Labour and to maintain as much continuity of policy as possible, because he was alive to the administrative difficulties of doing otherwise. It was the view of a man with essentially an administrator's mind. Loreburn favoured the same course, but in his opinion, 'whether the necessary amendments are to be made in favour of amendment to Lyttelton's Constitution, or by entirely new letters patent superseding Lyttelton's, is a detail'.[2] This was essentially a lawyer's view, and it was probably wrong. Discussion had taken place mainly among purely official minds, often in terms of administrative expediency and legal convenience. This was not surprising: Elgin and Loreburn were both peers, taking no part in the election.

---

[1] Ibid. 22 Feb 06. The question of a second chamber had not yet received any consideration by public opinion in the colony. There was no proposal before H.M.G., except a mere suggestion from Selborne that it should be nominated. The Cape legislative council was elective, Natal nominated. 'It seems impossible to form a judgment as to what form of second chamber would be suitable and acceptable to the people of the Transvaal without full materials, which cannot be improvised at short notice. ... The inevitable delay in coming to a ripe decision as to second chamber appears to preclude the possibility of making provision for it in the [amended] Constitution' (African (S) 808, memo. by Just, Jan 06).

[2] EP, Loreburn to E 21 Jan 06.

Parliament was not sitting during the first two and a half months of the life of the Liberal government, the period of their policy deliberations. It was left to Campbell-Bannerman, the man with essentially a political mind, to consider the party political implications of the decision, and, at the same time, to lift it to the level of an act of statesmanship. On both levels, a gesture making a clean break with Unionist arrangements seemed called for. It was, he believed, necessary to scrap the Lyttelton Constitution in order to prevent the disappointment, both of his radical and very vociferous supporters, and of the Boers. It was at once the shrewd tactic of a still insecure party leader, and the magnanimous strategy of a statesman. The magnanimous aspect of the gesture profoundly impressed Botha and Smuts, and has always been recognised by historians; but the party-political aspect was probably equally important in his calculations, and it was this which impressed Lloyd George and Lord Carrington. Lloyd George congratulated him 'on the way you saved the government from inevitable disaster'.[1] Carrington, president of the board of agriculture, congratulated him 'on having so magnificently saved the South African situation today. The Party would have been in arms if we had capitulated to Lyttelton and the mine-owners – and you pulled us through entirely, and alone'.[2]

The disaster from which the prime minister was thought to have saved the party, and very probably did in fact save it, was division – a split among the back-benchers. The cohesion of the Liberal party was still fairly gravely in doubt. The issues opened up by the split over the conduct of the Boer War were not yet settled. Moreover, Campbell-Bannerman may have been attracted by the possibility of consolidating his victory over the 'Liberal Imperialists'. Only a month before, they had tried to force him to take a peerage. Now he could retaliate by striking a blow against their preoccupation with maintaining some continuity of policy.

[1] CB. 41239/36, Lloyd George to CB 9 Feb 06.
[2] CB. 41212/310, Carrington to CB 8 Feb 06.

In any event, the result of Campbell-Bannerman's intervention in the planning of his ministers was remarkable. Though it was not a habit of his, it was not the only occasion, of course, on which the chairman of a parent body has played havoc with the recommendations of a sub-committee. To those who disliked the intervention, it was more than this. The policy of responsible government had been preached by the Liberals in Opposition. Its actual adoption by a Liberal government was quite a different matter. It could not be adopted simply as a matter of course. Indeed, it took more than a month for their resolution to harden upon it. There was a mass of expert advice to be countered. With the responsibilities of office, warnings could be set aside only with deliberate calculation. Risk had to be weighed against risk. To grant responsible government to the Transvaal at all after the Unionist decision was in itself a sufficiently bold course of action for men like Elgin and Asquith, and even for Loreburn the Radical, and Churchill the bold and daring junior minister. Campbell-Bannerman tried to persuade his colleagues to go further, cut the umbilical cord which tied them to their predecessors, and, in effect, to abandon all semblance of continuity of policy. To this principle many ministers attached great importance, either on its merits, or as a condition of solving the Transvaal problem successfully. The result of the action and psychological insight of Campbell-Bannerman was to turn Smuts from 'an absolutely unreconciled Afrikander Republican' into a loyal servant of Crown and Commonwealth. Campbell-Bannerman made Liberal policy seem whole-hearted and unequivocal. Yet the abrogation of the Lyttelton Constitution was chiefly intended as a gesture only. Elgin helped to ensure that it remained no more than this. The Lyttelton Constitution was abandoned. A committee of inquiry was sent to the Transvaal and Orange River Colony. Despite these significant and effective sops to Afrikaner opinion, the actual form of constitution granted by the Liberals did not really differ on the controversial electoral issues from that devised by their predecessors in office.

The Ridgeway Committee and the drafting of the new constitution, March to December 1906. At first, the Liberals had been swayed by the importance of an elected assembly meeting in the Transvaal in July 1906 as planned under the Lyttelton Constitution. Early in February they became convinced of the importance of not rushing. More information was needed. But how was it to be obtained?

At the cabinet on 8 February, a royal commission had been suggested. Elgin disliked the idea of sending a royal commission to the Transvaal. He defined the main difficulties facing the government as three. First, the principles on which the constitution should be based, which was a matter the government should decide for itself, and for which all the information was 'certainly more available' in England. Second, the feeling of the British and Boers towards these principles and other points of difference: ascertaining these by a royal commission would be 'directly calculated to increase political agitation and the dangers of the situation'. Third, the effect of 'the application of different principles to the actual facts': this was certainly something upon which they needed assistance, but the simpler method of a committee of inquiry would be more convenient for this.[1] It was the absence of any declaration of the wishes of the country which greatly influenced the decision to take time for further consideration and for the collection of information on controverted and disputed points.[2] The prime minister believed the government to be 'woefully in want of information' about the effect of decisions on the electoral basis, and did not hesitate to say so in public.[3]

The decision to send a simple committee of inquiry was made at the cabinet of 16 February. Selborne was notified privately by telegraph on 18 February:

We do not propose a roving commission to take evidence in South Africa regarding general principles of the constitution on which it is clearly our duty to decide – but we think a local enquiry, unostentatiously conducted, would usefully elucidate

---

[1] EP, cab. memo. 12 Feb 06.　　[2] Ibid. 6 Mar 06.　　[3] PD. 152/168, 19 Feb 06.

various points, especially as to topography and distribution of population.[1]

Elgin saw no objection to letting the Lyttelton letters patent stand until the registration of voters was completed in March 1906. 'Then we think the Letters should be recalled and the instructions to the committee will take the place of the instructions to the Commission [to delimit constituencies]. We no longer require executive action but a report.'[2]

Elgin explained to the cabinet that he thought it was of some consequence, in order to prevent fresh agitation in South Africa, to show in the terms of reference to the inquiry that they had fully observed their pledge to revoke the letters patent without prejudice to full consideration of the basis of the Lyttelton constitution. 'I suggest therefore that the first reference to the committee should follow *mutatis mutandis* the terms of the reference to the Delimitation Committee', on the understanding that they were to produce a report, not a decision. In addition to undertaking specific enquiries, they could be told 'to report generally on any point coming under their notice which illustrates the effect of the application of different principles to the actual facts, especially as affected by the numbers, distribution and social condition of the population'. Elgin emphasised that the committee

ought to be kept free from points of policy, and confined to ascertaining and reporting upon boundaries, areas, population, voters, machinery for recording votes, etc. And its main object should be to let us know how the country could be cut up into constituencies.

He believed the census of 1904, in regard to some localities, no longer reliable. Nevertheless, if at all possible it would be desirable to dispense with a fresh census, and the fresh registration of voters which a new census would make necessary. It might be possible to introduce such modifications as seemed reasonable and just, without superseding the general arrangements proposed for the representative constitution. 'And if that

[1] EP, tel. E to Selb. 18 Feb 06 (copy).   [2] EP, E to Selb. 22 Feb 06 (copy).

be so, under its provisions, especially that for automatic re-distribution, any minor discrepancies would soon disappear.'[1]

The composition of the committee was finally settled at the cabinet on 10 March. Lord Sandhurst, Sir Francis Hopwood (permanent secretary of the board of trade, shortly to succeed Ommanney at the colonial office), and Colonel Johnston, R. E. (of the delimitation committee) were appointed under the chairmanship of Sir Joseph West Ridgeway. All were men whom the cabinet thought to possess weight and authority while being reasonably detached from party.[2] Ridgeway was a distinguished soldier-administrator who had served in India during Ripon's viceroyalty; subsequently he had been a most successful under-secretary to Balfour in Ireland[3] and then governor of Ceylon. The terms of reference were communicated to Ridgeway towards the end of March. Urgency was stressed. Manhood suffrage was enjoined as tending to make the constitution generally more acceptable.[4] The committee was supplied with parliamentary papers relating to previous grants of responsible government in other colonies, together with the Durham report, maps, and books on South Africa by Fitzpatrick, Bleloch, Worsfold, Bryce and Lucas.[5]

In addition to their formal instructions, the committee were given to understand that, if a favourable opportunity occurred, they might attempt to negotiate a settlement on the basis of

[1] EP, cab. memo. 5 Mar 06.   [2] CAB. 41/30/48 and 49.

[3] As Balfour's under-secretary Ridgeway had contributed importantly to the success of the régime by being the engineer or operator of Balfour's policy: L. P. Curtis, jr. suggests recognition of this has been too long withheld (*Coercion and conciliation in Ireland 1880–92* (1963), p. 187). He was governor of Ceylon 1895–1903, then chairman of the Ceylon Company of Pearl Fishers. Ridgeway was defeated as Liberal candidate for the city of London in the 1906 election.

[4] CAB. 37/82/34, 'The general object of the inquiry is to inform H.M.G. as to the effect of the application of different principles to the actual conditions of the Transvaal, as affected by the numbers, distribution, and social condition of the population.' Enquiry should be made into the representation of different districts, the effect of manhood suffrage, how far the 1904 census could be relied on.

[5] J. P. Fitzpatrick, *The Transvaal from within* (1899), W. E. Bleloch, *The New South Africa* (2nd ed. 1902), W. B. Worsfold, *The problem of South African Unity* (1900), J. Bryce, *Impressions of South Africa* (3rd ed. 1899), C. Lucas, *A Historical Geography of the British Colonies*, iv, *South and East Africa*. See note in EP.

representation, subject to the approval of the government. Although he did not think it prudent to make it a prominent part of their instructions, Elgin certainly contemplated that they might with advantage confer with the various parties. The committee was left discretion to take such action as it found circumstances justified.[1]

Announcing the decision to send out a committee of inquiry, Churchill said that they could not be expected to take the assertions of their predecessors for granted:

whatever the amount of goodwill the government may have. ... We are not inclined to take all that they tell us so glibly on trust ... the decision we take should not only be the decision of fresh minds, but a decision based on freshly ascertained facts. ... It is an Imperial patrol sent out for the purpose of re-connaissance and not of action.[2]

Churchill did not oppose the despatch of a committee, but he was afflicted by 'a darkening anxiety' about immediate policy because of the evil effects of delay in deciding the fundamentals of the constitution. The prevailing and paralysing political instability and uncertainty led to economic difficulties and thus to actual physical hardship. Who are to be our friends in the Transvaal, he asked? His reply was significant:

I would do strict justice to the Boers; but when we remember that 20,000 of their women and children perished in our concentration camps in the year 1901/02, is it wise to count too much upon their good offices in 1906? And if we are to consider at all as one of the pillars of our power the loyalty of the British, are we not subjecting them to a terrible strain? ...

... We have to deal with the facts as they are. And the fact which glares me in the face is that a six months' delay in settling the fundamentals of the Constitution will, through economic pressure and political uncertainty, drive many British voters from the Transvaal, and alienate from the Mother Country the affections of the rest.

[1] EP, E to Selb. 18 May 06 (copy).   [2] PD. 155/843, 5 Apr 06.

These British could not know that the cabinet

while anxious to do what is fair and right between both races, while resolved not to lend themselves to anything like a trick, are absolutely determined to maintain, in the words of Lord Durham's Report, 'a numerical majority of a loyal and English population'.

Repatriation of the Chinese, and alienation through uncertainty. What was then likely to be left of the already precarious basis of British power? 'It would be far better to give the country back to the Boers as a great act of renunciation and of justice than to fritter it away piecemeal.'[1]

The committee arrived in South Africa on 24 April. During its nine weeks there, it examined nearly five hundred witnesses, and received more than seventy deputations. Ridgeway kept in close touch with Elgin. Sir Francis Hopwood wrote a few letters to Bryce, and Lord Sandhurst several to Ripon. Ministers were however imperfectly informed of the progress made, because Selborne, feeling himself snubbed, failed to maintain fully confidential and regular communication with Elgin.

The period during which the committee was in South Africa was a testing one for relations between Selborne and his new political bosses. Ridgeway lost no time in sending Elgin his impressions of the high commissioner. On the whole he thought that they were fortunate in having Selborne as their representative, if only because he would be hard to replace suitably. Though he was in Ridgeway's eyes saturated with 'an inveterate distrust of the Boers', he was popular with the rank and file. He was fairminded, but inclined to take exaggerated views of a situation, and he was, like Milner, pessimistic.[2]

As a result of its inquiries, the committee favoured manhood suffrage (as the cabinet had suggested), the retention of the voters basis and the old magisterial districts (which would save time and make a concession to Boer sentiment), a residential

[1] Minute by WSC 15 Mar 06: African (S) 834, 'Situation in South Africa', CO. 879/106 and CAB. 37/82/83. This was a highly secret document, and Churchill carefully removed all copies from the colonial office records. Photocopies are now available in the public archives through the good offices of the Chartwell Trust.
[2] EP, Ridgeway to E 14 May 06.

qualification of six months, single-member constituencies (the point on which the Boers gave the most strenuous resistance),[1] and automatic redistribution every five years. Het Volk accepted 'one vote one value' in exchange for manhood suffrage and other arrangements which would reduce the voting power of the over-mighty subjects of the Rand compared with the country districts. These arrangements included acceptance of the 1904 census figures as the basis for distributing seats and constituencies, instead of the voter's roll compiled under the Lyttelton Constitution.

The decisions to enlarge the franchise by establishing manhood suffrage, and to retain 'one vote one value', meant that it would not be possible to distribute seats and delimit constituencies on the basis of the Lyttelton Constitution voters' roll alone, because that was not based on manhood suffrage. Selborne suggested that the Lyttelton roll, which was completed in March, should simply be enlarged by the addition of those adult white male British subjects not hitherto included, and then the constituencies could be distributed accordingly. But as the committee wished to include an actual distribution of constituencies in their report, they could not wait for the enlargement of the roll. Using the census figures appeared to lead to an exceedingly small difference in results, except in the Rand, where, in the circumstances, the difference was material. The Rand would get three seats fewer. (Ultimately it was decided to make this only two by transferring one seat from the rest of the country.)

The committee at first proposed that the Witwatersrand (excluding Krugersdorp, with its Boer majority) should be represented by twenty-nine members in the assembly, Pretoria by five, and the country districts by twenty-nine. It calculated that on the basis of the 1904 census figures, a British majority of five might be expected in the general election. Het Volk and the Responsible Government Association accepted the committee's proposal, and at first, so did the Progressives. But on 14 May, Selborne asked to see representatives of the Progressive party.

[1] Ibid. 14 Dec 06.

He told them frankly that he was not going to agree to the scheme. As a result of his intervention, the Progressives withdrew their support, and the attempt to negotiate a complete agreement on the distribution of seats collapsed.

Elgin reported to the cabinet on 16 May that he had heard from Ridgeway a most hopeful account of the prospects of agreement between Boers and British, but unfortunately a subsequent telegram stated that the Progressives had withdrawn their assent to the proposed settlement. The cabinet instructed Elgin to enquire about the causes of the change of opinion among the Progressives, and to urge Selborne to use all his influence on the side of a harmonius settlement.[1] Elgin telegraphed an enquiry about Selborne's standpoint, remarking that the 'advantages of such an arrangement are obvious – and the proposals did not appear to us unreasonable'.[2] Elgin hoped that Ridgeway was 'not being too fond (?) of the Boers and showing it. That might account for a good deal'.[3] Selborne took his time in making reply, and his answer, which arrived only just in time for the next weekly cabinet, did not please Elgin.[4] Selborne explained that he had advised the Responsibles and the Progressives not to concur in a compromise which the committee had arranged between them and the Boers; and he told them to 'fix their principles and adhere to them and take the consequences'. The cabinet unanimously decided that Selborne had acted 'beyond his duty as high commissioner, that he was quite right to hear what all Parties might say, but ought not to have interfered to prejudice or upset a harmonious settlement, but should have reported what he heard to the Imperial government'.[5] Elgin had a delicate task. He was specially directed to communicate this decision in terms which indicated all possible consideration and respect. He did this as best he could, and suggested that Selborne and Ridgeway

---

[1] CAB. 41/30/57, 16 May 06.   [2] EP, E to Selb. tel. 16 May 06 (copy).

[3] EP, E to WSC 19 May 06 (photocopy).

[4] 'I am much concerned about this telegram of Selborne's – and will do my best for him in cabinet tomorrow – but I confess I do not think he has treated me quite as well as I expected. . . .' (EP, E to WSC 22 May).

[5] CAB. 41/30/59, 23 May 06.

should submit a joint statement on the points of difference.[1] Once again Selborne was in no hurry to reply. Eventually it became clear that the committee had not been taking Selborne completely into its confidence. This was because it found him so obstinately committed to his own opinion. He had never believed in the possibility of an all-round understanding.[2] Elgin had some sympathy with Selborne's pique.[3] Selborne continued to sulk. The telegraphic bill for the month of May, Elgin noted quizzically, would be much lighter in consequence.[4] The cabinet on 13 June again discussed Selborne's conduct at great length. They were anxious to spare Selborne as much as possible, but unanimously agreed that Elgin should follow up the telegraphic reproach by writing a temperate despatch remonstrating with him, and directing him again in future to use all his influence to bring about a harmonious settlement.[5] In effect, Selborne received a formal censure.[6] For his part, Selborne thought the rebukes undeserved, and contemplated resignation. But he decided that he could do more for the cause which he had at heart by staying in his post.[7]

The difference of opinion between Selborne and the committee was confined within what was perhaps, technically, a narrow compass, but the debate over the voting rights and delimitation of constituencies was crucial, because the British and the Boers were so nearly evenly balanced numerically that the electoral arrangements could virtually determine the out-

[1] EP, E to WSC 23 May 06 (photocopy).

[2] 'Both parties cannot have the majority which they both desire. One party must be disappointed, and a present understanding would turn I fear into a future misunderstanding and lead to bitter recriminations' (CO. 291/99/18103, Selb. to S/S tel. 19 May 06).

[3] 'One can easily see that a governor, who feels he is kept at arms length, may easily feel himself free to do more than if consulted. I am rather inclined to think that a full confidence would have put a man of Selborne's character on his honour not to oppose – and that this would have been the line of least resistance in the end. However that now is perhaps unprofitable speculation' (EP, E to WSC 3 Jun 06).

[4] Ibid. 6 Jun 06: 'It is very unfortunate. . . . But I do not see why he should have any feeling against me – and I certainly have no personal quarrel with him.'

[5] CAB. 41/30/63, 13 Jun 06.

[6] CO. 291/99/16 Jun 06. Extracts from relevant letters by Selb. and Ridgeway were printed in a cab. memo. (CAB. 37/83/53).

[7] Balfour papers 49708/160, Selb. to Balfour 13 Jun 08; EP, Selb. to E 3 Aug 06.

come of the elections. Selborne disagreed with the committee's attempt to bring about a general agreement, and in particular, he believed its proposed distribution unfair to Witwatersrand and Pretoria.[1] To the committee, Selborne's objections seemed based on 'very insufficient reasons'. He could only have arrived at his conclusions by the most pessimistic calculations and by refusing to believe in the pledge given by the Boer leaders that they would not contest seats in the Witwatersrand. Seats which the Progressives believed themselves to be certain, or almost certain, of winning, 'he summarily, without any sufficient data or reasons, declared to be hopeless'. So at least, Ridgeway thought. And he added, Selborne 'would not consider any majority to be sufficient which was not a large Rand majority'.[2]

Upon reflection Elgin doubted whether the failure to conclude 'a regular agreement' need delay matters much. Unlike Churchill he did not think that the work was all thrown away. After all, they had not staked everything on a compromise locally arranged. They would still get the report, they had some fresh knowledge of the feelings of the different parties, and they had the encouragement of knowing that the committee all but effected an arrangement.[3]

The committee suggested thirty-three seats for the Rand (excluding Krugersdorp Rural, a certain Boer seat), six for Pretoria, and thirty for the rest of the country (including Krugersdorp). It was finally agreed, with Selborne's concurrence, that the distribution should be thirty-four seats to the Witwatersrand (including Krugersdorp Rural), six to Pretoria, and twenty-nine to the remainder of the Transvaal. This was expected to give a British majority, but not necessarily a mining majority. Ridgeway did not want a Rand majority.[4] Elgin explained the position to his colleagues:

[1] EP, Selb. to E 21 May 06; Selb. to Balfour 13 Jun 08, loc. cit.
[2] EP, Ridgeway to E 19 May 06.   [3] EP, E to WSC 6 Jun 06 (photocopy).
[4] CAB. 41/30/70, 27 Jul 06, memo. by Ridgeway 14 Jul 06. The Boers wanted Krugersdorp excluded from the Rand arrangements as they had pledged not to contest Rand seats, but the Progressives wanted it included (EP, Ridgeway to E 4 Jun 06).

I do not deny that an agreement actually concluded would have been desirable, but its value might easily be over-estimated. The leaders who were negotiating had no real authority to bind the general public . . . we can take credit for an amount of agreement which under the circumstances is truly remarkable. The committee claim that all parties in the colony with the exception of the extreme wing of the Progressives, have approved of their last proposal. . . . I never expected this amount of consent and I plump for it.[1]

The report of the Ridgeway Committee[2] became available to ministers towards the end of July. It was never published, because the government found its emphasis on the desirability of British predominance a little too overt. The report contained two references to the Durham report. There was a final obituary notice for the Lyttelton Constitution: although 'honestly conceived and ably framed' (p.3), it would have produced friction and died quickly. That the report gave no evidence of 'a desire on the part of the government to truckle to the Boers',[3] is clear from the flavour of the following passages:

To the vital principle of British supremacy the Boers also profess their ungrudging and cheerful adherence . . . there is at this time no idea of questioning or undermining British supremacy in the Transvaal. While acknowledging that this is the case, we do not attach less value to the precautions which should be taken in order to maintain the supremacy . . . (p. 7).

We regard British supremacy as vital and essential, and we have also looked upon a British majority at the coming General Election as a desirable outward and visible sign of that supremacy, which should be, if possible, obtained (p. 8).

[1] EP, cab. memo. 23 Jul 06.

[2] African (S) 853, 'Report of the Committee appointed to enquire and report upon certain matters connected with the future constitutions of the Transvaal and Orange River Colony'.

[3] EP, Hopwood to E 19 Dec 07. Ridgeway admitted to Merriman that he considered 'a small British majority absolutely necessary in order to avoid an outcry in England' (*Selections from the Smuts Papers*, ii, Merriman to Smuts 26 Jun 06). Smuts wrote: 'The object of the Ridgeway Commission, as I saw early in their negotiations was simply to see how little they could give to the Boer without making the latter stand aside' (ibid. ii, 318, Smuts to E. Hobhouse 16 Aug 06); 'They are well-meaning but weak and I at any rate expect very little from them' (ibid. ii, 247, to Merriman 5 May 06).

Yet it is not in a majority, which must be more or less uncertain, that the most effective safeguards of British supremacy should be sought. A British majority in the Legislative Assembly, which is mainly the offspring of a precarious political alliance between capital and labour, will be but an unstable and transient guarantee of British supremacy. . . . Should at any time the Labour party throw in their lot with the Boers, a British majority is impossible (p. 10).

In our opinion a more trustworthy security for British supremacy will be found in an Upper Chamber, the referendum, federation, the increase in the number of British families, especially of the agricultural class, and above all, in a contented and prosperous community without distinction of races (p. 11).

Thus, in the light of these remarks, it is easy to understand the consternation when Mr John Burns discovered on 19 December 1907 that a copy of the Ridgeway report had been stolen, sold to the *Standard*, and that it would be published on 1 January 1908. The solicitor general, the crown lawyers and others advised the permanent under-secretary of the colonial office to see the editor of the *Standard* and extract a promise from him not to publish, on the ground that publication would be contrary to the public interest.[1]

To resume our account of the report: a second chamber, the committee believed, would act as a court of appeal for parties narrowly divided in the Assembly. The greatest importance was attached to federation. The report reflected the committee's conviction that Selborne was mistaken in his pessimism concerning the attitude of the Boers. 'We find them', Ridgeway wrote privately, 'reasonable and responsive to gentle and sympathetic treatment. Of course they may have dreams of a South African Republic in the future, but as regards the immediate future they have no inordinate ambition'.[2] This seems a reasonably accurate estimate.

---

[1] EP, Hopwood to E 19 Dec 07: 'I hate the idea of publication – there is a lot of *stuff* in the report. But the *Standard* could not say it was evidence of a desire on the part of the government to truckle to the Boers!'

[2] EP, Ridgeway to E 14 May 07.

The committee considered very carefully whether the new constitution should provide protection for Africans, pending the grant to them of representation. The committee was satisfied that public opinion on the native question was growing more liberal. Leading men seemed to see the necessity of dealing fairly and generously with questions of such gravity. It was an impression-judgment, not subject to proof. It agreed with Sir Godfrey Lagden, commissioner for native affairs, that ministers of the colony could be led but not driven in this matter:

if they are driven or hampered by restriction, there will be perpetual animus towards the Imperial Government. . . . No Imperial restriction or interference of [sic] administration methods will avail to promote the interests of the natives if sympathy towards them is checked.

The committee had little doubt that the question of representation for Africans would sooner or later be dealt with in a liberal spirit by the new legislatures:

the best and wisest policy . . . is to trust to their sense of justice. . . . It should be remembered that the native is indispensable in the social as well as the industrial economy of the two colonies. If he were ill-treated he might well leave the Colony, and certainly he would not migrate into it.

Hence the committee recommended that as far as possible the matter should be left to the new legislature (p. 33).

The committee was back in London by 14 July. The framing of the constitution and the writing of the report proceeded simultaneously because of the pressure upon time. The proposals for the new constitution were announced in both houses of parliament on 31 July 1906, just before the adjournment on 4 August.

In the course of his announcement, Elgin said that he could understand a logical mind like Lord Milner's considering a period of probation necessary; he could understand a denial of representative institutions; but he maintained that there was nothing more impolitic or cruel than to insist upon an intermediate period, 'which must be a period of unrest, uncertainty and intrigue'. Elgin was much concerned to minimise differences of policy between the two parties. On many of the details, he said, there was not much divergence of opinion; the proposal to rely on the 1905/6 voters' roll instead of the 1904 census figures in the distribution of seats, 'might be considered a very serious difference', but it might be a greal deal overstated.[1]

Churchill was allowed the honour of announcing the terms in the Commons. He defended single-member constituencies. Not to have them would only lead to the swamping of one or two local minorities. They would return 'just that very class of moderate, independent Dutch or British members whom we particularly desire to see represented in the new Assembly'. Churchill was ready to admit that the constitution did not rest

upon symmetry or acceptance, but it is very near symmetry, and very near acceptance, and in so far as it has departed from symmetry, it has moved towards acceptance. . . .

This is sheer rhetorical nonsense, but on the whole the speech seems to have been a great success. It was a measured performance; he appealed for a non-partisan approach to the solution of the problem: 'We can only make it the gift of a party; they [the Opposition] can make it the gift of England'.[2] The appeal

---

[1] PD. 162/612–21, 31 Jul 06. In defending the retention of magisterial districts he said: 'I have a prejudice, which would perhaps be more suitable if I sat on the other side of the House, in favour of the preservation of ancient landmarks . . .' (617).

[2] Ibid. 730–53, reprinted in WSC, *Liberalism and the social problem* (1909), pp. 16–44. It is surprising that the prime minister did not announce the terms in the Commons. About this speech, C. F. G. Masterman wrote: 'There have been moments [in the House of Commons] when a sentence or even a phrase has struck the right note and moved this strange audience to emotion. And this is usually the achievement of simplicity, that rarest and highest quality of the art of the orator. Such an example was the conclusion of Mr Winston Churchill's speech on the new Transvaal constitution; when after a long speech of fluent and clever exposition, he turned to the final appeal . . .' (L. Masterman, *C. F. G. Masterman: a biography* (1934), p. 84. Baroness Asquith recalls: 'There were no flights of rhetoric, there was no party challenge or provocation. There was measured weight and gravitas. He was persuasive, temperate, and restrained through-out, showing a perfect sense of the occasion' (V. Bonham Carter, *Winston Churchill as I knew him* (1965), p. 138.

fell on stony ground. The debate which followed was long and excited.[1]

They got through the ordeal of the Transvaal statements fairly well, Elgin thought.[2] After all, the prime minister wrote to wish him a happy recess, 'with the olive wreaths of South Africa around your brow'.[3] In the autumn, Carrington complimented him on 'soothing South Africa down in a most scientific and satisfactory way'.[4] Drafting of the new letters patent did not begin in earnest until just before parliament reassembled on 22 October. The process continued well into November. Elgin never seemed to be in a hurry, despite the need to avoid delay. He made smooth and thorough progress day by day and week by week.[5] Sir Richard Solomon, shortly to become agent-general for the new Transvaal government in London, gave assistance. Elgin found his help most useful.[6] The letters patent establishing responsible government for the Transvaal were issued on 6 December.[7]

To amuse his wife, Elgin likened the process to the preparation of a baby for baptism. His metaphor, elaborately sustained through several letters, is perhaps worth quoting, because it casts light on the more humorous side of Elgin which otherwise so seldom emerges from the archives. After the letters patent were laid before the cabinet on 28 November he wrote:

The baby was presented to its godparents this morning and they all were quite kind to it. One or two of the bows had been re-tied by the nurserymaids just before it was brought in – and the nurse was called upon to explain how and why this had been done – but I am glad to say that ordeal was successfully encountered. A 'counterfeit presentment' is now being des-

---

[1] Spender, *Life of . . . Campbell-Bannerman*, ii, 242.
[2] EP, E to Lord Grey 7 Aug 06 (copy).   [3] CB to E 4 Aug 06 (EP).
[4] EP, Carrington to E 13 Sep 06. Marlborough, formerly parliamentary under-secretary at the colonial office, told his cousin and successor in office, Winston Churchill, that he thought the Liberals had 'won all along the line and is full of rueful admiration for our statecraft' (EP, WSC to E 8 Aug 06).
[5] EP, E to Lady E 20 and 22 Nov 06.   [6] EP, E to Selb. 23 Nov 06 (copy).
[7] Cd. 3250.

patched to Sandringham,[1] and the nurse has received summons to proceed there on Saturday morning to take charge during the christening. . . .[2]

From Sandringham he described how

The ceremony went off quietly but with all proper dignity. The Royal Sponsor received the infant very generously and expressed his approval, audibly. Nothing now except the signing of the Register, which will be accomplished with due formality some day next week.[3]

Elgin was slightly apprehensive of the public reception. He did not think that anybody who was satisfied by the announcement in July need be very excited now. But general statements had become more particular, and their proposals for the Orange River Colony constitution would not, he thought, be popular in some quarters. Selborne for one would disapprove. On the whole, he did not, however, expect a dangerous attack. He was satisfied that, though under pressure, the work had not been done with undue haste or want of care. The timetable which he had set in the spring had been kept throughout almost to the day. The colonial office staff had been very good. Cox, especially, he thought, had served him well in this complicated business. Confiding to his wife, he thought that a minister had rarely 'more completely realised his ideas' than he had. The reflection is the more curious since Elgin did not normally blow his own trumpet, even to his wife.[4]

Newspaper comment was quiet, with little excitement either for or against the new letters patent.[5] The debates in both houses of parliament on 17 December were, like many important imperial occasions there, dull. Elgin had a sensation of anticlimax. Immediately before the debate in the Lords, the education bill which had absorbed so much Liberal attention throughout 1906 was wrecked by a motion put forward by

---

[1] Sandringham: a house in Norfolk, reputed one of the ugliest in England, much loved by the British royal family.
[2] EP, E to Lady E 28 Nov 06.   [3] Ibid. 1 Dec 06.   [4] Ibid. 2 Dec 06.
[5] Ibid. 13 Dec 06.

Lord Lansdowne. This preceding excitement over the education bill was fatal, for everybody went out of the chamber to talk over the crisis, except, as Elgin put it, 'those who remained and looked bored'.[1] The discussion was spoilt. Main principles were never touched. Milner was not involved.[2]

For a reader today, almost the only interesting feature of the debate in the House of Commons is Churchill's peroration:

We hope and profoundly believe better days are in store . . . the long lane which it has been travelling has reached its turning at last . . . the cause of the poor and the weak all over the world will have been sustained; and everywhere small peoples will get more room to breathe, and everywhere great empires will be encouraged by our example to step forward . . . into the sunshine of a more gentle and a more generous age.[3]

This may seem to bear little obvious relation to the grant of a constitution to a South African colony. Taken out of context, one might be forgiven for ascribing it to, say, a speech after a world war. But then it must be remembered that from his earliest days in ministerial office, Churchill tended to behave and to speak exactly as he would when he was conducting the Second World War.

The main features of the Transvaal Constitution

(a) *Manhood Suffrage.* Smuts had advocated manhood suffrage in place of the Lyttelton monetary qualification for the franchise.[4] The first hint that Liberal ministers were considering this alternative may be Churchill's question of 12 February: what would be the numerical difference between manhood suffrage and the Lyttelton suffrage?[5] The Liberals did not think Lyttelton's arrangements undemocratic: a franchise which yielded 89,000 voters out of a population of 300,000 was, making allowance for the abnormal conditions of a new

---

[1] Ibid. 18 Dec 06; see also E to Selb. 27 Dec 06 (EP, copy).
[2] PD. 167/940–73, 1066–138.   [3] PD. 167/1138, 17 Dec 06.
[4] African (S) 837: Under the Lyttelton constitution only the head of a family would have the property qualification needed to become a voter.
[5] CO. 291/96/4814.

country, a much more 'fertile' franchise than applied in England, or in some of the American and European states. But Churchill wondered whether the apparently artificial nature of the Lyttelton franchise, in combination with the unusual basis of distribution, might not give rise to the suspicion 'that something was intended in the nature of a dodge', artificially to produce a British majority; that would always rankle, for 'in dealing with nationalities, nothing is more fatal than anything like a dodge'.[1]

With the permission of the prime minister, Elgin introduced the idea to other ministers on 6 March:

> I think that a large step in the direction of an honourable compromise would be taken by the adoption of manhood suffrage in place of the £10 franchise proposed by the Lyttelton Constitution. It is probably true that owing to high scale of prices in the Transvaal a £10 franchise is not really so high as it would appear to be in this country, and therefore that manhood suffrage would not add so materially to the voters lists as might be supposed . . . [but it would] meet the principal requests of the Boers. . . .
>
> I submit that it could be defended in this country as a democratic constitution, and in South Africa as dealing fairly with the difficulties of race and condition, by admitting freely all Boers, and yet maintaining the basis of one vote one value and single-member constituencies to which the British attach supreme importance and which, it must be remembered, Het Volk itself was ready to accept, though with a preference for a population basis. We were told at one time that the parties would be nearly equal but I imagine that latterly the certainty of a British majority has been practically admitted, on the basis of the existing Letters Patent. The alteration to manhood suffrage must to some extent equalise, though I do not hesitate to repeat an opinion I have already expressed, that in the interests of all sides an actual Boer majority in the new parliament is not desirable.[2]

Elgin had received no indication of the lines on which a compromise could be achieved between rival views; the Boers seemed to prefer a population basis; and

---

[1] PD. 155/841–2, 5 Apr 06.   [2] EP, cab. memo.

they have also consistently claimed an amendment of the burgher lists and the enfranchisement of farmer's sons, and both of these claims seem to me to deserve fair consideration on their merits.

Might not a compromise be found on their admission? It would broaden the foundations of the Constitution and make it more intelligible and acceptable in this country, if manhood suffrage were substituted for the £10 franchise of the Letters Patent; the Boer claims above-mentioned would be effectually covered thereby and more satisfactorily than by special franchise.[1]

The introduction of the principle of manhood suffrage was important, because without this addition the electoral arrangements in the Elgin constitution would have been virtually a repetition of the Lyttelton constitution. When, at a much later date, Lyttelton asked why manhood suffrage – it did not exist elsewhere in South Africa – was established, Churchill replied that he was quite prepared to defend it on its merits, although he admitted force in the arguments against it (e.g. that it might not help federation). Many things the British contended for were granted to them. The Boers wanted manhood suffrage: 'while I do not say for a moment there was a bargain, I do say that there was a balancing of one set of considerations against the other in our Constitution'.[2]

(b) 'One vote, one value.' In most democratic countries it would have mattered little whether the distribution of seats was arranged on the basis of population or on the basis of voters only. But in the unusual conditions of the Transvaal, with its high proportion of unmarried British men on the Rand, compared with the large families of the Boer farmer in the country districts, it was thought to make a great deal of difference. The British contended passionately for the voters basis of the Lyttelton constitution, declaring that one vote ought to have only one value, since it would be to the advantage of the town-dwelling British.

[1] EP, E to Selb. tel. 9 Mar 06; CO. print 28 May 06.
[2] PD. 176/721-2, 20 Jun 07.

The principle of 'one vote one value' was upheld as the basis of the constitution. Indeed in view of what Selborne said about the importance of retaining it there was perhaps little alternative. He held 'as seriously as an opinion can be held, that under the peculiar circumstances of the Transvaal the principle of one vote one value is the only fair one to apply'; as it was 'the only system under which the whole connexion of the Transvaal with the British Empire will not be jeopardised', his resolution on the subject was 'a fundamental principle of policy'. It was 'the one standing political principle on which the British are solid. The solidarity in support of this principle is without crack or flaw.' It was the only principle which would give the British any effective share in the government of the country.[1]

Ripon opposed the adoption of 'one vote one value', because he doubted if there was any precedent for it in other colonies which had responsible government; moreover, it had 'about it an air of gerrymandering which ought not to commend it to us'.[2] Elgin was not particularly afraid of the charge of gerrymandering.

The principle of 'one vote one value' is a good democratic one. . . . There is a chance of introducing it here on the recommendation of the other side [i.e. the Unionists] . . . what does the charge of gerrymandering come to? Simply this, that under present circumstances the adoption of this principle will probably – not certainly – result in a British majority. Why should it not? It seems to me that the charge of gerrymandering would be still more applicable if we abandoned the principle we prefer to give the Boers a majority.[3]

Loreburn's opinion 'without entering upon the argument on its merits', was that the basis of one vote one value might be accepted as the only means of starting responsible government without delay. Even those who complained of it could hardly

[1] EP, Selb. to E 6 and 7 Jan 06.
[2] EP, cab. memo. by Ripon 26 Dec 05.
[3] Ripon Papers 43552/23–6, E to Ripon 28 Dec 05.

describe it as so inequitable that it ought to be abandoned at the cost of wasting a year.[1]

Churchill found serious and substantial arguments against 'one vote one value', but if this, the 'last and main line of resistance' of the British party, were abandoned in addition to all other concessions, the British population would accuse the imperial government of having betrayed them, 'bound hand and foot to their deadly foes', and would be able to cite in proof of this assertion the fact that in no single point in dispute was their opinion allowed to prevail. Smuts expected that 'one vote one value' would give thirty-six seats to the British and twenty-four to the Boers, while a population basis would give thirty-two to twenty-eight; but in both calculations Churchill thought that he took the gloomiest view and made the very lowest and most moderate estimate of Boer chances. Hence 'it may be assumed that, on a "population" basis, the parties will be numerically equal' and Botha would have to be sent for. 'Is this what H.M.G. desire?'[2] Hearing of Smuts' estimate, Selborne commented that the suggestion of a small British majority was 'nothing less than an impudent attempt to deceive you'. A population basis, he believed, would give the Boers a clear majority of certainly not less than thirty-four seats to twenty-six British.[3]

Smuts certainly played on the Liberal fear that the Transvaal might be dominated by the capitalist mining houses. He tried to scare the government away from 'one vote one value' by alleging that, although the Rand had only 39 per cent of the population, on a voters basis it would have 50·5 per cent of the votes, and by assuming that all the Rand members would be practically the nominees and servants of the mine-owners. 'Were that to be so,' wrote Bryce to Elgin, 'the mischief of the system we are asked by Selborne to sanction would be very serious.'[4] But the colonial office had evidence that Smuts was probably misleading them. They had a list of the members of the Johannesburg town council which showed that the great

---

[1] EP, Loreburn to E 21 Jan 06.
[2] African (S) 817, 30 Jan 06.
[3] EP, Selb. to E 10 Mar 06.
[4] EP, Bryce to E 5 Feb 06.

majority were independent-minded, disliking and distrusting the ring of financial houses which controlled the Chamber of Mines and the mining industry.[1]

The cabinet committee on 30 January decided to retain the voters basis, recognising that its abandonment would certainly be regarded by the British

as a mortal injury; and although their view of its actual importance is no doubt extravagant, the mere fact that nearly half the population of the Transvaal will *think*, however unjustifiably, they have been betrayed, will in itself prevent the resulting settlement from being accepted as fair and even-handed dealing between the two conflicting races.

It was pointed out that Selborne seemed to have committed himself so strongly in favour of the existing basis that he might find it difficult to recede. Although they believed it to give the advantage to the British and the towns, the result was to make the vote of the adult white male exactly equal all over the Transvaal irrespective of race or condition – 'a proposition not in itself indefensible'. A basis of population would have made the vote of the adult country Boer of considerably higher value than the vote of the adult British voter. The fact that the British paid nine-tenths of the taxes certainly did not prove that they should have less voting power. They decided that 'one vote one value' was, if not ideally the best settlement, probably upon the whole the best practical settlement then open to them.[2]

(c) *Protection for the Africans.* It is not in the least true that the African majority was ignored or forgotten in framing the Transvaal Constitution, although not a great deal could be done for it. The main reason for this was a promise in Article

---

[1] African (S) 827: six were listed as ex-burghers of the S. African Republic (of whom four were strongly anti-capitalist), thirteen were listed as aggressively independent, seven as independent, and only four as friendly to the mining houses (CO. 879/92).

[2] African (S) 823, memo. by Churchill, 4 Feb 06.

8 of the Treaty of Vereeniging (which ended the Boer war): 'The question of granting the franchise to natives will not be decided until after the introduction of self-government.'

The hands of the Liberal government were therefore tied. If they had dealt with the question of the native franchise, reported the Ridgeway Committee, in any shape, either directly or indirectly, the action would certainly have been regarded by British and Boer as a breach of faith.[1] The Liberal ministers were agreed that nothing would more embitter relations with the Transvaal, or embarrass future prospects, than this 'terrible accusation'.[2] Careful enquiry was made to ascertain whether Article 8 precluded action on behalf of the Coloured people. It appeared that white opinion in South Africa universally regarded the term 'native' as including the Coloureds. Therefore, although the committee felt these people undoubtedly deserved much consideration, they did not feel justified in putting on Article 8 a different interpretation from that generally accepted in South Africa. The Unionists had come to the same conclusion in preparing their letters patent in 1905.[3] Even Sir Charles Dilke publicly admitted the binding nature of the Vereeniging pledge.[4]

Elgin went out of his way to express his regret that the Treaty of Vereeniging should have embodied this policy.

I regret it [he told the House of Lords], because I am of opinion that a reasonable representation of natives would give

---

[1] *Report*, p. 32. Lord Hailey did not have access to the report when he wrote that the committee had 'to all appearance' neglected to raise the issue of African enfranchisement. See *The Republic of S. Africa and the High Commission Territories* (1963), p. 25.

[2] PD. 152/1233, Churchill 28 Feb 06, PD. 162/666, Ripon.

[3] CO. 291/81/8840, S/S to Milner, tel. 21 Mar 05.

[4] PD. 162/771: 'Unfortunately we were forced to continue' the colour bar; 'there probably was no alternative for the present'; PD. 167/1090: 'It might be inevitable, it might be impossible to resist it, but we were for the first time establishing a colour bar in the British Empire by the action of the Imperial Parliament.' Thomson, *Unification of S. Africa*, p. 27, rather unfairly describes the 1906 Constitution as 'a decisive step towards the triumph of the political colour bar throughout South Africa' on the ground that Vereeniging in no way bound H.M.G. not to admit to the franchise 'Coloured and Asiatic men as distinct from natives'.

strength and not weakness to the government of the country, and I cannot but hope that this will be recognised in some time to come. . . . It appears to me that if the rights of natives could be so regulated as to diminish the chances of conflict between black and white, it would be well to do so.[1]

His Indian experience was behind this attitude. He had sat in a council where there was native representation and he expected Lansdowne, as a former viceroy, to corroborate his view that they had gained much by their presence.[2]

Elgin began to explore the possible provisions for the protection of African interests in a long minute of 5 April 1906, starting from the assumption that the terms of the treaty of Vereeniging absolutely precluded the extension of Cape franchise rights to other Africans. But the necessity of safeguarding the legitimate rights of the natives (whether of indigenous tribes or of Indians or other Asiatic races) was undoubted.

Ommanney commented:

I am afraid that it is impossible to devise effectual means of controlling the native policy of a self-governing colony. When we decide to give that form of government to a colony where there is a large native population we deliberately accept the risk of having to save the white community from the consequences of its mismanagement of the natives.

'Even so', replied Elgin, 'it is better that we should take the risk with our eyes open.'[3] Elgin thought it certain that they must make some provision. He received a deputation headed by Dilke which left him in no doubt that they would be expected to be able to show that they had not neglected this side of the question.[4] To keep Swaziland under the high commissioner and outside the Transvaal for the time being 'would be a very effective demonstration of sympathy'. How could this be done? Perhaps some period might be fixed, thus

[1] PD. 162/623, 31 Jul 06.   [2] PD. 167/942, 17 Dec 06.
[3] CO. 291/97/11334, minutes 5 and 7 Apr 06.
[4] EP, E to Selb. 18 May 06 (copy).

showing that they did not distrust the new government, but wished to relieve them at the outset. Indeed there was a good deal to be said, in Elgin's opinion, for treating the native question in a provisional way at the start. The restriction on the grant of the franchise in the terms of peace might be a peg to hang this on.[1] Elgin held firmly to this projected policy for Swaziland, and secured its implementation, thus following the precedent of Basutoland rather than of Zululand.

On 26 June, Elgin saw another deputation of members of parliament (Dilke, Lehmann, Ramsay MacDonald, Molteno, Robertson). All of them acknowledged that Article 8 excluded the grant of the franchise, but they recommended sufficient reservations to give the British government power to safeguard native rights, pending reasonable enfranchisement, whereupon the reservations might be abrogated.[2] As a general statement of policy, Elgin saw no objection to such a proposition, but realised that there was considerable difficulty in giving effect to it. He considered the idea of setting up a separate department under a permanent secretary for native affairs, making the department directly subordinate to the high commissioner himself, at any rate until the right of franchise was granted. But he found that opinions of great weight were adverse to this suggestion, including those of the Ridgeway Committee, and he was thus reluctantly forced to admit that 'It would no doubt be an unprecedented restriction on the right of self-government, and to make it effective, it would be almost necessary to give the High Commissioner the independent control of some sort of police force'.[3] He admitted that to place Africans in the colonies, as well as those in Swaziland, more directly under the management of the high commissioner would almost inevitably lead to friction.[4] Active administration by the imperial government he always thought impracticable.

Believing that South African opinion on the native question was improving, and, if left alone, would continue to improve, the Ridgeway Committee recommended that as far as possible

[1] Ibid. 13 Jul 06. [2] CO. 291/111/23318.
[3] EP, cab. memo. 23 Jul 06. [4] EP, cab. memo. 12 Nov 06.

the whole question should be left to the new legislature. The British government could still veto legislation, and might appoint representatives of the natives to the legislative council. In addition, the committee suggested that the prime minister should take the native portfolio, perhaps assisted by an advisory board with some representatives of the African community on it. There should be reservation of all legislation concerning Africans, and strict prohibition of the alienation of reserves. Perhaps also, Britain should follow the Natal precedent and set aside money for education.[1] Elgin felt that an advisory council would at any rate give representatives of the African community an opportunity of influencing the management of native affairs. Hopwood was struck by the fact that South African authorities did not seem to have the least idea what the Africans were doing, or what their real aims and aspirations were. There was 'no conduit pipe between our people and the Natives'. A consultative committee of Africans sitting periodically with the commissioner of native affairs 'might help to make one'.[2]

The former editor of the *Cape Times*, F. E. Garrett, submitted a similar proposal, for governors' advisory councils of Africans and experts, to be formed by the governor of each colony partly by nomination, partly by election. Elgin had the proposal examined[3] in case it had a chance of satisfying African claims to representation of some kind, 'with which personally I have much sympathy'. The officials once again said 'when once you give self-government all these devices are necessarily worthless' and in support of their view recalled that Gladstone had said in 1852 that the salutary traditional principle of allowing colonists to judge the measures best adapted to secure their peaceful relations with aborigines, must be applied to New Zealand.[4] A sum for native

[1] *Report*, pp. 33–4.
[2] EP, Hopwood to E 8 Dec o6. Compare Morley's problem in India 'We do not know the minds of the Natives and the Natives do not know what is in our minds. How to find some sort of bridge? That's the question' (MM. 2/109, 16 May 07).
[3] CO. 291/113/30193, minute 2 Aug 06.
[4] J. Morley, *Life of Gladstone*, i, 645, gives the full reference which the officials quoted.

trust and for education and welfare was being reserved in the Transvaal draft; 'perhaps', they suggested, 'this is as far as you will care to go.'

Yes, I think so [Elgin replied]. I doubt the prudence of making elaborate provisions for administration by Natives at this stage. I have noticed some uneasiness as it is regarding 'safeguards' – and I should prefer to take my stand on the necessity of preserving all legitimate rights and property as they now stand.[1]

At a cabinet committee on 23 July, at which Sir J. West Ridgeway was present, it was pointed out that provision might at once be made for the representation both of Africans and Coloured persons, by allotting places in the legislative council [the second chamber] to members representing these interests. ('No one would advocate a manhood suffrage for natives without some qualifications.')[2] This idea also proved abortive since the upper house was to become elective after the first parliament.[3]

In the first draft of the Transvaal constitution, clause 58 set up a Transvaal native trust (consisting of the governor, the executive council and others) – a corporation to take, hold and dispose of lands 'for the support, advantage, or wellbeing' of the Africans. But the lord chancellor considered that any such provision should be left to the colony itself to enact. 'It could not work unless money were provided by the Colony, and if the Colony provided the money, it ought to have the control. I suggest the consideration of some method by which the natives may be allowed to choose representative spokesmen to communicate with the Governor in Council. This might perhaps be effected by a permissive clause.'[4] Sir Richard Solomon agreed with the lord chancellor, and accordingly all reference to such a trust disappeared.[5] Officials found it difficult to see what purpose the paraphernalia of a native trust, which was

[1] 30193, minute 19 Aug 06.   [2] EP, cab. memo. 24 Jul 06 by E.
[3] EP, E to Selb. 6 Sep 06 (copy).   [4] EP, Loreburn; comment on Draft B.
[5] African (S) 858, Draft Letters Patent, Nov 06.

really little more than another name for the government of the day, would have served.[1] Even Churchill's confident prediction in February, that a definite annual sum would be reserved for the special interests of the Africans and the maintenance of a native department,[2] was frustrated. Civil Service opinion insisted that similar reservations in Natal and Australia had proved worthless. In addition, Sir R. Solomon, who helped with the drafting in London, and Selborne, were opposed to the incorporation of a similar reservation in the Transvaal Constitution.

Elgin considered that the final terms were, under the circumstances, perhaps as far as they could safely go, despite his earlier hope that it would be possible to make proposals of a wider character. Four things were done: Swaziland was placed under the high commissioner by an Order-in-Council, the governor was retained as paramount chief,[3] legislation imposing differentials on account of race was reserved for imperial approval,[4] and a permissive clause provided for a native council.[5] Elgin welcomed the latter clause warmly, although it had not been possible to work out machinery in the letters patent. The governor in council was enabled to summon at any time an 'assembly of native Chiefs' to discuss problems of native administration. It could hardly be more than a suggestion. The idea was founded on the custom of South Africa. The records of what could be done, for instance in Basutoland, under the guidance of a sympathetic officer, by holding assemblies of this kind, made Elgin hope that the new government of the Transvaal might be willing and able to develop something useful on these lines.[6] In the House of Lords Elgin insisted on the impossibility of refusing confidence in Transvaal control of the Africans. By providing that the governor should continue to exercise his powers and authority as paramount chief, they would, he thought, be able to exert such influence as was proper and necessary on behalf of the Africans. This, he

---

[1] CO. 291/111/32059, minute by Lambert.　　　[2] PD. 152/1235, 28 Feb 06.
[3] Cl[ause] 39.　　　　　　[4] Cl. 51(1).　　　　　[5] Cl. 51(2).
[6] PD. 167/942, 17 Dec 06.

hoped, would be a better way of securing adequate provision for their needs than attempting to insert in the constitution itself definite sums of money, the sufficiency of which it was extremely difficult to estimate in advance.[1] The intention of this clause was to give governors a certain status in relation to African affairs, independent of ministerial action, and to enable Africans to have access to him. Elgin thought the intention clear and good; it was also politically expedient not to omit a provision which had been made in the Natal Constitution. It is, however, hard to argue that the provisions of the clause could be used very effectively. Although technically they made it possible for a governor to take action without his ministers, this was always a difficult, and sometimes a dangerous, proceeding.[2] It had not succeeded in Natal. The scheme was totally unrealistic.

The position of the Africans must in any case have been attended with difficulty, but it was complicated by the terms of peace, and the strong feeling in parliament, and accentuated by the recent events in Natal, which provoked unrest and distrust of Africans. The baleful influence of the Natal 'rebellion' may be seen from letters written by Hopwood whilst serving on the Ridgeway Committee:

All my hopes about the native question have for the time being evaporated. Events in Natal, and prejudices on all sides, make the moment inopportune to get concessions. Boer and Briton are both all agog to go native shooting in the sister Colony.[3]

The case of the Coloured persons, Elgin admitted, was in some respects a hard one:

Some of them are well-educated, estimable members of society. But so are many British Indians – and it is difficult to see how the position of the two is to be differentiated, while

---

[1] Ibid. 941. CAB. 37/85/105, draft desp. to Selb. Dec 06 argued that the effect of fixing an amount might discourage the legislature from voting a larger sum.

[2] CO. 291/128/34478 and 119/32934, see also L. P. Mair, *Native policies in Africa* (1936), p. 41.

[3] Bryce papers C. 5; Hopwood to Bryce 20 May and 18 Jun 06. See pp. 239 ff.

colonial opinion is bitterly hostile at present to the admission of Asiatics to rights of citizenship.

He felt that some of the provisions of the law which bore with extreme severity on Coloured people ought to be amended, but he found it difficult to see how a Coloured man could be treated as white in all respects, especially in the matter of the franchise.[1]

There was of course a strong Liberal predisposition not to dictate native policy from London. Ripon had long held:

In the self-governing colonies the more fully we can accept their self-government in its fullest sense, and leave them to deal with the natives in their own way and *on their own responsibility*, the better for our relations with them, and for the maintenance of their loyalty. But I doubt whether people in this country would accept the whole consequences of this doctrine – though anything short of it must lead to constant friction.[2]

After their patient search for an alternative, the Liberals had on the whole come back to this view.

(*d*) *Land Settlement.* Milner's scheme to strengthen the British element on the land by the introduction of settlers, went to the heart of differences between the two parties in their approach to the South African question. Campbell-Bannerman had denounced land settlement at the start as 'unnatural colonisation', promoted for avowedly political reasons. 'Economically, sentimentally, and politically alike, Ireland is at hand to show us what the result of a "plantation" policy may be.' The true solvents of the racial difficulties were social and economic relationships, community of interests. '. . . An unnatural state of society created by the use of British credit and British money can never bring peace and harmony into the country . . .'[3]

Unionist peers were sufficiently apprehensive of the Liberal attitude to these settlers (more than a thousand of them) to

[1] EP, cab. memo. 23 Jul 06. [2] Asq. 9/94, Ripon to Asquith 29 Dec 97.
[3] PD. 112/28–9, 29 Jul 02.

call a debate on land settlement in March 1906. No single act would be more calculated to reassure the British minority, declared Lord Milner, than the government's taking steps for the protection of this population on the land.[1] Elgin, in a sympathetic but non-committal speech, referred to the difficulties of land settlement, especially the extent to which success depended on the quality of the settler. He did not consider that the results had been quite comparable with those expected because the expenses had been greater and the number of settlers smaller. He thought land settlements, when successfully carried out, to be of great advantage, and was pleased to find that the government in South Africa had also set up a very large agricultural department to make much needed improvements in agriculture.

As to the position of the settlers, they have a definite legal status, and I cannot suppose that that legal status will be affected by any arrangements which may be made, or by any Government which we desire to see established in the Transvaal.[2]

Churchill made the first important announcement on land settlement policy. He began by noting that it had so far cost Britain £2,200,000. 'I do not think it is very encouraging', he continued, 'that we should have spent so much money upon the settlement of so few.' It was neither remunerative nor wise 'to try and change the character of a country by planting out farmers as if they were orchids'. But there was no reason for squandering such result as had been obtained. He thought it unlikely that they would provide for any further inflow of British settlers against the will or the independence of action of responsible governments, but they had a distinct obligation to those already settled if only because they would do a great deal to soften 'the harshness of contact' between the British and the Boer farmer.[3]

£3 million of the post-war loan of £35 million, guaranteed by the British government, had been set aside for land settlement purposes, and had not all been expended. In an important

[1] PD. 154/1036, 27 Mar 06.   [2] Ibid. 1026–30.   [3] PD. 155/845–6, 5 Apr 06.

ruling, the law officers said that money repaid by the settlers must either be devoted to further purposes of land settlement, or to the diminution of the total debt charge on the guaranteed loan. The government would have liked the money to remain devoted to adding to the population and development of the rural districts. An imperial land board independent of the local government was suggested. Elgin declared:

H.M.G. are not disposed to deny that a Land Board may supply the best machinery for administering these Colonies, but they are obliged to attach conditions. It seems to them that it would be entirely contrary to the general principle of responsible government, that an arrangement of that kind should be carried out except by general consent.[1]

Despite this feeling that it would be a 'considerable encroachment' on responsible government, Elgin thought that with the consent of all parties 'much might be overlooked', and a board be of real advantage. Milner he believed to have made a mistake in deriding the idea of consent. He was none the less convinced (he told Selborne):

It must be bona fide self-government as understood and exemplified in other Colonies, and every provision that differentiates it from the known type must expect criticism. . . . Well, it seems to me useless to put forward provisions which directly challenge attack on the above ground, but that does not mean that I ignore the possibility of dangers which you apprehend, or that I should not welcome anything which you would regard as a safeguard, and could be introduced with a reasonable prospect of acceptance.[2]

Selborne agreed to try to negotiate with the leaders of public opinion for the establishment of an endowed imperial and non-political land settlement board which would continue to introduce new settlers. He did his best, but, not unexpectedly, the result was most disappointing. Consent for expanding the scheme was not forthcoming. The only assurance he could

[1] PD. 162/621. [2] EP, E to Selb. 16 Aug 06.

obtain was that there should be an attempt to treat existing settlers fairly. Opinion was averse even to the substitution of fresh settlers for any of the existing settlers who might give up their holdings.[1] Elgin had for some time doubted the prudence of bringing in new settlers, but he was now convinced that it would be 'worse than useless' for the imperial government to introduce them without the general sympathy of the people.[2] This part of the original proposal was therefore dropped. The possibility of establishing, by at least tacit consent, an independent temporary land board, appointed by the governor, to administer funds, and to act as a sympathetic landlord, remained.

Churchill argued the case in an important memorandum.[3] There were obvious objections to the original suggestion that an imperial board should deal with the assets of responsible government colonies for the benefit of one particular class of colonists. They might dislike the objective of settlement, its lack of thrift and unsatisfactory result, but they were nevertheless confronted with six or seven hundred vulnerable settlers planted at much expense and trouble in the Transvaal alone. Asquith had suggested the desirability of interposing 'a screen between mortgagor and mortgagee'. Without this screen, Churchill thought it certain that a few bad years, and a rigid and severe administration would very easily sweep them all away 'like mushrooms before the scythe'. Although there was no conclusive evidence that harsh treatment would be meted out, such apprehensions were, he thought, real and widespread, and if, shortly after the new governments were formed, considerable numbers of those settlers were, or had to be, evicted, perhaps quite justifiably, for non-payment of rent, instalments or arrears, Churchill foresaw a succession of unpleasant incidents, each of which would give 'abundant opportunities for Tory appeals to prejudice, for constant attacks upon the new governments, and protracted feelings of irritation and unrest'. The question which the cabinet had to decide was whether reiterated charges of

---

[1] CO. 291/103/38688, Selb. to S/S 29 Sep 06.   [2] EP, E to Selb. 23 Nov 06.
[3] African (S) 859, 7 Nov 06: CO. 291/104/40044.

having 'deserted the settlers' would be less prejudicial to reconciliation and peaceful government in the two new colonies, than the unquestionable limitation upon the powers of a responsible government by the establishment of an imperial land board. In his opinion, the first alternative would be the worse, for the government had already been most accommodating to the Boers, and introduced into the constitution certain features, such as a nominated second chamber 'at variance with our general political conceptions'. 'In the interests of a broad-bottomed settlement which will reassure anxious minds, and prevent clear cut cleavages', he suggested a proposal which was 'the absolute minimum action possible, unless we are frankly to take the position of making no reservation of any sort or kind', namely a board to last only five years to enable existing settlers to take root. The 'absolute minimum' concept is an odd and early example of the influence of the terminology of the Webbs.

Elgin discussed these proposals with Churchill. Although there was not time to enter into all the details, he recommended the scheme to the cabinet, acknowledging Churchill's authorship. Elgin wanted to make some provision not only or principally because of the interest taken in the subject in Britain, but because from some points of view it was, he conceived, advantageous to the colonies. Not overlooking the fact that the ultimate object of some, if not of all, of these settlements had been political (i.e. the introduction of a large British population), he did not think such an object illegitimate, but they could not make special provision for it in a manner which would override the new responsible government. He felt

it would be disastrous for the Colonies if the settlers, many of whom are certainly bona fide settlers, did not receive fair play . . . because so far as these are bona fide settlers they are valuable to the Colonies. I am deeply impressed by the belief that the agricultural position of the Colonies was very unsatisfactory under the Boer regime; that it has now made a considerable advance, but that much more ought to be done. As matters stand, if there was a crash in the mining industry – and no one can say that this is impossible – it is difficult to see what there would be to fall back upon. We are advised that there might be a considerable future in the agricultural development of the country, and I deprecate anything which might retard it.[1]

The cabinet accepted this policy. The absence of consent forced them to retreat from the proposals of July, and adopt a more modest scheme. This was one of the few ways in which the final arrangements differed from those outlined in July.[2] All that could be done was to set up a land board to help existing settlers. The idea was to try to secure time, not only for the new government to form a fair estimate of the situation, but for the settlers to decide, with a knowledge of the new governments, whether to stay or to go.[3] Elgin regarded agricultural development of such obvious importance that the Transvaal government would surely see it to be in their interest not to dismiss or discourage useful settlers of any nationality but to increase their numbers.[4] This was placing undue faith in the power of reason. Land settlement funds and administration were to be transferred to a corporate board of three men, appointed by the governor. Churchill repudiated altogether any slur on the humanity or sense of justice of the Boers, whom he thought indeed the last people to be uncharitable to farming people; but it was represented to the government that they had an obligation of honour to relieve the settlers of anxiety and to deal with them directly.[5] The life of the land board was strictly limited to five years, and a proviso enabled earlier transfer of its functions to the government if the settlers were agreeable.[6] The board in fact remained for the full five years. Exactly parallel arrangements were made for settlers in the Orange River Colony.

(e) *Language policy.* The British community evidently wanted to make English the only recognised language in the Transvaal. However, the cabinet committee of 30 January 1906 recommended that absolute linguistic equality should be formally

---

[1] EP, cab. memo. 12 Nov 06.
[2] African (S) 858. Draft Transvaal letters patent. Nov 06.
[3] PD. 167/944, 17 Dec 06.   [4] EP, E to Selb. 23 Nov 06 (copy).
[5] Keith, *Speeches and Documents*, ii, pp. 20–1.   [6] Cl. 52.

established in the letters patent; that members should be allowed to speak indifferently in Dutch or English, and that parliamentary records and minutes should be kept in both languages. But in view of Selborne's arguments, ministers reconsidered their view.

Selborne wanted every sympathy to be shown to the colloquial Taal (Afrikaans), which had no literature, but he did not think that Britain should accede to the request to make Dutch an equal official language, though they might allow it to be taught in schools. The Boers could not understand Dutch, he said, and its advocates were those who cherished the ideal of an Afrikander republic. With all the optimism of a Macaulay, Churchill wrote a characteristic minute in favour of complete bilingual equality, if that was what the Boers wanted. In his view, High Dutch was not likely to oust English: 'No devices however costly and inconvenient will, in the present age, accomplish such a revolution.' He did not think that many artificial stimulants would be demanded once it was known that they would not be refused. If the Boers did not make a point of 'complete bi-lingual equality in its most pedantic forms', he would not suggest inconvenient methods to them, but 'follow calmly and trustfully the line of least resistance', which seemed to be, not separately to recognise the Taal, nor to make Dutch official to the same extent as English. This would be in accordance with Cape precedent. But if further recognition of the Taal or High Dutch was vehemently demanded, 'to their own detriment and at their own proper expense', he would not resist their wishes. Elgin noted that the considerations urged by Selborne had been mentioned by several other people from the colonies; they deserved attention:

To see that no man is at a disadvantage because he can only speak one language and that not English, is one thing – and involves full privilege for the Taal – to introduce another literary language on an equality with the language of the Empire, is an entirely different matter.[1]

[1] CO. 291/98/16845, Selb. to S/S 23 Apr 06, minute by Churchill 31 May (see also, Mansergh, *South Africa*, p. 49), minute by Elgin 4 Jun 06.

The use of Dutch was freely permitted in the new legislature. The Lyttelton constitution had allowed it only with the Speaker's permission; this the Liberals regarded as an invidious discrimination. 'The recognition of their language is precious to a small people' declared Churchill.[1]

English was made the language of the statute book, because it was thought there was very serious difficulty in using two languages for the purpose of final record. 'I think we all desire full opportunity for the use of their own language by the Boers', said Elgin, but in this particular instance it 'might introduce a dangerous element of uncertainty into judicial proceedings'. Solomon suggested the solution of the dilemma, which was to follow what had become the actual practice in the Cape: every law assented to in His Majesty's name should be printed in the 'Gazette' in English and Dutch for general information, and a fair copy of every law in the English language signed by the governor, should be enrolled on record in the office of the registrar of the supreme court.[2]

(*f*) *Second Chamber*. The Lyttelton Constitution provided for a single-chamber legislature. In his memorandum of 26 December 1905 Ripon argued for a second chamber, partly because it was normal in South Africa, and would therefore inevitably be required before federation, and partly because he believed 'that the true barrier against the great evils of race prejudice, is to be found in the creation of a well organised Senate or Upper Chamber, rather than in any manipulation of the electoral franchise.'[3]

Selborne believed that a second chamber would be necessary to secure stability in native policy, to safeguard African interests and ensure fair treatment. A carefully selected body of men, not known negrophilists, but of suitable and reflective character, might, he thought, gradually influence the chamber to consider itself specially charged with securing wise and just treatment

---

[1] PD. 162/744, 31 Jul 06.
[2] EP, cab. memo. 12 Nov 06; Letters Patent, cl. 44, 45.
[3] EP. By 'race prejudice' Ripon meant sweeping legislation in the Boer interest.

for Africans; such men might take a broader and more thought-ful view than the general white colonial view.[1] With the exception of Graham, officials did not receive suggestions of a second chamber with any enthusiasm. They remarked that it was not likely to be of any use in safeguarding African interests and could not be relied upon; that it would be foolish to set it up merely in the supposed interest of natives; that the tendency of the day was against nominated chambers; and that therefore they could not create one in the absence of a clear demand from the colony. This appeared to be missing; only Selborne seemed to want it.[2] Churchill described Selborne's anxiety about Africans as

a little too pronounced in his argument. One would think 'native interest' was the only function of the second chamber. No doubt it is the only argument which would commend such an institution to the present House of Commons. I do not think it is strong enough in itself.

Churchill disliked second chambers in general, and would have deferred the question of introducing one in the Transvaal until the fundamentals of the constitution were decided.[3]

Elgin had no such dislike of a second chamber in principle, but he could not make up his mind whether the Transvaal should have one. On the one hand, as was proper for a peer, he pointed out that there were able men in all communities who would not for various reasons undergo the ordeal of an election; 'I do not defend their position, but it gives a reserve on which we can draw in a case like this.' He was inclined to think that the establishment of a second chamber might perhaps meet some of the difficulties they were encountering, especially in the Orange River Colony, 'and help to counteract the fore-bodings of Lord Milner and others, and provide safeguards for

[1] CO. 291/96/6752, Selb. to S/S 5 Feb 06; 5406, tel. 11 Feb 06.

[2] CO. 291/88/1604, minute by Just 16 Jan 06; CO. 291/96/5406, minute by Keith 15 Feb 06; memo. by Graham, African (S) 818.

[3] WSC, minute 10 Mar 06 on CO. 291/88/1604. Four years later he was to argue 'the time has come for the total abolition of the House of Lords' (CAB. 37/102/3, 14 Feb 10).

the interests of the natives'.[1] It might be that in such a chamber, the true barrier against the great evils of race prejudice might be found, as Ripon had said. On the other hand, to create a second chamber in one or both colonies might produce a danger of confusion, and even a lack of properly qualified members. It might also be argued, that with a view to the possibility of a confederation of the South African colonies at no distant date, it was desirable not to multiply the arrangements which would require alteration when the time for such a system arrived.[2]

However, the Ridgeway committee looking towards confederation concluded that it would be 'highly convenient that ... the bi-cameral system should prevail'. It found a function for a second chamber: it could act as a court of appeal (as the assembly would have a close division of parties), it could redraft crude legislation, and it might secure fair consideration for African interests.[3]

One of the main problems was that nomination could only be a temporary expedient, for under responsible government the constitution of the second chamber (the legislative council) ought to be decided by the legislative assembly, over whom it was the special function of a second chamber to exercise a moderating influence – a state of things not expected to secure an unbiased decision.[4] A compromise was evolved, whereby the first house, with fifteen seats, should be nominated, but subsequent houses elected. It was thought better that the exceptional nominations should be made on the responsibility of the British government.[5] The recommendations were made by Selborne and accepted by Elgin, in the middle of February 1907. Nomination of the first house had the additional advantage of avoiding the confusion of two sets of elections simultaneously. Despite special efforts, there was not much success in finding men with special knowledge of, and interest in, Africans.[6]

[1] EP, cab. memo. 5 Mar 06; Elgin's constant attempt to accommodate the views of the other side emerges clearly here.
[2] CO. 291/97/11334, minute 5 Apr 06.   [3] *Report*, pp. 23, 26.
[4] EP, E to Selb. 22 Feb 06 (copy).   [5] EP, E to Selb. 6 Sep 06 (copy).
[6] CO. 291/115/5241, tel. Selb. to S/S 10 Feb 07.

(g) *Indentured Labour*. Clause 39 of the new letters patent declared: 'And whereas it is Our will and pleasure that all persons within Our dominions shall be free from any conditions of employment or residence of a servile character, the Governor shall reserve any law providing for the introduction under contract, indenture or licence, of labourers into the Colony from places outside South Africa.'

The idea of making a declaration against slavery originated in the Ridgeway Committee. They thought it possible that British public opinion might compel the British government against its will to listen to protests about native labour, and perhaps to comply with its demands. 'From such interference, especially if it should prove to be unjustifiable, grave complications may arise.' Therefore it seemed to them desirable to anticipate and provide against such a contingency in the new constitution, by a declaration prohibiting slavery. 'We think that any constitution which does not provide, so far as is possible, against such unfortunate collisions, would be defective to a very regrettable degree.' The Sand River and Pretoria Conventions of 1852 and 1881, recognising Transvaal independence, had declared that slavery would not be tolerated.[1] There was undoubtedly a strong desire for such a declaration among the anti-Chinese Labour group in the House of Commons. Opinions in the cabinet committee differed, and so Elgin asked the full cabinet

to decide whether, as a matter of policy, under existing circumstances, a statement of a principle, however indubitably a tradition of the British Empire, is to be for the first time inserted in the Constitution of an individual colony. That this may be resented as invidious is, of course, obvious.[2]

In the first draft of the Constitution there was a declaration in the preamble that 'All persons therein [in the Transvaal] shall possess full rights of personal liberty, and that no system of apprenticeship or indentured labour in derogation of such rights shall be at any time established within Our said Colony.'[3]

---

[1] *Report*, p. 27.   [2] EP, cab. memo. 24 Jul 06.   [3] EP. Draft A.

175

This declaration was abandoned. Elgin's private secretary, Bernard Holland, was alarmed by the suggested preamble and argued cogently against it. Non-Europeans would think such a reference, he said, either a bitter mockery, or regard it as a promise from the imperial government of which they could claim immediate fulfilment. 'It will be, to them, almost an incitement to insurrection.' It was not, he suggested, worth-while to enunciate a principle at variance with the facts and realities of South Africa 'in order to please sentimental politicians'. There was, he added, no surer way to unite white South Africa against Britain, while stirring up coloured peoples against white South Africa.[1]

Maybe as a consequence of this letter, Elgin wrote to Cox, who had drafted the preamble, describing himself as 'a little nervous' about the declaration. He had never been much in favour of these general propositions, which might easily give rise to a number of questions with non-Europeans. 'But no doubt it was decided to have a declaration – only according to my recollection this draft carries us further.' Elgin remembered how Asquith had suggested certain words which were not so specific. Presumably these were conditions 'of a servile character', a phrase Churchill had taken up on 31 July 1906; he thought that it would be more effective, because more precise and restrained, than 'slavery'.[2] Cox fully concurred in the view that the preamble was without precedent and un-desirable for the reasons given by Elgin.[3]

The declaration actually made was placed in a clause requiring reservation of legislation concerning Asiatics and Chinese labourers. A further clause provided for the termina-tion of Chinese Labour.[4] Elgin did not strongly favour any of these references to Chinese Labour. At first he thought reserva-tion of legislation concerning Chinese was superfluous. Even at the end of August 1906 he was not prepared to commit himself

---

[1] EP, Holland to E 4 Oct 06.   [2] PD. 162/749.

[3] EP, Cox to E 6 [sic] Oct 06; the letter begins by thanking E for his letter of 8 [sic] Oct.

[4] Clauses 39 and 50.

to the provision about termination.[1] And in December he felt bound to admit publicly that the Chinese Labour clauses, though justifiable in the circumstances, were abnormal.[2] He was satisfied that the references to Chinese Labour would entirely fulfil their obligations.[3]

THE ORANGE RIVER COLONY CONSTITUTION

There was no possibility of taking a holiday after the question of the Transvaal constitution had been settled, because the settlement of a constitution for the sister colony was now urgent. Elgin worked every day during the Christmas recess. Ommanney's retirement as permanent under-secretary may also have helped to make it certain that there could be no relaxation of the pressure upon him. By 11 January 1907 he described himself as feeling 'a bit done up.'[4]

The Orange River Colony constitution was a question full of difficulty.[5] The decision to grant full responsible government here too was an even more remarkable demonstration than in the Transvaal of the policy of trusting the Boers. For in the Orange River Colony there was no possibility whatever of a British majority, and the Orange River Colony had the reputation of being the most 'disaffected and illiberal' portion of South Africa. Indeed, one of the commonest objections to granting responsible government to the Transvaal had been that it would make it difficult to refuse it to the Orange River Colony.

Selborne was determined to try to prevent this dreadful eventuality. Under responsible government, he wrote, the

---

[1] EP, E to Selb. 31 Aug 06 (copy). [2] PD. 167/942.
[3] EP, cab. memo. 12 Nov 06. From the commencement of the letters patent, no licence could be issued for the introduction of labourers under the ordinance of 1904, which was to be repealed and cease to have effect at the end of one year from the date of the first meeting of the legislature, 'and the system of labour deriving effect from the said Ordinances, Rules and Regulations shall accordingly be determined' (Cl. 50).
[4] EP, E to Selb. 8 Feb 07, E to WSC 10 and 11 Jan 07 (copy/photocopies).
[5] EP, E to WSC 6 Oct 06 (photocopy).

whole power would be permanently vested in two or three men such as Fischer, Hertzog and de Wet, who were 'bitter enemies of the British connection' and far more hostile to it than the farmers of the colony generally. Selborne believed that they would use their power 'remorselessly to diminish British influence in their country'. These evils could, however, be greatly mitigated, or altogether obviated, by the restoration of the country's old independent constitution.[1] He submitted his scheme first in August 1905, officially arguing the unsuitability of ordinary self-government to the Orange River Colony, but privately aiming to retain maximum power in the hands of the governor and to keep the road of public influence open to the British party.[2] The major way in which he proposed to modify the old constitution was replacement of the elected president by a governor appointed by the king. According to Selborne's expectations, the people of the colony would receive the grant of responsible government with satisfaction, but the restoration of the forms of their old constitution with 'unfeigned, surprised delight'. His rather curious opinion was shared by the lieutenant-governor, Sir Hamilton Goold-Adams, and the executive council. Ommanney thought their support conclusive, and favoured the plan. Some of the other officials doubted the validity of Selborne's argument.[3] The most powerful critic was Keith, who thought the proposals naïve and ill-informed, hybrid and unworkable.[4]

The King's Speech from the throne on 19 February 1906 had promised that a constitution granting responsible government to the Orange River Colony would be framed.[5] Selborne was very much hurt by what he conceived to be the flagrant and casual rejection of his advice.

Strangely enough, the Ridgeway Committee found wide support for Selborne's suggestion in the colony, although it was decisively opposed by the leaders of Oranjie Unie. Neverthe-

[1] African (S) 813, memo. by Selb. 14 Dec 05 (CO. 879/91).
[2] Balfour papers, 49708/89, Selb. to Balfour 23 Aug 05 and 94–96, 12 Nov 05.
[3] CO. 224/18/31680, 42856, Selb. to S/S 13 Nov 05.
[4] CO. 224/18/6404, minute 23 Feb 06.   [5] PD. 152/23.

less, the committee recommended a plebiscite on this issue.[1]

Selborne took up his scheme again privately in June 1906, more convinced than ever that only his plan would really solve the problem and avert danger. He asked Elgin to ponder his conclusion that the whole history of South Africa proved the Boers 'very bad winners' – hence the state of alarm among the settlers and the civil servants at the prospect of responsible government.[2] Elgin indicated his considerable sympathy with Selborne's view, but:

The difficulty is that the arrangements suggested cannot, by any subtlety, be described as 'responsible government'. Personally I should not be restrained by regard for a 'fetish' – but you will understand that to have that feeling oneself, and to persuade the House of Commons, are two very opposite processes.[3]

Selborne then asked why, with his proposals before them, the government had made an 'unnecessary pledge' in the King's Speech. Why did they commit themselves first and enquire afterwards? Elgin did not admit giving an 'unnecessary pledge'. He could see nothing in the history of the colony to make it less qualified for self-government than its neighbour, rather the contrary. He felt the extreme difficulty of refusing the Orange River Colony a government really parallel to the Transvaal. 'An elected president is one thing – a nominated governor is another', and in his judgment the constitution Selborne proposed was 'neither more nor less than a form of Crown Colony government'.[4]

Elgin prepared the matter for submission to the cabinet in a memorandum dated 19 November 1906.[5] In the Transvaal, he explained, the chances of political contest must remain doubtful, but in the Orange River Colony one interest (the agricultural) and one race (the Dutch) enjoyed an acknowledged and overwhelming preponderance. The only doubtful point in

---

[1] See Le May, *British supremacy in South Africa*, p. 206.
[2] EP, Selb. to E 11 Jun 06. [3] EP, E to Selb. 13 Jul 06 (copy).
[4] Ibid. 6 and 28 Sep 07. [5] EP.

any election would be the size of the minority. Elgin thought an important feature of any constitution would be the amount and nature of any protection to be afforded to that minority. Undoubtedly protection of some sort was favoured by many; Elgin did not think this altogether unreasonable. It was true that the old constitution of the Free State did afford some of the protection required, and as it worked well on the whole, it was not surprising to find a demand for the renewal of at least some of its provisions. The Ridgeway Committee proposed only a 'limited form of self-government'.[1] This Elgin thought impracticable, for two main reasons:

(1) That it is not a reproduction of the old Dutch Government,... but (2) and still more important, that it is in no sense 'responsible government'. It is true that in our original announcements we carefully guarded against a definite promise to reproduce in the Orange River Colony every one of the provisions of the Transvaal Constitution in identical terms. But we did promise responsible government, and the form presented to us cannot be so described, for it lacks the essential characteristic of the responsibility of ministers to parliament, and the reasons which obliged us to set aside the Lyttelton Constitution for the Transvaal are still applicable here. That there are risks is a self-evident proposition which I do not think the Cabinet will expect me to argue; but as against these, we have the fact that, not only with a view to peace within its own borders but also in view of federation, to which many of us look forward, it is necessary that the Orange River Colony should be given a position of substantial equality with the other South African colonies.

The cabinet accepted this argument, and so the provisions of the Transvaal letters patent were largely reproduced in the second constitution, although there was a different distribution of constituencies. The Ridgeway committee proposed the separate representation of towns. This had the support of the Boers, and indeed the final scheme of the committee differed only in minor details from that of Mr Fischer. Elgin commented:

[1] African (S) 854.

If I understand the Committee's scheme aright it will give to men like Sir John Fraser, who may be said to represent both the British and the Moderate Boer, a better chance in the town constituencies i.e. in about twelve out of the 28, whereas if no such arrangement is made, I am told that Sir John Fraser himself might find it difficult to get a seat except in Bloemfontein.

He thought this the best system of minority representation in the existing circumstances of the colony. The British minority was so small that proportional representation would not help them. Elgin believed that under any such system the minority in order to succeed had to be carefully organised, which would mean an organisation on racial lines.

Nothing more disastrous could be devised. The Committee's Report speaks of a division of opinion amongst the Boers, and I have reason to believe that this means that, in the judgment of the Committee, a strong Moderate party exists. The worst thing that could happen would be that the British should be so organised as to prevent co-operation with any such party.[1]

Selborne regarded the constitution adopted as perhaps the next best thing to the one which he recommended. But he still believed it unsuitable.[2] Elgin quite understood Selborne's apprehensions though he could not accept them:

I can only say that we remain of the opinion that we practically had no alternative under all the circumstances, in which I mean to include not only those for which you may hold us to be responsible ourselves, but also the natural sequence of historical events.[3]

In justifying the decision in parliament, both Elgin[4] and Churchill[5] made use of Chamberlain's declarations that he would give representative government to the Orange River Colony before the Transvaal. If the Liberals had a different order of priorities, this was largely because of the Chinese

[1] EP, cab. memo. 19 Nov 06.   [2] EP, Selb. to E 28 Dec 06.
[3] EP, 31 May 07.   [4] PD. 167/945, 17 Dec 06.
[5] See Keith, *Selected speeches and documents on British colonial policy 1763–1917* (1918), ii, 3–24.

Labour problem. The letters patent for the Orange River Colony were issued on 5 June 1907. The general election was held in November. Thirty out of thirty-eight seats were won by Oranjie Unie.

COMPARISON WITH UNIONIST CONSTITUTIONAL POLICY

The Liberals based their policy upon a concept of equality and a demonstration of trust. One of the main reasons why the Liberals handled the Transvaal and Orange River Colony constitutional problems in a different spirit from the Unionists stems from the way in which Campbell-Bannerman had educated his party in opposition. He carefully fostered an attitude of mind which regarded the Boers equally British citizens with South Africans of British descent. The Transvaal Dutch, he declared in 1899:

are every whit as much our fellow subjects as the English colonists. . . . It is by letting it be seen that neither race shall have an advantage over the other that they can be brought into harmony.

In exactly the same spirit, Gladstone had said in 1885 that he could not treat the Irish as foes or aliens, or advise that less should be done for them than would in like circumstances be done for the inhabitants of any other portion of the United Kingdom.[1] To Campbell-Bannerman, the cardinal fact upon which the whole difficulty of the South African war turned, was that it had the nature of a civil war. Hence after the war, the Transvaal should be consulted and conciliated and not treated like a conquered state.[2] Among his notes for speeches, the following statement occurs:

[1] D. G. Hoskin, *The genesis and significance of the 1886 Home Rule split in the Liberal party* (unpublished Cambridge Ph.D. dissertation 1961), p. 159.

[2] CB, *Speeches*, pp. 34–5, 77. 'If we are to maintain the political supremacy of the British power . . . it can only be by conciliation and friendship; it will never be by domination and ascendancy, because the British power cannot . . . rest securely unless it rests upon the willing consent of a sympathetic and contented people' (quoted by Le May, op. cit. pp. 39–40).

Lord Durham did not try to make Frenchmen into Englishmen. He did not propose to . . . swamp them with new settlers and to break their spirit by a course of Crown Colony government. . . . Nor did he take the emotions of the loyalists as the test of statesmanship. . . .

Durham, he wrote (though it seems an unduly favourable interpretation) did not differentiate between French and English, 'nor penalise or pet' the one race or the other. As a result, 'Canada remains as the greatest triumph of British statesmanship, of broad and liberal views, and nobly instructed imagination.' Campbell-Bannerman also copied out Durham's passage about the 'two modes by which a government may deal with a conquered territory', and deduced that Durham would have recommended respecting the rights and nationality of the pastoral peoples of South Africa, recognising their existing laws and giving no encouragement to an influx of the conquering people, instead of regarding them as subordinate and to be assimilated rapidly to imperial institutions.[1]

Campbell-Bannerman thought of Milner as 'the partisan whose thoughts are only for the British, whose idea of making peace in South Africa, is to turn the Dutch into English'.[2] Liberal ministers deplored the 'excessive note' of distrust of the Dutch which pervaded Milner's speech on 26 February 1906. If Milner had been a chief secretary or viceroy of Ireland, remarked Crewe, he would have found that efforts to improve the condition of the people and advance material progress had been continually hampered by a state of feeling ingrained in the Irish, arising out of past attempts 'to establish in a community of mixed blood, an absolute and unreasonable ascendancy of one race, even though that race be our own. . . . We are not going to declare ourselves anti-Boers.'[3] Milner's approach was utterly different. In 1901 he described the Liberal attitude as

---

[1] CB. 41243 A/117–8; see Mansergh, *South Africa*, p. 29.
[2] CB 41243 A/59.
[3] PD. 152/995, Crewe 27 Feb 06.

thoroughly wrong headed. . . . I never lose sight of the fact that the 'conciliation' of our former enemies ought never to be our *first* object, [which ought to be] . . . to make sure of the position by strengthening the British element whether the Boers like it or not.[1]

And he regarded the Liberals as 'having given South Africa back to the Boers'.[2] He thought it was 'quite ludicrous', the way in which 'all their interest seems to centre in the enemy'. To Selborne also, it seemed that the impression the Liberals gave was one of hostility to all British people in South Africa, relying instead on the 'soft words' of the Boer leaders.[3]

Churchill declared that although the Liberals desired equally with the Unionists to maintain British supremacy in South Africa, they sought to do it by a different method. There was indeed, he said, a profound difference between the schools of thought which existed upon South African politics in the House of Commons. Liberals believed, he continued, that British authority in South Africa had got to stand on two legs. Their opponents had laboured for ten years to make it stand on one: this was the inherent vice of Lord Milner's policy. As Milner was regarded as 'the inveterate enemy of the Dutch, and the prime author of all their miseries, he was condemned to fall back entirely on the support of the British'. The Liberal government suffered from no such disability, and were free to hold the scales even, and work on terms of impartial justice with both sides.[4]

Churchill's sympathy for the Boers was genuine. When one of the officials described the Boer politicians as 'slim', Churchill asked 'Why are they "slim" to do what every Englishman would do under the same conditions?' He found them much more reasonable in their complaints, and much more ready to co-operate, than colonists in Kenya.[5] His sympathy extended ungrudgingly to Boers who had trekked into East Africa.

[1] *Milner Papers*, ii, 290–1, Milner to Chamberlain 20 Dec 01.
[2] Ibid. ii, 534, 17 Apr 07.   [3] EP, Selb. to E 28 Mar 06.
[4] PD. 155/848, 5 Apr 06; African (S) 817, 30 Jan 06.
[5] CO. 224/20/16064, minute 1 Jun 06.

Detecting a prejudice against them there, he insisted that the Commissioner should be enjoined 'to show consideration and patience. He will not be called unpatriotic. The war is over....'[1]

Given this generous insistence on equal rights of citizenship, it was inevitable that Selborne should have been reproached for presenting the government with vast quantities of information about British wishes, whilst giving almost no indication of Boer wishes. 'It might be prudent', suggested Elgin, 'not to press further your personal advocacy of British views on the constitution. We all understand the policy you prefer....'[2] Elgin explained further about support for the Lyttelton constitution:

You have not ceased to impress upon us the strong feeling of the British in this matter. As I have said before, I think you would have strengthened your own position in sending us this information, which it was your undoubted duty to send, and in supporting it, if it had been accompanied by some reference to any feeling in any opposite direction. That this exists, I am aware you recognise, e.g. from what you told me in anticipation of the visit from Smuts.[3]

In correcting this pro-British bias, the Liberals fell back upon the memorandum which Smuts had left with them, local inquiry by the Ridgeway Committee, and letters which Bryce received from various South African correspondents.

Although the guiding principle of the Liberal approach was to make no difference between Boer and Briton in their grant of responsible government, and although they viewed this principle as necessary to the permanent inclusion of South Africa in the empire, there was no intention of denying the British race any numerical preponderance which might properly belong to them. Announcing the constitutional proposals on 31 July 1906, Elgin saw no reason to speak the language of British supremacy, but added: 'I shall not be satisfied with my share in this work if British interests, in their widest sense, are not safe in the government we establish.'[4] Some such reassurance was clearly necessary, but there was a definite limit to the amount

---

[1] CO. 533/18/42084, minute 2 Dec 06.   [2] EP, E to Selb. tel. 2 Feb 06 (copy).
[3] Ibid. 22 Feb 06.   [4] PD. 162/625.

of reassurance the Liberal government felt able to give to Unionists and British colonists. An important indication of this was the refusal to publish the report of the Ridgeway Committee. The real reason for withholding it was never given: it was the pro-British tenor of the report.[1] There were some passages which 'simply from a desire to avoid any recurrence of dissensions' they would wish to omit or qualify before publication.[2] During September 1906 Elgin corresponded with the committee about revisions, but he was not able to get anything settled. It might be necessary, Elgin thought, 'to publish more than one would like, to escape from the too obvious retort of garbling'.[3] Selborne agreed that it would be difficult to withhold publication, as they might 'be accused, most unjustly, of acting contrary to their recommendations; but I do hope you will be able to induce the Committee to use the scissors'.[4]

The policy of trusting the Boers involved two distinct calculations. Could they be trusted to be loyal to British interests? Could they be trusted to treat the African majority fairly? Unionists and Liberals gave different answers to these questions because they interpreted human nature differently.

Balfour defined one question they must ask themselves:

Human nature, be it Dutch or English, being what it is, can the political institutions you are now going to give them, be made a substitution for the military organisation, cannon and all the rest of it, which brought them honourably into the field . . . ?[5]

Selborne never ceased to repeat his view that 'it would not be human nature' for the Boers to be reconciled to the British flag

---

[1] See pp. 146–7. In general, Loreburn thought the report very able and good, but: 'it is a great mistake to set forth the motive, viz, to secure a British majority . . . so repeatedly and in so marked a way. I very earnestly suggest that every trace of this anxiety to get a British majority should be eliminated. In fact I believe the Commissioners meant to be and were impartial, but in reading the Report an outsider might think they meant to have a British majority *coûte que coûte*. I am sure they did not mean that' (EP, to E 22 Jul 06).

[2] EP, E to Selb. 30 Aug 06 (copy).   [3] Ibid. 28 Sep 06.
[4] EP, Selb. to E 23 Oct 06.   [5] PD. 162/802.

so soon after defeat. Their objective was remorselessly to diminish British influence in every way. It was 'the same sentiment we ourselves would be inspired with under similar circumstances'.[1] Milner did not think complete self-government would bring about harmony between the two white races.[2] He could not regard with equanimity the prospect 'that the very hand which drafted the ultimatum of October 1899' would so soon be tendering advice which the British governor would have virtually no option but to accept.[3]

The traditional Liberal attitude stands in striking contrast. It was an article of this Liberal faith that men would act as you showed you expected them to act. Liberals believed in self-government, not only on the grounds of justice and effective administration, but on the ground that it exercised 'a wholesome influence on the people who enjoy the privilege'. Liberals believed, not only that, on the whole, the good forces were strongest in human nature, but that free institutions on a fair basis encouraged the good forces. Men were likely to be better men, 'through the mere fact of being voters' in a self-governing state.[4] They could hardly conceive that democratic government exercised by people of European stock might not prove beneficial to the governed. Just as they believed that the solution to the Congo problem was most likely to be found in control by the Belgian parliament, which 'may well be trusted to . . . extend the rights they themselves enjoy, so far as that is possible, to the . . . natives',[5] so they believed that the Dutch in South Africa would take full measure of their responsibilities. 'No nation is devoid of a conscience. . . .'[6]

The decision to trust the Transvaal in these two directions was to some extent an act of faith, reflecting a traditionally optimistic interpretation of human nature. Selborne left the

[1] African (S) 812, memo. 14 Dec 05.
[2] CO. 291/74/1547, Milner to S/S 24 Dec 04.
[3] PD. 152/707-21, 26 Feb 06.
[4] CB, *Speeches*, p. 181; PD. 152/571, Churchill; Fisher, *Bryce*, i, 287; Samuel, *Liberalism*, p. 225; J. Morley, *Indian Speeches 1907-1909* (1909), p. 42, 21 Oct 07.
[5] PD. 184/1297, Fitzmaurice 24 Feb 08.
[6] Morel papers F. 8; H. Samuel to Morel 6 Sep 05.

government in no doubt at all that he did not trust the Boers to act responsibly. Hopwood was cautious about the prospect for the natives, merely regarding it as 'true to some extent', that in normal times the attitude of Briton and Boer had greatly improved towards the native.[1] There was no real evidence that the Boers could be trusted, apart from their promises, and the opinions of local observers, whose judgment the Liberals trusted. J. X. Merriman's opinion, for instance, was always esteemed by the Liberals; he assured them that 'the old Boer – the so-called "tak haar", of whom Paul Kruger was the idol and the most prominent representative, has practically disappeared as a factor'. Merriman became prime minister of Cape Colony in 1908. He honestly believed that if the Boers were treated as equals they would become as law-abiding citizens as any in the world. His reasoning, like that of the Liberal government itself, owed much to Canadian analogy.[2] J. G. Kotzé (formerly Chief Justice of the Transvaal) had seen Botha, de la Rey, Smuts and others, and was persuaded that the pursuit of a fair and just policy, under which the Dutch realised and felt they were respected and trusted, would bring satisfactory understanding; 'given such a policy, there will be no doubt or fear about the future'.[3] The absence of direct evidence of Boer trustworthiness at that time did not worry the Liberals unduly. The assertion that Boers were not loyal in 1906 was to them, in the last resort, irrelevant. Self-government could make disloyal people loyal. Gladstone, preaching Home Rule for Ireland in 1886, stated the Liberal theory: Canada did not get Home Rule because she was loyal and friendly, but she had become loyal and friendly because she got Home Rule.[4] By analogy, Ireland, he thought, could safely be given self-government. His successors extended the same analogy to South Africa.

Most of the Liberal ministers had no illusions about the risks

[1] Bryce papers C. 5, Hopwood to Bryce 18 Jun 06.
[2] Ibid. C. 2, Merriman to Bryce 21 Jul 02, 2 Jul 05.
[3] Ibid. Kotzé to Bryce 22 Apr 05.
[4] PD, 3rd Series, vol. 305, 10 May 86.

involved. Their advisers saw to that.[1] Elgin thought that Indians might be worse off under responsible government in the Transvaal. In Churchill's opinion, doubts about native policy were legitimately entertained in 1907. Crewe was to admit that the schedule to the South Africa Bill implied distrust of the Union as possible protectors of Swaziland, Bechuanaland and Basutoland. Ridgeway was not blind to the fact that Boers dreamed of a future South African republic. There was widespread ministerial doubt whether the traditional Liberal nostrums and the Canadian analogy would work in South Africa. The remarks of Ripon, Churchill and Ridgeway on a second chamber show that whether trusting or not, they at least accepted safeguards as necessary. After the sufferings of the Boers in the war so little time before, Churchill asked whether it was 'wise to count too much upon their good offices in 1906?' He seems to have placed little genuine trust in the Boers.[2] In a sense the Liberals could afford to speak the language of trust because it could do no harm and might do good. They were confident that adequate safeguards for loyalty existed in the British section of the Transvaal, and that there were more British voters than Dutch. Churchill's public utterances were more sanguine than his private views. Political exigencies required him to affect more confidence than he felt. But he rapidly became persuaded by his own speeches into believing that reconciliation was actually taking place, into believing that the grants of self-government had removed all reason for anxiety, and that the Orange River Colony had 'definitely abandoned' the old ambition of creating an independent republic.[3]

The Boers, said Churchill, asked to be trusted with re-

[1] Graham for example: 'I should be quite willing to trust the Boers, if I were sure that they were not at the present time liable to be influenced by a small gang of dishonest, unscrupulous and self-seeking politicians, who can never hope to wield the same power in a British colony as in even a small independent state, not to speak of a great Dutch South African Republic' (CO. 224/20/6404, minute 26 Feb 06).

[2] CO. 879/106/834.

[3] Keith, *Speeches and documents*, ii, 11; CO. 291/126/22367, Selb. to S/S 1 Jun 08.

sponsible government. Let them be trusted! For the Orange River Colony, M. T. Steyn (president of the Orange Free State, 1896–1900), declared: 'the key to contentment in South Africa is mutual trust'; the British government, 'where they trust us in the least, they must trust us altogether, otherwise new difficulties in the future are to arise for them too'. Steyn admitted that they had no love for the British, but they intended to abide by the treaty of Vereeniging, and a man's word of honour was 'stronger than the so-called bond of love'. They simply asked to be justly treated. Churchill commented:

A very fine speech. I agree with nearly all of it: and what I do not agree with, I understand.

We may have great confidence in the future. These people mean what they say.[1]

Here then, it seemed, was a collaborating class which might be called into action by a generous gesture of trust. The Unionists had always denied the existence of a latent collaborating class. They had tried to create one by constructive measures. Feeling that the Johannesburg oligarchy of capitalists and mine-owners was not entirely suitable, and too narrowly based, to fulfil the functions of a collaborating class,[2] they had made the achievement of British numerical preponderance, especially by the strengthening of the British element in the rural population, the pre-condition of granting self-government. To the purest theory of Liberal meliorism, this proceeding was unduly pessimistic, too slow, doomed to failure, and possibly unnecessary. Unionists would have deferred responsible government until the process of fusion between Briton and Boer was well advanced. The Liberals preferred to try to precipitate fusion by a magnanimous gesture. There was no need for an educative stage of representative government. There was no

[1] CO. 224/21/41474, speech by Steyn at Bloemfontein 4 May 06, minute by Churchill 13 Dec 06.

[2] Chamberlain wrote in June 1896: 'whatever defects may exist in the present form of government ... the substitution of an entirely independent Republic governed by or for the [cosmopolitan] capitalists of the Rand would be very much worse, both for British interests in the Transvaal and for British influence in South Africa' (quoted in J. S. Marais, *Fall of Kruger's Republic*, p. 251).

need to populate the country with more British immigrants. So at least their reasoning in ideal theory ran. But did they really believe it?

There was more willingness to try the theory than confidence that it would succeed. They reposed their trust in a general theory of government rather than a particular set of men. The Liberal object was to divert the Boers from their republican ideal while it was supposed to be dormant, to prevent their dream hardening into a policy for action. One cannot call this an optimistic approach to the problem. One cannot assert that the Liberals did in fact trust the Boers. Their argument was that unless they showed or simulated trust, they were never likely to reconcile to the empire a people who were so sensitive to being thought untrustworthy. Nor would they be able to achieve improvements for the Africans unless they trusted the Boers as responsible adults. At any rate, Elgin clearly understood the paramount importance of avoiding any indication of any lack of trust in the Boers. When Selborne approached him with apprehensions about the possible fate of civil servants under the new government, Elgin appreciated the force of Selborne's observation, but what did it mean?

Surely nothing more nor less than that the Boers cannot be trusted. Pray believe me, that I am most anxious to prevent injustice – but it is a little hard to ask me to so frame the Constitution as to shew on the face of it that I cannot rely on justice being done.[1]

Liberal policy, the policy of trust, was a gamble. It might succeed. It might equally well fail. Liberals would not have claimed more. This was nonetheless a sufficient basis for action, because they were absolutely sure that the alternative policy, the Unionist policy, could only have one result – failure. Unquestionably in the short-term, the gamble came off. The South African settlement was at first a success, giving the government much prestige and bidding fair to become an almost classic textbook illustration of the political prudence and justice of

[1] EP, E to Selb. 16 Aug 06 (copy).

magnanimity. In the long-term it appears much less successful. But any Liberal in 1906 would have been surprised and well satisfied if he could have known that his policy would result in the retention of South Africa in the commonwealth for another 55 years, with appreciable advantages to Britain and to the evolution of the commonwealth ideal.

Perhaps the last word in a comparison of the policy of the two parties might be left with Lyttelton. Lyttelton was ready to admit that in some ways the Liberal constitution was an improvement on his proposed constitution. He welcomed

a second chamber which is a reality . . . this is a substantial point. I think also the Government have done well in making English the official language of the Transvaal state. I think that the whole of the provisions with respect to the Dutch language being spoken in the Assembly – which was always the intention of the late Government – are more happily dealt with. I express our obligations in some sense for the policy of land settlement.

He approved of the establishment of a land board, although the funds available to it did not seem to him sufficient.[1] When the Act of Union was before the British parliament, Lyttelton again tried to be fair to the Liberals, and said frankly:

I am perfectly ready, and always have been, to confess that His Majesty's Government in granting that responsible government, did obtain the speedier and more spontaneous goodwill of the Dutch race than anybody I think could have anticipated.

He could however find 'no real essential difference' of policy between the two parties:

Both were in favour of responsible government. The only difference was – I am not denying a somewhat important, but not an essential difference – the only difference was as to the exact time at which it should be granted.[2]

It was natural and proper on that occasion to minimise the difference between the parties. The difference was undoubtedly one of method rather than substance. Although it is true that

[1] PD. 167/1078-9, 17 Dec 06.   [2] PD/HC. 9/972-3, 16 Aug 09.

the form of the two constitutions did not differ much (apart from the introduction of manhood suffrage and a second chamber, and the incorporation of arrangements for land settlement), the difference of timing and the generous manner of the concession were factors of tremendous importance in securing the adhesion of at least some of the Boers to the British flag, and those who were for the time being the leaders of the Boers, Smuts and Botha. They had no grounds for describing the Liberal constitution as having 'the trail of distrust all over it', as they had the Unionist one. The Liberals, moreover, actually granted responsible government, whereas there is no telling how long the Unionists might have continued to deny it.

5 West and East Africa: Aftermath of the Partition

In South Africa the Liberals thought that an imperial problem of long standing had been profoundly aggravated by the Unionist government. But they were also disturbed by the multiplication elsewhere in Africa of entirely new formal responsibilities which resulted from the partition of Africa in the previous twenty years. The colonial office by 1905 had acquired responsibility for Northern and Southern Nigeria, Nyasaland, Uganda, Kenya and Somaliland. The ministers who were now in power had, on the whole, been no more than mere observers of the partition. None of them liked it. It was to them irrational and undesirable. Gladstonian Liberals were not, of course, in all circumstances rigidly anti-expansionist. Campbell-Bannerman expressed their feelings accurately in 1899:

We do not shrink from adding to it [the empire] if duty or honour compels us; but we abjure the vulgar and bastard imperialism of . . . provocation and aggression . . . and of grabbing everything even if we have no use for it ourselves. . . . I should be sorry to set any limit to the governing capacity of our people and race, but at the same time, it is with no small relief and satisfaction that we must see . . . the partition of Africa pretty well brought to an end.[1]

He was, in short, sceptical of any trend towards a pre-emptive imperialism of taking territory, whether for immediate strategic reasons or remoter economic ones, in order to deny it to European rivals.

[1] CB, *Speeches 1899–1908* (1908), p. 10, 9 Mar 99.

By 1906 all parties conceded that British territorial expansion was over.[1] No extension of responsibilities occurred under the Liberals. There was no annexation in the New Hebrides, no desire to be the residuary legatee of King Leopold's Congo.[2]

Elgin went out of his way in his speech on the Transvaal constitution in July 1906 to draw attention to the danger of multiplying contacts between European settlers and Africans, and thus revealed perhaps one of the deepest underlying Liberal fears about the results of the partition, and also one of their objections to the manner in which it was carried out. He discerned 'something very peculiar' in the relations between Europe and Africa during the partition:

I can understand an overflowing population from one country having a right to take possession of unoccupied and vacant lands, but during the last twenty years or so, the European nations have divided up Africa amongst themselves, so far as I can see on absolutely arbitrary lines, and at any rate, there was never any pretence whatever of consulting the desires or wishes of the millions of inhabitants of that great continent. I am not disputing in any way that there were difficulties which required a remedy, and very likely this was the only remedy which could have been adopted. But I do say that there is a risk in multiplying what we call white man's countries, where there are a very small number of whites in the midst of an overwhelming number of blacks.[3]

The reference to absence of consent in the partition was to a fact rarely admitted among British politicians. What were these 'difficulties which required a remedy'? Elgin, elusive as ever, did not say. A digression in a speech on the Transvaal constitution was hardly the place for making that systematic interpretation of the partition which has eluded sixty years of subsequent

---

[1] Even Milner admitted in 1907, 'the time had passed for looking for any greater extension' (*Nation and the Empire*, p. 264).

[2] 'The Congo question would have been a very simple one if we were prepared to say that unless things were put right within a certain time we would ourselves take the place in hand and put things right. But so far as I am aware, no government, no party and no organ of the press has ever advocated a course of this kind' (GP. 50, Grey to WSC 5 Nov 09).

[3] PD. 162/623, 31 Jul 06.

analysis. But it may be suggested that in Elgin's conception, British rule in Africa had been extended formally in order to maintain peace there, and because Africa had been caught up in European politics, an entanglement which in turn made it all the more necessary to bring peace and stability to Africa, in view of the constant friction involving especially Britain and France, and potentially other nations too. In common with most of his contemporaries, he did not view the partition as a purely African phenomenon. In 1894 he spoke about the 'struggle between civilisation and barbarism which is going on more or less all over the world'. Three years later, he wrote of 'an era of delimitation, all over the world'.[1] In this process, he would have preferred to bring the unstable non-European countries into the modern world by 'the gentler methods'. He doubted whether Britain derived much advantage from controlling primitive tribes, but it was 'impossible to stand still', because Britain had a 'mission as pioneers of civilisation'.[2] The Liberals habitually persuaded themselves that the British empire was justified chiefly as a contribution to the international task of bringing about peace. Elgin's view, then, was that Britain was in Africa primarily to maintain peace,[3] the essential prerequisite for the development of civilisation. He had no conception of anything like an economic interpretation of the partition.[4]

On the whole, despite their early apprehensions, the Liberals accepted the legacy of the partition with good grace; they tried to do the best they could for Africa. They pressed ahead with railways, the investigation of tropical diseases and transport

---

[1] VRP. 88/92, speech 30 Nov 94; 15/App. 95, E to S/S for India 15 Sep 97.

[2] Ibid. 13/48, 10 Apr 95.

[3] See p. 213. This is in line with Grey's declaration in 1910: 'We are trustees in Egypt, in the first place for the natives of Egypt themselves.... We are also trustees, because we have no other title to remain in Egypt, of good order and public security there. We are trustees for the interests of Europe as well as for the natives.... The maintenance of good government and order in Egypt is the first object of the British government and British parliament' (PD/HC. 17/1153, 13 Jun 10).

[4] For some further reflections on the partition see R. Hyam, 'The partition of Africa: a review article', *Historical Journal*, vii (1964), 154–69.

problems, the development of tropical products, especially cotton, with a vigour which would not have disgraced Chamberlain, and which certainly impressed even so ill-disposed a critic as Milner.[1] They were fully supported by the colonial office staff, who by 1906 conceded that 'every great power now recognises it as essential that it should control some portion of the tropics' and would not relinquish any control it had. The reason for this, they thought,

can only be found in the usefulness of the tropical possessions as a source from which can be drawn the tropical products which are more and more necessary as the food or raw material of every industrial nation, and in their value as a field for the commerce of the controlling power. From this point of view, it cannot be denied that the Home country is deeply interested in the development of the colonies.[2]

Whether or not the partition was caused by hope of economic benefit, such hopes were clearly the way in which many Liberals came to reconcile themselves to the possession of these new territories. No one doubted that European powers had a right to make Africa contribute to their conception of the general welfare of mankind, and in particular to supply the world with the produce which it needed. Africa attracted left-wing social theorists as a possible field for experiment. Even Churchill was to ascribe his deep interest in Uganda to its unusually favourable conditions for 'a practical experiment in State socialism'. The tropical territories commended themselves also as providing at least an opportunity for the Liberals to exercise a benevolent native policy unhampered by the obstacles which an entrenched and recalcitrant white settler community had placed, and would continue to place, in the way of a truly Liberal policy in South Africa. Without such new territories, it would have been thought much harder to redeem the reputation of British imperialism, to rescue it from a bastard phase.

[1] Lord Milner, *The Nation and the Empire*; he spoke in 1910 of great developments in tropical Africa in recent years, which showed recognition of their great potential value, which destined them to play a very essential part in imperial development (pp. 462–5).
[2] CO. 96/477/37402, minute by Butler 30 Sep 08.

South Africa had receded beyond imperial control. The only practical field for a liberal colonial policy was in the tropics. Their favourite regions proved to be those least like South Africa: Uganda and Nigeria.

REVIEW OF RESPONSIBILITIES

The Liberals were not grateful for the administrative complications which resulted from the partition, but they resigned themselves to them as anomalous and inconvenient things in an already anomalous empire.[1] Churchill's early comments on the post-partition situation in West Africa show clearly that ideas of informal control died very hard. In his view the scope and character of British activities in Nigeria needed to be more definitely confined, the total situation and policy brought under review. British responsibilities in Nigeria were, he said, 'serious, indefinite and ever-expanding', and threw a heavy burden on British finances.[2] He had no partiality for Lugard's procedures: 'Nigeria seems to be a sort of sultry Russia', he said when Lugard took time by the forelock with a proposal for a press law before there was a press.[3] The presence of Lugard and Sir Walter Egerton (of Southern Nigeria) in London during the summer of 1906 seemed to afford the opportunity he desired for a reconsideration of British liabilities and activities in Nigeria, from the point of view of policy, not administration. Elgin, however, was doubtful whether the policy as distinct from administration could now be reviewed. It was too late. Churchill's greater eagerness, rather unrealistic, to diminish Nigerian responsibilities, emerges from minutes at the time of the rising in Sokoto:[4]

I am inclined to the opinion that we should withdraw from a very large portion of the territories which we now occupy

---

[1] CO. 446/76/46301, minute by Crewe 24 Feb 09.
[2] CO. 520/32/353, 30 Jan 06.   [3] CO. 446/53/13023, 10 Jun 06.
[4] CO. 520/39/6993, minutes 17 and 19 May 06, and see p. 209 below for Sokoto rising.

nominally, but really disturb without governing; and that we should concentrate our resources upon the railway and economic development of the more settled and accessible riparian or maritime regions. . . . I see no reason why our occupation should be made immediately effective up to the French frontier line; or why these savage tribes should not be allowed to eat each other without restraint, until some much more suitable opportunity than the present shall arise for 'pacifying' them. At present we are simply drifting along upon the current of military enterprise and administrative ambition.

Elgin did not seriously entertain such a wide attempt to change British policy:

We engaged in the game of grab in the African continent and we cannot escape the consequences, of which this is one. It is sometimes, but not often, possible to decline responsibilities in a hinterland – but I much doubt if this is really a hinterland.[1]

Churchill also wanted 'a grand inquest' into the administration of the East Africa Protectorate.[2] This protectorate, he wrote,

has been handed over to us by the Foreign Office in confusion. . . . The administrative machine gives me very little confidence.

Sleeping sickness was spreading from Uganda in face of inadequate preventive measures. 'Great possibilities seem to be balanced by great anxieties.'[3] These misgivings led him to advocate a thorough reorganisation of its local government and its home control.[4] Elgin did not take quite so unfavourable a view.

Neither in Nigeria nor in the East Africa Protectorate (the future Kenya) did any reduction of responsibility result. The pacification of Nigeria was completed; the settlement of East Africa by white colonists continued. Substantially there was continuity of policy in the indigenous colonial empire.

[1] CO. 446/52/5712, minutes by Churchill 24 Feb 06, by Elgin 28 Feb 06, partly quoted in M. Perham, *Lugard* (1960), ii, 248–9.
[2] CO. 533/18/42278, minute 21 Nov 06
[3] CO. 533/25/24001, 11 Jun 06.　　　[4] Ibid. 40751, minute 17 Nov 06.

On the other hand it was possible to allow control over certain parts of Africa to remain imperfect. The Nile Province of Uganda, for instance, seemed to hold out little or no prospect of successful development, save at a cost which would be out of all proportion to the results. The governor considered that the effectual administration of this country would be purely a humanitarian work; the existing policy of hesitation alternating with punitive expeditions, he added, only wasted money on unproductive work which might eventually involve the government in having to govern properly a vast territory reaching to the very borders of Abyssinia, the commercial value of which would never pay for one tithe of the cost of its administration. He therefore recommended no further advance until other and more promising parts were developed. Elgin thought this sound analysis, and accepted the proposed policy.[1]

When the Liberals came into office, British troops were stationed in the Liberian Republic at Kanre Lahun and Walude on account of raids which had been made into Sierra Leone by subjects of the badly administered Republic. The governor of Sierra Leone suggested withdrawal from Walude, but Elgin agreed with his advisers that troops should not be withdrawn hastily, although he thought that there should be safeguards against indefinite occupation. He suggested an attempt to promote some organisation of the local chiefs for their own protection, if that was at all practicable. It was expected that withdrawal would be followed by tribal anarchy; the maintenance of peace was advantageous to Sierra Leone, for the terminus of its railway was only twenty miles from the frontier. The governor was therefore informed that troops should not be withdrawn until a further effort had been made to put matters on a more satisfactory and stable basis, and that Britain thought it quite worthwhile for the Sierra Leone government to continue for the present to incur the comparatively small expense involved in keeping the troops there.[2] If Britain

---

[1] CO. 536/7/38374, Govr to S/S 13 Sep 06, minute by E 29 Nov 06.

[2] CO. 267/483/11103, minute by Elgin 5 May 06; S/S to Govr 22 May 06. The western hinterland was immensely fertile; large forests of rubber were being

withdrew, officials argued, the French would absorb all Liberia. And so it was suggested that arrangements should be made with France for the delimitation of respective 'spheres of influence' and maintenance of order. Elgin accepted this – 'we must not have any conflict with the French. . . . But I regret any chance of an extension of our liabilities.'[1] The troops remained, but it was a situation he would have liked to terminate as soon as possible.[2] Although the governor saw no alternative between annexation and withdrawal, he was told positively enough that annexation could not be entertained, but as the government had no wish to hand the country over to the French, withdrawal did not take place. They wished to increase British influence in Liberia as much as legitimately possible, but unlike the French they intended to stand by their declarations to maintain the independence and integrity of Liberian territory. Two British officers were officially engaged in helping the Liberian government to organise the customs service. The Liberian government needed a gunboat to put the customs service in order. Grey was not anxious to incur any responsibilities in Liberia, but the gift of an old gunboat seemed a cheap way of helping British trade without incurring any obligation. If, however, it could not be done without a vote in parliament, he would not press it, as it would give rise to the impression that they were incurring some obligations or had some political designs in Liberia, which Grey no more entertained than Elgin.[3]

Although the Liberals were prepared to defend existing interests, they were fully determined to avoid being dragged into further commitments. In his early letters to Minto, Morley made repeated warnings on this head. For example:

---

exploited by British companies, largely with British capital. Chiefs were asking for British protection. The French were pushing into Liberia from the north, also to preserve peace, and there was a distinct danger of collision between natives who attached themselves to the two different spheres of influence being created and thus of collision between British and French soldiers (CO. 267/499/31079, CO to FO).

[1] CO. 267/486/29190, minute 15 Aug 06; 448/38237, S/S to govr 30 Nov 06.
[2] CO. 267/499/31079, minute 6 Sep 07.
[3] GP. 62, Grey to Asquith 18 Jan 07.

The new Parliament, and the new Cabinet, will be in the highest degree jealous of anything that looks like expansion, extension of protectorates, spheres of influence and the like; and of anything with the savour of 'militarism' about it.

He thought the centre of gravity utterly changed by the amazing election, especially touching frontier matters, and wars on tribes. 'Nobody, of any party or section of a party, means to give anything up, but taking new responsibilities will be watched with sharp suspicion for the present at any rate.'[1]

Even the Gambia was retained. Cession to the French had been considered by Conservatives in 1876 and 1903–4. In 1907 the French proposed an exchange of British and French rights in the Gambia and the New Hebrides respectively. The foreign office was prepared to entertain the idea. Elgin was not. 'From the political standpoint H.M.G. cannot lightly enter upon a negotiation to sell or exchange a British colony.' If the storm of criticism and misrepresentation which would be aroused by such a proposal was to be faced, the arrangement must have a propriety, expediency and equity placing it beyond legitimate criticism. To give up the Gambia would run the risk of prohibitive duties closing the trade of the whole Senegal area to British manufacture. Even if carefully drawn fiscal stipulations could safeguard trading interests to some extent, such stipulations would do nothing for the African inhabitants who had been encouraged to place themselves under British protection. It would be impossible therefore, said the colonial secretary, to contemplate the cession of the Gambia without providing ample safeguards for the rights and position of the African inhabitants.[2] However, the cabinet decided on 24 June 1908 not to refuse in all circumstances to give up the Gambia, though thinking the terms then offered quite inadequate. The question was referred to an inter-departmental committee in July 1908. On 29 July the cabinet resolved to open negotiations with France for the possible cession of the Gambia, if she would abandon her rights in the New Hebrides and Muscat, her

[1] MM. 1/22, 16 Jan 06; 1/28, 25 Jan 06.
[2] CO. 87/178/10001, CO to FO 24 May 07.

claims in connection with St Pierre and Miquelon, and grant Britain a coaling station in the Pacific. France would not agree. The cabinet eventually decided, on Grey's advice, that France was not offering returns of sufficient value to justify the cession, and so the negotiations were, 'for the time being at any rate', at an end.[1]

Throughout British Africa, only in Somaliland was it eventually decided to limit British responsibility. This was not an issue of continuity of policy raised in the first eighteen months of office, and so its treatment is deferred.[2]

The Liberal government was genuinely anxious to co-operate with European powers, especially, in view of the *entente cordiale*, with France, in maintaining peace in Africa; the government persevered in this policy even when it was obvious that France was not impressed by the appeal to extend the *entente* into Africa.[3] Concern for international obligations retarded withdrawal from the interior of Somaliland. As a result of the circumstances of partition, African policy tended always to be seen in terms of political co-operation and peaceful economic competition with European powers. Obstacles were so great to economic development that there must be mutual forbearance.[4] The principle of international co-operation tended to take precedence over the limitation of British responsibility.

LUGARD'S SCHEME FOR ADMINISTRATION OF WEST AFRICA

In July 1905 Lugard submitted a memorandum on the administration of Nigeria, together with notes on tropical administration in general. He put forward what Miss Perham has described as a 'scheme for continuous administration'. The main point was that the governor should spend more time in London, during which time he should remain responsible for

---

[1] Asq. 5, Asquith to the king 28 Apr 09.   [2] See pp. 359 ff.
[3] E.g. CO. 535/17/13667, CO. 267/488/38237.
[4] CO. 535/17/5419, CO to FO 13 Mar 09.

administration, and undertake more important work than he had done hitherto, such as putting legislation into final form, and discussing development with various experts.[1]

Lyttelton was 'disposed to make, as an experiment, a trial' of giving the high commissioner of Northern Nigeria about five months at home out of the year, and assigning to him during his residence at home the duty of carrying on his work as high commissioner at the colonial office. This improvement in the position of the governor might, he thought, mitigate domestic hardship, promote continuity, and substitute personal intercourse in the office for much detailed correspondence. Such a 'modest reform' could not wholly remove the inherent difficulties of West African administration, but if climatic conditions made it essential that the principal officer had to spend considerable time at home, they should try to 'secure a utilisation of inevitable waste'. The plan could easily be abandoned if its working disclosed obstacles of a serious character. 'If successful, it might be cautiously extended.'[2]

Lyttelton's willingness to accommodate Lugard to this extent was not, however, shared by any of his officials, who spoke of 'the innumerable fallacies' on which the scheme was based.[3] The central point of their objection was that it envisaged administration from Downing Street; the impossibility of doing this had been established as an axiom, on the basis of experience; they dismissed the proposal that Lugard should spend half his time in England as hardly deserving serious notice. But they were also prejudiced against it from a suspicion that the scheme took its origin in the desire of the newly married Lugards to spend more time together. They thought the process by which it had been allowed to assume definite shape indefensible. The scheme could not be considered of limited application.[4]

[1] See Perham, *Lugard*, ii, 225–36.

[2] CO. 446/50/25244, minute 25 Sep 05, African 789. Lyttelton thought Lugard had 'qualities, and I may add defects, which I think would respectively expand and be improved by closer personal touch with the Office'.

[3] CO. 446/50/43564, minute by Ommanney, 30 Jan 06.

[4] Ommanney remarked tartly: 'the wives of other governors would, we may perhaps venture to assume, be no less desirous of keeping their husbands at home during seven months of the year. All the West African Colonies, the less healthy

Lyttelton told Lugard verbally in November what he proposed to do, but in deference to the wishes of his officials did not send a communiqué of his intention to the press as he had intended. When Lyttelton came to consider exactly how effect was to be given to the proposal embodied in his minute, it revealed itself as more than a 'modest reform', and he left office without coming to any conclusion on what steps should be taken.

It devolved upon his successor, therefore, to determine whether the experiment should actually be made. One of the officials observed that the objections were obvious, and neither Lugard nor Lyttelton had explained how they were to be overcome; they had not indeed even alluded to them in what they had written.[1] Churchill thought Lugard's plan undesirable. The reasons against it had been fully and conclusively set out by the officials. An officer of Lugard's high position and capacity should in matters affecting his personal convenience always be treated with exceptional consideration and especially with generosity in respect of leave from an unhealthy post. But he added: 'We shall not simplify the labours of the Colonial Office by converting it into a pantheon for proconsuls on leave.'[2] Elgin wrote privately to Lugard rejecting 'even the modified scheme of Mr Lyttelton'. If it had been possible to treat it as affecting Northern Nigeria alone he might have been tempted under the circumstances perhaps to let the experiment be tried. But it seemed to him that general principles of administration were involved far too important for it to be so treated.[3] This view was clearly reflected in the choice of title for the confidential print on the subject: 'Papers relating to the administration of Tropical Colonies.'[4] The official reply of 9 March remarked the absence of any attempt to show that the established principles, whereby the administration of a colony was always in the hands of the man on the spot, were unsound. The secretary of

---

West Indies, British Central Africa and even Mauritius would have to be considered and the Treasury would have a good deal to say on question of salary and passage allowances' (ibid.).

[1] Ibid. minute by Antrobus 28 Jan 06.   [2] Ibid. minute 31 Jan 06.
[3] EP, E to Lugard 14 Mar 06 (copy).   [4] African 841.

state did not find in practice that the government of the West African colonies had suffered under this system; inconvenience was probably felt more by the governors than by the countries which they governed. The argument that continuity was broken was answered by pointing out that acting governors were carefully chosen, and that it was the constitutional function of the colonial office to secure continuity in policy. *If* the protectorates were administered directly from Downing Street there would have been advantages in having an officer in the colonial office for half the year, but it would be dangerous to accept such a new principle. The responsible officer on the spot would still need authoritative power. How then could administration be said to remain vested in the high commissioner? Following the wording of Churchill's minute, the despatch continued:

the arrangement seems likely in practice to lead to the establishment of a third authority between the Secretary of State and the responsible officer on the spot, which would be inconsistent with the constitutional position of the Secretary of State.

It was considered only reasonable that, as in recognised practice, a head officer on leave should be kept fully informed, see despatches, and be consulted before important decisions were taken, but it was not desirable that he should relieve the colonial office of duties which must be discharged by the department when the governor was at his post in the colony, as this would involve a breach of continuity in the work to be done in England, and would take up time which might be devoted by the governor either to work of a more useful kind or to necessary recreation.[1]

Here then was a reversal of policy. Historians think the Liberal action a wise one. Professor Kenneth Robinson describes Lugard's scheme as fantastic, over-centralising and not very sensible.[2]

[1] CO. 446/50/43564; African 841.
[2] Review of Perham's *Lugard*, ii, *Journal of African History*, ii (1961), 336. The rejection of Lugard's scheme has to be seen partly in the context of his reputation. He was not regarded by the officials as a first class governor. Antrobus described

PROBLEMS OF PACIFICATION IN WEST AND EAST
AFRICA

Nigeria. The Liberals not only thwarted Lugard's scheme for
the administration of Northern Nigeria, but, initially at any
rate, they were also highly critical of his methods of opening the
country up rapidly by military means. Lugard was inclined to
see more interference than under the Unionist government.
Any change of policy from the previous government, was,
however, perhaps more apparent than real, although the
Liberals were more anxious than their predecessors about
'pacification', and they certainly placed a stronger emphasis on
'peaceful penetration'. This shift of emphasis was perhaps the
biggest specifically Liberal contribution in West Africa. They
kept a closer watch on deviations from what was widely accepted as the ideal: peaceful and gradual establishment of
control.[1]

Churchill called for a complete examination of the question
of military operations in Nigeria. He wanted to know the policy
in pursuit of which a vast 'pacification' work was to be undertaken, and what relation its cost bore to the other needs of the
area and to the claims of the more settled districts.[2]

Opportunity for expressing doubt at the whole forward policy
and the departure from methods of informal control presented
itself almost at once. On 31 December 1905 the Munshi, the
only large and important tribe which had never been subdued,
burned down the Niger Company's station at Abinsi. As a result

---

him as 'very fairly good' but not first rate like Maxwell or Nathan (CO. 446/50/
43562, minute 28 Jan 06). Ommanney described him as 'a gentleman of great
intelligence, but rather a quick temper'; a man who would not be ideal for the post
of governor of Natal, but good enough to justify an appointment (EP, minute on
Selb. to E 27 Nov 06).
[1] Unionists also disliked punitive expeditions. When commissioner Stewart of
Kenya had sent what amounted to a punitive expedition against Sotik who had
raided the Elburgu Masai, Lyttelton minuted, 'the cabinet regard these expeditions
with great suspicion' (CO. 533/2/22482, 20 Jul 05). Lugard knew civil police were
more efficient in getting in touch with the people (C. W. Orr, *Making of Northern
Nigeria*, p. 84).
[2] CO. 520/32/353, 30 Jan 06.

the River Benue was closed to navigation. Lugard proposed reprisals. Churchill was perturbed:

We are about to be committed to operations of indefinite character and considerable extent without any substantial information. . . .

Of course, if the peace and order of the Colony depends on a vigorous offensive we must support him with all our hearts. But the chronic bloodshed which stains the West African seasons is odious and disquieting. Moreover the whole enterprise is liable to be misrepresented by persons unacquainted with Imperial terminology as the murdering of natives and stealing of their lands. H.M.G. seems to have only a nominal control over these grave matters, and yet bear the direct responsibility. I do not think we ought to enter upon these expeditions lightly or as a matter of course.

Elgin shared his perturbation. It was, he wrote,

most unsatisfactory that we should not be consulted in the case of military expeditions. I do not know what the practice has been, but according to my Indian experience, the sanction of the government ought to be necessary in the case of all punitive expeditions, unless the raiders can be caught red-handed.[1]

In his view, the government had a right to be fully informed of even all the possible objects when asked to sanction a military expedition.[2] Hence on 27 January a telegram was sent to Lugard, opposing the despatch of a large expedition without knowing more of the objects proposed; if these could not be explained by telegram, the advance should be limited to what was necessary to open the Benue navigation and to protect any property; but it should not be carried further without the

[1] CO. 446/52/2224, minutes 23 and 25 Jan 06.
[2] CO. 446/59/30528. M. Perham, op. cit. p. 249. seems to find Elgin's response puzzling in an ex-viceroy of India, but as early as 1894 he had expressed his detestation of punitive expeditions, their expensiveness and ineffectiveness. He could not 'subscribe to a policy that includes them as a probable, if not necessary result, unless and until I am satisfied that no other expedient exists' (VRP 12/60; see above, p. 24). Furthermore, at the time of the Chitral expedition in 1895, he vowed that if ever again he had responsibility for an expedition, he would 'take good care not to be left in the dark' from want of information from the scene of operations as he had been on that occasion (ibid. 13(i)/74).

sanction of the secretary of state. Lugard was very angry at this,[1] and telegraphed his belief that it seemed the favourable opportunity for settlement of the Munshi question once and for all.[2] Elgin and Churchill reluctantly admitted that the expedition was too far launched to be stopped, but told Lugard that they regarded it most desirable not to carry it further than the immediate object rendered necessary.[3]

In the middle of February the situation was greatly complicated by a Mahdi rising in Sokoto. This appeared serious enough for Lugard to be given considerable discretion, but although agreement with transferring troops from the Munshi expedition, to stop the *jihad* spreading, was telegraphed on 26 February, it was not without considerable misgiving. The situation was not clear, and so further enquiries were made. 'The events at Sokoto', minuted Elgin, 'may, when fully reported, show a connection with the French to the north – and that we have duties to our allies.'[4] Elgin generally refused to extend control into fresh territory prematurely. When it was clear that there were no international complications there seemed no reason to do this until tribes such as the Okpoto became more aggressive.[5] Retaliation began in March. At the end of March the extermination of about two thousand almost unarmed people of Satiru was reported. What would happen, asked Churchill, if this attracted parliamentary attention? He did not see with what face they could put pressure on the government of Natal over the hanging of a dozen natives, while this sort of thing was done under the direct authority of the Liberal government.[6]

Elgin reassured a deputation of the West African Trade Association on 4 April 1906 that the process of assuming absolute control up to a boundary with a foreign government had been growing, and would doubtless 'at some future time,

[1] Perham, op. cit. ii, 251.   [2] CO. 446/52/3443, to S/S tel. 30 Jan 06.
[3] Ibid. minutes 1 Feb 06.
[4] CO. 446/52/5712, 28 Feb 06. *Jihad* is the name given to Muslim war against unbelievers, which is the duty of the community as a whole.
[5] CO. 446/52, minute 24 Mar 06.
[6] CO. 446/53/13475, minute 29 Mar 06.

make expeditions less likely than they are at present'.[1] On the same day, Churchill, in answer to a parliamentary question, declared: 'Most certainly the government wish to discourage . . . all forms of military operations' in all parts of the empire.[2]

In a letter of 15 August Lugard explained that the Munshi had fired on canoes on the Benue in June last, and Britain was responsible under the Berlin Act for the safety of the navigation; the river was much used by the Germans for access to the headquarters of their Upper Kamerun possession at Garua, and the French for despatch of supplies to their Chad territories. In a minute, Olivier expressed himself very sceptical of 'the ultimate profit of the method of marching through these countries trailing our coat with a view to impressive retaliation, when it is trodden on'. Elgin was, however, more impressed with Lugard's point about international obligation: if Britain was responsible to Germany and France for this route she did not go into the country simply for the purpose of 'trailing our coat' but to prevent the much more serious position of an outrage on German or French subjects occurring.[3] But he described himself as the last person to wish to teach Africans the effect of Maxim guns;[4] he would not undertake military expeditions against African tribes simply in response to the pressure of the Niger Company who wanted to push trade.

Towards the end of 1906 acting commissioner Wallace proposed a military expedition against the Okpoto (who had been raiding British territory), to be followed by a march through Munshi country to Katsena Allah. The question of imposing order on these tribes received careful attention; the reply rejecting punitive measures embodied an important declaration of policy. The secretary of state considered it necessary that any tribe which committed overt acts of violence, as was reported to be the practice of the Okpoto, should be promptly punished. The punishment should be followed by such occupation as would ensure that the effects of the punishment

[1] CO. 520/39/16028. [2] CO. 446/57/11607.
[3] CO. 446/59/30528, Aug 07. [4] CO. 446/55/44219, minute 21 Dec 06.

would not be lost. It was also necessary that the navigation of the Benue River should be kept safe from molestation.

I desire that no outrage or aggression on the part of the natives should be tolerated, but that your government should also abstain from any action which may constitute an aggression, or a cause of grievance, to the native tribes. If aggression is punished, and suitable posts are established for the continued preservation of order, I should look to the recognition of the benefits of secure trading by the natives for the further extension of pacific influences.

Approval was therefore given to the Niger company's proposal to establish a post at Katsena. However, the secretary of state was not prepared to sanction the proposed march through the Okpoto and Munshi countries, on the ground that it was useless to send a military force through a country unless they were prepared to remain in effective occupation.[1] The subsequent definition and firm adoption of the policy of pacific penetration owed much to this despatch. The conviction that trade was the instrument of peace indicates that Victorian optimism about the extension of civilisation by informal means was not dead yet.

When the measures against the Okpoto were being planned, Elgin minuted:

I am afraid that we must recognise that 'punitive expeditions' cannot conform in all respects to the rules of civilised warfare. I have always opposed them for that very reason. . . . But we must use the weapon occasionally in an unsettled hinterland, and then the burning of villages and crops – and the carrying off of stock are not 'reprehensible' [a word used by an official] – they are part of the machinery.[2]

Elgin also advocated making expeditions overwhelmingly strong, so that the tribes would see the impossibility of resistance; the object was to prevent fighting and to persuade Africans to see the advantages of establishing friendly relations with Britain. His insistence upon peaceful penetration in

[1] CO. 446/55/44219, desp. from S/S 4 Jan 07.
[2] CO. 446/62/14060, minute 3 Aug 07.

Nigeria arose directly out of his experimental attempt to sponsor a similar policy in Waziristan and Chitral as viceroy.[1]

After Elgin's declaration in favour of peaceful penetration, and insistence upon effective occupation to follow it, the Northern Nigerian government sanctioned a patrol of Okpoto and Agatu with the object of bringing the remaining areas into submission and stopping the raiding of trade routes. By July 1907 Girouard had written out a set of regulations expanding and clarifying the procedure governing military operations. These were approved by the colonial office, and applied to Southern Nigeria, the Gold Coast and Sierra Leone.[2] The terms 'patrol' and 'expeditionary force' were abandoned, because henceforth all active operations were to be considered duties in aid of the civil power, at least until martial law was proclaimed.[3] The process of bringing Munshi country under control and opening it to trade, without use of force, proceeded well. In January 1908 a further patrol was approved, subject to a reminder that it must be possible to remain in peaceful and effective occupation. According to John Holt, Elgin succeeded in stopping the punitive expeditions, involving so much bloodshed, which had hitherto been prevalent in Nigeria, but some of the old abuses crept back again later, until it seemed as if the local governments were simply calling punitive expeditions by another name.[4]

When Egerton, governor of Southern Nigeria, foreshadowed a military patrol into Ikale country, Elgin noted that the report of the provincial commissioner referred to those who were averse to their country being opened up for trade, and he minuted:

[1] See above, p. 24; VRP 13/48, 152; 88/413.

[2] CO. 446/62/14024 and 63/29574. There was also an attempt to adapt them to Uganda and the East Africa Protectorate (CO. 533/43/15165, S/S to govrs. 14 May 09). It was explained that these patrols comprised a respectable number of soldiers who advanced through a portion of country making sure of every inch of the ground as they went, explaining to the natives why they were there, making it clear that they were not raiders, explaining the advantages of roads, peaceful trade, order and justice, and the meaning of British administration; then they settled down at an important spot in the heart of the country, which they made the jumping-off ground for further action of the same kind. Not a shot would be fired.

[3] CO. 446/63/29574.

[4] Dilke papers 43921/16, John Holt to Dilke 27 Feb 09.

I am not quite sure about this case ... while I do not for a moment say that they should be allowed to continue barbarous practices – I am not prepared to say that because they are 'averse to their country being opened up to trade', therefore they ought to be subjected to severe coercion measures.

Eventually the governor was authorised to send a political officer, escorted by troops, with authority to arrest disaffected chiefs.[1]

The Liberal government was prepared to use force to defend trade, but doubtful whether it should extend trade, just as it was ready to defend existing territorial commitments, but not to add to them. It is clear that despite the dislike of using force, the government was prepared to use it to fulfil international obligations to maintain peace. Nigeria indeed illustrates clearly the importance attached by the Liberals to international obligations. 'Both the French and ourselves', wrote Elgin, 'are interested in the peace of these countries: indeed we are there for that purpose.'[2] Priority was given to the pacification of Northern Nigeria rather than Southern Nigeria, so that effective control might be established along the French boundary.[3]

Elgin was warmly credited by the *West African Mail* with inaugurating a 'change of policy' by firmly putting 'a stop to the unnecessary use of force' in Nigeria. The year 1907 was an unusually peaceful one.[4]

Lugard's successor in Northern Nigeria, Sir Percy Girouard, suggested in 1908 the reorganisation of the constabulary. Elgin felt that as Britain held these vast territories with so small a military force, its efficiency was all-important. And so, while he approved generally of the scheme, he wanted to take advantage of the presence of the high commissioner in London

[1] CO. 520/50/2049, S/S to Egerton 23 Mar 08.
[2] CO. 446/53/18617, minute 18 Jun 06.
[3] CO. 520/37, Egerton to S/S 7 Sep 06.
[4] 'Under the previous government there was a great display of energy. . . . It was a period of wasteful finance and domineering employment of force for political and commercial objects in Africa. . . . Lord Elgin deserves the utmost praise and support in his decision to develop the resources of Nigeria and to obtain administrative control thereof, peacefully and without undue haste . . .' (17 Jan 08).

to have conversations with him before committing himself on the points affecting the West Africa Frontier Force.[1]

Elgin's caution in problems of defence also comes out strongly in his consideration of plans for the reduction of the military establishment in Ashanti, and its abolition in the Northern Territories of the Gold Coast. Readers familiar with his temperament will note without surprise that Elgin's first reaction was: 'I should like to increase the administrative staff and to decrease the military establishment, but in both cases I think it is prudent to move cautiously.'[2] A few months later he still found the Northern Territories a complicated matter to decide without a conference; he could not profess to a full comprehension of the financial effect of the scheme. There seemed no point in maintaining a force of 150 men to meet the French. In the case of Ashanti, the reductions seemed to leave only an extremely small force to deal with the danger of a possible rising, for the people were more turbulent than in the Northern Territories. Nevertheless, sanction was given. The government accepted the view that 'the more diffused and less purely military force which is suggested would be sufficient for the requirements of internal security, while it would certainly be more useful in the execution of new works of settlement and development.'[3] When one of the officials observed that Britain could not have as many soldiers in West Africa as France, who but Churchill would have used *this* as the occasion to echo a famous remark of Canning, and to declare: 'We should have to call in the old world to redress the balance of the new' in order to equal France? It was a typical example of his delight in dignifying the mundane with grandiloquent historical analogy.[4]

---

[1] CO. 446/65/40574, minute 16 Feb 08.　　[2] CO. 96/440/16854, 14 Jul 06.
[3] CO. 96/444/28533, minute 2 Oct 06, S/S to govr 16 Oct 06.
[4] CO. 96/451/21286, minute 17 Jul 06. Another example is provided from the Canadian files. In a dispute about the amendment of the British North America Act concerning British Columbia, the dominion government was supported by all the other provinces except British Columbia – hence: 'It is British Columbia (like Athanasius) *contra mundum*' (CO. 42/912/14962, minute by WSC 21 May 07).

Kenya. Pacification problems were much less prominent in, though not completely absent from, East Africa. One episode in particular, the Kisii revolt, attracted attention. After the decisive defeat of the Nandi at the very end of 1905 there were no more British expeditions in the Kisumu province of the East Africa Protectorate until the beginning of 1908. The Kisii (Gusii) were almost completely isolated, and regarded by the British as a truculent people. The Kisii resented white rule and thought to end it by getting rid of the first British officer stationed among them. This luckless officer, an assistant collector whose name was G. A. S. Northcote, was wounded by a spear attack on 17 January 1908, whereat several clans broke into open revolt.

Two and a half companies of the King's African Rifles were despatched to the trouble-spot. Although the Kisii sued for peace, as a result of the operations, by 30 January, 160 Kisii had been killed; the death roll was ultimately 250. 6148 cattle and 3500 sheep had been captured. There were no further British casualties.[1] When reports were received in the colonial office they were examined very critically. Naturally Churchill was quick to seize upon the unseemly side of the affair:

I do not like the tone of these reports [he wrote]. No doubt the clans should be punished; but 160 have now been killed outright – without any further casualties on our side, and the main body has not yet been encountered. . . . It looks like a butchery, and if the House of Commons gets hold of it, all our plans in East Africa Protectorate will be under a cloud.
    Surely it cannot be necessary to go on killing these defenceless people on such an enormous scale.

A telegram was sent to the governor. The drafting was done by Churchill himself. He expressed the hope that the governor would confine the bloodshed within the narrowest limits consistent with the safety of the British force and the restoration of order. The governor was asked to make every effort to obtain

---

[1] Northcote himself thought the expedition 'most shockingly mismanaged' (see J. M. Lonsdale, *A political history of Nyanza 1883–1945*, Cambridge Ph.D. dissertation (1964), p. 132).

peaceful submission after this most severe lesson the Kisii had received. Mercy should at once be extended to all who were not personally concerned in the original outbreak.[1] In fact, Churchill was quite right to question the justification for such violent retribution. This was no revolt, in the usual sense of the word, but a protest against the forcible intrusion of strange Europeans to whom the Kisii had never submitted.[2] There was a parliamentary question on 27 February 1908. What would happen to the cattle which had been captured? In reply, Churchill mentioned a proposal gradually to restore the cattle as pacification of the district proceeded, and also in return for the making of roads by 'tribesmen under their tribal chiefs', work which would add to the future civilisation, prosperity and accessibility of the country.[3] But on 12 March, the governor telegraphed that he proposed to auction 3000 cattle to the settlers. Churchill insisted that this proposal should be countermanded in view of the pledge which he had given. Elgin agreed rather reluctantly. He thought it a little hard upon the governor, because the arrangements he had made were quite in accordance with precedent – and he would have difficulty with the settlers. For the future they must decide whether it was to be ruled that no contribution towards the cost of punitive expeditions caused by the 'misconduct' of tribes was to be enforced. Several other points also needed to be considered carefully. Churchill had his way. The secretary of state indicated that he would prefer the cost of the expedition to be paid for out of protectorate funds. It was.[4]

Arising out of the Kisii episode, detailed instructions were issued in 1910 to all district officials in East Africa and Uganda. They called for a much more careful approach to any further operations. These instructions were copied from those used in Northern Nigeria since Elgin's directive on the Munshi

[1] CO. 533/41/3648, minute and tel. 3 Feb 08.
[2] CO. 533/43/15165, Sadler to S/S 1 Apr 08, minute by R. Popham Lobb 6 Mar 09.
[3] CO. 533/62/33415; PD. 185/41, 27 Feb 08.
[4] CO. 533/42/8988 and 9628, minute and tel. 18 Mar 08.

question, when he had insisted that there should be no punitive expedition unless it could be followed by effective administration and control.[1]

[1] CO. 533/43/15165, S/S to the officers administering the governments of Uganda and East Africa protectorate, 14 May 09. See above, p. 212, n. 2. There are references to the Kisii episode in Miss Perham's introduction to *History of East Africa*, ii, ed. Harlow and Chilver, xxix and xxxii.

6 Ceylon: Aftermath of the decline of the Imperial Factor

WITH the possible exception of the West Indies under Chamberlain, from the outbreak of the Boer War in 1899 until the fall of the Unionist government in 1905, South Africa nearly monopolised government attentions. The decline, or non-assertion, of the imperial factor may be widely observed in many parts of the world. Among the Liberals, Churchill represented a school of thought which regarded colonial governments, both Crown Colonies and responsible governments, as having been allowed too much discretion, and given too little supervision, as a result of a slackening of metropolitan control. Perhaps the best illustration of the Liberal attempt, or rather the attempt of a section of Liberalism, to tighten control, is provided by Ceylon, where the imperial factor was challenged by the indigenous inhabitants for abnegating responsibility for the pearl fisheries, and frequently complained of for failing to secure strict justice for its employees.

THE LEASE OF THE PEARL FISHERIES: CONTINUITY OF POLICY

Pearls had been recovered from the north-west coast of Ceylon for thousands of years. The fishery was centred on a hutment town at Maduchchukaddai, near the Gulf of Mannar. At the beginning of the twentieth century the pearl fisheries were under government control. In December 1904 the colonial office received from Ridgeway, formerly governor of Ceylon, acting on behalf of Lt.-Col. Foss and Mr Carl Derenberg, an offer from a 'reliable financial firm' to take a lease of the fisheries from the government. The syndicate would be prepared to expend a large sum of money in developing and improving the fisheries on lines approved of, and recently recommended to the government by Professor Herdman, who had considered scientific culture of the pearl oyster. By February 1905 the Ceylon government were prepared to negotiate on the basis of a twenty-year lease at a rental of £15,000 per annum (Rs. 225,000), provided that the syndicate paid the expenses of maintaining facilities and that it paid for the scientific advice already given to the government, and from which the syndicate could be expected to benefit. Historically, the fishery had been precarious and unpredictable, but there seemed no reason to apprehend a failure in future years, said the governor. In the 1905 season, nearly eighty million oysters were recovered by five thousand divers. The net profit of the government was £150,000. The governor therefore rightly considered a rental of £15,000 as 'very moderate'.[1] The colonial office considered it insufficient, and proposed to Derenberg and Co. an increase of rent to Rs. 310,000, which represented the approximate income over a twenty years' average after taking into account the record fishery of 1905.[2] The firm agreed. The operating company would be known as the Ceylon Company of Pearl Fishers Ltd. Their lease was to date from 1 January 1906.

When the Liberals took office the question of leasing the pearl fisheries to the company being formed by the Gulf Syndicate Ltd. was in its final stage. After lengthy negotiations conducted both in England and in Ceylon, Lyttelton had approved the signing of a preliminary agreement and the drafting of the lease and of an ordinance. The approval of the secretary of state had therefore been formally signified by Lyttelton; documents bearing his sanction had been remitted to the colony. The terms of lease he described as representing the result of 'the most anxious and laborious consideration'.

[1] Govr to S/S 14 Jun 05: Cd. 2906 (May 1906).
[2] CO to Derenberg & Co. 19 Aug 05.

He commended them to the Ceylon legislative council as conceived in the best interests of the colony.[1] By a large majority (12 : 4), the council approved the lease.

The Ceylon pearl fisheries was exactly the kind of question to attract a romantic like Churchill: a fishery famous for thousands of years, a fishery which had inspired Bizet's opera *Les pêcheurs de perles* in 1887: it demanded investigation. After studying the negotiations, it was to the rental in particular that Churchill directed all the ruthlessness of argument springing from his general distrust of Lyttelton's decisions. When private enterprise took over from government, Churchill said, it was reasonable to expect that the government would be offered in the first instance more than it had been able to make for itself. Elgin did not agree with this proposition. But Churchill's main attack was against the fundamental principle that the government, and hence the colony, were to gain no more in the next twenty years than in the last twenty. Of course he admitted that the previous twenty years included twelve blank years. There was, however, in his view, no reason for despondency in regard to the future of the pearl industry if treated scientifically, as it would be, following Herdman's report. He noted the 'immense and persistent rise' in the price of pearls.

But from all these possibilities, actuarial, scientific and financial, the Colony is to be cut off, and cut off I am sorry to say upon the initiative and careful shepherding of the Colonial Office. It is to bind itself to receive no profit as the result of the investigations of the scientist it employed at heavy expense; no profit from the application of science to an industry hitherto conducted haphazard; no profit from the enhancement on the value of pearls. . . . The new Parliament will not, to put it mildly, be inclined to view with favour projects for transferring State assets to a private monopoly.

According to his information, another company which was anxious to come forward had been 'curtly silenced' without even being accorded an interview.

After a careful reading of the files, Elgin did not feel able to

[1] S/S to govr 1 Dec 05.

agree with Churchill's condemnation of the bargain. This conclusion arose chiefly out of his 'profound disbelief in the ability of any government to work a commercial undertaking', a respectable Liberal doctrine of fifty years earlier. A government might, in his opinion, own properties which must be so developed, but it must enlist the aid of private enterprise where it entered the market. Such was the lesson he drew from his experience with Indian railways, where the government now retained the working only where strategic considerations were involved.

But this principle applies most of all to a case like that of the Ceylon fisheries, where annual capital expenditure must be incurred, and where the revenue is fluctuating, and at the mercy to a large extent of natural or climatic conditions. I do not think the comparison of the proposed rent with the average return of former years is fair without reference both to the extreme fluctuations of those years – and also to the distinct bargain that the company, in addition to their rent, expend an annual sum – determined within certain limits by the government – on the improvement of the fisheries. I am quite certain that unless the fisheries are so improved, no such average as the coup of the abnormal fishing of last year brought about, can be expected. And I venture to predict that if the fishery remained in our hands and a couple of bad years follow, as I see is now thought probable, the government will not be able to face the charge of capital expenditure on what will be termed a disappearing industry.

In any case, Elgin added, in view of the late stage which the arrangements had reached, further progress could only be stopped by direct orders, either to withdraw the ordinance or to use the official vote against it. In either case he thought that there would be 'a breach of faith', a charge, which, though he did not say so, he would hardly have wished to be made against him twice in his career. He was sorry to differ from Churchill, but decided to allow the ordinance to proceed without being disallowed, and to confirm the lease.[1]

[1] CO. 54/699/4627, minutes 12 and 14 Feb 06; on 16 Feb the S/S formally declared that he found no valid reason for intervening to prevent the legislative council deciding upon acceptance or rejection of the lease.

Reports now began to come in of Sinhalese protests at a public meeting in Colombo on 3 February. There were two main complaints. A lease on any terms was contrary to the interests of Ceylon. The lease now before them was at an inadequate rental. The memorialists said that if the government was really so incompetent as it professed to be in running the fisheries, 'the sooner it is done away with in all public departments the better in the interests of the colony'. It was a fair point. So too, was the observation that as 'the tendency of modern times is towards national proprietorship' it was strange to give up a 'valuable national property'. They expected the 1906 fishery to bring more than a million rupees to the company. Churchill had a large hand in drafting the despatch which replied to these public criticisms in Ceylon. It was he who devised the formula:

But although it would not have been my duty, and not, I apprehend, within my power, even had I so desired, to arrest the contract in its final stage, and although the Colonial Office had practically spoken the last word in the matter before I became cognisant of it, I feel, nevertheless, inclined to comment upon the controversy which has arisen, with the desire of removing some misapprehensions.

These comments included a reminder that in twenty years the fishery would revert to the government: and twenty years was a short time in a 2000-year old fishery. Moreover, the scientific operations were of 'a highly technical and experimental character' and it was very doubtful whether any machinery could be set in motion by the government 'which would be suited to develop processes at once so doubtful and so delicate'. Finally, there was the reflection that time alone could show how far the bargain had been wise or unwise. The secretary of state disclaimed personal responsibility for the transaction.[1]

Several protests against and questions about this business were put before the colonial secretary in England as well as from Ceylon. In reply to a parliamentary question by Sir John

[1] CO. 54/700/12300, desp. to govr. 9 May 06.

Jardine on 14 June 1906, Churchill commented on Lyttelton's decision to allow the legislative council merely to accept or reject the scheme as a whole, its own views never having been formally sought:

I confess I have formed views somewhat different from those which appear to have actuated Mr Lyttelton throughout the arrangements connected with the lease – views which have become more adverse the more I have had to deal with the matter. I think there are grave objections to the procedure which was followed and that the results have not been at all satisfactory.

Elgin must have been furious at this expression of a view contrary to his own, by one who ought to have been acting as the mouthpiece of the known views of the secretary of state. It was one of the most flagrant instances of Churchill's insubordination which Elgin encountered in their association.

Critics repeatedly alleged that the calculation of rent had been done on the wrong basis, because there was the probable expectation of enormously increased profits following the application of scientific methods and processes. The annual rent had been fixed at £20,666; everybody knew that the net profit in 1905 had been £150,000. Sir John Jardine specifically raised the point in the House of Commons. Churchill began his draft reply with the observation that the average annual net profit over the past twenty years was the basis of calculation. Although he was satisfied that Professor Herdman had conducted his scientific investigation and report with good faith and integrity, he could not speak 'with the same assurance of the wisdom of the bargain or of its results to Ceylon'. Elgin's blue pencil went straight through this. 'I hope Mr Churchill will not object to omit the last sentence;' he wrote, 'it is his opinion and he has stated it in the House – but it is not mine.'[1] A later questioner elicited the information that the profit in 1903 had been £42,000 and in 1904, £61,000. Elgin insisted on the necessity of bringing out in the reply

[1] CO. 54/704/22387, 25 Jun 06.

the precarious nature of the fishery. When a business fails utterly in twelve years out of twenty, to state three successful years as the basis of a new arrangement is simply to mislead.

Hence, the questioner was told, three successful years, the last of which was a record fishery, 'do not of themselves afford a basis for computing what would be a fair rental'.[1] This standpoint was open to the retort that it seemed to ignore the possible decrease in the speculative nature of the fishery in the future. On balance, however, it seems that Elgin was right. The 1905 season remained a brilliant exception in a consistently downward trend in the early twentieth century. It was the most successful fishery in at least the last three hundred years.

On the whole, it seems that belief in continuity of policy was strong enough to preclude Elgin's reopening of any questions where it was not absolutely necessary. In his opinion, the right decision had been made, but even if he had been doubtful, it is unlikely that he would have sought to alter it. Support for this interpretation comes from his attitude to another far eastern issue involving possible commentary on the decisions and actions of his predecessor. During Lyttelton's colonial secretaryship, the government of the Straits Settlements had acquired certain docks at Singapore from the Tanjong Pagar Dock Company by an arbitration award. Sir Charles Schwann asked in the House of Commons 'whether the present government approve of the acquisition and of the reasons assigned therefor by their predecessors'. Elgin hated questions like this: they were 'destructive of all business'. He refused to comment on the grounds that the transaction was wholly concluded before the accession of the Liberal ministry to office, and that it had been the subject of a legally constituted tribunal of arbitration.[2] The matter could not be quite so finally disposed of. In September we discover Churchill studying the case again, and reporting that although it was a very complicated affair, his impression was strongly that it was 'another Lyttelton-Lucas muddle' resulting in disastrous loss to the colony, like the Ceylon case.

---

[1] Ibid. 23333, 2 Jul 06. [2] CO. 273/322/24879, 11 Jul 06.

He wanted Elgin to make both transactions the subject of a parliamentary inquiry:

That would be a course which would win for you and for the government a great measure of public respect and approval, and which would put a stop once and for all to the innuendos and suspicions of which the action of the colonial office – believe me – is very widely the object.[1]

This was not the kind of argument which made much appeal to Elgin, and nothing came of it.

JUSTICE IN ADMINISTRATION: THE ASSERTION OF CONCERN

Liberals felt that Unionists did not attach sufficient passion to their concern with securing justice in the British empire. It is true that the Curzonian view looked to strict and inflexible justice between races and good treatment of non-Europeans as part of good administration, but it was 'a job to be done, not a duty to be fulfilled'.[2] Churchill was the spokesman of a Liberal view which stressed the duty of using imperial power to secure the highest standards of justice in administration everywhere.

Churchill repeatedly commented on the Ceylon government's 'ignorance of judicial procedure', its 'disgraceful' administration of justice, and the invariable tendency of the office in 'these scandalous personal cases' to uphold the colonial decisions, right or wrong. He constantly refused to accept responsibility for the administration of justice in Ceylon. He once described it as 'the vilest scandal of the colonial service'.[3] Elgin, by contrast, while he would criticise their methods as unsatisfactory, refused to allege injustice against the government of Ceylon. He simply could not see that any injustice was done in many of the cases to which Churchill drew his attention. The discussions between

[1] EP, WSC to E 14 Sep 06. [2] Gopal, *British policy in India*, p. 261.
[3] CO. 54/708/20564, minute 21 Jun 07.

Elgin and Churchill on these Ceylon cases are thus highly significant to any analysis of their relationship, and to their differing interpretations of the priorities to be observed in the conduct of imperial administration. Elgin was more inclined to side with the governor, Churchill with the governed. There were two *causes célèbres*, both concerning employees on Ceylon government railways, David and Serasinghe.

Towards the end of 1905, the colonial office received a memorial from Mr A. E. David, formerly a head guard on the Ceylon government railways. David petitioned for reinstatement in his job, from which he had been dismissed about eighteen months earlier on a charge of theft. Lucas, thinking the matter within the discretion of the local government, advised declining to interfere. Churchill seized upon the neglect of Colonial Regulation 87 to question this advice:

Mr David is formally charged with one offence, and actually dismissed for another; for another upon which he has had no opportunity of defending himself, and concerning which the evidence – purely circumstantial – is admitted to be insufficient to sustain a prosecution.

A charge of theft must either be made openly and brought to trial according to law, or dropped altogether. . . . Only a recognised tribunal can pronounce. . . . Reasons of the gravest public importance alone can justify action on suspicion. We must be specially careful not to be influenced in the administration of justice and in the observance of law by any criticism which may be passed on our action in a Colony. The *facts* in this case and in many similar cases are wholly irrelevant. Our duty is to insist that the principles of justice and the safeguards of judicial procedure are rigidly, punctiliously and pedantically followed. . . .

Although the case was in itself so petty that it had not hitherto been submitted even to the parliamentary under-secretary, Churchill, regarding the principles involved as very important, submitted the matter to Elgin. Lucas remained convinced that the decision should be upheld, and gave nine reasons. None of these satisfied Churchill, especially the appeal to inconvenience.

'The inconvenience inseparable from the reparation of injustice or irregularity is one of the safeguards against their recurrence.' Notwithstanding the confirmation of David's suspension by Lyttelton, Churchill pressed Elgin into sending a despatch requesting fuller information, and the explanation of several points before a final decision was taken.[1]

Churchill commented viciously on what he described as the incoherence of the governor's reply:

such a jumble of confused argument, such indifference to ordinary principles of justice and fairplay are intellectually contemptible if not morally dishonouring.

Elgin would have winced at this outrageous minute. He asked Churchill to remove at least part of it 'in order to avoid any record of a wide difference of opinion' between them. He did not ask Churchill to abandon his contention, merely to conceal it:[2]

I am not personally touchy in these matters, but you know that my successor in India was eloquent as to the inconvenience of notes by junior officers – and Kitchener upset the Army system on the same question. Now whatever force there may be in these objections, there is certainly as much in sending through an office like this, for the perusal of successive relays of juniors, minutes which reflect so severely as yours does on the conduct of a governor of a colony. In the interests of discipline I hold very distinctly that, while of course *I* should desire to hear your opinion without reserve – it is not expedient to record all and every opinion, strongly expressed.

Elgin had one further general comment on the case. It was equally characteristic. He found it difficult to follow Churchill's argument: he did not see why a servant employed on state railways should be in so essentially different a position from a servant in the employment of a company or individual that he could be dismissed only if actually convicted of crime. The right of summary dismissal was, he held, a necessary one. David

[1] CO. 54/696/45379, minutes 31 Jan 06, S/S to govr. 15 Feb 06.
[2] EP, E to WSC 25 May 06 (photocopy).

was inefficient and unsatisfactory. Elgin did not feel that he could condemn the governor for getting rid of him, as he would have concurred in a similar dismissal when he was a director of a railway company. The upshot of the discussion was that Elgin recorded his belief that David should have a further trial. His record was not good, but Elgin did not think that this precluded his being given this chance, as Churchill pressed for it. David was re-employed, but Elgin objected to allegations that he had 'acquitted' David or superseded the ruling of his predecessor. He adhered to the right of summary dismissal, but wished it to be exercised 'in a less bungling fashion'.

In view of the number of similar cases Churchill prepared an elaborate memorandum in order to get a ruling by the secretary of state. He did not propose that railway servants should become immune from dismissal, only that before they were adjudged worthy of dismissal, they should have some opportunity of knowing the charge made against them and of furnishing such defence or excuse as might occur to them:

The very modest safeguards of the Colonial Regulations do not prevent dismissal, do not enjoin anything in the nature of a regular trial, still less do they prevent immediate interdiction from duty, which is of course vitally necessary in railway management. The power continues absolute and summary; and it is strengthened not weakened by being clothed in some vestments, however scanty, of justice and formality. Are we seriously to be told that a Railway manager cannot maintain his authority unless he enjoys the right of 'sacking' his subordinates *without assigning any reason*? How then do military officers maintain their much more important authority, when there is no man under their command not protected by elaborate apparatus at every point from the arbitrary exercise of power?

Having produced the inevitable army analogy, Churchill propounded a splendid aphorism: 'Authority is disgraced when it claims to stand with equal right upon caprice or reason.' It was quite true, he continued, that in business, private persons exercised the right of arbitrary dismissal without even having the need to give a reason. No one could prove that there was any justice in such an arrangement, however. Still less could it be taken as the model for state action. That it was not so taken was evident from the existence of the Colonial Regulations. These, unfortunately, did not cover persons in the Ceylon railway service, which was not in existence when the regulations were framed. The situation was 'evidently absurd and improper', productive of 'much carelessness and callousness' in the railway management of Ceylon. It was high time that the position of the railway service was regularised and established on the same footing as any other class of government employees.

Elgin's angle of approach was quite different. He read the papers on the file with great care, as he was anxious to give full weight to Churchill's minute, 'the high motive' of which he expressly recognised. But he could not agree with its conclusions, or consent to bring these subordinate officers under the Colonial Regulations: it would be a mistake to do so from the point of view both of employer and employed. A remarkably large number of definite opinions had been recorded by different secretaries of state. Sir Michael Hicks Beach, Lord Derby, Lord Knutsford and Mr Chamberlain had all had the point before them and were agreed on their conclusions. The power of summary dismissal by the general manager must be retained especially in cases where public safety was imperilled. Otherwise it should be made rather a power of suspension subject to the decision of the governor or executive authority as to dismissal. He decided to inform the governor that if he wished to exercise the right of summary dismissal, it would not be necessary to proceed under Colonial Regulations, and get the decision of the secretary of state before removing an officer. It was, however, to be understood that every case must be investigated by the governor as fully and as carefully, and with the same help from advisers, as if he were acting under those regulations.[1]

The case of Serasinghe was a particularly interesting one. Serasinghe was a railway clerk who had been acquitted of a

[1] CO. 54/705/36699, minutes 18 and 22 Nov 06, desp. to govr 5 Dec 06.

229

charge of theft by the High Court, and on that score had pressed for further departmental enquiry, bringing a charge of perjury and conspiracy against the temporary station-master who had discovered the ingenious system of frauds and mis-appropriation of funds at the station where Serasinghe worked, and who had blamed Serasinghe. But the departmental committee dismissed Serasinghe for bringing what it considered a false charge against the station-master. The committee believed Serasinghe to have been guilty. The governor confirmed his suspension. Whereupon Serasinghe appealed for another trial. Churchill dipped his pen once more into the magisterial ink:

To try a man again upon the original charge, to review without any of the safeguards of justice a case already decided in a court of law, to overthrow the acquittal pronounced by judge and jury, and stolidly to assert upon departmental authority, that the man is guilty after all, is to commit almost every impropriety possible, and to commit them all in the stupidest way.

The frequency with which this kind of irregularity appeared to be committed in Ceylon rendered action imperative, he added. Sir Henry Blake, the governor of Ceylon, admitted that the question of re-employment must be considered. Churchill had wished to instruct re-employment, but Elgin thought advising reconsideration sufficient, because he suspected that Serasinghe was almost certainly unfit for the public service, and therefore it would not be wise to retain him merely to mask the irregularity of the procedure of the Ceylon government.[1]

It was wrong, Churchill thought, to assume that a government could do with its servants whatever a private employer would do:

The proper punishment for a thief is not dismissal but imprisonment . . . a trial is not a punishment but a privilege. To deprive a person of that privilege in the name of clemency is absurd. . . . Serasinghe should be given option of standing trial.

[1] CO. 54/702/36778, minutes 19 and 27 Oct 06.

Elgin knew the dangers of reversing the disciplinary decisions of governors in eastern lands, but he also had, on this occasion, considerable sympathy with Churchill's championship of the law. However, he did not think that a colony like Ceylon was the sort of place where they could say that no government servant was to be dismissed on a suspicion of dishonesty or the like unless the charge could be proved in a court of law. If dismissed by a departmental inquiry, Serasinghe should be able to bring an action for wrongful dismissal, but not appeal against the decision. Elgin therefore decided to uphold the governor's decision and to confirm the suspension of Serasinghe. Suspecting that Elgin was reluctant to embarrass the governor, Churchill retaliated:

I do not see what connection there can be between the irritation of Sir Henry Blake and an abstract question of law and justice affecting a humble person who has appealed to you. Nothing could well be more indefensible than the impropriety committed in this instance: and to offer the man the option of a criminal trial in open court is in my view the only step that can safeguard our position without infringing that of the governor. The right course would have been to say that the acquittal of the Supreme Court was final in respect of the charges of peculation against Mr Serasinghe; and that if the governor had not taken the trouble to present his case ... in its full strength, he had only himself to blame for the consequences. But I was anxious to find a middle course which would, I thought, harmonise with your administrative methods in these sort of disciplinary questions.

Churchill was very disturbed. He took a tough and reproachful line with his chief:

You now inform me that you intend to brush aside altogether the argument which I have set out ... and to confirm with your approval the shocking violation of elementary principles of law and justice which has occurred ... as if I ought to agree to this man being treated with wanton illegality and flat injustice in order to save Sir Henry Blake's face and to justify his impatience under correction. I cannot think you mean this.

I do not know what to do. You can of course overrule me *with* reasons or *without* them. But any of these cases may at any moment be brought before the House of Commons – the brick-bats will be about *my* head. ... The Liberal party cares very much for the rights of individuals to just and lawful treatment and very little for the petty pride of a colonial governor. I can only say that a determination not to consent to such impro-prieties which are cruel to individuals and fatal to good government has always actuated me, and that I will never depart from it because it is expedient in the supposed interests of discipline.

Churchill believed the man innocent, but the argument was to his mind the same whether he was guilty or innocent, which was something they had no right to jump to conclusions about. He explained to Elgin that he had no reason to suppose when he wrote his minute that Elgin would differ from it, 'as the action proposed was essentially moderate and in the nature of a compromise'. Yet even in this difficult case Churchill managed to retain some of the attitudes appropriate to a subordinate, and wrote to thank Elgin for the kind and considerate reply he received to his diatribe:

I am most grateful to you for the patience with which you treat me on all occasions. I did not mean to write bitterly, and cer-tainly I have always written in a spirit of profound respect; but I do most deeply regret the view you take of these questions, and that matters in themselves of very small importance relatively, should make such inroads upon our time and strength.[1]

Having taken full account of Churchill's views, and having taken no final action, Elgin decided on 24 January to adhere to his decision to confirm the suspension, on the ground that the man had been proved to be unfit for the public service. He did not think Serasinghe should have the option of compelling the government to undertake a fresh trial. But he proposed to make clear to the governor their belief that the case had been mis-managed, and to comment on the system which permitted such long continued frauds. A fresh prosecution would, Elgin sus-

[1] EP, WSC to E 23 Jan 07.

pected, almost certainly have led to Serasinghe's conviction. It would therefore be unwise to intervene on his behalf.[1]

This decision did not pass without one final challenge from Churchill. He let his 'profound disquietude' be known. He complained rather bitterly of being overruled without any reason being assigned, or without any attempt to do justice to the 'grave arguments' he had so earnestly submitted. But he did admit also that 'these sort of questions fall so largely within the legal zone that I recognise that a lay opinion like my own may be at fault'.[2] Elgin, not unnaturally, felt Churchill's persistent nagging rather unfair. After all, he had deliberately abstained even from recording a minute until he had corresponded privately with Churchill telling him how he saw the case. He had consistently followed his profound conviction that differences of opinion should not appear on the official record. Churchill seemed to admit that Serasinghe was presumably guilty of frauds. Elgin wrote to Churchill:

But your point is that he had not been convicted by a Court. My view may be coloured by the fact that I also had been a 'man on the spot' – but I cannot see why conviction by a Court should be a *sine qua non* for this class of servant. The Governor's despatch seems to me to state fairly the reasons why he did not appeal a second time to a Court, (and observe he also frankly admitted the justice of the first acquittal). I do not think it is fair in this case to allege the 'petty pride' of a Colonial Governor. No doubt petty pride exists among them as amongst other men. . . . I am not convinced . . . that the Ceylon government intends anything less than just and lawful treatment.[3]

So constantly did Churchill intrude into Elgin's room that for several days Elgin had some difficulty in disposing of other business. Fortunately there was a lull in other matters; perhaps that was partly the reason why Churchill had been 'roaming about', as Elgin described it. Churchill felt very strongly, and Elgin realised that a discussion could not be avoided.

[1] CO. 54/703/47474, minute by E 24 Jan 07, desp. S/S to govr 1 Feb 07.
[2] EP, WSC to E 26 Jan 07.
[3] EP, to WSC 28 Jan 07 (photocopy).

It took nearly two hours yesterday evening [he wrote to his wife], much to the inconvenience of ... others who wanted to see me! But it interested me much – he was thoroughly in earnest – impassioned and excited at times – and at the end in spite of my sticking to my guns, he calmed down and expressed this conviction: 'Well Lord Elgin – no one can ever have a conversation with you without advantage'!! I am afraid that Hopwood is also suffering a little from what he H. terms his 'pugnacity' – but is very pleasant and anxious to do all he can to keep things smooth.[1]

Elgin wrote privately to tell the governor that the confirmation of Serasinghe's suspension was a decision only arrived at with difficulty. The procedure by which his conviction was arrived at seemed unfortunate. Elgin did not question Serasinghe's guilt, nor did he contend that a man employed in the public service might not be dismissed after an inquiry by a special commissioner as well as after a public trial. But in this case both methods had been used, and Elgin did not think this wise. Some means, he thought, should be taken to find out whether Serasinghe realised that he had better accept the sentence of suspension than run the risk of another prosecution, which he would lose. Elgin therefore hoped that he would not appeal. Even if there were reason to doubt whether Serasinghe would accept this view, he ought to be given the option of accepting the decision or of standing his trial. It is interesting to note that Elgin made this request privately to the governor, and would not impose it upon him in an official despatch.[2]

Elgin certainly regarded the procedure adopted in Ceylon in these insignificant cases as faulty. But he carefully dissociated himself from adopting the 'whole of Mr Churchill's trenchant criticism'. To the governor he expressed his reluctance at being compelled to interfere with his decisions. In future such cases would, he hoped, be dealt with in a manner which would obviate the necessity for his intervention.[3]

[1] EP 30 Jan 07.   [2] EP, E to Sir Henry Blake (copy) 31 Jan 07.
[3] Ibid. 26 Feb 07.

Problems of Relationship with the White Self-Governing Colonies

Problems of Relationship
with the White Self-Governing

*If the characteristic problems of the first phase of the Liberal
government arose from reviewing the legacy inherited from the
Unionists, and if the decisions hinged principally on the issue of
how much continuity of policy was possible, the typical preoccupation of the second phase was the relationship between the
imperial government and the white self-governing colonies. This
preoccupation was made unavoidable by the imminence of, and
reached its climax in, a colonial conference, which was the chief
focus of public interest in imperial problems during 1907.
Though typical of the middle phase of the work of the ministry,
the problem had arisen explicitly in Natal as early as the
beginning of the third month of Elgin's colonial secretaryship,
and it was still in progress when he left office.*

7 South Africa: The Temptation to Intervene

THE question of how far self-governing colonies could be allowed unfettered control of their domestic affairs and especially of their native policy, posed a dilemma which was particularly embarrassing for British Liberals. They were torn between their desire to uphold and extend self-government and their desire to secure fair treatment for natives. In the early twentieth century, most people at home would have agreed with Bryce, when he wrote that self-governing colonies were never interfered with in internal affairs, 'unless in the rare case where a matter primarily local may affect the general relations and interests of the whole Empire'.[1] Interference in such circumstances was thought legitimate, but there was ample room for debate where the frontier line between matters of purely local concern and those of imperial magnitude should be drawn. There was widespread apprehension in Unionist circles in 1905–6 that a Liberal government would draw a frontier line favouring imperial control rather than local autonomy. So strong was Lord Cromer's apprehension, that it was a major reason why he declined the offer of the foreign secretaryship in Campbell-Bannerman's cabinet in December 1905. He feared that the government 'would not improbably lash the English party in South Africa into fury; that they would endeavour to govern South Africa from London; and, whilst proclaiming the principles of self-government on the house-tops, would themselves violate self-governing principles when the colony wished to run counter to their preconceived ideas'.[2] Cromer

[1] Bryce, *Impressions of South Africa*, p. 475.
[2] Cromer 8/418–21, Cromer to J. St. Loe Strachey (editor of *Spectator*), 3 Apr 06.

expressed himself privately, but similar fears were voiced in the House of Commons by Chamberlain and Wyndham.[1] Yet strangely enough, as a result of the way in which the Liberal government in practice determined the frontiers of imperial control, criticism swung from a belief that Liberals would violate self-government in order to protect African and imperial interests, to the charge of sacrificing these interests to an 'excessive deference' to self-governing colonies.[2]

Elgin's fullest public statement on the relations between the mother country and the colonies was made early in July 1906. His conception of the 'compact on which our relations depend' emphasised the reciprocal duties and obligations of the mother country and the colonies. Subject to the conditions of the instrument by which it was conferred, he believed that the right of the colony to self-government was irrefragable and complete, and that the mother country could not infringe it except by an act of force, which would always bring with it the risk of the penalty 'which history had recorded', the forfeiture of allegiance. They were bound to recognise that British colonial citizens, and those of British race, had a right to the full trust and confidence of the government. On the other side, there was, he believed, a correlative duty – the colonies must be true to the traditions of the empire. The British flag was everywhere the emblem of hatred of wrong and oppression, of justice and of protection of the weaker races, of national and individual freedom – and that boast was common to both the mother country and the colonies.[3]

---

[1] PD. 150/663 and 152/1245.

[2] PD. 183/669, Curzon's comment, 4 Feb 08, on the handling of the Transvaal Asiatic Ordinance, 1907, discussed below.

Schreiner, the South African lawyer: 'some of us in South Africa, who have never favoured unnecessary or ill-informed interference or intervention in the internal affairs of self-governing Colonies or independent States, discern in these contrary days a very real risk that the doctrine of non-interference may be carried to a most dangerous extreme at a time when both the great political parties in the Mother Country appear to be united in a weary feeling that Africa is "a Beast", and inclined towards handing over all trusts and responsibilities to the European section of our population on such terms as these may design. This is the "elimination of the Imperial Factor" with a vengeance' (E. A. Walker, *W. P. Schreiner* (1937), p. 321, Schreiner to Dilke, 1909).

[3] *Westminster Gazette*, 3 Jul 06: speech at the Canadian Club.

These were days when the rights and privileges of self-governing colonies were claimed with ever-increasing insistence.

NATAL: THE NATIVE DISTURBANCES, 1906–1908

Disputes between colonial governments and the British government have been remarkably few, and seldom pushed to extremes. Colonial ministries had in the nineteenth century normally acquiesced in a governor's acting on imperial instructions, and merely concentrated on seeking to have instructions reversed. Natal provided a notorious example of a more drastic mode of conduct, and in 1906 its ministers threatened mass resignation.[1]

The background was as follows. On 7 February 1906 there were disturbances among the Zulus south-west of Pietermaritzburg, and on the next day, two white policemen were killed. As a result, martial law was proclaimed on 10 February. Two Africans were punished by death on 15 February. The Liberal government agreed to the temporary despatch of a battalion of infantry to Pietermaritzburg, recognising that this would reassure the colonists and demonstrate to Africans the support of the imperial government for the Natal authorities. Elgin was not convinced by the governor's explanation of the cause of the outbreak. The governor stressed the role of a seditious Ethiopian Church movement, and mentioned rumours that Dinizulu, the Zulu chief,[2] was commissioned to kill off all the Europeans. Elgin's impression from incomplete information was that the causes were 'more local and particular'. Churchill thought that the poll tax had played a major part.[3] It was made

---

[1] A. B. Keith, *Responsible government in the dominions*, ii, 214.

[2] Dinizulu (*c.* 1869–1913). Son of Zulu paramount chief Cetewayo (*d.* 1884). Exiled 1889. Returned at end of 1897, not as paramount chief, but simply as a local chief and government *induna* at a salary of £500 p.a.

[3] CO. 179/233/10386, minute 7 Apr 06. The 'official mind' never evolved a full theory of causation. Governor McCallum said the outbreaks were engineered by a body of Ethiopians who had lately had preachers among them sowing seeds of sedition (EP, to E 10 Feb 06). Selborne ascribed the cause to the influence of Ethiopianism on idle, lusty men, though he did not think the Natal government altogether free from blame (EP, Selb. to E 13 Apr 06).

clear in parliament that the Natal government was responsible for measures to re-establish order.[1]

Censorship was also instituted in Natal as well as martial law. The colonial office did not like this. Churchill minuted:

The action of governor and ministers is preposterous. The proclamation of martial law *over the whole colony*, causing dislocation and infinite annoyance to everyone, because two white men have been killed, is in itself an act which appears to be pervaded by an exaggerated excitability. The censorship exploit descends to the category of pure folly.[2]

Elgin did not think a censorship judicious:

it certainly increased the apprehension here, especially as newspapers in self defence published vague and alarming rumours. A censorship may be of use against a civilised foe who can make use of early information, but surely against a native rising it must be useless.

However, in general Elgin did not disapprove of the firm action of the Natal government.[3] The colonial ministers reluctantly consented to abolish the censorship, but martial law remained.[4]

At the beginning of March 1906, tension appeared to be diminishing. The lull was deceptive. Further disturbances occurred. A police force was ambushed by Bambata, who withdrew into the forest and rallied massive support. On 28 March the colonial office received a telegram stating that twelve more Africans were to be executed under martial law for the murder of the same two policemen on 8 February for which there had already been two executions. Probably upon Churchill's insistence, a reply was telegraphed requesting the suspension of the sentences, pending the receipt of detailed information. The draft of this notorious telegram was by Churchill. In view of its importance, the text had best be quoted in full:

[1] CO. 179/233/11034.   [2] CO. 323/522/5096, minute 12 Feb 06.
[3] EP, E to McCallum 3 Mar 06.   [4] CO. 323/514/5323.

Continued executions under martial law certain to excite strong criticism here, and as H.M.G. are retaining troops in Colony, and will be asked to assent to Act of Indemnity, necessary to regularise the action taken, trial of these murder cases by civil courts greatly to be preferred. I must impress upon you necessity of utmost caution in this matter, and you should suspend executions until I have had opportunity of considering your further observations.

No one in the colonial office expected that the Natal government would treat this telegram as conveying more than friendly advice, and embodying a fully justified request for information.[1] But the Natal ministry reacted with extreme sensitivity, and alarm was registered even in Australia and New Zealand.[2] The Natal ministry tendered resignation *en bloc* on the ground of interference with the decision of the executive council of a self-governing colony. Undoubtedly the Natal ministers were surprised by the telegram of 28 March. None of them had ever imagined that the British government would consider participating in responsibility for the further executions. It was for this reason, or so he alleged, that the governor had not provided fuller information in the first instance.[3]

Before the resignations took effect, the governor sent information which the British ministers chose to regard as satisfying their doubts. A further telegram was sent on 30 March admitting the responsibility of Natal and denying any intention of interference. Again, this must be quoted:

[1] Keith, *Responsible government in the dominions*, ii, 217, alleges that this telegram was 'hastily despatched without consultation with the experts' (i.e. Mr Keith), and as a result it was, he said, peremptory. It may be true that officials did not see the final wording of the telegram, but it embodied their recommendations. Keith himself had urged staying the executions, see CO. 179/233/10712, minute 28 Mar 06.

[2] Governor-general of Australia to S/S 31 Mar 06: 'Since an intervention of H.M. ministers . . . with the administration of the self-governing colony of Natal would tend to establish, even in regard to prerogative of pardon, a dangerous precedent affecting all states within the empire, your excellency's advisers desire most respectfully to appeal to H.M. ministers for reconsideration of the resolution at which they are reported to have arrived in this subject' (CO. 418/44). New Zealand ministers also wished to be 'relieved of anxiety' (CO. 209/268/11624, tel. govr to S/S 3 Apr 06).

[3] CO. 179/233/14033.

H.M.G. have at no time had the intention to interfere with action of the responsible government of Natal, or to control governor in exercise of prerogative . . . [but were] entitled, and were in duty bound to obtain full and precise information. . . . In the light of the information now furnished, H.M.G. recognise that the decision of this grave matter rests in the hands of your ministers and yourself.

The Natal ministers then withdrew their resignations; the Zulus were executed on 2 April. The official telegram of 30 March was accompanied by a private telegram from Elgin to the governor, in which Elgin emphasised the sincerity of his approval of the governor's action. He would have regretted it very much if the governor had thought the telegram of 28 March conveyed any suggestion of censure. Elgin emphasised that the absence of information was the cause of the first telegram. He admitted that 'the unnecessarily precipitate action' of the Natal ministers could not have been foreseen by the governor. If they had not so acted, the governor could have given the explanations Elgin desired when he asked for them.[1] Yet another telegram was sent on 3 April, drafted by Ommanney, stressing the 'necessity of avoiding any action which may revive or accentuate the feeling already so strongly manifested here'. The governor was not to confirm any further capital sentence without giving the secretary of state previous information, 'except possibly in a case of great emergency where you consider delay impossible'. This exception was added by Elgin personally.[2]

Inevitably there was strong criticism from opponents of the Liberals. On 2 April the government was asked in the House of Commons whether they had sanctioned the executions of 15 February. Supported by officials, Churchill suggested replying that the decision rested with the governor and ministers of the colony, but Elgin commented:

The difficulty of this answer is that it might be taken to mean that we deliberately decided not to intervene. This is not the case, because we never heard of the matter, officially at all

[1] EP, E to McCallum, tel. private and personal 30 Mar 06 (copy).
[2] Ibid. 3 Apr 06 (draft).

events, till the execution had taken place. On the other hand, to state that fact might seem to imply that if we had heard, we should have intervened – which is not probable. I think the safest answer is the plain 'No sir',

– which was in fact given.[1] Later the same day, Churchill defended the Liberal government in an exceptionally excited debate. He admitted that more than once during the unrest, the government had 'felt grave misgivings as to what our duty should be, and in what direction we might properly exert ourselves to safeguard the interests of the vast native population'. He contended that the government had acted consistently, and with a desire to support Natal, but 'no colonial secretary for fifty years confronted by such a telegram under such circumstances could have acted otherwise'. It was absurd to say that they had no right 'to fullest information and to avail ourselves of every opportunity of tendering friendly advice' in a situation where martial law was in force. Churchill explained that as soon as the cabinet had received detailed information and was satisfied upon the correctness of the methods of establishing guilt, the governor was instructed to settle the matter locally with his responsible ministers. Churchill denied a 'climb down'. If Natal ministers had not resigned, the Liberals would not have prevented them acting on their discretion, once satisfied, that upon the whole, the regular forms of justice had been observed; but ten resignations, he said, would not have deterred the Liberal government from obtaining the information necessary to do their duty to the House and to their African subjects.[2]

The colonial office debated throughout April whether a despatch of explanation should be sent to Natal. Churchill favoured such a despatch, and assumed control of drafting. He made some notes which were then drafted into alternative despatches by two officials. Simultaneously, Keith was prepar-

[1] CO. 179/238/11256, minute 2 Apr 06.
[2] PD. 155/267-75, 2 Apr 06. Lord Lovat, a Unionist, publicly defended Elgin for maintaining a correct, dignified attitude, worthy of best British traditions; the telegram of 30 Mar was not a climb-down, but 'the acquiescence of a strong man to an act of the equity of which he had made himself certain' (*Morning Post* 26 Apr 06). No more favourable gloss can be made.

ing an eight-page memorandum on 'The right of H.M.G. to interfere in the Executive Government of a self-governing Colony'. But Ommanney and Graham declared themselves opposed to any despatch on these lines; when the time came for Elgin's decision, he accepted their argument. Churchill wished to declare that the power and rights of the crown in regard to self-governing colonies were 'latent and paramount', and had been called into actual being by the request of the Natal government for the support of British troops; though H.M.G. had the right, it had at no time had the intention, of interfering with the complete discretion of the Natal government. In Ommanney's view, a reasoned despatch was an impossibility, because they had continually asserted that the responsibility rested with the Natal government; moreover, if they hinted at heavy responsibility for, and therefore the right to effective control over, native policy in South Africa, they would unite every section of the white population there against them, and involve a heavy imperial expenditure. Such a policy he thought quite impracticable.[1]

Everyone in the office, however, agreed that the action of the Natal government, in resigning and giving publicity to their attitude, was unreasonable. Retrospectively, it might be admitted that the wording of the telegram of 28 March was perhaps unfortunate, but on the whole, the colonial office attitude was one of surprise and disgust. The episode left a general public impression that the Liberal government had been thwarted by Natal.

In mid-April 1906 proclamations were issued announcing rewards for the capture of Bambata and other supposed ringleaders in the disturbances, dead or alive. If parliament had been sitting, Elgin imagined that there would have been questions about 'blood money!' He disliked the proclamations exceedingly. He remembered stopping a similar proclamation in India 'most peremptorily'. Sadly he mused that he supposed he had no power to do the same in Natal. Even if he had, he added ruefully in a letter to Churchill, it would only provoke a

[1] CO. 179/233/11034, minute by Ommanney 6 Apr 06.

244

second resignation.[1] All the official papers he went through at this time he described as 'full of the most savage feelings'. The temper of the colonists, he wrote, was 'getting very dangerous'. But, he told Churchill, he did not see what could be done unless they were prepared to take the whole matter out of the hands of the colonial government.[2] 'The state of mind in the Colony is very serious', he noted on 22 April, 'and we must keep very cool here to prevent an explosion.'[3] Unless they acted with great reserve, the pressure for increased protection in Natal would become excessive.[4] Elgin was faced with a deputation of M.P.s on 30 April. He did not think it necessary to give any further reassurance to the Africans, in view of the government's acceptance of Mr Byles's motion on 28 February.[5] A study of evidence from various parts of Natal led Elgin to doubt the idea of general unrest. The demand of the Aborigines Protection Society for resumption of direct imperial control he refused very positively. Nor would he make any pronouncement on the Native Affairs Commission Report before the termination of the Natal crisis and the formulation of the new constitutions for the Transvaal and Orange River Colony.[6]

By the middle of May, three of the prisoners had not been tried because they were wounded; the governor tried to get a civil court for them. Churchill wanted to encourage him to 'persevere in restraining his ministers from giving us a ferocious and belated encore'. Elgin would not commit himself to such epithets on the official files. He could imagine an argument for a court martial, though he did not agree with it.[7] Resistance in Natal was stamped out during the summer. Three thousand Africans were killed. In October Elgin received a letter from

---

[1] EP, E to WSC 16 Apr 06 (photocopy).
[2] Ibid. 17 and 19 Apr 06. He wrote to his wife: 'There is also bad news from Natal – a regular rebellion apparently'; to Churchill: 'I will consider a warning to the governor, but after recent experience one is naturally unwilling to be accused again of interference – while a private telegram might only increase the difficulties of the governor's position without preventing the conduct which we deprecate' (19 Apr).
[3] Ibid. 22 Apr 06.   [4] CO. 179/233/12460, minute 17 Apr 06.
[5] See p. 373.   [6] EP, E to WSC 29 Apr 06 (photocopy).
[7] CO. 179/235/18017, minutes 26 May 06.

Mr Norman, M.P. requesting imperial enquiry into alleged atrocities in Natal. Elgin decided to dismiss this letter without further ado:

I must positively refuse to be a party to ordering an imperial enquiry, especially on evidence which is entirely anonymous. I cannot imagine anything more provocative not only to Natal but to Colonial sentiment. The governor wrote the other day in the most emphatic terms that he had been unable to trace anything of the kind. That war in the bush must mean things that no humane man can absolutely defend is unfortunately the fact – but the only charge which could justify investigations such as Norman and the Tribunal demand, is one that the Colony and the Colonial troops went into this with a pre-meditated object – and that a murderous one. I decline to father that accusation on the authority of nameless soldiers and the like. . . .[1]

The Liberal government had publicly proclaimed their desire to support the Natal government. Privately, Elgin repeatedly assured the governor that it was their first object to maintain a sympathetic attitude. Nevertheless, resolutions of protest against the British government flooded in from Natal, and also from the Transvaal, Orange River Colony, Southern Rhodesia and elsewhere. 'The great difficulty in all cases of this kind', reflected Elgin in a letter to the governor,

must be the responsibility of making people at home realise the position in the Colony – and making people in the Colony appreciate the feeling – sometimes intense, though quite possibly not sufficiently informed – which prevails at home.[2]

He was sorry to see so much comment in Natal on the supposed indifference of the British government to the troubles of the colonists; the governor must understand that they were not indifferent.

There always have been, and always will be, men in public life

---

[1] EP, E to WSC 6 Oct 06 (photocopy). Churchill described the chief difficulty in Natal as one of preventing 'our colonists (*who so thoroughly understand native war*) from killing too many of them' (EP to E 14 Sep 06).

[2] EP, E to McCallum 5 May 06 (copy). Selborne also protested at the apparent interference of H.M.G. (EP to E 7 May 06).

who dislike military operations – especially against natives – so much, that they cannot do justice to the real peril of the situation. But I cannot conceive that responsible men in the Colony can have believed that H.M.G. took this view: I am sure nothing was said to justify such a suspicion. So far as I am concerned, I think I had perhaps more right to complain than to excuse myself. But you are well aware that my sympathy was with you throughout.[1]

As a result of the prolonged disturbances in Zululand, by the end of 1906 the Natal government had some 4000 prisoners on its hands, and decided to seek the co-operation of the British government in deporting twenty-five ringleaders. The Natal government were in a serious difficulty. Their request put the British government in a dilemma. Elgin decided to give some confidential indication to the governor for his own guidance, while avoiding any appearance of interfering with Natal ministers' discretion. It seemed to Elgin that the obvious solution was the further reduction of the number of prisoners by exercise of clemency. He had a rooted objection to employing these prisoners in mines.[2]

At the beginning of 1907 Elgin decided to keep imperial troops in Natal for several months more, calculating that their presence put the Natal government under an obligation which might be used as a lever for the exercise of a restraining influence upon treatment of Africans.[3]

Churchill was all for using this leverage, or any other, to make help in disposing of prisoners conditional. If the Natal ministers did not care for the conditions, he minuted, 'they can dispense with our assistance. We cannot help unless we also mitigate.'[4] Elgin had expressed himself in favour of the deportation of the twenty-five ringleaders on the assumption that deportation would 'approach somewhat to political exile'. But under the law as it stood, no modification of sentence was possible. Elgin did not expect to help the governor much:

[1] Ibid. 24 Sep 06.
[2] EP, minute by E on proposed private tel. to McCallum 7 Oct 06.
[3] CO. 179/237/47159, 1 Jan 07.   [4] CO. 179/240/1138, 16 Jan 07.

there being a good deal of feeling here on the subject of the sentences of these prisoners, there would, we think, be strong objection to their being enforced outside your jurisdiction. . . . Of course a reduction in the number of prisoners would be your most effective argument, but I do not urge that against your anticipation of renewed trouble.

He knew well from his Indian experience, he added, how important it was to remove former leaders of disturbance to a reasonable distance. Hence he sympathised with the governor's anxiety about these twenty-five men.[1] But he could not recall the government of India encumbering itself with 4000 inferior prisoners.[2]

Elgin took the question before the cabinet on 13 February. He was asked then to submit a memorandum to clarify the position.[3] He had to explain that there were about 4000 prisoners under court martial convictions, made fully legal and unimpeachable by an indemnity act to which the secretary of state consented in October 1906. There was no prison accommodation in Natal for so great a crowd. The secretary of state had already objected to a proposal to deport the ringleaders on court martial sentences to the Seychelles, because it would require special legislation. He had refused to employ some 2000 rank-and-file prisoners on the Premier diamond mine, because the Transvaal was a Crown Colony still, and so the secretary of state would make himself directly responsible for an arrangement whereby prisoners were employed for profit by a private undertaking. He had also refused to employ them on Singapore harbour works, because these were not going to start for some time and would eventually be executed by contract. The objection to deportation to a foreign state such as Mozambique was insuperable. The only possibility seemed to be the transfer of twenty-five ringleaders to Mauritius under the Colonial Prisoners' Removal Act of 1884. Transfer to Mauritius would 'impress the native mind'. The difficulty here was that the Natal government were not prepared to ameliorate

[1] EP, E to McCallum 15 Feb 07 (copy).   [2] Ibid. 22 Feb 07.
[3] CO. 167/778/4787, minute 13 Feb 07.

their lot considerably, and to treat them as political prisoners, as Elgin thought proper, especially in view of the health risk in sending them to a strange land. The Natal government maintained that such conditions would have a deplorable effect in the colony. The question before the cabinet, then, was: could the Natal government be assisted as they wished to be – in carrying out legalised sentences which the British government had accepted?[1]

The cabinet confirmed the desirability of removing ring-leaders, but viewed the arrest of so large a number as 4000 as a mistaken policy, which had the effect of turning many people in England against Natal. Elgin wrote to the governor:

> while we have done all we could to prevent interference with the functions of your ministers, your ministers have, I imagine, no idea how greatly we are hampered in maintaining the sympathetic attitude, which is our first object, by the feelings, not altogether unnatural, excited by this crowd of prisoners.

He explained that any qualifications to British assistance were not reflections upon the Natal ministers, but 'were necessary to satisfy public opinion here that we were not unmindful of what would be required of *us* in respect of the treatment of prisoners removed from your jurisdiction'.[2] In his official telegram on the subject, Elgin explained that although they would have preferred to deal with the ringleaders as political prisoners under a special act, deportation would not be refused, in view of the urgent representations made by the Natal government. The basic qualification to British assistance was that punishment should not be made more severe than it would be for political prisoners, for, in the opinion of the British government 'the fact of banishment justifies such amelioration of conditions as is consistent with safe custody'.[3]

Churchill was not at all happy about this policy, and opposed the principle of deportation. He would have preferred not to have accepted charge of the prisoners, for it seemed to him that

---

[1] Cab. memo. by E, 'Natal Rebel Prisoners', 19 Feb 07 (CAB. 37/87/20; EP).
[2] EP, E to McCallum 22 Feb 07.   [3] CO. 179/240, 22 Feb 07.

Britain assumed responsibility for Natal methods of native administration by undertaking deportation – an interpretation which Elgin denied.[1] Churchill wrote:

At present we may say 'Natal is a responsible self-governing colony. We cannot interfere'. It is not a good defence, but it stands a lot of battering. We are now asked to leave that shelter and to accept a measure of direct responsibility for a system which keeps nearly 4,000 rebels in penal servitude.

Again and again he repeated his disagreement with the policy: 'We should take no responsibility unless we can plead a sensible amelioration.'[2] Members of parliament, he predicted, would be bound to express repugnance at Natal methods. This, he thought, would be only natural. There was nothing to be done, 'but to await some better disposition on the part of Natal'.[3] When the cabinet did not share his view, although Elgin mentioned it as Winston requested, Churchill became really peevish. He would not even suggest a draft answer to a parliamentary question on the subject, petulantly minuting that his share in the business would be limited to reading out on the authority of the secretary of state any answer he might give.[4] Churchill was convinced that the dangers of rebellion had passed.[5] Some months later, Churchill objected to a remark made by the Natal ministry. Elgin agreed that it was foolish and improper, and he was prepared to ask the governor to point this out. But he would follow Churchill no further. Surely, he asked him, 'you do not want another "incident"?'[6]

As far as the critical question of the prisoners was concerned, Elgin would not bluntly refuse to help the Natal government, because they would undoubtedly feel deserted by the imperial government, and would not conceal their opinion. 'They will therefore take the measures they think necessary without consulting us – those measures will probably be more severe even than before – and our difficulties with critics in this

[1] CO. 179/241/18285, minutes 25 May.
[2] CO. 167/778/2786, minutes 30 Jan and 1 Feb 07.
[3] Ibid. 4787, 11 Feb 07.   [4] CO. 179/243/19829.
[5] Ibid. 9424 and 20047.   [6] EP, E to WSC 2 Jun 07 (photocopy).

250

country will be increased, not diminished.' Whereas, if the Liberal government secured more favoured treatment for the twenty-five rebels in Mauritius, this would not only be all to the good in itself, but would strengthen the British position with the Natal government.[1] Clearly Elgin stood by the principle of non-interference far more staunchly than Churchill. For instance, in June 1907, representations were made to the British government that a magistrate had inflicted an illegal and unjust fine on an African for a pass law offence. Churchill wanted to intervene, 'to bring this wretched Colony – the hooligan of the British Empire – to its senses'. Elgin dissented: 'The Colony has the right of self-government, and the responsibilities attaching thereto – and I sincerely hope we shall respect that position.'[2] To Churchill the 'disgusting butchery of natives',[3] and what he conceived to be miscarriages of justice, revealed 'the kind of tyranny against which these unfortunate Zulus have been struggling'. Elgin's view was more sympathetic to the Natal government,[4] 'where there are small white communities in the midst of large coloured populations, the former are liable to panics, and the vindictiveness which accompanies panics. But that does not mean that the Government is tyrannous.' Churchill and Elgin were, however, united in their efforts to secure a reduction both in the number of prisoners and in the severity of their sentences.

These prisoners were sent to St Helena instead of Mauritius because of an outbreak of beri-beri in Mauritius. Once they were there, Churchill insisted on checking their diet, as the House of Commons had been definitely informed that it would be on a 'liberal scale'. An inspection of the proposed dietary scale led him to denounce it as more 'suited to the lowest animals than men'. Elgin wondered whether this was the correct interpretation of the dietary. He made a brief comment: 'Nothing is more misleading than to apply a scale of diet, understood and accepted here, to the circumstances and con-

[1] CO. 179/243/2605, minutes 22 Jan 07.
[2] Ibid. 21853, minutes 27 and 28 Jun 07.
[3] CO. 179/241/18285, minute 25 May 07.   [4] Ibid. 20385, minutes 18 Jun 07.

ditions of natives of other lands.' But he was ready to deal further with the problem of sickness among the prisoners if a satisfactory telegraphic explanation was not forthcoming from the governor of St Helena.[1] The reply did seem to him to contain unfortunate expressions, certainly indicating that the governor had not properly appreciated the position. Although the prisoners had been deported as convicts, Elgin wished them in practice to be treated as political prisoners, and had declared in parliament his intention that they should be treated leniently. If time had permitted he would have secured the passage of colonial legislation to effect this. Having now read the report of the Natal Native Affairs Commission, he felt still more doubt than before 'as to the abstract justice of these sentences', and felt fully justified in giving directions for any amelioration of their lot that could be made without inconvenience. After all, they were 'chiefs among their own people'. He explained to the governor that it was an open secret that the British government did not approve of the methods adopted by the Natal government. One of the reasons for sending the prisoners to St Helena was the fact that it did not boast a convict prison. Their treatment should approach as nearly as might be to that of political prisoners. This did not mean giving them the right to ask for anything and everything, but the governor should let them have what they were accustomed to use.[2]

Churchill had written to Elgin on 1 September 1907:

I wrote a sour minute on Galloway's despatch about the Zulu prisoners in St Helena; but knowing your views in these matters, I have had it pasted all over.

I do not like his tone at all. It is quite clear he has no sympathy with these unfortunate men. We seem to have the spirit of Sir Hudson Lowe revived again in a most petty and prosaic form over these dusky captives. I do not look upon them as murderers, although no doubt that is their legal status.

Churchill's interest in prison reform can be seen emerging here:

[1] CO. 247/168/26220, minutes 24 and 25 Jul 07.
[2] CO. 247/168/30435, minute by E 16 Sep 07; E to govr, private 17 Sep 07 (copy).

After an allotted daily task – they should be able to cultivate their own vegetable patch, or taught to make baskets or carve wood or make shoes – and allowed to sell them.[1]

The Natal question now moved into a third phase. In the initial phase the Liberal government had been attacked in the colonies and by the Unionist Opposition for having interfered too much. In the second and more vigorous phase of the troubles after 4 April 1906 it was attacked by the radicals for not interfering enough. This criticism was maintained in the third phase during which Natal again became a major preoccupation of the Liberal ministers. 'Loyal' Zulu chiefs were murdered in the summer of 1907. Towards the middle of September 1907, the Natal ministry decided that the Zulu chief and government *induna*, Dinizulu,[2] must attend an inquiry. They wanted the concurrence and the co-operation, in the shape of support by imperial troops, of the British government in taking the necessary steps. Therefore, they invited the opinion of the colonial secretary on the evidence for charging Dinizulu with complicity in the disturbances. The demand was unexpected, and it had a certain curiosity. In his last letter as governor, McCallum described Dinizulu and the rebels as 'flattened out'. His successor was Sir Matthew Nathan, whose first telegram described the situation as so menacing that Dinizulu's probable deportation was imminent; an inquiry was to be held. The point for immediate decision was whether the British government would agree to a movement of imperial troops to Eshowe to overawe Dinizulu. So far not a man had been moved. It was just the sort of issue which would have come before the cabinet had parliament been sitting. As it was, Elgin would not decide without reference at least to Haldane and the prime minister. Elgin's first instinct was to demand fuller information. Simultaneously, Elgin received the report of the Native Affairs Commission, which he discovered condemned the Natal native administration 'from beginning to end'. He recalled Churchill's

<hr />

[1] EP, WSC to E 1 Sep 07.
[2] For some details see E. A. Walker, *W. P. Schreiner* (1937), pp. 272–303.

continual criticism, for which he could not have wished a more striking illustration. It showed that the ineptitude had gone further than Elgin had imagined. But he would not depart from his fundamental proposition that in 'the relative positions of white and black, such things must happen'.[1]

After his experience of the previous year, Elgin hesitated to interfere with the course proposed in Natal. As his view was invited, however, he thought they could scarcely complain if he, in reply, pointed out the undoubted fact that public opinion in Britain would certainly demand the redress of grievances, to accompany, even if it could not supersede, the repression of disloyalty.[2] The colonial office opinion, and Elgin agreed with it, was that the evidence against Dinizulu was of a very indifferent character, and inconclusive. Having looked through the mass of papers before him, Elgin was left with the impression that the evidence on which to found an accusation of high treason was very weak. As to the chief charge, 'the harbouring of rebels',

the rebellion was put down with a heavy hand – thousands were punished severely – and it can scarcely be matter of surprise that any others who may have been conscious of complicity did not dare to return to their ordinary life. I do not defend the action of D. if he drilled these men, though if I was right in my reading of the evidence above, this came voluntarily to an end. And if the Natal Government was blameless, their right to complain would be indisputable. But who can say that after reading the report of their own Commission?

All that could be distilled from the narrative of events was 'a certain amount of suspicion of hopes or fears which might, unless discreetly handled, result in desperate enterprises'. Such views he would not himself express in public, though he expected others to do so, even men of moderate opinion.[3]

His official reply of 14 October was very carefully prepared and redrafted. It constitutes a most important policy statement.

[1] EP, E to WSC 25 Sep 07 (photocopy).
[2] CO. 179/241/32533, minute 28 Sep 07.
[3] African (S) 887, 'Alleged disaffection of Dinizulu', minute by E 28 Sep 07 (EP).

The chief criticism was that consideration by the colonial government of the report of the Natal Native Affairs Commission was entirely set aside or postponed. This official reply also expressed the opinion that the evidence against Dinizulu was weak. It declared that the British government could not become parties to a policy of police inquiry, behind closed doors, into questions of Dinizulu's conduct and complicity in the later rising, followed by further repression. On the other hand, Britain was prepared

to concur in the policy of [an open] inquiry, and, if necessary, to move the troops as desired, if the inquiry is to be into the best means of securing the peace of the country, including the redress of grievances, and if the Natal government will pledge itself to do its best in consultation with H.M.G. to carry out the reforms

– reforms recommended, that is, by the Native Affairs Commission.[1]

The telegram was approved in draft by Campbell-Bannerman, Grey, Haldane and Asquith. Haldane in particular, felt very strongly that it was monstrous of Natal to ask the imperial government to commit itself to the consequences of sending troops, without a careful and impartial inquiry. Haldane entirely agreed with the course Elgin proposed.[2] Thus fortified, Elgin sent off his reply, accompanied by a private letter to the governor, in which he stressed the hope that the Natal government would make the recommendations of the commission the basis of its policy. He thought this would be a very strong position to take up. 'I can honestly say that I would far rather approve and support a strong and benevolent policy initiated by the Natal government, than forward any criticism or suggestions from this country.'[3] In view of events in the last rising, it was 'essential to show there was a policy we could not support'. The governor and he must try to achieve as much

[1] CO. 179/241/32533, tel. 14 Oct 07.
[2] EP, Haldane to E 7 Oct, Asquith to E 7 Oct, Grey to E 8 Oct, CB to E 12 Oct 07. Churchill recommended driving 'a hard bargain' (EP, 4 Oct 07).
[3] EP, E to Nathan 14 Oct 07.

agreement as possible out of the opposite tendencies of the home and colonial governments.[1]

Elgin felt that the Natal case really raised the general question of policy towards Africans in South Africa, and demonstrated the difficulty of giving effect to the policy of the British government. The 'really effective reason why Natal should consult us at all,' he wrote, 'instead of rejecting our counsel, as on the last occasion, is that she knows she cannot stand alone'. It might not be necessary to use imperial troops in any active operations, any more than last year:

But their presence in the Colony is represented, legitimately enough, to count for a great deal, and I may add that it was for that reason that I so strongly desired not to lose the opportunity of clearly indicating certain directions in which we could not support the native policy proposed by the Natal Government.[2]

As a result of the declaration of policy by the Liberal government on 14 October 1907, the Natal government decided to withdraw the appeal for imperial assistance, and to proceed against Dinizulu on its own account. Consequently, the governor was informed on 2 December that the determination of the policy rested entirely with the Natal ministers; the British government could not interfere.

Martial law was again proclaimed on 3 December. Elgin commented privately: 'This wretched Natal Government is on its hind legs again after all! Still I am glad to have stated my view of the matter.'[3] This reveals a much less sympathetic attitude than he had adopted a year earlier. The Natal government elected to take its own line in spite of carefully enunciated British policy. It was now very difficult to conceal the very grave difference of policy between the two governments. At the direction of the cabinet on 6 December the secretary of state telegraphed to the governor, asking to be kept informed by private and personal telegrams of the position of the troops and of all matters of importance from day to day, because there was 'grave anxiety here as to situation'.[4]

[1] EP, E to Nathan 31 Oct 07 (précis).   [2] EP, cab. memo. 13 Oct 07.
[3] GP. 52, E to Grey 4 Dec 07.   [4] CAB. 37/88/111.

Loreburn, the lord chancellor, was appalled by what he called the

> dreadful alacrity with which the Natal government seems disposed to proclaim martial law. . . . It revolts me to note the ferocity (for really it is that), which seems to see nothing out of the way in using this weapon,

which he thought the 'most deadly and dangerous one' which could be used in the colonies, one which had done much to lose Britain the American colonies and to estrange affection in Cape Colony.[1] It was really no law at all, exercised by men totally inexperienced and often totally incapable of the judicial function. Greatly dissatisfied by its continuation, Loreburn wrote again a month later, stressing the 'wholly indefensible' conduct of Natal in professing 'to resent interference, if we, who are the people really to pay if a great war comes, so much as remonstrate.'[2]

On 6 December the governor had requested mitigation of the effect of the telegram of 2 December by a statement that the secretary of state fully sympathised with the colony in its desire to restore order, and in its expressed intention generally to put native affairs on a more satisfactory footing. The reaction to this request shows the intensity of feeling which had been generated against Natal. The permanent under-secretary, Sir Francis Hopwood, had no confidence in the Natal government and could not give them 'any testimonial, express or implied'. Elgin was convinced that if he sent an official reply such as the governor wanted, he might as well submit his own resignation at the same time.[3] However, in a private letter to Nathan, he excused himself by explaining that he did not possess the information which would justify expressing satisfaction with the methods adopted. Proceedings against Dinizulu under martial law would be 'unjust and impolitic'. Elgin added an assurance that he would do anything to help the governor that did

---

[1] EP, Loreburn to E 14 Dec 07. [2] Ibid. 10 Jan 08.

[3] CO. 179/242/42826, minutes 7 and 8 Dec 07. Hopwood to E 15 Sep 07: 'My confidence in the Natal government is small, not because they are bent on mischief, but because their fears govern their judgment' (EP).

not conflict with his own duty to the imperial government.[1]

Elgin despatched a strongly worded confidential telegram shortly after Christmas:

I consider that it is unjustifiable to maintain martial law for the purpose of arresting criminals and searching for arms. Martial law ought never to be extended to any district where there is not armed resistance to the authority of the Crown, which cannot be dealt with by the military, acting merely in aid of the civil power in the ordinary manner. It is at least doubtful whether on the present occasion this condition has obtained anywhere, but it certainly disappeared with the demobilisation of the military forces, and I had confidently expected that martial law had now been withdrawn.

He added a personal annexure: 'It is necessary that I should record this opinion, as there is strong feeling here, which I myself share, and which will find expression when parliament meets.'[2]

Although Elgin hoped that a first-rate lawyer would be appointed by the governor as paramount chief to defend Dinizulu, who had given himself up on 9 December and was now in custody, he realised that there could be no overt pressure from London to achieve this.[3] Towards the end of January 1908 he learned that Natal ministers considered it necessary to suspend Dinizulu's salary as an *induna*, pending the result of his trial.[4] Elgin regretted this: 'if we could detect any deviation from ordinary practice in the Colony, I should be inclined to draw attention to it at once.'[5] The chief object seemed to be to create a prejudice against Dinizulu. Fair dealing would be demonstrated by having outside personnel at the trial. Dinizulu should be defended by a lawyer of weight and recognised standing, preferably from outside Natal, such as Schreiner.[6] The governor was also told that the withdrawal of the salary was unacceptable in Whitehall. Dinizulu must be assumed to

---

[1] CO. 179/243/43231, 9 Dec 07.   [2] EP, E to Nathan tel. 27 Dec 07.
[3] CO. 179/243/44700, minute 24 Dec 07.
[4] CO. 179/244/3373, govr to S/S tel. 28 Jan 08.
[5] Ibid. minute 5 Feb.   [6] EP, E to Nathan 14 Feb 08 (copy).

be innocent until proved guilty. It was reasonable, politic and a most important factor in giving him a fair trial to leave him in possession of means to pay the heavy costs of adequate defence.[1] The British government regarded it as a matter of highest importance, not only in Dinizulu's interest, but in that of Natal, to secure for him from the outset the support of the best legal assistance in South Africa.[2] They felt directly responsible for the procedure adopted in the trial: the obligation was 'one of honour'.[3]

The Natal ministers suspended the salary without the assent of the secretary of state. At this point in the story, Crewe succeeded Elgin as colonial secretary. Crewe protested at the Natal attitude, deciding that the British government must be prepared to pay the arrears of salary, though not the full charge of his defence.[4] Asquith had agreed in February 1908 that, if necessary, the treasury should make a payment.[5] The decision to pay arrears from imperial funds was announced in the House of Commons on 21 July 1908. The government's motive was to terminate a situation which, besides being detrimental to the interests of the prisoner, whose resources were almost exhausted, tended to prolong the 'unfortunate and embarrassing conflict of opinion between H.M.G. and the government of Natal'.[6] This conflict threatened to be publicly canvassed in a court of law because Dinizulu's solicitors in England threatened action against the British government as co-guarantors for payment of the salary.[7] Thereupon, the Natal ministers, in effect, climbed down, by announcing their willingness to provide a sum of money to assist Dinizulu in his defence.[8] The British govern-

[1] CO. 179/244/5256, S/S to govr 15 Feb 08.

[2] Ibid. 5489, S/S to govr tel. 15 Feb 08.

[3] CO. 179/249/6243, S/S to govr tel. 20 Feb 08: 'I must remind you that not only in virtue of the conditions of Dinizulu's return to South Africa, but from the fact that it was through this Office that Mr Colenso's message inviting him to surrender peaceably on promise of a fair trial was conveyed, H.M.G. are directly responsible for the procedure adopted in the trial. The obligation is therefore one of honour.'

[4] CO. 179/245/19129, S/S to govr 30 May 08.

[5] CO. 179/244/4584.

[6] CO. 179/249/25750.

[7] CO. 179/246/26523 S/S to govr 23 Jul.

[8] Ibid. 27925, govr to S/S 31 Jul 08.

ment therefore no longer expected to pay the arrears of salary.

However, in October 1908, Dinizulu's friends reckoned that even with £500 from the Natal government, and funds raised privately, he would still need more money. The governor was asked to enquire whether his ministers would object to the British government's undertaking to ask parliament to pay up to £1000. Professing that there was no wish to embarrass the Natal ministers, the British government was anxious not to make such application without their concurrence.[1] There appeared to be no prospect of obtaining sufficient funds except from one of the two governments.[2] It was eventually arranged that Schreiner, the defence counsel, should be paid by the British government through the Natal government at the end of the trial. To avoid the possibility of the Africans' interpreting this as imperial sympathy for Dinizulu, the arrangement was, rather quaintly, not to be made public until the time of payment of the fee. But Liberal ministers refused to accept a further condition that they would not entertain an application for funds beyond 2000 guineas, because they were committed to the principle that the trial should not break down for lack of funds. The understanding between the two governments had therefore to be subject to this central consideration.[3] In fact the British government paid only the 2000 guineas. The defence did not at any moment break down, though this was owing partly to the generosity of Miss Colenso.

In April 1909 the Liberal government accepted the sentence of four years imprisonment and a fine of £100 against Dinizulu for harbouring rebels, and agreed that he had forfeited the position of government *induna*. Crewe gave his consent to the withdrawal of this position with a qualification: 'I wish to place it on record, that I take it for granted that when the time comes, suitable provision will be made for his maintenance.'[4]

How are we to sum up relations with the self-governing colony of Natal? Though the early declarations and actions of

---

[1] CO. 179/249/36597, S/S to govr tel. 6 Oct 08.   [2] CO. 179/247/36857.
[3] CO. 179/248/42226, S/S to govr tel. 21 Nov 08.
[4] CO. 179/252/10761, S/S to govr 7 Apr 09.

the Liberal government lent some justification to Unionist fears of undue interference, critics of the government were probably wrong to interpret the telegram of 28 March 1906 as evidence of a vicious determination to interfere, maybe with the desire to reverse the decision of the Natal government. The limits of Elgin's claim to intervene seem to have been reached with information full enough to tender useful advice. At any rate, it seems that in Natal, Elgin had to concede more than any previous colonial secretary to the principle of non-interference.[1] Ministers won their point against the British government in April 1906; though they were less successful in the second round, they had already virtually succeeded in getting it laid down that they, and indeed they alone, were responsible for the conduct of native policy. Throughout, the Liberal government had, in the last resort, power to enforce their views, because the Natal government depended on them for imperial troops. The Liberals did not use the leverage thus given them in any way which was unfair to the Natal government, despite the in-defensible readiness of the latter to rely on imperial aid whilst turning a deaf ear to imperial advice. Natal was handled with remarkable tolerance.

An understanding of the Liberal attitude towards events in Natal helps to explain much of British policy in South Africa in this period. The effect of the Natal situation on attempts to secure protection for African interests in the new constitutions has already been noted.[2] The Natal government completely lost the confidence of every British civil servant and minister, and outraged every liberal sentiment. Natal was a continuous source of serious anxiety. The most serious and blatant failure of the Natal government was in its treatment of Africans. As Elgin said, their own Native Affairs Commission report con-demned the government 'root and branch'.[3] But in other ways

[1] CO. 179/248/43579, minute 8 Dec 08; Lambert argued that for all essential purposes Elgin abandoned the instructions of Lord Knutsford to the governor in 1892, to the effect that 'The ultimate decision in every case, however, rests with the governor' – a principle which he admitted, however, Britain had never succeeded in living up to.

[2] See p. 164.   [3] GP. 52, E to Grey 5 Oct 07.

too, the government was found wanting. Its treatment of Asiatic immigrants was intolerant. In 1906 Natal proposed to withdraw from the customs union in South Africa, thereby hoping to force the inland colonies to approve an increase in tariff. It assumed a generally obstructive attitude in the South African railway rates disputes, an attitude Elgin found so impracticable he did not see what suggestion could be made.[1] When discussions for federation were begun, there was widespread irritation at the parish-pump views of Natal.[2] As early as April 1906, Churchill publicly ventured the opinion that the enormous liberties and responsibilities of self-government were perhaps too light-heartedly confided to a small white community.[3] Selborne felt privately that responsible government was being made 'simply ridiculous' there.[4] Officials believed that the only solution to the problem of Natal was to submerge this 'weak spot' in South Africa into the wider form of federation. Experience with Natal thus quickened and confirmed the British desire for closer union in South Africa.[5]

TRANSVAAL: NATIVE AND ASIATIC POLICIES OF THE NEW GOVERNMENT

The first elections under responsible government were held in the Transvaal on 20 February 1907. Thereafter, the Liberals tried to help General Botha's ministry, based on an overall majority of five, all they could. The cabinet agreed to the request for an imperial guarantee on a loan of £5 million to establish a Land Bank, rehabilitate farmers and build railways, proposals which, while generally speaking for the benfit of the Boers, were not thought unreasonable in themselves. An imperial

---

[1] CO. 179/237/35825; on railway disputes, see Thompson, *Unification of S. Africa*, pp. 55–60.

[2] EP, Hely-Hutchinson to E 10 May 08. [3] PD. 155/268, 2 Apr 06.

[4] EP, to E 18 Jan 07. Natal experience confirmed Selborne in his belief that parliamentary government was the worst possible form for unrepresented Africans, that Orange River Colony ought not be given responsible government, and that Swaziland ought not to be handed over to the Transvaal (EP, to E 27 Aug 07).

[5] See p. 283.

guarantee would release the new government from dependence on the gold-mining capitalists.[1] There was a remarkable episode when, in May 1907, a detachment of imperial forces helped bring a Rand strike under control.[2] The Liberals accepted a request for help in bringing an amendment to the Arms and Ammunition Ordinance into operation, Elgin putting in a caveat to the effect that 'though under the special circumstances of this year we have desired to assist the Transvaal government, the general practice must follow the strict rule'.[3] They refused to be moved by Selborne's complaints about retrenchments in the civil service, or by his plea that the colonial office should find alternative employment for the men who were axed. Elgin was not unsympathetic towards these men, but he declined

to stand in a white sheet on their account. These retrenchments are the result of a reckless policy in the past, which induced men to abandon prospects elsewhere by extraordinary promises . . . the new governments of the colonies have not been ungenerous in their dealing with these cases: and I am not inclined to share in any outcry that would throw a slur upon their action.[4]

Policy towards non-Europeans is the most important aspect of Liberal relations with the new government. Chinese Labour has already been dealt with.[5] Three other aspects of the whole question came before the Liberal government: Botha's request for the transfer of Swaziland, legislation about native administration, and legislation concerning Asiatic immigrants.

Botha was very anxious for the re-incorporation of Swaziland. The Liberals did not doubt that ultimately it would have to come under the Transvaal government. Churchill did not think that such a transfer could be proposed to the present House of Commons without exciting a great deal of disappointment.

[1] African (S) 880, memo. by Churchill 28 Apr 07; EP, typed memo. by Elgin, 30 Apr 07. It was wrongly suspected by the Opposition that the loan was a bribe to get rid of Chinese labour.
[2] CO. 291/117/18380.
[3] CO. 291/119/29161, minute 17 Aug 07.
[4] CO. 291/135/5247, minute 19 Feb 08.   [5] See pp. 89 ff.

Time may however promote a more assured confidence in the character and policy of the new Transvaal government; and if they were found in the course of the next year or two to be administering native affairs with success, and carrying out a faithful and enlightened policy in regard to the supply of native, Indian and Chinese labour, many of the doubts which are now legitimately entertained, would perhaps be removed.[1]

The matter was discussed with Botha while he was in London for the colonial conference, and considered by the cabinet. Afterwards, Elgin wrote to explain to Botha that some of his requests, especially the more important ones concerning Africans and the Chinese, involved modification of the letters patent, a fact which raised great difficulties:

it seems to me that it would be the height of imprudence for us at this moment, while your government is still, if I may say so, only settling into your places, to initiate a process of revision, which I fear might easily prove to be infectious, and if so, could not fail to be dangerous.

It had been impossible in framing the constitution to ignore the native question, in which many people in Britain took a lively interest, and it was decided that the reservation of Swaziland

was necessary to meet the necessities of the case. We are not prepared at this early date to abandon a proposal which certainly was generally approved here, especially in view of the settlement of the concessionaires and natives which is in progress. I do not mean to say that the arrangement cannot be altered on cause shown, and the time may come when it might be possible to reconsider the matter.

In the meantime the Liberal government would wish to co-operate in any measure for improving the general condition of the country, such as the development of railways.[2]

---

[1] African (S) 880. Swaziland had been a protectorate of the South African Republic for four years before the outbreak of the Boer War. At one time in 1906 Botha was saying that if Swaziland were separated from the Transvaal, his party would take no part in the Constitution (*Selections from the Smuts Papers*, ii, 307).

[2] EP, E to Botha 4 May 07; see also EP, E to Selb. 4 May 07. See below pp. 381 ff.

In August 1907 Botha's ministry set about reconsidering the administration of justice among Africans, defining more clearly the powers of persons concerned, from white paramount chief to Bantu chiefs. They proposed to substitute the governor-in-council for governor in all matters of native administration. This was contrary to the letters patent, for as Elgin remarked, 'I meant, and H.M.G. meant, to retain the control in the hands of the Governor. Nor do I yet think that we were wrong.'[1] However, he instructed a thorough consideration of the whole native problem in the office, and planned to submit a statement of views for the consideration of the cabinet.[2] Then on 20 March 1908 he wrote to ask Selborne if it would be possible to postpone the re-introduction of the bill on this subject in the Transvaal Assembly.

It would be difficult to imagine a moment when the obstacles to a general agreement could be more numerous or more serious than the present. The proceedings (I hesitate to say trial) of Dinizulu must prejudice any consideration of the native question in Natal.

I read some of the election proceedings in the Cape to mean that many candidates there are afraid of losing native support, and at any rate 'speak' accordingly.

And in the Transvaal, whatever may be the case in the [Orange River] Colony, I am afraid that, until the Chinese are definitely a thing of the past, any native question will be apt to be distorted in the House of Commons.[3]

Asiatic Legislation. The Indian problem is of special interest. Not only were two of the leading members of the British government, Ripon and Elgin, ex-viceroys who had looked at the problem from India as well as from England, but the question provided the most rigorous test of the sincerity of the Liberal grant of self-government to the Transvaal.

British governments had always disliked the restrictive legislation of the Transvaal on Asiatic immigration, but were pledged to maintain the *status quo* of the South African Republic

[1] CO. 291/119/32934, minute 24 Sep 07. [2] See p. 368.
[3] EP, copy.

until a responsible government could decide a matter of such fundamental importance. On the very eve of responsible government, Selborne and the Crown Colony government proposed fresh legislation to close the Transvaal to new Indian immigrants, and to compel registration of all resident Asiatics, in order to clear out those deemed illegally resident. Churchill's reaction was: 'The new [Transvaal] parliament may shoulder the burden. Why should we? Dawdle or disallow – preferably the former.'[1] Elgin was led to understand that the passage of a new ordinance before the advent of responsible government would be an advantage to Asiatics, as it would give them practically an indefeasible vested right. Selborne's intention apparently was not to prejudice the position of British Indians legally qualified for residence. Elgin did not feel he could raise objections except in so far as existing rights might be inadequately safeguarded. The legislation was in accordance with Lyttelton's policy of July 1904, that whilst the colony might restrict the influx of Asiatics, the rights of those already there should be respected.[2] Elgin felt bound to maintain this policy. He insisted that Britain should not waste effort in trying to obtain unrestricted immigration. Much as they might regret it, there was nothing that could be done if the colony was determined to keep Indians out.

The Indians agitated violently against this Asiatic Law Amendment Ordinance, which they called the 'Black Ordinance', on account of its stringent penalties. Elgin received a deputation (led by Gandhi) on 8 November 1906. He made to the deputation what he described as 'really a deliberate defence' of Selborne's action, because he thought the agitation ill-advised; he was inclined to think that the Indians might fare worse under a responsible government. But he came unwillingly to the conclusion that the opposition was too strong for him to sanction the proposals of the Crown Colony government.[3] As the Indians contended that it actually aggravated their disabilities, and as the Liberals felt bound to maintain the

[1] CO. 291/103/39670, minute 4 Nov 06.
[2] CO. 291/105/42335, memo. by Just 7 Nov 06.   [3] EP, E to Selb. 24 Nov 06.

policy of their predecessors in this matter, the government believed that they could have allowed the ordinance to be brought into operation only if it had been 'a pressing matter of practical expediency at the present time'.[1] Elgin explained to Selborne how he had originally accepted the draft proposals in July on the understanding that they would improve the position of resident Asiatics, 'not indeed to the extent which I would have desired, but in an appreciable degree'.[2] Selborne was embarrassed by the decision to disallow. Elgin repeated his belief that he had no alternative:

The Ordinance passed is widely different from the drafts which I approved, and I am sure that you will realise that H.M.G. cannot of their own initiative pass legislation which is regarded rightly or wrongly by a large number of those mainly affected as aggravating the restrictions against which H.M.G. have in the past consistently protested. . . .[3]

Elgin declared in the House of Lords that he acted with great regret, because he felt sure that the intention was to 'amend rather than to harden' the position of the Indians; in some ways, he added, Indian apprehensions were surely exaggerated.[4]

Almost the first act of the new Transvaal government was to pass (with unanimous support) an ordinance which was in all essential matter identical with the ordinance disallowed in 1906. The colonial office officials were unanimously agreed that if this second ordinance was disallowed something more stringent would be passed and a deadlock ensue.[5] The British despatch

[1] CO. 291/103/39670, draft despatch to Selb. n.d.
[2] CO. 291/105, S/S to Selb. 29 Nov 06.
[3] CO. 291/105/44213, S/S to Selb. tel. 10 Dec 06.
[4] PD. 171/628, 19 Mar 07.
[5] Whilst a clerk in the colonial office, Keith, and Keith alone, had wished, under Crown Colony government, to repeal the Transvaal law of 1885. The other officials felt this would unite all white colonial opinion against Britain; moreover 'H.M.G. could not in justice stop at the Indians. The "Cape Coloured" people have far more grounds of complaint' (CO. 291/84/26270, minute by Graham 13 Mar 06). This should be borne in mind in evaluating Keith's later judgment, that Elgin ought to have taken a stand on the principle of equality for Indians (A. B. Keith, *Responsible Government in the Dominions* (1928), ii, 828).

on the subject opened with the assertion that the previous ordinance had been disallowed because of objections and because the decision of a nominated legislative council could not be taken as final. It proceeded to state a doctrine of administrative modification such as had also been employed over Chinese Labour:

H.M.G. do not consider the position of Asiatics lawfully resident in the Transvaal, as settled by this Act,[1] to be satisfactory; they . . . hope that it may be carefully considered how far practical effect can be given to [relaxing restrictions]. But they feel that they would not be justified in offering resistance to the general will of the colony, clearly expressed by its first elected representatives.

Therefore they would not disallow. At the same time Botha was asked to see if other methods of registration could be adopted in place of those the Indians regarded as degrading. 'This would be an opportune concession to Indian sentiment.'[2]

Elgin wrote privately to Botha criticising the very hasty passage of the Act, without apparently any consideration of certain amendments which he had suggested when the ordinance of the late government came before him.

I hope you will recognise in our action our determination not to create difficulties. But I believe it would be possible to remove some of our objections by modification of the regulations under the provisions of the Act, and I think I may without impropriety ask you to look into this question.[3]

Botha gave assurances that he would do his very best to mitigate the sharpness of the ordinance. These, according to Morley,[4] were the unwritten conditions of the financial favour the British government agreed to do for him, namely guaranteeing the interest on the addition of £5 million to the existing loan of £35 million which was already guaranteed by the British government.[5]

[1] The Law took effect from 1 July 1907.
[2] CO. 291/116/13940, S/S to Selb. 9 May 07.   [3] EP, E to Botha 4 May 07.
[4] J. Morley, *Recollections* (1917), ii, 214, MM. 2/100, 9 May 07.
[5] CO. 291/123/15509, E to Botha 9 May 09.

In defending government policy, on more than one occasion, Elgin argued that to have refused assent would have been 'a very serious matter indeed', and contrary to precedent. He quoted Chamberlain and Curzon in support of the attitude he had assumed.[1] 'What we really have to deal with in this question, is not the admission of Asiatics, but their fair treatment when they are in the country', which could only proceed by the legislation which the self-governing colony adopted. He even defended the Transvaal government against the charge of undue haste; there was an unauthorised and illicit influx of Asiatics which it was desirable to check quickly. He would have preferred to have seen further deliberation, and several things altered. On the other hand, he was inclined to think 'that if you argue the thing out, you come to a variety of distinctions, and this seems to me to diminish the seriousness of the objections to the regulations'. In this connection he pointed out that the Indians had not objected to thumb-mark registrations under the old ordinance, because they persuaded themselves that it was voluntary, but they objected to compulsion under the new ordinance.[2]

In general the Liberals strove hard to meet the wishes of the new Transvaal government. The Asiatic problem did not prove an exception. Elgin was in fact always consistent on this question. Even as viceroy he had never believed it would be possible to do much officially for the Indians against a self-governing determination to exclude them.[3] And in 1907, he accepted the existence (or in 1906 the imminent existence) of a fully responsible self-government as the dominant factor in the situation.

Reflecting upon these events in a letter to his friend Lord Grey, Elgin wrote:

You know South Africa so well, that I am sure you will not want any argument from me to prove how impossible it was to refuse assent to the Registration Bill in the Transvaal. In spite of all the differences of opinion on this Bill, there was unanimity

---

[1] PD. 171/630, 19 Mar 07. [2] PD. 174/1592–5, 29 May 07.
[3] VRP. 15/105, 1 Jun 97.

in the new Parliament. That I had every predisposition in favour
of the Indians – against whose treatment I had myself protested
when Viceroy, goes without saying, and I should be the last
man to deny them any privilege which is legitimately theirs in
virtue of their being British subjects. But I cannot follow the
patriots who would break down the self-government we have
ourselves given, and introduce by force into white communities,
what they unanimously regard as a dangerous and discordant
element. Surely even if we claim to have inherited the doctrine
of 'Civis Romanus sum', this is a new and unnatural development of it. And yet Ampthill, last session, thundered something
very like it across the House, and even seemed to suggest that
the fleet might be sent to Pretoria.[1]

The Transvaal Immigrants Restriction Act 1907 proposed
the total exclusion of Asiatics by reason of race. Elgin persuaded
himself that in the interests of the Asiatics themselves, it was
probably desirable that further immigration should be prevented. The only chance of making the attitude of the white
colonists towards the Asiatic residents more tolerant, seemed to
lie in a policy which would assure them that the danger of
future Asiatic immigration was no longer to be feared.[2]

The total exclusion of Asiatics was, Elgin recognised, 'an
extreme provision for which no direct precedent exists'. But
then the circumstances in the Transvaal were exceptional. 'The
really serious objection', he thought, was to form rather than
practical effect, because Asiatics were excluded by reasons of
race. This could be justified only on the ground that the hands
of the British government were tied by the previous law of the
South African Republic. This ground would have to be alleged
if any other self-governing colony desired to imitate the legislation of the Transvaal. He proposed to invite the Transvaal
government to amend only the provision which empowered the
government to expel any dangerous person, by limiting this
power to cases backed by a court conviction or confirmation.

[1] EP, E to Lord Grey 30 Dec 07 (copy). For Ampthill's remarks, see PD. 174/591
29 May 07.
[2] African (S) 891, 'The Transvaal Immigrants Restriction Act', cab. memo. by
E 14 Nov 07 (CAB. 37/88/94).

The other provisions he thought justified by exceptional circumstances, or at any rate to be such that the British government could not very well refuse to accept, in view of the unanimous opinion of the white population. To placate the India office, he tried to get the Transvaal government to give their definite assurance that Asiatics of distinguished position, and high officials, would be admitted by temporary permits.[1] Elgin's telegram commented on provisions which were 'in some respects unusual', and indicated regret that the colonial ministers had not been content to rely on an education test for the exclusion of undesirables. He stated quite explicitly his hope that the exclusion of further immigration would result in more favourable treatment of Asiatics already lawfully resident in the colony.[2]

This policy was criticised by Curzon for showing 'a strange lack of imagination'. It would be hard to refute the charge. Elgin did perhaps underestimate the significance which could be attached to matters of form, and, as Curzon had said, with his Indian experience, and 'such an excellent reputation as an administrator and friend of Indian peoples', he might have been expected to foresee rather more clearly the dimensions which this problem would reach.[3] Elgin sometimes seemed to forget how much more powerful the emotional attitudes are in politics than the rational. His tendency towards over-rationalisation is plain in his treatment of this question.

At the end of January 1908, settlement was reached on the registration of Asiatics legally resident in the Transvaal. Finger-print identification was to be used only when no other form (for example, the signatures of those who were educated, had property, or who were well known) was practicable. Elgin communicated these points to the cabinet on 29 January, commenting on the removal of the humiliating effect of the registration regulations originally proposed.[4] Elgin had indicated to the governor that it would be 'a triumph for your government' if these two points most open to attack – finger-

[1] Ibid.
[2] EP, E to govr tel. 27 Nov 07.
[3] PD. 183/669, 4 Feb 08.
[4] CAB. 41/31/39.

prints and deportation – could be settled before parliament met. All those who were in prison for non-compliance with the Act passed in 1907 were released. Elgin and Churchill were delighted. 'Few colonial governments would have shown so much consideration for imperial interests', wrote Churchill. Elgin agreed 'that we are under obligations to the Transvaal Government. They have always been willing to give courteous consideration to our representations. . . . All's well that ends well. . . .'[1] He testified to this co-operative spirit in the House of Lords. He also made some remarks relevant to the general problem of relationship with self-governing colonies:

Self-government means a devolution of responsibility, and especially the responsibility for law and order. . . . I should like to ask how small white communities can undertake to perform the duties that fall upon them in virtue of undertaking self-government if they are not allowed to have within their bounds an adequate number of white inhabitants. If that is conceded to me, I proceed to say that in the competition between the East and West, the economic forces would inevitably turn the scale in favour of the east, and thereby prevent free competition. . . .

Hence the exclusion of Asiatics, not, as Curzon had said, because of any bad qualities, but because of their good qualities:

It is their patient industry, their frugal and temperate habits, that make them such formidable competitors to the white man. . . . Surely it will be evident that if there was an influx of Asiatics that would, on account of the economic forces to which I have alluded, tend to destroy the political equilibrium which is necessary for the development of the colonies themselves.[2]

Clearly the government did not feel its obligations to Indian immigrants to be as great as to the indigenous Africans.

'All's well that ends well. . . .' Elgin had written in February 1908. The Asiatic problem did not end in 1908. True, it became

---

[1] CO. 291/125/3464, minutes 30 and 31 Jan 08.
[2] PD. 183/674–9, 4 Feb 08.

the concern of the local government rather than the imperial government, though Crewe gave considerable thought to the problem. Crewe's approach followed Elgin's closely:

The whole question is one of the greatest difficulty, not only as concerns South Africa, and I know of no subject upon which Imperial discussion is more peremptorily required. We are all obliged to admit the right of self-governing Colonies to exclude, but we are bound to see that no needless hardships are inflicted, and to make representations when we are not in a position to give orders.[1]

Crewe interviewed Gandhi in 1909. Although the Indian leader held out for full theoretical equality, Crewe considered that the Transvaal government would do well to make concessions which would remove all practical hardship, and put themselves right with a considerable section of public opinion.[2] He told the Transvaal that it would, for instance, be very reasonable to allow the admission of six professional men a year to supply the wastage which must take place in the Indian community. The Transvaal 'Black Act' was repealed in 1913. Thereafter the power of the Union to restrict immigration was based exclusively on economic and social grounds.

Crewe became increasingly disturbed by the treatment accorded the Indians. Towards the end of 1908 he doubted whether the Transvaal government was showing the consideration in small matters which he thought it generally wise to exercise.[3] By 1910 his patience was exhausted. The honeymoon period with the new government was at an end. Crewe described the Transvaal government as behaving with 'crass stupidity'. When the Transvaal government offended Indian religious scruples, Crewe directed the colonial office to make a formal complaint, 'so that they may at any rate know what we think of them'.[4]

---

[1] CO. 291/133/34983, Crewe to Ampthill 13 Sep 08.
[2] CO. 291/142/30008, minute 16 Sep 09; PD. 194/1127, Crewe 21 Oct 08.
[3] CO. 291/132/39318, minute 30 Oct 08.
[4] CO. 291/145/8735, minute 30 Mar 10.

SOME REFLECTIONS

In situations which threatened to make divergent claims upon their liberalism and their humanitarianism, the amount of protection for non-European interests given by the Liberal government was determined, less by their good intentions, or by public opinion, than by the strength of imperial administrative control in each local situation.[1] Thus the frontier line between interference and non-interference varied from place to place, and did not necessarily reflect the policy ministers would have implemented, given a free hand. Wherever they had the power, the Liberal government exerted themselves for the humanitarian policy. In general, they accepted the hard fact that the grant of self-government deprived them of such power. Assent to measures in self-governing colonies did not necessarily mean approval. Thus they did not disallow the Asiatic Ordinance in the Transvaal in 1907, although they had disallowed almost the same ordinance when it was promoted by the previous Crown Colony government of the Transvaal. Nor would the government assent to a draft Southern Rhodesia Ordinance in 1908, which, though less stringent, was modelled on the Transvaal Ordinance. The secretary of state's refusal in this case was based on the contentions that it was open to grave objection in principle, that it was likely to lead to serious complications, not least in the Transvaal, and it could not be imperatively required as there were only 900 Asiatics in the colony. Crewe refused to reconsider his decision when pressed. Opinion in the Southern Rhodesia legislative council was unanimous – but it was not self-governing, and could not therefore prevail.[2]

The Liberal government did not waste time fighting the stubborn facts of recession beyond imperial control. They made no attempt to force either Asiatics – or British settlers – on an unwilling Transvaal. They confined themselves to fulfilling

[1] See Churchill's declaration, quoted on p. 374
[2] CO. 417/452/20559 and CO. 417/454, S/S to Selb. 12 Dec 08.

their obligations of honour to Asiatics – and settlers – already established in the colony. As if to ease their consciences, they proved capable of acting with determination whenever the facts were in their favour. They would make no attempt to provide for the protection of Africans under the future Union government, but took endless time and trouble over a schedule to the Union bill to protect the future of Africans in territories remaining outside the Union. Sometimes the needs or mistakes of self-governing colonies gave an opportunity for turning facts in imperial favour. The fact that Natal was self-governing, but not wholly self-dependent, increased the possible area of imperial interference. The financial needs of the new Transvaal government made it possible to ask Botha to mitigate the practical application of the Asiatic ordinance. But in neither case was the self-governing colony pressed unduly hard. In South African policy there was a fear of uniting all white South Africa against the British government, coupled with a recurrent belief that if colonial wishes were thwarted, the result would inevitably be the substitution of even less reasonable demands.

The rights of self-government were thus firmly upheld. Liberal treatment of the Chinese Labour question exhibited a high degree of deference to the self-governing principle. All the heart-searchings during the framing of the Transvaal constitution led to the clear conclusion that grants of self-government must be in effect absolute. The Liberals justified their reconciliation to an almost axiomatic non-interference in self-governing colonies by saying that it was really in the interests of the non-European peoples. Not all the Liberal ministers reconciled themselves to the principle in equal degree. Ripon in every case held firmly to non-interference, Elgin slightly less so. Churchill would have overridden the principle before Elgin. Loreburn might have drawn a frontier line much less favourable to self-governing colonies even than Churchill's.

Elgin was convinced that having freely granted self-government to the South African colonies *as white communities*, to demand from them, or from a federation of them, better terms for the Africans by 'any peremptory interference', would be 'an arbitrary act only to be justified, if at all, by military pre-dominance'. It would almost certainly wreck federation:

But it has over and over again been evident, that a certain section of the House of Commons takes an entirely different view of the situation, and the question is whether knowledge or sentiment is to prevail.[1]

The more radical Liberal ministers seem to have differed from Ripon and Elgin. Loreburn, for instance, wrote at the time of trouble with Natal:

There are I think indications that public opinion in this country is being roused, and will support us in making it clear (as we did in Newfoundland[2] with general approbation), that we are not going to pay pipers while our colonists call tunes. This view of mine is in no sense hostile to keeping together the British Empire. On the contrary, I wish that, and believe the best way of preserving the connection is quite plain speaking on a subject, which, if not put on a just footing now, will lead us to friction and disruption.[3]

On the other hand, Loreburn was quite firmly determined that no unnecessary interference should take place. The original draft of the Transvaal Constitution contained the following clause: 'The power to suspend or remove any Civil Servant from his office shall be vested in the Governor.' Loreburn opposed this clause on the ground that it perpetuated the interference of home ministers with the administration of the colony. It was dropped.[4]

Sometimes ministers exerted themselves to make a verbal protest, 'when we are not in a position to give orders', 'so that they may at any rate know what we think of them', as Crewe put it. This technique was also applied outside South Africa – to Western Australia for example.[5]

[1] EP, E to Crewe 7 May 08 (draft). [2] See p. 289 ff.
[3] EP, Loreburn to E 10 Jan 08. [4] EP, Drafts A and B, cl. 67.
[5] CO. 418/49/12746, minutes by Hopwood and Churchill 7 and 14 Feb 07: they agreed that the government of Western Australia should be worried and

This type of treatment of the problem was eventually to lead to a declaration by Lewis Harcourt, colonial secretary 1910–15, that part of the magnificence of the British empire was the renunciation of the right of the imperial government to interfere even when the measures of the dominion governments were repugnant to its views. Tolerance and restraint alone could maintain continuing unity.[1]

At the parliamentary level, there were a number of Liberal M.P.s, usually looked upon by ministers as sentimentalists, who protested against the way in which their government was apparently allowing the frontiers of imperial control to recede further. If native policy was much to the fore in these years, some of the credit lies with these men, led by Dilke, for keeping up the pressure. All the ministers who were bothered by their parliamentary questions – Grey and Morley,[2] as well as Elgin – whilst complaining among themselves of the trouble thus caused by simple-minded and excessive zeal for non-European interests, treated them with great caution. 'In dealing with this class of critic', wrote Elgin, 'the direct denial and defiance, which is one's natural instinct, might only too probably, in many cases, defeat its own object.'[3] So long as their critics remained fair and not malicious, ministers tried to keep on good terms. They recognised that not to make some effort to conciliate them would only create further difficulties. And so it came about, that the government was sometimes forced to adopt more radical postures than perhaps it wished. Elgin had not, for example, intended to disallow the first Asiatic ordinance from the Transvaal. Nor, it may be suggested, would he have modified Chinese Labour policy as much as he did, without

---

harassed, and left in no doubt as to the opinion held in England about their conduct of native affairs. So Western Australia was asked if it was true that aboriginal prisoners were made to wear neck chains for a journey of over 300 miles.

[1] PD/HC. 63/353–78.

[2] Morley would not let 'perverse simpletons' in England 'gratify their philanthropy at the expense of India' (MM. 1/139).

[3] EP, E to Selb. 1 Jun 06, referring to critics of government policy towards Natal. See also Cromer papers, 13 (ii)/8–9, 22 and 27, Grey to Cromer.

parliamentary pressure.[1] Some of the sting, in fact, was taken out of 'anti-imperialism' by government policy.[2]

Creation of a strong federation in South Africa was desirable as a means of escape from all the residual difficulties which stemmed from the existence of small-scale or inexperienced colonial governments. The ultimate solution of the problem of the recurrent temptation to interfere in South Africa, a temptation which could sometimes be hard to resist, was, it was thought, to promote closer union and imperial disengagement.

FEDERATION: THE ULTIMATE SOLUTION?

The major long-term objective of both British parties was the withdrawal of the 'Imperial Factor' from South Africa on conditions which would safeguard British and native interests. From the very moment they took office, the Liberals kept the objective of eventual federation clearly before them. The first ministerial memorandum on the Transvaal Constitution, by Ripon, began:

It is generally held, I believe, and I entirely coincide with the opinion, that one of the best modes of bringing about a more satisfactory state of things in South Africa will be found in the establishment, at as early a date as may be possible, of a confederation of the South African colonies on the same general principles as those on which the Dominion of Canada and the Commonwealth of Australia have been founded.

Ripon was therefore very anxious that nothing should be done in framing the new constitution which might prove a hindrance

[1] The influence of public opinion was at least alleged several times to explain government policy towards Natal. The Liberal government was certainly vulnerable to attack from its critics. The principle of acting where there was power to act led to anomalous situations. It was easier to tackle the Chinese problem in Crown Colony Transvaal than the Indian problem in self-governing Natal, and so the government intervened on behalf of non-British subjects, but not on behalf of British subjects, which of course led to the criticism that they had not got their priorities straight. Similarly, they were much more lenient to a strong Afrikaner ministry in the Transvaal after 1907 than they were to a weak British ministry in Natal (see Ampthill, PD. 189/41-2).

[2] See B. Porter, 'Radical and Labour attitudes to Empire, 1896-1914' (Cambridge University Ph.D. dissertation, 1967, to be published by Macmillan).

to confederation, and recommended for example a two-chamber system because it would be more easily adapted to a federal constitution.[2] Then the Ridgeway Committee supported this view, and was confident that men could be nominated to a second chamber who would materially further the negotiations for federation.[2] Campbell-Bannerman justified the appointment of the Ridgeway Committee by the argument that as the government looked to federation, everything they did for one of the colonies they did for all, and so they must proceed with great care.[3] In deciding the form of the Orange River Colony Constitution, it was argued that it was impossible to restore the old constitution:

We must give responsible government, not only or principally because we have so promised, but because unless we do so we raise up once more the serious obstacle to the ultimate federation of the South African colonies.[4]

When the prime minister and the governor of Cape Colony proposed that the title 'Lord Mayor of Cape Town' should be granted to mark the centenary of annexation, Ommanney and Churchill supported the idea, but Elgin feared that it might prejudicially affect federation, and Selborne agreed. And so the proposal was dropped.[5] Reflecting upon the railway rates quarrel, Elgin's chief anxiety was not to disturb the joint management of railways, for once the joint management of the Central South African Railway was dissolved, 'new separate interests' would, he expected, be created, and the difficulty of unification immensely increased.[6] Nor did he welcome in 1906 a report of rapid progress in a movement to unite Natal and the Transvaal: he was

sceptical of its taking any definite shape at present – and I cannot say that I particularly desire that it should do so. It

---

[1] EP, cab. memo. 26 Dec 06.   [2] *Report*, p. 26.
[3] PD. 152/169, CB 19 Feb 06.   [4] PD. 167/945, Elgin 17 Dec 06.
[5] CO. 48/588/45850, minute 28 Dec 06; EP, Selb. to E 8 Jan 07, E to Selb. 8 Feb 07.
[6] EP, E to Selb. tel. 19 Sep 06.

seems to me that a partial federation might add seriously to the obstacles in the way of a complete federation of the South African colonies, and that the latter is so desirable from every point of view that the smaller union ought not to be encouraged.[1]

All ministers recognised that Lord Carnarvon's premature attempt in the 1870s threw back the question for a generation.[2] Federation must now be the work of the South Africans themselves. The British government would do anything they could to help combination, but they would not insist on or compel it.[3] In general Elgin approached the subject believing in the necessity of restraining Selborne's enthusiasm for federation. He did not mean to discourage him, for if it could be arranged on proper lines, it could not come too soon. Nor did he deny that Selborne must be better able to judge than he, whether the local governments or people were ready for the next step in political development. He recognised that very cogent arguments arose out of the railway situation, which he admitted affected Selborne's case in 'a very peculiar if not unprecedented way', but he wished to have stronger evidence that they were generally accepted. He preached caution to Selborne, because he was not sure from his discussions with South Africans during the colonial conference that any of them, except Jameson, expected any very early development, and Solomon was distinctly of opinion that time must be allowed to elapse.[4]

Selborne prepared his famous memorandum at the request of the Cape government. Elgin did not think that a written statement on the subject of federation should be made by Selborne as high commissioner without at least submitting it to the cabinet in the first instance. Indeed, he was extremely doubtful whether such a statement should be made at all, in case it should seem they were endeavouring to promote the movement for federation, which should spring from below. The subject would receive ample discussion; Selborne ought not to do more than furnish materials confidentially to various governments if invited, and to assist and influence them by private

---

[1] Ibid. 6 Sep 06.
[2] EP, Ripon cab. memo. 26 Dec 05.
[3] EP, E to Selb. 28 Sep 06.
[4] Ibid. 15 Feb and 31 May 07.

discussion.[1] It was his view throughout, that Selborne would have been better advised if he had allowed the various governments and parliaments to advance further on the road to federation before he intervened.[2] Churchill was also at first highly sceptical about Selborne's activity:

Selborne is running great risks in entering this dangerous ground. . . . Cheap living on the Rand is in itself of greater Imperial importance than federation. . . . Further, in our zeal for federation and unification, let us not forget the old maxim, 'Divide et Impera'. Do we want an ill-tempered confederation against Downing Street interference? . . . *We* cannot go too slowly in this.[3]

But he was completely converted by a perusal of the Selborne memorandum and inconsistently pronounced an exaggerated eulogy upon it such as few in the office were prepared to endorse.[4]

Selborne was anxious to publish his memorandum before the Transvaal elections, lest from ignorance, candidates pledged themselves against federation. Elgin ruled conclusively against publication, as it would certainly be liable to misinterpretation. It was important in this election, above all others, that the high commissioner should not appear in such a way as to run the risk of an accusation of a desire to influence the elections:

Moreover, the Transvaal elector will have before him a number of important issues, and I doubt the expediency of raising another, or the probability of a pledge regarding federation being given in any definite form, unless the subject is unduly forced to the front.[5]

[1] CO. 417/428/45222, S/S to Selb. tel. 13 Dec 06, Cd. 3564 (1907), 'Federation'. An edition by B. Williams was published in 1925.
[2] CO. 417/442/23517, minute 5 Jul 06; EP, E to Selb. 5 Jul 07.
[3] CO. 417/442/1330, minute 12 Jan 07.
[4] Ibid. 3463. 'The publication of this impressive and noble document can, in my opinion be productive only of good. It contains truths, the appreciation of which is indispensable to the progress and peace of South Africa. It is animated throughout by a lofty spirit of statesmanship and tolerance, and expressed in language of grace and power which in some passages achieves high literary quality' (minute 15 Mar 07).
[5] CO. 417/428/46563, minute 26 Dec 06; EP, E to Selb. 13 Dec 06 (copy).

Uncharitable accusations would, Elgin believed, do more mischief than ill-informed votes, and embarrass the British government in their support of federation. He did not think it prudent to encourage the idea of federation actually taking place during the first parliaments of the new colonies.[1]

Elgin withdrew his objection to the preparation of a memorandum for confidential submission to the governments concerned.[2] Selborne asked for publication after the elections were over. He wanted the cabinet to consider the matter, and so he thoughtfully sent twenty copies of his despatch covering the memorandum. Elgin still preferred to defer publication. The practical difficulties, owing to constitutional changes in some colonies, and the electoral position in others, seemed to him to involve some delay if the evolution towards federation were to proceed naturally.[3] However, Elgin's inclination was to allow Selborne to publish on his own responsibility, as this would be in accordance with Selborne's appeal to personal experience of the facts, which he said induced him to undertake the task.[4] Campbell-Bannerman agreed that publication had better rest on Selborne's own responsibility: 'The less meddling from here the better.'[5] Consequently Selborne was notified on 19 February that publication was entirely at his discretion. The responsibility of the British government was expressly excluded. Elgin did not mean that he disapproved. The earlier interposition of the secretary of state he represented as solely due to Transvaal elections.[6] Selborne did not hurry, as the elections were over; he did not reply to the telegram of 19 February until 24 June. Churchill suggested publication of the memorandum in England as a parliamentary paper, simultaneously with South African publication. Elgin vetoed the proposal. He was doubtful whether the effect would be good. Simultaneous publication might be read as indicating suggestion from England.[7] The memorandum was published by the

---

[1] EP, E to Selb. 27 and 29 Dec 06 (copy).
[2] CO. 417/428/46563, S/S to Selb. tel. 29 Dec 06.
[3] EP, E to Selb. 8 Feb 07 (copy).
[4] Ibid. 15 Feb 07.
[5] EP, CB to E 18 Feb 07.
[6] CO. 417/442/5533.
[7] Ibid. 22627, minutes 26 and 27 Jun 07.

South African governments on 2 July 1907. Churchill complained that it had been disrespectful to parliament not to publish it in London at the same time. Elgin and Hopwood, however, thought that publication had been quite properly deferred. They continued to doubt the wisdom of publication until opinion in South Africa found more definite expression. But they agreed in July that publication would have to take place as early as possible.[1]

Federation commended itself with renewed force to the Liberal government from the beginning of 1907 very much as the result of their current experience with the separate colonies, especially Natal. Liberals had long believed that federation was the means – perhaps the only means – to improved native policy in South Africa.[2] This belief was confirmed by experience with Natal. On the same day, Elgin received similar letters from Campbell-Bannerman and from Haldane: Campbell-Bannerman wrote: 'Those Natal people of yours are tiresome to the last degree. I hope federation will soon squelch them'; Haldane agreed with Elgin's dislike of the Natal government's attitude, and concluded: 'We want federation badly for these native questions.'[3] Campbell-Bannerman praised 'the estimable Dinizulu, who seems to have taken it all with quiet dignity'.[4] Ministers later hoped that his ultimate destiny would not be decided by Natal, but the Union government.[5] It was believed that the smallness and weakness of the Natal community led inevitably to narrow-minded parochialism. Natal's native policy would never have been so bad, men said, if she had been unequivocally given undivided responsibility, and known that she would have to defend herself entirely alone against the consequences.[6]

[1] Ibid. 23517, minute 5 Jul 07.
[2] The instructions to Sir P. Colley in May 1880 stated: 'One of main objects of Confederation to secure good treatment for natives. Federal government to deal with native questions and might be expected to be more impartial, have larger views, etc.' (Gladstone papers 44225/176, Kimberley to Gladstone 25 May 80).
[3] EP, to E 21 Sep 07.   [4] EP, CB to E 2 Jan 07.
[5] CO. 179/252/7907, minute by Crewe 6 Mar 09.
[6] CO. 291/119/32934, minute by Lambert 20 Sep 07.

Panics [wrote Elgin] not unnaturally affect small white populations surrounded by coloured and more or less savage races. The ultimate remedy in South Africa would be federation, whereby white sentiment would be steadied, and white government would gain confidence.[1]

Elgin intended the reservation of Swaziland in 1906 to indicate that they would not be satisfied to leave the Africans permanently without some more adequate recognition than they were then able to give. Federation, he hoped, would perhaps be 'a fitting opportunity for an endeavour to obtain for them greater sympathy than is practicable in separate colonies and comparatively weak white populations'.[2]

All Liberals agreed that confederation would provide a more stable platform for the transaction of native affairs. The good sense of one part might redress hasty or excited feelings in another. The more advanced views of the Cape would influence Natal. Knowledge and experience would be pooled, and make a somewhat wider outlook and a more statesmanlike view possible. They looked to the evolution of a more consistent and enlightened policy, to a 'satisfactory development' of the native question, development because 'solution' seemed to be too strong a word to use.[3]

African interests, therefore, seemed to require federation. British interests, it seemed, would be safe. The new Transvaal government seemed to show the good results of trusting a fully responsible self-government.[4] Men quickly persuaded themselves that the Transvaal and Orange River Colony were becoming reconciled to the British connexion. The new governments behaved much better than Selborne had expected. At the end of the first session of the Transvaal parliament he was able to register pleasure. He was struck by the abilities of Botha and Smuts. Botha created a highly favourable impression, even among Unionists, when in England for the colonial conference.[5]

[1] EP, cab. memo. 23 Jul 06.   [2] Ibid. 13 Nov 07.
[3] PD. 167/1134, Churchill 17 Dec 06; PD/HC. 9/1010, Asquith 16 Aug 09; Dilke papers 43921/193-4, J. H. de Villiers to Dilke 31 Jul 09.
[4] See p. 272.
[5] A. Chamberlain, *Politics from inside* (1936), pp. 72, 76.

Botha and Smuts, wrote Morley, 'are behaving well. They have shown none of the intractable sort of temper of the Australians'.[1] 'They are really treating us in a thoroughly frank and reasonable manner', wrote Churchill.[2] Sir H. Goold-Adams reported favourably on the Boer response in the Orange River Colony. All parties there had accepted responsible government and seemed prepared to do their utmost to work honestly towards reconciliation, and to justify the trust placed in them. Though he had opposed the granting of responsible government as 'rather premature', Goold-Adams had come to the conclusion 'that it is the only thing which would have satisfied the majority of these people and that it is going to have satisfactory results'.[3] Elgin found this report most encouraging. The governor thought racial animosity much less marked than when hostilities ceased.[4]

Reports from the Cape were also reasonably encouraging. Hely-Hutchinson told Elgin that, although not inclined to be enthusiastic, 'I do really think that now ... there is every chance that, at last, things may come straight'.[5] By the end of 1907 he had visited almost all the villages in the Cape Colony. His impression was that, although there was still a certain amount of racial feeling, it had certainly diminished, and it seemed likely to diminish still further now that there was no centre, such as existed when there were independent Dutch republics, around which Dutch feelings could rally. The proceedings of the national convention seemed to him to afford evidence of a general desire to settle down in peace and quiet.[6]

There were also apparently some strategic arguments in favour of federation. Selborne and Seely believed that if Germany were at war with Britain she would make an attack on South Africa one of her prime objects, and that such an

[1] MM. 3/29, 30 Jan 08.   [2] CO. 291/120/26267, minute 24 Jul 07.
[3] EP, to E 15 Jul 07 and 12 Aug 07.
[4] CO. 224/26/29965, to S/S 27 Jul 08.
[5] EP, Hely-Hutchinson to E 18 Dec 06; CO. 48/588/669.
[6] CO. 48/596/4730, to S/S 20 Jan 08; CO. 48/598/286, to S/S 16 Dec 08.

attack would provoke a general rising of the Boers. Crewe passed this opinion to Grey, though he does not seem to have been convinced by the argument. Seely's recollection was that this consideration made it urgent to strengthen South Africa.[1]

In the event, the Liberals preferred a unitary to a federal constitution. 'It is not for me to interfere', Elgin wrote. 'If I did, on behalf of this Office, I should certainly go for unification. The Canadian precedent has, for us, many attractions which the Australian lacks.'[2] Canada was 'the strongest and best example of federation',[3] and in comparison with Australia, seemed virtually a union. It was not simply that the Commonwealth of Australia had been inaugurated under the auspices of Chamberlain. Canada was to the Liberals 'the greatest triumph of British statesmanship'.[4] The British North America Act had been the basis of Gladstone's Home Rule Bills. This predisposition for the strong central government of Canada was reinforced by current experience with the loose Australian federation. Elgin was highly conscious of the difficulties resulting from the constitution adopted in Australia, and referred to them when preaching caution to Selborne in approaching South African federation.[5] One of the difficulties was a dispute over the channels of communication in Australia, the State premiers complaining that the colonial office treated them contemptuously and exalted the Commonwealth government. Elgin minuted:

... I remember thinking at the time, that the Constitution adopted for the Commonwealth was not complete – and it may be that it was a mistake to accept so partial a union. ... Its weakness is mainly due to the want of loyalty in those who combined to demand it – but I do not see how anyone can doubt that one government and not six must ultimately prevail in Australia.

[1] CO. 417/413/32485, Selb. to S/S 21 Aug 05; GP. 52, Crewe to Grey 22 Jun 08; J. E. B. Seely, *Adventure* (1930), p. 133, quoted by Thompson, *Unification*, p. 399.
[2] EP, E to Hely-Hutchinson 3 Apr 08 (copy).
[3] EP, cab. memo. 5 Mar 06.   [4] CB. 41243A/62.
[5] EP, E to Selb. 15 Feb 07, Selb. to E 8 Mar 07.

Elgin stood firmly by the Australian Commonwealth government in this irritating dispute.[1]

It is possible that preference for Union as opposed to federation might have been reinforced by the fact that Natal preferred federation. The views, policy and objectives of the Natal government were so entirely discredited, that the very fact that they alone of the governments wanted federation may have been sufficient to damn federation irretrievably in the eyes of the British government. Desire for improved native policy strengthened the other reasons for preferring Union. In a federation, the states would have the power to pass laws which might irritate the Africans. In a Union, with one large parliament, the influence of the Cape might induce the other states to modify their illiberal arrangements.[2]

The Liberal government clearly intended Southern Rhodesia eventually to become a constituent part of the Union. The intention was foreshadowed by Churchill as early as May 1906, in a minute on General Booth's scheme for the colonisation of Southern Rhodesia, a scheme to which the Salvation Army would be a party. The minute is characteristic of Churchill's rhetorical enthusiasm for a romantic venture. The colonial office had received the scheme with scorn. Churchill hit back:

It is very easy to choke a scheme like this. But Rhodesia with its British population may ultimately be the weight which swings the balance in South Africa decisively on the side of the British Crown. Gen. Booth is the most practical idealist the world can show today. He can exert forces not at the command of ordinary commercial agencies. The difficulties of the wilderness, its loneliness and inaccessibility are not perhaps to be surmounted without the aid of some super-economic influence. I should be very sorry to see this plan shrivel into a polite official reply.

[1] CO. 418/47/1590, Jan 07. Thompson, *Unification of South Africa*, p. 482, criticises the makers of the Union for arguing partly from 'false prophecies' that Australian states must either adopt a unitary constitution or break up; but it seems as if they could have been arguing from actual experience of acute friction in Australia between 1906 and 1909 which might well have led to reasonable prophecies.

[2] Bryce papers C. 2. Merriman to Bryce 6 Oct 08.

I hope the secretary of state will consider very carefully whether £20,000 a year might not be well invested here.[1]

At Churchill's instigation, Elgin wrote to say that they believed the scheme full of interest and great possibilities. More definite proposals were invited. Elgin even went so far as to ask Hely-Hutchinson, who had just returned from Rhodesia, if he considered it a country 'well suited for general settlement purposes'.[2] The scheme, however, never seemed to shrug off its vagueness; the matter vanished from official interest with Hopwood's report which concluded that it was 'purely philan-thropic and visionary, and in no sense a business proposition'. If the treasury were asked for money, he warned Elgin, they would cut the prospectus into shreds, and so for that matter would any M.P. with business experience.[3]

Any proposal which might conceivably affect the future of Southern Rhodesia was considered most carefully. In 1907 Selborne was reminded, at the time of his discussions with representatives of the British South Africa Company, that a financial settlement between the company and the settlers would have to precede any change in the form of the administra-tion. Any arrangement would be scrutinised with an eye to the permanent interests of Southern Rhodesia, both as an individual territory, and as a constituent part of a federal South Africa. Its entry into a federation, 'now a possibility of the early future', must not be prejudiced by the insufficiently assured financial position of the territory.

In saying this I do not leave out of sight the fact that any very material change in the form of government is hardly justified by present circumstances, and that self-government will probably have to be reached by several stages.[4]

---

[1] CO. 417/434/16276 17 May 06.   [2] EP, 22 Jun 06 (copy).
[3] EP, Hopwood to Elgin 5 Apr 07.
[4] CO. 417/449/28399, S/S to Selb. 8 Aug 07.

8 Colonial Problems in an International Context

THE Liberals, it has been said, were imperialists because they were internationalists.[1] We have already seen how concern for the fulfilment of international obligations was prominent in the determination of their policy in tropical Africa. We have also observed a temptation to intervene in the domestic affairs of South African self-governing colonies, where problems of wider imperial concern seemed to be raised.[2] We should therefore expect to find, and we shall, that the Liberals had little compunction in overriding colonial views in problems of external policy, or in situations where the demands of allies and colonists conflicted. Good relations with friends and allies, American, French, Japanese, were of great importance in a decade of incipient international anarchy. The Anglo-Japanese alliance of 1902, the Anglo-French *entente* of 1904, and perhaps above all the unwritten, nearly tacit, nearly unilateral, and probably mythical, idea of a 'special relationship' with the United States, an idea developing since the 1890s – all these had important implications for imperial policy. In the period under review, Newfoundlanders and Australians became aggrieved by being treated in a way which emphasised their secondary or tertiary importance in the power evaluations of the imperial government.

NEWFOUNDLAND: UNITED STATES FISHING RIGHTS[3]

United States fishing rights off Canada and Newfoundland date from the successful assertion, in the treaty of 1783, of

[1] A. F. Madden, *C.H.B.E.*, iii, 345.   [2] See pp. 237–78.
[3] For background see A. M. Fraser 'Fishery negotiations with the United States' in R. A. MacKay (ed.), *Newfoundland: economic, diplomatic and strategic studies* (Toronto 1946), pp. 333–410, and the *Annual Register for 1905*, pp. 471–2.

rights formerly enjoyed as subjects. The rights were modified after the war of 1812 by a convention of 1818. Interpretation of this convention was debated by Britain and the United States throughout the nineteenth century. The two governments differed fundamentally about the nature and extent of American fishery rights in Newfoundland waters. The United States government claimed that the treaty conferred upon American fishermen a right to fish in the specified waters of Newfoundland free from any control by the government of Newfoundland, or at most subject only to such regulations and restrictions as existed when the treaty came into force. The British government refused to admit this claim. They contended that the Americans were subject to all reasonable enactments and regulations for the preservation of the fishery which were applicable to the fishermen of Newfoundland. Newfoundland was a self-governing colony from 1855. Towards the end of the nineteenth century, Newfoundland had been trying to reach a separate fisheries agreement with the United States, independently of Canadian and British partnership. In pursuit of this objective, Robert Bond, who had recently become prime minister, undertook a mission to Washington in 1902, with the approval of the British government. Canada had consented to the resumption of fishery negotiations between Newfoundland and the United States. As a result, a convention with John Hay, the United States secretary of state, was signed on 8 November 1902. But to become binding upon the two countries, the Hay-Bond convention had to be ratified by the governments of Britain and the United States. The American senate refused its assent, chiefly because of the opposition of New England fish merchants, whose interests were threatened by the proposed free entry of Newfoundland fish into the United States market. Disappointment and resentment were aroused in Newfoundland.

Bond now toughened his tactics against the United States by passing the Foreign Fishing Vessels Act in 1905, which abolished the system of licences in force since 1888, under which, on payment of a moderate fee, United States fishermen enjoyed extensive privileges, including that of purchasing bait for the herring fishery. The new law forbade the sale of bait and supplies to foreign fishing vessels. It was enforced against the Americans with extreme vigour. The Newfoundland government professed that the sole purpose of the regulations was to protect the fishery: failure to enforce them would be tantamount to an abdication by Newfoundland of her sovereignty in her own territorial waters. To evade the prohibition of bait purchase, the American fishing captains hired Newfoundlanders to fish for them as members of the ships' crews; thus they obtained bait without breaking the letter of the law. Bond accordingly decided to change the letter of the law, and strove to check the circumvention of his previous bill by carrying a second Foreign Fishing Vessels Act in 1906. This act forbade Newfoundlanders to engage their services to any foreign fishing vessel. Vigorous representations were made in London by the United States. Consequently imperial assent was withheld, and the measure never became operative. The United States government became convinced that the legislation was designed for retaliation rather than for the preservation of the fishery. The object of the Newfoundland government seemed to be to make the fishery so expensive and troublesome to the Americans, by depriving them of every facility, as to make it impossible for them to use it. The British government could hardly follow Newfoundland as far as this. It was a common fishery. The Americans could not be excluded. Bond's legislation affected the herring fishery, which was not of vital importance to the economy. The Newfoundland fishing industry centred more on dried cod-fish than herring. The whole herring export was only about 3 per cent of her total exports. This would be a ridiculously insignificant consideration, the British thought, on which to base a serious misunderstanding with the United States. The governor, Sir William MacGregor, wondered indeed whether Sir Robert Bond was acting more from personal motives than from political ones. It seemed to be a personal point of honour with the prime minister to push his policy with or without reason. Although his government was not unanimous in support of obstruction, Bond could easily get a following by adroit use of the 'platitudes of patriotism'.[1]

The governor set the whole tone of the ensuing negotiations with the remark in August 1906 that he would

not be forced into any act that would tend to precipitate a rupture [with the United States], even should it mean the dismissal of ministers. I hope this may not be necessary, but it would be a small matter compared to a serious quarrel with the United States, the memory of which would long survive our day.

Elgin was glad to know that MacGregor recognised the gravity of the situation, which was simultaneously being impressed upon him by Sir Edward Grey. An awkward business, wrote Grey:

We have got to choose between a row with Newfoundland, and a row with the United States. Newfoundland is the little boy who would very much prefer that the row should be between his big brother and the other big boy, rather than be kept in order himself. He thinks he will then get his own way, and have all the fun of looking in at the row into the bargain.[2]

From the first, Grey saw that this was a matter for arbitration. Elgin rather preferred to try diplomacy first, and to see what could be done at least temporarily by the conclusion of a *modus vivendi* for the imminent fishing season. Elgin and Grey agreed that there must be no rupture with the United States. The Newfoundland government would not co-operate in making temporary arrangements with the United States. Despite this, as Elgin explained to the governor:

We have no alternative but to go on with them, for to do otherwise might mean an international complication of considerable gravity. So far as I am concerned I am most anxious to stand up for the rights of the Colony in every reasonable particular, but when it comes to insisting on the enforcement of the provisions of the Bill of 1906 – to several of which we have steadily objected – as the one and only point of importance, I think too much is asked of us. I sincerely hope that the fishing season may pass off quietly.

[1] EP, MacGregor to E 2 Apr 07.   [2] EP, Grey to E 23 Aug 06.

Elgin believed that if Bond continued to obstruct by demanding this legislation and the ratification of the Hay-Bond commercial convention, there would be nothing for it but to overrule him.[1] Elgin was rather surprised at Bond's supremacy in the colony, because as far as he could see, 'his policy has no better foundation than an obstinate determination to get his own way'. In one telegram Bond had actually offered to give up every other point if Britain would accept the Bill of 1906. Elgin thought Bond 'entirely wrong'. All they asked of Newfoundland was that the colony should discuss the terms of an arrangement with the United States.[2] Newfoundland would not agree, and wished to bring the Foreign Fishing Vessels Act into operation at once. This would be a direct challenge to the United States.

A *modus vivendi* for the regulation of the fishery in the coming winter was concluded between the governments of Britain and the United States on 6 October 1906. The Americans were allowed to employ Newfoundlanders in the bait fishery. They were also allowed to use purse seines,[3] but were required to pay light dues, and to abstain from Sunday fishing. The *modus vivendi* was essentially a temporary arrangement intended to avoid untoward incidents during the discussion which Bond's animus against the United States had made necessary. It followed the precedent of Lord Salisbury's action in 1890 with respect to the dispute with France over the Newfoundland lobster fishery.[4] The British government intended it as a truce. The legislation of 1905 and 1906 was therefore in abeyance. Drawing a distinction between the internal affairs of the colony, and those of international interest, the British government could not place the Foreign Fishing Vessels Act in the former category.[5] The Newfoundland ministers now complained that the action of the imperial government was 'subversive of the Colony's constitutional rights and calculated to work severe

---

[1] EP, E to MacGregor 24 Sep 06 (copy).   [2] EP, E to Grey 29 Oct 06.

[3] The purse seine was much easier to use than the gill net, for which the skill of Newfoundlanders was required. The purse seine freed the Americans from dependence on Newfoundlanders.

[4] CO. 194/266/39509, answer to parliamentary question 30 Oct 06.

[5] CO. 194/263/30854, S/S to govr 3 Sep 06; 34470, tel. S/S to govr 19 Sep 06.

injury to the fisheries of the Colony'. They seemed to think that the action embodied an intention to 'override statutes'.[1] Naturally enough, Elgin directed that a brief protest should be made against this charge.[2] The government were sure that they had acted correctly, and had a good case. Lyttelton gave Churchill to understand that he would support them.[3]

Bond attempted to frustrate the operation of the agreement, but only made himself look increasingly ridiculous. Churchill allowed himself an unyielding minute on 22 November 1906:

> We must unhesitatingly enforce the *modus vivendi* by superior power. Sir R. Bond should be so informed; and that if we encounter further opposition of a mischievous and irresponsible character, we shall submit the whole question to arbitration – and enforce the decision of the tribunal.[4]

Elgin's private opinion was that the Newfoundland ministers were indulging in 'gratuitous mischief'. They did not respect the bounds of reason. Altogether it was 'a stupid business'. He could not say these things formally.[5] His advisers described Bond as petulant, blustering and ill-mannered.[6]

The fishing season passed off without serious mishap. Bond's endeavours were frustrated. He was not supported by the fishermen of the west coast, who resented both the prohibition of their profitable bait trade with the Americans and also the attempt to prevent them from obtaining employment on board American fishing vessels. The feeling there was so strongly against Bond's policy that the captain of H.M.S. *Brilliant*, ordered by the admiralty to enforce the *modus vivendi*, was able to arrange on the spot a satisfactory agreement between the local fishermen and the Americans as to use of purse seines.

The next phase in this difficult and delicate contest took place during the colonial conference of 1907 when Bond was in

---

[1] Ibid. 37760.   [2] Ibid. tel. S/S to govr 23 Oct 06.
[3] Ibid. 40161, minute by WSC 1 Nov 06.   [4] CO. 194/264/42763.
[5] Ibid. 44668, minute by E 6 Dec 06; CO. 42/915/19773, 4 Jun 07; EP, E to Lord Grey 26 Nov 06.
[6] CO. 194/264/48121, minute by WSC 1 Jan 07; CO. 194/271/197, minute by Cox 4 Jan 07.

London. Rather unexpectedly, he urged the necessity of submitting the interpretation of the convention of 1818 to the Hague Tribunal. Formerly, it had been expected that he would have to be coerced into arbitration. Churchill seized his opportunity to produce a memorandum.[1] He was anxious to make the point that they should not react to Bond's unconvincing and undiscriminating partisanship by assuming that the colony had no genuine grievances:

It is intolerable that the unique skill of Newfoundland fishermen should be hired year by year to catch fish for American companies, which fish are to be smuggled in free through the American tariff as if they were American-caught fish, to the detriment, even to the total exclusion, of the fishery catch of Newfoundland. No government, however small, could be expected to acquiesce in such a state of things, more especially when its unfairness has been plainly admitted by United States ministers. . . .

Churchill based the opinion in the last sentence on their readiness to accept the Hay-Bond convention (although the senate refused to ratify it). It was only natural, he considered, that the government of Newfoundland wished to restrain its fishermen from aiding a process injurious to the colony. On the other hand, he did not accept Bond's contention that Newfoundland was entitled to make laws which regulated or restrained the Americans in their resort to the fishery, because the treaty of 1818 had expressly provided for a 'common fishery', which, clearly, must be governed by common regulations, made by both parties to it, Great Britain and the United States, acting together. Having stated that the Americans had no treaty right to use the services of Newfoundland fishermen, and that the government of Newfoundland was entitled to refuse such services, and punish fishermen who did not comply, Churchill hoped that the government of Newfoundland would not risk 'a strenuous assertion of this undoubted right'. The first essential was to obtain a complete understanding and agree-

[1] CO. confidential print, North American, no. 211, 13 Nov 07: 'Newfoundland fisheries: United States Treaty Rights.'

ment between the British and American governments as to the interpretation of the treaty of 1818. What were or were not the regulations for the conduct of the common fishery?

At Elgin's suggestion, Grey joined the colonial secretary for an interview with Bond on 11 May. Churchill was also present. Grey took the initiative in the discussion. Elgin made only three remarks.[1] The session was inconclusive. Elgin was anxious to have another talk with Bond, this time alone. Grey welcomed this. The meeting took place on 17 May. At first Elgin thought that Bond was going to be quite immovable. All the old arguments were trotted out. But in the end Elgin persuaded him to submit his regulations to Britain. Bond was even willing to consider any criticism the government thought it right to make, and eventually agreed also to allowing his readiness to do this to be communicated to the United States, as it might possibly lead to an agreement which would be an alternative to the *modus vivendi*. If he could see the draft note to the United States, he promised to give it every consideration. He even suggested trying simultaneously to get an agreement on some of the practices on the Labrador coast.[2] Grey was most impressed by the concessions into which Bond had been led, and wrote to Elgin:

Admiration takes my breath away; it is wonderful that you should have been able to move Bond even so much. How did you do it? Do you possess the faith that can move mountains? We will endeavour to work your suggestions into the draft. . . .[3]

This enthusiastic tribute to Elgin's skill as a negotiator is all the more remarkable coming from Grey, who was usually so cool in his appraisal of men and events.

In spite of the hopeful expectations of mid-May, Bond proved irreconcilable once he got back to Newfoundland.[4] Elgin complained that Bond had not given all the weight which he and Grey thought was deserved, to the possibilities of international conflict:

[1] CO. 194/270/33388.   [2] Ibid. 21846.
[3] EP, Grey to E 19 May 07.   [4] EP, E to MacGregor 21 Jun 07.

We are extremely anxious to act in concert with the government of the Colony – and to do nothing to impair its authority. But it is the duty of H.M.G. to deal with international relations, and while we should prefer in a matter of this kind to rely upon Colonial legislation, we shall not hesitate if necessary to use such other means as are open to us to obtain sanction for the arrangements which we consider essential for the preservation of relations of peace and amity with a friendly nation and for the settlement of disputes in an orderly fashion.[1]

An approach to the government of the United States with a proposal for arbitration was made by the British government on 20 June 1907. It was still essential to conclude a *modus vivendi* for the season of 1907, for arbitration could not be established before the fishing season opened. The proposed terms were drafted before Bond left England. Under these proposals, the United States would abandon on behalf of their fishermen the claims to use purse seines, and to fish on Sundays; they would recognise the Newfoundland claim to prevent Newfoundland fishermen from serving aboard American fishing vessels. These were not such good terms for the Americans as they had had under the previous *modus*, but two concessions were made to them: Britain would not insist on American vessels reporting at Newfoundland customs houses, and there was the possibility of some United States vessels obtaining partial exemption from payment of light dues. Bond, however, would not approve these terms because he was opposed to any concessions whatever, pending submission of the whole question to arbitration.

The Americans were to be asked not to use purse seines because Elgin had become convinced that their use was destructive.[2] As the British government probably expected, the United States declined to acquiesce in the proposed *modus*. To accept it, they replied, would be equivalent to yielding on all vital questions in dispute. It would render their treaty rights worthless. Britain therefore had to decide which requirement

[1] CO. 194/270/21846, E to Bond 18 Jun 07.
[2] CO. 194/271/18398, minute 29 May 07; CO. 42/915/19052, 30 May 07.

to drop. The government of Newfoundland was asked in July to give an opinion about the points to which the United States took exception. The Newfoundland government replied in effect that they did not consider themselves called upon to decide the relative importance of the prohibition of the use of purse seines and the prohibition of the employment of Newfoundland fishermen. In view of this unco-operative attitude, on 10 August 1907, therefore, the British government notified Newfoundland that it had been decided to propose a *modus vivendi*, on the lines of that for 1906, but excluding the right of using purse seines. Two main reasons were given for conceding the right of Americans to use Newfoundland fishermen rather than purse seines. In the first place, if deprived of the help of Newfoundlanders, the American vessels would be forced either to return empty, or to attempt to use purse seines. The effort to do so would lead to disputes between American and Newfoundland fishermen, both parties thinking their means of livelihood threatened by the action of the other. In the second place, the use of purse seines was definitely forbidden by the law of Newfoundland, and the government was alive to the possibility that in sanctioning their use they would be charged with deliberately overriding an enactment of the colonial legislature. As it was, the Newfoundland ministers complained of being ignored, and treated with lack of courtesy, complaints with but little foundation, if any. While still declining to accept the *modus vivendi*, on 20 August, the Bond ministry for the first time put forward an alternative suggestion which might be proposed to the American government. This would have allowed American fishermen to buy fish from Newfoundlanders at a fair price. Elgin doubted whether the United States would accept this, but reckoned it to be a better offer than many people assumed.[1] The United States could not accept the offer, since the fishing fleet had already sailed. Early in September the Newfoundland government again declared their unwillingness to carry out the proposed *modus vivendi*, and repeated their readiness to permit

[1] CO. 194/269/30202, 23 Aug 07.

the Americans to purchase fish if the proposed *modus* were withdrawn. What a pity it was, Elgin thought, that the ministers had not shown a disposition to negotiate earlier. It was now too late. Having rejected the purchase proposal on this ground, the British government now had no alternative but to conclude the *modus vivendi* as planned with the United States. This was done on 6 September 1907.

The *modus vivendi* had proved workable in the previous season, partly because of the tact of the naval officer commanding the Newfoundland station, but partly because of the forbearance of the ministers in not pressing proceedings against Newfoundland fishermen employed by the Americans. Repetition of restraint could not be expected. It was therefore decided to issue an Order-in-Council on the authority of an Act of 1819 empowering the issue of directions which would ensure United States fishing rights under the convention. The Order-in-Council was effective against colonial legislation; it would help naval officers in their enforcement of the *modus vivendi* by ensuring that process against Newfoundland fishermen would not be served on American vessels and that American vessels or tackle would not be subject to seizure. The Order-in-Council was dated 9 September 1907. The problem was discussed by the cabinet in mid-August. Campbell-Bannerman's report to the king provides a convenient and amusing summary of the stage the Newfoundland question had reached at this date:

The dispute between Newfoundland and the United States has become again critical. The Colony has agreed to refer the quarrel to the Hague Tribunal, but it cannot be dealt with for some months, and the interval includes a new fishing season. Sir R. Bond is obstinate in refusing to consent to a renewal for this interval of the *modus vivendi* at present in force; and it becomes necessary to override this objection by an Order-in-Council. . . . It is to be hoped that the movements of the herring, which are not under official, or even human, control, will not precipitate the fishing season before that time. The Newfoundland government are most unreasonable, seeing that all we ask is that in the interval before arbitration, the same facilities should be given to American fishers as Canada willingly concedes: but there will no doubt be some commotion in the Colony.[1]

A long explanatory despatch carefully emphasised that while the British government claimed the right to act in 'imperial interests of the gravest moment', they did not assert any right to regulate the relations between the colonial government and its people. The old protest that the imperial government had not received 'all the assistance which they were entitled to expect', was repeated. Should the Newfoundland government change its mind, and adhere to the *modus vivendi*, the Order-in-Council would at once be revoked.[2]

The Order-in-Council could not remove all difficulties. Grey noted that Bond was already trying to frighten his people from engaging with American fishing vessels by threatening to punish those who did so. If he succeeded, the Americans would find that no Newfoundlander, though otherwise willing, would dare to engage because of Bond's action. Steps must be taken to overcome this difficulty. Grey insisted that Britain could not honourably let the United States suppose themselves to have a *modus vivendi* enabling them to hire labour as in the previous year, and then let Bond frustrate the arrangement. Britain could not simply shrug her shoulders if the Americans failed to get labour. Grey wondered whether they might tell the Newfoundlanders that the British government would pay their fines if they incurred any. Or perhaps pressure could be put on Bond by threatening to saddle him with the entire cost of the expenses of arbitration.[3]

The Newfoundland government again refused to accept the *modus vivendi*, and disputed the validity of the Order-in-Council as 'intended to override both international and local laws'. They pointed out that the imperial Act of 1819 had been passed prior to the grant of responsible government. Two draft telegraphic replies were submitted to Elgin, and as usual he pre-

[1] CAB. 41/31/32, 14 Aug 07; see Spender, *Life of Campbell-Bannerman*, ii, 336.
[2] Keith, *Speeches and Documents*, ii, 167–81, S/S to govr. 19 Sep 07.
[3] EP, Grey to E 18 [?] and 21 Sep 07.

ferred the shorter one. He never much liked telegraphic arguments. And he thought it a mistake to show such a distinct hostility as Keith had displayed in the longer draft to the Newfoundland willingness to sell fish. This willingness gave an opening to negotiations which the Americans had themselves suggested. Nothing could be more satisfactory than the success of such negotiations, enabling the government to withdraw the Order-in-Council.[1] Elgin tried to delay publication of the Order as long as possible.

At about this time, Elgin described Newfoundland and Natal as 'our two spoilt children'. Writing to Churchill, who had embarked on his voyage to East Africa, he compared the two problems:

The first pursues the even tenor of its way: i.e. vehement protest against anything and everything we attempt. I thought at one moment that there were better symptoms – when Bond actually proposed a 'modus' of his own! And I am not clear still that the case is hopeless. .... I think I have managed to keep the door open – if Bond means to be reasonable. If, as I fear is more probable, he means to follow the same impracticable policy as last year – we must disregard him as we did then . . . this case . . . is full of annoyance – but I don't fear any serious challenge to our policy.
Natal is a much bigger business. . . .[2]

Churchill replied from Malta congratulating his chief on the way he had handled Newfoundland:

The course of events seems fully to justify your views and action. Even 'The Times' for once is friendly and straightforward, and Bond is clearly coming to be regarded more and more as an impracticable person.[3]

Elgin was quite right. The problem fizzled out with a whimper, not a bang. The Americans, having secured special privileges to assist them in fishing, preferred to purchase. While the fishing was in progress, everything went smoothly, and there was no friction. At the end of the herring fishery after the middle

---

[1] CO. 194/269/33917, minute 22 Sep 07.   [2] EP, 25 Sep 07 (photocopy).
[3] EP, WSC to E 4 Oct 07.

of January 1908 there was a move among the officials to send a letter winding up the *modus vivendi* and attempting to score off Bond. Churchill and Elgin firmly quashed this proposal. Interest was dying. No one would bother to make much trouble for the Liberal government over it. They would say nothing. Let facts speak for themselves. Bond had completely discredited himself with all responsible people. Churchill quoted the Bible in support of a policy of silence: 'Blessed are the meek'....[1] The loss of confidence in Bond in the colony was reflected in the electoral débâcle of his ministry in 1908. His fall from power forestalled the development of any further crisis on the constitutional issue. Bond had never ceased to protest against the *modus vivendi*. But before he resigned he had at last approved the terms of reference to the Hague Tribunal, terms which Britain had proposed. As far as the Liberals were concerned the conclusion of their experience with Bond's Newfoundland was similar to that with Natal: absorption of Newfoundland into the Canadian confederation was 'a consummation devoutly to be wished'.[2]

The terms of reference were negotiated during the fishery of 1907–8. Elgin feared that Bond would put forward 'somewhat extravagant propositions', but felt that it was only right and fair to give the colonies of Newfoundland and Canada the first word, provided that they did not delay.[3] Bond, intransigent as ever, was only too anxious to delay. However, all was eventually agreed, and the Order-in-Council withdrawn. The Hague Tribunal sat from June to September 1910. Seven questions were put to it, and *mirabile dictu*, it virtually settled the century-old controversy to the satisfaction of both Newfoundland and the United States. It was decided that Britain, that is to say in practice Newfoundland and Canada, had the right to make regulations (subject to the treaty of 1818), without the consent of the United States. It was also decided that the United States could employ persons not inhabitants of the United States, but

[1] CO. 194/272/1996, minutes 27 and 28 Jan 08.
[2] EP, E to Lord Grey 29 Oct 06 (copy); see also below, p. 327.
[3] EP, E to MacGregor 7 Nov 07 (copy).

302

such fishermen would not get any benefit or immunity from the treaty. This seems rather ambiguous, but Newfoundland was not actually prohibited from forbidding her nationals to obtain employment in United States fishing vessels. It seems, then, that Churchill had correctly forecast that Newfoundland had, intrinsically, a substantial case.

AUSTRALIA: THE GENESIS OF THE ANGLO-FRENCH CONDOMINIUM IN THE NEW HEBRIDES[1]

The status of the Pacific islands in the New Hebrides group had been indeterminate since 1888, when the French and British had warned off other powers. It was difficult for Britain to share Australian fears that France might add the New Hebrides to her existing bases in the Pacific. They were the last remaining territories in the South Pacific unclaimed by any other power. By the end of the nineteenth century the islands were in grave disorder. The discussion of land claims emphasised the very dubious nature in international law of any exercise of Franco-British authority there. Britain proposed a joint protectorate in 1903, possibly as a generous gesture to conciliate Australian anxieties which she did not share. Britain would have preferred to do nothing, but was willing to take some action to placate the insistent Australians. The Australians would have preferred that Britain should annex the New Hebrides. This was impossible. Unilateral action was out of the question, because French interests in population, investment and so forth exceeded British, though both were negligible. The governing factor in the situation was that it was impossible to discuss the future of this group of islands except on the basis of an admitted equality of interests between Britain and France. The subjects of the two powers were so scattered that a reasonable partition could not have been arranged. In any case this would not have satisfied the Australians. The Anglo-French

---

[1] See J. A. La Nauze, *Alfred Deakin, a biography* (Melbourne, 1965), ii, chap. 19; Cd. 3288 (Jan 1907).

entente of 1904 had not managed to settle the question, but Britain and France had announced in April 1904 their intention to discuss arrangements to settle jurisdiction and land claims in the New Hebrides by a commission, and pledged themselves to deal in concert with difficulties arising from the absence of jurisdiction over the natives. Negotiations had been delayed since 1904 owing to the necessity of consulting the governments of Australia and New Zealand, and the impossibility of getting a reply from the French government to a British note of January 1905. When the Australians complained of these delays, there were pompous comments in the office on colonial naïvety and diplomatic inexperience, leading the Australians, it was remarked, to think of treating France 'as if she were Tonga or Samoa'.[1] However, the colonial office did remind the foreign office several times in 1905 about the dissatisfaction in Australia and New Zealand over the delay.

Then in December 1905, three delegates of each power had been appointed, to be known as the New Hebrides Commission. By the time of their first meeting on 1 February 1906, the scope of their talks had been considerably enlarged to discuss not only land tenure claims, as originally proposed, but also the best ways of terminating difficulties arising from the absence of jurisdiction. In practice this meant discussing the question of a joint protectorate. This was undertaken at the suggestion of both parties, the French government and the colonial office. No information about the new terms of reference, the more formal nature of the meeting, or the course of the negotiations was sent to Australia or New Zealand. This may have been a genuine oversight arising from the pressure and confusion of work during the change of government.[2] A draft convention, definitely asserting joint 'paramount rights', neither power being preponderant, was signed in London on 27 February 1906. It was forwarded to Australia by telegram of 5 March and

[1] CO. 418/44/8653, minute by Cox 19 Mar 06.

[2] Keith, *Responsible government in the Dominions*, with typical unfairness puts the whole blame on Elgin: 'it was a lamentable blunder on the part of the maladroit Lord Elgin when in 1906 a new Convention was arranged . . . without consulting the Dominions in advance' (i, 870).

despatch of 9 March. The attempt was to make the protectorate as little as possible a joint one in order to minimise friction. The joint authority would be 'restricted within the narrowest possible limits', leaving intact, as far as possible, separate jurisdiction over its own nationals by each power. This met the Australian desire for elasticity, so as not to make impossible difficulties for getting all the islands under British sovereignty in the future. Everybody in the colonial office thought that friction would be unavoidable if New Zealanders or Australians themselves were allowed into the negotiations or appointed resident commissioners. The colonists were supposed to be brusque in manner and overbearing in tone. Few men at the antipodes were thought capable of speaking fluent French, which was essential in such work.[1]

When the terms of the convention were announced early in March 1907 there was a good deal of discontent in Australia, despite Elgin's conviction that 'so far as difficult circumstances permit, H.M.G. have done their utmost to safeguard the interests of the [Australian] Commonwealth'.[2] The British government had got much more out of the negotiations than appeared possible at one time. They owed this, he thought, to the tact and firmness, combined with the conciliatory manner, of the British representatives.[3] It was probably true that Britain had secured the best bargain that was in fact practicable. And Ommanney was personally convinced that if delegates from Australia or New Zealand had been present the negotiations with France would have broken down at the outset.[4] Deakin's chief complaint, however, was of not being kept informed. He made it clear that he thought Australian ministers felt themselves to have been treated with some lack of consideration, since they had learned first from the press both that there had been an Anglo-French meeting at all, and that agreement had been reached. He did not dispute Britain's right to settle the question with France if she preferred to do so, but he held that

[1] CO. 209/268/8696, minute by Cox 15 Mar 06.
[2] CO. 418/44/8653, desp. 20 Apr 06.
[3] CO. 225/74/8162, minute 9 Mar 06.   [4] La Nauze, *Alfred Deakin*, ii, 451.

Australia should have been kept posted as to what was being done.[1] It was easier to defend the terms of the convention than the charge of failing to inform:

I scarcely hope [Elgin wrote to the governor-general] that your government will not look at it from a narrow point of view. I assure you that it was with the greatest difficulty that we got all that we have secured. At one time it looked as if the French would stand out for very much larger claims, and it was only the tact and ingenuity of our representatives that carried the day. I can speak with confidence on this point, for I had more than one conference with them, and during the critical part of the negotiations they reported progress to me every day.[2]

The Australian and New Zealand governments were informed in the despatch of 9 March that the draft convention would not be confirmed until Britain had had an opportunity of considering their views. But although minor details might be modified, as there seemed no prospect of getting an agreement with the French which would 'in general be more acceptable', they were told frankly that the draft convention 'must therefore be confirmed or rejected practically as it stands'. This was hardly an ultimatum. Deakin[3] made certain comments, which Elgin agreed to forward to the foreign office, with the recommendation that they should try to obtain the agreement of the French government to such of the amendments as could properly or usefully be submitted to them. He suggested the appointment of a fresh joint commission.[4] Elgin hoped that the foreign office would let them 'carry Australia with us as far as we can'.[5] But by October the government felt it to be very important to ratify the draft convention as the only means of preventing undesirable complications. Although still willing to recommend some of Deakin's amendments, further delay would necessarily be involved, and the French might make counter-proposals.

---

[1] EP, Northcote to E 5 Mar 06.   [2] EP, E to Northcote 6 Apr 06 (copy).
[3] Deakin, Alfred (1857–1919), prime minister of Australia 1903–4, 1905–8, 1909–10.
[4] CO. 418/45/30912, to FO 25 Aug 06.
[5] CO. 225/74/32385, minute 5 Sep 06.

In themselves, the amendments seemed of secondary importance, or at least not sufficiently important to be worth the
danger of delay. As the speedy settlement of the convention was
desirable, the British government concluded that immediate
ratification of the convention as it stood was on balance the
most advantageous course.[1] It was signed on 20 October 1906.

This procedure was in fact pressed by Deakin, who had
heard that German firms were buying plantations in the New
Hebrides. Sir Edward Grey concurred in recommending immediate ratification. He foresaw dangerous complications
otherwise. Signing the convention as it stood might make
another awkward row with another colony, but the row would
be much more severe if the Germans got into the New Hebrides.
Australia, he argued, would then have a worse and a standing
grievance. He referred to the row currently proceeding with
Newfoundland. Both in the case of Newfoundland and
Australia he thought that they had done the best possible for
the colonies, better than they could have done for themselves.
Their protests he thought unreasonable.[2]

A despatch to governor-general Northcote, dated 16
November 1906,[3] made some comments and attempted to
answer criticisms. The new system would not be easy to work
in practice. It was necessarily complicated. The convention
was not regarded 'as in any sense a final solution of the problem',
but it provided a fair settlement of the most difficult question
between Britain and France in the New Hebrides, the adjudica-
tion of land claims. The convention was represented as 'a clear
and important advance on the system, or lack of system, by
which the affairs of the islands have been hitherto governed'.
It was a reasonable claim, though in practice the administration
of the islands had become stuck in a deplorable rut. One of the
justifications of the system of joint institutions was that for the
first time the native inhabitants had a regular and recognised
authority to whom they might appeal for help and direction.
The arguments against the suggested amendments were mostly

[1] CO. 418/45/36426, tel. S/S to govr.gen. 4 Oct 06.
[2] EP, Grey to E 12 Oct 06.   [3] CO. 225/74, Cd. 3288.

effective, and there was no possible answer to the contention that a single code of law must be the work of years even for trained lawyers, and 'would assuredly be far beyond the powers of any legislative body which could be set up for the New Hebrides'.[1] The defence against the charge that Australia and New Zealand had been faced with a *fait accompli* was less strong. The despatch defended the course taken, of consulting the French officials already in London, as 'the one most natural and convenient'. Since making enquiry was done at the request of Australia,

it did not occur either to my predecessor or to myself that it was necessary to send an interim answer, merely saying that the enquiries desired would be made of the French official mission. . . . The draft convention of the 27th February last is, therefore, the answer to the tentative enquiries which your government suggested.

It was adopted as the clearest method of stating the terms on which an arrangement might be expected to commend itself to the British and French governments. When signed, it was still absolutely subject to the approval of the two governments. Thus the colonial office persisted in its assertion that 'no definite and important step has been taken, and no important information received, without its being at once communicated'.

When the final terms of the convention were announced at the beginning of 1907, there was a good deal of grumbling in newspaper comment about the way it had been concluded, although there was not much attack on the actual terms. 'How very ill-natured the press have been about the New Hebrides,' Churchill wrote to Elgin, 'I am making the office look up the numberless detailed communications which, in the last five years, we have had with the Australian governments on this subject.'[2] Such an attitude wholly ignored the fact that when the subject reached its critical stages there was a gap in communication, between August 1905 and March 1906.

[1] W. P. Morrell, *Britain in the Pacific Islands* (1960), pp. 358–60.
[2] EP, WSC to E 10 Jan 07.

The government came under heavy fire in parliament during the debate on the address in February 1907, not only for their tactlessness in allowing Australia and New Zealand to feel that they had not been adequately consulted, but also for devising a scheme of indentured labour for the New Hebrides which, it was alleged, resembled Chinese Labour.[1] Lyttelton contended that the government had given the maximum of offence with the minimum of information. In reply, Campbell-Bannerman described the government as 'saturated with the views of the Colonies', though he admitted that he had not read the blue book on the New Hebrides. Churchill concentrated on the labour question, and endeavoured to show by quotation that the regulations were better than those in the Chinese ordinance; in addition, the British government were not 'free agents' in this matter, because they were working with the French; as the regulations were being applied to a primitive situation, they therefore represented at least an advance towards more humane conditions of labour; it was, he concluded, a tribute to government success, that on the whole of the address the Opposition could only attack them in 'antipodean archipelagoes', where they were able to 'bring home nothing more fruitful, or more advantageous, than a homely mare's nest'.[2] The Opposition, however, was not to be placated by alliteration and analogy. By the first of March, Churchill was wishing fervently that they had prohibited recruiting for labour outside the New Hebrides. But the colonial office rejected all idea of

[1] One of the main differences was that the New Hebrides convention had not the force of law, binding upon the natives, but the Transvaal law compelled the Chinese to return: there was no such compulsion applicable in the New Hebrides.

[2] PD. 169/133–42, 12 Feb 07; Austen Chamberlain noted in his diary: 'The government has got into a mess (and an awkward one) over the New Hebrides Labour Ordinance. Their people do not like it, but swallow it. Winston was very poor and lame in his reply' (*Politics from inside*, p. 52, 13 Feb 07); and a month later: 'Well, we have had a very pretty day at the House. From 4 o'clock to 11, one speaker after another has rubbed the noses of the government in their New Hebrides dirt. . . . I have not heard our boys cheer so for a long time. And the other side! Dumb dogs, beaten curs and they knew it. . . . Winston was flippant and thin: Grey was grave but very weak; and C.-B. was pitiable' (ibid. 57, 11 Mar 07).

prohibition on the argument that it was contrary to native interests to limit competition for their labour.[1]

Deakin's biographer points out that of all the sources of grievance which Deakin had against the colonial office, the question of the New Hebrides rankled most and longest. In his irritation he was inclined to do less than justice to the officials, who were complacent rather than hostile. He could never see that Britain had no choice but to compromise with France on the New Hebrides.[2] Deakin pressed some of his observations on 5 January 1907. Officials intended to make reply if these were published. Elgin disagreed with them. To continue haggling over these details, he told them, would be ruinous. Deakin's despatch did not entirely climb down, but it came further towards them than he had expected. He preferred not to continue the argument on points of detail, but to look gratefully to the Australian promise of cordial co-operation with the officials who would administer the condominium, a promise which Deakin had made at the end of his despatch.[3]

Some modifications were made in the arrangements after discussions with Deakin at the time of the colonial conference. The New Hebrides question was raised at the conference session on 9 May 1907.[4] Deakin used it as 'the strongest possible impeachment of the methods' of the colonial office. A correspondence had, it was true, been proceeding for many years, but, he said, that was quite irrelevant to the making of this convention. Deakin certainly made some telling points. He proved that Churchill's reply to a parliamentary question on 19 February was contrary to the facts. Churchill apologised, and hoped that any inaccuracies in statements made could be withdrawn. Elgin was forced into the platitudinous, though correct, observation that 'if we could all meet across the table like this, these unfortunate happenings would be avoided'. In a lengthy but quiet defence, Elgin said that Liberals were not blind to the importance of the Pacific, or to the strength of Australian

[1] CO. 225/73/5081, 1 Mar 07.   [2] La Nauze, *Alfred Deakin*, ii, 487, 491–2.
[3] CO. 418/52/5141, minute 27 Feb 07, reply S/S to govr.gen. 7 Mar 07.
[4] Cd. 3523/554–63.

interest in it. Other powers, however, could not be excluded. And it was not quite justifiable to impute to the British government a desire to cause 'a sense of aggravated loss' to Australasia. In view of the sensitive feelings of the Australians, it had been indeed a serious fault not to give their government more information about the discussions, and Elgin made no attempt to pretend otherwise. Although he regretted the exasperation which Deakin suffered, he could not altogether admit to being quite so guilty as Deakin's eloquence made him appear. Their predecessors started the commission; Elgin could not, without further enquiry, explain why Deakin was not informed. If it was his fault he apologised, 'but on a change of government sometimes these things may occur'. Despite having taken the most careful precautions to prevent a leak to the press, 'an accident did happen'. Elgin next discussed the passage in the notifying despatch: 'the draft convention must therefore be confirmed or rejected practically as its stands.' Taken by itself, this might seem a very peremptory statement, 'but it really means if you are to accept the convention at all, it is obvious we cannot do very much more with the French in the matter.' At the same time, an opportunity was given to the governments to submit amendments, and they did so. The British government were prepared to negotiate with the French again, and were on the verge of doing so, when circumstances arose which induced the Australian government to advise immediate ratification. If Britain had been negligent, he would make every effort to avoid giving cause of complaint again. Finally, he dealt with Deakin's complaint that the English representatives had lacked the relevant local knowledge. He admitted that the French representatives had the advantage of closer knowledge of the New Hebrides, but he believed the British government had nevertheless done 'rather well'. Deakin replied tartly: 'You did exactly what they expected you to do. I do not say you did badly on that account.'

To finish this section off, we may leave the last word with Elgin:

The convention itself, though the Opposition made use of it for the purposes of a party attack on the Government, was a great advance on the conditions previously existing, and went as far as it was practicable to do in agreement with France. But the instructions to the High Commissioner bring the provisions regarding the regulation of labour and the like into conformity with British practice, and can, I think, be fully defended. ... I had an interview with a number of missionaries and others from these islands, who raised certain points, most of which are now met, but otherwise [they] were distinctly in favour of, and grateful for, the Convention itself.[1]

WHITE AUSTRALIA POLICY AND THE ANGLO-JAPANESE ALLIANCE

'The first thing which was demanded from its first parliament was a permanent guarantee that the country would remain for ever "white".' Professor Hancock thus aptly indicates the strength of feeling in favour of a 'white Australia' policy in the new Australian commonwealth. In Deakin's opinion, no other aspiration or interest so profoundly stimulated coming together in a federation as 'the desire that we are and should be one people, and remain one people, without the admixture of other races'.[2]

The attitude of the British government towards Australian legislation against Asiatics had been for many years, and remained, definite and consistent. They followed Chamberlain's general declaration in 1897. This stated that while the government sympathised with the determination of white inhabitants in colonies comparatively close to Asia to discourage an influx of people alien in civilisation, religion and customs, especially as such an influx might seriously interfere with the legitimate rights of existing labour populations, the British government preferred this determination to be carried out without placing a stigma upon any British subjects on the sole ground of race

[1] EP, covering note 7 Aug 07 to CO confidential print, *Australian*, no. 186, 8 Aug 07.
[2] W. K. Hancock, in *C.H.B.E.*, vii, pt. 1, *Australia* (1933), 500–1.

or colour. In other words, the British government agreed in substance with the colonial policy of restricting the immigration of Indians, Chinese and Japanese, but asked that it should not involve an express discrimination against coloured races. As Australian acts did not so discriminate, they could not be regarded as contrary to the settled policy of Britain. The policy became much more significant with the conclusion of the Anglo-Japanese alliance in 1902.

Several Australian states had passed legislation other than immigration laws which contained incidental provisions imposing disabilities on Asiatic immigration. The British government had generally failed to secure amendment. Hence Lyttelton on 11 November 1905 sent out a despatch to all self-governing colonies except Natal (where the provision was already written into the constitution), requesting governors to reserve for imperial consideration all bills containing provisions based on race and colour distinctions. This circular was most unpopular. It should not be forgotten that it was not only a Liberal government which was capable of upsetting the susceptibilities of colonial governments. The New Zealand ministers considered that Unionist policy, thus proclaimed, limited powers previously exercised by them; by holding back a decision from the people of New Zealand the despatch was 'subversive of first principles affecting self-governing colonies'. The governor-general of Australia suggested the withdrawal of the circular despatch. His ministers objected to a procedure whereby a mere letter added to the list of specified bills which had to be referred home. He noted 'a great jealousy of Home interference', and an Australian feeling that Englishmen did not appreciate Australian difficulties in dealing with coloured races, who would never swamp Great Britain, but who might swamp Australia.[1] Elgin's reply is interesting:

I may say to you personally that the intense jealousy of Home interference (if it is really genuine, which I sometimes doubt) seems to me to ignore the true relations of the Colonies to the

[1] EP. Northcote to E 4 Mar 06.

Mother Country. I do not suppose there has ever been a desire on the part of any Government at Home to 'interfere' with Colonial affairs. But if the colonies are to remain parts of a great Empire, there surely must be occasions when the action of a Colonial Government may conflict with Imperial interests. Are we not then to be consulted, or to be allowed to ask for information? ... No one would dream of swamping Australia with Japanese or any other coloured race – but I do think it is reasonable that we who are responsible to our allies should be consulted when legislation which may affect them is promoted.[1]

Officials disliked the idea of withdrawing despatches. Cox propounded the general principle that it was essential in the interests of the empire for the British government to have the right to see before it was enacted legislation which might involve them in trouble with other powers. Churchill considered that Lyttelton ought not to have sent a generalising circular despatch, but he counselled against quarrelling now on a matter of form:

We may have some more serious cause of difference later on. H.M.G. do not want to begin with rows all round; and no-one increases his dignity by standing on it. . . . But let us seek peace for the present and ensure it. Withdraw despatch.

Elgin did not feel sure. He agreed that the circular was probably a mistake. An alteration of procedure ought to have been made by royal instructions:

if so, it seems to me an untenable position to maintain the despatch. On the other hand, if 'to stand firm' on the principle involved is of high importance – and I do not say it is not – would it not be possible to do by Royal Instructions what we sought to do by despatch simultaneously with the withdrawal of the despatch? To withdraw the despatch *simpliciter* is to abandon the contention.

And this was done.[2]

Protests were received from the India Office that recent Australian amendments to immigration laws had been 'objectionable and unnecessarily harsh'. The colonial office

[1] EP, E to Northcote 12 Apr 06 (copy).
[2] CO. 209/268/7004, minutes 1 and 2 Mar 06.

legal expert, Cox, went right to the heart of the matter with typical incisiveness:

We simply shall be unable to amend the law save by Imperial legislation, which would be impossible if we wish to keep Australia in the Empire, and to urge what we know they will refuse, will cause friction and do no good.

In themselves, the suggestions of the government of India about modifications were fair and reasonable, but the British government was far too deeply committed to retrace its steps. The Liberal ministry continued the inherited policy. Elgin would very much have liked to do something for the Indians, but he agreed with his advisers that it was impossible.[1] On this question, Cox wrote a little later, they would have the whole of Australia and New Zealand against them; Canada and South Africa would sympathise with Australia. Britain did not question their white Australia policy:

All we ask is that the methods adopted shall be such as not to injure the feelings of civilised Asiatic races such as the Japanese, and such as not to involve us in diplomatic difficulties. In asking this, we are asking as trustees for the whole Empire, its safety and its credit, that local politics shall not be so conducted as to damage imperial interests. The Newfoundland fishery question is another case of the same kind.

Cox proceeded to sum up the government's attitude:

We shall have a much stronger case if foreign powers actually take objection to the provisions of the acts passed, and I would not actually disallow any act unless this occasion arises. When the question is fought out, as it must be if the Empire is to hold together, we must have a strong case and be able to fight on broad lines. Things have dragged on so long as regards these particular acts, that it will look as if we wanted to pick a quarrel if we disallowed any act now.[2]

There was nothing Elgin could add to this statement.

No serious protests were made to the imperial government by the Japanese in this period, but the colonial office was always

[1] CO. 418/50/17500, minutes 25, 26, 29 May and letter to India Office 16 Jun 06.
[2] CO. 418/54/11675, minute by Cox 26 Jun 06, endorsed by Elgin.

on the alert. The position was studied in a long memorandum by Lucas in July 1908.[1] He noted that the constantly growing colonial determination to exclude Orientals was a fixed commitment. The record of the imperial government showed three features. First, a general sympathy with the determination to keep the self-governing colonies for the whites; secondly, a great reluctance to interfere in immigration policy on the ground that it was a matter for the colonists to decide; but, on the other hand, and thirdly, constant pressure to try to obtain good treatment for the East Indians as they were British subjects, and in other cases, notably the Japanese, to safeguard treaty rights, and to ensure that a policy of exclusion should be pursued without specifying particular peoples or wounding their self-respect. Lucas thought it noteworthy that Chamberlain, who was in full sympathy with the self-governing colonies, had been especially outspoken in protesting against giving offence in methods of exclusion, and against harsh treatment of coloured British subjects. Lucas's conclusion was a serious one. The policy of exclusion, he wrote, derived its strength from being based on a natural antagonism, from receiving the solid support of all the working classes, and from being presented, with, as he thought, a strong element of truth, as conducive to the interests of the empire through maintaining 'the purity of the race'. The danger was obvious:

We may conceivably have to choose between our self-governing Dominions and the Japanese alliance; we may conceivably have to choose at some future date between India and the self-governing Dominions; and the matter is now, and will always be, one which may give cause or pretext for complaints against us by the United States, and for attempts at interference on the part of the United States in our relations with the Dominions.

[1] 'The self-governing dominions and coloured immigration', memo. by C.P.L., Jul 1908: CO. 886/1/1 or CO. 532/9/34812.

9 The Colonial Conference of 1907

A COLONIAL conference was due to meet in 1906, and Lyttelton had made plans accordingly. At the end of November 1905, owing to local political circumstances in Australia and New Zealand, it was necessary to postpone the meeting of the next conference from 1906 to 1907. The conference was held at the colonial office from 15 April to 14 May 1907, sitting on three days a week. It was the last one to be called 'colonial' rather than 'imperial'.

It is not difficult to detect a slight undercurrent of impatience over the colonial conference among liberal ministers. As Professor Thornton has said, they were more interested in the Hague conference on disarmament than the colonial conference.[1] The conference gave an opportunity for airing projects of imperial federation in which the Liberals had no interest. It gave tariff reform propagandists a field day for fêting their colonial allies. In addition, as Elgin complained, it disorganised all other arrangements and made it impossible to keep up regular correspondence.[2] In its train it brought a number of interviews which kept him occupied until well into June 1907, together with innumerable ceremonial functions, and the wedding of Botha's daughter.[3] All participants suffered from the frenzy of an incessant stream of faces and talk, at luncheons, dinners, receptions and the like.[4] The high-noon of Edwardian

[1] A. P. Thornton, *The imperial idea and its enemies* (1959), p. 140.
[2] EP, E to Selb. 4 May 07, to Northcote 7 Jun 07 (copies).
[3] The marriage was not to WSC, as gossip had earlier suggested.
[4] The premiers received the freedom of the City of London, were entertained by the Eighty Club, dined with the Prince and Princess of Wales, had a brilliant banquet at the Albert Hall given by the Tory 1900 Club, on an immense Union Jack carpet. They had luncheons given by the Imperial Industries Club and the

hospitality became oppressive in its profusion. Some ministers had a good deal of prejudice against colonials, who were thought swaggering, boring, impudent. Morley described the whole thing as 'the greatest bore that ever was known'. He had no partiality for the boisterous colonials of 'the Kangaroo breed', and of the Australians, he found the federal prime minister, Alfred Deakin, intolerable. 'Our robust young Colonials', he wrote,

are apt to be frightful bores, and if you had been condemned to eat twenty meals day after day in their company, and to hear Deakin yarn away by the hour, I believe you would be as heartily glad to see their backs as I am.[1]

Deakin was the *bête noire* of the Liberals. He had the reputation of being neither fair nor realistic in his criticisms, of twisting the lion's tail for the fun of it. Elgin regarded as satisfactory his unofficial relations with Deakin, whose nickname, after all, was 'Affable Alfred'. On the other hand, he thought that Deakin's official political attitude at the conference was unfortunate, even from the Australian leader's own point of view, since his extraordinary eloquence sometimes led to points being obscured in exuberance.[2] Deakin undoubtedly spoke too much, more than any other member of the conference. Elgin was very patient during this conference, but it was not the sort of occasion which suited his gifts, as he was expected to give more of a personal performance than he had done as chairman of commissions of inquiry. His desire to stand aloof from colonials was not as pronounced as Morley's – indeed he was ready to consider schemes for an imperial senate which would incorporate them more fully than ever before contemplated, into English life and government. Colonial representatives 'of high

---

Benchers of Gray's Inn; there was also a luncheon in Westminster Hall. They had dinners given by the Pilgrims, the Goldsmiths' Company, the National Liberal Club, the Canada Club; they also dined in Oxford, at No. 10 Downing St., and at the Colonial Institute. They escaped a review at Aldershot owing to the ground's being spoiled by heavy rain. See *Annual Register for 1907*, pp. 97–100.

[1] MM. 2/73, 90 and 115, 12 Apr, 26 Apr, 24 May: 3/255, 26 Aug 08; 4/147, 15 Jul 09.

[2] EP, E to Northcote 7 Jun and 30 Sep 07.

character' might be made members of the House of Lords or Privy Council.[1]

There was some disappointment among the overseas visitors when they realised that the conference was not taken so seriously in London as they would have liked.[2] Conferences often tend to be valued more by visitors than hosts.

THE COMMONWEALTH IDEAL

I am no fanatic on the subject of what is called 'Imperial Federation', but it is plainly our interest to maintain and strengthen the bonds of union with our colonies so far as may be possible and they are willing.

Ripon's opinion 1892[3] is a good statement of the Liberal attitude to the government of the empire. It was echoed some years later, by Bryce, when in Toronto he declared:

the Liberals in England were just as desirous of maintaining political connection with the Colonies as English Tories aimed to be. . . . [There was no] indifference to Canada's welfare or the imperial connection.[4]

The Liberals were beginning to find the term 'empire' embarrassing. The term 'commonwealth of nations' had first been used among them by Rosebery. Campbell-Bannerman described the empire as a 'commonwealth of free nations', 'the British Commonwealth' (the term officially adopted in 1921) before 1903. The name of course implied a theory, and Campbell-Bannerman always stressed the importance of the rights of self-government for white colonies, rights which gave vigour and loyalty to every colony which enjoyed them.[5] J. L. Hammond had in 1900 written of a Liberal preference

[1] EP, E to WSC 10 Jan 07 (photocopy), cab. memo. 22 Mar 07. But he once wrote about the honours lists: 'In the colonies, premiers and chief justices fight for stars and ribbons like little boys for toys, and scream at us if we stop them' (EP, E to WSC 3 Nov 06).

[2] *Fortnightly Review*, lxxxi (1907), 992.   [3] CB. 41224/14, to CB 16 Sep 92.
[4] CB. 41211/285, to CB 7 Oct 04.
[5] Spender, *Life*, i, 283; S. R. Mehrotra, 'On the use of the term "Commonwealth" ' (*Journal of Commonwealth Political Studies*, ii (1964), 1–16).

for applying the term commonwealth to the 'confederacy of states which makes up the dominions of the Crown'. Liberals, he said, must see that colonial autonomy was not suffocated. 'The attachment of the colonies to Great Britain depends upon conditions which imperialists are more likely than anyone else to disturb.'[1] Liberals regarded spiritual ties and loyalty to the Crown as the real basis of imperial unity.[2] Churchill was to declare that the empire was a family, not a syndicate; he approved Rosebery's description of it as a 'defensive league of communities under the august headship of the English Crown'.

When the conference of 1907 opened, Campbell-Bannerman, rather than make too effusive a protestation of friendly attachment, followed what he thought really the more significant course of taking it for granted. Then he said:

We found ourselves upon freedom – freedom and independence. That is the essence of the British Imperial connection; freedom of action on the part of the individual state, and freedom in their relations with each other, and with the Mother Country. Anything which militated against that principle would be wholly contrary to the genius of our race and our political ideals, and would sooner or later be disastrous.

Campbell-Bannerman then employed the favourite Liberal device of quoting Chamberlain who 'perfectly expressed' what he had in mind when he had spoken of gladly strengthening the sentimental link which had proved so strong that they would not wish to substitute for it a change which might be galling in its incidence.[3]

Asquith took up this theme in his remarks to the imperial conference of 1911, declaring that each of them intended to remain masters in his own house, but they would also remain 'units in a greater unity', aspiring to equality, combining 'local autonomy – absolute, unfettered, complete – with loyalty to a common head, co-operation, spontaneous and unforced. . . .'

[1] Hammond in Hirst, Murray and Hammond, *Liberalism and the Empire* (1900), pp. 207, 209.
[2] A. M. Gollin, *Proconsul in politics*, p. 125 and *passim*.
[3] EP, draft speech to conference.

This then, was the ideal towards which the Liberals were working. In retrospect, the conference of 1907 marks an important stage in the evolution of the commonwealth. As Professor Hancock has observed: 'In spirit it was far closer to the Commonwealth Club of 1926 than to the Colonial circus of 1887.'[1] It is now authoritatively regarded as probably the most important of all the conferences held before the outbreak of the First World War. All these conferences were in varying degree affected by the difference of opinion between the advocates and the opponents of federalism, between those who wished to formalise the ties of empire, and those who did not; between those who believed that imperial unity was possible only by maintaining the vague ties of friendship and those who believed that they must organise themselves with formal machinery in order to survive. Although the conflict was not finally settled in 1907, it is clear that the anti-federalists won a very important victory. The conflict between the two conceptions of imperial organisation was tacitly decided. Negative decisions are never very exciting, but they can be very significant. Much more than half the work of government consists in securing the quiet lapse of unwelcome proposals, which is what the Liberals achieved in 1907, with decisive support from the Canadians. Imperial unity as an ultimate goal was silently rejected. In the view of their opponents, the Liberals had opted for autonomy and disintegration, rather than centralisation and integration.[2] If Elgin was described as 'unimaginative' it was largely because he did not share the 'imaginative' – but impracticable – visions of the federationists.

THE QUESTION OF MEMBERSHIP

As the date of the conference approached, there were moves to secure the representation of India in any discussion of preferential tariffs. Next, Australian state premiers pleaded that

[1] Hancock, *Smuts*, i, 234.
[2] J. E. Tyler, 'Development of the Imperial Conference, 1887–1914' chap. xi, *C.H.B.E.*, iii, 420, 436–7; J. A. La Nauze, *Alfred Deakin, a biography* (Melbourne, 1965), ii, chap. 22.

they should be summoned. Elgin treated all such representations firmly as undesirable departures from the former rule, under which the only members of the conference were the secretary of state for the colonies, and the premiers. The presence of others would lead to endless confusion, and might easily change the whole character of the conference.[1] India would be represented, as on the previous occasion, by what he called an assessor. That point was quickly disposed of. Not so the Australian claims. In 1902 the states composing the commonwealth of Australia had not been members of the colonial conference. Despite the absence of any change in the relations between the Australian commonwealth and the component states, they now demanded representation. Churchill seemed to regard the claim as self-evidently reasonable, and contented himself simply with a single-sentence comment on it: 'They should certainly be represented.' From that tiny beginning evolved a prolonged and mammoth debate between Elgin and Churchill, reflecting a most bitter controversy between the colonial office in general, and Australia, with Churchill taking the Australian side. Elgin took refuge in the contention that he must follow strictly the practice of former conferences. In any case, he was anxious not to involve the colonial office in the dispute between the Australian commonwealth government and the federal states governments about channels of communication.[2]

Next it appeared that Sir Wilfrid Laurier, prime minister of Canada, would like to bring some of his ministers to the conference. Canadian provincial premiers requested that each colony should be at liberty 'to send such members of its government as it may think fit'. Churchill could see no reason why they should not all come if they wanted to. Elgin possibly overstated the difficulties, formidable though they were. He pointed out that this was not a vague congregation of chambers of commerce, but a conference of premiers, as expressly re-affirmed in 1902. His chief objection was that the larger the

[1] EP, E to Lord Grey 7 Aug 06 (copy).
[2] CO. 323/514/24708, minutes 14 Jul 06.

membership, the more difficult it would be to deal thoroughly with the business in the strictly limited time available. Prolonged discussion by many members was impracticable. The entire arrangements would be dislocated if any particular discussion exceeded the time allotted to it. There were two subordinate difficulties. It would become harder to agree upon a convenient date, a difficulty which again suggested the need for strictly limiting the duration of the conference. The proposal would also give an undue advantage to the colonies which were nearest London. It would be easier for half the Canadian ministry to come over and be absent for about a month, than it would for Australia and New Zealand ministers, who would have to be away for several months. He did not forget that the membership of the conference was in any case expanding as a result of the establishment of responsible governments in the Transvaal and the Orange River Colony. Although chiefly alarmed that the transaction of business would become impeded, for the time being he stood firmly on two points. First, that the last conference came to what was apparently a unanimous decision on this particular subject. Secondly, that the conference must be master of its own proceedings, or, as Mr Chamberlain put it, a change in composition could not be made unless there was a unanimous feeling in its favour. Elgin took the view that the one chance of a workmanlike solution was to discuss the issue only at the conference table itself.[1]

The Canadian proposal envisaged that any of the colonial prime ministers' colleagues who accompanied them should be members of the conference. In one sense, this seemed to Elgin reasonable, but not very meaningful, for they were admitted to the last conference freely when necessary. But it really concealed an important and more general issue. He felt perfectly certain that if they overloaded the conference it would break down. As the whole conception of the conference 'depends on consents', he wished to do nothing hastily which would imperil the unanimity which had hitherto prevailed.[2]

[1] CO. 323/515/40604, minutes 12 and 17 Nov o6, desp. 29 Nov o6.
[2] EP, E to Lord Grey 26 Nov o6 (copy).

Then in December 1906 a protest arrived from the prime minister of New South Wales against possible exclusion. Churchill thereupon launched a trenchant minute in favour of the attendance of the Australian state premiers:[1]

The hold of the state prime ministers upon their people is much more real and intimate than that of the Federal premier upon the loosely-knit and sullenly united Confederation over which he presides. The state premiers were represented at the first Colonial Conference; so that our construction of the Commonwealth Act virtually disfranchises them in the councils of the Empire, and deprives them of a privilege they already possessed. If a severe logic is to rule – how are we to justify the possible representation of South Africa by four ministers, and of Australia by one: or the grant of a representative *each* to Natal and Newfoundland, conjoined with the refusal to allow even one to New South Wales, with five times their aggregate population.

But of course, Churchill was not suggesting that logic should rule these things. Here were powerful persons, the heads of large communities whose co-operation and goodwill they earnestly desired and had few opportunities of winning:

Instead of conciliating them, we rebuff them, and most improvidently try to lean all our weight upon the Federal Government. I had always hoped that the creation of the Commonwealth meant the addition of a new strand to the ties which joined Australia to the Mother Country, that the parts might reinforce the combination, and the combination fortify the parts. We now decide that it shall mean not an addition, but substitution of one weak strand for six solid ones which have been cut.

It is no doubt a good debating reply that the Conference is master of its own procedure – and I cannot hope to prevail against it. But I feel bound to express in the strongest possible manner the regrets I feel at the course to which we are committed.

After this rather over-blown minute on the official papers, the matter was, in accordance with Elgin's maxim 'No quarrel-

[1] CO. 323/515/44358, 7 Dec 06.

ling in school', argued out largely in private correspondence between Elgin and Churchill. It was easy enough to complain that Elgin's attitude was a weak one. But he really did believe it necessary to abide by the constitution as it had hitherto been defined. To increase the numbers now 'would be to forestall the decision on the most important question that will come before the Conference'.[1] He thought the case for refusal a conclusive one, and he was supported by the governor-general of Australia.[2] Churchill admitted that the defensive position, 'the Conference must be master of its own procedure', was quite strong. He merely regretted occupying it. If the state premiers came, and Laurier was allowed to bring three of his ministers, it would mean only seven extra members. The question of Asiatic labour and immigration would certainly have affected the state premiers. These would automatically oppose Deakin, who was the most hostile of all the Australians to the British connection. Therefore, wrote Churchill gleefully, 'Divide et impera!'[3]

Although he disliked it, Churchill recognised that Elgin's decision about state premiers must stand. He was, however, pleased when Elgin agreed to accept his suggestion[4] that the cabinet should discuss the matter, since this might lead to support for his view against Elgin. Indeed Churchill had pressed the prime minister to let the cabinet hear both sides of the question.[5] Churchill admitted the difficulty of the question, and mentioned to Elgin that he had discovered a good many arguments in favour of Elgin's view. Hence he was prepared to suggest a compromise. The state premiers should be parties only to the conference discussion of the questions of their admission in future, and of immigration. In other words, they should take part in discussions which affected them in their state authorities, without too precise a definition of what those discussions would be. Refusal to invite them might have unexpectedly unfortunate results: 'It is hard to measure the importance of such

[1] EP, E to WSC 10 Jan 07 (photocopy).   [2] Ibid. 11 Jan 07.
[3] EP, WSC to E 8 Jan 07.   [4] EP, WSC to E 15 and 17 Jan 07.
[5] EP, CB to E 24 Jan 07.

matters when they first appear on the horizon. Some turn out to be cockle-shells, and others Cunarders.'[1]

By the end of January 1907, Elgin had a memorandum[2] ready for the cabinet. He began it by pointing out that, contrary to all the misrepresentation, and the unfounded allegations of innovations and restrictions, the one rule which he had in fact followed had been the precedent of the last conference. The case against the Australians was stronger than that against the Canadians since the governor-general advised him that the views of the state premiers were not generally supported in Australia. Elgin denied bias or prejudice against them. He thought it right to remember, however, that the commonwealth of Australia had already begun to legislate on trade, copyright, naturalisation, immigration and shipping. As a matter of fact, none of the many subjects on the programme for discussion at the conference, with one unimportant exception, was a subject which fell wholly within the purview of Australian state legislation as distinct from commonwealth legislation. True to himself, Elgin was not prepared to commit himself to any dogmatic pronouncement on the questions of 'status'. Nevertheless, he appealed to the list of subjects which he had mentioned, by no means exhaustive, now transferred to the commonwealth government. From this list he maintained that what was left to the states governments was exactly that class of powers and duties which was currently being connected with the idea of devolution. Therefore, he did not think Churchill's idea of partial admission a good one. It would be insulting to offer admission to the states premiers only when state affairs were under discussion. He had thought of this as a possible, though probably unpalatable suggestion, if a compromise had to be effected. But he had learned from Ramsay MacDonald, who had just returned from Australia, that it would be certain to be rejected. Elgin had satisfied himself that the states could not claim, on the merits of the question, a full right of admission. There was a further difficulty in practice. Very grave inconvenience would result from so material an alteration

[1] EP, WSC to E 17 Jan 07.   [2] EP, cab. memo. 29 Jan 07.

at so late a date in the arrangements. The position of Canadian ministers would possibly have to be reconsidered, and the subjects of discussion revised. All this might endanger the success of the conference. Elgin made one final observation. Envisaging a possible federation of South Africa before the next conference:

To my mind, a conference of Canada (including as I hope, Newfoundland), South Africa, Australia and New Zealand, would be better able to deal with large Imperial questions, and I consider that we should do nothing now to prevent at least its possibility.

Next day, Churchill produced a memorandum[1] arguing the opposite case, starting from the bland proposition that the main reason for inviting the state premiers of Australia was that they wanted to come. Assuming that the business of the conference was not likely to lead to large practical results,

there is one set of benefits of immense practical convenience and solid value which we hope this conference may secure or help to secure, to wit, the establishing of good personal relations between the new Liberal ministry and the leading men in the various Colonies; the friendly discussion of difficulties, mutually comprehensible if frankly stated; and above all, the object lesson that the affections of the British people for the Colonies are not a matter of party at all, but proceed on a plane above the ebb and flow of domestic politics.

A Liberal government had to encounter in imperial affairs what he called 'the steady and malignant detraction of a most powerful press service'. Every action or inaction was represented overseas in the most odious light. The conference would be a fine opportunity for dispersing these unhealthy vapours which hindered the working of the colonial office. He therefore submitted that it was an object of high policy, good in itself, to invite as many of the colonial premiers as possible, and to make the amenities of British hospitality effective throughout the widest possible circle. To exclude them would run the risk of

[1] CO. 885/18/Misc. 198, 30 Jan 07.

'a costly and elaborate function resulting in a net balance of ill-temper and misunderstanding'. Turning then from the ceremonial aspects of the conference, to which he attached so much importance, Churchill tackled the supposed precedent of the previous conference. That conference, he argued, was not formal and authoritative like earlier conferences, because it arose fortuitously out of the gathering for the coronation of King Edward VII. Hence the states did not then protest against exclusion, because the invitations were to the coronation, not the conference. Churchill's view was partly governed by his sympathy for the states in their quarrel with the commonwealth. Appearance, he thought, strongly favoured the states' claim. The creation of central authorities ought not to be allowed to alienate the loyalties of the subordinate or contributory governments. Still less, he continued, should they pronounce on the outcome of the dispute, but remain neutral and bring both parties together, showing to both an equal measure of courtesy and respect. In essence, Churchill, by making the excuse that their attendance was desirable in order to discuss membership, was pleading for an eleventh-hour compromise which might gratify the state premiers without derogating from the status of the commonwealth government.

Elgin flatly refused to have this memorandum printed. He wrote to Churchill:

I am sorry not at once to accept any proposal from you, but I really cannot circulate this memorandum on the Premiers. *I* know that it does *not* mean that you and I are not at daggers drawn on this subject – or any other. But this is a direct negative to the reasoned proposal which I am putting forward on behalf of the Colonial Office – and no-one would ever believe me if I said that behind that blast of defiance there was the calm which prevails. I will take it with me [to the cabinet], and shall not fail to mention that you take a different view – but you will I hope forgive me if I cannot do more.[1]

Elgin's determination to stand his ground succeeded. At the cabinet meeting on 2 February, it was agreed to uphold the

[1] EP, E to WSC 31 Jan 07 (photocopy).

decision already announced, according to which invitations were issued to the same governments as attended the conference of 1902.[1] And so, for all Churchill had written about the unwisdom of allowing 'legal technicalities and the pedantries of etiquette' to rule the decision,[2] he did not convince his superiors.

With one possible exception, that is: King Edward VII shared Churchill's opinion, and questioned the wisdom of the decision of his ministers. As the interventions of the king in colonial policy were very rare, this episode ought perhaps to be mentioned for the benefit of those who are interested in the vestigial influence of the Crown. The king's protest was very mild. Loyalty to the Australian commonwealth was not, he thought, a very deep-rooted feeling. Could it bear the strain of so vital an attack upon the states' *amour propre* as the language used seemed to indicate?[3] Elgin defended himself by sending a copy of his memorandum to the king, so as to make it plain that he was neither making an innovation nor being actuated by any prejudice; 'the whole existence of the conference was at stake.' The unpopularity of the commonwealth government was, he plausibly suggested, one very good reason for not diminishing its authority.[4] The king was not completely convinced, and dictated a memorandum at Biarritz. In his view, the states ought to have a certain amount of latitude where their interests were concerned; their protests were deliberate, official, responsible and plain. The composition of the conference of 1902 was hardly of so distinct a character as to form an unalterable precedent; it was, therefore, not so much on technical grounds as on those of general policy that the king hoped for a solution which might modify the grievance felt by the states, although it need not give all they asked. But as Elgin considered that such a course would diminish the authority of the Australian Commonwealth, he 'naturally does not wish to express a consideration which would involve such a result'.[5]

[1] CAB. 41/31/1; CO. 323/516/3436, minute by E 2 Feb 07.
[2] Ibid. 1592, minute 19 Jan 07.
[3] EP, Sir A. Davidson for the King to Holland for S/S 19 Mar 07.
[4] EP, E to the King 21 Mar 07 (copy).
[5] EP, memo. dictated and signed by the King 26 Mar 07.

And there the matter rested until it reached the conference table itself.

THE QUESTION OF AN IMPERIAL SECRETARIAT

In April 1905 Lyttelton had sent out a despatch in preparation for the next colonial conference. He probably regarded it as the most important despatch he was responsible for.[1] He and his Unionist colleagues proposed to rename and reorganise the colonial conference. The Imperial Council, as it would in future be called, would have new institutional backing in the form of a permanent commission. This body would have the powers of a royal commission, together with its own staff and offices. Its function would be approximately probouleutic, and probably executive. It would prepare the preliminary work for a coming Council. It would examine and report upon the best means of giving effect to the resolutions of the last Council. The cabinet agreed that this machinery would supply continuity between conferences and make them in all respects more fruitful of results,[2] although Balfour had found it difficult 'to form a very clear image ... of how this somewhat anomalous machinery is to work'.[3]

Underlying this despatch was a political object. Lyttelton privately hoped to establish a body which would perform a similar function to the Committee of Imperial Defence. Like that body, it might help to secure continuity of policy through a change of government. The Imperial Council would stand to the Commission as the cabinet did to the Defence Committee.[4]

The senior officials in the colonial office disliked this scheme as they disliked all Lyttelton's major proposals. They thought the Commission unnecessary as a preparatory body and potentially dangerous in its powers, especially as it was not 'responsible to the people'. They thought it unlikely to be

[1] E. Lyttelton, *Alfred Lyttelton*, p. 310.   [2] CAB. 41/30/15, 18 Apr 05.
[3] Balfour papers 49775/23, Balfour to Lyttelton 13 Jan 05.
[4] Balfour papers 49775/33–40, 1 Feb 05, Lyttelton to Balfour.

efficient. It was rather too confidently assumed, they thought, that the formal establishment of a Council would tend to promote unity of sentiment. They could discern no demand for a Commission. Ommanney summed up their apprehensions by urging that the proposal should not be carried further. Lyttelton, however, was not persuaded that the existing preparation for the conferences was as adequate as the office naturally liked to assume. The whole point of the suggested change was to inform, not the secretary of state and the British government, but the colonial conference and the colonial prime ministers, who had not the staff available to do the work for them, and could not, he thought, be expected to accept the material which the colonial office submitted. As to the supposed incapacity of colonials to keep secrets, he was prepared to safeguard the requirements of security by withdrawing the suggestion that they should have the powers of royal commissioners, and to withhold from them subjects for discussion unless these were referred to them by the Council, or by one or more of the colonies acting jointly with the secretary of state for the colonies. As usual, Lyttelton thought that his staff had rather magnified the whole proposal. His response was typical of the politician who tries to push through a change by minimising its significance: it was simply, he said, a 'cautious and tentative plan to give reality to the periodical conferences'.[1]

Colonial reactions to his despatch were not uniformly favourable, especially in Canada. This strengthened the hand of the officials. Once the new Liberal ministers took over, Ommanney lost no time in pressing his objections upon them:

I think it very desirable that the secretary of state should assume an attitude of detachment, for the present, in regard to the scheme for a Permanent Commission in connection with future Conferences. The objections raised in the office minutes were based on wide and practical knowledge: they were strong, and have never been met, and the manner in which the proposal has been received by the Colonies makes it necessary to proceed with caution.

[1] CO. 885/17/Misc. 184, minutes Apr 05.

He met with a sympathetic reaction. Churchill completely agreed with Ommanney. Elgin added his initial. It is exactly this kind of issue upon which Elgin has been accused of weakness and relying overmuch on his officials. If this was so, then it should be remembered that on such issues Churchill, whom everyone quite rightly thinks of as being independent-minded, also agreed with Elgin. A despatch sent out in February declared the dissociation of the new secretary of state from Lyttelton's suggestions:

I do not feel myself called upon to adopt the recommendation of those proposals in view of the expressions of opinion received from the Colonies, but I think that it will be desirable that the scheme should be freely discussed when the conference meets.[1]

Privately Elgin thought that they must be on the watch for powers being claimed for the conference, or for some council representing it, which might seriously hamper Britain in her international arrangements.[2]

Just before the conference, Elgin produced a memorandum on the 'Organisation in connection with colonial conferences'.[3] The name 'Colonial Conference' had, to his mind, accurately expressed the nature and purpose of the gathering. If the word 'imperial' was to be introduced, this must, he thought, imply presidency of the prime minister. Personally he would welcome this change with relief, but it would follow that the whole scope of the proceedings would be enlarged. Then, the cabinet as a whole, and not a single department, would in fact become in charge. He agreed with Canada in wishing to reject the use of the word council, especially as there was no real concurrence in the resolutions submitted by the colonies who nominally took a more favourable view of this change. While he was convinced that the proposal for an imperial council which would exercise

---

[1] CO. 323/514/2854, minutes 10, 12 and 13 Feb 06, and desp. 22 Feb 06.
[2] EP, E to WSC 10 Jan 07 (photocopy).
[3] EP, memo. for cabinet 22 Mar 07. This memorandum should be some answer to the assertion that Elgin 'appeared not to have applied his mind to the subject of imperial organisation, and to be merely the mouthpiece of the permanent officials', an opinion quoted in La Nauze, *Deakin*, ii, 500.

authority was bound to excite objections from both sides, he was far from saying that no advance from the present position was practicable. If practicable, it was certainly desirable:

Something is widely demanded both in this country and in the Colonies, and not now for the first time. It was in the attempt to satisfy that demand that Mr Chamberlain put forward his scheme of colonial preference, mistaking, as I have always thought, the true bond that united us. I would wish to proceed on less sensational, but, as I believe, sounder lines.

Elgin entirely distrusted the idea of a joint permanent commission not under the direction of a responsible head, especially when the business would be largely of a confidential character. Instead, he proposed to create a distinct branch of the colonial office, whose head would be secretary of the conference. This would not only bring the proceedings of the conference more directly into relation with the programme of its successor. It would also enable the necessary steps to be taken without delay if, in any direction, the discussions of the conference pointed to further investigations or preparations. Outside assistance could be enlisted in the work if necessary. In conclusion he wrote:

In my judgment the time has not yet come when H.M.G. or the Colonial Government can concede any part of the responsibility or authority belonging to either to an intermediate body. But I do think that the time is approaching when means might be devised for securing the intercommunication throughout the great divisions of the empire of ideas on which united action must so largely depend.

The cabinet discussed the arrangements for the conference on 27 March 1907. It was unanimously agreed to discard the proposal for a standing imperial council. But they authorised Elgin to mention two of his proposals when refusing the Lyttelton scheme. First, an official of the colonial office should be given the duty of seeing that the proceedings of the conference were recorded and tabulated. Secondly, the colonists should be represented in England by persons of weight and experience who would be able to speak with authority for the

333

colonies. The want of such intermediaries was deeply felt at the time when the New Hebrides convention was discussed.[1]

In his opening speech at the conference, Campbell-Bannerman planned to express approval of Elgin's proposal for a permanent secretary to the conference. He told Hopwood that he had read Elgin's memorandum, and 'was all for giving effect to it'. Hopwood wisely told Elgin of the prime minister's intention, urging Elgin to ask Campbell-Bannerman to omit this reference, because it would take from the secretary of state the one thing with which he could bargain when he came to deal with the resolutions on the imperial council.[2] The prime minister accepted the force of this point when it was put to him.

PROCEEDINGS OF THE CONFERENCE

The conference was in session on fifteen days between 15 April and 14 May 1907. The first problem dealt with was the organisational one. Deakin laid before the conference a resolution for a joint imperial secretariat. Behind the proposal was the conception of something like an imperial conference permanently in session even between its actual meetings. The proposal inevitably got confused with Lyttelton's original suggestion of a standing commission. However much Deakin might stress that his body would have no independent powers or functions, it was suspect as being somehow beyond ministerial control. His scheme blended two conceptions in a way likely to provoke misunderstanding: the secretariat as a body to prepare information, as a link between conferences, and the secretariat as a link between the governments, controlled by the prime minister, superseding the colonial office for that purpose. He seemed to believe that one might grow into the other. Although he could not state the aim openly, he hoped to see the elimination of the colonial office as the formal link between Britain and the self-governing dominions.[3]

[1] CAB. 41/31/12, 27 Mar 07. [2] EP, Hopwood to E 14 Apr 07.
[3] La Nauze, *Deakin*, ii, 478, 503–4.

Campbell-Bannerman had no enthusiasm for Deakin's plan for making the British prime minister directly responsible for the self-governing colonies. The prime minister, after all, had no staff or office, and could not undertake such work. There would, he felt, be an obvious disadvantage in breaking all connection between the two classes of colony. No drastic action was needed to meet criticism:

The real point is that the Crown Colonies have to be administered, or at least their administration has to be supervised; whereas the others should be left alone except in the cases where consultation and advice are required. The Colonial Office is alleged to have a tendency to apply to the latter the more meddlesome practices which they are accustomed to use in the former case.

If there is truth in this, it will be corrected (a) under the new influence of Hopwood – his predecessor, having been concerned entirely with Crown Colonies, may have had the tendency complained of – and (b) by your new division of the Office into two parts, one dealing with the Colonies to be administered, the other with those which require only correspondence, information and advice.[1]

In his opening address, Campbell-Bannerman stuck to generalities, as had been agreed. 'We found ourselves upon freedom. . . .' Freedom did not necessarily mean letting things drift. Some provision should be made for 'maintaining the impetus' which the conferences gave to the consideration and settlement of the questions discussed at them.

On 17 April Elgin made a long statement upon organisation. Having written out in full, well in advance, a draft of his remarks, he was disconcerted to find that he had not correctly anticipated the attitude of the premiers or interpreted the substance of some of their resolutions in the right way. What was said in discussion indicated that the vague New Zealand resolution was not intended to establish a permanent imperial council in place of the conference. Rather lamely, he continued to make remarks based on the assumption that such an inter-

[1] EP, CB to E 17 Apr 07.

335

pretation could be read into the resolution, and declared that the government could not agree to establish a body with independent status or authority. This would be 'a danger to the autonomy of us all'. Government was entrusted to ministers responsible to parliament. Any body interposing itself 'might almost endanger the liberties which ought to be inviolate'. On the other hand, it might be possible to improve the methods whereby the machinery of the conference operated. After Deakin had denied attempting to change the constitution of the conference, Elgin rather awkwardly explained that in what he had said, he had 'no doubt rather assumed that I was speaking of what I imagine possibly might be the idea underlying the New Zealand resolution as to an Imperial Council in place of the Conference'.[1]

The extent to which Elgin had prepared his remarks on premises which were made to seem false, may be judged from the lengthy cuts he made in speaking from his draft. His redundant reasoning is nevertheless of some interest.[2] He would have deprecated the introduction of the council, partly on the ground that it would destroy the influence of the governor and circumscribe his sphere of influence. As a result, it would become impossible for Britain to obtain men 'of a standing and calibre that any service would be proud to own'. He would not say that an imperial council would never be practical. One passage in his draft looks like a prophecy of the aeroplane revolution:

In these days it is hazardous to be positive as to any limits to the triumphs of science and the inventor. The time may come, perhaps much more speedily than we imagine, when what we now deem the insuperable obstacles of distance may disappear. If so – it is probable that, with the change of circumstance, solutions of the problems of representation and responsibility may present themselves which we cannot now conceive, but would readily accept.

[1] Cd. 3523 (1907), Minutes of proceedings of the Colonial Conference, 1907 p. 37.
[2] Compare draft in EP with version recorded in Cd. 3523, pp. 35–9.

The Latest Delicacy at the Carlton

'Repatriation (in the New Hebrides) had peculiar difficulties. . . . It was like repatriating the Under-Secretary for the Colonies to the other side (*Laughter*). If they popped him down on one side of the island he was admired, respected, and cheered; but on the other side he was eaten (*Loud laughter*)' — Sir Charles Dilke's speech

An Elgin Marble

To achieve greater continuity in the intervals between conferences, the colonial office itself, Elgin announced, would respond with alacrity to any call that was made upon it. He pledged himself to provide for continuity under ministerial responsibility. Laurier strongly supported the contention that an independent secretariat was inconsistent with ministerial responsibility, which must be maintained.

Having succeeded in obtaining authority from the conference for the colonial office to provide secretarial staff, Elgin logically enough treated an attempt by Deakin to elucidate some details as an unwarranted interference in the task of the imperial government, which should be allowed a free hand to determine how the scheme was to be implemented. The government would try to establish

a distinct division dealing with the affairs of the responsibly governed colonies. I will not say it will be exactly apart, because there is, and must be, at the head, at any rate, a connecting link between the several parts of any office. . . .

In his final remarks, Elgin protested, in as friendly a way as he could, at the attitude Deakin had attributed to the colonial office. Deakin had complained that the office gave a general impression of having made up its mind upon matters before discussion began. Its whole tendency was to become imbued with principles which might be appropriate to the great countries for which they were directly responsible, but which were 'very foreign, and in some cases antagonistic, to the principles on which the affairs of self-governing colonies are conducted'.[1] Elgin said mildly that they had no wish to be dictatorial or uncivil in correspondence, nor to infringe freedom and independence. He claimed to be offering 'a great advance on former practice' by his promise to set up a secretarial branch within the office. It would involve him in difficulties, but he believed it right to strengthen the process of getting and communicating information. Although the proposal

---

[1] An official at the time, G. V. Fiddes, later recorded that the colonial office 'was quite unable to recognise itself in the description given of it' by Deakin (*The Dominions and Colonial Offices* (1926), p. 245.

that the permanent secretariat should be in the colonial office was opposed by Deakin and Jameson, they seemed to be mollified as a result of Elgin's frank admission – as it practically was – that the colonial office needed bringing up to date.[1] Deakin was, however, to describe the creation of the dominions department in the office as merely a reshuffle of the old cards.

Other ministers besides premiers did in fact attend the conference, without being described as members. The rule of the 1902 conference which confined membership to premiers was abandoned. These ministers were allowed to the table as advisers; it was an honourable understanding that not more than one minister from each colony should assist his premier at any given session. For the future it was resolved that the name of the conference should be the Imperial Conference. Campbell-Bannerman thought the change innocuous. The members would be premiers and the secretary of state for the colonies. Other ministers would be members also, it being understood that normally each discussion would be conducted by only two representatives from each government.

One further matter of organisation was discussed at the conference. Although this was not put before the conference until the end, it will be convenient to treat it at this stage. This was a proposal by Deakin for the interchange of permanent staff. Deakin invited the secretary of state to frame a scheme creating opportunities for civil servants to acquire more intimate knowledge of circumstances and conditions in the colonies, whether by appointment, temporary interchanges, periodical visits or similar means. In reply, Elgin stressed the practical difficulties. As the colonial office was staffed from open competitive examination, 'it would be, perhaps, a little difficult to arrange exchanges on equal footings'. Their plans to make a

[1] Hopwood to Bryce 23 Apr 07: 'The government has done very well so far, although they have received a good deal of provocation from Deakin and Jameson, and of gross misrepresentation from the press, the other ministers, especially Laurier and Botha, have been most helpful. . . . The fact remains that the Colonies want to govern us and to take charge of our affairs! . . . They went so far as to claim that the senior colonial prime minister should take the chair when the prime minister could not be present' – instead of the secretary of state (Bryce papers E 28).

departure from the geographical division in the office by establishing a branch to deal with the dominions, 'may make even a fresh difficulty in the question of delegation as between offices and different parts of the world'. His reasoning thus far does not seem to have been very clear. It did not become any clearer when he dealt with a theoretical objection. The office dealt 'in no way with the local administration . . .' therefore:

the business which actually comes here from you depends more upon principles than upon local characteristics. I am not quite sure, I admit, that it is absolutely necessary for the performance of these duties that the men who are in charge of them should journey over the world.

He argued that they would have to go to several colonies, 'in order to qualify themselves in all'. No ex-viceroy of India had yet become secretary of state for India. He quoted this as an illustration of his belief that in dealing with certain questions it was not absolutely necessary for a man to be chosen because of his knowledge of the place from which those questions came. Nothing could be more mid-Victorian than this exposition.[1] Palmerston would have dismissed a similar proposal with the same argument, though Palmerston would have dismissed it more contemptuously.[2] Despite the old-fashionedness and confusion of Elgin's doctrinaire argument against it, the resolution for the interchange of permanent staff was allowed to drop. However, the hint was not entirely lost sight of. In 1909 Sir Charles Lucas became the first member of the colonial office staff to make an official tour of the empire.[3] But next year he retired.

[1] Cd. 3523/619–20.
[2] In 1859 Palmerston suggested that though the 8th earl of Elgin had been to China he was not necessarily better qualified to judge the possible effect of military operations on the Chinese Empire than he was himself.
[3] Yet as recently as Dec 06 Ommanney had successfully pressed on Elgin the view that they should rely on governors to promote the interests of colonies, and therefore no-one should be sent from the colonial office, as was requested, on an expedition to the West Indies to investigate cotton growing. The expedition was sponsored by the British Cotton Growing Association. Elgin thought there were some advantages in an official having such an opportunity, and enlarging his experience, but he did not like the idea of sending an official representative (CO. 318/315/45206, minute 15 Dec 06). Rapid tours around the world did not enable men to get to the bottom of big questions (EP, E to WSC 10 Jan 07, photocopy).

Sir Almeric Fitzroy, clerk to the privy council, correctly understood the significance of this conference in the field of imperial organisation. He noted that though lip-service to the imperial idea was forthcoming in abundance, the efforts of Deakin and his supporters to give it substantive form met with but little response. He made a very astute observation: 'Things are in fact tending to the free association of independent communities as the ideal of Empire, with no link apart from the Crown, but a common origin and an assumed parity of political development.'

Fitzroy also recorded in his diary a tribute to Elgin's chairmanship. Deakin tried to establish an imperial court of appeal. The lord chancellor firmly rebuffed this, though couching his remarks in terms of great deference to colonial aspirations. 'Outwardly Deakin took the rebuff in good part, but there was clearly in his mind an under-current of chagrin.' He strove to secure some affirmation of his resolution merely as if it were a recommendation to the imperial government. Elgin then interposed the remark that this would be out of place, as the government were a party to the conference. Deakin finally accepted the chairman's proposal simply to record the fact of his resolution's having been discussed. 'Elgin's intervention thus got over what might have proved a serious obstacle to harmony upon a subject involving one of the most important bonds of imperial unity.'[1]

Emigration, defence, and the promotion of uniformity in merchant shipping legislation were discussed. Apart from the procedural questions, the other item of major interest discussed by the conference was the issue of imperial preference.[2] At the conference, Asquith was the chief government spokesman on preference. Churchill was not a member of the conference, but succeeded in insinuating himself. He does not appear to have

[1] Fitzroy, *Memoirs*, i, 320, 25 Apr 07.
[2] E to Selb. 4 May 07: 'On the whole the Conference is proceeding smoothly. On preference of course there was bound to be a difference of opinion and some plain speaking, but otherwise I think more has been done than some expected. It has been anxious work and I cannot say I shall be sorry when it is over, though my relations with my colleagues have been very friendly' (EP, copy).

been invited to speak, but personally to have asked permission to address the conference.[1] Introducing him, Elgin explained that Mr Churchill wished to deal with a 'particular side' of the subject, of which the parliamentary under-secretary was 'specially in charge'. The particular turned out to be in fact the most general, namely, the political aspects of preference in relation to parliamentary government.

Churchill's main thesis was, as even Jebb admitted,[2] a perfectly tenable one: the addition to parliamentary business and the more extensive friction of commercial interests. If preference, said Churchill, was to be given effect to in 'any symmetrical, logical, complete or satisfactory, or even fair and just manner', it must involve new taxes on seven or eight staple articles of consumption in Great Britain. Apart from this remarkably comprehensive string of favourite Churchillian adjectives, a catalogue of the political virtues as he saw them, the speech was chiefly memorable for the dictum that the British Empire exists on 'the principles of a family and not on those of a syndicate'. A system of reciprocal preference must at its very outset involve conflict with the principle of self-government ('which is at the root of all our colonial and imperial policy'), because British M.P.s would refuse to vote preference tax until their views on native policy were met. The imposition of duties could lead to a 'deep feeling of sullen hatred' (another most characteristic phrase) among the poorer people, and to the emergence of an anti-colonial party in the House of Commons. Even if economically desirable, preferences would, in his opinion, prove an element of 'strain and discord' in the structure of the empire. He resisted it as positively injurious to the unity of the empire. And so to his peroration:

We may find a more convenient line of advance by improving communications, rather than by erecting tariffs – by making roads, as it were, across the empire, rather than by building walls.

[1] Cd. 3523/400.   [2] R. Jebb, *The Imperial Conference*, ii, 242.

He hoped that the conference would be remembered in the future,

> when imperial unification has been carried to a stage which it has not now reached, as a date in the history of the British Empire when one grand wrong turn was successfully avoided.[1]

Deakin cuttingly attacked Churchill for insisting on a complete, uniform and scientific system. This was clearly impossible. There must, he thought, be a gradual and experimental beginning. Asquith gave the final and decisive answer of the government quite bluntly. The government would not treat the 'foreigners and the colonies as it were differently'. Thus was the whole world, and not just the empire, to be considered as a family. In the end, the resolutions of 1902 were reaffirmed, the United Kingdom alone dissenting. As Asquith pointed out privately to Elgin, there was no real objection to this reaffirmation, because the resolutions did not invite, still less encourage, Britain to make any change in her fiscal system.[2]

REORGANISATION OF THE COLONIAL OFFICE: CREATION OF THE DOMINIONS DEPARTMENT

The conference resolved that it was desirable to establish a system by which governments should be kept informed between conferences about matters which had been, or might become, subjects for discussion. This would be obtained by means of a permanent secretarial staff within the colonial office, charged with the duty of obtaining information for the use of the conference, attending to its resolutions, and conducting correspondence on matters relating to its affairs.

The reorganisation of the colonial office was, however, something which, though it necessarily followed from the resolutions of the conference of 1907, would have come even without the

[1] Cd. 3523/400–7, 7 May 07.   [2] EP, Asquith to E 6 May 07.

pledges then made. Elgin had, to use his own words, 'something of the kind' in contemplation before the conference:[1]

Therefore, though from one point of view it was a counter-check to the, as I think, dangerous movement for the establishment of an authority outside the control of the Minister who is responsible for Colonial affairs, on the other hand something of the kind had become necessary to cope with the current work of the Office.[2]

Elgin found the internal arrangements antiquated and inefficient. When the new arrangements were in fact announced, Elgin and Hopwood insisted on the omission of any reference to the colonial conference in the title of the circular despatch. 'This is a much bigger thing than the mere arrangement for the Colonial Secretariat', wrote Elgin.[3]

Business had originally been distributed on geographical lines, but these divisions had become obscured by 'the gradual accretion of spheres of duty in many parts of the world'. Although there was also a general department, each geographical department settled its own concessions. The result was infinite complication. It was impossible to define any very distinct principle on which the office was organised. The lack of co-ordination produced some curious discrepancies and inconsistencies of policy, as well as overlapping. Elgin decided to strengthen and enlarge the general department. Otherwise his principle was 'to make the line of division in the Office one of status rather than of geography'. In particular, the business of the self-governing colonies was to be separated into a new

---

[1] In December 1906 Elgin argued for a financial secretary or adviser to be appointed, and foreshadowed his later scheme: 'We have concessions and contracts coming to us for consideration from every part of the world. At present all the four under-secretaries have to deal with them. There is no fixed principle, nor even co-ordination. It is true that at a certain stage they are referred as a rule to the Crown Agents – but even then the decision may be come to in entire ignorance of the decision on a similar case in another branch the previous week. That at least might happen.... Just as all legal business would go from all branches to the Legal secretary – so all financial business would go to the financial secretary from all the geographical branches' (EP, memo. [n.d.] on Ommanney's and Sir G. Murray's scheme and notes on colonial office reorganisation).

[2] EP, E to Crewe 7 May 08 (draft).   [3] CO. 532/3/34119.

Dominions department, self-contained, but within the colonial office. The head of this branch, it was originally envisaged, would also act as secretary to the conference. His duties were to be 'retrospective and prospective alike, imposed or contemplated by the periodical conferences'.[1] Eventually it was decided to appoint a separate secretary and head of department, posts which were first occupied respectively by Just and Lucas, perhaps the two officials most highly regarded by Elgin.[2]

The actual relationship of the conference secretariat to the Dominions department was left somewhat vague. It was described as being linked to the Dominions department without being entirely merged; as having its own functions, but necessarily connected with the department. Administratively at least, it was in fact fully integrated as part of the department. Its staff performed ordinary departmental duties in addition to secretariat functions.[3]

The scheme of course had to have the sanction of the treasury. In presenting the proposals to the treasury every argument had as usual to be strained to the limits. Elgin argued that his scheme would satisfy pledges without making the further call on the public purse which would have been involved in the creation of a separate new department. The colonial office would be divided into three departments: one to deal with the self-governing colonies (also including possessions adjacent thereto, for example Fiji, the native territories and protectorates in South Africa, and the British South Africa Company possessions), another to deal with the Crown Colonies (where the work would no longer be divided on a geographical basis), and a third department called the Legal and General Department, to deal with audit, personnel, currency, education, immigration, concessions, returns and so forth. Elgin explained how he had been much influenced by the want of co-ordination and concerted investigation in dealing with certain very

[1] Ibid. minutes by E 17 and 20 Sep 07, circular desp. 21 Sep 07.
[2] PD. 181/1070–1, 22 Aug 07.
[3] J. A. Cross, 'Whitehall and the Commonwealth', *Journal of Commonwealth Political Studies*, ii (1964), 192.

important questions, especially the consideration of applications for land and other concessions, of railway schemes and financial proposals. He proposed to establish four standing committees, to deal with patronage and promotions, railways and finance, concessions, pensions. The colonial office had been consistently overworked for years. One of the chief objects of the reorganisation was to decentralise, and to try to reduce the amount of work hitherto falling on the under-secretaries. The committees were designed to reduce the 'unnecessary duplication of work', to relieve the Crown Colony department of some of its work and to treat important business questions in 'a more systematic and matured manner than at present'. Retaining the imperial secretariat as an integral part of the establishment of the colonial office was desirable on financial and other grounds.[1]

Both the prime minister and Asquith as chancellor of the exchequer were in favour of the scheme in principle. When the treasury criticised details, Asquith soothed Elgin's alarm by saying that this was its duty. Otherwise he thought Elgin's scheme 'in all its main features admirable', and would be extremely sorry to see it hampered.[2] The scheme was approved.

Elgin was satisfied with the first few months of the working of the new arrangements, which was all he was to experience. He would have liked, at the time of his departure in April 1908, to supervise them a little longer, but felt that the arrangements were on the right lines. The main object was achieved: 'the great evil of overlapping or duplication of work' had been lessened.[3] It was a valuable contribution to obtaining greater consistency of policy in the Crown Colonies. As far as the self-governing colonies were concerned, there was never any pretence that the changes were even remotely revolutionary or likely to lead to vital results.[4]

---

[1] CO. 323/534/29255a, CO to treasury 15 Aug 07; CO. 323/528/30095, CO to treasury 16 Sep 07.

[2] EP, Asquith to E 29 Jul and 10 Oct 07.

[3] EP E to Crewe 7 May 08 (draft).

[4] Hopwood thought Lord Grey 'far too sanguine' in his views as to the results of the reorganisation; there seemed to be extraordinary interest in Canada 'in a matter which seems to me comparatively unimportant' (EP, Hopwood to E 23 May 07).

Problems of the Dependent Empire

On *12 June 1907 Elgin was in Cambridge to receive an honorary degree, in company with Campbell-Bannerman, Haldane, Curzon and Milner. He was buttonholed in a crowd by 'a medical professor', who tried to persuade him that African fleas and mosquitoes could be dissected and classified, with a view to discovering their influence in various diseases, as well in Britain as in Africa, or even better. The receipt of an honorary degree in company with Curzon and Milner might be said to symbolise the movement of imperial problems into a less contentious phase, the quaint incident with the professor to symbolise the increasing impossibility of escape from the problems of tropical Africa.*

South Africa was the chief fount of imperial policy throughout 1906. The colonial conference absorbed most of the attention in the first half of 1907. In the last phase of Elgin's colonial secretaryship, the Crown colonies and African protectorates had their turn. Elgin spoke of the 'ever increasing importance and value' of the Crown colonies in August 1907. Their emergence to a position of public prominence in colonial policy was heralded, and expedited, by Churchill's tour of East Africa in the autumn recess of 1907.

10 Churchill's Tour, Autumn 1907, and its Consequences

ELGIN welcomed Churchill's plan to make a tour of East Africa in the autumn of 1907. For one thing, it would put Churchill safely out of the way. (Or so he thought. He was to discover that it took more than a few thousand miles' distance to reduce the pressure Churchill tried to exert upon affairs.) For another, it would be of the greatest advantage that one of them should see a region which was the seat of so many difficult problems. In particular it would give a splendid opportunity for a study on the spot of the problem of race relations. It is of great interest to see that this was how Elgin interpreted Churchill's opportunity. He commended the subject to him as 'well worth study on the spot'. He looked forward 'with the greatest interest' to learning first-hand from Churchill the result of such a consideration by 'so acute an observer'. In a letter to wish Churchill *bon voyage*, he set forth at some length his own speculations upon native problems; he wanted to profit by the unique opportunity 'of your being able to look at them with all your great powers of observation and your knowledge of official information'.[1]

Unfortunately the African tour did not turn out quite as Elgin had expected when he blessed it. Elgin had understood that it was intended to be 'a purely sporting and private expedition'; he was rather at a loss to know 'how it drifted into so essentially an official progress'. But such a character it assumed, much to Elgin's discomfort and chagrin. It is possible that thereafter his opinion of Churchill was not as good as it

[1] EP, E to WSC 5 Jun and 25 Sep 07 (photocopy).

had been before. In addition to tourist accounts contributed to the *Strand Magazine*, Churchill sent back memoranda on every possible subject: Malta, Cyprus, Somaliland, railways in East Africa, the Nile. Elgin was very sceptical about this spate of paper. He dismissed most of the proposals as 'impracticable, at least as they stand'.[1] Churchill also sent private letters direct to Hopwood, as well as a minute to the treasury about the Cyprus tribute. Hopwood was embarrassed by the letters he received, especially when Elgin saw them. Hopwood realised that they 'would not either in style or substance be pleasing' to Elgin. Hopwood disapproved of the flood of memoranda which Churchill was despatching. Churchill, he thought, should have reserved his points until he returned home. Anybody else would have done so out of caution and personal convenience: 'Marsh gives a vivid description of 14 hours work in one day upon these memoranda in the heat and discomfort of the Red Sea.'[2]

As far as Churchill was concerned, the tour confirmed the development of his imperial thought in a constructive direction. The initial phase of iconoclasm, the hankering after systems of minimum concern, was abandoned, except for Somaliland. Chamberlain's doctrine of developing Britain's 'great estates' overseas received a new and whole-hearted advocate.[3] The special message Churchill brought back from East Africa was 'concentrate upon Uganda', especially by building a railway extension: 'Uganda is the pearl.'[4]

MALTA AND CYPRUS

Churchill left England in September 1907, and first spent some weeks in Europe. Then, in Malta, he visited schools and

---

[1] EP, E to Crewe 7 May 08 (draft). [2] EP, 27 Dec 07.

[3] WSC, *My African Journey* (1908), p. 52, hereafter cited as *MAJ*. He speaks of 'these great estates' on p. 215. 'That Uganda will become one of the greatest centres of tropical produce in the world seems to me indubitable' (WSC to Grey 29 Feb 07, FO confidential print 9125, Jan 08).

[4] *MAJ*, pp. 197, 209–13.

the Corradino prison just outside Valetta. Certain features of Maltese law shocked him, especially those relating to adultery and debt. This was probably the beginning of Churchill's strong interest in prison reform, which was to animate him as home secretary a couple of years later. He made a speech to the elected members of the Executive Council on 4 October 1907. Five years earlier Chamberlain had curtailed their power of making their views effective. Churchill told them that they would have to confront the colonial secretary with clear evidence that a new situation had arisen before he would be induced to reconsider the present state of affairs. Churchill urged them to co-operate with the government and avoid a constitutional struggle with the imperial authorities. For the maintenance of order, for security reasons, the authorities must have a predominant voice in all matters which could be considered to touch imperial interests. On the other hand he would be glad

if it be possible, to make some arrangements which would be more in accordance with your wishes, and secure to you a more effective voice in purely local affairs . . . the door is not closed upon the constitutional question.

Elgin was quite happy with this statement when he read it. He thought that Churchill had given them sound advice.[1] Churchill received a deputation and had conversations with the leader of the elected members, Mr Azzopardi. He also saw the president of the Old Nobility, the leader of the Malta Bar, and the president of the chamber of commerce. Privately, he felt that their grievance was 'a very real, and . . . a very painful one. . . . I do not like to feel that we are behaving in a high-handed and arbitrary fashion – even with the best inten-tion. . . .'[2] His conclusions were recorded in a minute on 15 October, forwarded home on 2 November, and revised in a memorandum of January 1908.[3]

[1] CO. 158/356/36812. [2] EP, WSC to E 4 Oct 07 from Malta
[3] CO. 158/360/3351, typed memorandum.

351

All these Maltese leaders, said Churchill, agreed in complaining that on purely Maltese questions their opinion was not even effectively consulted, let alone allowed to prevail. They were being made to feel 'strangers in their own land'. They were never conquered by England; they were not allowed any sort of control in the spending of their money.

Upon the whole I am not prepared to deny the essential justice of the complaint made to me. The saying that 'Malta has no more right to a constitution than has a battleship' is widely known, and I venture to think it is an extremely inadequate argument upon which to dismiss the claims to any measure of self-government, even in respect of their own purely local affairs, of an ancient and highly intelligent community of more than 200,000 Europeans, who entered the British Empire of their own free will, who have been and are unquestionably loyal, and who support the whole burden of an elaborate administration from the resources of their industry. We should further remember that although it is within our power by brute force to deny to the Maltese all share in the government of their island, and to rule with an arbitrary if benevolent autocracy, it is in their power – travellers and traders as they are – to give us a bad name, much to our disadvantage, from one end of the Mediterranean to another.

Churchill recommended allowing them management of their own purely local affairs. It was a modest proposal. Churchill referred to it as his 'suggested "eirenicon" for Malta'.[1] The governor-in-council would determine in each case whether the question at issue was imperial or local. If imperial, means could be found to ensure an official majority.

Elgin directed consideration of Churchill's 'eirenicon', and after some sort of precedent was revealed in Jamaica, thought it possible that some plan could eventually be made for forming a kind of separate chamber of unofficials to deal with purely local affairs. The matter came before Crewe shortly after he took over from Elgin. Crewe agreed with Hopwood that they must proceed cautiously. There seemed no need for immediate

[1] EP, WSC to E 2 Nov 07.

change.[1] In November 1908 he decided not to change the existing form of the 1903 constitution in the direction desired by the elected members; but to facilitate its harmonious working and to meet the biggest objection to it – that the executive council was composed exclusively of unofficial members – he would provide for the addition to the executive council of two members to be chosen by the governor.[2]

After Malta, Churchill's next stop was Cyprus. He arrived in Famagusta on 9 October, and was confronted with *enosis* demonstrations. The mayor, on behalf of the Greeks, begged Churchill to see that Cyprus was immediately handed over to the king of Greece. The Moslem leader then urged him not to do this. In official discussions in the legislative council Churchill discussed union with Greece and especially the tribute to the sultan of Turkey. Every effort was made to impress Churchill with the strength of *enosis* feeling in Greek circles. Greek flags were specially manufactured by the thousand. School-children were organised and drilled to wave the national standard effectively. Addresses were prepared in which Churchill's visit was likened to the arrival of Mr Gladstone in the Ionian Islands in 1858, which led to their union with Greece. Arrangements were made for the simultaneous despatch of telegrams to him from all parts of Cyprus. Everywhere large assemblies of people called for union with Greece. Churchill decided that the demonstrations, 'though aggressive', were not hostile to the British government.[3] The governor was pleased with the visit, feeling it to be of the greatest advantage to the island from every point of view. The Greeks, he thought, were pleased by Churchill's sympathetic recognition of their patriotism, and both Greeks and Turks were satisfied by his assurance that Britain would remain in occupation and try to start economic improvement.[4] Churchill believed that the island had been 'terribly starved' by the treasury, and as a result 'bore deep marks in moral and material conditions'.[5]

[1] CO. 158/360/3351, minutes by Hopwood 21 Feb and 1 May 08, Crewe 4 May.
[2] CO. 158/359/24261, minute by Crewe 20 Jul 08; 35461, S/S to govr 9 Nov 08.
[3] EP, WSC to E tel. from Limassol, Cyprus 13 Oct 07.
[4] CO. 67/149/38671, govr to S/S 21 Oct 07.   [5] To E 13 Oct 07.

His inevitable memorandum on the condition of Cyprus was concerned to find a means to free Britain from a position he thought morally, politically and economically indefensible. Europe and the House of Commons would never allow it to be given back to Turkey. Churchill himself would also feel deep regret if the question of giving it to Greece were raised, as this would be unfair to the loyal one-fifth minority of Moslems. He found its condition lamentable, owing to its having been held in 'intolerable financial trammels' before 1906, when the treasury for the first time agreed to give a fixed grant-in-aid each year of £50,000. Under the terms of the original transaction in 1878, which Churchill described as improper, Britain had been collecting an annual tribute, theoretically due to the sultan of Turkey. Thus it looked as if Britain was using Cyprus as a milch cow. This should cease. 'Let us have only one measure for treating people subject to our rule, and that a measure of justice.' It was worth while to make a success of Cyprus. 'Great and signal success in Cyprus as in Egypt invests the British name with dignity and even lustre in the eyes of the world.'[1]

EAST AFRICA

Churchill could not bring himself to use the next stage of his voyage through the Red Sea for relaxation, but was busy drafting memoranda on what he had seen so far. After a day at Aden, several days in North Somaliland, and five more days at sea, he arrived at Mombasa on 28 October 1907. Here he received deputations from planters and local communities, and discussed all manner of development problems. From Nairobi he made a visit to Fort Hall and Embu. After this he proceeded

[1] WSC, memo. 'Condition of Cyprus', 19 Oct 07, confidential print, *Mediterranean*, 65, Nov 07. Hopwood told E: 'the chancellor of the exchequer and the officials are vastly amused at the Cyprus memorandum, for Churchill has not understood the financial basis of the arrangement' (EP 27 Dec 07); 'Sir George Murray says it is amazing that any man who could write such an insane minute as that on Cyprus could within a few days deliver himself of such a weighty and statesmanlike pronouncement as that on Somaliland' (ibid, 9 Jan 08). Yet L. S. Amery describes this memorandum as 'a convincing document couched in all the exuberant eloquence of an earlier Churchillian style' (*My political life*, ii, 367).

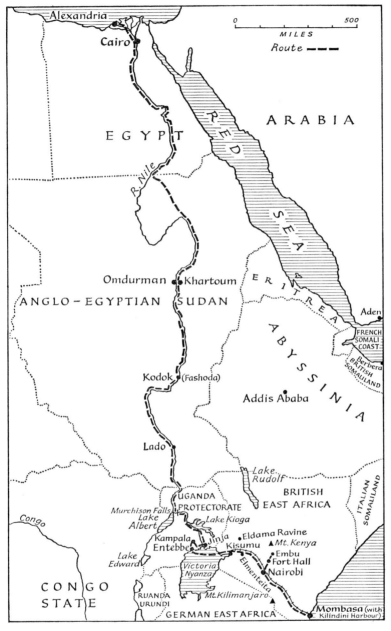

Churchill's African Journey

on the Uganda railway from Nairobi, met Lord Delamere at Elmenteita for pig-sticking, and then arrived at Kisumu, where he was greeted by hundreds of Kavirondo 'in their fullest undress'.[1] Then on to Entebbe, which already had that homely and characteristic mark of British rule, a golf course. From there he travelled by rickshaw to Kampala, where he was delighted to hear the little black schoolboys in white English cotton clothes singing 'Oh dear, what can the matter be?' This seemed to please him almost more than anything else in East Africa, apart from the highly-coloured butterflies.[2] He had tea with the young Kabaka of Buganda, who apparently liked football more than anything else. Steamboat took Churchill to Ripon Falls on the Victoria Nile. Next he went on trek, travelling on foot, by bicycle and canoe, coining the memorable phrase about his safari: 'sofari, sogoody'. He saw the Murchison falls and shot a white rhinoceros. His secretary Eddie Marsh, himself reporting for the *Manchester Guardian*, noted that Churchill had been in magnificent form, leaving everybody gasping at his quickness and power of seeing what ought to be done and how. 'I can never get over the wonder of it myself. And nothing ever pumps him dry.'[3] Churchill followed the proposed railway route to connect lakes Victoria, Kioga and Albert. This part of the trip lasted from 23 November to 14 December. He came back via Lado and Fashoda, and then stopped in Cairo. He was back in England on 17 January 1908.

At Nairobi he received persons of all classes and positions, and gave them a chance of airing their grievances, which proved to be 'as numerous as the sounds of the sea'. In Nairobi, wrote Churchill, every white man is a politician, and most of them are leaders of parties.[4] The dominant question, he noted, was colour.[5] At Fort Hall he made a speech to African chiefs, having first taken the precaution of previously discussing his remarks with the secretary for native affairs. He promised them

---

[1] *MAJ*, p. 83.
[2] *MAJ*, pp. 7, 116, 133, 152, 154–6, 163, 178 (all references to butterflies).
[3] C. Hassall, *Edward Marsh, a biography*, pp. 132–40.
[4] *MAJ*, p. 21. There were 580 white men in Nairobi.   [5] Ibid. p. 45.

that enough land would always be reserved for them and their children. But he rather spoiled the effect of this by nobly exhorting them to shew proper respect to the white man and to encourage their people to go to work.

Churchill conceived a very high confidence in the economic future of East Africa. Politically it was more disturbing:

The white population here, though small in numbers, is loud and vehement in its opinions. English people dislike being governed so intensely that they shut their eyes to all the advantages they derive, and I must say many of their complaints have appeared to me to be most ungrateful. At the same time there are a good many grievances and petty annoyances which might easily be swept away.[1]

As far as the Africans were concerned, he suggested methods of regulating the recruitment and protection of contract labour. In particular he recommended that Africans should be provided with facilities for obtaining food on journeys to and from work:

Nothing can tend more to bring discredit on the Administration and to discourage the native from offering himself as a labourer, than the spectacle of skinny scarecrows crawling back to their tribes after a few weeks' contact with Christian civilisation.

These facilities he considered absolutely necessary unless some very shocking scandal in the employment of contract labour were to occur.[2]

In Uganda, the energetic and capable governor, H. Hesketh Bell, found him very pleasant and stimulating. Churchill, he thought, got to the kernel of things with great rapidity, but he also noted in his diary that 'he seems to have a good many preconceived ideas about Uganda which I shall have to knock out'. Churchill asked him how old he was. On learning that Bell was 43, Churchill declared that by the time *he* was 43, he would be prime minister. It was not the only one of his forecasts which was to be proved wrong. Bell found that Churchill did

[1] EP 14 Nov 07 from Gilgil, British E. Africa.
[2] CO. 533/33/44976, minutes 11 Nov 07 and 26 Feb 08.

not always agree with his views, but seemed willing and able to help.[1]

A clear example of the way in which Churchill frequently tended to allow rhetoric to obscure reason was his advocacy of a dam across the Victoria Nile at Jinja to harness the Ripon Falls. 'It is possible that nowhere else in the world could so enormous a mass of water be held up by so little masonry. . . .' All that was required, apparently, was 'two or three short dams from island to island across the falls'; the cost would be 'inconceivably small'.[2] Yet the Owen Falls dam, which eventually realised his vision in 1954, cost £22,000,000, took six years to build, was 2725 feet long and 85 feet high.

Churchill advocated the dam in his published account, *My African Journey*, worked up from letters originally published in the *Strand Magazine*. Churchill never thought much of this book, believing its construction too jerky.[3] For understanding Churchill's attitude to African problems it is of course indispensable reading. Only a few snippets need be quoted here. He was particularly impressed by the intelligence of the Baganda, whose system of government he thought vital, powerful, and popular. Nevertheless, the British officer class was, 'in all that constitutes fitness to direct, as superior to the Baganda as Mr Wells's Martians would have been to us'.[4] Churchill's attitude towards Africans reminds one strongly of the characteristics of the mid-Victorian gospel of improvement, its paternalism, and its optimism. He was patronising and condescending. The Kikuyu tribes he described as 'light-hearted,

[1] H. H. Bell, *Glimpses of a governor's life* [n.d.] 167–71, diary 19–26 Nov 07. On 25 Nov: 'Last night he kept me awake for some time by what appeared to be a long soliloquy in his bath . . . while performing his ablutions he was dictating to a clerk', descriptions for the *Strand Magazine*. When Bell said that if he visited one bishop in Kampala, he would have to visit the other two then there, Churchill said, 'I'm not going here, there, and everywhere! And I'm damned if you're going to turn me into a blasted starfish!' (Ibid. p. 170).

[2] *MAJ*, p. 31.

[3] P. de Mendelssohn, *The age of Churchill*, i, 330. A reprint of *MAJ* was issued by the Holland Press, Neville Spearman Ltd, in 1962, with revised pagination and the inclusion of far fewer illustrations and photographs. I have quoted from the original Hodder and Stoughton edition of 1908 (226 pp.).

[4] *MAJ*, pp. 125 and 31.

tractable, if brutish children ... capable of being instructed and raised from their present degradation'. All Africans must be made to work: 'No man has a right to be idle, and I do not exempt the African.' Churchill perceived them to be more industrious than was often supposed. He was above all anxious that the African should be encouraged to wear clothes, which would make him 'less crudely animal' – and, incidentally, make him more useful and more profitable to the cotton manufacturers of Churchill's Manchester constituency. By developing a taste for civilised attire, and with just and honourable discipline and sympathetic education, many of the Africans could be raised to a higher social level.[1]

SOMALILAND: THE REDUCTION OF RESPONSIBILITY

One of the major results of Churchill's tour was to initiate a reconsideration of policy in Somaliland. His brief visit there led eventually to an important attempt to reduce British responsibility.

A protectorate in Somaliland had been declared in 1884. From 1902 to 1910 and beyond, the problem of governing it was continually before the cabinet. Somaliland had been an extremely costly liability since 1899, when British authority was challenged by the nationalist *jihad* of the so-called 'mad' Mullah, Sheikh Muhammad 'Abdille Hassan,[2] who was crushingly defeated in January 1904. It was one of the most unpopular of all African possessions, and because it was so barren, it became a symbol of the irrationalities of the partition.[3] The Unionist government in 1905 considered the possi-

---

[1] *MAJ*, pp. 37–8, 63–4, 103.

[2] Sheikh Muhammad (1864–1917) was not, of course, mad; nor was he merely a clan or tribal leader. He was turbulent and tyrannical, but the hero and forerunner of modern Somali nationalism, who wrote religious poems and theological works; he was clever, eloquent and exercised a magnetic leadership (see I. M. Lewis, *The modern history of Somaliland* (1965), chap. 4, 'The Dervish fight for freedom, 1900–1920'; pp. 63–91).

[3] John Burns in a speech at Battersea said he 'would continue to fight against that orientalised Imperialism of which Somaliland was a fruit and South Africa the rotten ripe product. ... Their money had been wasted in Africa, Tibet, Somaliland, the Soudan – all the stony places of the earth' (*The Times*, 28 Dec 05).

bility of concentrating authority on the Somali coastline, but decided that it was not practicable so to limit control without creating the very difficulties which by withdrawal to the coast it was hoped to avoid. They aimed ultimately at making the friendly tribes take care of their own safety, but realised that it would take considerable time to accustom them to doing this, and to organise them into a militia.[1] Meanwhile the Mullah had retired to Italian territory to recuperate. In August 1908 he again began to challenge British authority, helped by the weakness of administration in Italian Somaliland and the inflow of arms from French Somaliland. It was the resurgence of disturbance led by the Mullah which eventually persuaded the government to accept the reasoning which Churchill had already laid before them, and to withdraw from the interior. Throughout the whole range of British interests in Africa, it was only in Somaliland that the Liberals deliberately diminished the area of responsibilities they inherited. And the reversal of policy was a delayed one – withdrawal from the interior did not take place until 1910. It was preceded by very close ministerial reappraisal of the situation.

In passing, Elgin wondered during June 1906 whether the whole position in Somaliland ought not to be reconsidered,[2] but it was not until Churchill visited the region in 1907 that the situation there was examined closely.

His memorandum[3] upon the subject expressed dissatisfaction with the financial and military situation. The revenues of this 'wilderness of stone and scrub' did not, and most likely could not, support the forces necessary to rule the interior. Existing policy required a grant-in-aid of £60,000 a year, yet even this failed to afford any real security to the tribes within the demarcated British border. The military force there would be quite incapable of resisting a determined advance by the Mullah; British obligations to 'friendly' (*Isaq*) tribes were already plainly in default; even the small portion of the country which *was* held could not be maintained against any very

---

[1] CAB. 41/30/30, 1 Aug 05.   [2] CO. 535/5/18059, minute 3 Jun 06.
[3] African 896, 28 Oct 07.

serious attack. In short, in spite of a military expenditure utterly disproportionate to the resources or the value of Somaliland, no effectual security was obtained against the perpetual threat of a wave of rifle-armed Moslem fanaticism. Churchill would not seriously entertain the policy of effectively occupying Somaliland and crushing the Mullah. The only alternative was to withdraw to the coast, as the Italians had done since, and as Britain did before the rise of the Mullah's power. Accordingly he recommended discharging the bulk of the Indian troops, which would reduce the cost of military expenditure by half. The other advantages of concentration on the coast were two-fold: that

it does all that it pretends to do, viz to exercise peaceful penetration in the interior, and to hold the coast effectively . . . that being essentially self-contained and final, it limits precisely the liabilities of the British government, and closes altogether the vistas of expenditure and expeditions which now lie pain-fully and even deliberately exposed. It gives no hostages to fortune; it in no way compromises future policy. It safeguards absolutely the coastal line, by customs duties along which practically the whole existing revenue is raised.

If the Mullah advanced, provided that he treated the friendly tribes properly, Britain should allow his trade to come through their posts to the sea, but 'if he misbehaves we will blockade him completely. This is not a heroic policy, but it finds much justification and many examples in Indian frontier experience.'

Here was an important issue indeed. Elgin had not come to a decision before he left office, although he was deeply interested. He obtained the opinion of the commissioner,[1] and the former commissioner, on Churchill's minute. On 20 February 1908 the matter was referred to the foreign office, for an opinion on the international implications of Churchill's proposals. Elgin seemed inclined to let the decision rest with the foreign office. Grey, who was in no hurry to commit himself,[2] considered that the governments of France, Abyssinia and Italy would all have just cause of complaint if the new scheme of

[1] African 904.   [2] EP, Grey to E 3 Feb 08.

administration led to the chaotic results forecast by the commissioner. Britain could not withdraw from the hinterland without first coming to an understanding with Italy. The position hitherto enjoyed by Britain in Abyssinia and the surrounding countries could not fail to be seriously prejudiced by the adoption of the new policy, which would be likely to decrease British influence and prestige in East Africa, and to involve Britain in serious difficulties with both the Italian and Abyssinian governments. Crewe in his turn admitted that the purely military and strategic aspects of the question demanded careful consideration, and he agreed that Somaliland was not a very attractive or useful possession; but the foreign office memorandum seemed to him 'to set the balance definitely against any change of policy under present circumstances'.[1] In August 1908 a sudden revival in the Mullah's hostility was reported. Crewe telegraphed that his threatening attitude should be dealt with by diplomatic methods; at all costs Britain must not precipitate action.[2] There was grave reason for fearing an attack would be made upon the tribes under British protection, and upon British military forts.

At a meeting on 25 November 1908, the cabinet decided not to send an expedition against the Mullah,[3] but hoped to establish an understanding with him; if this was impossible, the only prudent alternative would appear to be withdrawal in time to the coast.[4] A general outline of the government's decision was sent to the commissioner on 30 November. They were anxious lest action should be taken which might entail the despatch of an expedition to extricate troops in the interior. They approved continuing to hold Burao, and so were prepared to order reinforcements from neighbouring British territories if these were necessary for its safety and for the line of communi-

---

[1] CO. 535/12/17451, FO to CO 13 May 08, minutes by Crewe 22 and 25 May 08.
[2] CO. 535/11/30805, tel. 24 Aug 08.
[3] H.M.G. recognised that an organised campaign against the Mullah was out of the question in view of the inconclusive results of the last expedition which had cost 2½ millions sterling.
[4] Asq. 5; Asquith to the King.

cations between Burao and Berbera. This left the government freedom of action should they decide to withdraw from Burao. They had discussed the possibility of adopting a policy towards the Mullah which was used on the North West frontier of India – persuading him to refrain from raids on British territory in return for the payment of an annual subsidy. It was clear, however, that the present moment was not favourable, as it was difficult to obtain direct access to the Mullah.[1] In March 1909 the situation was still obscure, as no trustworthy evidence about the effective strength and real intentions of the Mullah could be obtained, but every effort was being made to prevent Britain from drifting into fresh difficulties.[2] On 10 March the general opinion of the cabinet was strongly in favour of withdrawal to the coast, making any provision that might be found practicable (by agreement with the Mullah or otherwise) for the proper treatment of the tribes with whom Britain had entered into engagements.[3] The existing situation threatened to continue indefinitely, but the indefinite continuation of such heavy expenditure would be impossible to justify. The commissioner was reminded that a forward movement against the Mullah was 'quite out of the question'. Reinforcements could not be retained indefinitely. Would it be possible to arm the friendly tribes to a point where they could hold their own? In view of the possibility of withdrawal, the commissioner's earnest attention was directed to the possibility of a subsidy. The government were prepared to accept within reason any financial arrangement he might make.[4]

In April Sir R. Wingate was asked to make a report on the situation from the point of view of his special knowledge of the whole of north-east Africa, and of his experience of similar difficulties during his administration of the Sudan. The government wanted a purely defensive and cautious solution to a problem of almost unbelievable complexity. He was asked to recommend either complete evacuation or withdrawal to the

[1] CO. 535/13/42293.   [2] Asq. 5; Asquith to the King 5 Mar 09.
[3] Ibid. 10 Mar 09.   [4] CO. 535/17/8863, tel. 12 Mar 09.

363

coast, and to consider the effect of any increase in the Mullah's prestige on the powerful and turbulent Somali tribes in adjoining British territories.[1] His report was not published, because its recommendation was unwelcome to the government. He favoured a full expedition against the Mullah, as the only policy with a hope of finality. Withdrawal to the coast would be premature.[2]

Somaliland was thoroughly discussed at the cabinet on 18 September 1909. It was resolved that in view of recent raids by some of the Mullah's followers against some of the 'friendly' tribes, the commissioner should be instructed to tell them that as the Mullah continued to attack and had broken off negotiations with Britain, they must take such measures as they thought proper to protect themselves – but the government would not undertake any responsibility for the consequences of their actions. Crewe's object in recommending cancellation of the prohibition on tribal reprisals was not simply to bring the Mullah to reason, but to relieve British responsibility, for 'the surest way of settling the Somaliland difficulty is to educate our tribes up to providing for their defence against the Mullah'.[3]

It was felt that if future policy was to have any stability, this was the principle upon which it must be based. The Mullah had been considerably discredited recently and the tribes had shown on more than one occasion that they could hold their own against his raiding parties. Military force was therefore gradually and cautiously reduced. The tribes were also allowed more responsibility in the settlement of their own questions, to relieve the government of some of the administrative burden.[4]

In October a cabinet committee recommended withdrawal at the earliest possible moment of all British posts in the

[1] Ibid. 13667, CO to Wingate 15 Apr 09.

[2] CAB. 37/100/107, 'Summary of recommendations contained in Sir R. Wingate's report of 12 and 17 June 1909'. Withdrawal to the coast should not, said Wingate, be resorted to except in the event of some great national emergency involving the immediate reduction of all overseas responsibilities, because there were undoubted obligations to the tribes who had identified themselves with Britain in hostilities, and the Mullah was not yet a negligible quantity.

[3] CO. 535/15/30335, memo. 14 Sep 09.

[4] CO. 535/17/22505, tel. S/S to commissioner, 2 Sep 09.

interior, and concentration on the coast. The full cabinet approved this on 27 October. The exact time and method of withdrawal were to be left to the discretion of the officer appointed for the purpose. Asquith explained to the king that the time had come 'when it is necessary to avoid the indefinite risks of a prolonged and for the most part ineffectual occupation of a disturbed and valueless area'. Early in March 1910, the military advisers were satisfied that the time for withdrawal had arrived. No attack on friendly tribes by the Mullah was expected, but they appeared to be in a position, in case of possible raid, to give a good account of themselves.[1] The retirement to Berbera, Bulhar and Zeila was successfully carried out by the end of the month.

In defending this policy in the Lords on 6 April 1910, Crewe said that he had never been able to regard Somaliland as a proper subject for the administration of the colonial office; regular, orderly administration was 'an idle dream'; the tribes did not in the least want British administration – their main desire was to be left alone. The whole proceeding now proposed was to be regarded as

a piece of military strategy or policy . . . not in the least as a great political event, and only so far political because the attempts at a political administration of the country have in our opinion broken down.

No disgrace was involved to the empire, he added. The policy was the only possible course in relation to a country

into which we went as we do sometimes, without thought of the consequences, and without considering whether we were doing either ourselves or the inhabitants of the country any real service, in taking the course we did. In our opinion it is time to put a stop to that. . . .[2]

So much for the official line. In fact, Crewe had never been convinced, it seems, by Churchill's argument that a line of observation could be permanently maintained by leaving the

[1] Asq. 5, Asquith to the king 9 Mar 10.   [2] PD/HL. 5/573-83.

political officers where they were after the garrisons were withdrawn. He doubted whether they could be lucky enough to have it both ways, and to maintain the British hold over the protectorate without effective occupation.[1] Events proved him (and Wingate) correct. The results of the compromise policy adopted at Churchill's suggestion can only be described as melancholy and even catastrophic. The policy of coastal concentration was an ignominious failure, because it was based on a complete misunderstanding of the Mullah's unique position as a national figure appealing to the patriotic sentiments of Somali as Muslims irrespective of clan or lineage allegiance. The friendlies who were given arms to protect themselves against the Mullah used them in an orgy of intertribal pillaging. The interior lapsed into unparalleled confusion; a large proportion of the population was reduced to near-starvation. The Mullah continued to harass the British until 1920, when an expedition finally overcame him.[2]

[1] Crewe's covering note circulating minute by Cordeaux 8 Dec 08 (CAB. 37/96/165).

[2] Another change of policy was devised to combat the anarchy in 1912: a camel constabulary of 150 was raised, a civil force, to keep the peace, but it was practically annihilated in August 1913. A military unit of 500 called the Somaliland Camel Corps was set up; this, together with an increase once more of the Somaliland Indian contingent to 500 kept the Mullah in check for six years, and ultimately encompassed his destruction. The problem was not solved till Amery, colonial secretary, 'polished him off for £77,000, the cheapest war in history' (Amery's own description). Almost all the Mullah's personal following was killed in the expedition of 1920. The Mullah fled to Ethiopia and died of influenza before the year was out (Gen. Lord Ismay, *Memoirs* (1960), pp. 23–34; Amery, *My Political Life*, ii, 202). The decision of 1910 stemmed from an impossible attempt to control costs (A. Hamilton, *Somaliland* (1911), xiii, and Lewis, *The Modern History of Somaliland*, pp. 76–7).

11 Towards the Definition of a Native Policy for British Africa

'It is a curious coincidence', Elgin wrote to Churchill on 25 September 1907, 'that this question of the treatment of Natives is coming to the front everywhere in Africa.' He had before him at that moment the crisis in Zululand, the despatches from the Transvaal on native administration, a letter from Girouard about education and nationalism in Northern Nigeria. A little earlier, he had been confronted with a racial incident in Nairobi, and the problem of forest concession in West Africa. He therefore directed that there should be 'a comprehensive and exhaustive consideration of the whole subject', and commended it to Churchill as a subject 'well worthy of study on the spot' during his tour of East Africa. The subject was only at an elementary stage of investigation, he added, and he rightly predicted that it was 'destined to cover reams of paper'.[1] Perhaps this was the most significant directive Elgin ever gave on his own initiative as colonial secretary. It deserves to be quoted in full:

I do not know any question which raises more important issues for South Africa – or indeed for Africa generally: and I think that it is highly important that we, in the Colonial Office should discuss it: not on a single despatch, but reviewing the position as a whole. For instance, how can we answer these brief and for the most part conjectural arguments from the Transvaal until we have digested the very solid food presented to us by the Natal Native Affairs Commission? ... In view of the *present* position: not in the Transvaal only – not in Natal only – not in Federated South Africa only – but in West and East Africa also,

[1] EP, E to WSC 25 Sep 07 (photocopy).

367

where similar problems are emerging – I should like the great subject of the government of the native populations to be thoroughly discussed in this Office during this winter, in order that we may be ready with a policy when we are challenged as we most likely will be next year.[1]

This minute represents a superb attempt to widen the significance of piecemeal discussions.

A few weeks before Elgin left the colonial office early in April 1908, the officials had completed a memorandum summarising Selborne's despatches on the native question and referring to the report of the South African Native Affairs Commission.[2] Lucas had prepared a further comprehensive memorandum containing suggestions for future policy.[3] This was followed by a complementary long paper on the special question of the self-governing dominions and coloured immigration.[4] In addition, Elgin circulated a copy of the report of the Natal Native Affairs Commission to every cabinet minister. He fully intended to lay the whole matter before the cabinet. Asquith removed him from the colonial office before this could be done. In retrospect, the absence of cabinet consideration seems one of the most significant results of Elgin's dismissal. It was therefore in effect still true in the middle of 1908 that no official view on native races existed.[5] Even in South Africa no 'developed or conscious system of African administration' had been worked out.[6] What clarification Elgin might have achieved in this vital sphere of colonial policy is a matter for speculation. A new colonial secretary could not possibly master so vast a subject at once. As a result, the matter lapsed, the First World War intervened, and the 'comprehensive and exhaustive' attack on the problem which Elgin had planned never took place.

[1] CO. 291/119/32934, 24 Sep 07.
[2] CO. 291/125/3907, memo. 6 Mar 08.
[3] CO. memo. confidential print, *Miscellaneous*, 217, 31 Dec 07 'Native races in the British Empire'.
[4] CO. 532/9/34812 or CO. 886/1/1, Jul 08, by C.P.L. See p. 316.
[5] CO. 417/458/19782. minute by Crewe 14 Jun 08.
[6] M. Perham, introduction to *History of East Africa*, ii (ed. Harlow and Chilver), xli.

"PARTING IS SUCH SWEET SORROW."

Lord Elgin. "WELL, MY BOY, YOU SEE I'M HELPING TO GET YOU OFF, THOUGH I SHALL MISS YOU TERRIBLY. YOU MUST BE SURE TO HAVE A GOOD REST, *AND, WHATEVER YOU DO, DON'T HURRY BACK!*"

[The Colonial Secretary has expressed a desire that Mr. Churchill should visit Uganda and British East Africa in the recess.]

Mr Churchill and the rhinoceros at Simba

Two decisions seem to have evolved in practice out of the policy of Elgin's colonial secretaryship. The first was a resolve to try to find out more about African political views, especially by devising machinery for the representation of these views other than by grants of franchise. The government's basic problem seemed to be essentially one of penetrating the native mind. The second decision was to support all attempts to secure 'the development of native institutions on native lines' throughout Africa, partly as a means of realising the first objective and coping with the basic problem. The fact of the survival of tribal institutions was thought to prove their worth.

The general context within which the question was discussed had two aspects. In the first place, Africa had been brought under European rule at a time when European attitudes towards non-Europeans were perhaps harsher than they had ever been before. In the second place, there was a conditioning undercurrent of fear, a belief that future African risings against Europeans were inevitable.

There were perhaps three general assumptions upon which all discussion was based. The primary one was that nothing could be done for Africans if it involved regular spending of the British tax payer's money. But for a treasury limitation, more would have been done. The colonial office undoubtedly could not do all that it would have liked to do. The secondary assumption was the belief that change must be slow, because it was supposed that, above all things, Africans hated to be hurried and hustled. Lugard was not the only person to take as his maxim in this matter *festina lente*.[1] Finally, it was firmly and

[1] Lugard, *The Dual Mandate*, p. 164; see also C. W. Orr, *Making of Northern Nigeria* (1911), p. 224: *festina lente* must be the motto in 'every case where circumstances do not actually clamour for a speedy solution to the native problem'. For understanding government policy in this period, one of the most interesting statements is that of the commissioner for native affairs in the Transvaal 1901–7, G. Lagden, who wrote in 1909: 'It is unwise to wander off into the bye-paths of experiment with coloured races who are capable of being moved to indiscretion or madness by violent changes, even when contemplated for their betterment. . . .

'The native races can be brought into the general polity and contribute their share to the commonweal in proportion as their administration is in harmony with their evolution. But they are maturing under conditions totally different to those which governed the western world in its rise from medievalism. . . . It is folly

uniformly assumed that Africans were irremediably inferior to Europeans, much further down the scale of civilisation than Asiatics. Asquith was probably typical in thinking only some of the African races capable of progress;[1] privately he was probably doubtful about even these. Churchill did not think that they could treat Egypt, in inverted commas, as a separate responsible power, whose views about her own interests could be accepted as final.[2] If the Egyptians were treated thus, what hope was there for the Egba?

SOUTHERN AFRICA AND THE GENERAL DISCUSSION

Although many of the Liberals realised in 1897 that, as Ripon said, the native question was the abiding difficulty in South Africa,[3] in terms of practical politics the native question was not much to the fore during the course of the next eight years. This was not simply because of the overriding nature of the Anglo-Boer difficulty, but because the problem was still, to a large extent, latent. South Africa had not yet become an arena of acute racial tension comparable with the Southern States of North America. In 1899 Bryce observed:

therefore to impose upon them laws and traditions that have grown slowly into Europe in the course of several hundred years. . . . It would be a fatal error to encourage or set a pace suitable to the standard of a few who have shown capacity for higher education. The pace of the mass must and ought to be slow. . . .
    'The bulk of the people are content to be governed and guided, to be allowed to live in their own quiet way so long as they are not hunted by ardent reformers. The best reforms will come from within as the outcome of intellectual growth. . . . What the Basuto want above all is a sense of security in their possessions and permanence of control by a government they confide in. If not perplexed and frightened by changes they will accommodate themselves to the exercise of any judicious restraint. . . . Their tribal system has been buttressed up because, together with chieftainship, it provided a useful discipline required by untutored people. It is a great power for good - the cornerstone on which government rest. Should it be recklessly disturbed before in the fitness of time another system is ready to replace it effectively, the foundations of our rule will be undermined (*The Basutos: the mountaineers and their country* (1909), ii, 647-9). These views have innumerable parallels in official thinking about Africans in general at this time.
[1] PD/HC. 9/1009, 16 Aug 09, speech on South Africa Bill.
[2] GP, WSC to Grey 29 Oct 09.
[3] Asq. 9/94, Ripon to Asquith 29 Dec 97.

There is at present no serious friction between the black and the white people in South Africa. . . . Each race goes its own way and lives its own life. . . . The social and political troubles which the juxtaposition of the two races has caused in North America . . . have as yet scarcely shown themselves in South Africa. Neither in the British colonies nor in the Boer Republics is there any cause for present apprehension.[1]

Three years later Bryce listed the major areas of racial friction: the United States, Egypt and the Philippines; South Africa was not mentioned.[2] As confidence in the prospects of fusion between Briton and Boer grew, Bryce warned the House of Commons that 'the permanently abiding difficulty will be the reconciliation of the black race and the white race, and it may prove in South Africa in the future as great or a greater danger' as in the Southern States of U.S.A., because the whites were in a smaller minority.[3] Nevertheless, as late as 1 September 1910 Morley was writing: '. . . Talk of India and other "insoluble problems" of great states. I declare the American Negro often strikes me as the hardest of them all.'[4]

No clear policy for the future of African races existed in 1905, but from the moment when the Liberals had set in motion their attempt to solve the Anglo-Boer antagonism, and especially after the grants of responsible government, the problem became a topic of interest. In view of the difficulty of the problem, the prevailing tendency was simply to try to safeguard tribal lands and to protect Africans from the temptations of civilisation. In practice the existing 'native policy' of the British government was based on belief in personal and paternal administration, and in the preservation of the civil jurisdiction and authority of chiefs. Taxation was adjusted to African means with a view to securing a fair contribution towards the cost of government, but not specially increasing it for the purpose of forcing Africans to work. Land was set apart in reserves or locations for the Africans as tribal land. Education was assisted only by means of

[1] Bryce, *Impressions of South Africa*, pp. 361–2.
[2] Bryce, *The Relations of the advanced and the backward races of mankind* (Romanes Lecture, 1902), p. 31.
[3] PD. 132/317, 21 Mar 04.   [4] MM. 5.

371

grants to missionary bodies for ordinary subjects.[1] But there was no planning for the future. The Report of the South African Native Affairs Commission did not really get to grips with the roots of this problem.[2] It advocated territorial separateness, and separate voting in elections instead of the Cape franchise. It reflected the tendency of the time to deplore the presence of blacks in what ought to have been a white man's country. British Liberals shared this view. Elgin would not condemn the report.[3] Samuel declared in the House of Commons that white and black would no more mix than oil and water, and that they should aim 'to make the Transvaal as far as possible a homogeneous white country';[4] Seely added that they 'wanted to arrive as far as possible at a white South Africa'. Such views help to explain the dislike of Chinese Labour as well as the readiness to accede to the local demand to stop further Indian immigration. Seely was able to quote Herbert Spencer in support of both policies: immigrant Asiatics must either mix with the whites, in which case a bad hybrid was produced, or not mix, in which case they occupied a position of slavery.[5]

The Bantu were regarded as being much further down the scale of civilisation than the Asiatics. Col. Seely, who succeeded Churchill as under-secretary, claimed to have seen a good deal of both Maoris and South African Bantu, and had no hesitation in describing the latter as 'below the average' of dark races.[6]

The problem of adapting and evolving free institutions in a community where two races were intermixed in totally different stages of civilisation, was, said Asquith in 1909, 'essentially a modern problem and at the present moment remains unsolved'. He thought that

the experience we have gained in Cape Colony itself shows that differences which are certainly implanted by nature, and some-

---

[1] CO. 291/125/3907, memo. by Lambert, Lucas and Just 6 Mar 08.

[2] Cd. 2399, Hancock, *Smuts*, i, 315.

[3] 'There is a tendency in some quarters to indulge in a wholesale condemnation of the report of the Native Affairs Commission. I do not share in that view' (EP, E to Selb. 18 May 06, copy).

[4] PD. 129/1511–17, 16 Feb 04.   [5] Ibid. 1524–6; 193/2032, 31 Jul 08.

[6] CO. 417/463/38204, minute 30 Oct 08.

times seem as if they were intended by nature to be permanent, may yield in a greater or less degree to judicious treatment, and to wise and humane arrangements. There is, in fact, in many of these races, I do not say in all, but certainly in some of those who inhabit South Africa, a capacity for, or potentiality of progress, which it ought to be the object of every wise government and representative free institution to encourage and stimulate.[1]

Here then was a Liberal objective, but what was the Liberal government doing to put it into practice? The problem occupied much ministerial attention from 1906, and Elgin in particular encouraged the attempt to formulate a coherent policy.

The new Liberal government had been quickly called upon to give assurances about its attitude towards African interests. Mr Byles, a radical M.P., put down a motion about recognising British responsibility for South African native races, on 28 February 1906. The task of stating the view of the government fell to Churchill.[2]

The under-secretary of state for the colonies opened by fully accepting an imperial responsibility for the protection of African races not represented in legislative assemblies, and in particular assured the House that there would be no derogation in the slightest degree from the existing position of Bechuanaland and Basutoland. Wherever there was positive cruelty, and especially where Africans were exploited for gain, the government

should not be deterred from speaking our mind by any fear of Colonial susceptibilities. . . . H.M.G. will do all in their power – perhaps will run the risk of attempting something beyond their power – to bring the opinion of the House to bear upon those concerned.

[1] PD/HC. 9/1009, 16 Aug 09, South Africa Bill second reading.
[2] PD. 152/1232–44. 'That in any settlement of South African affairs, this House desires a recognition of imperial responsibility for the protection of all races excluded from equal political rights, the safeguarding of all immigrants against servile conditions of labour, and the guarantee to the Native populations of at least their existing status, with the unbroken possession of their liberties in Basutoland, Bechuanaland, and other tribal countries and reservations.' (Byles's motion.)

He would certainly not support taxation designed to force Africans to work. In practice there were, however, several limitations upon interference which had to be observed. The fact that it was other people who had to live up to the standards they set, emphasised the necessity for caution in applying principles to the existing circumstances.

... There are many things in the laws of the colonial governments which frankly we do not like ... and we wish they were not there. . . . But harsh laws are sometimes better than no laws at all, and unless we carry public opinion with us in procuring the removal of any of these objectionable provisions, the result would only be their lawless assertion, which I believe, would impose more injustice and tyranny on the natives, than the regulated assertion which is contained in a statute of law.

The second limitation was the principle of self-government, a fundamental maxim of Liberal policy. It was not a moral principle, and 'when it comes into collision with moral principles I think upon occasion it should be overborne'. But it was 'the master-key of many of the problems which embarrass and perplex us. . . . Once it has been given, it is not good to grudge it, and it is impossible to limit or restrict it.' As conditions in the empire varied greatly, so the power of intervention varied greatly. The general foundation upon which he intended to approach South African problems was 'that our responsibility in this matter is directly proportionate to our power'. Our power, our foothold for intervention in South Africa was stronger than elsewhere. But a warning was added: 'circumstances of the time impose upon us an extraordinary degree of caution.' Fear of the black peril, Churchill pointed out, was 'the one bond of union' between British and Boer; he hoped that this would draw them together and that the new charity which might come from this feeling of union might lead them, not to crush the African, but to raise him 'to his proper position as an inheritor in what is, after all, a great estate'. The course of the government was clear. Rhodes's principle of equality for the civilised was invoked to explain it:

374

The government believe that in those wide lands there is enough for all. As far as we have any right or power to intervene, whenever our intervention will be useful or will not be positively harmful, we will labour to compose the racial differences and animosities by which South Africa has been distracted. We will endeavour as far as we can to advance the principle of equal rights of civilised men irrespective of colour. We will encourage as far as may be in our power, a careful patient discrimination between different classes of coloured men.

Attempts to formulate a practical policy for the protection of Africans arose during the drafting of the Transvaal Constitution. On 5 April 1906 Elgin rebuffed an official who said that nothing could be done for the Africans:

The native question in South Africa is no doubt a difficult one, but it is admitted on all sides that it will certainly have to be faced some day. I want a paper showing what has been done – what can be done – and the difficulties, but not show on the face of our instructions that we do not like to do anything effective.

Having looked at Selborne's despatch on the subject (12 March) and the Report of the South African Native Affairs Commission he thought it evident

that the time must come when there will be danger of a collision between the white and coloured races, unless the relations between them are fair and equitable. If that collision takes place, it is beyond doubt that an appeal for Imperial assistance is inevitable – and the strain even on Imperial resources may be severe. It is not too soon even now to take the future into account, and to consider what steps are open to us to secure the just interests of the Natives.[1]

For the moment consideration stopped short at what could be done in the Transvaal, though ultimate federation was always borne in mind. Elgin took the matter up again in the autumn of 1907, when the Transvaal Native Administration Amendment Bill stimulated him to remark:

[1] CO. 291/97/11334, 5 Apr 06.

375

I have some sympathy with the view, which I believe Selborne to hold, that so long as the Native is excluded from the political rights possessed by the white man, he is better left under a personal rule. There is no doubt some difficulty in combining the 'personal' rule of the Native (which must almost of necessity rest with the governor) – and the 'self-government' accorded to the Colony as a whole, and exercised by the white inhabitants. But I am not satisfied that a compromise is impossible.[1]

It will be seen that Elgin did not rule out the achievement of political rights for the Africans, and he regarded his policy as an interim one. He was, however, not very enthusiastic about the Cape native franchise as a model for immediate application. As early as April 1906 he had refused in any way to commit himself to the Cape system of franchise without further critical consideration.[2]

The fullest statement of Elgin's view of the Cape franchise and the native question in general is to be found in a long letter which he wrote to Crewe, on handing over the colonial secretary-ship. He very much hoped that the question would not be raised in the House of Commons too soon; discussion there was 'certainly premature'. He had no illusions about the possibility of exercising any control over native policy in self-governing South Africa. But, assuming that this difficulty could be surmounted, he could see two possible ways in which the rights of Africans might be safeguarded:

(*a*) by making the individual native so far as possible equal in rights and privileges to the individual white man;
(*b*) by distinct legislative provisions for the protection of native interests.

Both of these have supporters: (*a*) appears, at any rate in an elementary form, in the Cape Constitution, and I have no doubt would find supporters in this country. (*b*) has much support from those who know the native best, and especially in the latest documents: the Report of the Natal Commission on Native Affairs, and the last despatch from Selborne. . . .

For myself, I claim that I entertain and have shown a sincere desire to befriend the native – but having seen some-

---

[1] EP, E to WSC 25 Sep 07 (photocopy).   [2] Ibid. 29 Apr 06 (photocopy).

thing of him, I must say that I doubt (*a*) being practicable, or in his interest if it were practicable.

Generalising about 'the native' as if he possessed the same characteristics the world over is not much to our taste nowadays, but we must nevertheless recall the reasons which Elgin adduced for his statement:

In the first place, it means the gradual growth of a class of natives who would oust the class of whites represented by the smaller traders, as the imported Indian and other Asiatics have done, and where you have a small white community in the midst of a large native population, such a process means the destruction of all sense of security;

Secondly, although so far we have only the Cape precedent, where the number of natives admitted to the franchise is still within bounds: the population figures compel us, if we admit the principle, to contemplate a time when the natives will control the elections. Are we prepared to subordinate the whites to native rule under such circumstances?

It is not difficult to guess that his answer to the rhetorical question would be the same as Morley's; he would 'not submit to be governed by a man of colour'.[1] Pseudo-Darwinism influenced his next point:

Thirdly, it is argued that native subjects of the King have a right to the same treatment as all others. I am tempted to ask whether nature itself so permits. We have absorbed Frenchmen and Dutchmen, and individuals of every European race, because they have amalgamated with us, and there have been association and intermarriage, and their descendants have become as ourselves. But is that conceivable in the case of coloured races? So far as I know, there is no historical foundation for any such proposition. I do not venture to propound scientific theories, but the half-caste (certainly the Eurasian in India in my experience), does not hold out much expectation of favourable results.

He admitted that this was an argument which could not well be pressed far in public, but in the form of an unconscious belief, it probably accounted for a good deal of the prejudice

[1] A. Chamberlain, *Politics from inside*, p. 60, 15 Mar 07.

which undoubtedly existed in the colonial communities. It was to a large extent, he added, an unconscious belief with him, until he found Lucas making a very strong claim for equal rights, and 'began to think out all that this meant'.[1]

It is hardly too much to say that the reasoning here, unhappily, may in effect stand as a definition of the basis of British policy for the next forty years. Elgin expressed a 'strong preference for the development of native institutions on native lines, which is urged by those on the spot'.

It appears to me [he wrote], that when you have two parts of a community differing in race, religion, manners, customs and wants, you cannot amalgamate them simply by conferring upon them equal 'rights', politically or otherwise. On the other hand, the inferior race has common sentiments, and perhaps aspirations, which it is possible to conserve and develop: (*a*) by sympathetic administration, and (*b*) by preserving and utilising any of their own customs which lend themselves to such objects.[2]

Hence he favoured a reformed native administration in South Africa, under the 'personal government' advocated by the Natal Commission, in combination with the preservation or formation of native councils. 'No doubt some day, not in our time, the claim of the native generally to equal political rights may, probably must be reached.' In the meantime, he agreed with Selborne that Africans would be better off under separate native departments, not directly responsible to white parliaments, together with wise and sympathetic development of native councils and other indigenous institutions, until further assimilation could take place, than they would be under 'hasty admission . . . to political rights, for which neither they, nor the whites, are as yet prepared'.[3] This he considered a more

---

[1] EP, E to Crewe 7 May 08 (draft).

[2] EP, E to Selb. 20 Mar 08 (copy).

[3] EP, E to Crewe. The idea of native councils was a popular one at this time; for example Sir William MacGregor as governor of Southern Nigeria in 1901 sought to provide funds for developing them as instruments of administration, though his ordinance was largely a dead letter (C. W. Newbury, *Western slave coast and its rulers* (1961), p. 196.

effectual safeguard, because only a minority could obtain the franchise, and because it might be easier to get the whites to agree at that time to native councils than to any other form of African representation. He wondered whether the Cape franchise arrangements would be so effective:

They are said to have succeeded so far – but after all only a comparatively small number of natives have been admitted – and the time of trial will come when the whites begin to realise that political power is passing out of their hands. If the struggle on that issue is taken prematurely, it may prejudice the just expectations of natives – whereas the time may come when the two races stand more on an equal footing, a treaty may be concluded between them, fair to both. I call it a treaty, for I have doubts if amalgamation is practicable. White races amalgamate . . . but where is there an example of successful intermixture of black and white ?

He might perhaps have thought of Brazil as just possibly an example, but he did not.[1]

Elgin agreed generally with the views which Selborne set forth in his memorandum of 9 January 1908, prepared at Botha's request. So did the colonial office as a whole. Selborne had a typically British combination of humanitarian fervour and racial complacency. He had no fear at all that the black man could ever rival the white, and so there was in his view no reason to deny the African the 'freest opportunities to evolve himself under the best conditions'. He would not absolutely refuse Africans admission to some franchise rights, but it would be absurd to give them the same rights under the same conditions as whites. The gradual destruction of tribal systems must be ensured as 'incompatible with civilisation'. The worst form of government for Africans was direct government by a

---

[1] Elgin did not favour any extension of the principles of Europeanisation implicit in the Glen Grey Act. He noted from the Cape blue book for native affairs 1905 that several officers condemned it, and bore out the opinion expressed by the select committee of 1903 that there was a marked reluctance among Africans to come under its operation (CO. 291/113/30193, minute 19 Aug 06). The Glen Grey Act encouraged Africans to take land on quit rent, subject to the expensive system of European systems of land tenure and individual tenure.

parliament of white men. Native councils should be established to give them freedom to express their views.[1]

The whole discussion set out above forms an interesting and comprehensive statement of the classic conception of British policy in the earlier part of the twentieth century. It was influential on British thinking rather than relevant to the needs of Africa. Advocacy of development on native lines was mostly abstract and academic theorising, with little attempt to relate it to the sociological realities of Africa, of which Elgin was, like most of his contemporaries, almost totally ignorant. There was little new in this theory of native development. It sounded enlightened, but it frequently reflected more concern with segregation than differentiation.[2]

Any discussion of the future of South African natives was likely to bear little fruit, as Elgin always admitted. It is therefore all the more remarkable and impressive that so much time was devoted to it.

Throughout the self-governing parts of South Africa, the chief difficulty was to give effect to any native policy which the British government might approve. Hence, when the question of the reduction of the South African garrison was before the cabinet, Elgin pointed out that if it were withdrawn, or was too weak to give assistance such as Natal required,

the last opportunity for bringing the influence of the Imperial government to bear except indirectly through the governor, is at an end. I state the fact without attaching too much importance to it.

It seemed to him desirable not to diminish any means of controlling native policy in the near future, even though the control might be indirect, because increased hostility between whites and Africans in any part of South Africa would increase the difficulties of coming to agreement in federation; and because, if federation were deferred, the British government

[1] CO. 291/125/3907, Selb. to S/S 13 Jan 08, minute by E 3 Mar 08; see also Hancock, *Smuts*, i, 317; for full text, see *Selections from the Smuts Papers*, ii, 374–94.
[2] See Hancock, *Smuts*, i, 312, and G. and M. Wilson, *The analysis of social change* (1954), p. 104.

would have to be prepared to face two sets of critics. The self-governing colonies might demand control of Africans in the adjoining territories, especially Swaziland. In that event,

and indeed, I apprehend, in any event, the supporters of native rights in this country and in the House of Commons are bound to intervene. I have always felt that they accepted our arrangements in the Transvaal Constitution with some hesitation, but I gratefully acknowledge that they were not unfriendly. Agreeing in many points with them, I should wish to keep faith and in no way diminish, or even appear to diminish, any protection for natives which we were able to secure.[1]

The particular decisions taken by the Liberal government concerning African interests in the self-governing parts of Africa have already been discussed. From the areas not under white self-government, Swaziland and North-western Rhodesia were the subject of decisions which throw some light on Liberal government attitudes to the native problem. Like their advisers, Liberal ministers found the administration of the protectorates a welcome relief from the burdens of colonial South Africa. In general Basutoland seemed to them the model for native administration. It was taken to represent clear evidence of the superiority of a bureaucratic government for Africans, free from interference by colonial communities.[2]

Swaziland. From about 1887 a prodigious number of concessions and industrial monopolies was granted to Europeans by Mbandzeni (Umbandine). Almost all sources of revenue, land and minerals were granted away together with every conceivable right which could be made a source of profit: the right of

---

[1] EP, cab. memo. 13 Nov 07.

[2] CO. 417/439/18594, minute by Lambert, 29 May 07. In July 1906 Graham said reading the loyal addresses welcoming Selborne on his tour of the protectorates, 'amidst our innumerable difficulties in South Africa is like drinking a bottle of champagne after a course of Harrogate waters'. Graham's comment was followed by the note: 'Pula! W.S.C. 7 July.' Basutoland, wrote Lambert in 1908 'is a legitimate subject of pride to Crown Colony administration' (CO. 417/455/11870, minute 24 Apr 08). Crewe also found accounts of its recent progress 'a very pleasant story' (ibid. 19756, minute 27 Jun 08). Selborne on Basutoland: EP 13 Dec 07 and 3 Aug 06.

tanning, minting, collecting customs, the importation of machinery, oil, tobacco, the right of establishing pawnbrokers and orphanages, the use of steam, even the right to apply for concessions. Land and mineral rights frequently overlapped. Boundaries were vague because there had been no land survey. All rights over future development were signed away. The Swazi came to speak of 'documents that killed us'.[1] The total land area granted to concessionaires was believed to exceed the actual land area of Swaziland.

In 1894 colonial secretary Ripon agreed to the assumption of a protectorate over Swaziland by the South African Republic. The British government acquired responsibility on conquest of the Transvaal during the Boer War, and steadfastly refused to hand it back to Botha's government.[2] Concessions were in a state of unparalleled confusion. Milner appointed a commission in 1904 to separate the rights of the Swazi and the concessionaires, and to allocate reserves to the Swazi. It was considered impossible to annul concessions which had been recognised by a legal tribunal. The commission was therefore to define boundaries, decide the exact nature and priority of claims where these conflicted, and to expropriate at pre-war value the monopoly and industrial concessions. Selborne decided to change the character of the commission and make its function purely advisory. He requested final discretionary authority to settle the matter himself. Elgin agreed to this procedure in principle, though with misgivings about the pressure on the high commissioner's time, misgivings which were well founded, for Selborne eventually discovered that the matter was too complicated and too important for him to settle alone. Elgin accepted the fact that something had got to be done to sort out the concessions, but rightly understood that a policy of inaction presented great advantages, the greatest, perhaps, being that it, and it alone, would satisfy completely the wishes of the Swazi themselves, who hated the idea of being restricted to reserves. But he was impressed with the belief that inaction could only

[1] See H. Kuper, *An African Aristocracy: rank among the Swazi* (1961), pp. 19–31.
[2] See pp. 263–4

result in increased trouble to the Swazi in after years, and in a still greater burden to the administration. He agreed with Selborne's recommendation that there should be a definite separation of the rights of the Swazi from those of the concessionaires by a process of compulsory partition. Every concessionaire was required to give up one-third of his concession without compensation; it was represented to him that he would gain by the substitution of a certain for an uncertain tenure. Land allocated to the Swazi was to be in every respect of a suitable character, sufficient to provide not only for their present needs but for reasonable and natural expansion. Reserves were not to be unduly concentrated, or scattered in too many pieces. There would be as little disturbance as possible of existing kraals. Ample rights of way were everywhere to be reserved, and attention paid to securing for the Swazi sufficient access to water and a full share of the best land and timber. Elgin also agreed that no pressure should be put upon the Swazi to move from lands remaining in private ownership after partition had taken place, into the inalienable reserves prepared for them, until five years had elapsed from the date of the partition, and only then in the absence of a special agreement satisfactory to both parties. During the five-year period, the Swazi need pay no rent, and after five years he might still stay on the concessionaire's land if an arrangement could be made.[1]

The partition proclamation was announced in 1907. On the whole it satisfied the Europeans, but Swazi peasants were aghast. To lose any of their land struck at the roots of the economic and political system. Land was the focal point of their communal sentiment. They were not consulted. Their attitude to land was not understood. Despite their bitter feeling, the partition was carried out with little friction, under the expert and sincere direction of George Grey, brother of Sir Edward Grey. The most important chiefs were not at once affected. Because the concessionaires were restrained from immediately ejecting Swazi many of the latter remained as

---

[1] CO. 291/107/42552, S/S to Selb 30 Mar 07.

squatters. By 1943 slightly under two-thirds of the land was owned by about five hundred Europeans.[1]

Elgin agreed with Selborne that it would be most undesirable to allow the Swazi to carry their protests as far as a deputation to London on behalf of the Swazi Queen Regent. On the other hand, he did not want to be too peremptory: 'The rights of natives are much to the fore at present. But . . . you can certainly say with emphasis that I consider the only proper mode of communication is through yourself', he told Selborne.[2] However, the Queen persisted, and Selborne reluctantly came to the conclusion that a deputation to England seemed inevitable. Elgin was still very doubtful of the expediency of allowing a deputation: it would be impossible to prevent them raising all their grievances. But the deputation could not be prevented. Fortified with full memoranda prepared by his staff, and entrenched in chilliest official manner behind his enormous desk, Elgin received the deputation on 21 November. He told the Swazi representatives that one-third was 'a very exceptional and indeed enormous deduction' from European claims. As a result they would get half the land area. He did not intend to increase the share of the Swazi beyond an ample provision for their wants, but, he added, power was reserved to take more land in future from the concessionaires if required. He made it as plain as he could that their clear decisions would not be reversed.[3]

[1] Selborne described the separation as the most 'tiresome and intricate piece of administrative work' in the history of the empire.

[2] EP, E to Selb. 18 May 06.

[3] CO. 417/441 and EP, E to Selb. 21 Nov 07: Elgin's account of the deputation is as follows: 'I was determined to make my interview essentially a statement by them and reply by myself and to avoid all question and answer. Accordingly when they came this afternoon they found me entrenched behind my writing table. . . . There was no possibility of shaking hands, but after the formal salute and presentation they were seated on chairs opposite me. I asked who was spokesman and Vilakasi was named and spoke for some time. Malunge made a few observations, and I then had my say. . . . I think that you will admit that I gave them no ghost of a chance for hoping that the decision would be reversed. . . . I impressed upon them the necessity that they should take the [written] reply back to Swaziland as rapidly as possible. . . . However I don't think that they could do much mischief if they delayed. All of us – the government – will have disappeared after Tuesday –

Two curious by-products of this disentanglement of concessions may be mentioned, one concerning a European, the other
concerning the Swazi royal family. Churchill took up the case
of Mr Sheldon, who had a bad legal title to his concession (it
was technically an 'unconfirmed concession'), because Sheldon
had spent a lot of money in Swaziland, and everything else
about him was 'solid and *bona fide*'. It was not, said Churchill,
in a spirit of narrow legal technicality that they had dealt with
the concessions of King Mbandzeni. The whole spirit of their
policy had been 'a rough and ready, but essentially fair
consideration of their merits'. The House of Commons, he
wrote, would very much like the arbitrary dispossession of
concessionaires to the advantage of the Swazi people; but he
objected to the mixture of arbitrary confiscation and legal
technicality in Sheldon's case. Churchill was in his naughtiest
mood as he penned the following sentences:

What a pity Mr Sheldon is not an ex-Councillor. His vested
rights would receive a much more respectful consideration. But
the colonial office is a department of many moods, and
promulgates principles which would delight the House of
Lords or the Revolutionary Convention with equal grace and
facility.

In accordance with Churchill's suggestion, Sheldon was given
access to a court of law.[1] The supreme court decided against
him, though saying that his case was a hard one. Churchill
fulminated about the 'wide divergence between Law and
Justice, always deplorable, but never presented in such an
abrupt form. . . .' Having cut through various doubtful legal
tangles in these concessions, the authorities were suddenly
whipping round, 'like a squirrel', and tripping up Mr Sheldon

---

and M.P.s are otherwise engaged, e.g. fighting suffragettes, in the Provinces.
But so far as we are concerned, we shall do all we can to ship them off'. Selborne
seemed satisfied with this. Elgin replied: 'I hope the result will be to strengthen
your hands – for so far as I am aware, in spite of their long stay they did not manage
to enlist any champions in this country' (EP, 24 Jan 08).

[1] CO. 291/107/36826, minutes 25 Oct and 1 Nov 06.

with a legal technicality.[1] It was a 'very grave case of injustice – almost amounting to robbery'.[2]

The other by-product concerned the personal private revenue concession which King Mbandzeni had granted to J. R. Harington in 1889, and which was not subject to investigation by the commission. The government of the South African Republic had taken it over on setting up the protectorate. Milner in 1905 proclaimed the private revenue to be part of the general revenues of Swaziland. Legally payment could not continue thereafter, although payment was requested, together with arrears, by the Swazi royal family. The concession had been worth £12,000 a year to them. Graham was firmly opposed to making these payments. 'The Swazi royal family is about the most worthless in all South Africa', he wrote. They were, according to him, all drunkards. The £12,000 was more likely to be spent on champagne than in the interests of the Swazi people, or at all events it would disappear in 'gross extravagance and even waste'. In any case the sum far exceeded what other African chiefs of higher standing enjoyed. It was suggested that in compensation an allowance of £1000 a year might be paid. Elgin thought it prudent 'to err in the direction of liberality' and give this allowance. He thought the despatch setting out this policy one of 'considerable importance'.

The possibility of establishing a native council in Swaziland was briefly considered, but Selborne dismissed the suggestion as not yet practicable. In principle he was strongly in favour of such councils: through a much larger recourse to such machinery, South African natives might thereafter be given an opportunity of making their opinions understood and their wants felt. The Basutoland council, established in 1903, was rated a distinct success, but the Basuto were considered the most able and advanced tribe in South Africa, while the Swazi were thought to be the least advanced, the least intelligent and reasonable. Elgin, and Crewe following him, agreed that such

[1] CO. 417/450/23732, minute 13 Jun 07.
[2] Ibid. 25262, 29 Jul 07. It was proposed to give Sheldon a lease, and Elgin agreed to approach Selborne about this.

386

a council would not represent the Swazi nation, but only the Queen Regent and her immediate reactionary adherents. Meanwhile, the resident commissioner was reminded of the importance of ascertaining and paying regard to Swazi opinion, especially upon legislation affecting African interests and rights.[1]

North-western Rhodesia. The policy of creating native reserves was much to the fore in the period before 1914, especially in Kenya, but plans were also made for Rhodesia; there were also reserves in Bechuanaland, and Basutoland in a sense was one large native reserve. Native reserves are often now regarded as illiberal measures to restrict African development, but at this date they were not the product of sinister intention. They were genuinely regarded as necessary and beneficial to the tribal Africans; they provided adequate areas of absolutely guaranteed security of tribal possession, with a real attempt to bear future needs in mind.

Notwithstanding a willingness in general to accept a policy of reserves, the government, for significant reasons, refused to create one for the Barotse. The Barotse had achieved some degree of economic sophistication as a trading people of the plain, and were fairly co-operative towards their British overlords. Lewanika, the paramount chief of the Lozi, ruled over most of what became North-western Rhodesia, and what became part of Eastern Angola and Northern Bechuanaland. Fearing the Ndebele, Lewanika agreed to accept British protection in 1890. A resident agent was appointed in 1897. In 1899 Lewanika conceded administrative rights to the British South Africa Company. Lewanika went to the coronation of Edward VII in 1902. He was impressed by British power, and by attention shown to him, as many others have been on similar occasions, and he in turn impressed Londoners with his excellent manners, aristocratic bearing and shrewd realism.[2]

The proposal to create a Barotse native reserve was made by Selborne in a despatch dated 17 June 1907 discussing the

[1] CO. 417/456/13884, S/S to Selb. 6 May 08.
[2] L. H. Gann, *A history of Northern Rhodesia: early days to 1953* (1964), p. 103.

387

administration of North-western Rhodesia by the British South Africa Company. He would have attempted to delimit the area over which chief Lewanika exercised a real authority and to which the British South Africa Company were likely to attach the least value commercially. He envisaged that the reserve would be administered by the imperial government on the lines of Basutoland, that is to say, without wrecking the power of the chief. He suggested that the rest of North-western Rhodesia might be amalgamated with Southern Rhodesia.

Elgin considered the argument against these proposals a strong one, and gave his ruling against Selborne's scheme. His despatch recognised that the present position of affairs was not entirely satisfactory; doubtless an imperial protectorate would provide an administration less likely to clash with African interests and more satisfactory from the standpoint of relations with Lewanika; but the secretary of state was not convinced that either party would welcome the proposals, or that they would not involve the British government in further expenditure (a dreadful bugbear). Administration of a reserve would depend financially entirely upon native taxation, which was incapable of sufficient extension. Britain would be expected, in conformity with international stipulations, to suppress slave-raiding and illicit trading, which could hardly be achieved without a considerable outlay of money.

Even more serious than these financial objections, was the infringement of the arrangement whereby the British South Africa Company had been placed in possession of the assets of a wide area because it administered that area without cost to the British tax payer. Good reasons had from time to time been urged for placing this or that part of the interior under imperial control, but had always been turned down:

However much there might be to recommend it on intrinsic grounds, your proposal would involve a departure from the settled policy of H.M.G. in this matter, and could not but react on the solution of the problem which lies before us in regard to other parts of their territory where a change in the position of the Company is more urgently needed than in North

Western Rhodesia. It would I think be a pity in these circumstances to complicate the problem by relieving the Company of
the cost of the administration of the least valuable part of
North Western Rhodesia, whilst leaving them in full possession
of the really promising portion.

Furthermore – and how unfortunate the wording! –

Southern Rhodesia already suffers from an excess of black as
compared with white population: and the addition of even a
slice of North Western Rhodesia would be to increase the
disproportion, and to add to the difficulty of including the territory as a constituent member of a South African federation.[1]

This reply was unanimously supported in the colonial office.
It reflects the reluctance to extend responsibilities, the primary
importance of economical considerations, and the compulsions
of the wider strategy of South African federation. Though there
was a reference to the high commissioner's being bound in an
especial degree to exercise his powers for the protection of
African interests, the dominant preoccupation was the attempt
to secure a strong federation in which Southern Rhodesia
would eventually act as a counterpoise to Boer predominance.

This was not to say that the Liberals approved of the British
South Africa Company. In 1893 Ripon, as colonial secretary,
had reluctantly sanctioned its charter, realising that

These companies are really speculative, got up mainly for stock
exchange purposes and a good deal blown up in that aspect of
their existence . . . they are not pleasant instruments of
administration.[2]

But the British South Africa Company, in particular, was a
useful device for administration without expense to the British
tax payer, and consequently its administrative powers were
defended in the face of continual complaint from the small
settler community that the commercial policy of the Company
was detrimental to the development of Rhodesia.[3]

[1] CO. 417/436/23910, minute 5 Aug 07; S/S to Selb. 10 Aug 07.
[2] R. E. Robinson and J. Gallagher, *Africa and the Victorians* (1961), p. 252;
Ripon to Gladstone 4 Nov 93.
[3] The colonial office attitude was that 12,623 whites probably could not sustain
the burden of representative government; that if they were to be governed direct

WEST AFRICA: INDIRECT RULE AND CONCESSIONS

In common with most other politicians and administrators of his day, Elgin had a poor view of the capacity of non-Europeans for governmental work. He also had an unshakeable belief in the superiority of everything European. It was no surprise to him to learn that the colonial office doubted whether the natives of West Africa would make good district officers. Africans had been tried as district officers in the Gold Coast quite often during the past thirty years. According to official assessment, although two or three of them had done well, there had been some bad failures. Elgin thought this quite in accord with Indian experience.[1]

A curious illustration of Elgin's uncompromising devotion to European ideals is provided by his adoption of a policy upon African marriages in Sierra Leone which was contrary to the judgment, not of Lyttelton only, but of Churchill, the entire colonial office staff, and of Crewe and Seely. Marriages between Europeans and Africans under native law Elgin put in the category of immorality only, and refused to allow such marriages to act as disqualifications for subsequent Christian marriage, thus reversing Lyttelton's decision, which would have recognised African marriages as constituting a disqualification for white marriage, and made the latter punishable as bigamous. Elgin believed it unsatisfactory to condemn a man as a bigamist for entering into a connection which was not marriage in the eye of the British law: 'to class these connections, where women are bought and sold, alongside a Christian marriage, is degrading

---

from London it would involve a substantial addition to the estimates, though the longer the transfer could be delayed, the less this was likely to be. In the meantime, they dismissed complaints with the argument that those who were discontented would also grumble against the colonial office; with the belief that the 'general efficiency' of company administration was striking, and with the fact that the settlers went out in full knowledge that the company had a perfect right under its charter to run their property on commercial lines (CO. 417/425/43531. Selb. to S/S 5 Nov 06; minute by Harris 13 Dec 06).

[1] CO. 267/487/33891, minute 21 Sep 06. The proportion of Africans holding senior posts in the civil service was decreasing (D. Kimble, *A political history of Ghana*, i, *1850–1928* (1963), 94–123; C. Fyfe, *History of Sierra Leone* (1962), p. 615.

to Christian marriage.' Thus Sierra Leone received a law which was not in force anywhere else in British Africa, and which Crewe refused to extend to Kenya in 1910.[1] Poor Elgin! It is a sad commentary on the total state of British official knowledge of Africa that a colonial secretary should have been guilty of such a crude misunderstanding. He did not even begin to understand that the transfer of cattle signifies not purchase of a wife, but legalisation and even insurance of the union.

Elgin did not discourage such attempts as there were to increase anthropological knowledge of Africans. He supported the projects for a classification of African marks,[2] and for a questionnaire about African customary law in West Africa; he arranged for the replies to the latter enquiry to be indexed and deposited in the library of the Royal Anthropological Institute.[3] But merely to list these projects is to realise how pitifully inadequate they were.

Indirect Rule. The policy of indirect rule was worked out by men on the spot in various parts of Africa. It is not clear that the Liberals saw any difference between what Lugard was doing in Northern Nigeria and what had become settled policy in Basutoland, between the versions which were constructive rather than *laissez-faire*, between those which, like Lugard's, stressed the 'rule' and those which stressed the 'indirect', and exercised only a minimum of control.[4] They understood it basically as a system of ruling through native chiefs, or sometimes even less precisely as 'governing people according to their own ideas', as Hopwood once wrote. The Liberal government decisively accorded its support to the theory. This support was not given simply, or perhaps even mainly, because of its administrative expediency, although it is of course unlikely

---

[1] CO. 267/479/27838, minute by E 16 Feb 06; CO. 533/76/28567, S/S to govr 24 Oct 10. In Nyasaland too, Elgin said they 'must be careful in giving State recognition to "modified" forms of marriage.' It was too soon for legislation, he added (CO. 525/9).

[2] CO. 96/442, circular desp. 12 Jul 06.

[3] CO. 87/174/34648, circular desp. 20 Mar 06 and CO. 446/82/9521.

[4] M. Bull, 'Indirect Rule in Northern Nigeria, 1906–1911', in *Essays . . . presented to Margery Perham* (ed. K. Robinson and F. Madden, 1963), p. 49.

391

that the Liberals would have approved the expense of direct rule (any more than they approved the expense of coercion in Ireland), which, on the surface at any rate, appeared greater. Indirect rule in West Africa commended itself to the Liberals as part of the general policy of making as few political changes as possible, respecting and preserving indigenous customs and institutions, and working through African chiefs. The policy was strongly reinforced by Indian experience. Furthermore, wherever the Liberals wished to limit imperial administration, they at once fell back upon the policy of organising tribal leaders, as for example in Liberia and Somaliland.[1] As viceroy, it will be recalled, Elgin had not believed it impossible to turn native forms of government to good account. Like Lugard and E. D. Morel, he was impressed by the popularity and stability of non-oppressive princely rule as compared with the British.[2] He formulated carefully a policy of encouraging native rule in Waziristan, a policy he believed capable of wider application. Firmly believing that 'a plant derives more of its strength from the fibre in itself than from any adventitious or foreign aid from the watering-pot', he aimed at consolidating and strengthening native authority in alliance with Britain, rather than superseding it, and at limiting in every way direct administration by British officials.[3]

With this background, it is not surprising to find Elgin lending quick and firm support to the policy of indirect rule in Northern Nigeria. Girouard, the governor who succeeded Lugard, had grave misgivings about the success of Crown Colony government in West Africa; he thought Nigerians incapable of understanding even the lowest form of constitutional government; Britain would have to find some more reasonable system, something more in accord with native ideals, whether Mohammedan or negro: Accra, Lagos, Sierra Leone might be fitted for municipal government of some kind, but their hinterlands did not appear ripe for anything but the personal supervision of Europeans, ruling the Africans by their

[1] See pp. 200 and 363.   [2] VRP. 14/191.
[3] Ibid. 13/153 and 88/176, 194, 472.

own laws and customs, and through native executive heads.[1] Elgin assured him that his Indian experience gave him some familiarity with the Mohammedan problems of Northern Nigeria, and that in addition:

you may count on my support in a policy of dealing with these 'ideals' (Mohammedan or Negro) with great caution and even with sympathy.

I agree that if we look forward to union of the provinces [i.e. Northern and Southern Nigeria], it would be absurd to introduce into these states the procedure which suits (I am not sure that is the right word even there), and has been adopted on the coast. But again I turn to India, and I can imagine a Governor-General of Nigeria, who kept under his own administration or control the Native States possessing governments of their own, and left to the provinces capable of modern self-government the control of their own affairs under the Lt.-Governor – and yet remained the acknowledged head of all.[2]

Elgin was fully in favour of amalgamating Northern and Southern Nigeria.

In education too, the old Anglicisation process, which had hitherto governed policy in India and on the West African coast, was abandoned. The educational policy which began with Macaulay was under fire from most of the governors in West Africa at this time. They believed that it was probably the source of the grave difficulties confronting the government of India in the early twentieth century, and did not wish to see similar developments in Africa.[3] However, in September 1906

[1] EP, Girouard to E 27 Aug 07.

[2] EP, E to Girouard 19 Nov 07 (copy). Another example of Elgin's using Indian analogy for Nigeria occurred in his remarks about licensing law. Liquor-sellers in Ibadan and Abeokuta did not have to be licensed; licensing law, he said, had not been enforced there for those districts claimed a certain amount of independence by treaties. 'I do not know the details but it strikes me that they are somewhat in the position of Indian Native states; and we should certainly not, in that case, have introduced into a Native State, the liquor laws of British India' (PD. 181/6, 19 Aug 07).

[3] CO. 96/473/686, Rodger to S/S 22 Dec 08. For Nyasaland, Elgin laid 'great stress on the encouragement of industrial education amongst natives'; hitherto the education had been 'too exclusively literary' (CO. 525/22/23717, desp. from S/S 23 Aug 07).

Lugard recommended allowing Dr Miller's scheme to give secular instruction to the sons of emirs and Moslem chiefs and leaders. Miller's ultimate objective was Christianisation, but he agreed not to give religious instruction in official school hours. The office staff had no objections. Churchill remarked that it would never do to prejudice the beginnings of education in Nigeria by suspicion of Christian proselytising, but he relied on Lugard's judgment of the risk. Elgin recalled the Roman Catholic and Wesleyan schools in South India which were attended by Indians without change of religion, and he allowed the plan to be cautiously tried under careful government observation.[1] But Elgin quickly withdrew government support when it was clear that Miller was in fact not only aiming at conversion, but also wanting to put pressure on the emirs to obtain acceptance of his scheme. Elgin ruled this out of the question. He regretted that Lugard had misled him into countenancing the project. In his minute on the subject, he once again recalled his Indian experience. He was impressed by

the supreme importance of not separating the rulers from their people – and ... even with the precautions, which the Government of India invariably prescribes, it is almost inevitable that the influence of even a secular education, should weaken the bond between the young Chief and his subjects.[2]

Nor did he think that an English education would make a native ruler more contented or useful.[3] Thus he was happy enough to approve Girouard's policy of gradually improving facilities for Moslem education. Girouard planned to abandon the aim of turning Africans into European lines of thought, and instead to raise the African intelligence on native or 'national' lines.[4]

[1] CO. 446/60/36412, minutes 28 Oct and 11 Nov 06.
[2] CO. 446/62/15068, 20 Jul 07. When Girouard reported that Bishop Tugwell of the C.M.S. had baptised an African Moslem openly, Elgin said: 'We must certainly stop these practices', and sent a telegram asking Girouard if the action was so dangerous to the peace to require immediate action by the secretary of state (CO. 446/66/130, tel. govr to S/S 31 Dec 07, minute 9 Jan 08).
[3] VRP. 15/38, 24 Feb 97 and 15/App. 109, 13 Oct 97.
[4] CO. 446/74/30542, Girouard to S/S 22 Jul 08; ibid. 75/39688, 25 Sep 08.

Following the policy laid down by Elgin, Crewe gave decisive impetus in the Gold Coast to the effectual implementation of the Native Jurisdiction Ordinance of 1883. This aimed at strengthening the position and responsibility of chiefs, but it was largely a dead letter, and the chiefs were in a degraded condition. The real question at issue in 1908, when the governor again pressed the matter on the attention of the government, was whether Britain was to rule through the chiefs, and in order to enable them to be instruments of British rule, to give them an exclusive legal jurisdiction over tribal Africans in certain cases – or, as had been the case in practice, gradually to deprive their courts of all power and make government purely European in purpose and method. The opinion of successive governors and secretaries of state for nearly fifteen years had been in favour of the former alternative – but it was not until 1908 that anything was determined finally. Part of the reason why practice had gone in an entirely opposite direction from agreed theory, was to be found in the hostility of the chief justice to native courts.[1] The government despatch of 25 October 1908 represented virtually a decision in favour of the principle of the bill. Crewe thought it right

to give a full and fair chance to the plan of native jurisdiction, combined with [educational] efforts towards improvement of individual chiefs and their sons. I dare say that the conditions are less favourable at the Gold Coast than at some other places: but we must proceed on these lines.[2]

Full governmental support was also accorded to the new Northern Nigerian land policy[3] propounded in 1908, which likewise based on the same general principle of respect for African custom. This policy was also related to the encouragement of African production of raw materials. Indirect rule was apt to check the European capitalist in a hurry to push ahead with development; missionaries tended to regard it as a

[1] CO. 96/473/47182, minute by Ellis 30 Jun 09.
[2] CO. 96/486/36881, 26 Dec 09; see also D. Kimble, *A political history of Ghana*, i (1963), 462–9.
[3] See pp. 425–7.

stumbling-block. In all cases of European economic activity the consent of the Africans had to be obtained.[1]

The Lever palaver. The long-drawn out palaver surrounding Lever's attempt to obtain concessions from the Liberal government in West Africa seems to indicate a difference of treatment from that earlier accorded him. William Lever, the grocer turned soap-manufacturer, had formed a limited company with his brother in 1890, and aimed to provide the raw materials for his own trade. He was elected a Liberal M.P. in Cheshire in 1906. He had obtained a generous concession in the Solomon Islands from Chamberlain. In the summer of 1906 his proposals came into the colonial office for extending, from 99 years to 999 years, the certificate of occupation held by Lever Brothers' Pacific Plantations Ltd in the Solomons. The proposed rental for the first 99 years was only £60 a year. Officials were anxious to increase this, otherwise the colony would obtain no benefit for 99 years. Cox wrote sensibly:

We want more in the present and less in the future. The British Empire certainly won't last another hundred years, if so long, and it is, it seems to me, laughable to talk of £3,000 a year three hundred years hence.

This attracted a Churchillian rebuke: 'Such pessimism is unworthy of the Colonial Office!'[2] It is tempting to believe that this remark was not jocular. After all, Churchill was quite serious when he later said he did not become prime minister in order to preside over the liquidation of the British empire.

The company was asked to pay an increased rent after seven years, in view of the necessity of raising funds for development.

[1] It is interesting to note that Morley was concurrently following a not dissimilar line of thought with regard to India. He said he would spare no pains to improve relations with native governments, potentially of increasing value, and would make them independent in administration. If he had to frame a new system of government for India, he would 'multiply the Baroda system of government, rather than have an Imperial Duma and universal suffrage' (Morley, *Indian Speeches*, pp. 21, 53).

[2] CO. 225/71/27566, minutes 1 and 3 Aug 06; this entire correspondence has been incorrectly bound up in the files for 1905.

Lever protested against this. On reconsideration, Elgin did not think it wise to quarrel with Lever on that score. 'After all,' he wrote, 'it is not every day that we find a millionaire tenant in the Solomon Islands, and I think we may assume that the rental he pays is the lesser part of the advantage the protectorate will derive from him.' Elgin thought it reasonable to try to get some benefit for the present and two succeeding generations, and so a small increase was suggested to Lever.[1] Levers would not pay more in total over 999 years. Lever offered a compromise of an immediate increase of rentals by 10 per cent, which Elgin gladly accepted.[2]

Times were changing. This is a transitional episode, a last manifestation, perhaps, of sympathy towards Lever, closer to Chamberlain's attitude than to Harcourt's determination not to open under-developed areas to unrestricted exploitation by those whom he dubbed pejoratively in 1913 as the 'soap-boilers of the world'.[3]

In West Africa, Lever from 1907 seems to have received much less sympathetic consideration than he had done with the Solomon Islands.[4]

The Liberals aimed at the economic development of West Africa, and also, probably, of Uganda, by the indigenous inhabitants.[5] By supporting their institutions and improving their capacity to undertake development themselves, it would be easier to keep out the unpopular European capitalists. Africans were to be assisted by European technical knowledge, by the supply of seeds and instruction where necessary. This policy by no means excluded individual European enterprise;

[1] Ibid. 29904, minute by E 17 Aug 06, S/S to Lever 27 Aug 06.

[2] Ibid. 32416, Lever to S/S 30 Aug 06, minute by E 2 Sep 06.

[3] PD/HC. 66/786, 31 Jul 13.

[4] On Lever's schemes for West Africa, see W. K. Hancock, *Survey of British Commonwealth Affairs*, ii, part 2 (1942), 190, and C. H. Wilson, *History of Unilever*, i (1954), 165–7.

[5] This was not peculiarly a Liberal policy. Lyttelton had declared: 'The best way of fostering the cotton industry within our colonial empire was to educate the natives in the production of that commodity' (PD. 144/565). Egerton, governor of Southern Nigeria, also favoured peasant agriculture (CO. 520/65/35818), and so did Sadler in Kenya (CO. 533/17/39572). There are however confusing cross-currents in an opposite direction.

indeed, such enterprise was essential the to success of the policy, though the government did not always seem to realise this as clearly as it might. But it did preclude conferring upon individual European companies exclusive territorial or other privileges calculated to interfere with what was coming to be recognised, at least in the regions not suitable for white settlement, as the first duty of government in Africa: to preserve the land for the people. It was becoming clear that ownership encouraged production. According to E. D. Morel, in Southern Nigeria by 1911 there were several hundred thousand people exporting nearly four million pounds' worth of tropical products every year. At the suggestion, and with the technical help, of the newly established forestry department, Africans established communal plantations, especially for rubber, in 700 villages in the Benin district.[1] Harcourt declared in 1913 that it was 'extremely satisfactory' to note that the increased cultivation of cocoa in the Gold Coast in the previous seven years, was 'entirely due to native industry and energy, and that the great bulk of the plantations are native-owned and worked'.[2]

The colonial office was always prepared to encourage *bona fide* schemes for the development of West Africa, but very few *bona fide* schemes were put forward. They declined to help any scheme in which it appeared that government recognition was really wanted for the purpose of raising money which would go more into the pockets of the promoters than into development.[3] Lever's plans were given serious consideration.

In October 1907 Lever attended a meeting in the colonial office at which he outlined a scheme for the 'modern treatment of the fruit of the oil palm in the Colony and Protectorate of Sierra Leone upon a scale of considerable magnitude'. From the outset Lever made it clear that his proposed undertakings would have to be on a very extensive scale in order to make it worth while embarking large capital; he therefore regarded the sanction and encouragement of the government as essential.

---

[1] Morel papers, F. 8, Morel to Lever 19 Apr 11.
[2] PD/HC. 56/790.
[3] Morel papers, F. 9, Antrobus to Morel 21 Feb 03.

Officials were not unsympathetic to his application. Apparently without consulting the secretary of state, they informed the governor that Lever's representative, Alldridge (formerly a district commissioner), would negotiate with the chiefs, and asked him to consider the project carefully, confer with Alldridge and give him whatever assistance he might require. They were satisfied that the firm was in a position to carry out the scheme; if it were found practicable, and provided that the interests of the Africans were duly safeguarded, it might, they thought, prove advantageous to Sierra Leone.[1] Alldridge eventually proposed to offer, in effect, a sum which represented threepence per carrier-load for ripe nuts brought to the crushing mill. The governor believed the project impracticable on these terms, and the officials agreed with his opinion that the proposed remuneration was inadequate. Africans could not be advised to accept these terms. The fact that Levers were a firm of good reputation, very much in earnest, and that it was admittedly very desirable to exploit the resources of Sierra Leone, did not prevent the government scrutinising proposals most carefully.[2] Alldridge's proposals were considered at a conference in the colonial office in June 1908, as a result of which the proposal to acquire land on which actually to cultivate the oil palm was abandoned. As Lever subsequently explained to Morel: they found

the system of land tenure in Africa did not readily admit of Companies coming in and planting large areas. . . . We also came to the conclusion that the government would not be favourably disposed to this method of development in Africa.[3]

At the end of the conference Lever said that he wished to have only an exclusive right of erecting oil-expressing power mills and the exclusive privilege of laying down monorails over a radius of twenty miles from the mills. The colonial office thought the obligation of chiefs (under the agreements drafted by Alldridge), to provide native labour, most objectionable; they

[1] CO. 267/500/39693, S/S to govr 15 Nov 07.
[2] CO. 267/502/13708, Govr to S/S 3 Apr 08; minute by Butler 7 May 08.
[3] Morel papers, F. 8, Lever to Morel 29 Aug 10.

also disliked the virtual perpetuity of lease, the low rate of pay suggested, and were suspicious of the 'slobbering' eulogy of the benefits which it was alleged would accrue to Africans. The matter was discussed further on 27 October, with the under-secretary of state in the chair. Seely disliked the request for a 99-year lease, and was clearly apprehensive lest Lever should eventually establish a monopoly of the whole palm oil belt of the Protectorate, which he thought could result from an extension of the principle implied in the demand that there should be no monorail running nearer than twenty miles to any part of Lever's monorails. Lever was asked to submit proposals of a more moderate nature.[1] The government was determined to prevent interference with the Africans obtaining the full benefit of competition between European firms.[2] When Lever assured them that Africans would be absolutely free to carry their produce to his mill or elsewhere as they pleased, doubts began to recede. He submitted revised proposals on 31 October 1908, still insisting on protection from possible competition to the extent of having the sole privilege of laying monorails over an area of twenty miles radius. The government would not permit an area of more than ten miles radius. There were still doubts about the adequacy of the proposed remuneration. Their final terms were communicated to Lever on 6 February 1909. They were prepared to grant the exclusive right of erecting power mills for the expressing of oil from the palm fruit within the area agreed upon, 'subject to the consent of the natives concerned having been obtained in a manner satisfactory to the government'. These rights were to be for twenty-one years. This proved to be the fatal blow, because Lever wanted the security of tenure which a 99-year lease would give. 'A reasonable payment to the native authorities concerned . . . would be a necessary part of the agreement with them' for the site of the mills. The government would not agree to the remission of duty on building materials or to preferential rates on the railway.[3] Lever rejected these counter-proposals as

[1] CO. 267/505/35351.   [2] CO. 267/508/782.
[3] CO. 267/520/2578, Hopwood to Lever Bros 6 Feb 09.

they would preclude the successful operation of the scheme.[1]

The colonial office remained sympathetic,[2] but did not, on the other hand, rate the prospects of advantage to Sierra Leone so high that they need make further overtures. Lever then began to consider operations in Southern Nigeria, but found it difficult to approach the colonial office again. He secured the intercession of Morel to clear up what he thought had been misunderstanding. Morel was fully in favour of Lever's plans for Southern Nigeria, and did not think that they interfered with the native policy which was rightly being followed by the government. Application was made, and after a delay of three months, the government of Southern Nigeria replied offering terms (i.e. five miles radius), which, Lever observed, were worse than could have been obtained in Sierra Leone.[3] Attempts to work within the limits imposed were a fiasco. Lever, thus thwarted, found an opening in the Congo.

It is noteworthy that the government appeared more sceptical even than Morel of the advantage to the Africans of Lever's scheme. The guiding principle being evolved was that the palm oil industry, of such potential importance to West Africa, would 'largely remain in the hands, and for the profit of the natives'.[4] It is not, however, clear to what extent Lever's failure was due, less to fears on behalf of the Africans, than to horror of monopoly and to the pressure of European merchants. The governor of Southern Nigeria favoured Lever's plans and thought them advantageous to Africans, but expected difficulties in giving him guarantees that other mills would not be established, because of the opposition of merchants, who provided the government with most of the revenue.[5]

Attitude to the Congo scandals. During the years under review, the tropical African territory attracting most attention in Britain was not a British possession, but Leopold's Congo. Removal of

---

[1] Ibid. 5255, to under-secretary of state 12 Feb 09.
[2] Morel papers, F. 8, Strachey to Morel [?] 20 Aug 10.
[3] Ibid. Lever to Morel 27 Apr 11.
[4] PD/HC. 56/785, Harcourt 31 Jul 13.
[5] Morel Papers, F. 8, Egerton to Morel 28 Aug 10, Morel to Lever 1 Sep 10.

Leopold's 'uncontrolled and irresponsible' régime was a major object of British policy,[1] and the attitude of the Liberals to the Congo situation throws light on their conception of proper African policy.

Where did the Liberals think Leopold had gone astray? The real root of the trouble, said Grey, was that the state itself was a trader, and private trading companies had administrative powers. Britain had always looked with suspicion upon the combination of trading rights and administration. There had always been anxiety about British chartered companies, which had been sanctioned only because the colonial office and parliament were behind them. 'Even so', Grey added, 'we do not much like the system, and gradually it has been contracted.'[2] While the state remained a trader there was no real guarantee that offenders would be brought to justice in the Congo.

Britain had trading and material interests to assert – not very extensive, as Katanga was not yet a great mining district – but wished for no political advantages. Grey always put the first grounds of objection as moral and human,[3] even in private discussion. His only desire was to see the abuses in the Congo ended, and the state placed under a government which did not exploit it for private profit, and which would spend all revenue on public services.[4] Privately, Liberal ministers were entirely in sympathy with the strong public feeling on the Congo question.[5]

In 1908 Grey prepared a drastic policy for the approval of the cabinet. If control of the Congo did not pass to the Belgian government, he would announce that if there had been no improvement within a year, Britain would cease to recognise the existence of the Congo state, because the system of forced labour, undoubtedly amounting to the enslavement of a great part of the African population, violated the conditions on which Britain originally recognised it. To make such declarations

[1] GP. 50, Grey to WSC 5 Nov 09 (copy). [2] PD. 160/322, 5 Jul 06.
[3] Morel papers, F. 8, Grey to Morel 6 Jan 07.
[4] GP. 60, Grey to Ripon 11 May 07.
[5] GP. 62, Grey to Lloyd George 11 Nov 08; Lloyd George to Grey 12 Nov 08.

effective two gunboats would have to be sent to the Congo.
The system was

> so scandalous, that if neither Belgium nor any other Power
> will act, we must use all the means at our disposal, short of
> undertaking the administration of the Congo ourselves, to put
> an end to it. . . .[1]

Grey insisted that Britain should receive definite assurances
from Belgium that if the Belgian government assumed responsibility, improvements would be introduced quickly, and
grievances remedied within a reasonable period of time. This
was necessary if only because of the manner in which the situation in the Congo reacted on kindred tribes under British rule.
The essential point was that the African should be enabled to
trade in the natural products of the soil and forest. A return
to African communal tenure in land and rights in produce as
they existed before all lands were declared state property,
regardless of African rights, in 1891–2, 'would lead to a sensible
and immediate alleviation' of the unhappy conditions of the
Congolese.[2] Grey had given instructions that Morel's points
should be used as far as possible in drawing up the despatch.[3]

It is clear that the Congo situation had considerable influence
on the African policy of the British government. This influence
was reflected especially in the new land policy for Northern
Nigeria,[4] and generally in vigilance against the occurrence of
similar oppressions and misgovernment in British territories.
The fear that the case against the Congo would be compromised
if Leopold could point to similar abuses under British rule was
a powerful factor leading to better treatment of Africans.
Compromising parallels came to light in Zululand, North-
eastern Rhodesia, and the East Africa Protectorate. On the
whole the servants of the British government were a little too
ready to assert parallels, and critics even more so. Undoubtedly
one of the things the Liberals disliked about Chinese Labour
was that it tended to compromise Congo protest, and for the

[1] EP, cab. memo. by Grey 16 Mar 08.
[2] Cd. 4396 (1908), Grey to Count de Lalaing 4 Nov 08.
[3] Cromer 13 (ii)/48, Grey to Cromer 20 Aug 08.   [4] See p. 426.

same reason, they were embarrassed by the punishment both of the Zulu disturbances by the Natal government, and of the Denshawai affray by the Egyptian government.[1] Forced labour was employed in Uganda, but the government justified this with the argument that the work the Africans were required to perform was for the benefit of their own country, and not for kings and concessionaires in Europe.[2] Seely had to assure Dilke in 1910 he did not think that there was then the slightest reason for anxiety on the score of the labour being forced for cotton growing. The African grew it for himself on land which he held from a chief, sold it himself, and received the whole of the proceeds.

The compulsion necessary was merely to induce him to cultivate an unfamiliar product, and it was only the normal degree of authority which the chiefs in Uganda habitually exercise over the natives belonging to their own tribes. The compulsion was never exercised by our direct authority, and has now ceased altogether.[3]

It seemed impossible to prevent all forced labour in the East Africa Protectorate, but the colonial office was determined to prevent the enforcement or administration of the system in such a way as to cause scandal. In 1907 there was a suggestion that Africans of the Kasempa district of North-western Rhodesia should pay increased hut tax in rubber. No one in the colonial office seemed to notice the significance of this point, but Elgin asked:

Is it safe to authorise the collection of taxes in rubber, without some warning to secure that care is taken that the amount, if levied, does not exceed in local value the tax payable? We must not let the Congo State system creep in.

Whilst making this proviso, the ensuing despatch did not discourage discussion of the principle.[4]

[1] Morel papers F. 8, Samuel to Morel 6 Sep 05; PD. 152/693-4; PD. 155/250 and 160/273, 312. For attacking a provocative sporting party of British officers at Denshawai in 1906, four Egyptians were hanged, after being forced to watch five others flogged.

[2] CO. 536/21/37925.   [3] Dilke papers 43922/43, Seely to Dilke 25 Apr 10.
[4] CO. 417/435/16808, minute 21 Jul 07; desp. 26 Jul 07.

404

EAST AFRICA: AFRICANS, INDIANS AND EUROPEANS
IN KENYA

Everybody in Britain wanted to see East Africa developed as
rapidly as possible and made to pay its own way. It was difficult
for Britain to avoid the conclusion that the only way to develop
East Africa and to pay for the Uganda railway was through
white settlers. The extension of white settlement in America and
Australasia had been one of the triumphant facts of the
nineteenth century, one of the most remarkable achievements in
human history. Export production by indigenous peasants was
a system virtually untried in tropical Africa when the twentieth
century opened. In any case, it seemed better suited to West
Africa than to East, partly because control over many of the
East African peoples was still tenuous. There seemed to be
ample physical space for Europeans without damaging African
needs. White settlement in Kenya had therefore been begun
while it was still the responsibility of the foreign office.

The early settlers in Kenya tried to follow the traditional
colonial occupations of wool and wheat, to which the Highlands
were not really suited. The production of both suffered severe
set-backs. Coffee production was as yet insignificant. The chief
social and economic problem was not land, but the provision
of an adequate labour force. The need for plantation workers,
road and railway builders and safari porters created a demand
which placed an impossible strain upon the voluntary supply.[1]
By the beginning of 1908 a general crisis had arisen. The inflow
of capital had almost ceased. At one time in 1907 there was an
actual efflux of Europeans, and land began to go out of cultivation.[2] An ugly demonstration took place outside the governor's
house. The colonial office seriously thought of repatriating the
settlers. This proposal, though it came just after Elgin's
departure, deserves inclusion here, because it is essential to
understanding Liberal policy after 1905.

[1] C. C. Wrigley, 'Kenya: the patterns of economic life, 1902–1945', *History of
East Africa*, ii, ed. V. Harlow, E. M. Chilver and A. Smith (1965), p. 229.
[2] E. Huxley, *White Man's Country*, i, 226.

British governments, whether Unionist or Liberal, certainly did not accept Sir Charles Eliot's view of East Africa as a clean slate, a place 'in which native questions will present but little interest', and in which 'white interests must be paramount'.[1] Far from it. Even the foreign office had carefully instructed the commissioner, Sir Donald Stewart, in 1904 to watch African interests with the greatest care:

How best to harmonise their indisputable rights with the requirements of white settlers is a problem which will require your closest attention. . . . It is only by a most careful insistence on the protection of native rights that H.M.G. can justify their presence in East Africa, and the imposition of the taxes which are levied from the natives on the grounds of such protection. . . . The collection should be exercised with the greatest care, for whilst the development of the Protectorate revenues is of great importance on behalf of the taxpayer of this country, the primary duty of Great Britain in East Africa is the welfare of the native races.[2]

Officials doubted if white population would ever be numerically important; they considered East Africa as 'the natural outlet for Indian immigration',[3] as Sir Harry Johnston had done in speaking of it as the 'America of the Hindu'. When Stewart was succeeded in 1905 by Sir James Sadler, the choice was governed by the fact that Sadler had an exhaustive knowledge of East African languages, and because, in the words of Ommanney, he had

those qualities which are essential for dealing successfully with native chiefs and tribes. During the next few years the policy to be adopted towards native tribes in British East Africa will largely govern the progress and peaceful development of the Protectorate.[4]

Sadler certainly proved not to have the qualities necessary for winning the confidence of the settlers. It may be conjectured that Girouard was appointed to succeed him in 1909 partly for

[1] C. Eliot, *East Africa Protectorate*, pp. 302, 310.
[2] CO. 519/1/26334, copy of Lansdowne to Stewart 8 Jul 04.
[3] Ibid. 26065, minute by Lambert.   [4] CO. 533/3, minute.

similar reasons to those which had led to Sadler's appointment: his Nigerian governorship seemed to prove him sympathetic to Africans. In practice he proved to be even more sympathetic to the Kenya settlers. But his appointment does not mean that the colonial office was changing course, merely that it backed the wrong horse.

Although these remarks are intended to suggest that there was much more recognition of the paramountcy of African interests at this date than is usually assumed, or than there was to be after the First World War for a spell, it is however difficult to be sure what the imperial priorities were in East Africa in the early twentieth century. 'The whole story of this period is one of precipitate government action, followed up by no clear definition of policy, no considered scheme of action. . . .'[1] The confused intention and frequent contradictions in East African affairs are well illustrated by the way in which some British politicians were prepared to consider a Zionist settlement there. Joseph Chamberlain made an offer in 1902. The Colonists' Association in Nairobi petitioned against the proposed land grant. The officials were strongly opposed to it. Zionists were divided. Fortunately, the Zionist commissioner did not report favourably. Lyttelton was relieved by this, regarding it as an obligation which ought never to have been incurred.[2] 'No opportunity should be spared of judiciously pouring cold water on this plan', he minuted in 1905; circumstances had changed so much since the offer was made that it would hardly have been possible to give effect to it.[3] Nevertheless the idea of a Zionist settlement continued to crop up. As is well known, Churchill was a convinced Zionist. Elgin probably did not discourage him. There is in the colonial office files a draft in Elgin's own hand of a letter he sent to Mr I. Zangwill. Elgin expressed sympathy with the general aspirations for a Zionist settlement. He did not take any exception to the construction of the Jewish Territorial Organisation. On the other hand, he could not agree with them that the general political sanction of the government should

[1] W. McGregor Ross, *Kenya from within* (1927), p. 65.
[2] CO. 533/1/1511.   [3] CO. 533/10/19381 and 43150.

precede the elaboration of Zangwill's proposals in sufficient detail to enable it to be discussed in a businesslike manner. Elgin insisted that in dealing with any large proposal of the kind it would be necessary, first to be satisfied that it came from responsible people, and secondly, to have submitted at any rate the outline of a definite plan, and thirdly to have evidence of adequate financial backing.[1]

What was the attitude of the Liberal government towards white settlement? In fact, the Liberals were apprehensive about the expansion of white settlement in Africa. They disliked capitalist exploitation and were generally prejudiced against commercial companies. They were also turning towards peasant proprietorship in preference to plantation economies.

Elgin spoke of the 'risk in multiplying what we call white men's countries, where there are a very small number of whites in the midst of an overwhelming number of blacks'. This was not because he thought his fellow countrymen abroad in the least less humane than those who remained at home, 'but they were nearer the danger', and they had fewer means of meeting the difficult circumstances.[2] He understood very clearly that the white community in Natal was almost inevitably subject to panics. It was a matter of self-preservation to keep up the existence of white shopkeepers and skilled artisans, in other words, a self-sufficient white community.[3] There was widespread relief that in Uganda at least, climate ruled out any possibility of settlement.[4] The government, advised by Selborne, thought that it would be a mistake to introduce white settlers in North-western Rhodesia.[5] Elgin and Crewe were well aware of the danger of laying themselves open to the charge of having allowed white settlers to take up land which might thereafter

[1] CO. 533/24/11657, S/S to Zangwill 8 May 06.
[2] PD. 162/623, 31 Jul 06.   [3] EP, Lucas to E 2 Mar 08.
[4] E.g. W. S. Churchill, *My African Journey* (1908), p. 213.
[5] They would not as a rule succeed. 'They will consequently . . . try to live on the natives, in itself a great evil. . . . They will not support the revenue; . . . they will look to politics as a remedy of their economic distress, and exactly the same movement as has existed in Southern Rhodesia will be reproduced' (CO. 417/437/42336; Selb. to S/S 11 Nov 07).

be utilised by the Africans, while opportunities were still available in the self-governing colonies; hence Crewe refused in November 1908 to consider settlement in Bechuanaland, recalling that the government had pledged itself in February 1906 not to alter the *status quo* in the Protectorates.[1]

This was no irrational prejudice. The dangers of reproducing the social structure of South Africa or the southern states of the U.S.A. were obvious. The Indian question in Natal or the Transvaal alone would have been sufficient to point the moral; it was already regarded in the colonial office as insoluble in any manner at once satisfying justice and practical requirements. There was, in fact, no example of success in ruling satisfactorily a community where one part could put continual and powerful pressure on the colonial office to repress the other part.[2]

Since 1903, the settlement of Kenya, then known as the East Africa Protectorate, had proceeded steadily. The Liberals regarded this protectorate as one of the most troublesome of the new responsibilities. When he handed over the colonial secretaryship to Crewe in 1908 Elgin wrote:

Just because it has advantages in natural resources . . . every sort of man from Peers downwards flocks there. The Foreign Office methods were lax: an indifferent type of settler was established under them: and men like Delamere, who might have been expected to help us in the absolutely essential task of introducing regulation and order into all departments, have taken the extreme 'settler' side and actually headed restive mobs![3] To my mind, to give in to these pretensions is to fail in our duty to this magnificent country, and especially to the natives who inhabit parts of it, and I suppose formerly owned the whole.

Elgin concluded that this early and urgent attack on the government by the settlers had taken place because they foresaw that the better organised the government became, 'the less chance

---

[1] CO. 417/454/37915, S/S to Selb. 3 Nov 08.
[2] CO. 533/28/13999; CO. 533/43/15172, minute by Ellis 1 May 08.
[3] See p. 412.

they have of securing their inordinate and unjustifiable demands'.[1]

At this date there was considerable doubt whether it would prove possible for white men to flourish and breed successfully in this part of Africa.[2] Elgin was very much inclined to take the view that it would not prove possible. At any rate, he was convinced that it was no place for settlers of indifferent character or small means, and he doubted whether it was ever destined to become suitable for them. Officials did not think, however, that the government was strong enough to adopt a policy of the 'Protectorate for the Indian and the native. No white except capitalists need apply.'[3]

Elgin strove to keep the fact of the large African population to the foreground in public discussion of the future of Kenya. He stated his aim simply: to administer the protectorate on lines which were just, not only to the settlers, who no doubt benefited the country by taking possession of lands they could make best use of, but to the country as a whole, because it was not a country only of the white man. He could imagine no statement having so little foundation as that which spoke of a 'white man's country'. According to his information, there was an estimated total of not more than 2000 white men in a population of four million Africans.[4]

Churchill was very keen to initiate rapid development in Kenya. This led him to protest against a tendency towards indiscriminate distrust of settlers in the colonial office. Land grants to *bona fide* settlers would, he hoped, be expedited: 'I cannot feel the slightest sympathy with a policy which tends to preserve the East Africa Protectorate to officials, capitalists

[1] EP, E to Crewe 7 May 08 (draft).

[2] WSC, in *MAJ*, pp. 58–60, wrote that it was still quite unproved that a European could make the Highlands his permanent home, and until proved, 'white man's country' would 'remain a white man's dream'.

[3] CO. 533/24/40275.

[4] PD. 177/20–8, 27 Jun 07. The information was on CO. 533/5/43423, and probably overestimates the African population to the extent of doubling it. Lansdowne considered Elgin had not spoken at all too strongly of British obligations as trustees.

and Big Game.'[1] Elgin agreed generally, but was more inclined to see difficulties: too rapid progress in a new colony could not be expected, potential colonists were not tough enough, trusteeship doctrines and protection for African interests must come first. Although Churchill favoured allowing white settlement of the selected portions of the Highlands to proceed steadily, he would not encourage a rush of persons unsuited to the conditions, and unacquainted with the difficulties of East Africa.[2]

There were two incidents which took place in Nairobi, very much a frontier town; both of them attracted a great deal of attention in Whitehall. The first was in March 1907, associated with the name of Capt. E. S. Grogan, president of the Colonists' Association, famous for his journey from the Cape to Cairo some years before. The second was almost exactly a year later, and was led by Lord Delamere.

Legal proceedings were taken against Grogan and two of his friends for flogging three Kikuyu servants, right in front of the Nairobi court-house! The Kikuyu had offended by a trivial impertinence to white ladies, and by jolting a rickshaw. 'It is clear', declared the secretary of state, commenting on the floggings,

that such flagrant acts of lawlessness and injustice ... [are] the surest way to provoke an outbreak [of African violence], and in the interests not only of the natives (constituting as they do an immense majority of the population), but also of the innocent white inhabitants, I am determined to restrain and punish those who commit such acts.

The ordinary law was accordingly to be rigorously enforced. There was to be no hesitation in deporting anyone who conducted himself in a manner dangerous to the peace and good order of the protectorate.[3] Churchill supported a policy of backing the governor fully in such matters.[4] He wrote a memorable minute:

[1] CO. 533/24/40275, minute 29 Nov 06.
[2] CO. 533/33/43714, minute 16 Nov 07.
[3] CO. 533/28/15409, S/S to Sadler May 07.
[4] Not that WSC had any opinion of Sadler personally: 'a poor old "qui hai" at the end of his tether' (EP, to E 8 Jul [07]).

We must not let these first few ruffians steal our beautiful and promising protectorate away from us, after all we have spent upon it – under some shabby pretence of being a 'responsibly governed colony'. This House of Commons will never allow us to abdicate our duties towards the natives – as peaceful, industrious, law-abiding folk as can be found anywhere.[1]

The Grogan incident was the subject of local investigation, and of several long despatches. Correspondence was still flowing thickly upon the subject at the end of August 1907, by which time the colonial office began to be heartily sick of the business.[2]

The second incident was more obviously directed against the government. The administration had put forward a code of rules or conditions on which the Native Affairs department was willing to help find labour for the settlers. Violent and compulsory means of obtaining labour had already been proscribed. Labour supply diminished. At a meeting of the Colonists' Association in Nairobi at the end of March 1908, Lord Delamere passed a motion requiring the withdrawal of the new rules. The governor would not take immediate action, but promised to consider the relaxation of some of the conditions. There followed a demonstration, marked by calls for the resignation of the governor, by over one hundred settlers outside government house. Next day, Sadler gave his replies to a deputation led by Delamere. He refused to withdraw the rules, but agreed to appoint a board of inquiry. Sadler was thoroughly taken by surprise by this unseemly incident,[3] involving most of the settlers in Nairobi. He was inclined to think of the labour rules as a mere excuse: Delamere used them to appeal to the discontented, frustrated and unsuccessful settlers:

[1] CO. 533/28/13999, minute 27 Jun 07.
[2] CO. 533/31/29649. There is a possible Indian comparison: when a British corporal shot an Indian in 1908 Morley posed the fundamental question, 'whether the excited corporal and the angry planter are to be the arbiters of policy. . . . If we claim to be men of large views, it is our duty not to yield without resistance to the passions and violences of a public that is apt to take narrow views' (MM. 3/253–4, 26 Aug 08).
[3] EP, Sadler to E 28 Mar 08.

the whole thing is due to political agitation working on certain amount of distress among poorer settlers. The demonstration was the result of Delamere's ungovernable temper and of excitement of meeting after lunch at which he presided, subsequently conducting the mob up to my house. At this meeting a resolution was framed but afterwards withdrawn, calling on me to resign unless I immediately acceded to their demands.[1]

When the situation in Kenya was assessed in May 1908 by the colonial office, as it had to be after this incident, it was noted that so far no-one in the Highlands had made any money, and many had lost what they had. In these circumstances, the tendency to force Africans to work, either by direct compulsion, or by taking their land or cattle, had grown. Applying the inherited historiography of his department, one of the official minds observed:

These methods have led over and over again to wars in the Cape and Natal: and it would probably pay the British taxpayer to repatriate all the whites and forbid their entry except on payment of a heavy poll tax. Such a course is however, impracticable. . . .[2]

Modestly safeguarding himself by saying his suggestion was impracticable did not prevent Ellis having his repatriation proposal taken up by the politicians. Seely, recently appointed parliamentary under-secretary, determined not to be outdone by his predecessor, took the large view of a social engineer:

From conversations I have had with officials, and others recently returned from East Africa, I am sure that a wholesale repatriation of these indigent settlers is the only policy; it would cost surprisingly little money.

Crewe endorsed this minute, and a secret despatch was sent to the governor on 15 July 1908. It read as follows:

There can be no doubt that the presence of a number of white settlers who are either unwilling or unable to earn a livelihood by their industry, is a source of danger to the order and good

[1] Ibid. tel. 26 Mar 08.   [2] CO. 533/43/15172, minute by Ellis 1 May 08.

government of the Protectorate. . . . I should be glad if you would furnish me with an expression of your opinion as to the desirability and feasibility of a policy of repatriating them, together with an estimate of the probable expenditure involved.[1]

The idea of a possible, maybe only partial, repatriation was thus seriously entertained. It marks a clear difference in Liberal African policy from Unionist. It is inconceivable that Lyttelton or Chamberlain would have been prepared to consider repatriation.

The proposal lapsed quite narrowly. The governor replied after a long delay, because he was not convinced of the necessity for such a measure and wished to see for himself how matters were proceeding. Perhaps his real fear was of the impeachment kind. He had already incurred more hatred and wrath among settlers than was comfortable. After undertaking several tours, he elected to be agreeably impressed with a great deal of the work being done on the farms. He professed to see fewer loafers in Nairobi. The latest harvest was an abundant one, and would, he thought, go some way to repay the farmers for the losses they had incurred for the previous two seasons. He therefore concluded that any general scheme for repatriation need not be considered at present (February 1909). There would doubtless be individual cases of distress where repatriation would be desirable. He asked to deal with such cases at his discretion.

Liberal ministers naturally accepted his recommendations.[2] No more was heard of repatriation for the time being, and then of course it became too late even to be spoken of. Optimism had, however, been dissipated. 'Settlement in this difficult country should not be made too easy', wrote Crewe in October 1908.[3] Entry of Boers was also made harder, for it was thought that their treatment of Africans complicated the difficulties of the government. No formal discrimination against them was applied, but the provisions of the Restriction of Immigration Ordinance relating to persons without visible

[1] CO. 533/44/22385.
[2] CO. 533/58/9702, to S/S 25 Feb 09; S/S to govr 30 Mar 09.
[3] CO. 533/47/36067, minute 10 Oct 08.

414

means of support, were strictly enforced, and shipping companies were warned of the penalties for landing prohibited immigrants.[1] The emphasis was henceforth upon trying rather to ensure the success of settlers already established than to encourage an addition to their numbers.

An effort was made to increase white participation in government. A legislative council was established in 1907. Europeans were also encouraged to take a more active part in local government and in organising agricultural activities. The purpose was to strengthen the administration by preventing, it was hoped, the settler community from becoming solidly opposed to the government.[2] Lyttelton had thought some form of representation on a council a reasonable request.[3] The petition requesting such representation was also considered by his successor. The officials were agreed that numerically the Africans must always so enormously preponderate, that the idea of ever giving responsible government over the whole area to a handful of white settlers in Nairobi was highly unwise. They did not think that the Colonists' Association was a body whose views were entitled to much weight. 'Anything except Crown Colony government cannot be a matter of practical policy for many years to come,' Elgin replied to the Association in accordance with official advice submitted to him. This reply effectively commented on the argument that the existing system of government was equivalent to 'taxation without representation': only a small proportion of the revenue raised by taxation in Kenya was in fact contributed by the European colonists. Although the secretary of state did not consider the time ripe for the introduction of electoral institutions, he agreed to establish a council to assist the officer administering the government in making laws. The unofficial members of the proposed legislative council would be chosen by the British government

[1] CO. 533/45/22476, S/S to Selb. 10 Jul 08. Compare Churchill's opinion in 1906: 'The Boers would make most desirable settlers in East Africa, and all encouragement should certainly be offered to them' (CO. 533/14/15859).

[2] CO. 533/28/14395, minutes by Churchill and Elgin, 27 and 29 Apr 07; CO. 533/74/24546, Crewe to Girouard 3 Nov 10.

[3] CO. 533/10/27738.

415

'to represent as far as possible the different interests of the community'.[1] In 1907 Churchill used a word pattern familiar to us, in a speech in Nairobi to the Colonists' Association: 'Never before in colonial experience has a council been granted where the number of settlers is so few.'[2] The council first met on 17 August 1907, with five official, and three unofficial members nominated by the governor. It needs to be stressed that this grant of a legislative council does not imply a blessing of the white community by the Liberal government. Rather it reflects their general belief that the only chance of improving men's conduct is to give them responsibility. It was regarded chiefly as a safety valve, which might meet a good deal of the agitation of the Colonists' Association.[3] It could criticise, but not control, the administration. Throughout these years the government left the settlers in no doubt what it thought of their attitudes to the Africans.

Two examples of their disapproval may be quoted, one from 1906, and the other from shortly after Elgin's departure. The East Africa Protectorate showed an incipient tendency to follow South Africa in attitudes towards Africans, and into legislative racial discrimination. The tendency was held in check as far as possible. In 1906 a Masters and Servants Ordinance came before the secretary of state. It allowed both payment in kind and imprisonment of labourers for breach of contract. Some of its provisions appeared to be derived from a similar ordinance in the Transvaal. Elgin was very doubtful if this ordinance should be adopted, and insisted on 'a more distinct assurance' to allay his suspicions before he would approve it. His despatch noted objections to six sections, and requested a full report on the conditions which rendered such provisions necessary, and on the general policy and scope of the ordinance.[4] The dis-

[1] CO. 533/5/43423, S/S to commissioner 8 Jun 06. See also House of Lords Papers, no. 208 (Aug 07). The despatch also refuted the claim to have the English Common Law established as of right as ill-founded, 'inasmuch as the East Africa Protectorate is not, as they suppose, a colony of settlement, but a foreign country in which, by treaty, H.M. has the power to legislate'.

[2] Quoted by G. Bennett in *History of East Africa*, ii, 176, n. 2.

[3] CO. 533/14/19303, commissioner to S/S 7 May 06.

[4] CO. 533/16/34203, minute 2 Nov 06, S/S to Sadler 21 Nov 06.

approval of the secretary of state was also conveyed when it was alleged that the conservator of forests had said: 'Natives did irretrievable damage to the forests, and whilst the natives themselves could always be replaced, with trees it was different, for it cost much money to plant a forest.' Such a remark by a government officer could only incur severe displeasure.[1]

The Indian problem. The Liberals recognised that the movement of Asiatics posed for the empire important and even menacing problems which were almost wholly unstudied, and that Indian immigration was rapidly establishing itself as the hardest problem in the empire, becoming recognised as a question which would 'grow to be more and more, a world question if ever there was one'.[2] Kenya had its Indian problem as well as the Transvaal.

White prejudice in East Africa was probably greater against immigrant Indians than native Africans. The Indians were there before the white settlers, and had done much of the pioneering work. Churchill described the apparently hopeless antagonism of interests as 'the Sphinx's riddle in its newest form'. Since several South African and all Australian colonies would undoubtedly refuse access to large numbers of Indians, it was all the more desirable that the government should afford them scope in the tropical protectorates, which were 'big enough for all'. If the whites had the Kenya Highlands, the Indians should be encouraged to trade and settle in tropical regions.[3]

Lyttelton had been afflicted with some doubts about the expediency of imposing any restrictions on the holding of land in Kenya by coloured races, especially British Indians,[4] but he had made no pronouncement, and in practice discrimination was exercised against them. In 1906 Elgin made a written statement which the white settlers interpreted as implying that the Kenya Highlands should be reserved to them. It had never

[1] CO. 533/43/16451, desp. S/S to govr 11 Aug 08.
[2] Morley: MM. 3/5, 3 Jan 08.   [3] WSC, *MAJ*, p. 50.
[4] CO. 519/1/26065, CO to FO 15 Aug 04.

in practice been policy to grant land in the uplands to Indians, except within municipal limits, and the report of the lands committee of 1905 firmly supported this. When the Indians protested, Elgin directed that the Colonists' Association should be informed:

It would not be in accordance with the policy of H.M.G. to exclude any class of H.M. subjects from holding land in any part of a British Protectorate, but that in view of the comparatively limited area in the Protectorate suitable for European colonisation, a reasonable discretion will be exercised in dealing with applications for land on the part of natives of India and other non-Europeans.

Approval of previous practice was confirmed.[1] The dominant consideration behind this declaration was the belief that a relatively small area was suitable for European settlement, but enormous tracts suitable for Indians, who were in any case regarded as insanitary neighbours.[2] The settlers now proceeded to try to obtain actual legislative discrimination. Then came the so-called Elgin Pledge, which slightly qualified the earlier statement:

It is not consonant with the views of H.M.G. to impose *legal* restriction on any particular section of the community, but as a matter of administrative convenience, grants in the uplands area should not be made to Indians.[3]

The attempt to solve problems and circumvent the law by administrative practice is a *leit motiv* in the imperial policy of the Liberal government. The files do not suggest that there was any heart-searching among officials or ministers about either of these declarations, which later came to assume so great and controversial a significance. Certainly there was no official prejudice against the presence of Indians in East Africa.

When the representation on the newly established legislative

---

[1] CO. 533/14/21797, S/S to Sadler 17 Jul 06.

[2] CO. 533/3/33231, Commissioner to S/S 14 Aug 05.

[3] CO. 533/33/44998, S/S to Sadler 19 Mar 08. G. Bennett describes this as a 'yet more specious reason for breaking with an imperial policy . . . and clearly demonstrated the continued settler pressures . . .' (*Kenya, a political history* (1963), p. 24, and *History of East Africa*, ii, ed. Harlow and Chilver, 278).

council was being reviewed, Churchill urged the case for Indian participation: 'There can be no reason for excluding this large and meritorious class. Begin early to instil good principles in the East Africa Protectorate!' The governor could, however, find no suitable person to represent them at that time. The secretary of state then replied that Indian interests must nevertheless not be overlooked.[1] In April 1908 the governor recommended A. M. Jeevanjee, Indian head of a firm of contractors, shipowners and general merchants to be a member. Crewe approved his 'important decision'.[2]

Plans were afoot in July 1908 to set up a committee to consider the whole question of encouraging emigration from India to the Crown Colonies.[3] The colonial office wanted to encourage coolie emigration, but after all the trouble over Chinese Labour it could not sanction ordinances for the purpose until more fully advised about conditions.[4] Announcing the appointment of the committee, Crewe told the House of Lords that it must be of advantage to the empire as a whole to promote healthy interchange between the Indian empire and the African territories, which were in certain respects akin to India, and in many cases governed in a similar way, and which had such 'immense possibilities of development'. He found no difficulty in defending indentured labour. Politically, many non-European races were treated as though they were minors, and in labour questions, since they did not possess such power of organisation as white labour possessed, it seemed to him 'that they may fairly be subjected to some conditions of apprenticeship as if they were minors', provided that these conditions were fair and reasonable, and the operation of them was watched very carefully, to prevent conditions nearing the borderline of servility.[5]

---

[1] CO. 533/29/18135, minute 11 Jun; desp. 26 Jun 07.

[2] CO. 533/43/13249, tel. govr to S/S 13 Apr 08.

[3] CO. 323/546/27719, minute by Crewe 29 Jul 08. For terms of reference, see CO. 323/554/4116.

[4] Ibid. 9590, minute by Crewe 23 Mar 09.

[5] PD/HL. 1/611–2, 21 Apr 09. The Sanderson committee rejected renewed charges that indentured labour was a veiled form of slavery.

LAND POLICY: TOWARDS UNIFORMITY

Perennially important, the land question in Africa sprang into particular importance under the Liberals from the conjunction of a variety of circumstances. It was a question attracting radical attention at home. The theories of Henry George's *Progress and Poverty* (1897) were well known. In circumstances of financial stringency it was thought desirable to maintain an 'economic rent' by ensuring the 'unearned increment' on land values, as Henry George had advocated. The example of Leopold's Congo helped to provide further incentives towards caution in the concession of land grants. Railway development was expected, wrongly it proved, to lead to applications for land in Northern Nigeria, and thus to make the question urgent there. The policy of respecting African custom and encouraging African enterprise unavoidably implied some definition of land policy.[1] Elgin found himself called to deal especially with problems in Kenya, Crewe with the application of Elgin's Kenya principles over a wider area, and with the important report of the Northern Nigeria Lands Committee, which was set up in 1908. By this time, land problems occupied a large proportion of the minister's attention.

Elgin was well equipped as an estate-owner and ex-viceroy to tackle these questions. Indian experience led him, even before the Nigerian committee's report, to reject the application of European forms of land tenure in Africa. In his opinion, the permanent settlement, with its English methods and English law, worked well in Bengal, but he did not advocate its extension anywhere else, because it upset the possibility of the government's retaining a substantial share in the unearned increment from land.[2]

---

[1] From land tenure 'there is a common origin of many serious Native problems. It dominates and pervades every other question, it is the bedrock of the Native's present economic position and largely affects his social system' (Cd. 2399, Report of S. African Native Affairs Commission 1905).

[2] VRP. 15/107, 1 Jun 97.

Kenya (*East Africa Protectorate*). When the Liberal government came into office, a new Lands Ordinance to replace that of 1902 was under discussion. The change of government resulted in delay in settling land policy. A lands committee had been appointed in May 1905, became controlled by Delamere, and presented a report which strongly reflected settler criticism of the existing legislation. Officials agreed to accept its recommendation of a land board, to be set up under the chairmanship of a land commissioner. One of Elgin's very first decisions as secretary of state was to endorse this proposal. Naturally he felt that the best chairman might be a good officer from India with some knowledge of land settlement work. Such a man was found in the person of Colonel J. A. L. Montgomery. The new commissioner was instructed to make another report on the whole position. This was because the secretary of state did not feel able to pass orders on the conclusions of the previous committee's report. Elgin believed the evils of unrestricted speculation in land to be much more serious than the committee realised. He would not abolish restrictions on transfers as requested, because, although anxious to encourage settlement and development, with unfortunate Australasian precedents of the 1840s and 1850s before him he could not assent to any legislation which facilitated the holding of large areas of land for speculative purposes.[1]

The delay in settling a revised ordinance was much criticised, and Elgin had to defend himself in the House of Lords. He explained that he did not reject the report of the lands committee, but criticised it from one particular point of view: whether it was expedient in the interests of the country that land should be held in large areas by single individuals, or combinations of individuals, and whether there was to be free transfer in regard to those areas. The distinct proposition he put forward was that the government could not agree to the holding of land for speculative purposes; he did not believe, as the committee did, that to allow free transfer of land would not lead

[1] CO. 533/3/33231, commissioner to S/S 14 Aug 05, minute by E 13 Dec 05, reply 23 Mar 06.

to this abuse. He denied being unreasonably obstructive. Postponing decisions on the practical matter raised in the report arose out of reconsidering the general condition of the protectorate.[1]

Colonel Montgomery made his report towards the end of November 1906. A conference was held in the colonial office with Sadler in March 1907, and a major despatch issued on 23 April 1907. The objections to free transfers in leasehold property were re-stated; they would tend to encourage people to acquire land as a speculative counter, and to enable persons of larger capital to amass large estates of which they made but little use, with the same evils which had followed in the Australasian colonies. Such a result might possibly be prevented by the covenant implied in the lease, to develop the land in a businesslike way, but this had not been found very easy to enforce even in small holdings, and would be still less likely to be observed when the small holding had been swallowed up in a vast estate. The second main point in the despatch was the recommendation that leases for pastoral purposes should be in general reduced to not more than 21 years, with the option of renewal for another 21 years, at the rent then prevailing for such leases. This was subject to much contention, as the settlers insisted on 99 years, which Montgomery had also recommended.[2]

By March 1908 no decision had been arrived at, owing to the need to reconcile the considerable divergence of the views of the Land Board (supported by Sadler) from the views set forth in the despatch of 23 April 1907. The colonial office insisted on 21-year leases in order to obtain an 'unearned increment'; the precaution was considered specially necessary in East Africa because resort to customs duties, usually the most important branch of revenue in newly settled countries, was partially

---

[1] PD. 177/22–4, 27 Jun 07.

[2] CO. 533/19/1199, S/S to Sadler. See HL. 158 (Aug 07). The criticisms of this despatch in E. Huxley, *White Man's Country*, i, 194–5 do not seem adequately justified, e.g. to speak of its decisions as those of 'urban-minded men who were not interested in farming', is to forget Elgin was a landowner much interested in estate management.

barred by the operation of international agreements, whilst at the same time, it was clear that the existing state of things, under which so large a proportion of the expenditure was borne by the Africans and by the tax payers of the United Kingdom, was not defensible as a permanent arrangement.[1] This policy was determined by the new concessions committee of the colonial office under the presidency of Churchill, who looked forward to the time when all revenue should be raised by taxation from land revenues.[2] A draft ordinance was then prepared in East Africa to give effect to these instructions. In August 1908 Crewe rejected the land commissioner's suggestion of giving administrative powers to the Land Board, and adhered strictly to Elgin's decision that it should be advisory only.[3]

Crewe's analysis was: 'The difficulty in all these cases is to steer between the laxity which was so disastrous', and mischievous in Australasia, (leading to the accumulation of land in the hands of a few farmers and the loss of the unearned increment to the state), 'and a rigidity which hampers enterprise', and it was a very real difficulty. The government proposed that at the time of revaluation, the increased rent should not be levied on the improvements made by the lessee, but only on the unearned increment resulting from the growth of organised society,

an increment which even in countries with an old established land system, is coming to be regarded as proper to be resumed, in whole or part for the benefit of the society which created the value.[4]

By the middle of February 1910 governor Girouard had come to the conclusion that there was no alternative but to throw over the conditions imposed by the secretary of state, namely, that if leases were granted for 99 years there should be revaluations at the end of the 33rd and 66th years, and that there should be a surtax on large holdings.[5] The question was

[1] CO. 533/33/44998, S/S to Sadler 19 Mar 08.   [2] CO. 96/475/5835.
[3] CO. 533/43/19551, S/S to Sadler 11 Aug 08.
[4] CO. 533/48/minute 21 Dec 08; S/S to Govr 9 Jan 09.   [5] CO. 533/71/7672.

referred back to a small departmental committee, chaired by Seely, which advised adherence to Elgin's policy. Girouard then requested discussion during his leave, the result of which was adherence to Elgin's land policy, although the governor's wishes prevailed on certain subsidiary points.

Attempts were made to apply to other parts of Africa the policy laid down by Elgin on 23 April 1907. For example, an ordinance regulating Crown lands in Southern Nigeria submitted in 1908 met with the reply that something 'more comprehensive and more precise' was needed. A copy of the East Africa despatch was transmitted in the hope that it might provide useful suggestions; 'it should be laid down in the law that land will not be granted on any other tenure' than leasehold.[1] In November 1907 Elgin enquired about African rights over land in Uganda,[2] and in 1909 the situation there was tackled with determination. It was a fairly bold move to interfere with the system of disposing of Crown Lands in Uganda, for the governor and the land officer believed the system (which contemplated the grant of freehold interest), to be reasonable, and suited to local conditions. But the position in Uganda could not be reconciled with the policy adopted for the East Africa Protectorate after mature deliberation. No freehold land was being granted there. It was pointed out that the East African system applied even in the lowlands, where conditions approximated to those prevailing in Uganda, and reference was also made to the opinion of the Northern Nigeria Lands Committee in a similar sense – and Northern Nigeria was no more a settlers country than Uganda. The governor was asked to take these points into consideration. The governor of the Gambia was urged to consider whether a system of leasing Crown lands would not be an improvement on selling them outright.[3]

In July 1908 a report was forwarded on the disposal of Crown Lands in Nyasaland; in acknowledgment, Crewe drew attention to the fact that it did not recommend the introduction

[1] CO. 520/59/13016, S/S to Egerton 11 Jun 08.   [2] CO. 536/20/28172.
[3] CO. 536/25/7392, S/S to govr 18 Apr 09; CO. 87/181/23736.

of any changes based on the new régime in the East Africa Protectorate, and asked if this meant that such modifications were felt to be unnecessary.[1] The governor did not however recommend material alterations in the system, as, with comparatively few exceptions in Ngoniland, there was nowhere where Europeans could reasonably hope to settle permanently. In reply the secretary of state noted that in agricultural leases, instead of the indefinite renewal which was allowed, the planter usually availed himself of the very favourable option of purchase; he directed that this should be stopped. And again following the Northern Nigeria Report, it was declared inadvisable to grant town freehold – treatment should be on the same lines as agricultural leases.[2] But the governor agreed with the unanimous legislative council in clinging to freehold tenure. Crewe reflected:

> It is unfortunate that we cannot get a uniform system in the African Protectorates, but the conditions in Nyasaland do not admit of a complete adoption of the better principle. So we must be content for the time with this modification.

The secretary of state was convinced, said the despatch, that 'leasehold without the option of purchase is the right policy', but he would not insist on it at present 'on the understanding that, pending a return to the subject, no tracts of Crown Land of unusual extent will be alienated'. He agreed to allow freehold to be given in towns.[3]

Northern Nigeria. The colonial office was anxious to profit by catching the land system in Nigeria while it was young, and to apply negatively the experience of the older West African colonies, and, both positively and negatively, Indian experience. The Northern Nigeria Lands Committee sat in London in 1908 at the suggestion of governor Girouard. It began to take evidence on 1 June. The committee worked fast, and reported on 29 July of the same year. It recommended that the funda-

[1] CO. 525/24/32528, S/S to Sharpe 31 Dec 08.
[2] CO. 525/28/12334, S/S to Sharpe 18 Jun 09.
[3] CO. 525/29/40232, minute 23 Dec 09; S/S to govr 31 Dec 09.

mental basis of land law ought to be (a) the paramount power and authority of the government over the whole land, (b) the preservation, with such definitions and modifications as locally necessary, of existing African customs concerning use and occupation. Legal conceptions borrowed from non-Nigerian law ought as far as possible to be excluded. The first principle in the exercise of governmental control ought to be the interest of Africans, providing for their security, the needs of shifting cultivation and population growth; development should come second to this. The administration should give security to the occupier rather than attempt to create the new and strange idea of an estate or property in the land itself. The state should get an increment as the land increased in value, even though this was not an indigenous principle. Useful hints might be obtained from studying the manner in which similar revenue and taxation problems had been solved in India; but the success of a Nigerian system would depend upon the extent to which it was in harmony with the customs and sentiments of the people. All grants of the occupation, use, or enjoyment of the land, should be in the form of leases, not grants of the absolute property of freehold interest. No distinction should be made in this respect between urban and rural land: the principle that no grant of a freehold interest should be permitted by law, ought to be universal.[1]

Crewe thought the scheme 'undoubtedly one of nationalisation, not of the creation of Crown Lands'.[2] In an interesting passage, Girouard compared Congo policy; he thought the difficulty there had arisen from the claim by the state to 'vacant lands', defined to include all lands outside the actually cultivated holdings of the villages. The inhabitants had been forced to gather for the concessionaires sylvan produce they had always looked upon as the property of the community.[3] In his reply (drafted in July 1909) Crewe indicated his complete

[1] Cd. 5102 (1910); CO. 446/79/27838.
[2] CO. 446/75/42884, minute 23 May 09. The word 'nationalisation' hardly seems appropriate today.
[3] Ibid. Girouard to S/S 17 Oct 08; Cd. 5102.

sympathy with the view that Africans should have first claim on use and enjoyment of the land. In practice it would follow that the interests of the Africans should rank before those of immigrants in any question involving the revocation of a title of occupancy.[1] The main objective was to control alienation of land.

The importance of this unequivocal statement of policy, and its subsequent legislative enactment,[2] was soon grasped by Morel, who described the declaration that the whole land, whether occupied or not, was 'native land', as consecrating a great and far-reaching principle:

No act of such wise and far-seeing statesmanship has been recorded on the part of any European government in Africa since the political absorption of Africa by the powers of Europe began.[3]

In Morel's view, the new policy formally marked a complete change in the treatment of the land question in Crown Colonies; the application of English concepts was abandoned in favour of indigenous concepts. Morel thought that the land law had its part to play in training the Africans to govern themselves; it was not an innovation or an experiment, but designed to preserve the *status quo*.[4] The importance of the Lands Committee indeed lies in the fact that the policy and practice were formally approved by the government, who became anxious to extend its principles. And so in 1912 the West African Lands Committee was appointed, to deal with the problems of the other colonies.[5]

[1] Ibid. to govr 22 Mar 10.
[2] The Land and Native Rights Proclamation, 1910.
[3] Morel papers, F. 9, to S/S 23 Oct 13.
[4] E. D. Morel, *Nigeria: its peoples and problems* (1912), pp. 143–4.
[5] This Committee was also under the chairmanship of Sir Kenelm Digby. It was dissolved owing to the war, and never reported.

12 The Development of Dependencies: The Contribution of the Government

IT is often assumed or implied that the Liberal government neglected the empire outside South Africa, and that once the partition had taken place, African possessions were forgotten.[1] But the years after 1905 saw, as Milner recognised,[2] a remarkable growth in understanding the value and possibilities of tropical territories, a strengthening of the sense of duty towards them, and a 'great change' toward a progressive policy which regarded them as integral to imperial development.

Several years before the Liberals took office, the colonial office already accepted the general principle that it should assist and stimulate development,[3] because of the usefulness of the tropical possessions as a source of food and raw materials for industrial nations, and as a field for commerce.[4] Despite their grumblings and apprehensions the Liberals came to accept African responsibilities with good grace. As early as 1902 Grey had said 'our business now is to develop what we have got, wisely and with discrimination'.[5] The new government had in Churchill, once he got over his initial phase of iconoclasm, a whole-hearted advocate of the 'great estates' doctrine, a phrase he often used in speaking and writing about Africa. The new possessions would, he expected, unquestionably prove an invaluable, if not indeed a necessary, feature of the British

[1] For example, W. M. Macmillan, *The Road to Self-rule* (1959), p. 187, R. Oliver and J. D. Fage, *A short history of Africa* (1962), pp. 196–7.
[2] Milner, *The Nation and the Empire* (1913), p. 462, speech 7 Jun 10.
[3] *C.H.B.E.*, iii, 382.
[4] CO. 96/477/37402, minute by Butler 30 Sep 08; see p. 197.
[5] H. Samuel, *Memoirs* (1945), p. 37, Grey to Samuel 10 Aug 02.

empire.[1] After his journey to East Africa, he noted that 'all those new products which modern industry insistently demands are offered in measureless abundance.'[2] Elgin was also very interested in tropical Africa, even once giving part of an after-dinner speech to the Corona Club on the discovery of a preventive medicine for 'Malta fever', which he described as a very good piece of medical research.[3] With his Indian experience he was perhaps more at home in dealing with the dependent empire than the self-governing, and among officials he acquired an excellent reputation in this field.[4] Neither in India nor Africa did Elgin neglect the problems of development. One of his last acts as viceroy was to send Dr Voelcker on tour to collect facts and figures about agriculture, and as a result of Voelcker's recommendations, one or two experts were appointed, forming the nucleus of an Imperial Institute of Agriculture at Pusa, aided by a grant from the imperial government in 1905.[5] Like their predecessors, the Liberals were especially impressed by the example of the French and Dutch governments in developing their great estates.[6] The British government, and particularly perhaps a Liberal government,

[1] WSC, *MAJ*, p. 215.   [2] Ibid. p. 52.

[3] EP, E to Lady E 20 Jun 07.

[4] For example, Antrobus wrote to him on his departure from office, acknowledging Elgin's interests in the Crown colonies (EP, to E 14 Apr 08; see also the opinion of Sir Cecil Clementi Smith, below, p. 519). An avenue in Entebbe, Uganda, was named after Elgin as an expression of gratitude for 'the great interest he evinced in the welfare' of Uganda (CO. 536/19/17729, govr to S/S 16 Apr 08). See also Cosmo Parkinson, *The colonial office from within, 1909–1945* (1947), 47–8: 'The most lasting impression left upon me from my early years in the Colonial Office is admiration for the constructive work which was in progress all the time . . . there was a steady advance in every sphere of administration', most notably in tropical medicine, and sanitation, despite financial restriction.

[5] Research, experimental farming and an agricultural college for post-graduates were instituted at Pusa. Curzon followed Elgin's initial moves by setting up in 1905 a department of commerce and industry in the central government to guide the activities of provincial governments in promoting new industries and technical education. These developments, stressing science and efficiency, gave rise to misgivings and it was not until 1918 that the policy was fully accepted in India. But these developments could have had some influence on African projects in a general way (V. Anstey, *The Economic development of India* (4th ed., 1952), pp. 7 and 165; *Cambridge Economic History of Europe*, vi (2), 912).

[6] PD. 144/564–5, Lyttelton 5 Apr 05: the example was one it was 'almost necessary' to follow.

could not afford the charge of being left behind in twentieth-century developments. Before 1914 there was no slackening of the effort to continue the 'constructive imperialism' initiated by Chamberlain, the Liberals being especially ready to assist the progress and development of railways, tropical medicine and sanitation, despite sore financial restriction. Agriculture and education were not so high on their list of priorities.

CO-ORDINATION: EXTENSION AND DIFFUSION OF INFORMATION

One of the most pressing tasks before the government was to find out more about tropical Africa, and to make information and experience gained in one part of Africa readily available in other parts. The extension of knowledge about tropical diseases and economic products was especially necessary. Expert advice was already being obtained from the Scientific and Technical Department of the Imperial Institute,[1] the British Cotton Growing Association, the Royal Botanical Gardens at Kew,[2] and the Schools of Tropical Medicine at Liverpool and London. Increasing use was made of all these agencies after 1906. In addition, a number of colonial office advisory committees was set up, in each case on the initiative of one of the officials, with the warm encouragement of the secretary of state. Each was financed largely on the principle of colonial contributions to supplement a treasury grant.

In 1906 great efforts were made to relieve the Scientific and Technical Department of the Imperial Institute from its financial troubles, caused by the cessation of payments from the Commissioners of the Exhibition of 1851. The problem became urgent because staff threatened to leave. The treasury and the colonial governments were persuaded to contribute to its upkeep, meet its deficit of £2000, and provide for future expansion, in the proportion of £1500 and £3000 a year. A

---

[1] Founded in 1896 to create new openings in trade, and promote agricultural and industrial development.

[2] The director of Kew since 1902 had the title 'Botanical adviser to the secretary of state'.

circular despatch was sent out on 31 July 1906. It observed that the Crown Colonies and Protectorates had, it seemed, as yet hardly received the attention to which their position in the commercial system of the empire entitled them:

If these great and growing dependencies are to be fully developed in the coming time, the fact must be recognised that, under modern conditions, the business of the Colonial Office can no longer be confined to questions of politics and administration; but ... there must be a department to deal with the material development of the Colonies, and funds must be forthcoming for this purpose.

France, Germany and the Netherlands, none of whom had interests approaching those of the British Empire in variety and magnitude, were spending large annual sums on the scientific investigation of colonial products for commercial development – an example it was necessary to follow if the British colonies were to compete on even terms.

While very large sums are being spent upon the administration of new territories, it would seem worth while to expend the further comparatively small sums required in order to enable the resources of those territories to be investigated, and to secure the best return for the money laid out upon them.

The Scientific and Technical Department provided the nucleus of what was required.

These proposals were experimental, and the secretary of state looked to their future expansion into a more complete scheme than he was then able to present. He urged them for acceptance as a step forward in building up a suitable scientific organisation for the commercial and industrial development of the whole empire and more especially of the tropical dependencies.[1] Elgin was pleased by the generous response.[2]

[1] CO. 323/518/24163.
[2] Ibid. 22844, 28448. On 1 Oct 07 the CO took over control of the Imperial Institute, although the Board of Trade retained nominal control. In Apr 08 a further circular was sent to colonial governors asking them to put their contributions on a 'more permanent' basis. The Treasury agreed to renew its grant, as the importance of the Institute to the empire had increased so much (CO. 323/548/43331 and 554/7819).

Elgin welcomed the proposals for courses of instruction to be given to officers appointed to serve in tropical Africa, a scheme devised by officials and Professor Dunstan (director of the Imperial Institute), towards the end of 1907. Taking a close interest in planning the arrangements, Elgin suspected that some waste of time and money was involved in the scheme as presented to him. He pointed out that as they received candidates every day of the year and demands from the various colonies for appointments at uncertain intervals, it would be impossible to avoid inconvenience if the arrangements followed university sessions, and if they were for a period of three months' training after the selection of a candidate. Furthermore, men were often on the list of candidates for a considerable time, during which they had no stated occupation. Elgin decided to let them attend courses, thus enabling them to take up their full duties immediately they were appointed.[1] Instruction was given in tropical hygiene and sanitation, law, government accounting procedures, and especially in mineral, agricultural and commercial products.[2] The first session began in the Imperial Institute, in May 1908. Plans were made for including anthropology among the courses after 1911, as a contribution towards promotion of the study of the subject, an object for which Crewe professed a warm sympathy.[3]

The express purpose of the establishment of the colonial office advisory committee on tropical agriculture (March 1909),[4] and of the investigations of the Mechanical Transport Committee of the war office (on which two members of the

[1] CO. 96/476/1769, minute 17 Feb 08.

[2] Three courses were held every year, each course lasting three months. The object was to provide officers with facilities for acquiring general knowledge and principles, to enable them to take an intelligent practical interest, for example, in the work of developing and utilising tropical resources, co-operating with technical officers (ibid. 12596).

[3] CO. 323/547/41418, minute 4 Mar 09: the courses did not begin as soon as planned.

[4] CO. 96/477/37402. Its functions were to consider the general policy and expenditure of colonial agricultural departments, and to select and train candidates for them. Crewe expedited the formation of this committee. (See also CO. 323/547/41315.)

colonial office sat from the middle of 1907),¹ was to prevent waste of energy through ignorance of what had been tried in other colonies. Circular despatches on these and other matters familiarised governors with three ideas: that the development of tropical colonies was 'now a pressing matter', that it was as necessary to the government as to the merchants that their great agricultural and economic potentialities should be recognised, and that knowledge not then readily accessible should be diffused.² A steady stream of enquiries and directions was sent to governors. At one time or another almost all tropical products were the subject of enquiry by the secretary of state, and information gained from one colony was supplied to others.³

Elgin and Crewe were keenly aware of the extreme importance and urgency of the problem of tropical disease, and encouraged the officials with full support for their proposals. A circular despatch encouraging the investigation of tropical disease was sent out in 1906.⁴ Elgin agreed to ask the Tropical Diseases Research Fund Committee to compile a return showing what had been done against malaria, and in order to help them, he approved a circular inviting reports on the subject to be made to the Committee. The Committee prepared a report which Elgin agreed to publish, Churchill describing publication as an earnest of the government's interest in 'this most important and promising work'.⁵ In 1907 Churchill negotiated treasury sanction to doubling the £500 annual grant to the Liverpool School of Tropical Medicine.⁶ The treasury

¹ The committee investigated the situation with respect to the use of motor cars in 31 colonies (CO. 323/547/40033, circular desp. 15 Aug 07).

² The secretary of state, for example, recommended to the governors concerned, Prof. Dunstan's scheme to prepare a series of handbooks on the products of West Africa (CO. 96/476/2312, circular desp. 20 Mar 08).

³ E.g. CO. 520/50/36549; CO. 267/502/10005. A report on methods of collecting and preparing rubber in Southern Nigeria was requested, and then circulated to Sierra Leone, Gold Coast and Northern Nigeria. A West Indian report on agricultural education in schools would, it was hoped, give valuable guidance elsewhere (CO. 318/318/4865, 17 Mar 08).

⁴ CO. 323/522/13837, Cd. 3306.

⁵ CO. 323/516/15768 and 524/46963. The Fund, and Committee to administer it, was set up in 1904 to provide salaries for University lecturers.

⁶ CO. 323/534/26708.

contribution to the Research Fund was also doubled to £1000 in the same year.[1]

Liberal secretaries of state sanctioned the establishment of several advisory committees, including the committee to investigate the veterinary aspect of tropical diseases (1907), and the Medical and Sanitary committee for tropical Africa (1909).[2] Elgin superintended the initiation of the Sleeping Sickness Bureau (1908) which acted as a central agency in London for distributing information.[3] This was followed in 1909 by the formation of the Tropical Diseases Research Bureau (to perform for other diseases the same functions as the Sleeping Sickness Bureau),[4] and the Tropical African Entomological Research Committee.[5] In both cases, Crewe's personal interest ensured treasury grants and the appointment of leading experts to the committees. He presided at the conference in March 1909 to plan the Entomological Committee, remarking: 'I will cheerfully do anything I can to give the project a start, because I can imagine nothing more useful.'[6] To place the co-ordination of research on a permanent and business-like basis, Crewe secured the services of Lord Cromer as president, and was delighted by his keen interest.

Medical measures were not undertaken solely for the benefit of Europeans. Throughout these years, Africans were treated

[1] CO. 323/554/13564. The grants paid in 1909 by the Research Fund (from a combination of Treasury, colonial and Indian sources) were: £1333 to London School of Tropical Medicine, £750 to London University, £1000 to Liverpool School of Tropical Medicine, £100 to Cambridge University (CO. 323/547/41296).

[2] On the recommendation of a committee, led by Prof. W. J. Simpson, appointed to investigate the sanitary conditions, and the effectiveness of the medical services, in West Africa (Cd. 4718). The Colonial Veterinary committee was established with the co-operation of the Board of Agriculture and Fisheries.

[3] CO. 323/543/23681 and 544/3399 and 545/9453. This arose out of a conference with German delegates arranged by the CO. The managing committee was a sub-committee of the Research Fund; Sir J. West Ridgeway was chairman of both. A paid director controlled the work of distributing literature (some of it obtained by exchanges with foreign governments), and of preparing a map of tropical Africa showing the distribution of the disease.

[4] CO. 323/554/29383.

[5] This was expanded into an Imperial Bureau of Entomology in 1913 with a £500 annual government grant.

[6] CO. 323/562/3541, minute 24 Feb 09, and 554/15794.

for syphilis and sleeping sickness. The spread of these diseases was very much on the British conscience.[1] Local investigations and measures to check them involved the expenditure of large sums annually, especially in Uganda, where the governor undertook vigorous preventive action against sleeping sickness on a very large scale, with the sanction of the secretary of state in August 1907. Crewe read the governor's report on the effectiveness of the measures with the 'deepest interest'.[2]

STATE CONTROL AND CONCESSIONS TO PRIVATE ENTERPRISE

It was generally recognised that state action was necessary in African development, because England was confronted by the 'far-sighted and most formidable rivalry' of other European powers.[3] The Liberals realised the impossibility of rigidly up-holding *laissez-faire* doctrines; like the Unionists, however, they still applied the doctrine of financial self-sufficiency to poor and undeveloped areas without substantial modification, believing that given time, the improvement of health, communications and education, and the development of production would gradually increase wealth and government revenue.[4] In the attempt to avoid making continual calls on the British tax payer, African territories had to be made self-supporting by developing them as quickly as possible, by whatever means were available. Priority in development was given to three areas: Nigeria, East Africa Protectorate and Uganda, which, significantly, were the territories with the largest grants-in-aid.

[1] WSC, *MAJ*, pp. 95–103: 'What an obligation, what a sacred duty is imposed upon Great Britain ... to shield this trustful, docile, intelligent Baganda race from dangers which, whatever their cause, have synchronised with our arrival in their midst' (p. 103). See also L. Harcourt, PD/HC. 15/525, 27 Jun 12. There were no European cases of sleeping sickness to speak of after 1906.

[2] CO. 536/31/38571, minute 26 Dec 09. Sleeping sickness began to appear in Uganda in 1901. By the end of 1906, 200,000 had died. The governor established a segregation camp for the sick, and removed 100,000 people from the areas infested by the tse-tse fly (Cd. 4990).

[3] PD. 144/565, Lyttelton 5 Apr 05.

[4] A. Cohen, *British policy in changing Africa* (1959), p. 28.

Grant-aided Somaliland could never conceivably be made self-supporting, and was partially abandoned. Serious consideration was given to the part which private enterprise should be allowed to play, and in the East Africa Protectorate, even the dislike of creating further white communities had to be set aside, as European settlers were necessary to development.

The question whether the government should develop resources itself or allow private enterprise to take the initiative, was raised in various forms in almost all the dependencies. As far as the East Africa Protectorate was concerned, Churchill was inclined to think rapid development so important that concessions to private enterprise must be permitted.

> We want to develop East Africa as quickly as possible, and if we cannot get, and have not got *money*, we ought not to refuse to pay *land* for necessary and urgent services.[1]

He would have the government build Kilindini pier if money could be obtained, 'but if not, let us in any case have it built', by a company willing to build, 'so long as we provide for powers of expropriation. . . . But let us get on.'[2] In 1906 Sir F. Fryer submitted a scheme for electric railways in East Africa and proposed first to connect Nairobi and Fort Hall. Churchill supported him: 'The Nairobi–Fort Hall line is urgently needed and should be begun through *some* agency without delay. . . . Do not let us waste precious time.'[3] The arguments for state ownership of natural resources were, Churchill believed, strongest in Uganda. The introduction of the European businessman there would only bring difficulties and troubles. Private capital and enterprise should be 'carefully directed and narrowly controlled', for it would be hard to find a country where the conditions were more favourable to 'a practical experiment in State Socialism'. The economy of the world would certainly remain 'hopelessly incomplete' while these assets were neglected, but it would be 'wasteful and foolish to

[1] CO. 533/20/5474, minute 26 Mar 06 on Eldama Ravine railway scheme.
[2] CO. 533/24/7894, minute 12 Mar 06.
[3] CO. 533/20/11133, minute 11 May 06; see further, p. 473 below.

hustle'.[1] Churchill emphasised the importance of evolving a consistent, co-ordinated and harmonious system of development; then, he said, 'we should not have to choose between sacrificing valuable public assets to private firms on the one hand, and a dilatory dog-in-the-manger policy on the other'.[2]

With respect to railways, Chamberlain and Lyttelton followed the general principle that construction, ownership and control should be in government hands, although feeder lines catering for genuine interests might sometimes expediently be constructed and worked for a term of years under a concession.[3] Elgin did not simply continue this policy, but refined it in the light of Indian experience:

the accepted view there now is – at least it was when I came away – that on the whole the best thing for the country is that the ownership of the lines should be in the hands of Companies. It is sometimes difficult to bring that about, but if we look to private enterprise in a matter of this kind, we have of course, either to support it by some form of guarantee, of which we have had grievous experience, or we must support it, as has been done pretty frequently in other parts of Africa lately, by land grants, to which also there are considerable objections.[4]

Consequently government control over railway construction was largely maintained. Nor did Elgin believe that open competition was the best way to ensure cheapness of construction,[5] although he did not rule out private enterprise as an auxiliary.[6]

Dislike of speculative concessionaires and desire to preserve the resources of a territory in such a way as to swell the revenue of the government: these two things united to form a policy of strict control over the alienation of natural assets – land, forest rights, water power and oil. The following examples have been selected from the large number of instances.

Elgin refused to allow the forest on the slopes of Mount

[1] Churchill, *MAJ* pp. 121–5, 167.
[2] African 862, memo. on Uganda railway 30 Nov 06.
[3] Cd. 2325 (1904), circular desp. 5 Dec 04.
[4] PD. 156/1439, 10 May 06.   [5] CO. 520/39/16028.
[6] CO. 533/23/44909, minute 12 Dec 06.

Kenya to pass into the hands of Lord Warwick and Mr Moreton Frewen. Elgin insisted on knowing more about the forest before conceding,[1] and secured the services of Mr D. E. Hutchins, one of the ablest forestry officers in the world, to make a report, as a result of which Elgin was convinced that the forest must remain in government hands.[2] In fact no concessions of forest in East Africa were arranged during Elgin's tenure of office. He regarded it as absolutely essential for the government to keep control of the forests, for if they were destroyed, it might mean 'absolute ruin to many, if not all, of the interests of this great dominion'.[3] He had particularly strong views about the concession of water power, and refused to grant Col. Owen Thomas a concession to use the Ripon Falls, in case 'we may find hereafter that we have given away for a song an asset of the greatest value'.[4] He thought the granting of concessions in Southern Nigeria 'somewhat loose'; Mr Brown's attempt to obtain concession of 600 square miles at Ijebu Ode was 'preposterous' and rightly reduced by the governor, but even then, Elgin thought 100 square miles a large tract and stricter supervision seemed desirable. The governor was accordingly asked to submit a memorandum on the procedure in granting concessions, and to consider the possibility of adopting a more satisfactory system and a more effective supervision.[5] During this period, oil was discovered in Southern Nigeria and the Gold Coast; Elgin recognised its possible importance, and favoured further investigations. Steps were taken to place control of oil-mining fully in the hands of the government.[6] In the case of Southern Nigeria, the discoveries did not lead to paying quantities. The discovery in the Gold Coast turned out to be a fraud.

---

[1] CO. 533/13/19288, minute 5 Jul 06.
[2] CO. 533/28/11819, minute 28 Mar 07.
[3] PD. 177/25, 27 Jun 07.
[4] CO. 536/7/27052, minute 2 Aug 06.
[5] CO. 520/56/30490, minute 28 Aug 07; S/S to govr 20 Sep 07.
[6] CO. 520/39/33228, minute 28 Sep 06; CO. 96/456/12059, S/S to govr 16 Apr 07.

THE PROMOTION OF RAILWAYS IN UGANDA, NIGERIA AND CEYLON

One of the major African achievements of the Liberal government was the contribution to railway development. By the end of 1911, extensive additions had been made to the railway system in Nigeria (nearly 750 miles), and there were also extensions to the Uganda railway (58 miles), to the Gold Coast Railway (20 miles), and to the Sierra Leone Railway (25 miles). The Shiré Highlands railway in Nyasaland, begun in 1903, linked Blantyre with Port Herald and Chiromo by June 1908, making the total length of track about 100 miles. During 1911, a further 110 miles of railway were under construction in British East and West Africa.[1] Outside Africa there was railway building in Ceylon and in British Honduras. This achievement was not simply a continuation of the impetus given by Chamberlain to railway development. Elgin had a life-long interest in railways,[2] and his vice-royalty in India had been notable for the construction of more than 3500 miles of railway. He described himself as 'a thorough believer in railways', though not a fanatic: he also believed in proceeding cautiously.[3] Churchill threw himself quite as enthusiastically as Elgin into railway work; it was, he wrote, a waste of time and money to try to govern, or still more to develop big African territories without a railway: without it, 'all civilised government is extravagant and precarious, and all profitable commerce practically impossible'.[4] The jungle could not be tamed by naked fingers.[5]

In the development of newly acquired territories, priority was given to the construction of railways. With respect to Nigeria, Churchill declared succinctly

[1] PD/HC. 40/518, Harcourt 27 Jun 12.
[2] He had been a director of the North British Railway.
[3] EP, E to Sir H. Blake [governor of Ceylon] 10 Dec 06.
[4] Churchill, *MAJ* p. 217.
[5] Ibid. A striking passage on p. 78.

There really is no sensible middle course between developing N. Nigeria by means of a railway, and withdrawing from it. As the latter alternative is excluded, the former becomes imperative.[1]

When the commissioner of the East Africa Protectorate suggested a wide programme of public works, Elgin and Churchill agreed to concentrate their limited resources on 'indispensable railway projects', though Elgin stressed the importance of water supplies and sanitation in Nairobi.[2]

Uganda. Elgin and Churchill were thoroughly sympathetic to the Uganda railway.[3] Their attitude towards it was far removed from Liberal attitudes ten years before. Elgin fully supported the idea that the quickest and surest way of getting rid of the grants-in-aid, and of providing for the debt charge on the Uganda railway, was a progressive policy of extension – 'to starve this railway at this stage is a deplorable policy'.[4] He agreed with Churchill that cheap freight rates on the line were vital, and so long as the railway was not worked at a loss, ought to be granted.[5]

Initial mistakes [wrote Elgin] need not condemn a scheme for ever. I think it probable that the Uganda Railway will turn out a 'success' in the development of the country – and that it is possible . . . it may even become a 'great success' in every sense . . . [if extensions were made].[6]

The treasury refused to reduce rates for freight. Elgin commented: 'The Treasury do not go so far as to kill the goose that lays the golden eggs, but they delay the hatching.'[7]

---

[1] CO. 520/43/10503, minute 17 May 06.

[2] CO. 533/19/45221, minutes 11 and 12 Dec 06, and 1196.

[3] The Uganda railway was 582 miles long: it ran through the E.A.P. to Uganda, but not through Uganda. It cost nearly £8,000,000.

[4] CO. 533/15/27905, minute 15 Aug 06.

[5] CO. 536/10/3681, minute 21 Feb 07.

[6] CO. 536/6/15220, minute 3 Jun 06.

[7] CO. 533/22/26075, minute 2 Aug 06; see also PD. 182/366, 27 Aug 07: he went on record as believing there was 'a great future before the Uganda railway and its extensions'.

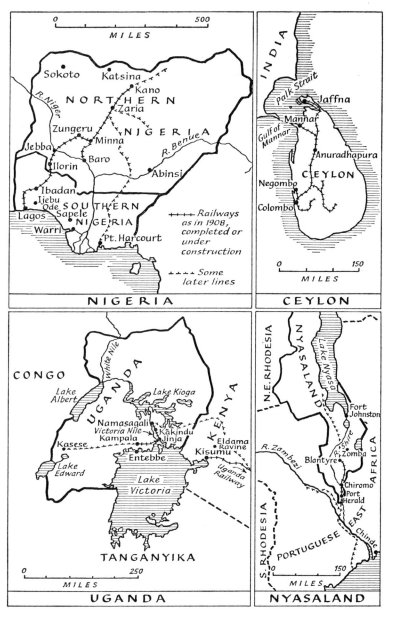

Sketch-maps of railway development

P2 H.E.C. 441

Churchill sketched out plans for railway development based on the Uganda line as early as 30 November 1906, in a memorandum[1] in which he remarked that the unexpected and excessive cost of the Uganda railway had tended to prevent public recognition of its immense potential value, even from a purely commercial point of view. There was of course no possibility of the railway's paying interest on all or any large proportion of its capital charge for some considerable time.

At present it is only a trunk without its feeder limbs, without a deep-water head at Kilindini, without its necessary tail of steamers on the Lake, and above all, without its prolongation to the Congo. But even thus undeveloped and restricted, its rapid and substantial progress has now become apparent.

The government, argued Churchill, should now plough all profits back into supplying the line with those ancillary services, extensions, developments and improvements which it urgently and vitally required, and by which alone could the traffic volume on the main trunk-line be expanded to dimensions capable of sustaining at some future date the interest on the capital charge. Only thus would the British tax payer secure a fair return upon his investment. Churchill was attracted to the idea of linking Lake Victoria and Lake Albert to the Uganda railway. It was the large accession of trade by which the Uganda railway would be flushed when inter-lake communication was established, that more than anything else might be relied upon to establish its commercial solvency. Its prolongation to the Congo by means of a line joining the two great lakes, establishing complete trans-African communication, was 'the natural and logical conclusion to which our efforts must be directed'. Elgin had this 'excellent memorandum' sent to the treasury in December 1906.[2] Meanwhile Churchill persuaded Grey and Gorst from the Egyptian point of view to prefer this Uganda-Congo route to a Nile-Congo railway which had previously been under discussion, as 'the Lado scheme'.[3] The Churchill scheme was realised in 1956.

[1] African 862.   [2] CO. 533/23/44909; EP, Grey to E 3 Feb 08.
[3] FO. 371/448/1796, minute by Grey Jan 08.

Elgin appealed again to the treasury on behalf of Uganda shortly before he left office. He asked them to consider whether a change in the policy hitherto pursued was not required, as much in the interests of the British tax payer as of the Protectorate itself. Uganda was rich in tropical produce of sufficient value to bear the cost of transport along the whole length of the Uganda railway. Only a small fraction of the resources had been exploited, because of poor communications. Such measure of success as had come to the railway was largely due to traffic from Uganda. Under the existing system which involved the construction of public works from current revenue and admitted only a slender programme being carried out each year, there was little hope of the resources being adequately developed at an early date. A moderate outlay could, however, make a rapid and certain difference. At that time half the labour force in Uganda was tied up in human porterage. Few other obstacles to development presented themselves. Elgin therefore wanted to spend a considerable sum on public and mostly reproductive works, with a view to making Uganda self-supporting at the earliest possible date, arguing that such a course was likely to be less expensive in the long run. Furthermore, the prosperity of the East Africa Protectorate was so closely connected with Uganda, that to make the latter self-supporting was the surest and quickest means of abolishing grants-in-aid to the East Africa Protectorate. He requested a £500,000 loan to the Uganda Government from the Local Loans Fund, to be spent during the next five years, by which time the grants-in-aid could be extinguished. This was much earlier than could be expected under existing arrangements.[1]

It seemed important to act quickly because the Germans were pushing a scheme for a railway which would tap the very part of the Congo Britain was aiming at. The treasury, however, refused to sanction such a large scheme as Elgin urged, but assented to a loan of £200,000 for the most important part of it, a railway linking Jinja on Lake Victoria and Kakindu, the nearest point on the Victoria Nile where the river became

[1] CO. 536/18/5711, S/S to treasury 9 Mar 08.

navigable, a distance of forty-six miles. Rapid development of resources was expected from this line, known as the Busoga Railway. 'This is as much as one could expect at first', commented Crewe. It was much more than officials had expected: they had put the chances of a treasury grant somewhere between the remote and the hopeless.[1]

Nigeria. Churchill's advocacy of the line to connect Baro on the Niger and Kano, 356 miles to the North, was based first on strategic and political justifications.

So great an extent of country cannot be conveniently held for an indefinite period by a considerable force of drilled troops in garrison, unless buckled together by at least one central line of rapid communication. Large military economies and greater security . . . are to be counted on. The effective occupation of a territory now precariously and loosely held, and the more complete fulfilment of our responsibilities to the natives, over whom we have declared a Protectorate, and to the foreign powers with whom we have made boundary conventions, are the political advantages. These are sufficient in themselves to justify a considerable amount of not directly remunerative expenditure; but additional to them, is the prospect of the speedier development of local trade, on which ultimately the capacity of the country to yield revenue depends.

The prospect of increasing the export of cotton by enabling the British Cotton Growing Association to open up new areas for cultivation, 'might almost of itself be said to be an adequate inducement to build the line'.[2] The growth of cotton trade, said Elgin, seemed the most likely way of making the protectorate self-suppporting.[3]

In 1903 Lugard recommended a temporary light tramway or railway with a 2 ft 6 in. gauge, from Baro to Kano. Lyttelton had deferred any decision, as he was not quite sure of the advantages of such a line over an extension of the Lagos railway

---

[1] CO. 536/30/15957, treasury to CO 11 May 09, minute 5 Jun 09; CO. 536/21/42421 gives officials' opinions.
[2] African 850, 14 Jul 06.   [3] PD. 156/1439–43, 10 May 06.

from Southern Nigeria.[1] Nor was Elgin, although he was anxious to respect Lugard's local knowledge and experience, and to support the efforts of 'that great pioneer of civilisation' to make Nigeria less of a 'pathless wilderness'.[2] Elgin referred to the scheme in the House of Lords in May 1906 before any decision was taken. He did not approve either the principle of a light tramway, or the departure from the 3 ft 6 in. gauge of the Lagos railway. Light railways might be useful in prairie or veldt country, essential in mountainous country, and advisable where only small traffic was expected, but they were not the most expedient or economical mode of construction where considerable works were required. The latest estimates showed that the extra cost of a 3 ft 6 in. line would be £600,000, which, 'though considerable, is not excessive'. And he thought it most undesirable to have two systems of gauge. The simplest method seemed to him to continue the Lagos railway into Northern Nigeria to meet Lugard's proposed route from the upper bank of the Niger to Kano.[3] He expressed misgiving about Lugard's idea of utilising the navigation of the Niger. This could be 'rather a dangerous experiment', since, although navigable by ships for two months, for eight months of the year the maximum depth of the river was only $3\frac{1}{2}$ feet. Transport would thus be made uncertain and expensive. By contrast, Churchill was in favour of giving Northern Nigeria separate access to the sea by combining rail and river transport. Northern Nigeria, he said, ought not to be forced to wait upon the progress of transport in Southern Nigeria.

Elgin and Churchill were determined to build a railway in Northern Nigeria. Part of the stimulus to this project came from the knowledge that the government of French West Africa had raised a loan of £2,600,000 for public works in 1903, and shortly afterwards a further £4,000,000 for the extension of railways and other public enterprises. 'The French West African railway programme', wrote Churchill, 'must be an essential portion of our case to the Treasury in support of our

[1] CO. 446/47/12976, minute by Antrobus 10 Nov 05.
[2] PD. 181/59, 17 Aug 07. [3] PD. 156/1439–43, 10 May 06.

445

Nigerian plans.'[1] An incidental, but by no means unimportant, reason why railway development appealed to the Liberals, as well as to the officials, was the prospect that it would end the trading monopoly in practice enjoyed by the Niger Company.[2]

Elgin was dissatisfied with Lugard's estimates for a tramway, based on a figure of £2000 per mile. Although Lugard had promised to make good his estimates to Elgin's satisfaction, he had not done so by September 1906, when Elgin returned to the problem, and Lugard himself was on the verge of resignation. Lugard's note of 22 July Elgin found 'entirely insufficient'. Elgin now requested the preparation of a statement on certain definite points on which he wanted more precise information, and he had asked the officials to ensure that if Lugard, who was in London, wanted expert assistance he should have it, *'not to criticise but to sympathetically elaborate* his project'. Unless he had more information he could not make a case with the treasury; it would not be fair to ask Asquith personally 'to take the responsibility of setting aside his expert opinion, when I have difficulty in my own mind and all *my* experts against me'.[3] Churchill was in complete agreement, and accepted Elgin's decision as a wise one.[4] Elgin arranged for two personal friends, majors Carmichael and Pringle to help Lugard. As a result, the revised estimate was placed at £2583 per mile, though this was still not a firm figure. Up to a point Elgin was satisfied, but not altogether.[5]

Sir Percy Girouard was appointed to succeed Lugard, specifically because of his experience in railway administration in Egypt, the Sudan and the Transvaal. Before his formal appointment in December 1906, he was invited to produce a statement on the transport problem. Elgin was disappointed

[1] CO. 96/451/18462, minute 2 Jun 06. For French mileages, see Cd. 2325 (1904).

[2] CO. 446/82/6063, minute by Antrobus 5 Apr 09; CO. 446/59/24994, minute by Ommanney 17 Jul 06. The desire of the government to encourage other traders was so great that they might even have been prepared to consider a proposal for a subsidised company to compete with the Niger Company.

[3] EP, E to WSC 10 Sep 06: CO. 446/58/26478, minutes 3 Aug and 10 Sep 06.

[4] EP, WSC to E 14 Sep 06, from Vienna.

[5] EP, E to WSC 17 (?) Oct 06 (photocopy): CO. 446/60/38481.

with this. Girouard had not been truly impartial, but committed himself to Lugard's idea without local knowledge:

I think he is at least doubtful on a number of points, and I have marked some with queries (in pencil that they may be rubbed out), e.g. take the navigation of the Niger – he seems to me either to ignore or to underrate the fact that there is no sea port – and that Lugard himself declared against Supele and Warri under existing conditions as a substitute or competitor for Lagos.[1]

Girouard continued to favour using the Niger as the primary access route to Northern Nigeria, and, unlike Egerton, was not in favour of bridging the Niger at Jebba to make the link with the Lagos railway. Unlike Lugard, he preferred the 3 ft 6 in. gauge.

On 28 February 1907 the treasury was asked to sanction a 3 ft 6 in. line from Baro to Zungeru only, though along Lugard's route, as a branch of the eventual extension of the Lagos railway running direct to Kano, at a cost of £375,000. This was essentially Elgin's scheme. The treasury refused. They demanded an exhaustive report from Girouard.[2]

Girouard completed his comprehensive report on Nigerian development in May 1907. When it was received in the colonial office, Churchill described it, with wit and over-dramatisation, as 'Napoleonic both in compass and precision'.[3] He launched a long memorandum in its support. In it, he pointed out that a population of seven millions was ruled by 300 civil servants and 3300 native troops, without a single white or Indian regiment. Hence it was, without a railway,

difficult to repress a sensation of political insecurity. . . . We are sprawled about this gigantic country without means of communication or concentration, without any trustworthy maniple of military force; without any revenue or trade proportioned to the cost of administration . . . at heavy annual expense to the British tax payer. . . . We are encamped in Northern Nigeria rather than in permanent occupation.

[1] Ibid. 8 Nov 06.　　　　　　　　[2] CO. 446/68/11468.
[3] CO. 446/63/23179, minute 8 Jul 07.

Churchill favoured the 3 ft 6 in. gauge. There must be strict economy of construction – it was unnecessary to have a railway of English standards 'through a wild and poor country just thawing into civilisation'. Above all, he wished to accept Girouard's case for combining the rail system with the navigable Niger waterway. Not to utilise the river would be 'a cardinal error'. This would mean that, instead of an extension of the Lagos railway, Northern Nigeria would be served by a separate railway system based on the Niger. The one system must for many years supplement and not supplant the other. He envisaged that the extension of the Lagos railway might carry troops, passengers, mails, perishable and high class goods, but that the bulk of trade would go on the rail-plus-river route.[1]

Lugard, Girouard and Churchill wanted this combination. Elgin swallowed his doubts. A re-submission to the treasury was now made on the basis of a line from Baro, not merely to Zungeru, but to Kano, as Lugard originally proposed, at an estimated cost of £1,230,000, or less than £3000 per mile. It was to be a pioneer line of 3 ft. 6 in. gauge. The treasury, guided by Asquith, while admitting the importance of the project, refused to sanction an imperial loan, and suggested the alternative of utilising the credit of Southern Nigeria for raising the loan, since amalgamation of the two had been agreed in principle.[2] In order to get the support of the governor of Southern Nigeria to this arrangement, Elgin promised that the Lagos railway should simultaneously be extended from Ilorin to cross the Niger at Jebba by a ferry, and later by a bridge, and to make a junction, now as a pioneer line, with the new Northern Nigeria railway, via Zungeru, at a point to be decided, which was eventually chosen as Minna. Thus confronted with alternative schemes for linking Northern Nigeria with the sea, Elgin chose both. This was because he preferred one scheme, and Lugard, Girouard and Churchill the other, and he did not like to disappoint them. Construction of the Baro to Kano line was approved in August 1907. The double

[1] CO. 446/69/29405 memo. 18 Jul 07. [2] EP, Asquith to E 14 Mar 07.

arrangement would cost £2,000,000. The Lagos–Minna and Baro–Minna–Kano lines were opened simultaneously on 1 January 1912. It proved probably a mistake to build both. History proves Elgin right and Lugard, Girouard and Churchill wrong. The Minna–Baro line became redundant and was closed.[1]

Ceylon. Ceylon already had 560 miles of government railway by the beginning of the twentieth century. Ceylon's Northern Railway line, from Colombo via Anuradhapura to Jaffna in the far north, was completed by 1895. Two further railway schemes were under consideration when the Liberal government took office. One was the Negombo railway project, a fairly orthodox and safe scheme, giving Colombo a link with Negombo twenty miles to the north. The other, known as the Mannar (Manaar) project, was based upon a long discussed scheme to connect Ceylon and India by rail and steamship, mainly to bring Tamil labourers from India. The Northern Railway of Ceylon would be connected with Mannar, which was about forty miles to the west of it. Both projects had been subject to delay. Something was at last decided by Elgin.

[1] The government of Southern Nigeria, as a colony, could raise loans in the open market, as the North could not, being a protectorate. The South already made a grant-in-aid to the North of £75,000 p.a., out of which it was proposed to meet the interest on the sum of £2,000,000 loaned by the treasury under the Public Works Loans Act, normally providing funds for loans to municipalities in the U.K. (PD. 182/364–8, 27 Aug 07). 'Pioneer' meant the railway would follow a proper survey, and be constructed with gradients and generally so as to suit a fully constructed line in the future, though it would not at first have signals or stations, which seemed hardly necessary for a line that would at most run two trains a day; 'pioneer' thus means a permanent line, not a light railway or a tramway, but a line without frills or refinements. When the bridge replaced the ferry at Jebba in 1916, and Lagos harbour was improved by dredging a sand-bar to allow ocean-going vessels to get into it without the transhipment of goods previously necessary, the Baro-Kano line became redundant (R. J. Harrison-Church, 'Transport pattern in British West Africa', in *Geographical Essays on British tropical lands*, ed. R. W. Steel and C. A. Fisher (1956), p. 70). In July 1908, when it was too late, Egerton returned to the scheme of February 1907, suggesting a realignment directly linking Lagos and Kano, via Zungeru (CO. 520/63/29951), which would have been more sensible. As Elgin foresaw, the all-rail route was preferred. CO. 520/52/27112, E to Egerton 6 Sep 07, and 34138, minutes by E 30 Sep 06, 1 Oct 06; S/S to govr 25 Oct 07.

The Negombo line was not thought to be a remunerative or developmental project, but it was hoped by it to placate an agitation 'manufactured by agitators appealing to Burghers and Singalese'. Everyone in Ceylon seemed to be complaining that the advance of the colony was being needlessly held up.[1] Elgin was not convinced that the nationalist agitations and Moslem intrigues were very serious:

It is difficult I think to form much of an idea about the working of these movements. I remember receiving similar reports when I was in India, and though nothing seems to come of the travels of these emissaries, it seems natural to suppose that they must indicate the existence of a recognised centre or a recognised sentiment. Beyond that we do not, I think, get far, and my feeling is that while of course we must be on the watch, we need not be too much alarmed.[2]

He was however impressed by the argument that the Negombo railway might benefit the 'natives and smallholders'. He would much rather take it up than 'a more ambitious scheme or one more directly in the Planter's interest'.[3] The governor approved giving this line preference. The Mannar proposals were then referred to consulting engineers, who were urgently requested to report.[4]

In an official despatch Elgin stated that he had only decided to sanction the Negombo scheme with some hesitation, and in coming to the decision he had been largely influenced by assurances that the line would be of great benefit to the natives, 'whose claims to consideration in respect of railway facilities are deserving of attention'. In addition, he approved of extensions to Colombo station, and sanctioned the extension of the breakwater. These three projects involved 11–12 million rupees. He would not therefore at that moment add to the liabilities of the colonial government by sanctioning the Mannar line as well. He was not convinced that a case of urgency had

[1] CO. 54/701/27681, minutes by Lucas and Ommanney, 8 and 14 Aug 06.
[2] EP, E to Sir Henry Blake 10 Dec 06.
[3] CO. 54/701/27681, minute 15 Aug 06.
[4] Ibid. tel. S/S to govr 17 Aug 06, and 30558, reply, govr to S/S 18 Aug 06.

been established for immediate construction of other works, or that fresh projects might not soon be put forward in competition with those then before him. His decision was criticised as 'an arbitrary curtailment of development'. Elgin would not accept this interpretation, and pleaded in extenuation the 'exceptionally unfavourable' conditions in the money market for some time past.[1] He apologised privately to the governor if he had seemed to be dilatory. That would not be his own wish or intention, as he was a thorough believer in railways. But cautious consideration had to be given to these railway schemes. He was still unsure about the India–Ceylon rail link:

I used to see it from the Indian side, and I had my doubts then, and entertain them still. But besides that, this is not an easy time for large financial operations – and although you have a large surplus, you cannot eat your cake and have it. If you spend your surplus too freely or too quickly, the issue of a loan may be forced upon you at an inconvenient moment. If there is such a risk, and I am advised that there is, the delay for even a year or two in the execution of this work (supposing it to be approved), is merely a trifle in the history of the Colony, as compared with the effect of the existence for many years of a loan contracted at an unfavourable moment.[2]

In July 1907, however, Elgin proposed to authorise a survey of the line to connect the Ceylon railway to Mannar.[3] A definite promise to construct the line would have been premature until the survey was finished, but Elgin did what he could to obtain the completion of the survey for this important project.[4] The branch to Mannar was thus completed by the outbreak of the First World War.

COTTON-GROWING IN AFRICA

The Liberals were fully alive to the importance of governmental aid to the Lancashire cotton industry. Churchill and

---

[1] CO. 54/703/43369, S/S to govr. 14 Dec 06.   [2] EP, E to Blake 10 Dec 06.
[3] CO. 54/709/26017, CO to India Office 24 Jul 07.
[4] CO. 54/713/29221, minutes by WSC and E 20 and 21 Apr 07.

Bryce had been early advocates of the systematic development of cotton-growing in the empire, especially in Africa. As early as February 1904, Churchill had declared that Liberal policy was to increase the sources of raw cotton, and the markets for cotton goods. 'A well-considered and thrifty policy of railway development in West Africa and in the Sudan would do more for the Lancashire cotton industry than will ever be gained by Mr Chamberlain's food taxes or Mr Balfour's tariff wars. . . .'[1]

Early in the twentieth century, raw cotton prices were rising steadily; demand was increasing for the first time in a generation. Shortage of supply led to a revival of interest in schemes to promote a raw cotton supply alternative to the American source, schemes which had been forgotten since the days of Palmerston and the American civil war.[2] The search for new sources in the British empire began after the short American crop of 1900, which caused great distress in Lancashire, at that time dependent on the United States for 85% of its supply. In 1902, a powerful pressure group, the British Cotton Growing Association was founded to promote imperial cotton cultivation. It was accorded the privilege of monthly meetings with colonial office officials, on account of its professed semi-philanthropic aims.[3] This privilege was continued under the Liberal government, the only difference being that instead of meetings chaired by a civil servant as formerly, the parliamentary under-secretary of state normally presided. Presumably Churchill had himself requested this arrangement, in view of his connection with Lancashire as an M.P.

In answer to a parliamentary question, Churchill declared on 1 May 1906 that their predecessors' policy regarding the British Cotton Growing Association would be continued. Ten days later, Elgin declared his personal adherence to that pledge.

---

[1] Bryce: PD. 144/563, 5 Apr 05; Churchill, *For Free Trade: speeches during the fiscal controversy preceding the late general election* (1906), pp. 54–6, at Manchester 19 Feb 04.

[2] C. Ehrlich, in *History of East Africa*, ii, 399.

[3] CO. 96/450/16561. In conjunction with the colonial office and African producers, the B.C.G.A. established ginneries, provided seed, gave advice, and organised indigenous cultivation, purchased or produced the lint and marketed the bales.

There was, he said, no possible reason for difference of opinion between the two sides of the House. The Liberals, quite as fully as their opponents, admitted the necessity of providing larger supplies for the great cotton industry, and he saw no reason why they should not, as cordially as their opponents, desire to find those supplies within the empire. He was prepared to assist the Association 'in the same way and to the same extent, and do more if possible' than the Unionists had done.[1] An improved transport system was the chief practical way in which the Liberal government proposed to show its support.

Gradually the Association became more commercial. The government accepted this development as probably inevitable. Towards the end of 1909 the treasury was asked to grant £10,000 to the Association for five years. As Southern Nigeria had contributed £40,000 it was argued that £10,000 for the other colonies must be worthwhile. Cotton showed good prospects of becoming a much-needed African staple. But the grant was not requested even mainly on the ground of the interest of exchequer-aided protectorates. The plea was made chiefly on the ground of the importance of Lancashire cotton interests.[2] By this time it was generally recognised that the experimental and instructional work which the Association had hitherto been subsidising for undertaking, should in future be done by the colonial governments concerned, though the Association might help in the establishment of ginneries, especially where they were built before they were commercially desirable.[3]

The interests of the cotton industry were prominent in the discussion of Nigerian railway development. The British Cotton Growing Association had concentrated its attention on Northern Nigeria. A great deputation to the prime minister, Lord Elgin and Lord Morley on 17 May 1906, representative of the whole force of Lancashire, pressed for a railway. Having made enquiries all over the world, the cotton manufacturers were

---

[1] PD. 156/1435–8, 10 May 06.   [2] CO. 323/561/36466.

[3] CO. 96/489/19869, circular desp. 23 Jul 09. Ginneries are places where machines are used for ginning, that is, separating cotton from its seeds.

convinced that the greatest opportunity was in Northern Nigeria. There alone 'lies the possible salvation of Lancashire'. The stumbling-block was that Northern Nigeria was, for all practical purposes, inaccessible. Campbell-Bannerman replied on behalf of the government. His remarks acquire a special interest, as he so rarely had anything to say about the tropical dependencies. He acknowledged that he was deeply moved on the matter. It was a national question, not just a Lancashire one. Perhaps there never had been a deputation to a government 'so important, so almost portentous, and so impressive as this one'. The government was all in favour of developing the empire. Territories like Nigeria were not mere prestige items:

We possess them to benefit ourselves to some degree, and in a great degree, if we can, but above all to benefit the inhabitants of the country and those who are interested on the spot in them. What can we do better for the people over whom we have some responsibility, than by introducing a new mode of cultivation, a new industry, a new means of raising themselves – not only acquiring money, but of raising themselves – among the peoples of the world?

He spoke of anxiety and a necessity for caution in proposals for the construction of railways, in view of their experience with the Uganda railway. But they would give reasonable assistance, because he was convinced that Northern Nigeria was 'a great possible source of supply'. The idea appealed to him because if it worked, it would deliver Lancashire from monopoly, 'from the real and natural monopoly and from the artificial and ill-intentioned monopoly of the speculator'.[1]

Churchill fastened tightly upon the representations of Lancashire. He did not mean to suggest that the interests of a single county, or of a single industry, however important, should receive special favour at the hands of the government. But when the case had been, as he thought, shown on strategic and administrative grounds to justify the construction of a railway:

these other considerations may fairly be urged for the purpose of showing the great commercial advantages which may be

[1] *British Cotton Growing Association pamphlet*, no. 10, 44–7 (EP).

454

expected to flow from such an enterprise, and the very large measure of public satisfaction among all classes with which its initiation would be acclaimed. . . . Cotton is the thread which more directly and palpably than any other unites the material interests of British industrial democracy with the retention and development of the tropical possessions of the Crown.[1]

The railway was built, but cotton did not prove to be as important in Nigeria as it became in Nyasaland, and even more in Uganda, where the Africans were successfully induced to take up cotton-growing. In 1907 the British Cotton Growing Association and the Uganda government agreed each to spend £1000 a year for three years to encourage the growing of cotton.[2] Many crops were tried in Uganda. There was nothing premeditated about the emergence of cotton as the dominating crop.[3] Between 1904 and 1907 many different varieties of cotton had been introduced. Some of them were so indifferent as seriously to threaten the reputation Uganda was trying to establish for cotton. In December 1907, the governor, H. Hesketh Bell, recommended drastic action. After the harvest, all plants would be exterminated, except the Upland variety, the seed of which would be supplied to all growers. To stop bad ginning, all hand-gins were to be withdrawn and destroyed. Regulations, based on Indian models, were to be introduced for controlling the sale of local cotton and for preventing the export of produce below a certain standard. Bell advocated instructing the Africans in the best method of cultivation, and setting up a government experimental seed farm. These Draconian proposals and recommendations were approved by the secretary of state at the beginning of February 1908. An ordinance of a very stringent character was promulgated in March 1908. By 1909 it was clear that the desired result was achieved. The governor's report on these measures to encourage a high-grade cotton production was published as a blue book. Publication was intended to check the pretensions

---

[1] CO. 446/69/29405, memo. 18 Jul 07, 'The Northern Nigeria Railway'.
[2] Ingham, *A history of East Africa*, p. 235.
[3] Ehrlich in *History of East Africa*, ii, 403.

of the British Cotton Growing Association, who advertised themselves as having done everything to save Uganda cotton.[1] The development of peasant-grown cotton was expertly directed. The chiefs proved an effective instrument in enforcing government orders.

Nor was Churchill's recognition of the possibilities in the Sudan proved inapposite. The Gezira cotton-growing scheme proceeded steadily throughout the period of the Liberal ministry. As it was not the responsibility of the colonial office, it will not be dealt with here. Suffice it to say that, in retrospect, this scheme appears 'perhaps the most constructive development undertaken in any colonial country'.[2] It ranks as one of the major achievements, in the imperial field, of the Liberal government. An Act giving an imperial guarantee for the interest on a £3,000,000 Sudan government loan at $3\frac{1}{2}\%$ was passed by parliament in 1913, and subsequently augmented to £6,000,000 in 1919.[3]

THE PROBLEM OF THE WEST INDIES

Colonial office staff and British politicians did not have a high opinion of either West Indian Negroes or planters. The former had the reputation of being ignorant and superstitious, abnormally excitable and prone to ferocious rioting, especially under the increasing influence of a 'disreputable and quite unscrupulous class of half-breed agitators'. The negroes of British Guiana were explicitly regarded as quite unfit for any share in the government. Officials had a poor opinion of the planters, as uneducated, narrow-minded and provocative.[4]

There were riots at Georgetown in British Guiana at the end of November 1905. The disturbances arose out of a general

[1] CO. 536/31/32860, govr. to S/S 14 Sep 09; Cd. 4910 (1909).
[2] K. Robinson, *Dilemmas of trusteeship* (1965), p. 85.
[3] For the Gezira scheme see A. Gaitskell, *Gezira: a story of development in the Sudan* (1959) and P. M. Holt, *A modern history of the Sudan* (1961).
[4] See CO. 318/315/309, CO. 111/553/47565, CO. 23/263/21685 and 262/42278, CO. 321/235/18829, CO. 295/436/17150.

strike of casual wharf labourers who demanded higher wages. Race issues between black and white soon became involved. Shops were looted, and government house was besieged for a couple of hours. Elgin noted that the governor had interviewed agents of certain planters and had insisted on the policy of resisting all demands for increase of wages. This could be criticised on the face of it 'as appearing to associate the civil authorities with the interests of the planters only, in opposition to any legitimate claims that the labourers might be able to put forward'. Nevertheless, Elgin complimented the governor for his firm and restrained conduct of affairs: 'It is evident that any want of firmness might have had very serious consequences.'[1] He and Churchill were anxious lest the governor should appear to use the armed power of the crown to assist private traders in securing larger profits. He could be defended only so long as he acted on grounds of public safety, preventing the spread of strikes and disturbances to other sugar plantations.[2] On the whole Elgin satisfied himself that complaints against the governor's suppression of the riots were unreasonable. This did not stop him from asking for fuller information 'as to the grievances of the labourers and your suggestions for their remedy, if they are well founded'.[3] The colonial office in general placed on the planters part of the blame for the riots.

Although it never reached a political level in this period, the long-term colonial office policy was certainly trying to move towards disengagement from the West Indies by means of a federation. Lucas was preparing the necessary memorandum. Hopwood minuted in May 1908 that this question 'must be seriously taken in hand'.[4] At all events, the West Indies were not a primary field of Liberal interest. Indeed they were sacrificed to considerations of wider imperial policy, both by

---

[1] CO. 111/547/45393, minute 29 Dec 05.

[2] CO. 111/549/3830, minute by WSC 5 Feb 06.

[3] CO. 111/547/902, minutes 11 and 13 Jan 06 by E and WSC, S/S to govr 18 Jan 06. See Cd. 2822 (1906).

[4] CO. 42/920/34302. There was talk of the possibility of committing the administration of the West Indies to the Dominion of Canada.

the reduction of defence forces and by the termination of British participation in the Brussels Sugar Convention. Chamberlain had already done all that could be done for some years by a comprehensive five-year plan and by grants-in-aid to make up revenue deficits, encourage and improve the sugar industry, modernise methods of cultivation, stimulate agricultural research, augment steamer services and roads in Dominica, and settle peasant proprietors in St Vincent.

Chamberlain had created the pressure for framing an international agreement to abolish the bounty system, as a major part of his effort to revive sugar-growing in the West Indies. When the original International Sugar convention was signed at Brussels on 5 March 1902, practically the whole of the Liberal Opposition attacked it, because, arguing that Britain was largely a sugar-consuming country, they did not want to enter any bargain which would enable sugar-producing countries artificially to restrict British sources of supply.[1] Churchill waxed eloquent on the joys of cheap sugar, 'comforting and strengthening our masses', and on its value as the basis of an imposing array of secondary industries, from sweets to soda water. 'In order that the West Indies should benefit effectually, it is necessary that the British consumer should suffer substantially. . . . We lose immediately; the West Indies may not gain for a great many years.' Even if the convention would save the West Indies, Churchill would not have supported it. The West Indies, however, could not, in his judgment, be saved, since 70% of their market was in the United States. The United States was destined within four or five years to obtain its supplies elsewhere, either from Cuba, or from home-grown sugar beet. 'We shall only prolong its dying agony, and by impoverishing ourselves we shall weaken our power to help them.'[2] In fact, Chamberlain's policy failed to bring about any expansion of the West Indian sugar trade as a whole. The convention was probably not very helpful. Though it might

[1] EP. Printed speech by Campbell-Bannerman to deputation of free-trade M.P.s on the convention 14 Jul 06, pp. 21–2.
[2] PD. 126/714–25, 29 Jul 03.

have revived confidence in the West Indies, no increase in prosperity can be attributed to it.[1]

Once in power, the Liberals were determined to reverse their predecessors' policy and to secure the abolition of what Churchill described as an 'insane convention'.[2] By 1906 it was clear that Britain would withdraw. In June 1907 Grey explained to the cabinet that their policy was to announce withdrawal of Britain from the provisions of the convention which required them to penalise sugars declared by the Permanent Sugar Commission to be bounty-fed. This would probably involve complete withdrawal from the convention, which could only take effect in September 1908, leaving ample time available for future arrangements to be made with the countries concerned.[3] The government announced its conclusion:

that the limitation of the sources from which sugar may enter the United Kingdom, whether by prohibition or by the imposition of countervailing duties, is inconsistent with their declared policy, and incompatible with the interests of British consumers and sugar-using manufacturers.

The interests of these were 'paramount'.[4] The governor of Jamaica, Olivier, felt bound to admit that from the point of view of imperial policy, the government's grounds were 'deep and far-reaching'. He admitted that the policy was primarily based upon consistency with their general and declared trade policy, for the maintenance of the convention would offer a weak spot in the argument against fiscal reform.[5] Many protests were received in 1907 from the West Indies, and from sugar-refiners in Canada and Australia asking for continuation of the convention. There were also protests from Hong Kong, Mauritius and New Zealand.

The troubles of the Caribbean region were further increased

[1] S. B. Saul, 'Economic significance of "Constructive Imperialism"', *Journal of Economic History*, xvii (1957), 178–9, 190.
[2] CO. 323/519/6880, minute 28 Feb 06.
[3] CAB. 41/31/22, 11 Jun 07.
[4] See Cd. 3565, *Papers relating to the Brussels Sugar Convention.*
[5] EP, Olivier to E 4 Jul 07.

by a violent earthquake which devastated Kingston, Jamaica, only three years after it had been struck by a hurricane. The earthquake occurred on 14 January 1907. After it, there was some pressure upon the government to make a free grant for rebuilding. Inflexibly, Churchill was opposed to meeting these pressures, in view of the existence of a Mansion House Fund. The total damage to property valued at £2,130,000 was £1,625,000. After hearing a deputation from the West Indies on 10 and 11 April 1907, Elgin came to the conclusion that he could not refrain from putting to the treasury the arguments for a free grant of £150,000. Among other reasons, there clearly was a large class of ruined people who could give no security for a loan. He suggested that if Churchill was not satisfied, he ought to see the archbishop of the West Indies, and test the strength of the case for himself. As a result, Churchill agreed that in the circumstances – the governor had discouraged contributions to the Mansion House Fund – he would acquiesce in the draft letter to the treasury, although he still thought from the point of view of general principles that there would be no justification for a grant, and that the island was perfectly capable of meeting the situation from its own resources.[1] In his submission to the treasury, Elgin represented that aid was not being asked lightly, and in his opinion, it was highly inexpedient that there should be any opportunity given for imputing a refusal to give adequate imperial aid:

the business centre and capital of the leading British West Indies Colony has been largely destroyed. There is no doubt as to the urgency and the extent of the need: there is no doubt as to its political expediency: it is not easy to see how a grant and a loan in the present instance can make an unfortunate precedent for future years.

Refusal to grant genuinely needed assistance would meet with the criticism that however grave the crisis, and however well founded the claim, Great Britain was indifferent to the fate of her West Indian colonies.[2] The treasury was persuaded. It was

[1] CO. 137/656/7697.   [2] Ibid. CO letter to treasury 22 Apr 07.

agreed to make a free grant of £150,000 in addition to a loan of £800,000, mostly for restoring public buildings.[1] Churchill still affected to be unable to see why the loan should not be made to cover the purposes of the grant:

'Free grants' ought not to be taken by force from the taxpayers of this country. Charitable enterprises should be the proper subject of Mansion House Funds. The subscriptions of the public have already been generous and would have been more so, had it not been for the strange discouragement administered to them.[2]

But nobody seems to have taken much notice of his pernickety disapproval.

Chamberlain's Imperial Department of Agriculture for the West Indies had done invaluable work under Sir Daniel Morris, in saving the West Indies. The colonial office under Lyttelton had already applied to the treasury for the continuation of the imperial grant to the department which Chamberlain had arranged for the ten years after 1897. Elgin completely accepted the view of his predecessor that the West Indian colonies ought not to remain a perpetual burden on the British tax payer at home. The letter to the treasury urged the view that any delay or indecision would increase the feeling of uneasiness which existed, militating against the investment of capital. In addition, it pointed out that the reduction of naval and military establishments had already greatly curtailed the total expenditure of the imperial government in the West Indies, and had compelled some of the colonies to incur heavy expenditure of their own to provide for the maintenance of internal order. Finally, appeal was made to the treasury on the argument that once the withdrawal from the Brussels Sugar convention had been arranged:

the work of the Imperial Department of Agriculture in giving what support may still be given to the sugar industry, and still more in encouraging alternative products, will be more important than ever. It is therefore of the utmost importance that the future of the Agriculture Department should be

---

[1] CO. 137/660/16277. [2] CO. 137/662/11680.

temporarily assured, and the scope of its operations unrestricted by financial disabilities.

The treasury decided to continue paying grants for five years from 1 April 1908, but on a diminishing scale.[1]

Transport problems were also difficult. Frequent communications between the islands had to be maintained if their economic progress was to be possible, or federation feasible. There had been many complaints of the inadequacy of single steamer service, which was all that had been provided from the autumn of 1906. The colonial office successfully persuaded the treasury in April 1907 to approve a contract with the Royal Mail Steam Packet Company to provide a second steamer service for ten years with a total subsidy of £25,000, of which half would fall on imperial funds.[2]

At long last a decision was arrived at to start railway-building in British Honduras. The colonial office had been criticised for taking twenty years to consider various proposals. Both Churchill and Elgin diagnosed an unnecessary prejudice against light railways of all kinds. Although Elgin thought it a mistake to construct a railway, destined to become a trunk line, in a form which could not readily be converted into a railway of a standard gauge, he saw no objection to narrow gauges and light construction for feeder railways, or short independent lines, especially in 'backward' countries.[3] A light railway, said Churchill, was better than no railway. To refuse to build any railway until you could build the London and North-western was to forbid enterprise altogether. He warned against frittering money away on small detached projects,[4] or 'a series of disjointed petty enterprises, in some cases of a more than doubtful character'. Nevertheless, after further consideration, he satisfied himself that they would be justified in spending not more than £40,000 upon the construction of a 'really light railway' to lead twenty miles into the interior from the town of Stann Creek,

[1] CO. 318/315/12963, CO to treasury 13 Aug 06.
[2] CO. 318/317/11025, CO to treasury 12 Apr, treasury to CO 29 May 07.
[3] CO. 123/253/21707, minute 14 Aug 06.
[4] CO. 123/254/14666, minute by WSC 27 May 06.

and in making the necessary pier.[1] The gauge was eventually fixed at 3 feet. In accepting the necessity of establishing a trade by cheap land grants to large companies, Elgin consented to the sale of land at £1 per acre.[2]

In the West Indies as elsewhere, the Liberal government assumed a cautious attitude towards concessions and evoked the usual criticism of retarding development thereby. Curtis, Campbell and Co. were prepared to cultivate rice on a large scale on crown lands in British Guiana, provided that the government would guarantee interest on the capital. As a general rule Elgin preferred an enterprise of this kind to stand on its own feet, but he agreed to let the Crown Agents work out a draft agreement on the distinct understanding that everything would be subject to the approval of the secretary of state and the legislative council.[3] A firm calling itself the British Guiana Rubber Corporation was supported by the governor and his advisers in its application for a concession. The colonial office took a dislike to the attitudes and methods which the company revealed during the negotiations. Especially damning was the issue of a misleading prospectus. As a result, while professing extreme reluctance to differ from the governor, and while anxious to do everything possible to develop the rubber industry of British Guiana, the secretary of state would not encourage the company. The company then brought an action against the government of British Guiana for a sort of breach of promise. The company had insufficient of the maidenly virtues to win its case, and the affair ended tamely with a decision in favour of the government. An impression got about the colony that by fighting off this company the government was courting capital in a most misogynistic way. In truth, it was hardly fair to say that the government was frightening away capital. Honourable and virile intentions were therefore confirmed by telegram in August 1907. The question could be considered again *de novo*:

[1] CO. 123/253/38486, minute 1 Nov 06.
[2] CO. 123/257/29461, minute by E 12 Sep 07.
[3] CO. 111/556/18851, minute by E 22 Jun 07.

Should you be satisfied that *bona fide* company had been formed with adequate paid-up capital and with *bona fide* intention to work, I shall be prepared to approve reasonable concession for rubber cultivation.[1]

The record of the Liberal government in the West Indies is hardly impressive. It did little more than shuffle its feet in embarrassment. Such action as it took was minimal and unavoidable. But in the post-Chamberlain era to have done much more would have been, in the full imperial perspective, unjustified.

LAND QUESTIONS IN FIJI

Outside Africa, the most prominent land policy questions concerned Fiji. There was even a discussion in the House of Lords. The general significance of land policy in Fiji was this. In Fiji the Liberal government, though preferring leases, was prepared to assist development by not entirely preventing the sale of land to Europeans, where the grants appeared not to prejudice indigenous interests.

In 1905 governor Sir Everard im Thurn passed an ordinance permitting long leases and sale of native lands for public purposes strictly defined, subject to the approval of the governor-in-council. In August 1906 Sir G. Des Vœux, a former governor, drew attention to the sale of lands in Navuso in which he considered the rights of the Fijians insufficiently safe-guarded. Elgin obtained a report. The circumstances it revealed did not seem such as to open the transaction to serious question. Officials, however, pressed him to reconsider the advisability of allowing sales, which Lyttelton had sanctioned. Elgin agreed with them that where possible leases should be preferred to sales. He would not, however, forbid all sales. The whole process was under the control of the governor, which was a safeguard. He did not see why, if the money realised from sales were invested on behalf of the natives, the native owners should not benefit. Elgin had more to say:[2]

[1] CO. 111/556/26151 S/S to govr. 6 Aug 07, tel.
[2] CO. 83/85/14594, minute by E 4 Jun 07.

464

It is material to observe that on the one hand the native population is small and decreasing – and on the other, the extent of *unoccupied* land is large. That means that there can be no question of natives being left destitute, without land, for many years to come. I understand that it is accepted that the whole of this unoccupied land is the property of the native community. If so, it must of course stand: but a very different state of things prevails elsewhere, e.g. in Africa, where we freely dispose of unoccupied lands. But would it not be legitimate to invest the price of unoccupied land and from the proceeds of the fund so created provide for purposes of general utility to the native community, e.g. education?

It was decided that the governor should sanction sales only in exceptional circumstances. Where possible he should arrange that lands were leased.[1]

An Australian sugar company wanted a 99-year lease of most of the Rewa delta. The inhabitants were almost unanimously opposed to this lease, despite strong bribing. The Acquisition of Lands Ordinance 1906 was therefore passed, in order to facilitate the desire of the Colonial Sugar Refining Company to build a road and tramway along the west coast of Viti Levu. This ordinance authorised the governor to acquire land for 'any undertaking, proposal or policy which may appear to the governor in council desirable as directly benefiting the colony'. It was not disallowed. But as the powers given to the governor were so wide, he was instructed to exercise them with considerable caution, and to refer every case to the secretary of state for approval. It was feared that the powers might be exercised to facilitate schemes, which, though they were of public utility, might also be in the interest of private persons or companies.[2] Elgin wrote one of his best minutes on this question:

A great deal is said in some of these minutes about the 'unearned increment', of which the new Ordinance will deprive the natives. Do not let it be supposed that an unearned increment is anything more than a speculation. It may never exist. It may even be on the wrong side, if such an expression is allowable –

---

[1] Ibid. S/S to govr. 9 Sep 07.   [2] CO. 83/83/45341, S/S 28 Jan 07.

as the case in these papers shows, for the deterioration of the land has halved its annual value. Assuming that the owner has perfect freedom of choice between lease and sale, it is simply a question of judgment and of terms, whether sale or lease is most favourable for him. This is a commonplace of estate management. I do not of course dispute that in the dealings of a Government other considerations must arise, indeed that would be the second branch of my argument – but that only means that a Government may not have the freedom of choice which I presupposed.

A lease was not necessarily a more provident arrangement for the community than a sale. That was the crux of his argument:

In the case of an undeveloped country, beyond a doubt the first thing is to attract capital. If capital will not come on a leasehold tenure – and if its not coming will forfeit an increment, not only in respect of a limited area, but of the various forms in which a new and growing industry affects prosperity – would it really be good government to be pedantic as to the form of bargain? . .

This was a sharp retort to the doctrinaire advice tendered to him by Keith that sales ought not to be permitted at all.[1] Elgin could not think that any injustice was done, or ought to result from, sales under the control of the governor in special cases. When there was a sale the protective clauses should be enforced. The general rule, however, should be to lease rather than to sell.[2]

The 1906 ordinance was criticised in the House of Lords by Lord Stanmore on 16 July 1907. He acknowledged that Elgin was 'a man who has at heart in the truest and fullest sense native interests everywhere'. The compliment was rather diminished by adding the implication that Elgin probably knew more about conditions in India than in Fiji. He appealed to the secretary of state to give the Fijians protection. The

[1] CO. 83/86/8332, minute by E 29 Jun 07: CO. 83/85/20527, minute by Keith 10 Jun 07. The minutes were written *after* the desp. of 28 Jan 07 had been sent.
[2] CO. 83/86/8332, 29 Jun and 16 Jul 07.

British government of Fiji had no more right to take communal land in Fiji, except under particular circumstances, than any of the land of the British peers. In reply, Elgin reminded their lordships that in 1875 Carnarvon had distinctly declared the whole of the land to belong to the Crown, and that in 1893 the chiefs were willing to accept government control of the land. From this he deduced that the government clearly possessed powers over the land. There was ample room for the introduction of settlers, who would undertake development, since the population was only 86,000. The Fijians cultivated only 4,250,000 acres out of a total of 4,800,000. It was the duty of the government to take what steps they could to promote the 'settlement of the islands with a view to increasing their prosperity'. Like Stanmore, Elgin declared his distinct preference for leases rather than sales.[1]

In June 1907, the governor forwarded yet another ordinance. This was the Native Lands Amendment Ordinance, permitting sale or lease of Fijian lands to other, individual, Fijians. The officials, without consulting Elgin, asked for further information before giving a decision, stating their anxiety lest such ownership should merely prove a device under which lands held individually by a native Fijian might be disposed of to a non-native.[2] Elgin was naturally very cross when he discovered the existence of this elaborate and argumentative despatch.[3] He disagreed with part of it.

Land questions in Fiji were settled, at least for the time being, by Elgin's successor. The governor lost his battle. His desire to make a distinction between occupied and unoccupied, or waste, lands was rejected. The two must equally be regarded the property of the Fijians. There was no wish in London to prevent the best possible development of the waste lands, but

[1] PD. 178/473–83, 16 Jul 07. Elgin described the provisions for dealing with land in Fiji as entirely different from elsewhere. In other colonies, 'we reserve land for the natives necessary to their maintenance, and the Crown is permitted to dispose of the surplus lands to those whom the authorities consider to be most likely to be good settlers and to promote the prosperity of the Colony as a whole.'

[2] CO. 83/85/25489, S/S to govr 26 Oct 07.

[3] CO. 83/86/42776, minute by E 13 Jan 08.

Elgin's decision that the sale of waste lands should be exceptional, was upheld. The proceeds of leases, or, rarely, sales, when permitted, should be invested, and 'held in trust' for the benefit of Fijians, as Elgin had suggested. The proceeds should not be paid direct to native owners, in order to prevent them from squandering the money, and so to make sure that the benefits of development went to the community, not to the individual, and that succeeding generations 'may not have their interests sacrificed in favour of the present generation'.[1] Tenure had been 'essentially communal'; so in no circumstances was it desirable that an individual Fijian should be in a position to sell the land and pocket the money himself. The governor complained that this position would retard development, but the secretary of state stood firm. He had taken, Crewe said, 'the only decision which can be adopted with justice to the natives of the Colony'.[2] So far as the unoccupied lands were not used by or wanted for the native communities, they should be as far as possible developed in the interest of 'the islanders as a whole'. Whilst the government would not delimit land in actual occupation, they would not prevent the unoccupied land being leased, with the consent of the council and chiefs, to those willing to develop it.[3]

As in Africa, so in Fiji, the government wished to facilitate development, but only subject to the paramountcy of native interests, paternalistically regarded.

SOME REASONS FOR THE CAUTIOUS ATTITUDE TOWARDS DEVELOPMENT

The Liberal government under Elgin was not inactive in promoting the collection and diffusion of information, in improving medical and transport facilities, in promoting cotton growing, and in extracting money from the treasury for the benefit of the dependent portions of the empire. Despite

[1] CO. 83/88/25329, S/S to govr. 15 Jul 08.
[2] Ibid. 36456, 16 Oct 08. See H.L. 205 (Oct 08).
[3] PD. 192/1000–1, Crewe 16 Jul 08.

considerable progress, however, the attitude of the government towards development was predominantly one of caution. Caution, but not inaction. The reasons for this reflect the inherent assumptions of Edwardian government.

The most obvious limitation on development was the desire to avoid spending the British tax payer's money. Britain's empire was ever an empire on the cheap. The economical considerations of the treasury determined the extent of colonial office action. There were many things ministers, officials and governors would have liked to do, if only money had been available. They were denied a free hand, and always had to argue with the treasury. Projects suggested by governors had continually to be cut down or shelved.[1] Any tendency to commit protectorates to heavy capital expenditure was carefully watched. One reason why the colonial office to some extent shared treasury reluctance to call upon the British tax payer might have been the fear that to do so would create an awkward prejudice against the African possessions. For apart from the interest of the cotton industry, there was very little pressure for African development in England. In the case of Uganda, the government discerned trading possibilities long before British industry.[2] It was hard to apply money to Africa while many urgent and deserving objects at home were being kept waiting because of the large demands upon the British exchequer.[3] Development schemes were best argued on the ground that they would save the British tax payer money. Milner once described the colonial office as the Cinderella of the great public departments, standing a poor chance in the estimates battle with the treasury. Amery called the treasury a 'surly watch-dog'. These remarks were made after the First World War. Their applicability to the pre-war period is even greater. The policy of development was not then a positive one. The chief reason for interest in economic growth was the desire

[1] See pp. 470, 474 below; also CO. 533/19/1196 – £134,931 wanted for public works; CO. 96/440/16854, proposals for additions to roads and civil staff.
[2] CO. 536/21/37925.
[3] FO. 371/661/10715, minute by Grey.

to relieve expense to the British tax payer, to get rid of imperial grants-in-aid, to make colonies self-supporting. Self-supporting, that is, in what Tawney called 'the idiomatic Anglo-Saxon sense' of supporting, not only themselves, but English troops and officials as well.[1] What is true of the period of Elgin's tenure had long been true and was to remain unchanged.[2]

The traditional reluctance of the treasury to spend money on the empire was reinforced during the year 1907–8 by exceptionally unfavourable conditions in the money market. It was not an easy time for large financial operations. For example: in 1907 the governor of the Gold Coast requested that a loan of £1,300,000 be authorised for public works; but the Crown Agents reported that it was quite out of the question that any loan should be issued,

since the money and stock markets are in an extremely difficult and uncertain position, and it is impossible to say when they are likely to improve sufficiently to render it possible to place a loan on other than very onerous terms.[3]

The colonial office was still reluctant to take initiative in the general formulation of a policy of imperial development. Its tradition was to act as 'the "governor" of the steam engine and not the boiler'.[4] It was nearly axiomatic that colonial governors

[1] R. H. Tawney, *Business and politics under James I* (1958), p. 208.

[2] Even Chamberlain admitted the force of the limitation: 'If I had my way, I should, as I have often told you, treat it [Nigeria] as a great estate which must be developed, in the first instance at considerable expense to the mother country. Unfortunately, taxation has reached so high a level that the cry is all for economy, and we must I expect wait for a favourable opportunity before we can make such progress' (quoted by Perham, *Lugard*, ii, 228–9). Nobody, wrote Crewe, took a keener interest in malaria prevention than he did, but he thought it impracticable 'to suggest at this moment to the Mauritius government any expenditure of any sort, even for so good an object as this. The matter can, of course, be laid before them, but not directly, as though we urged it in any way' (CO. 167/787/46084, 19 Dec 08, minute on receipt of Ross's report). The colonial office quashed proposed improvements in the Lagos railway over a twelve mile stretch between Iddo and Aro; Crewe minuted: 'There seems to be a tendency to commit Southern Nigeria to heavy capital expenditure, which must be carefully watched, though no doubt a large part of it may be ultimately remunerative' (CO. 520/80/27797, 25 Aug 09).

[3] CO. 96/461/31883, S/S to govr 17 Sep 07.

[4] The phrase is Goldie's. See J. E. Flint, *Sir George Goldie and the making of Nigeria* (1960), p. 275.

470

overseas did the work and the planning, while the colonial office exercised control and supervision. Administration from Downing Street was 'the one rank heresy' which all officials shuddered at.[1] If any mistake was to be made in the colonial office, the officials preferred that it should be one of excess caution rather than the opposite. They regarded their essential function as making cautious criticism to check local enthusiasm. Their guiding principle was decentralisation. The staff of the office had not the time, even if they had the training, to take initiative.

Ministers had even less time for thinking out problems and policy. Elgin 'most entirely' agreed with Selborne and Milner that 'one has to go on doing things without any real time for thinking'. They were not attracted to speculations about the future, when there were so many routine problems to engage them.[2]

Long-term planning did not emerge. There was no sense of urgency. At the same time, there was a desire to avoid mistakes at all costs. Excessive precipitancy was more dangerous than excessive slowness in reforming Egypt, said Grey.[3] No doubt it was desirable to develop East Africa, said Elgin, 'but sometimes most haste worst speed'.[4] He did not believe in 'forcing' either protectorates or strawberries.[5] When Girouard proposed to gather all the Masai into a single reserve, Crewe's response was typically Edwardian:

it is evident that nothing must be done without a searching inquiry, all the more as there is no conceivable urgency. The

---

[1] CO. 446/50/25244, minute by Ommanney 31 Jul 05.

[2] Hence when Girouard wished to draw attention to the wider implications of his Nigerian transport policy, saying that Lake Chad would be only 400 miles from the railways, which would cross a river from which vessels could get to the lake, just before Kano, thus giving rise to a great opportunity for securing trade beyond British territories, Elgin responded in an incredibly pedestrian fashion: 'Nothing arises out of this at present, though it may in the future. I reserve my opinion' (CO. 446/63/25915, minute 28 Aug 07). Milner: *Nation and the Empire*, p. 292. EP, Selb. to E 25 Nov 07, E to Selb. 24 Jan 08; see also Grey, *Twenty-five years* (1925), i, 6.

[3] FO. 371/452/26600, to Gorst 31 Jul 08.

[4] CO. 533/20/27274, 3 Aug 06.   [5] CO. 533/25/23381.

land won't run away, and if Sir P. Girouard can prove his case, some delay in acting on his advice would be immaterial, whereas unjust action could never be repaired.[1]

Development was, as the report of the Northern Nigeria Lands Committee declared, subordinate in the exercise of governmental control to securing the interests of the natives. In theory at any rate, Crown colonies were administered chiefly in the interests of the inhabitants of the territories, and only secondly in accordance with the views of the British people (and not the merchants, a small and interested section of them) as represented in parliament.[2] In Nigeria the demand for trade guns stopped in 1908 after the duty had been increased from five to ten shillings. This led to immediate protests about resulting unemployment in Birmingham. But guns were dangerous toys for Africans. Humanitarian considerations prevailed. The government must be prepared to face the likelihood of further unemployment in Birmingham. Ministers and officials agreed to do what was best for Africa.[3]

The idea of trusteeship was employed in argument against rapid development. Trying to push development too rapidly tended, it was believed, to evils such as forced labour.[4] There seemed to be no difficulty about looking to the future when the government wanted to be cautious. A striking example of the use of the argument of trusteeship arose when the British South Africa Company began to promote a project to transmit electrical power from the Victoria Falls to the Rand. Churchill of course supported the syndicate responsible: 'I would much rather use the water sensibly for power than let it splash over in a useless stream.'[5] Rather an insensitive comment on one of the splendours of Africa, but it was all part of his technique of advocacy. Elgin was anxious about the protection of life and property from the conductor rail. The government, he said,

[1] CO. 533/72/9075, 18 Apr 10.
[2] CO. 96/462/9590 and 464/11011, minutes by Antrobus 19 Mar and 4 Apr 07.
[3] CO. 96/480/18095, Jan 08.
[4] See Olivier's opinion, quoted by K. Robinson, *Dilemmas of Trusteeship*, p. 58.
[5] CO. 417/449/8195, minute 12 Mar 07.

must do what they could to meet 'both the present and the possible future position there ... the lonely wilderness may become populated and we ought to provide for the contingency.'[1] The company was therefore asked to furnish further assurances about its proposals. Elgin similarly was not quite satisfied about the East Africa and Uganda Corporation Ltd, and its proposed electric railway linking Nairobi and Fort Hall. He did not think that the government should commit itself further than to arrange for a survey in the usual manner.[2] The company, however, wished to make its own survey. Churchill saw no objection: 'No preliminary consultation – involving fresh delays – is necessary. Let the survey be undertaken at once.' Elgin opened his minute with a formula which could scarcely be described as novel:

I cannot agree. [He proceeded:] We are Trustees for the future of this territory and I do not think we could properly push the matter through as proposed in Mr Churchill's minute. I think the usual course – not a new one, but founded on experience – is the right one, and that the Survey must be a Government Survey. . . . As to electricity – the promoters may or may not know what they are about. . . .[3]

In February 1907 it was decided that the government should make the survey.[4]

One of the main reasons why there was an almost deadening fear of making mistakes was that decisions were often taken on the basis of defective information, especially in the new African lands. Even in November 1909 an official complained that both in Uganda and in Kenya the government still suffered from want of information regarding their natural resources. The situation was improving, but it would be some time yet before a thorough economic survey had been made.[5] In 1906 the difficulty was thrown into sharp relief. Alternative proposals for the Eldama Ravine railway were submitted. The office

---

[1] CO. 417/432/24387, minute 12 Jul 06.
[2] CO. 533/20/11133, minute 16 May 06. See above p. 436.
[3] CO. 533/24/21688, minutes 4 Jul 06.   [4] CO. 533/24/41402.
[5] CO. 536/30/37519, minute by Read 20 Nov 09.

did not know enough of the topography and natural features of the territory to judge between them. The colonial office was often forced to rely on maps made by the Germans. For this deficiency, more blame attaches to the foreign office than to the colonial office, for they had been initially responsible for the new acquisitions in East Africa.[1]

One further reason for the slow pace of development by later standards may be appended. It was not the kind of reason for which one can usually find documentation. It was revealed in one of Crewe's minutes. The governor of the Gold Coast wanted to start a general scheme of public works to be financed by a loan of £2,000,000. Rejecting this proposal, Crewe remarked that one of the subsidiary objections

to a large programme extending over a long term of years – though it need not be mentioned in a despatch – is that governors are not permanent and immortal. A new man arrives, and administration is dull for him, unless he can discover some new plan of expenditure, and is not tied down to somebody's previous inventions.[2]

[1] CO. 533/25/40751.
[2] CO. 96/471/30469, minute 12 Nov 08. The reply despatch said the programme might be out of proportion to the financial resources of the colony (S/S to govr 13 Nov 08).

Conclusion

13 Elgin and Churchill at the Colonial Office: The Conduct of Business

In this chapter we shall consider some general characteristics of the way in which Elgin and Churchill conducted their routine business, and explore the relations between the ministers and their colonial service staff, and between themselves.

ELGIN AND THE COLONIAL SERVICE

Essentially an administrator rather than a politician, and very much an official mind, Elgin established good relations with the men in the colonial service, both at Whitehall and overseas. He held some distinctive views about the management of the colonial service. His homilies about the right conduct of public business, while they do not quite add up to a compendium of the whole duty of an official, are worth looking at. Churchill learned much from them.

Relations with governors. Elgin made one of his more important speeches at the Royal Colonial Institute on 25 April 1906. *The Times* described this speech as 'eminently statesmanlike', the *Morning Post* praised it for its soothing grace and tact, and the *Scotsman* received it as evidence that Elgin was 'thinking imperially', and compared him with Chamberlain; both had the reputation of being practical men of affairs, and, like his illustrious predecessor, Elgin was now adding 'lofty ideals to the gift of practical efficiency'. In this, his first public speech as colonial secretary, Elgin enunciated a principle of hearty co-operation between those at home and those abroad, and promised government support to the man on the spot:

My own personal conviction is that we must look more than anything else to secure the sympathy and support of the 'man on the spot'. . . . I deprecate the use of the word 'interference' as introducing an element of active opposition which would be entirely foreign to my position or to that of the government. . . . In my opinion this Empire must be strong to do its work, and to be strong it must be united.

He warmly testified to Selborne's loyalty.

Elgin required the 'man on the spot' to be loyal to the greater interests of the empire,[1] as he had been himself as viceroy. His Indian experience had taught him to appreciate services which colonial governors rendered, and to sympathise with their outlook. Governors did indeed receive considerable support from Elgin, much more than they would have received from Churchill. They recognised this gratefully. One of the most notable governors, H. Hesketh Bell, found Elgin 'very pleasant and appreciative'.[2] Generally speaking, a governor had a large amount of freedom,[3] the colonial office exercising supervision

---

[1] 'My view is that a governor, responsible to the Imperial Government while entitled to freedom of judgment and freedom of expression of his opinion, must always so govern the latter as to avoid conflict with any overt act of the Imperial Government' (EP, E to Selb. 26 May 06). See also speech at the Corona Club, June 1907: 'Our colonial service was like that of a ship, a crew, of which every part had different duties, but of which the whole could not succeed unless there was a close association and confidence one with the other.'

[2] H. Bell, *Glimpses of a governor's life*, p. 162, 2 Jun 07.

[3] Governors usually got their way. For example, Bell was allowed to double the hut tax in Ankole for a year as punishment for the murder of a government official, Galt. Elgin wrote: 'I don't much like the increased Hut Tax, but as the Commissioner thinks it necessary, I will not refuse to sanction' (CO. 536/7/30229, 18 Aug 06). Another example is found on the Trinidad files. The much respected governor, Sir H. Jackson, proposed the remission of a punitive additional house tax imposed on Port of Spain after riots in 1904. The officials said 'no'. Churchill thought that it was a matter in which he should be guided by the governor, but he agreed they should telegraph to discover whether the burden of paying off the cost of damage would be transferred from Port of Spain to the general community of Trinidad. Elgin agreed. The governor replied that no injustice would be felt by such a transfer. This was considered a sufficient answer. The official approval was couched in these terms: the secretary of state had 'considerable hesitation as to the advisability of the proposed remission, and in consenting to it, I have been guided not by the merits of the case – as I apprehend it – but solely by your re-iterated recommendation in favour of remission' (CO. 295/437/41669, govr to S/S 26 Oct 06, minutes 21 Nov and 3 Dec 06: 438/912, govr to S/S 20 Dec, minutes 11 and 13 Jan 07, S/S to govr 15 Jan 07).

rather than control. Indeed one of the biggest headaches of the colonial office was its heavy dependence on the judgment of the man on the spot.[1] A governor's freedom and authority had its limits, however. Matters which might become dangerous politically, such as punitive expeditions, were watched with great care. If for any reason, a colony was attracting public attention, it was much harder for the governor to impose his will. Because of this, Selborne in South Africa never stood much chance of getting his way with the Liberal government. Almost every recommendation which he made was turned down, though Elgin was careful to show that he appreciated Selborne's sense of frustration, which he could do the more readily, having himself been gallingly overruled as viceroy. Any governor who wanted to spend too much money was liable to meet a rebuff, as Sir John Rodger of the Gold Coast discovered.[2] If the slightest suspicion once began to attach to a man that his judgment was becoming faulty, his independence was doomed. In this period, Sierra Leone was not of special significance, but papers on its files almost always went before the secretary of state when the governor, Probyn, appeared to be on the verge of a nervous breakdown.[3]

The Liberal government fell out decisively with only one governor – Sir James Alexander Swettenham, governor of Jamaica. A very curious incident arose out of the Jamaica earthquake. It throws light not only on the government's attitude towards governors, but also reflects the paramount importance it attached to maintaining good relations with the United States. The United States very generously sent some warships to Kingston, the seat of the disaster; some American sailors were landed, and tried to help victims. The governor

[1] For example, dependence on Lugard's judgment on the expediency of recognising Miller's school in Northern Nigeria, see above, p. 394.

[2] See pp. 470 and 474.

[3] Antrobus noted in October 1907: 'I am anxious that Mr Probyn is going out of his mind. He has written some odd things lately . . .' (CO. 267/496/34704); see also 34705, and p. 200 above. A further example: at the end of 1907 it was feared Sir Cavendish Boyle, governor of Mauritius had quite lost grip of his administration (CO. 167/781/38952 and 783/9826, minutes by Hopwood).

behaved with remarkable discourtesy to the American admiral, Davis, who had, it is true, cast doubts on the adequacy of protection to property. He wrote a sarcastic letter to the Admiral, rejecting his offer of help as needless interference. This letter was published in newspapers on 21 January 1907. Churchill was so excited by it that he telegraphed to his chief: 'Hopwood and I think it plainly indefensible and wantonly insulting. In the event of refusal to withdraw, we should recall him at once.' Elgin entirely agreed and immediately telegraphed to the office.[1] Next day an official telegram instructed Swettenham to withdraw the letter: 'both in tone and expression, it is highly improper and especially unbecoming to His Majesty's representative in addressing an officer of a friendly power engaged upon an errand of mercy.' The governor was also asked to telegraph an apology.[2]

Swettenham responded by getting on his high horse and tendering his resignation. Elgin found the whole affair 'very troublesome', and was at a loss to know what to do.[3] It seemed best to wait for a few days before deciding whether to accept the resignation. Then he consulted Grey, who agreed that Elgin ought to raise the matter with the cabinet. Churchill disapproved of this as equivocation. The governor, he wrote, should be relieved forthwith.[4] Churchill disliked the governor's bumptious attitude to the Americans. For his part, the governor seems to have acted partly from a fear of the expansive aims and diplomacy of the United States in the Caribbean. By the time the cabinet discussed the incident on 2 February, a telegraphic report on the affair had not been furnished by Swettenham. The governor was therefore peremptorily required to send such a report.[5] When it had been received, and with full

[1] EP, tel. WSC to E and reply tel. 21 Jan 07.

[2] CO. 137/661/2557, tel. S/S to govr 22 Jan 07. The text of Swettenham's letter is most conveniently read in the *Annual Register for 1907*, pp. 466–7.

[3] EP, E to Lady E 30 Jan 07.

[4] CO. 137/655/3699, minute 30 Jan 07. Elgin hoped to treat the governor more gently, but felt it was his own fault (for not telegraphing the fact that he had got into difficulties) if he now was reprimanded. He thought him a 'rather rough' man but a good officer (EP, E to WSC 25 Jan 07).

[5] CAB. 41/31/1, CB to King 2 Feb 07.

information before them, the cabinet concluded that the contretemps was 'due to a pure misunderstanding, with some hastiness of temper on one side and the other'. As the governor had withdrawn the offending letter, and as his conduct in the hurricane and in the earthquake crises had otherwise been creditable, the cabinet decided not to accept his resignation, but to ask him to remain in his appointment for the present.[1] This decision did not please Churchill who still wanted the governor's blood. To allow Swettenham to remain in Jamaica for the full term of his appointment would be, he said, 'detrimental to the public interest'.[2] Eventually the governor played into Churchill's hands. When Swettenham's full despatch was received in March, Elgin was far from satisfied with the governor's explanation for the delays in telegraphing particulars of the episode: 'It is absurd to say that he did not telegraph material facts regarding an international incident because of the expense.'[3] Elgin now decided to recall Swettenham. Still worse was to come. On learning his fate, the governor dared to accuse the colonial office of an unchristian attitude towards him. He tried to demonstrate the unfairness of the policy which 'seems to resemble that denounced in St Matthew, XXIII, 4'. Churchill refused to read the despatch in which this fulmination occurred. Elgin thought it his duty to read it. He did so with great sorrow. He would have preferred to suppress it, but he agreed that in all the circumstances it must remain on record.[4]

Swettenham left Jamaica in May 1907 and was replaced by Olivier. Elgin and Churchill decided not to send him a valedictory despatch, lest, as Churchill put it, they provoked a maledictory acknowledgment. Elgin was quite upset. He had never before parted on these terms with an officer who had served under him.[5] He was too sorry to feel any

[1] Ibid. /2, 6 Feb 07.   [2] CO. 137/655/5669, minute 20 Feb 07.
[3] CO. 137/656/9295, minute by E 20 Mar 07.
[4] CO. 137/657/14271, govr. to S/S 4 Apr 07, minutes by WSC and E 27 and 29 Apr 07.
[5] CO. 137/658/17945, minutes by WSC and E; 29 and 30 May.

481

resentment at such a sad ending of an honourable career.[1]

Not very long after Swettenham's disgrace, and when Olivier was installed as governor of Jamaica in his stead, a minute of the new governor attracted Elgin's attention. The ensuing correspondence contained a profusion of theorising by the earl. Olivier pronounced against the execution of capital sentences, 'save possibly in exceptional circumstances', as 'inexpedient in the best interest of civilised communities'. Elgin thought advocacy of abolition of capital punishment singularly improper, and went to great lengths to impress his view upon the idealistic, Fabian governor. Elgin admitted that a great many people disliked capital punishment. He also admitted that personally he had experienced the distaste which the duty of confirming such sentences inspired;

but I put it to you, that it is not expedient that a governor should thus declare himself in an official minute. It is his duty to carry out the law, and I do not see how he can be justified in allowing his personal feelings to prevail. It might be a positive danger in some communities, and perhaps Jamaica is one. I do not know how far these minutes become public property, but I do urge you to exercise more caution in the expression of personal feeling.

Olivier must have regarded Elgin as the stuffiest possible defender of discipline and established procedures. He defended himself quite ingeniously, but Elgin was not convinced, especially by the proposition that a governor, because in a sense he exercised the powers of king and minister, could, on his own judgment, set aside the statute law:

The governor is not shot into his position from the clouds – he voluntarily assumes it under all the existing conditions, and he cannot be justified in setting aside any one of these pre-existing conditions of his own motion. . . . Capital punishment remains the law throughout the British empire. No governor can possibly assume office without recognising . . . that he will be called upon to administer that law. . . .

[1] Ibid. 17940, minute 31 May 07. Churchill noted that the governor had made an unkind point about Admiral Davis's spelling the word thieves incorrectly: 'It is characteristic of all his writings – an irrelevant, petty and spiteful kink in his composition – literary and personal.'

Speaking as an ex-viceroy, he had no hesitation in saying that he thought Olivier had entirely missed the true point. A man's appointment as governor did not throw upon him the obligation of deciding what he would do if he had the powers of king and home secretary combined, but it did put upon him the obligation of observing the law which both king and home secretary must obey.

It would be a satisfaction to me, I will not put it higher than that, if I could hear from you, still privately, an assurance that you would, during the remainder of our association bear in mind the opinion (shall I say the ruling?) – which I have now given on this point.[1]

This highly characteristic letter reminds us once again not only of Elgin's punctilious sense of public propriety, but also of his essential modesty, his diffidence in casting his conviction in the form of a fiat.

Relations with the colonial office staff. Elgin got on well with all the senior officials. He admired Hopwood, the permanent under-secretary, because he never spared himself, never quarrelled, and had a judgment both quick and correct. Of the assistant under-secretaries, C. P. Lucas was the one he thought most highly of: popular, likeable, a man of long experience, of very high academic and literary distinction, he was perhaps 'a little lacking in decision'. R. L. Antrobus was very thorough and good, but worked rather slowly, and wrote rather short minutes. H. W. Just was almost the opposite, with a diffuse and rambling style, but with 'an unsurpassed capacity for work', an immense knowledge of South Africa, and a selfless willingness to help. He liked H. B. Cox, considering him a sound lawyer with clever diplomatic gifts into the bargain. Of the less senior clerks, he rated Fiddes, Read, Davis and Keith, in their various ways, the best.[2]

[1] EP, E to Olivier 26 Aug and 22 Oct 07.
[2] EP, E to Crewe 7 May 08 (draft). Elgin also praised Lucas and Just in the House of Lords, announcing their appointments in the dominions department PD. 181/1070-1, 22 Aug 07).

His business experience and his knowledge of Indian government, together with his Gladstonian belief in the serious nature of the responsibilities of public office,[1] made Elgin rather shocked at some of the practices and attitudes of the colonial office. It was an arrogant institution, an ivory tower of proud, patronising and precedent-ridden pundits. Officials had a very remarkable confidence in their own opinions, even when they were in opposition to the highest authorities. Hopwood, coming into the office as an outsider, was struck by this, and complained that a great deal of time was wasted every day in endeavouring to convince or coerce. It seemed to be a tradition of the office, and he suspected that Chamberlain, 'up to a certain point seems to have fomented contentiousness'.[2]

Arrogance manifested itself in one small way Elgin found most irritating. This was a habit of scribbling comments in the margins of incoming despatches, underlining portions of the text. Elgin stopped this practice, feeling it to be incompatible with proper respect to crown representatives. He also disliked officials passing pedantic and adverse judgment on despatches.[3] They must also, when dealing with subjects which specially interested them, restrain their enthusiasm, and not write unduly long minutes.[4]

On several occasions Elgin was annoyed by being led into making decisions which subsequently appeared foolish in the light of fuller information, especially when such information

[1] For example, commenting on Lord Carrington's 'deplorable want of knowledge' on a land bill under debate, Elgin wrote: 'He says such funny things that the house treats the whole thing as more or less of a joke – but that doesn't tend to edification or good legislation' (EP, to Lady E 14 Dec 06).

[2] EP, Hopwood to E 4 Jan 08.

[3] For example, he complained about the 'unjustifiable irritation' with which officials commented on Egerton's despatch concerning a penal code for Southern Nigeria (520/35/14841, Sep 06). He disliked reading a remark such as: 'Sir A. Swettenham's cloistral ignorance of the agricultural realities of his island trips him up repeatedly' on the Jamaican files (CO. 137/652/41019, minute by E 8 Dec 06).

[4] Ibid. Olivier wrote one minute which was nine foolscap pages long, and in addition he interleaved every page of the despatch on which he was commenting, with further remarks. Such commentary Elgin found far too long for practical purposes.

could have been supplied to him in the first instance. The Nigerian files provide a good example. A sum of £200 had been stolen from the guardroom at Ibadan, where it had been kept by Major Reeve-Tucker, instead of in his safe. Elgin inclined towards treating the major mercifully, and to writing off the whole loss, because, although he thought it incautious, he could not discover anything to suggest that it was unusual to keep cash in a guardroom. It then appeared that his advisers had assumed his familiarity with rule 130 of the financial instructions of the West Africa Frontier Force, which stated that wherever an officer had a safe he was to put public money into it. Elgin lectured his staff for their presumption:

This case is a good example of the manner in which minutes should *not* be written. The decision I gave was on the minutes as written. . . . It is reasonable . . . that the governor in his despatch took this knowledge for granted in the *officers of this department*; but it is wholly unreasonable that these officers should not inform me when they ask for my decision. What can I know of rule 130 – or rule 100 – of the West Africa Frontier Force – unless my attention is properly drawn to them?

Had the papers gone beyond the office he would have adhered to his original directive, but as he understood that no action had been taken, he agreed to the imposition of a penalty of £20, for, as his former minute indicated, he thought that Major Tucker had been careless.[1]

A further intermittent source of difficulty was the habit of committing the secretary of state to a view, on relatively important matters, without consulting him. For instance, Elgin was not shown an outgoing despatch to Fiji until several months after it had been sent. It was a reply to the governor of Fiji's defence against criticisms of his land policy, which were made in the House of Lords. Nor had he even been shown the governor's comments on the debate, although Elgin himself had spoken in it. Then, as it turned out, Elgin disagreed with part of the argument sent out in his name, because it was

[1] CO. 147/169/17398, minutes 26 May and 15 Jun 06.

inconsistent with his public utterance. He objected forcibly to a procedure which might land him in such inconsistencies. The official who drafted the despatch admitted that it went 'somewhat beyond' anything Elgin had said in the House of Lords.[1] At about the same time, it was discovered that a circular despatch concerning the submission of quarterly reports from Australasian colonies was sent out without Elgin's knowledge. Again he protested at not being consulted. Two of his predecessors differed in opinion. He was said to agree with one of them. In fact he did not agree with either.[2] The colonial office, it seems, had lapsed into slack habits under Lyttelton, who had hardly aspired to comprehensive mastery of business.

Elgin not only asserted himself against the arrogance of the office. He was far from automatically accepting drafts laid before him. He recast a despatch suspending all preparations for a school for the sons of emirs in Northern Nigeria, in order to make it more direct.[3] He criticised a draft on the withdrawal of the garrison of St Helena because it made two false assumptions. He removed words suggesting gratuitous pessimism about the difficulties which might attend withdrawal; he added words of sympathy and encouragement; he offered a practical suggestion for alternative employment in a new flax industry.[4] A despatch on religious catechism in Jamaican schools he cut to half its length, omitting much debatable matter.[5] He never accepted any advice upon railways without the closest personal scrutiny.[6] He overruled even the combined weight of Churchill and Hopwood when these two proposed to grant unconditional British nationality to Boers settled in Angola; he refused, lest they might raise up another uitlander question.[7] When the temperance committee of the United Free Church of Scotland complained about the supposedly deleterious effects of the liquor traffic in the Gold Coast, it was Elgin who saw most clearly what the reply should be. Officials suggested asking the

[1] CO. 83/86/42776, 13 Jan 08. See also p. 467 above.
[2] CO. 418/55/27973, 23 Feb 08.   [3] CO. 446/62/15068.
[4] CO. 247/165/25280, minute, 19 Aug 06.
[5] CO. 137/650/10465, 31 Mar 06.   [6] E.g. CO. 54/702/27681.
[7] CO. 417/443/23444, minute 19 Jul 07.

committee to prove its allegations, because in the office they had a mass of information which did not support the allegations. Elgin was convinced that this was not the best reply to make:

Anybody who knows anything of the working of causes which, like temperance, appeal to the emotional side of human nature, will recognise, I think, that if direct evidence is available it is better to produce it than to make a demand which will have no result.

And so he arranged for a concise statement of facts to be sent.[1] Sometimes Elgin decided not to send replies, a course of action which rarely occurred to any of the officials or to Churchill. Deakin was his favourite victim for this treatment. Correspondence which had become futile by being too long drawn out must be allowed to cool. Misrepresentations and self-congratulatory crowings should be ignored.[2]

Elgin was very properly cautious in making decisions; he did not make up his mind in a hurry. He tended not to do anything unless it was really unavoidable, frequently deferring a decision until he had fuller information, especially if he would otherwise have been relying on telegraphic reports. Sometimes he ended his minutes with a query instead of an order. Despite some tough phrases and taut argument, his minutes were quite often inconclusive. This does not mean to say that he was incompetent. Readers of these pages may judge for themselves how far it is correct to describe Elgin as finding the work of the colonial office beyond him, and therefore leaning heavily upon his officials.[3] Certainly this was not the opinion of his colleague Haldane, even at the beginning of their period in office. No man, Haldane realised, was less in the hands of his officials:

He is a man who will have his own opinions, but who will not form them till he has full material and will then carry them tenaciously into action. He is absolutely master of the colonial office.[4]

[1] CO. 96/452/15615, 7 Jun 06.
[2] CO. 418/45/43463, minute 6 Dec 06 on channels of communication; 60/11989 on visit of U.S. fleet, 532/1/44639, minute 14 Feb 08.
[3] As is alleged in C.H.B.E., iii, by R. B. Pugh, p. 746.
[4] Quoted by M. Perham, Lugard, ii, The years of authority, p. 241.

Did Elgin have the sort of mastery which can afford not to be dictatorial? Quite often, against his judgment, he let Churchill, or a governor, have his own way. The formula, 'if X considers it necessary, I will not dissent', frequently recurs among his minutes.[1]

RELATIONS BETWEEN ELGIN AND CHURCHILL

Elgin and Churchill were in closer accord upon Transvaal problems than any other; for the remainder, the secretary of state arrived at his decisions as often as not from disagreement with his parliamentary under-secretary; they diverged often on Kenya, invariably on Natal and always on Ceylon.

It has generally been supposed that the relationship between Elgin and Churchill was a difficult one.[2] Edward Marsh, who had good opportunities for observing things from Churchill's side as his private secretary, described Elgin, none too sympathetically, as 'a rugged old thane of antique virtue'. Winston regarded him, Marsh thought, with 'impatient respect, recognising his four-square stability and his canniness, but desiderating initiative and dash'. What Elgin thought of Churchill Marsh was never able to discover, but he conjectured that 'their qualified esteem was mutual'.[3]

[1] For example, Churchill felt strongly that the principal speeches in the Transvaal parliament should be published in the Chinese Labour blue book, so Elgin would not veto the idea. But he hoped publication would not be taken as a precedent. He thought too much was published anyway: it was unnecessary and wasteful. He appointed a departmental committee on official publications to cut down waste and costs in October 1907 (CO. 291/121/26386, minute 25 Jul 07; CO. 323/528/17848).

[2] Lugard told Austen Chamberlain about a discussion on Nigerian railways at which Elgin 'could hardly sit in his chair' when Winston spoke, 'snubbed him and interrupted him' (A. Chamberlain, *Politics from inside*, p. 79, 3 May 07). An exception to the general interpretation was 'Ephesian', C. E. B. Roberts, who writes that Churchill held Elgin 'in highest regard, thinking his consideration for him all the more remarkable because he knew Elgin was previously prejudiced against him: his relations with Lord Elgin are excellent' (*Winston Churchill* (1929) p. 126).

[3] E. Marsh, *A number of people: a book of reminiscences* (1939), p. 150. This statement is fair and very carefully considered, but C. Hassall, *Edward Marsh* (1959), p. 122, needlessly glosses the statement about 'qualified esteem' by suggesting it was a euphemism. P. Mendelssohn, *Age of Churchill*, i, 256, follows Hassall in this.

Undoubtedly Churchill sorely tried Elgin's patience. Like Gulliver he found 'by experience that young men are too opinionative and volatile to be guided by the sober dictates of their seniors'.[1] When Elgin accepted Churchill as under-secretary, he knew that he himself had no easy task. He resolved to give Churchill access to all the business,[2] but to keep control – and to curb his temper. When it was all over, he reviewed the relationship as it had worked out:

I think I may say I succeeded, certainly we have had no quarrel during the two and a half years, on the contrary, he has again and again thanked me for what he has learned and for our pleasant personal relations, and I have taken a keen interest in his ability and in many ways attractive personality. But all the same I know quite well that it has affected my position *outside the Office*, and the strain has often been severe.[3]

Elgin did his best to check Churchill's exuberance – not always with the success which so well-meaning and public-spirited an effort deserved. The real point of difficulty in the relationship was Churchill's ambition. He hoped to become a full cabinet minister as soon as possible. In his attempt to focus attention upon himself, unwittingly, perhaps, at least in part, he depreciated Elgin. He tended to maintain separate and direct contact with the men in high office. His public reputation grew at Elgin's expense. This difficulty for Elgin certainly did not escape notice at the time. Fitzmaurice, and even Lyttelton commented on it.[4] Three weeks before Asquith actually became prime minister, Churchill was laying his plans for obtaining cabinet rank. In the first instance, he asked unashamedly for the reversion of the colonial office, claiming that, during the past two years, 'practically all the constructive action and all the parliamentary exposition has been mine'. The first part of

---

[1] Swift, *Gulliver's Travels*.

[2] E wrote to Churchill when necessary at generous length: he seems to have written more to Churchill than Churchill did to him. On 3 Jun 06 he apologised for writing so much, 'but I wish as usual to show my whole mind to you'. Churchill complained that he was not seeing papers (CO. 54/700; Petrie, *Austen Chamberlain*, p. 198): if so the fault was not Elgin's.

[3] EP, E to Crewe 7 May 08 (draft). [4] See pp. 513 and 520.

the claim was unjustified. He also claimed, and fairly, to have the advantage of knowing the work thoroughly. In addition, he considered himself to have established excellent personal relations in the right quarters, and to be undertaking work which was 'well within the compass of my strength and knowledge'.[1] If this is a sample of Churchill's loyalty, no wonder Elgin suffered strain.

Ambition, however unpleasant its methods, was understandable. But there were two things about Churchill which Elgin found bewildering. One was the frankness of his minutes, sometimes involving an apparent indifference to concealing from the office his disagreements with his chief. Such indifference Elgin thought not merely disloyal, but unbecoming and destructive of the proper conduct of government affairs. The other characteristic mystifying to Elgin was the streak of levity and irresponsibility in Churchill, which probably resulted from a compulsion always to be doing something. Churchill could concoct a cause without always bothering to distinguish between the important and the unimportant.

The first characteristic has been remarked many times in these pages, and needs little further elaboration. The disagreements frequently concerned small personal cases about unfortunate individuals, upon which Churchill thought that the officials were taking much too harsh a line.[2] From the very beginning, Elgin asked Churchill to mention such matters to him directly, either verbally, or in a private letter, before minuting on the files officially. More explosive issues also, were

---

[1] Asq. 11/10–11, WSC to Asquith 14 Mar 08.

[2] Perhaps one further example may be given. The executive council of Mauritius decided to reduce the pension of Mr E. Labour of the police. Twice the decision was reconsidered. The officials were opposed to interference, but Churchill appealed to Elgin to help the accused: 'The system of saying that a man is inadequately punished, two years after his offence has been disposed of, and therefore making a purely arbitrary deduction from his pension – not warranted by any clearly expressed principle – is not in my opinion healthy.' Elgin minuted crossly: 'I have given a great deal more time to his case than its importance deserved. In the result, I cannot see any great principle involved, and I would accept the decision of those on the spot' (CO. 167/776/47425, minutes 1 and 3 Jan 07).

best minuted upon with great caution. In most minutes, Elgin pointed out, Churchill and he were compelled, as members of the government, to judge issues from a standpoint different from that of the office staff:

We must take political considerations into account. *They* are bound not to do so.

I want to put it to you that where the political element comes in, the less *we* write the better. I hope I may say that we know each other well enough now not to scruple to say what we think if we confer, or to hesitate to compromise if that becomes necessary. But I feel very strongly that nothing of that ought to appear on the Minutes, if it can be avoided.[1]

He urged the need for a pact 'only to quarrel out of school'.[2]

Churchill's apparent desire to create work was even more tiresome. Sometimes he seemed to write papers simply to amuse himself.

Winston is a curious impulsive creature [Elgin wrote to his wife]. He came in on Friday when I was looking at a paper on which he had written a homily about the duty of receiving deputations, which anybody would have thought directed to me. I said 'You have been rather hard on me here'. 'On you – Oh no – you always see them and they like to come to you.' So he seized the paper and tore it up – 'I meant that for what the Department had written.'[3]

It was always difficult to know whether or not to take Churchill seriously, but Elgin consistently gave him the benefit of the doubt. Churchill sprang to the defence of a detained African chief, Sekgoma, with one of his most teasing minutes, which seemed determined to make work and to invite trouble.

After a usurpation of twenty years' duration, Sekgoma had been removed from the Batawana chieftainship in Ngamiland, Bechuanaland. His suspension from office was in accordance with the wishes of the great majority of the tribe, among whom

---

[1] EP, E to WSC 3 Nov 06 (photocopy).
[2] Ibid. 21 Jan 08.   [3] EP, 16 Jun 07.

he had the reputation of being a bad character, whom they wished to replace by the legitimate chief Mathibi, who was now twenty-four. As Sekgoma was not taking his deprivation quietly, he was put into detention. Selborne thought that he should be deported to avoid a general disturbance. Only Churchill saw fit to question this recommendation fiercely:

We cannot imprison him or deport him without flat violation of every solid principle of British justice. As at present advised I could not undertake even to attempt a defence of the lawless deportation of an innocent man upon an informal *lettre de cachet*. If we are going to embark on this sort of law-breaking and autocratic action, where are we going to stop? What kind of injustice is there that would not be covered by precedents of this kind? If we are going to take men who have committed no crime, and had no trial, and condemn them to life-long imprisonment and exile in the name of 'State policy' why stop there? Why not poison Sekgoma by some painless drug? No argument, that will justify his deportation to the Seychelles, will not also sustain his removal to a more sultry clime. If we are to employ medieval processes, at least let us show medieval courage and thoroughness. Think of the expense that would be saved. A dose of laudanum, costing at the outside five shillings, is all that is required. There would be no cost of maintenance, no charges for transportation, no legal difficulties, no need to apply to the Portuguese, no fear of the habeas corpus. Without the smallest money or expense the peace of the Protectorate would be secured, and a 'dangerous character' obnoxious to the Government, removed.

If however, as I apprehend, Secretary of State would be averse to this procedure, the next best thing is to obey the law, and to act with ordinary morality, however inconvenient.

Secretary of State was very cross. He did not think it necessary to carry the argument so far as a five-shilling dose of laudanum – so Elgin's rejoinder begins. He did not mince his words. 'This man is a savage – and is said to be contemplating proceedings in defiance of all law to disturb the peace.' As he saw it, the measures which had only narrowly averted fighting had resulted inevitably in Sekgoma's detention. Elgin ended on a militant note: he at any rate, was ready to take his share of the responsibility for the preservation of peace. This responsibility was, of course, to a Liberal, the primary function of African government.

This minute on Sekgoma reflects many of Churchill's characteristics. It is audacious in the extreme. Indeed it is doubtful whether there could be found anywhere in the history of British government a more audacious minute than this by a mere under-secretary of state. Moreover it reduces the argument to absurdity. On the other hand, it shows an awareness of the necessity of safeguarding the fundamental principles of British life. It is a splendidly written piece of prose. It could scarcely have been more carefully prepared if it had been a draft for a major public speech, as in fact so many of Churchill's minutes were. It has the characteristic and favourite words, solid, courage, sultry. And it has the typical flash of impish humour – hell, the more sultry clime. Yet all this effort and brilliance had gone into an ephemeral issue of no intrinsic importance, at least at that date, concerning an insignificant and unpopular usurping chief: into an issue which was properly decided on the spot. No other minister, let alone an official, would have questioned whether Sekgoma ought even to be in detention, or have seized upon the case in order to squeeze out of it issues of major principle. It is a teasing minute. The humour and the irony call its seriousness into question. It is in this sense, irresponsible. Nobody ever contrived to get so much fun out of official business as Churchill.

It was decided to detain Sekgoma for such period as would enable the young Mathibi to establish his position completely. Elgin thought that Sekgoma could be more easily managed in a detention compound in the protectorate; setting him free would certainly result in the 'calamity of a breach of the peace'. He accepted Churchill's representations so far as to tell Selborne that Sekgoma's present detention was an act of state for which no actual legal authority existed, and so a special proclamation was issued, indemnifying the officers who had detained him. Elgin also agreed to veto deportation, as too troublesome, and objectionable in principle. Churchill, finally, succeeded in

493

adding to the despatch the observations that Sekgoma had not been formally condemned, and that his power to disturb the peace might prove transitory.[1]

One of the stories which has found its way into the folklore of political history describes how Churchill wrote a long memorandum for Elgin, ending with the words 'These are my views', and how Elgin calmly minuted upon it, 'But not mine'. This, and similar stories, is indeed well within the spirit of what happened. Elgin and Churchill had endless disagreements of a trivial sort.[2] Churchill suggested shipping goods to and from East Africa on German, instead of British steamship lines, because their freight rates were cheaper: Elgin denounced this as declaring war 'against the flag'.[3] Elgin's hypersensitive patriotism also surfaced in a clash of opinion after he had made arrangements for 7000 silver medals to be struck for the troops engaged in operations against the Zulus. Churchill described this as a 'silver badge of shame'; Elgin retorted: 'Emphatically No. This will be worn by men who did their duty in obedience to orders, and did it well.'[4] A fantastic number of hours was spent in drafting the answers to parliamentary questions alone. Elgin frequently deleted the more outrageous portions of Churchill's draft answers.[5] A notable instance was the drafting of an answer to Colonel Wedgwood's question whether the state, the African or the white planter would obtain the benefit of enhanced land values in the regions through which the Northern Nigerian railway would pass. Churchill deleted Ommanney's draft reply. Elgin then superimposed a cross on Churchill's deletion, commenting: 'some of this is a little

---

[1] CO. 417/434/38258, minutes 23 Oct 06, tel. S/S to Selb. 31 Oct, desp. 10 Nov 06.

[2] A. Chamberlain, *Politics from inside*, p. 459. A colonial office official told Dame Margery Perham that when Churchill minuted upon a certain proposal: 'I cannot take the responsibility for doing this', Elgin wrote underneath: 'I can' (*Lugard*, ii, 270). For instances of minor disagreements, see CO. 520/43/10503, CO. 418/47/1590, CO. 54/708/19620, CO. 533/35/44142. Churchill thought the governor of Jamaica's despatch on the restoration of Kingston after the earthquake 'very sensible'; Elgin added: 'Perhaps – I am not sure' (CO. 137/656/8166, 7 and 9 Mar 07).

[3] CO. 533/20/15345, 26 May 07.

[4] CO. 179/243/23725, minutes 5 and 6 Jul 07.   [5] E.g. CO. 179/238/17539.

dangerous', and substituting a briefer version of Ommanney's non-committal answer.[1] When a photograph of Kikuyu being flogged by Grogan was forwarded from Kenya, Churchill recommending publishing the photo: underneath his minute Elgin wrote: 'No – I do not care to publish.'[2] Shortly after the formation of the new Transvaal government, a question was put down in the House of Commons asking whether or not the Transvaal government would reduce the size of the South African Constabulary in the Transvaal. Churchill proposed to reply that substantial reductions were certainly to be expected; Elgin deleted this, because it unfairly forestalled the opinion the new government might come to: the answer should simply say that no instructions for reduction had yet been given.[3] 'I am sorry that I entirely disagree with Mr Churchill's minute' was a typical opening formula in Elgin's minutes.[4] They disagreed about censuring a dead man: Churchill called for 'a severe and measured reprimand' on the late Mr Crewe Read for flogging Africans in Southern Nigeria; Elgin, however, was horrified at the idea of censuring the dead.[5] Churchill read into an advance notice of a public meeting in Colombo to form a Labour Union, 'a serious and reasoned indictment of the Administration of Ceylon'; Elgin read the document carefully, but could not accept it as a reasoned, certainly not as a just indictment: 'No action seems necessary. . . .'[6]

Their disagreements, whether on drafting or policy, did not arise from animosity, and never grew into a quarrel. To some extent, each of them sometimes liked to argue a course of action simply as a means of being sure that they were arriving at the right answer. Both of them sometimes maintained a point of view without believing in it very deeply, in order to test the strength of the other's case.[7] Elgin never acted without

[1] CO. 446/57/45905; see also: Perham, *Lugard*, ii, 269.

[2] CO. 533/29/15843, minutes 31 May 07.

[3] CO. 291/121/18954, 5 Jun 07.

[4] E.g. Elgin on Churchill's opposition to the ratification of the International Wireless Telegraphy convention (CO. 323/520/42027, 29 Nov 06).

[5] CO. 520/38/2149.   [6] CO. 54/709/26989, minutes 5 and 7 Aug 07.

[7] EP, E to WSC 27 Dec 05.

Churchill's concurrence if he could see his way to obtaining it. Above all, he never forgot that Churchill in the House of Commons had 'the labouring oar in the defence of our policy'.[1] The tact with which Elgin handled Churchill must clearly have been prodigious. That very intelligent man, Haldane, often told Elgin how much he admired his management of the young Churchill.[2] These two men were much more appreciative of each other than might be supposed. At a moment when there was a chance that Churchill might have been promoted, Elgin wrote:

I have been dreading every post to find the rumours true and that I was to lose your help. You might think it unkind if I said I 'hoped' not to hear – but however it may turn out, I shall always look back on our co-operation during this year of toil and strife with peculiar satisfaction and with real gratitude to you, not only for the courage and ability with which you have fought our case – but for the invariable consideration you have shown for me and my opinions.[3]

The last remark is hardly ironical. Cynics may, however, wonder whether it indicates rather the way in which Elgin wished to be treated than the way in which he had been treated. Churchill was evidently pleased to have such a kind letter. He replied in a generous, if slightly patronising way, that he had learned from Elgin's instruction and example a very great deal in the conduct of official business which he might otherwise have remained permanently ignorant of, if he had gone elsewhere. He valued highly the words of approval which his indulgent chief had bestowed.[4] Towards the end of their association, Churchill wrote a short letter about a difference of opinion on retrenched official civil servants from the Transvaal, saying simply:

It would never be possible for me to quarrel with you because your frank and invariable kindness always removes at once from my mind any trace of vexation which may arise from the tiresome course of business.[5]

[1] bid. 2 Apr 07. [2] EP, E to Lady E 16 Nov 06. [3] EP, WSC to E 27 Dec 06.
[4] bid. 30 Dec 06. [5] Ibid. 22 Feb 08.

There is no reason to doubt the sincerity of these letters. They are not just formal exchanges. Sir Almeric Fitzroy, clerk to the privy council, asked Churchill about his relationship with Elgin, as he had commonly heard it said that their differences were acute, and as language not at all respectful to his chief was frequently attributed to Churchill:

I was therefore agreeably surprised to find him speak of him in terms of the most cordial loyalty and admiration. They did not know each other before they became colleagues, and Winston frankly admitted that Elgin probably had prejudices not altogether in his favour; but nothing he said could exceed the confidence and consideration with which he had been treated.[1]

For his part, Elgin undoubtedly admired Churchill's ability, found him most stimulating at all times, and often even attractive.[2]

CHURCHILL: AN ASSESSMENT

Churchill at the colonial office presents a curious combination of magisterial statesman and mischievous schoolboy. The Pitt in him jostled with the Puck in him. He was just as capable of producing a rash and unrealistic suggestion as he was of producing a reasonable and statesmanlike one.[3] Could anything be more different than his first memorandum on the Transvaal constitution question,[4] and his minute on the scheme for a Salvation Army settlement in Southern Rhodesia?[5] In the case of Booth's scheme, Churchill's talents were lavished ineffectually upon magnifying the importance of a very vague and eccentric proposal out of all proportion. In the case of the Transvaal constitution, his gifts were exercised on a matter of acknowledged high policy, with considerable effect. And yet

---

[1] Fitzroy, *Memoirs*, i, 290, 7 Apr 06. [2] See p. 489.

[3] Masterman: 'He is just an extraordinarily gifted boy, with genius and astonishing energy' (L. Masterman, *C. F. G. Masterman*, p. 97). Gardiner noted that 'he has the curiosity and animation of a child in fairyland' (A. G. Gardiner, *Prophets, priests and kings*, p. 106). For civil service opinion, see above, p. 354, n. 1.

[4] See p. 115 ff. [5] See p. 287.

he seemed to treat the two issues as equally deserving of attention, at least in the sense of devoting equally brilliant rhetoric to them. His eagerness to support Booth's scheme suggests that he was not always very good about distinguishing between what was practical politics and what was not.

His romantic support of Booth, or of Sekgoma, also suggests that he had not mastered the art of coming to terms with the mundane, repetitive routines of day-to-day human life. He was hardly the man for the humdrum round of ministerial duties. Churchill exaggerated the importance of everything he touched. Every speck on the horizon, he assumed, would turn out to be a Cunarder, not a cockleshell. As a result of historical instincts and histrionic tendencies, he treated too many issues indiscriminately as matters of fundamental concern or historic significance. If important issues did not exist he would invent them. Not even the work of one government department could satisfy his voracious appetite for improvement. He was as fruitful in producing ideas for other departments as he was for the one to which he had been allocated. He was congenitally incapable of relaxing, even on holiday abroad. His power of concentration amounted almost to obsession.[1]

Churchill extracted what entertainment he could from his work. A letter forwarded by the governor of British Guiana from Mr E. A. Burgess, who offered his views on various matters, was not so readily dismissed by Churchill as by the officials. He quoted Dr Johnson: 'The applause of a simple human being is of great importance', and went on to instruct the office not to be

too stiff and proud in answering this man's loyal and civil letter. By snubbing a would-be supporter you can nearly always make a bitter enemy. 'Earth has no rage like love to hate that's turned/Nor hell a fury like a Burgess spurned.'[2]

---

[1] V. Bonham Carter, *Winston Churchill as I knew him*, p. 20. Hopwood to E 3 Apr 07: 'Churchill full of energy at Biarritz – he has been writing and telegraphing to me day by day – but almost nothing important' (EP).

[2] CO. 111/550/17129, minute 3 May 06.

In perusing the estimates for the Seychelles, Churchill did not fail to notice that the income from unique postage stamps in the Seychelles was approximately the same as the annual expenditure on education and religion:

Observe that the caprice of the philatelist yields in a normal year sufficient to defray exactly the annual cost of education and religion: and thus Christianity is sustained by variations in the watermark! Such are the unseen foundations of society.[1]

It seems reasonable to deduce that Churchill felt some frustration in these years 1905 to 1908. He was not head of the department. He was not in the cabinet. The issues with which he had to deal, once the Transvaal question was out of the way, were insufficiently challenging, insufficiently matters of life and death. Possibly the fact that Churchill wrote less autobiographically about this phase of his life, with the significant exception of the account of his African journey, is symptomatic.

At this time, Churchill was one of the most unpopular politicians in Britain. One of the main reasons for this was his unhappy gift for putting people's backs up by an apparently gratuitous offensiveness of manner. Even before Churchill had taken office his biographer described him as 'probably the best-hated man in English politics' after Joe Chamberlain.[2] In office, no single episode did more serious or lasting harm to his reputation than his attack on Lord Milner,[3] the hero of the British Establishment. In April 1906 Mr Arnold-Forster moved to reduce Churchill's salary, accusing him of being a young man in a hurry, without the excuse which age gave for haste, short-circuiting the traditional courtesies of politics, and presenting his views in an unpalatable way. He criticised Churchill for using expressions deeply wounding to Natalians, and other loyal South Africans, for 'embittered and empoisoned

[1] CO. 530/4/13351, 27 Apr 06. The watermark was varied to ensure that no stamp was issued without one.

[2] A. MacCallum Scott, *Winston Spencer Churchill*, p. 241.

[3] See p. 85 and n. 4. Churchill described Milner as 'a man of fine profession and poor performance' who had 'ceased to be a factor in public events'. He made an invidious comparison with Parnell, adding that whereas Parnell was innocent, Milner was guilty.

language' on Chinese Labour, and above all for insulting Milner, 'a man whom so many of us esteem, honour and love'.[1] The other main reason for his unpopularity was his apparent inconsistency, his unpredictable changes of mood and opinion, his lack of stability, both personal and political. Elgin coined the phrase 'Churchill's latest *volte face*'. His career between 1901 and 1911 was indeed full of contradictions, or shifts of attitude. From enthusiastic war correspondent and prisoner of the Boers to denouncer of the war and sympathiser with the Boers, from protectionist to free trader, from foremost ministerial champion of peace and disarmament to builder of the biggest ships ever built so far: all these changes were accomplished in a little over one decade. And there were a hundred other little shifts of interest and emphasis. Confronted with evidence of this kind, contemporaries said that he seemed not so much concerned with the merits of a quarrel as to be at the thick of the fight. But the readiness with which he dropped some of his ideas cannot be explained solely by a desire to be at the centre of events. Nor can they be ascribed simply to ambition, which, it is supposed, led him to swim with the tide, or, chameleon-like, to change colour with the ground he stood upon, though there is doubtless some truth in each of these explanations. At a deeper level of interpretation, these changes of attitude may be seen as the result of a journalistic impulsiveness, by which he was sometimes attracted suddenly to ideas, not so much on account of their substance, as of their suitability for expression in a striking fashion. He seized on new ideas, wild or sober, without discrimination. His attachment to a particular view might, therefore, be quite superficial. It almost seemed that in these years his chief pleasure in life came from phrase-making.

[1] PD. 155/757–68, 5 Apr 06 (Civil Service and Revenue Departments Estimates 1906/07). By contrast with Churchill, Elgin was thought to be the one minister who stood up for Milner. Milner's popularity among Unionists was enormous. A large dinner for Milner was held at the Hotel Cecil on Empire Day 1906. The Address appreciating his services to the empire, presented to him by Lord Halifax, was signed by 370,000 electors. Despite this lionising, Churchill persisted in calling Milner 'the disconsolate pro-consul' (12 Oct 06, *Annual Register for 1906*, 75, 77, 138, 211, 218).

Contemporaries agreed that his basic weakness was that phrases mastered him, rather than he them. He tended to be carried away by the logic of his own arguments, by the beauty of his own rhetoric. He was indeed endowed with the most rhetorical mind of any British statesman in history. Not even Gladstone thought and lived Rhetoric quite as Churchill did. His behaviour was open to the interpretation that his real inclination was to conclude that a thing was right and true if it could be stated in a rhetorically effective manner. His friends agreed in 1908 that his temptation to see first the rhetorical potentialities of any policy was growing, and becoming a real intellectual and moral danger.[1]

At this time his style was much more antithetical, polysyllabic and prolix than it subsequently became.[2] As a result, it was occasionally quite difficult to understand what he was talking about. In his writing, the obscurity usually resulted from verbal diarrhoea, but he could also be extremely cryptic. Once he minuted merely with an exclamation mark. Such constipated restraint was rare, although he was not averse to the occasional single sentence.[3]

Few of his colleagues would have predicted unhesitatingly in 1908 that he was destined to enjoy a glorious future. They felt that there was a big question-mark written against his prospects. They were uneasy about his love of the limelight, his insensitivity to the feelings of others, to the atmosphere of occasions. They disapproved of his pugnacity and obstinacy in argument, his emotional response to situations, the element of levity and playfulness, the super-journalism of some of his phrase-making, his fluctuating sense of proportion. They noted the less than scrupulous sense of loyalty in his deference to Elgin, and the distrust he widely inspired. They thought that these tendencies might not be successfully checked, and that if they were not, he would never attain the heights.[4] Those men

[1] J. A. Spender, *Life, journalism and politics* (1927), i, 163. M. V. Brett (ed.), *Journals and Letters of Viscount Esher*, ii, 344.

[2] Amery, *My political life*, i, 393.

[3] E.g. CO. 417/422/17996, CO. 179/234/11604.

[4] E.g. Asquith (see R. Jenkins, *Asquith*, pp. 339–40).

with the largest ingredient of scepticism in their forecasts of his future were the civil servants, to whom he was an *enfant terrible*. Sir Francis Hopwood, permanent head of the colonial office, was one of those universally admired and respected public servants,[1] whose judgment was regarded as unusually sound. His considered judgment on Churchill was as follows:

He is most tiresome to deal with, and will I fear give trouble – as his Father did – in any position to which he may be called. The restless energy, uncontrollable desire for notoriety, and the lack of moral perception, make him an anxiety indeed!

Hopwood admitted that in all his dealings with Churchill, he fully respected Elgin's authority and judgment, but he could never understand that there was any better way of enforcing an argument than by intrigue and by pugnaciously overstating a case.[2]

Nevertheless Churchill's work quickly earned him a brilliant reputation. It was soon conceded that he possessed innate political flair. John Morley's assessment was penetrating. Next to Chamberlain, he wrote, Winston was (in forty years) 'the most *alive* politician I have ever come across – only he has not got Chamberlain's breadth nor his sincerity of conviction. But for ceaseless energy and concentration of mind within the political and party field, they are a good match. They make other folk seem like mere amateurs, flâneurs, etc.' He singled out Churchill as one of the cleverest, most original and keenly industrious of the Liberal ministers. He diagnosed in him a 'curious *flair* for all sorts of political cases as they arise, though even he now and then mistakes a frothy bubble for a great wave'.[3]

As under-secretary of state at the colonial office he was able to make a definite contribution to the work of the department. Not all his ideas were equally valuable, and his recommendations had always to pass the acid test of Elgin's canny common-sense and varied experience. Occasionally he seemed to see the

---

[1] He was recommended as permanent under-secretary by Grey, Bryce and Morley (EP, Grey to E 8 Jun 06, Bryce 18 Dec 05, Morley 14 Dec 05).

[2] EP, Hopwood to E 27 Dec 07.

[3] MM. 3/50-1, 19 Feb 08, and /67, 12 Mar and /129, 30 Apr 08.

right course of action more quickly and more clearly than others. On the parliamentary side of his duties, he was extraordinarily good at anticipating and representing the House of Commons view, even if he sometimes cleverly enlisted it upon his own side to fight a private battle. Three aspects of his achievement may be selected as standing out. First, there is his gift for writing arresting minutes and for expounding government policy effectively in parliament. His preoccupation with phrase-making left behind it a host of attractive aphorisms enlivening the ponderous archives of government. Some of the most trenchant and forceful writing of his life was done in these early minutes and memoranda. His skill and eloquence in the presentation and defence of ministerial policy in the House of Commons brought his talents in this direction before a much wider audience. Second, despite his subordinate position, Churchill was able, by the sheer power of his mind and his imagination, and by the force and persistence of his rhetoric, to take a real part in the formulation of policy. He played his part in the Transvaal settlement, the major work of the Liberal government in the Edwardian empire. He provided much of the written analysis and argument upon which the cabinet decisions were based and justified. He was himself the originator of specific points of policy, such as the establishment of the Land Settlement Board.[1] Third, he had a generous and sensitive, if highly paternalistic, sympathy for subject peoples, and a determination to see that justice was done to humble individuals throughout the empire. He had this sympathy to a degree which was rather rare among British administrators, and even politicians, at this time. Human juices must be injected into olympian mandarins. By vigilant reading of routine official files he frequently uncovered what he thought were 'flat' or 'shocking' violations of the elementary principles of law and justice. He insisted that the principles of justice, and the safeguards of judicial procedure, should be 'rigidly,

---

[1] See above, p. 168. He was also supposed to have been largely instrumental in securing the acceptance of the Cullinan diamond as a peace-offering from the Boers to the king (Marsh, *A number of people*, p. 152).

punctiliously and pedantically' followed.[1] He insisted on questioning the colonial office assumption that officials were always in the right when complaints were made against government by Africans, or as was more probable, by Asians. He campaigned for an earnest effort to understand the feelings of subject peoples in being ruled by alien administrators, 'to try to measure the weight of the burden they bear'.[2] The business of a public officer, he maintained, was to serve the people he ruled. The officer must not forget that he was as much their servant, however imposing his title, as any manufacturer or tradesman was the servant of his customers. It was a salutary but unpopular reminder. Churchill supported Hofmeyer's suggestion that British civil servants in South Africa should learn Dutch, for if the people

like to talk to him in Volapuk, he must learn Volapuk. If they have a weakness for Sanskott [sic], it must become his study. By humouring them, and understanding them, he will be able very often to make their wishes and their welfare coincide.[3]

At the same time he was also a watchful champion of the interests of the colonial service, more narrowly considered. He defeated the threat to make marriage a disqualification for candidates proposing to enter the civil service in Ceylon.[4]

In a sense, Churchill's interest in the empire was never more

[1] See above, p. 226. 'There is scarcely anything more important for the government of men than the exact – I will even say the pedantic – observance of the regular forms by which the guilt or innocence of accused persons is determined' (*MAJ*, p. 40). See also CO. 273/317/14811, 7 May 06.

[2] CO. 54/709/26989, minute 5 Aug 07. Officials opposed Churchill's demand for a telegraphic report on remarks by the colonial secretary of Mauritius, Mr Cameron, which had upset Mauritians. 'I totally disagree', he protested. 'A prompt and frank investigation is the least these people can ask for. Mr Stubbs seems to assume that they are children and that the whole incident can be safely burked. I am all for upholding the officer and authority, but at the same time we must remove any legitimate cause of grievance without delay or shirking' (CO. 167/782/27167, minute 2 Aug 07).   [3] CO. 48/592/23907, minute 29 Jul 07.

[4] The Ceylon government wanted to make a rule that future candidates should be unmarried, and not marry without the governor's permission until they had reached the fourth class in the cadet service. This was because early marriages had resulted in financial embarrassment and an alleged impairment of efficiency. Churchill of course denounced the proposed rule: 'The cadets must continue to

than circumstantial and tangential. L. S. Amery once observed that Churchill's patriotism had always been for England, not the empire or commonwealth. England was the starting-point, and the ultimate object of policy, enhanced by the prestige and power of an empire of beneficent rule. Commonwealth patriotism never seriously influenced his thinking, his eloquence or his actions.[1] There is a good deal of truth in Amery's view. It could hardly be claimed that Churchill's colonial office days left an indelible mark on all his future political development. His interest in the empire never absorbed him entirely at the colonial office, and it may indeed have been very nearly exhausted by it. At any rate he had already begun to devote much thought to domestic problems. When he reflected upon the 'fine homogeneous' majority conferred by the electoral victory, he dwelt chiefly upon its significance for domestic legislation: 'I do not suppose we are likely to attain the millennium; but a few Big Acts by way of instalment ought certainly to be put on the Statute Book.'[2] A speech at Glasgow on 11 October 1906 marks his emergence as a social reformer. Starting from the proposition that 'the whole tendency of civilisation' was towards the 'multiplication of the collective functions of society', he wished to see 'the State embark on various novel and adventurous experiments', increasingly assuming the position of 'the reserve employer of labour'. He much regretted that they had not got the railways in state hands. He looked forward to the 'universal establishment of minimum standards of life and labour'. The state must mitigate the consequences of failure in the struggle for existence and 'spread a net over the abyss'.[3] These thoughts were always at

---

solve the riddle of life for themselves. There is no objection to moral suasion and friendly advice being tendered them by persons of riper years and larger salaries. But no politician in his senses would put his name to such arbitrary, decadent and objectionable restrictions . . . they are much better married if they can keep out of debt.' The most that Liberal ministers would do was to raise objection to the issue of a circular stressing the imprudence of a young officer's marrying on a shoestring (CO. 54/699, 12 Feb 06: S/S to govr 23 Feb 06).

[1] Amery, *My political life*, i, 196.
[2] Dilke papers, 43877, WSC to Dilke, 24 Jan 06.
[3] WSC, *Liberalism and the social problem* [Speeches 1906–9] (1909), pp. 75–82.

the back of his mind while he was at the colonial office. He began a careful study of labour problems in January 1908, and wrote in *The Nation* on 7 March about his ideas of extending government action. Before he left the colonial office he had evolved the blue-print of state welfare action which was to occupy him in practice for the following three years:[1]

Youth must be educated, disciplined and trained from fourteen to eighteen. The exploitation of boy labour must be absolutely stopped. . . . Labour must be de-casualised by a system of Labour Exchanges. The resultant residuum must be curatively treated as if they were hospital patients. The hours of labour must be regulated in various trades subject to seasonal or cyclical fluctuations. Means must be found by which the State can, within certain limits and for short periods, augment the demand of the ordinary market for unskilled labour so as to counter-balance the oscillations of world trade. Underneath, though not in substitution for, the immense disjointed fabric of social safeguards and insurances which has grown up by itself in England, there must be spread – at a lower level – a sort of Germanised network of state intervention and regulation.

No other parliamentary under-secretary of state for the colonies has ever managed to evolve so important or comprehensive a programme of social reform.[2] In this post, Churchill was much more influenced by the Webbs and Lloyd George, and their schemes for domestic change, than he was by any of the theorists of empire.[3]

[1] Asq. 11/10–15, WSC to Asquith 14 Mar 08.

[2] There was more than a touch of paternalism about Churchill's attitude to the social problems of the time, just as there was in his view of how the 'natives' of the empire should be treated. To both problems he brought an attitude typical of the Victorian gospel of 'improvement'. All his social reform speeches are full of concern about the stability of society and the waste of resources.

[3] By 1909 Wilfrid Blunt thought that Churchill's interest in the empire had been nearly exorcised. Perhaps Churchill had only ever been affected by the vanity of the empire and by his military training. Now Blunt found him almost converted to the view that the empire would be the ruin of England; Churchill admitted that it was a lot of bother: it could only be justified if it was undertaken in an altruistic spirit for the good of the subject races. He had, he thought, as under-secretary, upheld an optimistic Liberalism whereby the British Empire was to be maintained in part by concession, in part by force, and in part by the constant invention of new scientific forces to deal with the growing difficulties of imperial rule (W. S. Blunt, *My Diaries*, ii, 287–95, 2 Oct–25 Nov 09).

14 The Departure of Elgin from the Colonial Office April 1908

Asquith did not want Elgin in his ministry. The departure of Elgin from the colonial office was an unpleasant episode in Edwardian politics, which were much less subject to ruthless cabinet purges than those of the new Elizabethan era. Gladstone's principle was not yet forgotten: one of the most serious decisions a prime minister could take was to leave out a man once in the cabinet.

It is just possible that Asquith might have believed that Elgin did not really want to remain in office. Certainly Elgin disliked the wider political aspects of being a cabinet minister. On this account he passed through a time of personal crisis in the middle of August 1907. He was having to spend several hours in the House of Lords for government bills, which were mostly being wrecked by the Unionist peers. His silence began to be commented upon there and in the press. At one moment he wondered whether it would not be better 'to throw up the sponge' in the fairly near future.[1] In particular he became very fussed and depressed about pressure upon him to speak on the unpopular Small Landholders (Scotland) Bill. It was opposed by his friends Rosebery and Lord Balfour of Burleigh. Rosebery's hatred of the measure may be gauged from his remark that not even Gladstone risen from the dead could persuade him to make 'so vast an experiment' as the extension of the Crofter Acts to all Scotland. It is hardly surprising, then, that Elgin did not care a straw for the bill. On the other hand he doubted whether he could refuse to speak. Having made such prepara-

[1] EP, E to Lady E 16 Aug 07.

tions as time permitted, he was twice on the verge of speaking, but was discouraged by Ripon, who led the Liberal peers. On the second occasion he lamented to Lady Elgin:

... I had screwed myself up. But again Ripon threw cold water, and I put my papers in my pocket. I think now I might have made something of it – but I hate this debating – and do it so badly that – well, it is no use talking. I foresaw the difficulty when the government was formed and I ought to have stood out then.[1]

Grey seemed to sense his discomfort, and a few days later spoke to him very kindly both of the amount of work done in the colonial office in 1906 and of the success and quiet of the current year. He agreed with Elgin that it was impossible in 'our big offices' to take up and master large outside bills. Elgin was soothed by Grey's remarks, but wrote: 'My knowledge of the *limitations* on my usefulness remains.'[2] On 19 August he made a short statement in the House on the licensing laws and policy for the restriction of the liquor traffic in Nigeria,[3] 'so I am no longer absolutely a dumb dog'. He felt that he managed it quite fluently for him. He was not yet out of his difficulties on Scottish bills. Another was coming up, again opposed by Balfour of Burleigh. Again Elgin did not feel at all inclined to speak on it. Again he feared awkward criticism of his silence which would be made by 'the violent men on our side in Scotland'.[4] On 22 August he made a statement on the re-

[1] Ibid. 15 Aug 07. First reading in Lords 9 August, second reading 13–14 Aug 07 (PD. 180/948–1035, 1203–59). The Small Landholders (Scotland) Bill was withdrawn, and came up again in revised form for second reading in the Lords on 10 and 11 Mar 08. Elgin spoke, following Balfour of Burleigh whose final remark was that if he were to agree to pass the bill as it stood, he would be ashamed to go back to Scotland. Elgin showed far more knowledge of the problem than enthusiasm for the bill: 'There is a want for a bill of some such character as this'; if there was a demand for smallholdings, this bill could meet it – if not, no harm would be done, because smallholdings could not be created without smallholders. He scarcely could be said to have demonstrated the necessity for the bill (PD. 185/1462–9, 11 Mar 08). The bill was defeated.

[2] EP, E to Lady E 17 Aug 07.   [3] PD. 181/5–9, 19 Aug 07.

[4] EP, E to Lady E 22 Aug 07; reference is to the Land Values (Scotland) bill, brought from Commons for first reading 21 Aug 07; second reading, 26 Aug 07: Elgin did not speak on it.

organisation of the colonial office, to a very small House. This went off satisfactorily.[1] Next day he wrote to Selborne: 'The end of the Session is, I hope, at last in sight. It has been a long and continuous strain.'[2] Three days later, he became distinctly upset once more, over the Scottish Land Valuation Bill. He wrote to his wife from the House of Lords:

I am in another hobble about this abominable speaking. Here is another serious attack on a Scotch Bill and everybody clamouring for me to speak, but I really cannot summon up courage to do so. I think the only thing for me to do [is to] come out to write to you – which at any rate is an undeniable duty. But the thing cannot go on, and though I shall not, unless it is suggested to me by my friends themselves, take any hasty steps while we are separating [at the end of the session] – I think I must reconsider my whole position before we come back. That is my feeling of the moment.[3]

The next day was the last of the parliamentary session. Before the cabinet Ripon tried to cheer him up by speaking warmly of the successes in South Africa, and Elgin's share therein. Elgin thought it to be almost too good to be true that he could turn his back on the House of Lords for several months. How he wished that it could be for longer![4]

Apparently Elgin decided against resignation. His little crisis was surmounted. It was not likely to recur. It must not be imagined, therefore, that in April 1908 Elgin was glad to leave office.[5]

Campbell-Bannerman attended his last cabinet on 12 February 1908. Thereafter Asquith deputised for him, until he himself became prime minister on 6 April. Campbell-Bannerman died shortly after his resignation, on 22 April.

[1] EP, E to Lady E 23 Aug 07; PD. 181/1067–72, 22 Aug 07.
[2] EP, E to Selb. 23 Aug 07.   [3] EP, E to Lady E 26 Aug 07.
[4] Ibid. 27 Aug 07; E to Selb. 30 Aug 07: 'I have at last escaped from London! It has been a long and trying session in many ways. The one relief has been that it has been exceptionally cool for London at this time of the year' (EP). Elgin's difficulty about parliamentary speaking seems to have been inherited: his father had not been accounted much use in debate or cabinet by his contemporaries (E. Fitzmaurice, *Life of 2nd Earl Granville* (1905), i, 345, 369).
[5] As J. E. B. Seely does in *Adventure* (1930), p. 128.

Asquith dropped Elgin from his new ministry. His intention leaked out in the *Daily Chronicle* as being a settled fact, three or four days before Elgin had heard even a whisper on the subject. Then Asquith wrote a very brief note to Elgin, dated 8 April, telling him that he had done good work. It was damning with faint praise. Asquith regretted not being able to ask him to continue to hold the post of colonial secretary. No reason was given. Insult was added to injury. Elgin was offered the dignity of a marquis, in recognition of the 'great services' which he had rendered to the state. Elgin was deeply shocked. Although not an intimate or admirer of Asquith, he had always tended to rely upon him as an old acquaintance.[1] He would not, perhaps, have minded so much, if he had not been succeeded by another peer, Lord Crewe. It was this that made his dismissal seem so personal. He drafted his reply to Asquith with solemn care. He did not conceal his disappointment: 'I was prepared to give you a loyal support. . . .' As regards the marquisate, he asked Asquith to obtain the king's permission for him to decline.[2] Asquith replied saying that he was extremely sorry about Elgin's refusal of elevation in the peerage, though he could appreciate the reasons. He had never, he added, undertaken a more disagreeable task than the process of ministerial reconstruction, involving, as it did, saying farewell to men for whom, both on personal and public grounds, he had the highest regard:

In your own case, I may say without exaggeration and with perfect sincerity that I faced the prospect with the most extreme reluctance. If in what I wrote to you, in the stress of a most embarrassing duty, I failed to make clear my sense, and the King's, and that (I believe) of all our late colleagues, of the splendid services which during two critical years you have rendered to the Empire, I beg you to forgive the short-coming and to believe that I could not help myself.[3]

[1] At the time of the controversy on Chitral policy (see above, p. 23), Elgin had written: 'I cannot conceive Asquith wishing to injure me' (VRP. 15/195, 7 Dec 97). They had known each other since Oxford days. In Nov 06 E described Asquith as 'very kind and helpful' (EP, to Lady E 20 Nov 06).

[2] Asq. 11/163–4, E to Asquith 10 Apr 08; draft in EP.

[3] EP, Asquith to E 11 Apr 08.

The letter did little to soften the blow. This is clear from Elgin's reply: 'I liked the work at the Colonial Office. . . . I am sorry to leave the Cabinet, where I have experienced nothing but good feeling and good fellowship. . . .'[1]

Elgin never wrote about his feelings to anyone else except Lord Tweedmouth, who had a rather similar experience. Asquith had dismissed Tweedmouth from the admiralty, but compensated him with the lord presidency of the council. He was informed in a two-line note, without comment or explanation. When Tweedmouth complained to Elgin about this scurvy treatment of the head of a great department of state, and expressed the view that Elgin had 'suffered grievous wrong',[2] Elgin could not resist a reply indicating an almost stinging contempt for Asquith's procedure:

I venture to think that even a prime minister may have some regard for the usages common among gentlemen. The letter I received was *mutatis mutandis* the same as yours, except that I was not wanted at all – for what reason I am still ignorant. I cannot conceive why both of us should not have had the situation explained, and if this had been done and the slightest appeal made to our loyalty – I should have cheerfully retired – as you would no doubt have accepted your new position. . . . I feel that even a housemaid gets a better warning. . . .[3]

Elgin's relations with Asquith had perhaps never been too easy, nor his opinion of him particularly high. Asquith indeed had little impulse to creative action, and he soon lost whatever moral fervour he might have had in his younger days. He was more deficient in ideas and doctrine than a Liberal prime minister ought to have been. Despite his serene composure and administrative skill, he was naturally irresolute, and sometimes slipshod. In many ways he was a Philistine.[4] The excessive sociability of his second marriage hardly attracted Elgin. The intellectual blandness did not impress him. Asquith gave the impression of being unduly casual in high office. Playing bridge

[1] Asq. 11/91–2, E to Asquith 13 Apr; draft in EP.
[2] EP, 17 Apr 08.   [3] EP 20 Apr 08 (draft).
[4] R. B. McCallum, *Asquith* (1936), *passim*.

continually was decidedly not in the best Gladstonian tradition, which Elgin revered.[1] The remark attributed to Asquith, that in cabinet-making one had to be a good butcher, was no joke, as Elgin and Tweedmouth discovered.[2] What happened to Elgin was a foretaste of the weak ingratitude Asquith was to display by sacrificing Haldane, a master mind, if ever there was one, among Liberal politicians, from his war-time cabinet. The element of brutality in Asquith was marked. He upset Deakin at the time of the 1907 colonial conference by the undue bluntness of his manner in refusing to consider preference in any shape or form.[3]

It was perfectly possible for intelligent men to form opinions of Asquith, which, for all his acknowledged gifts and experience as a debater, parliamentarian and administrator, were based upon neither liking nor admiration.[4] It was to this school of thought that Elgin inclined, and in which he was now confirmed.

By the spring of 1908 Elgin was politically isolated, even at the cabinet level. He had never had many friends. The best he had, Rosebery, had long ceased to count. His most powerful champion, Campbell-Bannerman, who had happily accepted his departmental preoccupation, was dying. Morley had never cared for Elgin.[5] Of all Campbell-Bannerman's team, no one had been on better terms with Elgin than James Bryce, but

[1] M. V. Brett (ed.), *Journals and letters of Reginald, Viscount Esher*, ii, *1903–1910* (1934), 308, 366. L. S. Amery's judgment of Asquith is harsh, but not wholly wide of the mark: he had 'a speciously transparent lucidity of expression, of saying nothing whatever in the course of half an hour, and yet leaving an impression of business-like conciseness.' Asquith's letters delight the eye more than the mind. Arrogance was one of his failings. 'More flexibility and humility', Churchill wisely observed, were necessary in modern prime ministers. (L. S. Amery, *My Political Life*, ii (1953), 79; WSC, *Great Contemporaries* (1937), p. 137).

[2] R. Jenkins, *Asquith* (1964), p. 181, n., reveals that Asquith also dropped Lord Portsmouth as under-secretary of state for war, although he had once tutored Portsmouth.

[3] A. Chamberlain, *Politics from inside* (1936), p. 78: 'Asquith seems to have been on this occasion, as so often, quite needlessly brutal.'

[4] See A. M. Gollin, *Proconsul in politics*, p. 221, Dicey to Milner. See also, A. M. Gollin, 'Asquith: a new view' (*A century of Conflict 1850–1950. Essays for A. J. P. Taylor*, ed. M. Gilbert (1966), pp. 107–13).

[5] VRP. 15/195, 7 Dec 97.

Bryce had gone to Washington as ambassador early in 1907.[1] Churchill could hardly be expected to put in a good word for Elgin, since he was angling for the reversion of the colonial office. Haldane and Grey admired his work, but were not personal friends. The remainder of the cabinet he had hardly ever come into contact with at all.

Thus Asquith could drop Elgin without provoking a ministerial rebellion. But why did he do it? Elgin would not ask for an explanation, and never received one. Fortunately for the historian, there were plenty of others who were curious to know. Elgin was regarded as a veteran, who had done excellent service to the state in many capacities. The hardness of the treatment accorded to him was plain to everyone, the want of consideration in point of form and manner disagreeably obvious. Fitzmaurice summed up the reaction of most of the ruling *élite*:

If he had been left out when the Government was formed, I do not see that he could have had much reason to complain, as he never came near the House of Lords during 'the long winter of our discontent'. Now it is otherwise. He has done his administrative work conspicuously well; although he had all the most difficult questions to deal with – Chinese Labour, the Transvaal Constitution and the Colonial Conference – and also had an under-secretary who did his best 'to queer the pitch'.

Searching for an explanation, Fitzmaurice conceded that Elgin was a bad speaker. So, however, was Tweedmouth. His shyness and silence made him an ineffective member of the cabinet. It was this which was used to justify his extrusion.[2] To justify. But did it explain? Crewe seemed to think so:

The reason for Elgin's removal [he said] was not discontent with his administration of the Department, which he believed to be admirable, but because he never opened his lips in

[1] EP, Bryce to E 24 Dec 06: 'May I say that there is no-one with whom I am more sorry to part than yourself? I have greatly enjoyed our consultations and opportunities of intercourse....' Bryce repeated that he was 'more sorry to leave no-one than yourself', 11 Feb 07. Elgin found him 'very friendly' (EP, to Lady E 21 Dec 06).

[2] Bryce papers, E. 28, Fitzmaurice to Bryce 20 Apr 08.

Council, except in regard to matters connected with his own office; and secondly, because he was no use in general debate,

which was at that moment the principal difficulty of the government in the House of Lords.[1]

Yet Elgin was not unique in either short-coming. It was not entirely true, as Morley also alleged, that Elgin was not 'of the slightest use for debate'.[2] He had spoken on the policy for the north-west frontier of India. He had even spoken eventually in the debate on the Smallholders (Scotland) Bill on 11 March 1908. Haldane had been very pleased with his major speech in the army debate, supporting the formation of a territorial force.[3] On the other hand, of course, no one could really represent him as adding much actual debating strength to the government front bench in the Lords, beyond the respect inspired by his character. But strength could not be added by replacing him by another peer who was already in the cabinet. Nor was Elgin the only minister who stuck chiefly to his own departmental work. Few of his famous colleagues knew what was going on outside their departments.[4] Morley flatly refused to speak about Irish matters, even though he had formerly been chief secretary for Ireland.[5] Looking back, Haldane felt that he himself ought to have taken a more active part in the general business of the cabinet.[6] None of them had Elgin's excuse, that his extra-departmental energies were absorbed in conducting a taxing commission on the Scottish ecclesiastical problem. Elgin, it seems, could have been the unlucky scapegoat for a collective failing.

The colonial office was the most expendable department, in Asquith's conception of politics in 1908. His interest in the

---

[1] A. Fitzroy, *Memoirs*, i, 348, 11 Apr 08, recording Crewe's remarks.

[2] MM. 3/160, 15 May 08.

[3] 'An admirable speech . . . your remarks were full of penetrating points . . . your anecdote very much in point' (EP); speeches on Territorial and Reserve Forces Bill, second reading PD. 176/1260–73, 26 Jun 07 and third reading PD. 178/1298–300, 23 Jul 07. For speech on NW. frontier see PD. 184/1728–30, 26 Feb 08.

[4] Bryce papers E. 28, Fitzmaurice to Bryce 2 Nov 07.

[5] CB. 41223/252, 20 Jun 07.

[6] Haldane, *Autobiography* (1929), p. 216.

empire was strictly limited. Unlike Elgin, Crewe, Asquith's nominee to the colonial office, had little special qualification to be colonial secretary. This landed magnate and millionaire coal-owner had, however, as lord president of the council, shown himself to be a good all-rounder, an excellent cabinet minister in every general sense.[1] Such men were hard to find. Elgin's dismissal in no way reflects upon his actual performance. Indeed, it was a measure of Elgin's success,[2] that the colonial office could be entrusted to a minister whose finesse was essentially in those activities which are now usually given to a minister without portfolio. The new under-secretary Colonel Seely, was, moreover, almost unknown and quite inexperienced. The dropping of the imperial pilot seems rather to reflect Asquith's fundamental lack of concern for the empire after the South African problem had been dealt with. This indifference affected many of the Liberals, including Churchill to some extent.

At all events, Asquith's dismissal of Elgin hardly seems the result of any personal animus or disapproval, except possibly in the social sphere. Elgin's lack of participation in the social life of the ministerial *élite* probably detracted from Asquith's desire to retain him as a colleague. It is an interesting fact that Crewe cut a no better figure in public than Elgin did. He too was a hesitant, and sometimes a stammering speaker. But Crewe House was the opulent social centre of the Liberal Party. Other things being equal, Asquith would have preferred Crewe to Elgin at the colonial office on this ground. But it can hardly have been decisive. Apart from such secondary social considerations, Asquith could not have found much else to worry him in Elgin apart from his silence. It is true that Elgin had modestly, and perhaps rather foolishly, told Asquith at the end of 1906 that he 'little understood' the work of the South African department of the colonial office.[3] This frank modesty

[1] Asquith came to rate Crewe top of the list of his order of merit in the cabinet (Jenkins, *Asquith*, p. 340).

[2] Success which did not go unremarked: as McKenna said in 1907 to Elgin: 'Yes, we are all attacked, except your department; you have got things quite smooth' (EP, E to Lady E 17 Aug 07).

[3] Asq. 10/208, 21 Dec 06.

515

was, however, not so damaging as it might seem. Such admissions were common enough among ministers in their first year of office. Morley made no secret of his initial bewilderment at the India Office.[1] Asquith was not so green in politics as to imagine that ministers could be expected even to pretend to universal competence. It has been conjectured that Elgin may have been dismissed because he was not sufficiently in sympathy with the left-wing and radical element.[2] Certainly he was never popular with the radical rank-and-file,[3] and he obviously had little commitment to the Scottish land policy to which the inexperienced secretary of state for Scotland, Sinclair, tied the government. Scottish issues formed a large part of parliamentary politics in 1907. But as far as the social welfare issues were concerned, if he was dubious about the doctrines and tendencies of Lloyd George and Winston Churchill, so were most of his colleagues, and so was Asquith himself. Elgin was no more sceptical of the Morley–Minto reforms than Ripon.

Intrinsically perhaps, there was no good reason why Elgin should not have been thought fit to continue as colonial secretary. He was not a perfect politician, but who was? Maybe Asquith was genuine when he professed to being unable to help himself. There was an unusually bright constellation of talent for him to choose from, and Elgin was the unlucky one among the old guard which had to suffer some depletion of its ranks to make way for new men, of whom Churchill was one.

Elgin received a very large number of appreciative letters

---

[1] MM. 1/81–99, 2/103, 136, 142: CB. 41223/242.

[2] *The Scotsman*, 13 Apr 08 described Elgin as representing 'a safe and moderate element in the government. But it may, without any injustice or unkindness, be said that he had played an ambiguous and ineffective part as a member of a cabinet with whose measures he was often not in sympathy. By remaining at his post he gave official sanction to these measures, while he was too honest publicly to advocate or defend them. He will be happier and more useful in an independent position, and the government will be more homogeneous.'

[3] The radicals were, for example, very dissatisfied with what they felt was a climb-down in favour of white colonial opinion in Natal (W. Blunt, *My Diaries*, ii, 140, 31 Mar 06). They also thought him lukewarm on Chinese Labour – but Haldane dissociated himself from them much more ostentatiously.

from a wide range of people, most of whom had never been in the habit of writing to him. I propose to quote from some of them at length, because they are first-hand evidence of what contemporaries really thought about Elgin and his fate; they are also nice examples of the sensitive dignity which had still not entirely disappeared from British political practice. The first to arrive were from the senior officials of the colonial office. The permanent under-secretary, Sir Francis Hopwood, indicated his 'very grievous' sense of shock:

I had read the gossip in the press and had sullenly disbelieved it . . . we in the Office have prided ourselves on the undoubted fact that your policy and administration have been dwelt upon by the party as the principal achievement of the Government. In acute contradistinction to the acts of any of your predecessors, you have applied a healing salve to the wounds and sorrows of South Africa. You have given to a continent a peaceful content based on the principles of truest liberalism. . . .

I shall always endeavour to make your methods of business and of administration a tradition and a guide.

He would miss Elgin's 'kind help and advice terribly'.[1] There could hardly have been a warmer tribute. Yet Lucas almost outshone his superior in feeling. He wrote almost emotionally:

When this Government came in, it was such a relief to me to know that I was to serve under you, and all the time I have felt such complete confidence in your administration – even when I ventured to think differently on any point – and in your constant friendship; I am as certain that the best interests of the country and the Colonies are suffering by the loss of your services, as that I am personally the loser in no longer having you for my chief. There will be very many who will be surprised and grieved at what is taking place. . . . I write this only to thank you once more for all your consideration for me, and to express my very great regret that more consideration was not given to you, when I know from inside of what great value your wise and

[1] EP 11 and 25 Apr 08.

fair management of colonial matters has been in the last two years.[1]

Other senior officials paid tribute to his kindness and patience, his readiness to listen to any explanation of their difficulties, to his power of seeing things from the point of view of governors on the spot. If there are two kinds of politician, those who commend themselves to the civil service and those who commend themselves to the public at large, Elgin belonged to the former category. And who is to say which commendation it is better to have?

There were some kind letters also from some of his ministerial colleagues. Fitzmaurice, under-secretary for foreign affairs, drew upon his historical knowledge,[2] and political experience to declare:

When Governments are formed and changed some absolutely incomprehensible things always occur, but I can certainly say that your retirement is one of the most incomprehensible of this order of events which I have ever come across. . . .[3]

There was a letter from Grey:

There has been so much inter-communication between the Colonial Office and the Foreign Office, that I should like to say how grateful I am for the way in which you dealt with difficulties and took the Foreign Office difficulties into consideration and helped to overcome them whenever we had to work together. I am very sorry that our official connection is broken, for to me in the Foreign Office work, it was very pleasant and helpful.[4]

Elgin's old friend Sandhurst, who had been on the Ridgeway Committee, wrote as follows:

[1] EP 11 Apr 08. Lest it be thought that Lucas and others were unduly moved by pity, it should be recorded that in a letter of 23 Oct 07 Lucas had written of 'so kind and good a friend as yourself', and that Ommanney in his retirement thanked Elgin for 'all the consideration which you have extended to me and which has made it such a pleasure to work for you' (EP 15 Jan 07).

[2] Fitzmaurice had written a three volume life of Shelburne (1875–6), *The Life of Sir William Petty 1623–87* (1895) and a two volume life of the 2nd earl Granville (1905), so he claimed knowledge of three centuries of British politics.

[3] EP 15 Apr 08.   [4] 14 Apr 08.

I really do not know whether I was more concerned or amazed at missing your name in the Cabinet list; amazed because of the work you have done in and out of office since 1894, especially in your late office – and concerned, from the point of view of Colonies and Mother Country.

He hailed Elgin as 'a man in whose mind self and self-interest and advancement had no place, but whose singleness of purpose and transparent honesty' those who had worked with him knew so well.[1]

Civil servants and colleagues could hardly avoid writing to him. Even more striking, therefore, are some of the tributes from unexpected persons, who need not have bothered to write, but who did so because they felt strongly. Sir Cecil Clementi Smith, for example, governor of the Straits Settlements 1887 to 1893, wrote:

I venture to assert that, so far as the Crown Colonies are concerned, no secretary of state has gained a higher reputation for impartiality, sympathy and wise guidance, from those serving under him in those Colonies – and of those alone can I write from a somewhat extensive knowledge – and your retirement will be universally regretted.

Elgin, it seems, had held his own even against Joseph Chamberlain. Even more remarkably, Elgin's predecessor in office, Alfred Lyttelton, wrote to him a typically warm letter, in which he compared him with Grey:

I venture at the risk of presumption to express my deep regret that you are leaving the Colonial Office.

I remember with gratitude how, coming into an arena of envenomed controversy you tried to maintain, where it was possible, both the substance and the form of continuity – emphasised the points in which you agreed with your predecessors, fairly set forth their arguments, when you differed from them, and opposed a tranquil but steady resistance to base, intemperate and unscrupulous exaggerations.

In such a spirit Edward Grey has administered his department, but he has not had the difficulties which confronted

[1] EP 16 Apr 08.

you, both in policy, and the circumstances of your office upon which I need not dwell. Indeed, these must have made the position sometimes very trying to one of your temper of loyalty.

I have every respect for Crewe, but I still profoundly regret that the colonial office loses a chief who never advertised, or thought of himself, but who was to those who *knew*, a guarantee of the wise and high-minded patriotism which we love to associate with Eton.[1]

Disregarding the *floreat Etona* element, this letter makes two very important observations, stressing Elgin's concern for continuity, and the difficulties arising from having Churchill as a subordinate.

In addition, there were letters of regret from I. Fowell Buxton, representing the opinion of the humanitarians, from the chairman of the British Cotton Growing Association, expressing thanks for Elgin's interest in and help for their work, and from the secretary of the West African Trade Association, praising Elgin's efforts in advancing the economic welfare of the West African colonies. Besides all these, there were letters from Selborne,[2] Sir Richard Solomon, Ommanney, Girouard, Balfour of Burleigh, Sinclair, and of course some very indignant ones from members of his own family. The receipt of so many appreciative letters made the dismissal even harder to understand.

Nor did Crewe shirk the delicate task of writing to him:

Knowing as I do, the interest you took in your work, and the devotion you gave to it, I think I can appreciate the keen regret with which you must have been affected by the change. . . . So far as I have been able to judge, as a colleague not specially cognisant of the circumstances, you have passed through a difficult and anxious time with courage and success. If I can leave so good a *souvenir* at the Office, I shall be more than content.

Crewe asked him if he would care to write something about the colonial office and the colonial service personnel which would help him to take over the reins.[3] Elgin welcomed this offer, and

[1] EP 14 Apr 08.
[2] 'I feel that you have backed me up in a way which I greatly appreciate.'
[3] EP 16 Apr 08. Elgin replied on 7 May 08.

his long, authoritative letter to Crewe was his final production in the service of the Liberal government.

This done, Elgin put the past resolutely behind him. His papers were gathered together into five boxes and put away and not reopened until fifty years had elapsed, in accordance with his wishes. He never again in his lifetime referred to his tenure of the colonial office. He never again spoke for the government in the House of Lords. His break with politics was absolute. Always the reluctant politician, he regarded himself as now entirely absolved from any obligation to the Asquith ministry. From the very moment of his retirement, he had made it quite clear that he claimed the utmost freedom in respect of party notices. He would not attend the Lords to order, and probably not even to invitation. He put his threat into practice with utter inflexibility, while avoiding any public indication of wounded pride.

Neither his public services, nor his worries, were at an end, however. Once again he immersed himself zestfully in parochial, Fifeshire and Scottish affairs, which had always been his first and deepest attachment. The Scottish Churches Commission still had not quite finished its labours. At the request of the founder, he became chairman of the Carnegie Trust for Scottish Universities, and he took a great interest in the application, to the best advantage for the Scottish Universities, of the large funds made available by Andrew Carnegie's generosity. In 1914 he became Lord Rector of Aberdeen University. In Scotland at least, his devoted and useful services were recognised and appreciated on all sides.

After the death of his ailing wife in 1909, he married again in 1913. The second Lady Elgin, Gertrude Lilian, widow of Capt. Frederick Ogilvy, R.N., was about the age of his eldest children, but it was a most successful marriage. The countess had a welcome talent for brightening Broomhall, and for soothing the earl in the anxieties of his last years.

For he was not to find peace. In his retirement he suffered a serious threat to his family estate from the Greater Dunfermline scheme, a development programme arising out of the expansion of Rosyth dockyard. The outbreak of war granted a reprieve which eventually proved final, but Elgin lived all his last years under the perpetual strain of an exceedingly bitter wrangle.[1]

'I had some unusual difficulties to encounter, – and I should be prepared to maintain [my work] was based on sound Liberal principles.'[2] This was Elgin's own modest estimate of his colonial secretaryship. His liberalism was in the tradition of Gladstone and his own father. He admired Macaulay, Bright, and Mayo. Hopwood recognised the justice of his claim. Like Campbell-Bannerman's premiership, of which it was a prominent facet, Elgin's tenure of the colonial office may be described as common sense enthroned. He seldom took any decision which can be criticised harshly in the light of history. His decision upon African marriage in Sierra Leone was bad, but it was not important or influential, and was an eccentric exception to his usual good sense. Wide experience, unwavering administrative courage, unimpeachable honourableness – these were his assets. Sometimes he was pedestrian, sometimes unduly cautious, sometimes unimaginative, but he was never weak, never lethargic, and never slavishly dependent on his officials. His mistakes resulted from a tendency to be over-rational and from a deficiency of imaginative foresight which might have enabled him to gauge more accurately what popular reactions to governmental activity might be. Perhaps he suffered from the typical fallacy or delusion of the administrator that political problems are amenable to administrative solution.[3] Certainly

[1] The Dunfermline Burgh Extension and Drainage Bill, a private bill, received royal assent in August 1911. Dunfermline Burgh applied for a provisional order extending its boundaries so as to include the Rosyth naval base. Elgin lodged an objection to the extension on the grounds that it meant extra taxation to him (PD/HC. 22/1404, 9 Mar 11, parliamentary question). After his death the land was valued for death duties at building value and taxed accordingly, but in general it is yet to be built upon.

[2] Asq. 11/91, E to Asquith 13 Apr 08.

[3] Compare Prof. Tawney's judgment on Lionel Cranfield: 'By nature a planner and executant, he was the victim, in the first place, of an illusion which may be called perhaps, the administrator's fallacy – the belief, that is to say, that efficient management, combined with public spirit and a logically unanswerable case, can hold its own against interests and ambitions wielding personal and political power' (*Business and politics under James I*, p. 292).

he had the typical limitation of the aristocratic landowner in national government: uneasiness in operating an impersonal relationship with a large public.[1] Yet in general, his work amply confirmed his reputation, at least as it existed in Scotland, as a man 'with a fine instinct for the essentials of a case, patient over details, and of sound judgment'.[2] In zeal he equalled Churchill. In tact he far surpassed him. Gladstone always used to choose a few ministers of his type to be in his cabinets – men who supplied an element of strong common sense, who could be trusted to work diligently at their administrative routines, and who had no love of personal display.

Sir Henry Campbell-Bannerman has usually received most of the credit for the South African settlement, probably because he died so soon after it had been made. Apart from one notable intervention, his share in the work has perhaps been exaggerated. At all events, Elgin deserves some of the credit. Sir Richard Solomon, agent-general of the Transvaal in London, testified at the time, having worked with Elgin on drafting the new constitutions, that it was Elgin's generosity of sentiment, and scrupulous respect for the susceptibilities of the Boers, which largely explained their reconciliation and readiness to co-operate with England for the time being.[3]

Elgin died on 18 January 1917. A son was born posthumously to his widow. The speeches made in the House of Lords to mark his passing were made in combination with tributes to Lord Cromer who died at about the same time. These orations were fair and just. Maybe Crewe was rather cool – 'a man, indeed, who did himself perhaps insufficient justice, either in public or in private discussion: but those who had the opportunity of knowing the work that he did in administration know

---

[1] See Lord Eustace Percy's reflections: 'Large private responsibilities do tend to form in their possessors a certain talent for public affairs. A certain talent, but one that is apt to be restricted in its range'; a landowner 'could manage men with whom he could talk, but he was uncertain in judging public opinion or in conducting public debate' (*Some Memories* (1958), p. 15).

[2] *Dundee Advertiser* 13 Apr 08.

[3] Fitzroy, *Memoirs*, p. 371, 9 and 11 Jan 09. Fitzroy's own view was that rapid progress towards confederation in South Africa was 'no small tribute to Elgin's statesmanship' (p. 370).

how valuable and solid that was.' Much warmer, and more significant, was Curzon's appreciation. Curzon mentioned that Elgin's Indian administration had been confronted with many difficulties. He testified from what he had seen and heard 'that he met those difficulties with cool imperturbability, with quiet sagacity, and with unshaken courage'. He concluded:

Elgin was one of those well-endowed, but unassuming men whose abilities and services are not the less useful because they are to some extent concealed by instinctive modesty from the public gaze. . . . He made . . . no effort anywhere to strike the public imagination, but he did his work, whether it was public or local, diligently and well; and he was one of those men who seem to be put into the world to maintain, instinctively and faithfully, the highest ideals of duty in public life.[1]

Elgin would have been well content with that epitaph.

[1] PD/HL. 24/12 and 19–20, 17 Feb 1917 (addresses in reply to the King's Speech).

15 The Watershed of the Empire-Commonwealth: The Imperial Policy of the Liberal Government, 1905–1908

I T could be argued that the years 1905 to 1908 represent a dividing line in the history of several of the main European empires. After parliamentary criticism in Germany, the rejection of the colonial estimates and the Herero uprising in South West Africa, a new era of total reconstruction began with the appointment of Dr Dernburg in 1907 as first colonial minister. From 1906 the French African empire was marked by growing decentralisation and a reaction against further expansion. The theory of assimilation to French civilisation and citizenship was under attack. The administration of French Equatorial Africa was reformed from 1906 and federated between 1908 and 1910. Fresh constructive interest in French African problems developed. In the same period, Leopold's Congo Free State was under fatal assault. Transfer to the Belgian parliament and people was achieved in 1908. By 1913 the entire Leopoldian system had been completely abandoned; the concessionaire companies had either vanished or been reduced to impotence, and the British government felt able to recognise the Belgian annexation.

The changes in the British empire were not so sweeping as in the German, the French and the Belgian empires. This was because there was no need for them to be. The changes were more of theory than of practice. The period is a watershed chiefly in that it marks the decisive rejection of the constructionist vision of imperial federation and consolidation. Lyttelton

525

in 1910 noted[1] how aspirations for a Greater Britain remained unfulfilled. The empire, he wrote, was then rather 'a confederation of independent nationalities', without a unifying force. Another of the leading advocates of imperial unity, George Wyndham, formerly chief secretary for Ireland, realised that a decisive watershed had been reached. In 1898 he was excited about prospects for the renewed quest of the British empire – 'the spread and consolidation of the sea-commonwealth of Free Peoples'. In January 1906, he saw in the election a critical choice between two possible ideals: between an insular socialism, and a grand imperialism. Imperialism demanded unity at home and throughout the empire. It prescribed fiscal reform to secure both. Imperialism looked to the past and the future. Socialism looked only to the present. In any case, old-fashioned liberalism was doomed – 'the bankers and hairdressers and "épiciers" are out of the hunt'. In the long run, he was right about the fate of the Liberals. But he was wrong about the prospects of imperialism, and he quickly realised this. By 1913 he was writing sadly: 'I think my Child – an Imperial spirit in England – is dead.' And so it was.[2] Professor Sir Keith Hancock has drawn attention to 'those important years from about 1887 to 1914 when it was decided, once and for all, that the Empire was going to become the Commonwealth, not an imperial federation or a memory'.[3] Perhaps it is not too fanciful to select the years 1905 to 1908 as the decisive years in this span. As Hancock says, in 1907 the empire was 'moving between two worlds'.[4]

There were other shifts of emphasis too. In 1906 the government was charged with interfering too much with self-governing colonies; in 1908 it was criticised for excessive deference to

[1] E. Lyttelton, *Alfred Lyttelton* (1917), pp. 363-4, Lyttelton to B. Holland 2 Oct 10.
[2] J. W. Mackail and Guy Wyndham, *Life and letters of George Wyndham* [n.d.] i, 329, letter to Percy Hurd 23 Jan 98; ii, 540, to his father 24 Jan 06; ii, 734, to his wife 11 Feb 13.
[3] W. K. Hancock, introduction to K. Sinclair, *Imperial Federation: a study of New Zealand policy and opinion* (1955).
[4] W. K. Hancock, *Survey of British Commonwealth Affairs*, i, 'Problems of Nationality 1918–1936' (1937), pp. 49-50. See also above, p. 321.

them. In 1906 Churchill urged the extension of settlement in Kenya; in 1908 Seely not only discouraged it, but wanted to repatriate existing settlers. The entry of Boers was encouraged in 1906, discouraged in 1908. In Nigeria, support shifted from a scheme of western education in 1906 to a programme of extending Moslem education in 1908. To some extent such changes were the result of growing experience, but they also reflect unresolved tensions between conflicting policies.

Paradoxes abound. Infuriation with self-government in Natal and Newfoundland, and disgust with the white settlers in Kenya, had not quite led to repudiation of any further grants of responsible government, or further settlements. Self-government was envisaged for Southern Rhodesia. It was not specifically or unequivocally ruled out for the Kenya colonists. Settlement was being allowed in Rhodesia while it was being condemned in Kenya. Doctrines of trusteeship were becoming more effective in certain circumstances in their protective aspect, but had not yet become positive and constructive. We may note a desire for retrenchment parallel with a determination to spend money. Between 1906 and 1914, the Liberals were more successful than any of their predecessors in prising open the tight fist of the treasury for imperial purposes. Yet economical administration was still much admired. Churchill attacked Milner's costly bureaucracy in the Transvaal, drew attention to 'very grave increases in the ordinary cost of the administration' in the Gambia,[1] refused to co-operate in an Anglo-Egyptian proposal for a through-telegraph from Alexandria to Mombasa – 'They are very free with their money in the Soudan'[2] – and vetoed an office proposal to spend £750 on a report on police in Kenya.[3] We may, moreover, contrast Churchill's plea for informal control in Nigeria in 1906 with his advocacy of 'state socialism' to develop Uganda in 1907. We may observe that the last hankerings for informal control in Africa fizzle out in Somaliland, where the attempt to operate the classical method of control from outside, or at least from

[1] CO. 87/196/1747, 11 Feb 07. [2] CO. 536/22/5236, 5 Mar 08.
[3] CO. 533/28/17426, minute 29 Jul 07.

the coast, proved a decisive failure. Elgin's optimistic remarks about the regenerative effect of the inflow of trade and civilisation co-exist with a deep suspicion of traders and capitalists. Lever was encouraged in the Solomon Islands up to 1906, and, in effect, discouraged in West Africa from 1907. The lease of the Ceylon pearl fisheries was one of the last examples of handing over to private enterprise.

All these things mark the period as a watershed. Some of the attitudes of ministers are inconsistent and irreconcilable. We need not attempt to reconcile them, but acknowledge that old and new attitudes coexisted.

A watershed may be predicated for parts of the empire where the colonial office writ did not run. Of Zanzibar under the foreign office, Dr Flint writes: 'In so far as administrative "policy" existed at all before 1913 it may be said that from about 1907 ideas of development began to override the earlier concern for preserving Arab dominance.' The number of British officials in Zanzibar increased.[1] The Morley–Minto reforms in India reflect admirably one of the paradoxes of the period. Morley strongly denied that they were the instalment towards self-government which they inevitably proved to be. 'For India, the year 1909 marks the watershed between 19th century paternalism and the national self-governing body of today.'[2]

Similarly equivocal and transitional attitudes may be observed in Liberal domestic policy in these years. Asquith as chancellor of the exchequer linked the old liberalism of economy with the new liberalism of old age pensions.[3] The younger men, Lloyd George and Winston Churchill, were evolving ideas which gave an even greater role to the state. This precipitated a 'crisis of liberalism' in which the fundamental question was whether the party could make the intellectual and moral reorientation demanded for successfully

[1] J. E. Flint, 'Zanzibar, 1890–1950' (*History of East Africa*, ii, 654).
[2] H. Tinker, *The foundations of local self-government in India, Pakistan and Burma* (1954), p. 88.
[3] A. Briggs in *Edwardian England, 1901–14*, ed. S. Nowell-Smith (1964), p. 81.

undertaking a new career,[1] or whether the attempt would be written off by the older men as useless and dangerous 'pandering to demagogism all round'.[2]

In the years under consideration, there is no doubt at all that South Africa was the major preoccupation within the empire. Indeed, at the beginning of 1906 it was one of the chief problems of the government, arousing the interest of every cabinet minister. But general ministerial interest in South Africa, and in the empire as a whole, declined sharply after the middle of 1906. Ministers not directly concerned never showed much interest in the administration and development of the tropical territories. Campbell-Bannerman does not appear to have made much impression on imperial policy after the middle of 1906. The colonial policy of the Liberal government was genuinely the policy of Elgin and Churchill. Even after their departure from the colonial office, it is difficult to see that Crewe, with less absorption in departmental affairs, and with a less able parliamentary under-secretary to help him, did much more than continue along the lines laid down by Elgin and Churchill.[3] If length and frequency of minuting is a reliable guide, Elgin showed a more comprehensive interest in the empire, and especially in Africa, than either Lyttelton or Crewe. With Churchill's fertile mind also at work, it is hard to resist the impression that tropical Africa, at any rate, received more ministerial attention between 1905 and 1908 than it did at any time between 1898 and 1911.

Taken as a whole, the continuity of policy between the Unionist and Liberal governments is striking. It was marked in foreign policy. Grey's Egyptian policy was coloured by attitudes similar to those of the Unionists. Legislation for Ireland in 1907 was of a kind which Balfour could have produced. As far as the empire was concerned, Elgin lent the weight of his support in the direction of continuity of administration wherever

[1] J. A. Hobson, *The crisis of Liberalism* (1909), p. xii.
[2] Bryce papers, E. 28, Fitzmaurice to Bryce, 11 Oct 07.
[3] The only matter on which Crewe differed from Elgin was on African marriages in Sierra Leone, see p. 390.

possible, as Lyttelton recognised gratefully.[1] The major changes were the constriction of Chinese Labour and the establishment of immediate (that is to say, without an intermediate stage of representative government) responsible government in the Transvaal and in Orange River Colony. In practice, some concessions were made to the principle of continuity in both policies. Apart from the eventual withdrawal from the interior of Somaliland, there were no changes of policy in other parts of Africa comparable in importance with those which took place in the Transvaal. Lugard's scheme for administration was probably bound to fail. Repatriation of Kenya settlers never materialised, but would have been tremendously important. No Unionist government could ever have contemplated such a step. It marks therefore a difference of approach. But Chamberlain's policy of development was continued. There was no difference on promotion of cotton-growing, or on treatment of the Asiatic problem. Land policy was clarified rather than altered. Such continuity does not conflict with the concept of a watershed, implying change. The significant point is that the Liberals were prepared to continue Unionist policies in certain ways: this constitutes a watershed in the evolution of Liberalism.

One difference can, however, be detected. The Liberals were inclined to rely much less than the Unionists on the advice of the 'man on the spot', and much more on their office staff. This was natural in so far as they had not appointed the men in politically important posts. There was a very wide divergence of view from Selborne, and his recommendations were very rarely approved.[2] Their much less subservient attitude to Lugard led to his resignation. On the other hand, apart from some difference of opinion on the question of the timing of self-government for the Transvaal, there seems to have been considerable harmony between Liberal ministers and their departmental advisers. By contrast, the Unionist cabinet had ignored civil service advice on Chinese Labour, on constitutional change

[1] See p. 519.
[2] See for example, pp. 142, 178, 263, 267, 280–2, 388.

in the Transvaal, on the name and constitution of the colonial conference, and on Lugard's administrative scheme.

After some initial uncertainty, the members of the Liberal government proved themselves to be as realistic in imperial policy as the Unionists, who had doubted whether the Liberals would prove fit to run an empire. Those who dealt with problems of race relations, Elgin, Grey, Morley and Crewe, resolutely refused, though not with uniform success, to be deflected from realistic courses of action by the pressure of their radical rank-and-file, whom they pejoratively referred to in their private correspondence as sentimentalists.[1] It was not sentimentality as such that they thought did the mischief. This Crewe regarded as a superficial view, because he believed

that Byleses and MacKarnesses are almost as scarce as the white rhino' (of which Mr Roosevelt killed too many, I fear), and that the harm comes not from a moral source, but from intellectual indolence, which misapplies political maxims in countries like Egypt by treating them as if they were fundamental truths.[2]

Ministers did not undervalue noble emotions and good intentions, but generally they would not arrange the whole duty of government on a catalogue of first principles, and apply them rigidly. They had little time for public opinion which manifested itself as sentiment divorced from full knowledge, impartial responsibility and a cool comprehension of realities – especially if it led to agitation which added to the difficulty of busy ministerial lives.[3] They were contemptuous of attempts to apply the doctrines of the equality of man, or 'Civis Britannicus sum', without qualification.[4] They eschewed writing general propositions into the Transvaal constitution. Elgin had long realised the importance of avoiding shibboleths. 'It is folly to

[1] See p. 176 and pp. 276–7.
[2] GP, Crewe to Grey 5 Jun 10.
[3] MM. 2/285; Morley, *Indian speeches*, p. 51; GP. 7, Grey to Gorst 6 Nov 07.
[4] E.g. PD. 193/2029, Seely 31 Jul 08.

legislate for India on the same lines as for Scotland', he once wrote.[1] He no more regarded responsible government as a fetish, to be applied without qualification to all white communities, than he regarded the full heritage of English law as a panacea to be imposed, as a *sine qua non* of progress, on all African territories.[2] Liberal ministers were not implacably opposed to state control of economic activity in the empire, or to plantations in West Africa, or to indentured labour, or to Indian immigration into Kenya, or to the freehold tenure of non-European land by Europeans. Almost the only principles they applied inflexibly were trade principles. Free trade was firmly upheld, caravan-tolls were abolished in the Gold Coast, the Brussels sugar convention repudiated, export duties everywhere discouraged,[3] and all forms of monopoly, 'the most retrograde and fatal of all policies for a commercial country' as Elgin described them, were opposed.[4]

While they managed not to be unduly doctrinaire, they tended to rely rather heavily upon analogy. Tropical Africa

[1] VRP. 13/189, 9 Dec 95, 16/178, 3 Nov 98.

[2] VRP. 13/189, 9 Dec 95; EP, E to Selb. 13 Jul 06. Elgin was uneasy about the general application of the law of a highly civilised country to a territory like Nyasaland, and suggested a declaration should be made that English statute law applied only 'so far as circumstances permit' (CO. 525/20/26316, minute 16 Aug 07).

[3] CO. 96/459/30214, S/S to govr 15 Apr 08. In 1914 only the Gambia had export duties among British West African possessions. In March 1907 assent was withheld to a bill to amend the tea duty in Mauritius, the object of which was to give further protection to tea planters, and so to relieve the colony from its precarious dependence on sugar. 'It is rank heresy', said Churchill. Like Hopwood, he was on the side of the consumer. The interests of a few individuals could not be allowed to impose a tax on the whole community for one of the necessaries of life. The principle of the bill was directly opposed to the declared policy of H.M.G. (CO. 167/778/5990, minute 4 Mar, S/S to govr 15 Mar 07). The government of the Leeward Islands advised an export duty on cotton to raise additional revenue in Antigua. Elgin and Churchill thought this had 'an ugly ring': it was undesirable to place any handicap on the expansion of the cotton industry. If it was absolutely necessary to raise revenue and no other means was available, a moderate increase of land tax (which the cotton planters would pay) was less objectionable (CO. 152/297/28041, minutes 20 and 24 Apr, S/S to govr 3 Sep 07).

[4] CO. 323/520/42027, minute 29 Nov 06. The dislike of monopoly extended to monopoly recruiting by the Witwatersrand Native Labour Association, which Elgin took steps to end (EP, E to WSC 3 and 9 Jun 06).

posed difficult and unfamiliar problems, and much could be, and was, learned by bringing Indian experience to bear, as Lugard and Morel advocated.[1] Whilst thinking in terms of Indian or Canadian analogy, or sometimes even Australian or Irish analogy,[2] gave them a frame of reference, helping them to understand the problems facing them in a different perspective, their decisions were not dependent solely, or even largely, upon the use of analogy. Aside from its relevance in working out administrative details, applied experience affected attitudes more than decisions, the exposition rather than the adoption of policy. Because of his intimate experience as viceroy, Elgin probably tended to think of Africa almost continually in terms of Indian comparisons, without distinguishing sufficiently the difference in social structure. It was standard practice for those who wished to persuade him to any course of action to appeal to his Indian experience.[3] Though this might be the way to engage his heart, he was no slave to analogy.[4]

Africa was big enough to permit the application of analogy between its constituent parts. The lessons of South African experience reacted on the approach to the whole continent. It is perhaps hardly to be expected that the Liberal ministers should have seen African policy as a whole. South Africa had been under the British flag for much longer than tropical Africa, and had been bedevilled by an entrenched white colonial community. Egypt was not only under foreign office

[1] E. D. Morel, *Nigeria*, pp. 152, 159; F. Lugard, *The Dual Mandate*, pp. 46–7, 530, 607.

[2] Irish analogies with the situation in Johannesburg were noted by Sandhurst (Ripon papers 43639/173, 194) and Merriman (Bryce papers, Merriman to Bryce, 20 Jun 99, 18 Oct 99). 'Through the difficulties of Ireland,' said Grey, 'we have learnt more sympathy and caution on being on our guard against oppression than we should have learnt but for that experience' (PD. 160/316, 5 Jul 06). See also p. 183.

[3] E.g. Egerton, CO. 520/43/5148; Stanmore, PD. 178/479; Marlborough, PD. 156/1424.

[4] See his minute on the question of introducing either the Indian penal code or the Queensland code (which Lyttelton had preferred) into Southern Nigeria. Elgin felt the Indian code more likely to be suitable for a mixed pagan and Mohammedan population, but: 'I have no prejudice for the Indian code ... and therefore I am disposed to postpone decision for a time (as Mr Cox thinks can be done) and to obtain more advice' (CO. 520/35/14841, minute 21 Sep 06).

control, but the problems of governing it were thought to have affinities with India rather than with the colonial office territories. Nevertheless, there was some attempt to secure uniformity of policy throughout the tropical regions.[1] Although there was nothing like an African studies branch, there was a beginning made with collating and reflecting upon experience in different parts. Foreign office policy in Egypt and Zanzibar was not inconsistent with African policy in general.

In the sense that the government had at its disposal a fairly mature accumulation of knowledge and experience, it was possible to treat the problems of empire with a greater degree of sophistication at the beginning of the twentieth century than ever before. Many Liberal ministers had governmental experience of India or Ireland, or had travelled widely. They were served by governors with long and varied experience all over the world.[2] Several ministers and officials had become deeply interested in the problems created by the expansion of Europe, and could not only see their work in intellectual and historical terms, but express it in books.[3] The resources before the government were neither rich nor adequate, but they were superior to anything previously available.

[1] See above p. 212, n. 2 and pp. 424–5. The tropical African Services Committee considered amalgamation of the East and West Africa services in its interim report, July 1910 (CO. 96/503/20964).

[2] Elgin, Ripon, Ridgeway and Cromer had all served in India. Crewe, Morley and Ridgeway had experience of governing Ireland. Before taking office, Bryce had toured South Africa, Churchill had visited South Africa, India and the Sudan; Samuel (under home secretary) had been to Uganda in 1902, Seely had travelled in New Zealand as well as South Africa. Whilst in office, Churchill visited Malta, Cyprus, Aden, Cairo, Somaliland, Kenya and Uganda. Just, Fiddes and Hopwood of the CO had been in South Africa, Olivier in Jamaica. None of the eleven governors of tropical Africa and Natal had experience of dealing with only African colonies. Lucas made an official tour of Australia and New Zealand in 1909.

[3] For example, works by Bryce: *Impressions of South Africa*, and his Romanes lecture on the relations of the advanced and backward races; see also *Modern Democracies* (1923), chap. lxxi, 'Democracy and the backward races'. See also Lord Cromer, *Modern Egypt* (1908) and *Ancient and Modern Imperialism* (1910), WSC, *My African Journey*. Of the civil servants, C. P. Lucas had started publishing his *Historical Geography of the British Colonies* in 1888; he also wrote two books on Canadian history in 1906 and 1909; the first edition of A. B. Keith's *Responsible Government in the Dominions* came out in 1909. See also, G. Lagden, *The Basutos* (1909), and F. D. Lugard, *The rise of our East African empire* (2 vols, 1893).

The combined result of their realism, their analogies and their sophistication was that the Liberals saw clearly what they ought not to do, but not what they ought positively to do. The pitfalls had been mapped. They could rehearse all the objections to action. The idea that this was a period characterised by a last flowering of easy self-confidence and unbounded optimism must be questioned. Pessimism stands out more clearly in India[1] than in South Africa. Maybe the Liberals became more optimistic about South Africa between 1906 and 1909, but it is difficult to believe that much of their apparent and publicly proclaimed optimism in 1909 was genuine. So often what looks like optimism might be no more than over-rationalisation.[2] 'The zeal of liberalism', wrote J. A. Hobson in 1909, 'is everywhere chilled by doubts and difficulties.'[3] At all events, they had unpleasant misgivings about the value of applying purely political solutions, such as the grant of franchise rights, to the problem of race relations. They were more likely to try to reduce the hardship resulting from legislation discriminating against non-Europeans, by mitigating the administration of the law than by striving to amend the law. Morley expressed a common view among cabinet ministers when he described himself as 'cool and sceptical about *political* change, either in India or other places'. He wondered whether a reform policy and 'virtuous deeds' would make 'a pin of difference' to Indian objections to British rule.[4] Elgin had felt the same. On the other hand, Morley also felt that although their reforms might not save the British *raj*, nothing else would:

Our liberal experiment may fail. The Tory experiment of grudging and half-and-half concession is sure to fail; sure to end in dangerous impotence. The only chance, be it a good chance or a bad chance, is to do our best to make English rulers

[1] M. V. Brett (ed.), *Journals and Letters of Viscount Esher*, ii, 344, 350–1; Ripon papers 43543/92, 43552/223.
[2] See for example pp. 148, 170, 187.
[3] *The crisis of liberalism*, p. 91; nor is there much optimism in J. R. MacDonald, *Labour and the Empire* (1907), p. 106; nor in Garvin's contribution to *The Empire and the Century* (ed. C. S. Goldman, 1905), p. 69.
[4] MM. 3/84, 28 Mar 08, 2/199, 15 Aug 07.

friends with Indian leaders, and at the same time to do our best to train them in habits of political responsibility.[1]

Liberal policy in South Africa and in Egypt shows parallel attitudes. The Liberals thought that the surest road to improvement of native policy must be the achievement of a right spirit within those who actually lived among and must rule non-European peoples, and consequently that the only effective way to deal with 'the native problem' was to await the conversion of local public opinion to more generous ideas.

Direct political action was therefore not undertaken with enthusiasm. It was avoided if possible. The colonial office was in fact steadily divesting itself, or preventing the accretion, of even administrative responsibility. This was partly because its resources had been strained by the increase in the number of territories under its control. Self-government was given to the Transvaal and Orange River Colony, and then to a united South Africa. Once given, the imperial government intervened with decreasing force and frequency. At the same time, efforts were made to prepare the peoples of India and of Egypt[2] to take a larger share in their own administration. White settlers were also still being encouraged to take part in their own government: Nyasaland and Kenya both received legislative councils in these years.[3] In tribal Africa, indirect rule was preferred to direct administration. Detailed control in tropical

[1] Ibid. 3/151, 7 May 08, 4/72–3, 2 Apr 09. Smuts' view seems to have been similar: see Hancock, *Smuts*, i, 221.

[2] The policy of Grey and Gorst (who succeeded Cromer) from 1907 was to prepare Egyptians for self-government by enlarging the scope and powers for provincial councils, appointing a new ministry, improving the conditions under which the legislative council and general assembly exercised their consultative functions, increasing the number of Egyptians in posts of responsibility (previously held by Europeans), and continuing the development of the educational system on 'national' lines (FO. 371/661/12738).

[3] Nyasaland obtained executive and legislative councils, although the European settler population was not much over 600 persons, for there was a strong feeling among them that they should be allowed some means of expressing their views (CO. 525/17/14033, 28 Feb 07, Sharpe to S/S). The new constitution was proclaimed on 21 Oct 07 and the name changed to Nyasaland from British Central Africa Protectorate.

administration from Whitehall was consciously slackened whenever possible.[1]

Twenty or thirty years earlier, Liberal recognition of and sympathy for nationalist movements was almost confined to Gladstone and Bright, but it was now becoming more generally and fully diffused among Liberals, as their discussion of the Transvaal constitution demonstrates.[2] This appreciation was mainly, though not exclusively, for white colonial nationalism. Even this would have been an advance on Unionist understanding, but there was also a groping towards talking in terms of African nationalism. Alike in South Africa, Ireland, and even in India and Egypt, the Liberal government tried to co-operate with moderate nationalist leaders. It was demonstrably effective in West Africa. They received deputations from non-Europeans, and gave private interviews; Morley saw Gokhale several times. Besides seeing Gandhi, Elgin granted interviews to some Africans, including the Rev. K. Egyir-Asaam, representing the Aborigines' Rights Protection Society of the Gold Coast.[3] There was a growing feeling that the continued appointment of British officials would lose more by the effect on popular content in Egypt than it would gain in administrative efficiency. The volume of nationalist feeling in Egypt was gauged more accurately by Grey than by his officials.[4]

[1] Lyttelton thought it impossible to manage the Uganda railway from Whitehall (CO. 533/2/22482, minute 10 Aug 05). Elgin agreed (CO. 533/4/37772, 31 Dec 05, and 6/45751, 2 Feb 06): the treasury had drifted into the habit of laying down rules about details of railway management. Crewe wanted changes in Uganda railway rates to be decided locally, and not approved by the treasury: 'To govern a railway on the Equator from here, is like conducting a war by an Aulic Council' (CO. 533/63/37269, minute 22 Nov 09).

[2] See especially pp. 153, 172, 182–4, 190.

[3] The society presented a petition signed by more than 70 chiefs against municipal house rates and demanding repeal of the Town Councils ordinance. It was agreed that the representative element on the councils might be enlarged when they had gained sufficient experience. Although the colonial office was not prepared to concede any immediate change, it treated the society with courteous recognition (D. Kimble, *Political history of Ghana*, (1963), 360–1).

[4] FO. 371/449/6182, Feb 08. On the death of Mustapha Kamel, an official minuted: 'It appears probable that the Nationalist party will collapse.' Grey wrote that the demonstration of feeling at the funeral was remarkable and showed the great volume of nationalist feeling which existed in Egypt.

The Liberal government, and the official mind generally, is frequently charged with insufficient awareness of racial problems, with forgetting their obligations to non-Europeans, with neglecting native interests, and with sacrificing them to European ideals, such as Anglo-Afrikaner reconciliation, or, in Kenya, white settlement.[1] This charge is unfair. Concern for African interests was central to their entire approach to African policy. They might legitimately be criticised for not doing enough to ensure their protection and progress, but it is ridiculous to assert that they ignored the problem. The word 'trusteeship' was frequently on their lips, and it meant something to them.[2]

They did not know much about Africans. Ignorance and dwindling confidence bred fear. Europeans were already on the defensive.[3] One of the most remarkable facts about the treatment of the native problem is that it was consistently discussed within the context of apprehended native risings against Europeans. This was not quite as strong in London as it was among the settler communities themselves, but it was present, even prominent, none the less. There was genuine concern for the well-being of non-Europeans too, as the medical measures in Africa indicate. But the conclusion that there was preoccupation in government with keeping peace among Africans and with obtaining security for Europeans in their midst, is inescapable. At the root of anxiety about white settlement, about missionary enterprise, about capitalist exploitation and about the system in Leopold's Congo, was the fear of provoking violent and widespread African reactions. Feelings of

[1] See for example, Pyrah, *Imperial policy and South Africa 1902–10*, pp. 93, 236; Thompson, *Unification of South Africa*, p. 24; Oliver and Fage, *A Short History of Africa*, p. 227.

[2] WSC spoke of India as a great trust in Feb 04 (*For Free Trade* (1906), p. 70). Asquith spoke of the trust at the imperial conference of 1911. Morley used it in July 1906 (PD. 155/571). For Elgin's use of the trust doctrine, see pp. 410, 473; for Crewe's, see CO. 417/468/21210, 31 Jul 09, etc.

[3] 'We have to recognise the fact', declared Elgin, 'that all over the world, there are difficulties arising on the part of white communities' (Cd. 3308, speech to Transvaal Indian deputation 8 Nov 06).

insecurity were pervasive.[1] Moreover, if they failed to keep peace, one of their main justifications for ruling African and other peoples would seem to collapse.[2]

The mid-Victorian objective of turning Africans into black Europeans had long been given up, and the question of educating them towards self-government of the European type relegated to the distant future. Gilbert Murray noted in 1900 that the question was distasteful to modern politicians: 'no political party with any prospect of holding office seems to have the faintest hope of achieving that end, or even much desire of working towards it.'[3] Fresh but partial advances were made in India and Egypt, but in Africa, Elgin's attempt to direct the redefinition of native policy in the light of existing circumstances, recent historical experience, and the teaching of pseudo-Darwinian science, led only to a policy of developing native institutions along native lines. The tendency was, perhaps, more than in traditional Liberal native policy, towards segregation rather than assimilation, though elements in the Liberal tradition had always believed in separate development.[4] Probably the main reason for this was the collapse of the old confidence that Europeanisation was inevitably beneficial. Elgin did not regard ready access to law courts as a boon to

[1] See above, pp. 159, 176, 214, 257, 375, 403, 411. WSC referred to the fear of a rising in African (S) 804, 2 Jan 06, Selb. in CO. 291/119/32934. See also cab. memo. by E 13 Nov 07, Merriman to Bryce (Bryce papers 6 Oct 08). There was a notable minute by Graham 14 Mar 06: 'South Africa always has been and will be for many a year yet, subject to the risk of a great native rising, and I fear that the most liberal policy possible will not remove this. On the contrary, I am disposed to think that for some time to come the danger will increase . . .' (CO. 179/233/8487). See also MM. 4/65. The Colonists' Association of Kenya in 1905 expected a 'black rebellion': 'We stand practically on the edge of a human volcano, which may at any time burst forth in uncontrollable eruption and destroy us . . . that it will come is an absolute certainty.' The colonial office replied that 'just treatment of the natives is the surest safeguard of the settlers' (House of Lords papers, no. 158 (1907), 34–5, 40).

[2] See above, pp. 196, n. 3 and p. 213.

[3] In *Liberalism and the empire*, ed. F. W. Hirst (1900), p. 151.

[4] 'John Bull' said W. P. Schreiner, is 'as good an Afrikander as any of us' (E. A. Walker, *W. P. Schreiner*, p. 311. See also Hancock, *Survey*, ii, part 2, 194, and above, p. 372.

natives;[1] nor did he think an Indian prince likely to be 'more contented or more useful if he has been an Etonian and an officer of a cavalry regiment'.[2] This disillusionment and uncertainty was well reflected by L. T. Hobhouse in 1911:

A specious extension of the white man's rights to the black may be the best way of ruining the black. To destroy tribal custom by introducing conceptions of individual property, the free disposal of land, and the free purchase of gin, may be the handiest method for the expropriator . . . perhaps our safest course, so far as principles and deductions avail at all, is to fix our eyes on the elements of the matter, and in any part of the world to support whatever method succeeds in securing the 'coloured' man from personal violence, from the lash, from expropriation, and from gin; above all, so far as it may yet be, from the white man himself. Until the white man has fully learnt to rule his own life, the best of all things that he can do with the dark man is to do nothing with him. In this relation, the day of a more constructive Liberalism is yet to come.[3]

The government was thus rather better at checking evils and stopping abuses, and preventing the emergence of fresh ones, than it was at devising a constructive programme for future development. Ministers were quick to embarrass the perpetrators of wrong by flashing the glare of publicity upon them whenever they could.[4] In this sense, they lived up to their

[1] CO. 179/239/32723, minute 9 Sep 06. Notice also his opinion that ardent reformers did not always 'allow sufficiently for the presence in human nature of wayward impulse, which cannot be brought under control in a day or by a stroke of the pen, and must be conquered by patience and the training of years, or perhaps of generations' (VRP. 88/350, speech 17 May 97).

[2] VRP. 15/App. 109, 13 Oct 97.

[3] L. T. Hobhouse, *Liberalism* (1911), pp. 43–4.

[4] 'There can be no question', said Crewe, 'that almost all the records of ill-doing in Africa, whether by individuals or companies, show that it has been very largely caused or aided by the absence of publicity' (PD. 184/1304, 24 Feb 08). Churchill was generally 'strongly of opinion that every officer against whom a definite charge is preferred should be brought to trial before a recognised tribunal. Endless inconvenience and often flagrant injustice is caused by good-natured attempts to hush up delinquencies and hustle the officer quietly out of the service without a scandal' (CO. 111/548/44167, 23 Dec 05). As an example of firm determination to prevent abuses, the files of Southern Nigeria may be quoted. Early in December 1906, Mr O. S. Crewe Read flogged some Africans aboard the launch *Otto*. In retaliation, Crewe Read was murdered, and encouragement given

intention of restoring the principles of morality and justice to the government of the empire. They insisted on public trials for Chinese Labourers as well as for Dinizulu. The disinfectant of publicity must wash over Leopold's Congo as well as over Milner's bureaucracy. There was as much concern for African interests as for the expediency of imperial rule and reputation. Beyond this, however, they scarcely ventured. Crewe and Seely agreed that:

it is all very difficult . . . there is no royal road, no golden rule, and that we here, who are far enough away to be impartial, must do the best we can, when and how we can, by safeguarding their lands and by protecting them from temptations, to save the subject race.[1]

If the imperial government, with all its accumulated historical and actual experience from all parts of the globe, was not clear what should be done, then how much the less qualified did it believe that non-Europeans themselves were to determine the direction of their own evolution. The Basuto and the Baganda, the Egyptians, and even the Boers, were all in these years described by various government advisers as, politically

---

to encroachments of the paramount chiefs of Benin. The governor ordered an enquiry, which found that though not cruel or severe, the floggings were illegal and improper. Secretary of state wrote: 'I have learned with great regret that the late Mr Crewe Read caused native chiefs to be flogged, and that much unnecessary and even useless work was demanded, provoking very great discontent amongst a population whose character I gather is not peaceable. . . .

'Steps should be taken to prevent, as far as possible, the recurrence of similar action on the part of any other officer; and it is in the highest degree important that any such abuse of authority would entail their instant dismissal from the service' (CO. 520/38/2149, S/S to govr 15 Mar 07).

Lugard was asked by telegraph to report by telegraph the number of floggings in the W.A.F.F. since 1905. 'Even Lugard, moderate and humane as he was for a man in his position, was the better for Liberal checks and questions, if only because they reminded him to control his own agents' (Perham, *Lugard*, ii, 199, 275).

The punitive cutting of women's hair in British Guiana was frowned upon (CO. 111/547/2418, S/S to govr 6 Feb 06). When it was alleged that part of the wages of Chinese miners in the Federated Malay States was paid in opium, immediate cessation of this practice was suggested, and other forms of truck condemned (CO. 273/321/39545, S/S to govr 9 Nov 06).

[1] CO. 417/463/38204, minute by Seely 30 Oct 08.

speaking, 'mere children',[1] whose views of their own good could not be allowed to prevail against British views (even when these did not exist). The regeneration of Africans and Egyptians[2] might be accomplished along native lines, but it was Britain who determined the shape and rate of advance. Only such customs and institutions as Britain did not think repugnant to civilised ideas were preserved.

If the future of non-Europeans was left open, if the future of Kenya was left vague, if the Egyptian advance to self-government was halted, the explanation is not one of wilful neglect, still less of churlish indifference. Questions of race relations, and the government of non-Europeans, were perhaps to some extent deliberately shelved. Ministers appear to have been anxious not to prejudice the interests of non-Europeans by undertaking fundamental consideration of such questions at a time they thought premature or otherwise unfavourable, or by making makeshift arrangements.[3] But the ultimate reason for the government's sins of omission, both in political treatment of the non-Europeans themselves and in economic development in their interest, does not rest here. Planning for the future was not yet regarded as very important, and in any case they lacked time and the energy to undertake it. The immediate and routine problems of administration absorbed most of their attention. They did not generally make elaborate calculations for the future, nor often mount to the high summits where long-term plans for the empire could be made. Crewe summed up the typical attitude:

---

[1] See above, p. 370; for Selborne on the Basuto, see CO. 417/459/29921, to S/S 27 Jul 08; for Cromer on Egyptians, see GP. 7, to Grey 26 May 06; for Graham on the Boers, see CO. 291/95/2011, minute 19 Jan 06.

[2] There is a parallel between the ideal in African administration and in Egyptian. Campbell-Bannerman hailed Cromer for, as he thought, understanding that 'the regeneration of Egypt could only be effected through the Egyptians themselves'. He sought 'to preserve what was vital and characteristic in their habits, laws and customs . . . employing as far as possible native agents, he hoped to enable them to develop along their own lines', rather than allow them to meet the civilisation of the West as hybrids (PD. 179/838, 30 Jul 07).

[3] See pp. 164, 265, 376, 378.

What will be the future of India, fifty, sixty, or a hundred years hence [he said], need not, I think, trouble us. It is on the knees of the gods, and all we have to do is to provide, as best as we can, for the conditions of the moment, having, of course, an eye to the future, but not troubling ourselves about what may happen in days when, to use Sheridan's words – 'all of us are dead and most of us are forgotten'.[1]

The worst of cabinet government, Morley remarked, was that ministers lived for the day, and were content to leave their successors to fend for themselves. The minister who presumed for a few minutes, he said, to draw attention to a possible day after tomorrow, was considered a bore of the worst kind, an irrelevant bore.[2] Elgin, to his credit, tried to break through this inhibiting barrier with the reminder in April 1906 that it was 'not too soon even now to take the future [of Africans] into account'. He had always tried to frame measures so as to guard as far as possible against the dangers of the future, but he too was the prisoner of his age, and at the same time, saw 'a danger in looking too far ahead and not observing the rocks that may be under the bows'.[3]

Liberal policy was not, however, simply the re-application of traditional policy. We have stressed that it contained more state aid, increasing segregation of Africans, less hankering for systems of informal control, a new attitude to land tenure, preferring leases where possible, and more construction, in the Chamberlain sense of actively promoting economic development. How did the differences arise? More, it would seem, from growing devotion to the principle of respecting continuity of policy through changes of government, or from on-the-spot practice and observation, or from the development of elements in the older Liberal policy, than from any inspiration from left-wing theorists or intellectuals. The only one of these whose influence can be traced with any certainty is E. D. Morel.[4]

[1] PD/HL. 1/215, 24 Feb 09; see also Grey, *Twenty-five years*, i, 6.
[2] MM. 2/290, 8 Nov 07; for further evidence of this attitude see MM. 1/32, 4/145, 2/25, 5/9 Mar and 19 Apr 10; Bryce, *Impressions of South Africa*, p. 368.
[3] See above, p. 375; VRP. 15/App. 94, 7 Sep 97.
[4] See p. 403.

As far as tropical Africa is concerned, there is little that can be called a distinctively Liberal policy. The striking features of policy were a paramount concern with peace, and a similarity with Unionist policy. The Trust is not distinctively Liberal. Lyttelton, Lansdowne and Selborne all professed it. Chamberlain had, before Elgin, favoured developing native institutions on native lines. In 1910 there was little policy in any part of Africa which the Unionists wished to quarrel with, except the reduced control over Somaliland, the one African issue which was in any sense controversial. The Liberal attitude, spirit and approach show more difference than their actual policy.

What then is the significance of these years in the history of British imperial policy? The principle of self-government was accorded increasing deference, as is especially evident with the Transvaal. The more complete acceptance of its limitations on imperial action marked a clear stage on the road to the Statute of Westminster. The 'magnanimous' grants of self-government to the Transvaal and Orange River Colony had their part to play in the evolution of the modern commonwealth.[1] A dominions department was established in the colonial office, as part of a modernisation scheme. The colonial conference of 1907 proved the decisive turning-point in the demise of schemes for more formal machinery of empire. The idea of a permanent independent secretariat or commission was rejected. The pacification of Africa was practically completed, with a sharpened emphasis on the gentler methods. The first seeds were sown of policies which would later germinate in a system of welfare and development. In the treatment of Africans, native interests were kept well to the fore, and the principle of ruling through tribal chiefs was becoming unequivocally established in imperial policy, now that Liberals signified their acceptance of it. The commercial development of Africa was pressed with plenty of enthusiasm and some incipient sense of urgency. The Liberal government spent more money and

[1] Mansergh, *South Africa 1906–1961*, 92–8; on p. 94 Gokhale is quoted: 'The cases of the French in Canada and the Boers in South Africa showed that there was room in the Empire for a self-governing India' (1907).

directed economic development increasingly readily as time went on. Some of the bureaucratic arrogance and heavy-handedness of the colonial administration of the Chamberlain era was diminished. Administrative standards were tightened up, and brought more into line with the practice of the Indian civil service. Trusteeship conscience revived. As a result, some of the sting was taken out of 'anti-imperialism'. In all these ways, the short and lively partnership of Elgin and Churchill was fruitful, and constitutes the watershed between the nineteenth-century empire and the twentieth-century common-wealth.

Bibliography

UNPUBLISHED MATERIALS

(1) *Colonial Office Records* (Public Record Office) [* denotes end of series]

Bahamas, CO. 23/261–3 (Jan 06–Dec 08)
Barbados, CO. 28/265–71 (Jan 06–Dec 08)
Bermuda, CO. 37/243–54 (Jan 06–Dec 08)
Canada, CO. 42/906–28 (Jan 06–Dec 08)
Cape Colony, CO. 48/581, 584–606* (Dec 05–1910)
Ceylon, CO. 54/696, 699–720 (Dec 05–Dec 08)
Cyprus, CO. 67/145–52 (Jan 06–Apr 08)
Falkland Is., CO. 78/107–13 (Jan 06–Apr 08)
Fiji, CO. 83/82–9 (Jan 06–Apr 08).
Gambia, CO. 87/173–84 (Jan 05–Dec 10)
Gibraltar, CO. 91/433–9 (Dec 05–Apr 08)
Gold Coast, CO. 96/433, 440–91 (Dec 05–Dec 09), 492–9
British Guiana, CO. 111/547–61, 564 (Dec 05–Apr 08)
British Honduras, CO. 123/251–8, 260 (Dec 05–Apr 08)
Hong Kong, CO. 129/333–6, 339–42, 346–7 (Jan 06–Apr 08)
Jamaica, CO. 137/650–63, 667–9 (Jan 06–Apr 08)
Lagos, CO. 147/176, 179* (1905–6)
Leeward Is., CO. 152/289–99, 301–2 (Jan 06–Apr 08)
Malta, CO. 158/351–60 (Jan 06–Apr 08)
Mauritius, CO. 167/774–80, 782–4, 786–7 (Jan 06–Apr 08)
Natal, CO. 179/232, 233–56* (Dec 05–1910)
Newfoundland, CO. 194/262–4, 266–72 (Jan 06–Apr 08)
New Zealand, CO. 209/267–9 (Dec 05–Dec 06; continues in CO. 418)
Orange River Colony, CO. 224/18–19, 20–33* (Jan 06–1910)

Western Pacific, CO. 225/71–81, 83–4 (Dec 05–Apr 08)

St Helena, CO. 247/165–72 (Jan 06–Apr 08)

Sierra Leone, CO. 267/472–520 (Jan 04–Dec 09)

Straits Settlements, CO. 273/317–45 (Jan 06–Apr 08)

Transvaal, CO. 291/68–145* (Jan 04–1910)

Trinidad, CO. 295/434, 436–44, 447–8 (Dec 05–Apr 08)

West Indies, CO. 318/314–19 (Jan 06–Apr 08)

Windward Is., CO. 321/230–40, 242, 244 (Jan 06–Apr 08)

General, CO. 323/513–62 (Dec 05–Dec 09)

South Africa, CO. 417/410, 413, 422–78 (Dec 05–Dec 09)

Australia, CO. 418/44–60 (Jan 06–Apr 08: includes New Zealand 1907–8)

Northern Nigeria, CO. 446/47, 50, 52–88 (Dec 05–Dec 09)

East Africa Protectorate (Kenya), CO. 519/1, CO. 533/1–70 (1904–Dec 09)

Southern Nigeria, CO. 520/32, 35–90 (Dec 05–Dec 09)

Nyasaland (British Central Africa Protectorate), CO. 525/9, 12–31 (Dec 05–Dec 09)

Seychelles, CO. 530/3–8, 10 (Dec 05–Apr 08)

Dominions, CO. 532/1–12 (Jan 07–Apr 08)

Somaliland, CO. 535/1–17 (Jan 05–Dec 09), 18–20

Uganda, CO. 536/1–31 (Jan 05–Dec 09)

Circular despatches, CO. 854/42–3, 45–6

Confidential print, CO. 879/91–2, 106: CO. 882/8, CO. 885/17–18

(2) *Cabinet Records* (Public Record Office)

Prime minister's letters to sovereign – CAB. 41/30–1 (Dec 05–Apr 08). (Photographic copies of original letters in Royal Archives made available by gracious permission of H.M. The Queen.)

Memoranda printed for the use of the cabinet – CAB. 37/80–108 (also EP).

(3) *Private Papers*

COLLECTION	LOCATION	PORTIONS REFERRED TO
Asquith	New Bodleian	Boxes, Dep. 5, 9, 10, 11, 12, 46, and first three boxes of cabinet papers (to 1911)
Balfour	B[ritish] M[useum]	Add. MSS. 49708, 49719, 49721, 49724, 49729, 49733, 49774, 49775, 49778
Bryce	New Bodleian	Vols 3, 17; boxes E. 27, E. 28; South Africa/C. 2, C. 5.
Campbell-Bannerman	B.M.	Add. MSS. 41207, 41208, 41210, 41211, 41212, 41213, 41214, 41217, 41218, 41220, 41222, 41223, 41224, 41225, 41230, 41231, 41238, 41239, 41240, 41242, 41243A, 41243B
Cromer	Public Record Office	FO. 633/8, 11, 12, 13, 14, 18, 18, 25, 26
Dilke	B.M.	Add. MSS. 43877, 43882, 43895, 43897, 43919, 43920, 43921, 43922, 49610
Elgin, Viceroy of India 1894–9	India Office Library	MSS. Eur. F. 84/12, 13, 14, 15, 16, 18, 29, 30, 31, 32, 33, 132 (letters etc.) and 88 (Speeches)
Elgin, Colonial Secretary, 1905–8	Broomhall, Dunfermline	All
Viscount Gladstone	B.M.	Add. MSS. 45988, 45997 46042, 46063, 46064, 46065
Grey	Public Record Office	FO. 800/41, 45, 46, 90, 91, 92, 97, 98, 99
Haldane	National Library of Scotland	MS. 5907/6, 7, 8
Morel	London School of Economics	F. 8 and F. 9
Morley (Letters to Minto)	India Office Library	MSS. Eur. D. 573/1, 2, 3, 4, 5
Ripon	B.M.	Add. MSS. 43518, 43541, 43542, 43543, 43552, 43579, 43580, 43589, 43603, 43639, 43640

PUBLISHED MATERIALS

(1) *Parliamentary Papers*

COMMAND NO.	SUBJECT	VOLUME YEAR	NO.
Cd. 2325	West Africa, construction of railways	1905	lvi
2399	South Africa: report of Native Affairs Commission	1905	lv
2906	Lease of pearl fisheries on the coast of Ceylon	1906	lxxvii
3250	Transvaal letters patent	1906	lxxx
3288	Convention with France respecting New Hebrides	1907	lvi
3523	Minutes and proceedings of colonial conference 1907	1907	lv
3564	Federation (the Selborne memo.)	1907	lvii
3565	Brussels Sugar Convention	1907	lxxxvii
4396	Congo	1908	lxxi
4910	Report on the introduction and establishment of the cotton industry in the Uganda protectorate	1909	lix
4990	Report on the measures for the suppression of sleeping sickness in Uganda	1910	lxv
5102	Report of the Northern Nigeria Lands committee	1910	xliv

(2) *Parliamentary Debates, 4th series*

L = Lords, C = Commons

VOL. NO.	HOUSE	DATE	SUBJECT
129	C	16 Feb 04	(Address in reply to King's speech) Chinese Labour
132	C	21 Mar 04	Vote of Censure, Chinese Labour
144	C	5 Apr 05	Cotton cultivation
150	C	27 Jul 05	(Estimates), Transvaal letters patent
152	L	19 Feb 06	Address in reply to King's speech
152	C	19–26 Feb	Ditto
152	L	26–7 Feb	Transvaal and Orange River colonies
152	C	28 Feb 06	South African Native races
153	L	5 Mar 06	Chinese Labour
154	C	21 Mar 06	South Africa (Milner, high commissioner)
154	L	27 Mar 06	Milner
154	L	27 Mar 06	Land settlement in South Africa
155	C	2 Apr 06	Martial law in Natal
155	C	5 Apr 06	(Estimates) Transvaal
156	L	10 May 06	Cotton cultivation (and Nigerian railway)
160	C	5 Jul 06	(Estimates) Egypt. Congo
160	L	6 Jul 06	Chinese on the Rand
162	L	31 Jul 06	Transvaal constitution
162	C	31 Jul 06	(Estimates), Transvaal constitution
167	L	17 Dec 06	South African constitutions
167	C	17 Dec 06	Transvaal and Orange River Colony (Constitution)

169	L	12 Feb 07	Address in reply to King's speech
169	C	12–20 Feb	Ditto
171	L	19 Mar 07	British Indians and the colonies
174	L	29 May 07	Transvaal Registration Bill
176	C	20 Jun 07	(Estimates) South Africa
177	L	27 Jun 07	British East Africa
178	L	3 Jul 07	Congo Free State
178	L	16 Jul 07	Fiji
181	L	19 Aug 07	Nigeria and licensing law
181	L	22 Aug 07	Business of self-governing colonies (reorganisation of CO)
182	L	22 Aug 07	(Public Works Loans Bill) Nigerian railway
183	L	4 Feb 08	British Indians in the Transvaal
184	L	24 Feb 08	Congo Free State
184	C	26 Feb 08	Ditto
188	C	13 May 08	Native Affairs (South Africa)
189	L	19 May 08	Indian traders in Natal
193	C	28 Jul 08	(Estimates) South Africa
193	C	31 Jul 08	(Adjournment) Asiatics
194	L	21 Oct 08	Indians in Transvaal

5th series, House of Lords, vol. 5, 6 Apr 09, Somaliland
5th series, House of Commons, vol. 9, 16 Aug 09, South Africa Bill, 2nd reading

(3) *Select list of published works**

(a) *General books*

AMERY, L. S., *My Political Life*, vols i and ii (1953).

Annual Register for 1904, 1905, 1906, 1907, 1908.

BELL, H. H., *Glimpses of a governor's life* [n.d.].

BENNETT, G., *Kenya, a political history: the colonial period* (1963).

BLUNT, W. S., *My Diaries*, part 2, 1900–1914 (1920).

BONHAM CARTER, VIOLET. *Winston Churchill as I knew him* (1965).

BRETT, M. V. (ed.). *Journals and letters of Reginald, Viscount Esher*, vol. ii, 1903–1910 (1934).

BRYCE, J. *Impressions of South Africa*, 3rd ed. (1899).

Relations of the advanced and the backward races of mankind (Romanes lecture, 1902).

Cambridge History of the British Empire, vol. iii, *The Empire-Commonwealth 1870–1919* (1959).

* All works published in Britain unless otherwise stated

CAMPBELL-BANNERMAN, H. *Speeches, 1899–1908* (selected and reprinted from *The Times*).

CHAMBERLAIN, A. *Politics from inside: an epistolary chronicle, 1906–1914* (1936).

CHURCHILL, RANDOLPH S. *Winston S. Churchill*, vol. ii, *The Young Statesman 1901–1914* (1967).

CHURCHILL, W. S. *For Free Trade: speeches . . . during the fiscal controversy preceding the late general election* (1906).

My African Journey (1908, repr. 1962).

Liberalism and the social problem (1909).

DE MENDELSSOHN, P. *The Age of Churchill*, vol. i: *Heritage and Adventure, 1874–1911* (1961).

FISHER, H. A. L. *James Bryce*, vol. i (1927).

FITZROY, A. *Memoirs*, vol. i [n.d.].

GANN, L. H. *The birth of a plural society: Northern Rhodesia, 1894–1914* (1958).

GARDINER, A. G. *Prophets, priests and kings* (1908).

GOLLIN, A. M. *Proconsul in politics: a study of Lord Milner in opposition and power* (1964).

GREY, E. *Twenty-five years, 1892–1916*, vol. i (1925).

Speeches on foreign affairs, 1904–1914 (ed. P. Knaplund, 1931).

GWYNN, S. and TUCKWELL, G. M. *Life of Sir Charles Dilke*, 2 vols (1918).

HAILEY, LORD. *An African Survey*, revised (1956).

HANCOCK, W. K. *Survey of British Commonwealth Affairs*, 2 vols. (1937–42).

Smuts, vol. i, *The sanguine years* (1962).

HANCOCK, W. K. and VAN DER POEL, J. (eds). *Selections from the Smuts Papers*, ii, 1902–1910 (1966).

HARLOW, V. and CHILVER, E. M. (eds). *History of East Africa*, vol. ii (1965).

HASSALL, C. *Edward Marsh, a biography* (1959).

HEADLAM, C. (ed.). *The Milner papers: South Africa 1897–1905* (2 vols, 1931–3).

HILL, M. F. *Permanent way: story of Kenya and Uganda railway* (Nairobi, 2nd ed., 1961).

HOBHOUSE, L. T. *Liberalism* (1911).

HUXLEY, E. *White Man's Country: Lord Delamere and the Making of Kenya*, vol. i (1953).

INGHAM, K. *A history of East Africa* (1962).

JEBB, R. *The Imperial Conference*, vol. ii (1911).

JENKINS, R. *Asquith* (1964).

KEITH, A. B. *Responsible Government in the dominions* (1928 ed.).

(ed.). *Selected speeches and documents on British colonial policy, 1763–1917* (1918, one vol. ed. 1948).

KIMBLE, D. *A political history of Ghana*, vol. i, *Rise of Gold Coast nationalism, 1850–1928* (1963).

KUPER, H. *An African aristocracy: rank among the Swazi* (1961).

LA NAUZE, J. A. *Alfred Deakin, a biography*, vol. ii (Melbourne, 1965).

LE MAY, G. H. L. *British supremacy in South Africa, 1899–1907* (1965).

LEWIS, I. M. *The modern history of Somaliland* (1965).

LOW, D. A. and PRATT, R. C. *Buganda and British overrule, 1900–1955* (1960).

LUGARD, F. D. *The dual mandate* (1929 ed.).

LYTTELTON, E. *Alfred Lyttelton: an account of his life* (1917).

MCCALLUM, R. B. *Asquith* (1936).

MACCALLUM SCOTT, A. *Winston Spencer Churchill* (1905).

MACDONALD, J. R. *Labour and the Empire* (1907).

MCGREGOR ROSS, W. *Kenya from within: a short political history* (1927).

MACMILLAN, W. M. *Road to Self-rule* (1959).

MCPHEE, A. *The economic revolution in West Africa* (1926).

MANSERGH, P. N. S. *South Africa, 1906–1961: the price of magnanimity* (1962).

MARSH, E. *A number of people: a book of reminiscences* (1939).

MASTERMAN, L. *C. F. G. Masterman, a biography* (1934).

MAURICE, F. *Haldane*, vol. i, 1856–1915 (1937).

MILNER, LORD. *The nation and the empire: speeches and addresses* (1913).

MOREL, E. D. *Nigeria: its peoples and problems* (1912 ed.).

MORLEY, J. VISCOUNT. *Indian speeches, 1907–1909* (1909). *Recollections*, vol. ii (1917).

MORRELL, W. P. *Britain in the Pacific islands* (1960).

MUNGEAM, G. H. *British rule in Kenya, 1895–1912* (1966).

OLIVIER, S., Lord. *White capital and coloured labour* (1929).

ORR, C. W. *The making of Northern Nigeria* (1911, 2nd ed., 1966).

PARKINSON, COSMO. *Colonial office from within, 1909–1945* (1947).

PERHAM, Dame M. *Lugard*, vol. ii, *The years of authority* (1960).

POPE-HENNESSY, J. *Lord Crewe, 1858–1945* (1955).

PYRAH, G. B. *Imperial policy and South Africa, 1902–1910* (1955).

ROBINSON, K. *The dilemmas of trusteeship* (1965).

ROBINSON, R. E. and GALLAGHER, J. *Africa and the Victorians* (1961).

SAMUEL, H., Viscount. *Liberalism: its principles and proposals* (1902).

Memoirs (1945).

SEELY, J. E. B. *Adventure* (1930).

SPENDER, J. A. *Life of Rt. Hon. Sir Henry Campbell-Bannerman*, vol. ii (1923).

Life, Journalism and Politics, vol. i (1927).

SPENDER, J. A. and ASQUITH, C. *Life of Henry Asquith*, vol. i (1932).

STUART, J. *A history of the Zulu rebellion of 1906* (1913).

THOMPSON, L. M. *The unification of South Africa* (1960).

WALKER, E. A. *History of Southern Africa* (1957).

W. P. Schreiner (1937).

WILSON, C. H. *History of Unilever*, vol. i (1954).

(b) *Works referring extensively to Lord Elgin*

ALDER, G. J. *British India's Northern Frontier, 1865–1895* (1963).

Dictionary of National Biography, 1912–1921, 'V. A. Bruce, 9th Earl of Elgin' by F. H. B. [Sir Frank Herbert Brown].

FOWLER, E. *Life of H. H. Fowler, 1st viscount Wolverhampton* (1912).

GOPAL, S. *British policy in India 1858–1905* (1965).

'India under Lord Elgin', in *Quarterly Review,* vol. 189 (1899).

SINGH, H. L. *Problems and policies of the British in India 1885–1898* (1963).

(c) *Essays, articles and reviews*

BULL, M. 'Indirect rule in Northern Nigeria, 1906–1911', *Essays in Imperial government presented to Margery Perham,* ed. by K. Robinson and F. Madden (1963), pp. 47–87.

CROSS, J. A. 'Whitehall and the Commonwealth', *Journal of Commonwealth Political Studies,* vol. ii (1964), 189–201.

FRASER, A. M. 'Fishery negotiations with the United States', *Newfoundland: economic, diplomatic and strategic studies,* ed. R. A. MacKay (Toronto, 1946).

GILBERT, B. B. 'The grant of responsible government to the Transvaal: more notes on a myth', Communication in *Historical Journal,* vol. x, no. 3 (1967).

HARRISON-CHURCH, R. J. 'Transport pattern in British West Africa', *Geographical essays on British tropical lands,* ed. R. W. Steel and C. A. Fisher (1956).

HYAM, R. 'Partition of Africa: a review article', *Historical Journal,* vol. vii (1964), 154–69.

'Smuts and the decision of the Liberal government to grant responsible government to the Transvaal, January and February, 1906', *Historical Journal,* vol. viii (1965), 380–98.

Review of Le May, 'British supremacy in South Africa, 1899–1907', *Historical Journal,* vol. ix (1966), 149–51.

TYLER, J. E. 'Campbell-Bannerman and the Liberal Imperialists, 1906–1908', *History,* vol. xxiii (1938), 254–62.

UNPUBLISHED DISSERTATIONS

HYAM, R. *The African policy of the Liberal government, 1905–1909,* Cambridge University Ph.D. dissertation (1963).

PORTER, B. *Radical and Labour attitudes to Empire, 1896–1914,* Cambridge University Ph.D. dissertation (1967).

ROBINSON, R. E. *The Trust in British Central Africa policy,* Cambridge University Ph.D. dissertation (1950).

Biographical Notes on the Policy Advisers

† (Titles are given as in 1908)

ANTROBUS, R. L. (1853–1942). Entered CO., 1877, asst. under-sec., 1898 (chiefly concerned with W. and E. Africa) to Jun 09. Senior Crown Agent for the colonies 1909–18.

ASQUITH, H. H. (1852–1928). Entered parliament, 1886. Home sec., 1892–5. Chancellor of exchequer, Dec 05 to Apr 08. Prime minister, 7 Apr 08–Dec 1916.

BELL, H. H. (1864–1952). Served in W. Indies 1882–3, 1894–1905. Commissioner and C.-in-C. Uganda, 31 Jan 06; title changed to govr, 18 Oct 07. Govr of N. Nigeria, 30 Dec 09–1912. Knighted, 1908.

BLAKE, Sir Henry A. (1840–1918). Govr of Bahamas, 1884; Newfoundland, 1887; Jamaica, 1888; Hong Kong, 1898; Ceylon, 1903–Jul 07 (retired).

BOND, Sir Robert (1857–1927). Prime minister of Newfoundland, 1900–8. Official Newfoundland delegate to London on fisheries, 1890; col. sec., 1889–94, 1895–7. Negotiated Hay–Bond treaty, 1902.

BRYCE, J. (1838–1922). Regius Prof. of Civil Law, Oxford, 1870–93. Entered parliament, 1880. Travelled in S. Africa, 1895. Chief sec. for Ireland, Dec 05 to Feb 07. Ambassador to U.S.A., 1907–13. Created viscount, 1914.

BUTLER, F. G. A. (b. 1873). Trinity Oxford. Entered CO, 1897. Private secretary to WSC. 1st class clerk, Jan 07.

CAMPBELL-BANNERMAN, Sir Henry (1836–1908). Entered parliament, 1868. Chief sec. for Ireland, 1884–5. Sec. for war, 1886, 1892–5. Leader of Lib. party, Dec 1898. Prime minister, 5 Dec 05 to 6 Apr 08. D. 22 Apr 08.

CARRINGTON, Earl of (1843–1928). President of board of agriculture and fisheries, Dec 05–Oct 11.

CHURCHILL, W. S. (1874–1965). Entered parliament 1901. Changed from Conservative to Liberal 1904. Parliamentary under-sec. for the colonies and spokesman of the department in House of Commons, Dec 05 to Apr 08. President of board of trade, 1908–10, subsequently home sec. 1910–11, first lord of admiralty, 1911–15; minister of munitions, 1917, sec. for war and air, 1919–21; col. sec. 1921–2; chancellor of exchequer 1924–9; 1st lord of admiralty 1939–40; prime minister 1940–5, 1951–5.

CORDEAUX, Capt. H. E. S. Entered Indian army, 1894. Asst. Resident Berbera, 1898. Deputy commissioner of Somaliland, 1904; administered the government from Jun 05; commissioner and C.-in-C., 15 May 06–Jan 10. (Succeeded by Brig. Gen. Sir W. H. Manning, who supervised withdrawal from interior 1910.) Govr of Uganda, 1 Feb 10.

COX, H. B. (1861–1930). Called to Bar, 1885. Legal asst under-sec. in CO from Nov 97 to 1911; head of general department, 1907.

CREWE, 1st Earl of, K. G. (1858–1945). Lord Lieut. of Ireland, 1892–5. Lord President of Council, Dec 05 to Apr 08. Colonial sec., 16 Apr 08 to Nov 1910. Sec. for India, 1910–15.

CROMER, Earl of, Evelyn Baring (1841–1917). Entered Royal Artillery, 1858. In India, 1872–6. Agent and consul-general in Egypt 1883–13 Jul 07. (Succeeded by Gorst.)

DAVIS, C. T. (b. 1873). Balliol. Entered CO, 1897. 1st class clerk 1905. Principal clerk, 1916; asst under-sec., 1921; permanent under-sec. for dominions affairs, 1925.

DILKE, Sir Charles W. (1843–1911). Voyage round world, 1866. Liberal M.P., 1868–86. Under-sec. for foreign affairs, 1880–2; president of local government board 1882–5.

EGERTON, Sir Walter (1858–1947). Served in Far East, 1880–1902. High commissioner, S. Nigeria, Nov 1903, and govr of Lagos from 30 Jul 04. Govr. and C.-in-C. of S. Nigeria (in which Lagos incorporated), 1 May 06 to 1912.

ELGIN, 9th Earl of, Victor Alexander Bruce (1849–1917). Commissioner of works, 1886. Viceroy of India, 1894 to Jan 99. Appointed chairman of royal commission to inquire into military preparations and conduct of South African War, Sep 02–Jul 03. Colonial sec., 11 Dec 06 to 8 Apr 08, when he was dropped on formation of Asquith ministry. Chairman of royal commission on Free Churches controversy in Scotland, 1904; and then of royal commission to administer the Scottish Churches Act, 1905.

ELLIS, W. D. (b. 1871). Winchester and New Coll. CO. clerk, 1895; 1st class clerk, 1899.

FIDDES, G. V. (1858–1936). Dulwich and Brasenose. Entered CO, 1881. 1st class clerk, 1896. Secretary to Transvaal administration, 1900–2; returned to CO as principal clerk, 1902; accounting officer, 1907; asst under-sec., 1909–16; permanent under-sec., 1916–21.

FITZMAURICE, Lord Edmond (1846–1935). Entered parliament, 1868. Called to Bar, 1871. Under-sec. for foreign affairs, 1883–5, 18 Dec 05–19 Oct 08.

GIROUARD, Lt. Col. Sir E. Percy C., D.S.O., R.E. (1867–1932). Railway traffic manager, Woolwich Arsenal 1890–5. Director of Soudan railways, 1896–8. President of Egyptian railway board, 1898–9. Commissioner of railways Transvaal and O.R.C., 1902. Appointed high commissioner of Nigeria, 12 Feb 07, largely because of his railway experience, to superintend Baro-Kano line. Govr of E.A.P., 16 Sep 09 (in succession to Sadler) to 1912.

GOOLD-ADAMS, Major Sir Hamilton J. (1858–1920). Royal Scots Fusiliers. Resident commissioner, Bechuanaland; deputy administrator, O.R.C., 1901; Lt govr, 7 Aug 01; govr, 1 Jul 07–1910.

GLADSTONE, H. J. (1854–1930). Youngest son of W. E. G. Entered parliament, 1880. Under-sec. at home office, 1892–4; first commissioner of works, 1894–5. Chief Liberal Whip from 1899. Sec. for home affairs, 1905–10. Created viscount, 1910, on appointment as first govr. gen. of Union of S. Africa, May 1910, to 1914.

GRAHAM, Sir Frederick (1848–1923). Entered CO, 1870. Asst under-sec., 1 Mar 97, chiefly concerned with S. Africa. Retired, Jan 07.

GREY, 4th Earl of (1851–1917). Director of B.S.A. Co. Administrator of Rhodesia, 1896–8. Govr gen. of Canada, 26 Sep 04–1911.

GREY, Sir Edward (1862–1933). Liberal M.P., 1885–1916. Under-sec. for foreign affairs, 1892–5; foreign sec., 1905–1916.

HALDANE, R. B. (1856–1928). Called to the Bar, 1879. Liberal M.P., 1885–1911. Sec. for war, 1905–12; lord chancellor, 1912–15, and 1924.

HAMILTON, Sir W. A. Baillie (1844–1920). Harrow. Entered CO, 1864. Principal clerk, 1894; chief clerk, 1896. In Dominions dept. from 1907.

HARCOURT, L. V. (1863–1922). Son of Sir W. V. H. Entered parliament, 1881. First commissioner of works, 1905–10. Colonial sec., 7 Nov 10 to 1915.

HARRIS, C. A. (b. 1855). Christ's College, Cambridge. Lincoln's Inn. Entered CO, 1879. 1st class clerk 1896; worked on Venezuela boundary arbitration; principal clerk, 1898.

HELY-HUTCHINSON, Hon. Sir Walter (1849–1913). Served in Fiji and West Indies. Govr of Natal, 1893. Govr of Cape Colony 1901–10 (retired).

HOPWOOD, Sir Francis J. S. (1860–1947). Permanent sec., board of trade 1901. Visited S. Africa as member of the Ridgeway committee. Permanent under-sec. at CO, 15 Jan 07 (in succession to Ommanney) to 1911. Created Lord Southborough, 1917.

JUST, Hartmann W. (1854–1929). Entered CO, 1878. Visited S. Africa with Chamberlain, 1903, and chiefly concerned with S. Africa. Asst under-sec., 10 Jan 07–1916. Sec. to imperial conference from 1907.

KEITH, A. B. (1879–1944). Entered CO, 1901. Sec. to Crown Agents, Jul 1903. Called to Bar, 1904. Re-transferred to CO, 1 May 05. Regius Prof. of Sanskrit and Comparative

Philology, Edinburgh, from 1914 and Lecturer on constitution of British empire from 1927; author of many books on both subjects.

LAGDEN, Sir Godfrey Y. (1851–1934). Entered G.P.O., 1869. Entered service of Transvaal government, 1878. Asst. commissioner, Basutoland, 1885; resident commissioner, 1893–1901. Chairman of S. Africa Native Affairs Commission, 1903–4. Commissioner for native affairs, Transvaal, 1901–7.

LAMBERT, H. C. M. (b. 1868). Eton and New Coll. Entered CO, 1892. Visited Australia, 1905. 1st class clerk 1898; principal clerk, Jan 1907.

LEVER, W. H. (1851–1925). M.P., 1906–10. Founded Port Sunlight. Created Lord Leverhulme, 1922.

LOREBURN, Lord (1846–1923). Called to Bar, 1871. Entered parliament, 1880. Attorney-general, 1894. Lord Chancellor, 1905–12, with title of Lord Loreburn. (Sir Robert Reid).

LUCAS, Sir Charles P. (1853–1931). Called to Bar, 1885. Entered CO, 1877. Asst under-sec., Jun 97, chiefly concerned with West Indies and Eastern colonies, and Somaliland. Author *Historical Geography of the British Colonies*. Head of Dominions department, 1907 to 1911 (retired).

LUGARD, Col. Sir Frederick J.D., D.S.O. (1858–1945). In India, 1878–9; in E. Africa, 1899–1902. High commissioner for N. Nigeria, 29 Dec 99; resigned, Sep 06. Govr Hong Kong, 29 Jul 07; Nigeria, 1912–18.

LYTTELTON, A. (1857–1913). Called to Bar, 1881. Entered parliament, 1895. Chairman of commission to inquire into concessions granted by Kruger in Transvaal. Col. sec., 9 Oct 03 (in succession to Chamberlain) until 5 Dec 05.

McCALLUM, Col. Sir Henry E., R.E. (1852–1919). Served in Far East from 1876. Govr Lagos, 1897; Newfoundland, 1898; Natal, 1901 to 1 May 07. Govr of Ceylon, 24 Aug 07.

MacGREGOR, Sir Wm, M.D. (b. 1847). Govr of Lagos, 1899; Newfoundland, Jul 1904. Formerly assistant government medical officer, Seychelles 1873; chief med. off., Fiji

1875; administrator of New Guinea, 1888; Lt govr 1895.

MARLBOROUGH, 9th Duke of, K.G. (1871–1934). Parliamentary under-sec. at CO., 1903–05.

MERRIMAN, J. X. (1841–1926). Offices in both British and Bond governments in Cape Colony 1875–1900. Prime minister of the Cape and leader of the South African party, 1908.

MOREL, E. D. (1873–1924). Editor *African Mail*, 1903–15. Founder and sec., Congo Reform Association, 1904–12. Visited Nigeria, 1910.

MORLEY, J. (1838–1923). Editor (e.g. of *Fortnightly, Pall Mall Gazette*), 1867–82. Entered parliament, 1883. Chief sec. for Ireland, 1886, 1892–5. Sec. for India, 1905–10. Created viscount, 1908. Lord president of council, 1910–14.

NATHAN, Lt Col Sir Matthew (1862–1939). Entered R.E., 1880. Govr Gold Coast, 1900; Hong Kong, 1903; Natal, 1 May 07 (in succession to McCallum) to Dec 09.

NORTHCOTE, 1st Baron (1846–1911). Sir Henry Stafford Northcote. Govr of Bombay, 1899; governor-general of commonwealth of Australia, Aug 1903–8.

OLIVIER, Sydney (1859–1943). Entered CO, 1882. Sec. of Fabian Society, 1886–90. Col. sec. Jamaica, 1900–4. Returned to CO as principal clerk, Oct 1904, chiefly concerned with W. Africa. Govr. of Jamaica, 20 Apr 07–1913. Created baron, 1924.

OMMANNEY, Sir Montagu F. (1842–1925). R.M.A., Woolwich. Entered CO, 1874. Crown Agent, 1877–1900. Permanent under-sec., 1900, till retirement, Jan 07 (succeeded by Hopwood).

PROBYN, L. (1862–1938). Called to Bar, 1884. Served in West Indies. Sec. to govr Southern Nigeria, 1901. Govr Sierra Leone, 14 Jul 04 to Oct 10, govr of Barbados, 1910. Knighted, 1909.

READ, H. J. (1863–1949). Principal clerk, 1 Apr 05, chiefly concerned with E. Africa. Sat on most of tropical African advisory committees. Asst under-sec. 1916. Govr of Mauritius, 1924.

REID, Sir Robert, see Loreburn, Lord.

RIDGEWAY, Sir Joseph West, P.C. (1844–1930). Indian Army until 1889. Under-sec. for Ireland, 1887–92. Govr of Ceylon, 1896–1903. Chairman of Committee of Inquiry in Transvaal and Orange River Colony, 1906. Chairman, Tropical Diseases Research Fund Committee.

RIPON, Lord (1827–1909). Entered parliament, 1853. Sec. for war, 1863–6. Lord President of Council, 1868–73. Created first Marquess of Ripon, 1871. Viceroy of India, 1880–4. Col. sec., 1892–5. Lord Privy Seal, 1905–Oct 08 and leader of Liberal party in House of Lords.

RODGER, Sir John P. (1851–1910). Called to Bar, 1877. Served in Far East, 1882–1901. Govr of Gold Coast, 21 Sept 03 to 19 Sep 10 (died).

SADLER, Sir James Hayes (1851–1910). Indian Army to 1899. Commissioner of Uganda, 1901. Commissioner and C.-in-C., E.A.P., 11 Dec 05; title changed to govr, 9 Nov 1906 until Sep 09. Govr of Grenada, 13 Oct 09–9 Jan 10 (died).

SAMUEL, H. (1870–1963). Entered parliament, 1902. Under-sec. at home office, Dec 05–Jun 09. Subsequently chancellor of Duchy of Lancaster, postmaster-general. Created viscount, 1937.

SEELY, Col. J. E. B., D.S.O. (1868–1947). Served in S. African War. Entered parliament, 1901; moved from Conservative to Liberal Party, 1903. M.P. for a Liverpool division, 1906. Under-sec. for colonies, 16 Apr 1908 to 1911. Under-sec. at War Office, 1911–12; sec. for war (in succession to Haldane), 1912–14. Created Baron Mottistone, 1933.

SELBORNE, Earl of (1859–1942). Entered parliament, 1885. Under-sec. for the colonies 1895–1900. First Lord of Admiralty 1900–5. High commissioner for S. Africa and govr of the Transvaal and O.R.C. (in succession to Milner) from 23 May 05 until establishment of Union government, 31 May 10. Minister of agriculture, 1915–16.

SHARPE. Sir Alfred (1853–1935). Magistrate in Fiji, 1885–6. In Nyasaland from 1891. Commissioner and C.-in-C.,

British Central Africa Protectorate, 1 Jan 02; title changed to govr of Nyasaland, 6 Sep 07 to Nov 10 (retired).

SOLOMON, Sir Richard (1850–1913). Called to Bar, 1879. Acting Lt govr Transvaal, 1905. Agent-general for Transvaal in London, 1907; high commissioner in London for Union of S. Africa, 1910.

SWETTENHAM, Sir J. Alexander (b. 1846). Clare Coll. Entered Ceylon service, 1868. Col. sec. of Straits Settlements, 1895; govr of Brit. Guiana, 1901, of Jamaica, 1904–7 (resigned). Not to be confused with Sir F. A. S., govr of Straits Settlements, 1901–4.

WALLACE, Sir William (1856–1916). Deputy high commissioner and senior resident, Northern Nigeria, 1900. Administered the government, Jul 06 to Apr 07 (in interval between Lugard's departure and Girouard's arrival). Retired, 1910.

WINGATE, Maj. Gen. Sir F. Reginald, D.S.O. (1861–1953). Sirdar of the Egyptian Army and govr gen. of the Sudan, 1899–1916.

(Sources: *Colonial Office List, Foreign Office List, Who's Who, Who Was Who, Dictionary of National Biography*, Debrett's *Peerage, Baronage and Knightage*.)

Index